OXFORD
UNIVERSITY PRESS

MW01129894

Complete
Business Studies

for **Cambridge IGCSE®** & **O Level**

Third Edition

Brian Titley

OXFORD

Great Clarendon Street, Oxford OX2 6DP

Oxford University Press is a department of the University of Oxford.
It furthers the University's objective of excellence in research, scholarship,
and education by publishing worldwide in

Oxford New York

Auckland Cape Town Dar es Salaam Hong Kong Karachi
Kuala Lumpur Madrid Melbourne Mexico City Nairobi
New Delhi Shanghai Taipei Toronto

With offices in

Argentina Austria Brazil Chile Czech Republic France Greece
Guatemala Hungary Italy Japan Poland Portugal Singapore
South Korea Switzerland Thailand Turkey Ukraine Vietnam

Acknowledgments

The publisher and authors would like to thank the following for permission to use
photographs and copyright material:

® IGCSE is the registered trademark of Cambridge International Examinations.

Cover images: Shutterstock; viii:Danishkhan/iStockphoto; p2 (TL):Asia Images Group/
Getty Images; p2 (TC):Eco Images/Getty Images; p2 (CL):Eco Images/Getty Images; p2
(C):Monty Rakusen/Getty Images; p2 (CR):SeanShot/iStockphoto; p2 (B):Steven Morris
Photography/Photolibrary/Getty Images; p3:S. Forster/Alamy Stock Photo; p7:Library of
Congress/Corbis/VCG/Getty Images; p8 (R):Tobias Schwarz/Reuters; p22 (R):Johnny Ha-
glund/Lonely Planet Images/Getty Images; p23 (B):Science Photo Library - IAN HOOTON/
Getty Images; p41:Kevpix/Alamy Stock Photo; p43 (L):JUSTIN LANE/EPA; p43 (R):Dario
Pignatelli/Bloomberg/Getty Images; p46 (B): Gareth Brown/Corbis/Getty Images; p60:Age
Fotostock/Alamy Stock Photo; p67 (T):Willy Matheisl/Alamy Stock Photo; p68:MyLoupe/
UIG/Getty Images; p78:Jonktm/Stockimo/Alamy Stock Photo; p79:G Keshav Raj/The India
Today Group/Getty Images; p81 (R):Arian Camilleri/Masterfile; p86: CribbVisuals/ E+/Getty
Images; p106:Juan Manuel Silva/Age Fotostock; p107 (C):ALLESALLTAG BILDAGENT/Age
Fotostock; p107 (R):Javier Larrea/Age Fotostock; p122:Mike Hutchings/Reuters; p125:Ahn
Young-Joon/AP Images; p144:Luis Galdamez/Reuters; p145 (T):Monkeybusinessimages/
iStockphoto; p145 (B): Jochen Tack/ArabianEye/Getty Images; p158:RICHARD DUGOVIC/
AFP/Getty Images; p159 (T): Jupiterimages/Photolibrary/Getty Images; p159 (B):Janine
Wiedel Photolibrary/Alamy Stock Photo; p166:Steven Senne/AP Images; p168:Jacob Wack-
erhausen/iStockphoto; p175:Andrew Ammendolia/Alamy Stock Photo; p180:Paul Brown/
Alamy Stock Photo; p185:Peter Erik Forsberg/Prague/Alamy Stock Photo; p189:Chris
Eriksson/Dreamstime; p193:Zhuangmu/Dreamstime; p203 (T): Jutta Klee/Canopy/Getty
Images; p203 (B):G-stockstudio/Shutterstock; p205 (TR):Leungchopan/iStockphoto; p205
(CL):imageBROKER/Alamy Stock Photo; p205 (BL): MIXA/Getty Images; p210:Janine
Wiedel Photolibrary/Alamy Stock Photo; p216:Al Freni/The LIFE Images Collection/Getty
Images; p229 (L):Oxford University Press; p229 (CL):Alamy Ltd; p229 (C):Getty Images;
p228 (L):BSIP SA/Alamy Stock Photo; p228 (C):Q28/Alamy Stock Photo; p228 (R):Patti
McConville/Alamy Stock Photo; p236:Javier Larrea/Age Fotostock; p239:Justin Sullivan/
Getty Images; p240 (R):Craig Stephen/Alamy Stock Photo; p243 (R):Ollo/iStockphoto;
p247 (T):Adem Yilmaz/Anadolu Agency/Getty Images; p247 (B):Caroline Penn/Alamy
Stock Photo; p257 (B):Kathy deWitt / Alamy Stock Photo; p260 (TC):imageBROKER/Alamy
Stock Photo; p260 (BC):Stephen Chernin/Getty Images; p261 (T): Jamie Grill/Getty Im-
ages; p261 (B):imageBROKER/Alamy Stock Photo; p267 (L):NetPhotos/Alamy Stock Photo;
p268:Lou-Foto/Alamy Stock Photo; p277 (R):Phil McCarten/Reuters; p278:Martin Lee /
Alamy Stock Photo; p294: CribbVisuals/ E+/Getty Images; p302 (L):Mevans/iStockphoto;
p302 (R):Ali Ali/EPA; p308:GM Photo Images/Alamy Stock Photo; p309 (T):Eye Ubiquitous/
Age Fotostock; p309 (B):Sean Sprague/Alamy Stock Photo; p311b:David Hancock/Alamy
Stock Photo; p311c: Monty Rakusen/Cultura/Getty Images; p311g: Matilde Gattoni/arabi-
anEye/Getty Images; p313 (T):Zhejiang Daily/VCG/Getty Images; p336 (L): Stewart Cohen/
Stockbyte/Getty Images; p336 (R):Geoffrey Robinson/Alamy Stock Photo; p337:Tomohiro
Ohsumi/Bloomberg/Getty Images; p342 (T):Art Directors & TRIP/Alamy Stock Photo; p342
(B):Markus Schreiber/AP Images; p360 (TL):Drimi/Dreamstime; p360 (TC): Silverstock/
Photodisc/Getty Images; p360 (TR):imageBROKER/Alamy Stock Photo; p360 (BL):CERN;

p369: Michael Heffernan/The Image Bank/Getty Images; p373 (CR):John van Hasselt/
Sygma/Getty Images; p373 (BL):SFL Life Style/Alamy Stock Photo; p381:Tim Graham/
Getty Images; p397 (TR):Dary423/Dreamstime; p424: CribbVisuals/ E+/Getty Images; p436
(C):Senior Airman Laura Turner/US Air Force; p438 (L):Louise Murray/Robertharding/
Getty Images; p439 (L):Age Fotostock/Alamy Stock Photo; p440:Andrew Holt/Alamy Stock
Photo; p449 (R):Holger Mette/iStockphoto; p460 (T):BSIP SA/Alamy Stock Photo; p460
(BC):ImagineGolf/iStockphoto; p460 (B):Andrew Biraj/Reuters; p467 (C):Albert Gea/Re-
uters; p468 (T):Maloy40/iStockphoto; p469:Pascal Parrot/Getty Images; p267 (R):NetPhotos
/ Alamy Stock Photo; :NetPhotos/Alamy Stock Photo; all other images by Shutterstock.

The authors and the publisher are grateful for permission to reprint extracts from the
following copyright material:

The Anglesey Sea Salt Company: Extract adapted from Exports case study: Anglesey
Sea Salt Co Ltd, http://www.fdf.org.uk/exports-anglesey-sea-salt.aspx.

Business Case Studies: Extract adapted from Creating quality customer care

A Zurich case study, http://businesscasestudies.co.uk/zurich/creating-quality-customer-
care/introduction.html#axzz2z8RK7IYa.

Solo Syndication: Extract adapted from Nike workers 'kicked, slapped and verbally
abused' at factories making Converse by Daily Mail Reporter, http://www.dailymail.co.uk/
news/article-2014325/Nike-workers-kicked-slapped-verbally-abused-factories-making-
Converse-line-Indonesia.html#ixzz3Uvu6tyMQ, 13 July 2011, MailOnline.

Startups.co.uk: Extract adapted from Government launches start-up loans for
young entrepreneurs by Steph Welstead, pub 27 May 2012, http://www.startups.co.uk/
government-launches-start-up-loans-for-young-entrepreneurs.

Telegraph Media Group Limited: Extract adapted from Government dishes out £3,000
broadband grants for small businesses by Sophie Curtis, 7 December 2013, http://www.
telegraph.co.uk. © Telegraph Media Group Limited 2013.

Telegraph Media Group Limited: Extract adapted from World's biggest music store
to close by Graham Ruddick, 12 January 2014, http://www.telegraph.co.uk, © Telegraph
Media Group Limited 2014.

Telegraph Media Group Limited: Headline 'Net loss: the decline of UK fishing', 25
November 2007, http://www.telegraph.co.uk/news/uknews/1570441/Net-loss-The-decline-
of-UK-fishing.html, © Telegraph Media Group Limited 2007.

YGS Group: Extract from U.S. Economy: Retail Sales Slide Signals Recession (Update1)
by Bob Willis and Timothy R. Homan, 15 October 2008, http://www.bloomberg.com/
apps/news?pid=newsarchive&sid=aZ0o8ZBt6hos&refer=home. Used with permission of
Bloomberg.com. Copyright © 2008. All rights reserved.

Although we have made every effort to trace and contact all copyright holders before
publication this has not been possible in all cases. If notified, the publisher will rectify
any errors or omissions at the earliest opportunity.

Introduction

Complete Business Studies will help you build the skills and understanding you need throughout your course and for future success

Whether you want to start your own business or work for a major international company, the study of how businesses operate, make decisions and affect our welfare, will provide you with the knowledge, understanding and critical thinking skills you will need to succeed.

By studying for Business Studies you will develop lifelong skills including

- the ability to make effective use of business terminology and ideas and to recognise the strengths and limitations of these ideas in business contexts;
- knowledge and understanding of how different types of businesses are organized, financed and operated, and how their relations with other organizations, consumers, employees, owners and society are regulated;
- knowledge and understanding of the major groups and organizations within and outside of businesses, and an appreciation of the ways in which they are able to influence business objectives, decisions and activities;
- the ability to apply your knowledge and critical understanding to current issues and problems to a wide range of business issues;
- confidence in using, calculating, interpreting and presenting business data including financial data;
- the ability to distinguish between facts and opinions, and evaluate qualitative and quantitative data in order to help build arguments and make informed judgments;
- awareness of the nature and significance of innovation and change within the context of business activities.

At the end of the Cambridge IGCSE or O Level course, your skills will be assessed in 2 examination papers. These are as follows:

	Paper 1	Paper 2
Time allocated	1 hour 30 minutes	1 hour 30 minutes
Number of questions	Four questions based on four different businesses requiring a mixture of short answers and structured data responses. All questions must be answered.	Four structured questions based on a business case study. All questions must be answered
Maximum number of marks	80 marks	80 marks

Complete Business Studies contains a wealth of examination-style questions for you to practise and develop all of the key skills. Sample answers to all the questions in this book are provided on the accompanying website: www.oxfordsecondary.com/9780198425267.

Good luck with your studies and exams!

Contents

1 Understanding business activity

1.1 Business activity

1.1.1 The purpose and nature of business activity — 1

1.2 Classification of businesses

1.2.1 Business activity in terms of primary, secondary and tertiary sectors — 15

1.2.2 Classify business enterprises between private sector and public sector in a mixed economy — 15

1.3 Enterprise, business growth and size

1.3.1 Enterprise and entrepreneurship — 28

1.3.2 The methods and problems of measuring business size — 37

1.3.3 Why some businesses grow and others remain small — 37

1.3.4 Why some (new or established) businesses fail — 48

1.4 Types of business organization

1.4.1 The main features of different forms of business organization — 54

1.5 Business objectives and stakeholder objectives

1.5.1 Businesses can have several objectives and the importance of them can change — 72

1.5.2 Differences in the objectives of private sector and public sector enterprises — 72

1.5.3 The role of stakeholder groups involved in business activity — 80

2 People in business

2.1 Motivating employees

2.1.1 The importance of a well-motivated workforce — 87

2.1.2 Methods of motivation — 93

2.2 Organization and management

2.2.1 Draw, interpret and understand simple organizational structures — 101

2.2.2 The role of management — 112

2.2.3 Leadership styles — 112

2.2.4 Trade unions — 122

2.3 Recruitment, selection and training of employees

2.3.1 Recruitment and selecting employees — 128

2.3.2 The importance of training and the methods of training — 144

2.3.3 Why reducing the size of the workforce might be necessary — 149

2.3.4 Legal controls over employment issues and their impact on employers and employees — 156

2.4 Internal and external communication

2.4.1 Why effective communication is important and the methods used to achieve it — 164

2.4.2 Demonstrate an awareness of communication barriers — 164

3 Marketing

3.1 Marketing, competition and the customer

3.1.1 The role of marketing — 181

3.1.2 Market changes — 187

3.1.3 Concepts of niche marketing and mass marketing — 198

3.1.4 How and why market segmentation is undertaken — 201

3.2 Market research

3.2.1 The role of market research and methods used — 207

3.2.2 Presentation and use of market research results — 207

3.3 Marketing mix

3.3.1 Product — 225

3.3.2 Price — 235

3.3.3 Place–distribution channels — 246

3.3.4 Promotion — 254

3.3.5 Technology and the marketing mix — 266

3.4 Marketing strategy

3.4.1 Justify marketing strategies appropriate to a given situation   274

3.4.2 The nature and impact of legal controls related to marketing   281

3.4.3 The opportunities and problems of entering new foreign markets   285

4 Operations management

4.1 Production of goods and services

4.1.1 The meaning of production   295

4.1.2 The main methods of production   307

4.1.3 How technology has changed production methods   307

4.2 Costs, scale of production and break-even analysis

4.2.1 Identify and classify costs   317

4.2.2 Economies and diseconomies of scale   317

4.2.3 Break-even analysis   317

4.3 Achieving quality production

4.3.1 Why quality is important and how quality production might be achieved   334

4.4 Location decisions

4.4.1 The main factors influencing the location and relocation decisions of a business   344

5 Financial information and decisions

5.1 Business finance: needs and sources

5.1.1 The need for business finance   357

5.1.2 The main sources of finance   361

5.2 Cash flow forecasting and working capital

5.2.1 The importance of cash and of cash flow forecasting   376

5.2.2 Working capital   376

5.3 Income statements

5.3.1 What profit is and why it is important   386

5.3.2 Income statements   386

5.4 Statement of financial position

5.4.1 The main elements of a statement of financial position   396

5.4.2 How to interpret a simple statement of financial position   396

5.5 Analysis of accounts

5.5.1 Profitability   404

5.5.2 Liquidity   404

5.5.3 How to interpret the financial performance of a business   404

5.5.4 Why and how accounts are used   416

6 External influences on business activity

6.1 Economic issues

6.1.1 Business cycle   425

6.1.2 How government control over the economy affects business activity   425

6.2 Environmental and ethical issues

6.2.1 Environmental concerns and ethical issues as both opportunities and constraints for business   448

6.3 Business and the international economy

6.3.1 The importance of globalization   464

6.3.2 Reasons for the importance and growth of multinational companies   474

6.3.3 The impact of exchange rate changes   480

Website includes:

- a range of assessment questions to support Parts 1-6
- interactive multiple choice revision tests, with answers provided
- a dictionary of business "buzzwords"
- sample answers to all activities and questions in the book
- a complete set of crossword puzzles for you to print and complete.

Access your support website at www.oxfordsecondary.com/9780198425267

Matching chart

The units in this book offer a match to Cambridge International GCSE Economics (0455) and O Level (2281).

Syllabus overview	Unit in Student Book
PART 1 Understanding business activity 1.1 Business activity 1.2 Classification of businesses 1.3 Enterprise, business growth and size 1.4 Types of business organization 1.5 Business objectives and stakeholder objectives	**PART 1 Understanding business activity** 1.1 Business activity 1.2 Classification of businesses 1.3 Enterprise, business growth and size 1.4 Types of business organization 1.5 Business objectives and stakeholder objectives
PART 2 People in business 2.1 Motivating employees 2.2 Organization and management 2.3 Recruitment, selection and training of employees 2.4 Internal and external communication	**PART 2 People in business** 2.1 Motivating employees 2.2 Organization and management 2.3 Recruitment, selection and training of employees 2.4 Internal and external communication
PART 3 Marketing 3.1 Marketing, competition and the customer 3.2 Market research 3.3 Marketing mix 3.4 Marketing strategy	**PART 3 Marketing** 3.1 Marketing, competition and the customer 3.2 Market research 3.3 Marketing mix 3.4 Marketing strategy
PART 4 Operations management 4.1 Production of goods and services 4.2 Costs, scale of production and break-even analysis 4.3 Achieving quality production 4.4 Location decisions	**PART 4 Operations management** 4.1 Production of goods and services 4.2 Costs, scale of production and break-even analysis 4.3 Achieving quality production 4.4 Location decisions
PART 5 Financial information and decisions 5.1 Business finance: needs and sources 5.2 Cash flow forecasting and working capital 5.3 Income statements 5.4 Statement of financial position 5.5 Analysis of accounts	**PART 5 Financial information and decisions** 5.1 Business finance: needs and sources 5.2 Cash flow forecasting and working capital 5.3 Income statements 5.4 Statement of financial position 5.5 Analysis of accounts
PART 6 External influences on business activity 6.1 Economic issues 6.2 Environmental and ethical issues 6.3 Business and the international economy	**PART 6 External influences on business activity** 6.1 Economic issues 6.2 Environmental and ethical issues 6.3 Business and the international economy

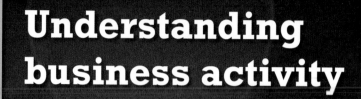

1 Understanding business activity

1.1 Business activity	1.1.1 The purpose and nature of business activity
1.2 Classification of businesses	1.2.1 Business activity in terms of primary, secondary and tertiary sectors
	1.2.2 Classify business enterprises between private sector and public sector in a mixed economy
1.3 Enterprise, business growth and size	1.3.1 Enterprise and entrepreneurship
	1.3.2 The methods and problems of measuring business size
	1.3.3 Why some businesses grow and others remain small
	1.3.4 Why some (new or established) businesses fail
1.4 Types of business organization	1.4.1 The main features of different forms of business organization
1.5 Business objectives and stakeholder objectives	1.5.1 Businesses can have several objectives and the importance of them can change
	1.5.2 The role of stakeholder groups involved in business activity
	1.5.3 Differences in the objectives of private sector and public sector enterprises

1.1.1 The purpose and nature of business activity

- Business involves organizing and combining resources into firms with the purpose of producing goods and services to satisfy needs and wants of consumers.

- Resources, or factors of production, are used to make goods and services.

- Resources are scarce. There are not enough to produce everything we need and want. We must choose between alternative resources.

- Resources include land (natural resources), labour (human effort), capital (man-made resources) and enterprise (the knowledge and skills people need to own and run business organizations).

- Resources are inputs to productive activity and products (goods and services) are outputs from productive activity.

- Specialization involves individuals and business organizations focusing resources on the limited range of productive activities they perform best. Without specialization, far fewer goods and services would be produced. There would be far fewer business and employment opportunities and incomes and living standards would be much lower.

- Business activity adds value to resources by using them to produce goods and services that are more desirable to consumers.

- Firms owned by private individuals are private enterprises. Most firms aim to make a profit but some, like charities, engage in non-profit-making activities.

Key POINTS

Business BUZZWORDS

Consumers – people and organizations who are willing and able to buy goods and services.

Consumption – the using up of goods and services to satisfy consumer needs and wants.

Production – using resources to make goods and services to satisfy consumer needs and wants.

Factors of production – productive resources used to make goods and services.

Firms – organizations that produce goods and services.

Entrepreneur – a person with the know-how and willingness to take the risks and decisions necessary to set up and run a business.

Opportunity cost – the benefit lost by not consuming or producing the next best alternative product.

Specialization – focusing production on a single or limited range of products in order to make the best use of scarce resources.

Division of labour – the dividing up of a production process into a number of sequential tasks, with each one completed by a different worker or group of employees.

Customers – consumers who buy goods or services from business organizations.

Revenue – proceeds from the sale of goods and services to customers.

Profit – a surplus of revenue over costs of production.

Value added – the difference between the price of a product and the cost of the natural and man-made materials, components and resources used to make it.

Look at the pictures below. Use them to discuss with your fellow students.

▶ Which pictures show items you need for survival and which show items you simply want to enjoy?

▶ Which pictures show someone consuming a good or service?

▶ Which pictures show someone producing a good or service?

▶ What do you understand by the term "business"?

What is business?

Have you used or bought any goods or services recently? Some food perhaps, new clothes, a book or a computer game? Did you buy these items from a shop or purchase them from an online retailer using the internet? Without business activity many of the goods and services we buy and enjoy would not be available.

Few people are self-sufficient and able to make all the things they need or want for themselves. Instead we rely on business activities to provide the goods and services we need and want. The food we eat, the houses we live in, the roads we travel on, the schools we attend, the television programmes we watch and the health care services we use are all examples of goods and services provided by business activity.

People and organizations consume goods and services

We are all **consumers** because we demand goods and services to satisfy our **needs** and **wants**.

When we consume food we are satisfying our need to eat. Similarly, when we listen to music we are satisfying our want for entertainment.

In the same way, business and government organizations consume power and use machinery and component parts to make other goods and services.

Consumption therefore involves using up goods and services to satisfy our needs and wants.

▲ Consumers

Productive resources are used to make goods and services

Production involves using resources to make goods and services that satisfy our needs and wants.

Resources are the **inputs** to productive activity while **products** are the **outputs** of productive activity. **Products** can be physical **goods** such as cars and clothes, or **services** including banking, health care and retailing.

The resources used to produce goods and services are also known as **factors of production**. There are four factors of production.

- **Land** or all natural resources, including plants, animals and fish, forests and water, oil and gas, metals and other mineral and ore deposits. For example, sand is used to make glass and oil is used in petroleum, plastics and paints.

- **Labour** is the human effort needed to make goods and services.

- **Capital** refers to man-made resources, such as machinery, computers and tools, that are used in the production of other goods and services.

- **Enterprise** refers to the knowledge, skills and desire some people have to own and run business organizations.

People who run or work in business organizations are **producers**.

▲ Producers

Resources are organized into firms to produce goods and services

One day you may want to start your own business and become an **entrepreneur**. If your business is successful it will earn you a **profit**.

Entrepreneurs are producers with enterprise. They have the know-how and willingness to take the risks and decisions necessary to set up and run a business. They combine and organize resources into firms to produce goods and services.

A **firm** is an organization involved in productive activity.

There are many millions of different firms in the world today. Some are small and run by just one person called a sole trader. Other firms may be very large and have many thousands of owners called shareholders spread across many different countries. ➤ **1.4.1**

◀ Resources are organized into firms to produce goods and services

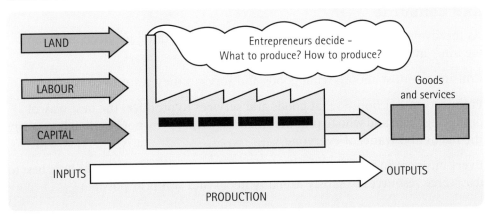

Private and public enterprises provide goods and services

Lilliana owns and runs a self-service laundry on a small island in the Caribbean. She used all her savings to buy the washing machines, laundry dryers and other equipment she needed to start her business. Lilliana's laundry is an example of a **private enterprise**.

In contrast, the government of her country supplies water to households and businesses using equipment and other resources it owns or employs. A government-owned water supplier is an example of a **public enterprise**.

Firms owned by private individuals are called **private enterprises** but some business organizations are owned and controlled by governments. Different local, regional and national government authorities may combine and organize resources to produce goods and services, including building roads and bridges, providing hospital care and national defence. Business organizations that are wholly or partly owned and controlled by government are **public enterprises**. ➤ **1.2.2**

The concepts of needs, wants and scarcity

Productive resources are scarce

World oil supplies are set to run out faster than expected, warn scientists

Business leaders complain of skills shortages among workers

Last remaining rainforests could be consumed in less than 40 years

Supply of computer chips not meeting demand, report business analysts

The news headlines to the left all highlight a major problem: there is just not enough land, labour, capital or enterprise in the world to make everything we need and want.

We all need food, clean water and some shelter from the extremes of weather in order to live safely and to survive. But we also want fashionable clothes, DVD and music players, cars, overseas holidays, insurance and banking services and much more. Just imagine if we could list everything that everyone in the world wanted. The list would go on forever!

Our wants are without limit, and as the world population grows so too our demands grow for different goods and services. Yet there is only a limited supply of factors of production available to public and private enterprises to make goods and services. That is, resources are scarce compared to our needs and wants.

People and organizations must choose what to produce and consume

As there are not enough resources to produce everything we need and want, we must make choices.

Consumers must choose what goods and services they want to consume.

Producers must choose what goods and services to produce, the best way of producing them and who to produce them for, as there will not be enough to satisfy the needs and wants of everyone.

Every business and every country in the world must therefore choose how best to use scarce resources to satisfy as many needs and wants as possible.

Human wants
UNLIMITED!

Resources
SCARCE!

Choices

What to produce?

Should more resources be used to produce consumer goods and services instead of using those resources to build roads or provide health care?

How to produce?

What tools and machinery will be needed? How many workers will be required and what skills do they need? Is it cheaper to employ more labour or more machinery?

Who to produce for?

Should people in the greatest need get the goods and services they require? Or should the goods and services be provided to people who can pay the most for them?

The concept of opportunity cost

Opportunity cost is the cost of choice

The true cost of something is what you have to give up to get it. This cost is called the **opportunity cost**.

For example, before Lilliana opened her self-service laundry in the Caribbean she had to choose between using all her savings and the small plot of land she owned to build a house and using them to build premises and buy the washing machines, laundry dryers and other equipment she needed to start her business. Before she decided to invest her savings in a laundromat, Lilliana had also considered opening a small bakery.

Lilliana therefore had to choose between a number of alternatives. First of all she decided not to use her plot of land and savings to build a house. She then decided against buying the mixers, ovens and other resources she needed to start and operate a local bakery. In both cases Lilliana gave up these opportunities to start a laundromat instead.

This is because Lilliana wanted to be her own boss and thought if she worked hard and provided a good service to local people she would make more money each year from her laundromat than she would from working in an office or a shop or from owning and running another business.

In exactly the same way, a government may have to choose between using scarce productive resources to build a new road and using them to build a new school. If the new road is built it will benefit many motorists and businesses, but many children will have to go without the benefit of a local school.

Because we do not have enough resources to satisfy all our needs and wants, we are always forced to choose between alternatives. The benefit we go without by not producing or consuming the next best alternative is our opportunity cost.

CHOICE   CHOICE

▲ Like Lilliana, we all must choose how best to use scarce productive resources

Day 1

▲ Chopping down a tree

Day 2

▲ Sitting on a rock whittling down a wooden shaft

Day 6

▲ Binding the parts together with rope to complete a spade

Day 7

▲ Using the spade to dig soil

The importance of specialization

Most modern producers specialize in the production of a single or limited range of goods or services

As resources are scarce it is vital that we make the best use of them to produce as many goods and services as possible and therefore to satisfy as many needs and wants as we can. To do this most modern producers specialize in the production of only those goods or services they are best able to given their skills and interests.

- Businesses specialize in the production of one particular good or service. For example, a car manufacturer specializes in the production of cars, a bank specializes in the provision of financial services and a supermarket specializes in buying and selling food and household goods to consumers.

- Workers specialize in a particular occupation or skill. For example, a teacher specializes in the provision of educational services, a bricklayer specializes in construction and a mechanic specializes in the repair of motor vehicles. In return they earn wages and salaries they can use to buy the goods and services they need and want but are unable to produce themselves. ➤ **2.1.2**

In contrast, many of our ancestors had to be self-sufficient, for example by growing and hunting the food they needed, making their own tools, building their own shelters, weaving cotton and wool to make clothes and producing cooking pots from clay. As a result they produced very little of each because it took so long to produce each item from start to finish and because they lacked all the different skills, equipment and resources they needed.

For example, just to make a spade our ancestors had to find, collect and cut the wood they required by hand, make rope to bind the different parts together or shape metal to produce the blade separately and make some nails to fix it to the handle. The entire production process was very slow and could take many days, even a week or more, before a finished spade was ready to dig soil to plant seeds to grow food.

It was not long therefore before people began to recognize how difficult it was trying to do so many different things at the same time. People had different skills and abilities and access to different resources. It was far better therefore for each of them to concentrate on the productive activities they were best able to perform.

For example, some people were better at making spades and pots while others were more skilled at hunting and fishing. Similarly, some villages were located on good farmland while others were located in woodland areas able to supply wood or in areas capable of being mined for iron and tin.

People and communities therefore began to specialize in different productive activities. As a result they were able to produce far more than they did before. They would then trade their different goods with each other so that each person or community could obtain the items they needed or wanted but could not produce for themselves.

Specialization therefore required trade and so businesses began to develop, such as bakeries that produced bread and cakes for sale, butchers selling meats and also toolmakers and shoemakers. As output expanded further and different goods and services became available, trade increased and more and more businesses formed and expanded.

Specialization is now widespread in every modern economy. It involves individuals and organizations focusing their resources on the limited range of productive tasks they perform best in order to maximize their productive efficiency. It is important because without specialization far fewer goods and services would be available to trade today, there would be far fewer business and employment opportunities, and incomes and living standards would be much lower.

Increased specialization in modern business has been made possible for the following reasons.

- We now exchange goods and services for money which has made trade much easier.

- Specialized machinery and equipment has been developed and is widely available to improve the quality of goods and services as well as the speed at which they are delivered. ➤ **3.3.5**

- The production of many goods has become automated using computer-controlled machinery and industrial robots to carry out specific tasks.

- People have developed more and more specialized skills.

- International specialization and trade means we are now able to buy many different goods and services from all over the world. ➤ **6.3.1**

Specialization involves the division of labour into specific tasks

Modern specialization involves dividing up the production process for any given good or service into a number of sequential tasks.

Doing this has helped increase the speed and quality of many production processes and greatly increased the amount of goods and services that can be produced with scarce resources. This is because each task in a given production process can be performed by different machines, equipment and workers devoted to that particular task. This is called the **division of labour**. ➤ **4.1.2**

By completing the same task over and over again each worker becomes more and more skilled at doing so. For example, in the early days of the car industry one employee would put together an entire engine. Then Henry Ford decided to divide up the work involved into 84 different operations, so that 84 employees were needed to build a whole engine instead of just one person. However, it meant many more engines and therefore cars could be built each day. The very first Model T Ford car was produced in 1907 and took over 12 hours to assemble. After Henry Ford had divided up his production process and labour into a set of sequential tasks, a completed Model T Ford rolled off the assembly line at the rate of 1 every 10 seconds each working day. As output increased, the price of cars came down and the wages of the workers and profits of the manufacturers went up.

While the division of labour has many clear advantages it also has a number of downsides that can harm production and profitability in modern businesses.

Component parts are delivered to the start of the assembly line

Workers program industrial robots to complete individual tasks

Each worker completes a different task, including fitting the engine, bumpers, headlamps and car interior

The finished car is tested and ready for delivery to car showrooms for sale

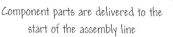

▲ The division of labour in a modern car factory

Advantages of labour specialization	Disadvantages of labour specialization
✓ Employees can make best use of their particular talents and skills.	✗ Individuals must rely on others to produce the goods and services they want but cannot produce themselves.
✓ Employees can increase their skills and experience by repeating tasks.	✗ Workers can become bored doing the same job or completing repetitive tasks. The quality and efficiency of their work may fall.
✓ Employees can produce more output and reduce business costs if they concentrate on the same job or tasks.	✗ Many repetitive manual tasks are now undertaken by computer-controlled machinery and robots. This has reduced job satisfaction for many workers and reduced employment opportunities for many low-skilled workers.
✓ More productive employees can earn higher wages.	

Adding value and how business can increase added value

Value is added by satisfying customer needs and wants

Business involves organizing and combining resources to make final outputs that are more desirable to consumers. Each business specializes in the production of a single or limited range of goods or services it is best able to supply to consumers given the skills and resources available to it. In this way, a business adds value to the resources it uses.

The **value added** by a business activity is the difference between the price paid for a product by a consumer and the cost of natural and man-made materials, components, tools and equipment used to make it.

For example, Java Crafts in Indonesia adds value to solid teak and mahogany wood, and to other resources such as tools, glues, waxes and varnishes, by making high-quality handmade and antique reproduction furniture that is sold to consumers all over the world.

The skilled designers and furniture makers at Java Crafts buy the wood, waxes and other resources they need to make furniture from other businesses. Imagine that it costs Java Crafts $400 to buy the resources it needs to produce a dining table and four chairs. If Java Crafts can sell the table and chairs for $1000 the business will have added $600 to the value of these resources.

The consumer who pays $1000 to buy the set of furniture becomes a personal customer of Java Crafts. However, there are many different businesses producing tables and chairs so Java Crafts must compete with them to attract customers. Offering better value and service than rival firms can help the furniture maker achieve this. ➤ 1.5.1

A business that fails to attract customers will be unable to sell its products and will not add any value to the resources it has used.

ACTIVITY 1.2

BP is one of the world's largest petroleum and petrochemicals businesses. It employs many thousands of people and owns drilling platforms, pipelines, oil tankers, refineries, petrochemical plants and retail outlets all over the world.

Crude oil is a raw product produced by drilling into natural reserves deep underground. It is a complicated mixture of different natural chemicals. These can be isolated and produced for sale by heating up or refining the crude oil. They include diesel fuel, jet fuel, gasoline, grease, heavy fuel oil (used in boilers and to "fire up" coal-burning power stations) and a product called "Naphtha" that is used to make many different petrochemical products including resins and solvents.

1 Give examples of natural and man-made resources used by BP to produce petroleum and petrochemical products.

2 What evidence is there about how BP "adds value" to the resources it uses to produce petroleum and petrochemical products?

When is a consumer a customer?

Consumers are people and organizations willing and able to buy goods and services. Consumers are potential customers for business organizations. Businesses compete with each other for customers. Consumers become **customers** of business organizations when they buy their goods and services.

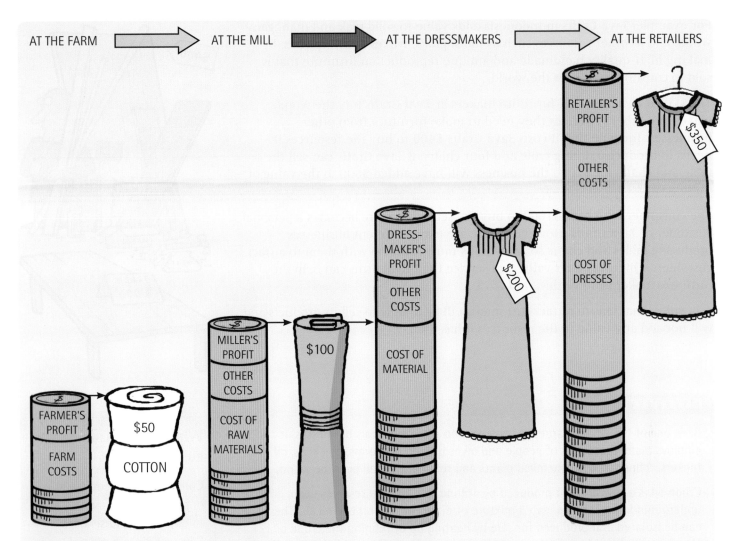

AT THE FARM ➡ AT THE MILL ➡ AT THE DRESSMAKERS ➡ AT THE RETAILERS

Stage 1: A farm spends $40 on seeds, fertilizers and other resources to grow cotton. After the harvest the farm produces a bale of raw cotton and sells this for $50 to a mill. The farm has therefore added **$10** to the resources it used to produce the cotton.

Stage 2: The mill spins and dyes the raw cotton to make a roll of cotton fabric. In addition to the cost of $50 for the bale of cotton it buys dyes, tools and other resources worth $20. The mill sells the roll of fabric to a clothing company for $100. It has therefore added **$30** in value to the bale of cotton and other resources used.

Stage 3: The clothing company has paid the mill $100 for the roll of fabric and spends a further $60 buying sewing and cutting equipment and some other materials. It uses these to make 10 dresses and sells these to a dress shop for $200. The clothing company has therefore added **$40** in value to the fabric and other resources it used.

Stage 4: In addition to the $200 paid for the dresses, the shop also faces advertising and running costs of $50. It sells each dress for $35, raising $350 from the sale of all 10. The shop has therefore added a further **$100** in value to the dresses.

In total the entire process has added **$180** in value to all the resources used to produce and sell dresses.

▲ Adding value – an example

Value is added by providing employment and incomes

If a business can sell its products for much more than the cost of the natural materials and man-made items used to produce them then it can use this money to employ workers and still make a profit for the business owners.

Business organizations pay people wages and salaries to work in their factories, offices, shops and other places of production to produce and sell their goods and services. In this way value is added to their labour. This is because if they were unemployed they would not be productive and would not be paid wages or salaries.

Business activity therefore "adds value" to labour by creating jobs and incomes for people.

Similarly, to obtain other factors of production business organizations must pay the owners of these resources to supply them. Owners of shops, offices and factories used by firms require rent to supply their premises. Similarly, people and organizations that produce natural or man-made resources must be paid to supply them.

How can businesses increase their value added?

A business can increase the value it adds by:

- increased specialization and using resources as efficiently as possible
- reducing waste
- reducing the costs of the natural and man-made resources it must buy or hire, for example by finding cheaper suppliers

- making products more attractive to consumers so they are willing to pay a higher price for them
- making its products more appealing to consumers through **advertising**
- creating a recognized **brand**, such as Coca-Cola, that consumers are willing to pay more for.

Motorola today unveiled a new line of mobile phones to meet the needs of mass-market consumers. All the new phones feature compact designs and easy-to-use keypads, with talk times of up to 700 minutes and up to 450 hours of standby, reducing the need for frequent recharging. Value added features also available on some models include a 65 000 pixel colour screen, a multimedia messaging service (MMS), zoom font, polyphonic ringtones, a built-in FM stereo radio and video camera.

Megamart is the retail business of India's largest textile manufacturer, Arvind Ltd. It adds value to the clothes it makes by providing them in a convenient way for customers.

Megamart's highly popular large-format stores offer a wide range of high-quality brand name merchandise in a concentrated space to consumers at competitive prices, and also include products such as luggage, footwear and lifestyle electronics.

▲ How two major businesses are adding more value in production

The purpose of business activity

Combining and organizing resources to produce goods and services

We have now looked at the reasons for business activity and what it does. Here is a summary of why business activity is needed:

- Few people are self-sufficient and able to make all the goods and services they need and want. We therefore rely on business activity to produce goods and services to satisfy our needs and wants.
- Productive resources need to be combined and organized to produce goods and services.
- Productive resources are scarce and we cannot produce enough to satisfy all human needs and wants. Business organizations therefore help to determine what goods and services to produce, how to produce them and who to produce them for.
- A business can add value to the resources it uses by specializing in the production and supply of one or more goods or services that consumers want and are willing to pay for.
- Businesses pay the owners of factors of production to supply their resources, including the payment of wages and salaries for labour. People use their income to buy the goods and services they need and want from different business organizations.

What do you think are the main goals or objectives of the business activities in each of the pictures and newspaper articles below?

The Royal Swaziland Sugar Corporation reports record profit

RSSC is one of Swaziland's largest businesses, producing two-thirds of the country's sugar. Last year the group announced a record profit of $200 million, principally due to rising sugar prices and increased ethanol production.

Recreation Ground

HESSINGTON

CRICKET & SPORTS CLUB

Telephone : 008 4321 567

Public health care in Brazil

Public health care is provided to all permanent residents in Brazil and is free at the point of need. The federal government aims to improve the overall health of the population, with particular emphasis on the reduction of child mortality through improved efficiency and delivery of universal health care.

Jakarta Animal Aid Network (JAAN) is a non-governmental, non-profit organization established to help protect Indonesian wildlife and to improve the welfare of Jakarta's stray dogs and cats.

▲ Profit is a surplus of revenue over total costs

The purpose of most business activity is to make a profit

How do entrepreneurs earn an income from owning and running a business?

Unlike labour, entrepreneurs do not get paid a wage or salary. Instead they aim to make a **profit** by selling the goods or services they make at a price greater than the total cost of producing them including wages and other payments to employees. Profit motivates entrepreneurs to run businesses.
➤ **1.5.1**

- **Costs** are incurred by a business because it must buy or hire the resources it needs in order to produce goods and services.

- **Revenues** are earned by a business when it sells goods and services to customers.

- **Profit** is achieved when revenues from selling goods and services exceeds the cost of their production.

- A business will make a **loss** if its revenues are not enough to cover its costs.

If an entrepreneur makes a loss he or she will be losing the opportunity to earn a profit from producing another good or service instead. Alternatively, an entrepreneur could close the loss-making business and earn a wage or salary as an employee of another business organization. ➤ **2.1.2**

Some business organizations do not aim to make a profit

Not all businesses aim to make a profit. Some businesses are non-profit making and have other goals or **objectives**.

- Charities aim to help people or animals in need, or to protect the natural environment. They rely on donations or gifts of money to pay for their costs.
- Local social or sports clubs are organized and run by their members. They may pay a small membership fee to cover the costs of newsletters and the hire of venues.
- Government organizations may provide **public services** free of charge, including free health care and bus travel for elderly people and people on low incomes. The cost of their provision is funded from tax revenues. ➤ **1.5.3**

Exam PREPARATION 1.1

Sanyu is an apprentice in a large manufacturing company. As well as training on-the-job, he must also attend college one day each week to learn engineering and business skills. Sanyu has read in his business textbook that for a business to be successful and profitable it must add value to the resources it uses. Table 1 is a task from his textbook.

Table 1: Adding value in production

Type of business	Raw materials	How value is added	Final product
Paint manufacturer	Minerals to provide different pigments (colours)	Grinding and mixing the minerals with solvents and other chemicals	Cans of paint
Food processor (ready-made meals)			Meal

a Complete table 1 by identifying **one** example of a raw material a food processor would use in the production of ready-meals and **one** example of an activity, method or process the business would use to add value to raw materials. [2]

b Define "added value"? [2]

Sanyu's uncle owns a small business that manufactures business shirts.

c If the cost of materials used by Sanyu's uncle to produce each shirt is $10 and each shirt sells for $30, calculate the value added. [4]

d Explain **three** ways in which Sanyu's uncle could try to increase the value added by his business. [6]

e If Sanyu's uncle is successful at adding value to the resources he uses to produce business shirts do you think that his business will be profitable? Justify your answer. [6]

Before you continue make sure you are able to

Understand the purpose and nature of **business activity**:

✓ the concepts of **needs, wants, scarcity** and **opportunity cost**

✓ the importance of **specialization**

✓ the purpose of business activity

✓ the concept of adding value and how **added value** can be increased.

Learning CHECKLIST

Clues down

1 Consumers' desires for goods and services. They are unlimited (5)
3 The term used to describe natural resources used in the production of other goods and services (4)
5 People must choose between alternative uses of resources because resources are scarce relative to consumer wants. One use of a given amount of resources therefore involves giving up another. What term is used to describe the benefit lost from doing so? (11, 4)
8 Term used to describe human resources used in the production of goods and services (6)
9 Business owners and employees who are willing and able to produce and supply goods and services (9)
11 A surplus of revenue over costs, and the main objective for many private enterprises (6)
12 The increase in the "value" of resources used up in the production of a good or service to satisfy a consumer need or want. It is measured by the difference between the price paid for the product and the cost of natural and man-made resources used to make it (5, 5)
14 Organizing and combining resources into firms to make goods and services (8)

Clues across

2 This involves producers focusing their resources on the limited range of productive tasks they perform best in order to maximize their productive efficiency (14)
4 The using up of goods and services by people and organizations to satisfy their needs and wants (11)
6 Another term used to describe goods and services (8)
7 Scarce resources are organized and combined into these organizations by entrepreneurs. It is another term used to describe business organizations (5)
10 Money raised by a business from the sale of goods and services to their customers (7)
13 The separation of a production process into a number of sequential tasks, each one completed by a different worker or group of employees (8, 2, 6)
15 The process of making goods and services to satisfy consumer needs and wants (10)
16 Term used to describe man-made resources, such as machinery and tools, used to make other goods and services (7)
17 People and organizations who are willing and able to buy goods and services (9)

1.2.1 Business activity in terms of primary, secondary and tertiary sectors

1.2.2 Classify business enterprises between private sector and public sector in a mixed economy

▶ The production or extraction of natural resources is the first stage of production for many products. Industries in the primary sector of an economy produce natural resources.

▶ The secondary sector of an economy includes industries engaged in manufacturing and construction.

▶ The final stage of production involves the distribution and sale of products to consumers. These and other services are provided by service industries in the tertiary sector of an economy.

▶ Most people in developed economies are employed in services. Manufacturing output and employment has been shrinking over time. In contrast, secondary and tertiary industries are growing rapidly in many developing economies.

▶ Production, consumption and trade take place within an economy. In a mixed economy these activities can be organized by private individuals and businesses as well as by government-owned and government-controlled organizations.

▶ Privately owned businesses are part of the private sector of a mixed economy while business enterprises owned by government are part of its public sector. The size and importance of the public sector has changed in many economies over time.

Key POINTS

PUBLIC SECTOR

PRIVATE SECTOR

Business BUZZWORDS

Industrial sector – a group of firms specializing in similar products or using similar production processes.

Primary sector – industries that produce or extract natural resources.

Manufacturing – the process of converting natural resources into other products.

Secondary sector – industries involved in processing natural resources, manufacturing or construction.

Tertiary sector – service industries.

Industrial structure – the relative size and importance of industrial sectors in an economy.

Developed economy – a country with a wide range of industries and a large tertiary sector.

De-industrialization – the decline of manufacturing and the growth of services in developed economies.

Developing economy – a country that is seeking to develop its resources, create jobs and increase incomes and living standards through industrialization.

Private sector – that part of an economy owned and operated by private individuals and privately owned businesses.

Public sector – that part of an economy owned and controlled by government and government-owned organizations.

Mixed economy – an economy that combines private sector and public sector ownership of resources and provision of goods and services.

The basis of business classification

Businesses can be classified by industry and how they are owned

There are many different types of business. It is useful therefore to identify and compare businesses according to:

- the types of goods and services they specialize in

- how they are owned and controlled.

Production involves a chain of different business activities

Rather than trying to produce many different goods and services, a business specializes in the production of one or a limited range of products. Specialization means a business can make the best possible use of the skills and productive resources it has and therefore add much more value to them. ➤ **1.1.1**

▶ The Toyota Motor Corporation specializes in making cars, buses and commercial vehicles and HSBC specializes in providing financial services

However, specialization also means that a business will need to obtain many of the other goods and services it needs for production from other firms, such as materials, machines, power, insurance and banking services. A business may also need to use the services of a recruitment agency to hire workers, a haulage company to transport its products, an advertising agency to promote them and many other businesses. This is because the production of any given good or service normally involves a **chain of productive activity**.

Each chain of productive activity links together many different firms and activities – from those businesses producing natural resources such as coal, corn and oil, to those that use these materials to make component parts and finished goods and services for consumers, and finally to those that operate warehouses, transport services and shops to distribute and sell products to customers.

For example, look at the chain of productive activity in the diagram on the next page. It shows there are different **stages of production** involved in making and selling bread.

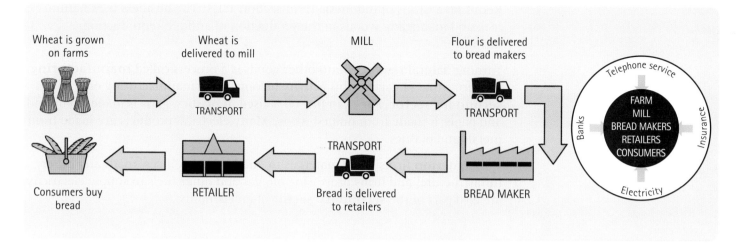
▼ A chain of production for bread

Similar business activities are grouped together into industries

It is useful to classify or group business activities into industrial sectors.

An **industrial sector** or **industry** is a group of firms specializing in the production or sale of the same or very similar goods or services or using very similar production processes. An industry includes small, local firms employing very few workers and large, national or even multinational firms employing many thousands of workers and selling products all over the world.

For example, the automotive manufacturing industry consists of all firms making and supplying vehicles and engines, tyres, body parts and components. Similarly, the air transport industry includes all firms providing air passenger and airfreight transport services and facilities, including airports and airlines.

Industries in the primary sector extract or produce natural resources

The production or extraction of natural resources is the first stage of production for most goods and services.

Industries in the **primary sector** of an economy specialize in the production or extraction of natural resources by growing crops, managing forests, mining coal and other minerals, and extracting oils and gases.

Some primary sector industries

- Crop and animal production
- Forestry and logging
- Fishing
- Mining
- Quarrying
- Oil and gas extraction

Industries in the secondary sector process natural resources

Recall Java Crafts of Indonesia from section 1.1.1. The business uses natural teak and mahogany woods in the production of antique reproduction furniture.

Turning natural resources into other goods is a process called **manufacturing** and firms that engage in this activity belong to the manufacturing or **secondary sector**. For example, oil is used in plastics, glass is made from sand and paper is made from pulped wood. Many electrical products are made from metals and plastics.

Construction firms using materials to build homes, offices, roads and other infrastructure, and firms processing oil, gas and other fuels to supply electricity are also part of the **secondary sector** of an economy.

Some secondary sector industries

- Food processing
- Textiles
- Paper, pulp and paperboard
- Chemicals
- Oil and gas refining
- Pharmaceuticals
- Rubber and plastic products
- Fabricated metals
- Computer, electronic and optical products
- Water collection, treatment and supply
- Electric power generation, transmission and distribution
- Construction

Industries in the tertiary sector provide services

In section 1.1.1 we learnt about a laundromat business owned and managed by Lilliana in the Caribbean. It provides a clothes washing and drying service for people in her town. Her business is part of the tertiary sector in the country in which she lives.

Firms that provide services are part of the **tertiary sector** of an economy. The distribution and sale of manufactured goods and the provision of services to consumers is the final stage in their production. Firms in the wholesale and retailing industries specialize in these activities.

However, there are many businesses providing services that are used at every stage of production such as banking, insurance and transport. Some firms also provide personal services such as hairdressing, decorating, health care and personal training.

Some tertiary sector industries

- Wholesaling, retailing and repairs
- Transportation and storage
- Accommodation and food services
- Publishing and broadcasting
- Telecommunications
- Banking and insurance
- Real estate
- Public administration
- Defence services
- Education
- Arts and entertainment
- Health care
- Legal services
- Internet services

ACTIVITY 1.4

1 Arrange the following list of industries into primary, secondary or tertiary sector activities.

Dairy farming	Ship building
Newspaper printing	Nuclear fuel processing
Investment banking	Licensed restaurants
Footwear manufacture	Freight rail transport
Grain milling	Newspaper publishing
Salt extraction	Motion picture distribution
Carpet weaving	Site demolition
Cement production	Motor vehicle repair
Cargo handling	Tax consultancy

2 Which of the following well-known global businesses are primary, secondary or tertiary sector activities? (Note that some may have activities in more than one sector.)

Royal Dutch Shell	Vodafone
Ford Motor	FedEx
Hewlett-Packard	Pfizer
Boeing	Google
Dell	McDonald's
PepsiCo	Mercedes-Benz
Walt Disney	Sony

Reasons for the changing importance of business classification

An economic system involves production and consumption

Every country has an **economy** involving all business activities and the exchange of goods and services for money between producers and consumers.

For example, the Kenyan economic system is the national economy of Kenya. In turn, the Kenyan economy is part of the African economy including all other African countries. Similarly, all national economies are part of the global economy. ➤ **6.3.1**

The mix of industrial sectors in different economies has changed over time

The **industrial structure** of a national economy is determined by the relative size and importance of its different industrial sectors and the industries within them. Industrial structures vary significantly between different economies and can change over time as their economies develop and consumer incomes and spending increase, thereby increasing demand for more and different types of goods and services.

Every economy has a primary, secondary and tertiary sector but in some countries the primary sector is the most important while in others the most important is the secondary or tertiary sector.

The two main ways to measure and compare the size and importance of different industrial sectors in an economy involve looking at:

- how much output they each produce as a proportion of national output
- how many workers they employ as a proportion of total national employment.

The most **developed economies** have a wide range of different industries, especially in the tertiary sector and in advanced or hi-tech, high value added manufacturing. Industries in these countries are supported by highly skilled workforces and modern technical infrastructure including road and telecommunications networks, airports and education and research institutions.

These countries were the first in the world to develop large-scale manufacturing industries around 200 years ago. However, more recently manufacturing output and employment has declined in many developed economies including the United States (US), Canada, France and the United Kingdom (UK). Mechanization and the ability to import cheaper raw materials from other countries has also reduced the importance of their primary industries to their economies. However, as average incomes have risen in these countries, consumer spending on many services has increased. As a result the tertiary sector has expanded significantly in these economies and now employs over 75% of all their workers and produces over 70% of their total output.

The decline of manufacturing and the growth of services in developed economies is called **de-industrialization**.

Consumers in developed economies now buy many of the manufactured goods they need and want from **newly industrialized economies**, also known as **emerging or developing economies**, including Brazil, China, India and Malaysia. Wage costs are much lower in these countries than in developed countries. This means they are able to produce many goods more cheaply than firms in developed economies. Manufacturing output and employment has therefore expanded significantly in these and other emerging economies through international trade.

In contrast, some countries have a low level of economic development. They have relatively few industries and lack modern infrastructure. Most of their workers are employed in primary industries, especially in agriculture. These countries have less-developed economies. Average incomes, and therefore consumer spending in these economies, are low. Many people also lack the skills and capital they need to start and grow businesses.

For example, the chart opposite shows the distribution of employment in the African country of Liberia, one of the least developed countries in the world. It shows that 70% of the Liberian workforce is currently employed in agriculture. This has changed very little over time.

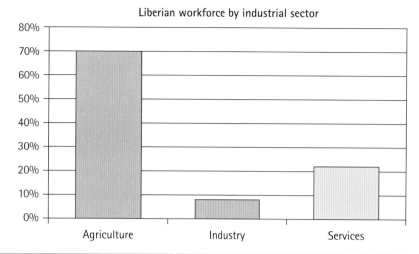

Liberian workforce by industrial sector

Developed economy	Rapidly developing economy	Less-developed economy
• There is a small primary sector. • Manufacturing output and employment have declined. • The service sector has expanded significantly. • Incomes and living standards are generally good for most people. People spend a large proportion of their incomes on services. • A wide variety of goods and services are available to consumers.	• There is a large but shrinking primary sector, especially in agriculture. • The manufacturing sector is expanding rapidly. Workers from agriculture and mining have been attracted to higher-paid jobs in manufacturing. • Service sector output and employment are also growing. • Incomes and living standards for many people are improving. • The amount and variety of goods and services available are growing quickly.	• Most workers are employed in agriculture and other primary industries. • There are very few manufacturing industries. • The service sector is small and growing only very slowly. • Incomes and living standards for many people are poor. • Few goods and services are available to consumers.

ACTIVITY 1.5

The charts below show the proportion of total output produced by different sectors in two countries.

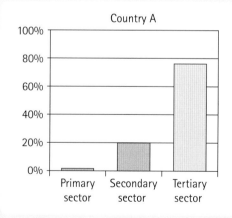

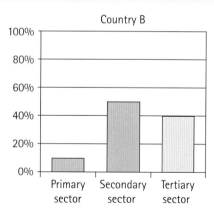

▶ Which country do you think has a developed economy?

▶ Which country do you think has a newly industrialized or rapidly developing economy?

▶ What do you think the chart for country B could look like in 30 years' time?

▶ Which chart do you think most resembles the industrial structure of the economy in your country?

What is a mixed economy?

Business enterprises may be privately or publicly owned and controlled in a mixed economy

Another way to classify business enterprises is by the way they are owned and controlled. ➤ **1.4.1**

Production in any **mixed economy** is organized by:

- business enterprises owned and controlled by private individuals and companies; they are part of the **private sector** of an economy

- organizations owned and controlled by government authorities; they are part of the **public sector** of an economy.

The public sector is a major employer, producer and consumer in many modern economies. For example, the public sector of Norway employs 35% of the total Norwegian workforce. This compares to public sector employment of less than 10% of the workforce in Chile.

Xian-Li is the Chief Executive of one of Hong Kong's public hospitals funded by the government. Her job is to ensure the objectives of the hospital and the government's health care policy are met.

"The hospital is not required to make a profit from the provision of health care" she explained, "but it does have to meet targets for patient care and satisfaction, treatment waiting times, hospital cleanliness, and surgical and running costs."

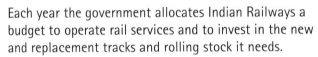

Indian Railways is the state-owned railway company of India, which owns and operates most of the country's rail transport.

Each year the government allocates Indian Railways a budget to operate rail services and to invest in the new and replacement tracks and rolling stock it needs.

Pradesh Verma, a regional manager, explained that all the railway managers are accountable to the Indian Parliament. "We are entrusted by government to spend public money efficiently", he said, "and to meet performance targets for punctuality, safety, passenger and freight traffic and more."

"Ticket prices are kept low to enable people on low incomes to use the rail service and to carry freight to rural areas where there may be no other means of getting goods to people who need them. However, the company is still expected to generate an operating surplus or profit each year for the government."

The two organizations above are owned and controlled by their governments. They are part of the public sector in the economies of Hong Kong and India and they have very different objectives from many private sector organizations. ➤ **1.5.3**

Public sector organizations include:

- **national, regional and local government authorities** and their administrative departments, ministries and offices responsible for economic policies, laws and regulations, taxation and government spending

- **government agencies** responsible for running specific administrative functions and services, such as an intelligence agency, statistical agency or food standards agency

- **public corporations** that are business-like organizations created to carry out particular public sector functions, such as a municipal water company, hospital or central bank. ➤ **1.4.1**

Public sector enterprises can provide goods and services people need that private sector firms are unwilling or unable to produce

Most private sector businesses aim to make a profit from their activities. They do this by producing goods and services that consumers want and are able to buy at prices that exceed their costs of production.

This profit motive encourages private sector businesses to:

- produce a wide variety of different goods and services to satisfy consumer wants

- respond quickly to changes in consumer wants and spending patterns, otherwise they would lose sales and profits

- develop new and innovative products and production methods to reduce costs, boost sales and increase their profits

- ensure their production is efficient by making the best use of scarce resources and keeping their costs as low as possible.

However, goods and services that are not profitable will not be produced by privately owned firms even if those goods and services are beneficial or even essential for people and other businesses to have. In a mixed economy these goods and services can be provided by public sector organizations. Unlike private sector firms, most public sector organizations do not aim to make a profit from their activities. Instead they provide many beneficial or essential services either free of charge or at prices even people on low incomes can afford to pay; for example street lighting, police services and national security are provided to protect public and economic interest.

Public services such as health care and education have significant social and economic benefits: a modern economy needs a healthy and skilled workforce. Some health care and education may also be provided for profit by private sector organizations but will only be affordable to people with the highest incomes and greatest ability to pay.

The full cost of providing public sector services considered essential or beneficial, including health care, education and street lighting, is financed from tax revenues collected by a government from the incomes and wealth of private individuals and businesses. ➤ **6.1.1**

However, some public sector organizations are **trading bodies** and, like Indian Railways in the article on the previous page, they produce and sell services to earn revenues that will cover their costs and for some, return a profit. For example, public sector trading bodies may sell rail and bus services, electricity and water supplies.

Trading bodies are run by **public corporations**. Any profits made by trading bodies can be either reinvested in improving the services they provide or used by their government to help fund the provision of other public sector services. ➤ **1.4.1**

▲ Public services are often provided for no direct charge

Cuba to cut one million public sector jobs

The Cuban government has started giving up its control of the economy. Inefficient and unnecessary public sector companies will close and those laid off will be encouraged to become self-employed or join new private enterprises.

The size and importance of the public sector has changed over time in many economies

In some mixed economies, the size of the public sector in terms of employment and contribution to national output exceeds that of the private sector.

For example, in 2013 the public sector in the Philippines was responsible for just 16% of the total value of output that year as measured by its total spending on goods and services. In contrast, the public sector of Cuba accounted for over 66% of the total output of the Cuban economy.

However, the government of Cuba has been changing the balance between its public sector and private sector. In 1991 the public sector of Cuba employed 91% of its total workforce and public sector spending accounted for almost 90% of total output. Today, the private sector of Cuba employs around 28% of the Cuban workforce.

The same is true in many other economies, even those with much smaller public sectors than Cuba. Many governments have been reducing their public sectors by:

- selling off or transferring public sector enterprises and activities to private sector firms – this is called **privatization**; for example, many governments have transferred the provision of electricity, mail delivery, refuse collection and rail and bus services from the public sector to private sector firms

- encouraging the private sector to create more output and jobs, for example by cutting taxes on businesses and providing grants and other support to business start-ups. ➤ **1.1.1**

▶ Many countries have been reducing the size of their public sectors to reduce costs and increase efficiency

Italy's new government targets ambitious public spending cuts

Pakistan plans privatization of state-owned Pakistan International Airlines Corporation to reduce losses

UK prime minister argues cuts to public spending will pay for lower taxes

Brazil to cut $18.5 billion in public spending

Reducing the size of the public sector in an economy and encouraging growth in the private sector is argued to have the following advantages.

➤ Running public sector organizations is expensive. They employ many people and consume many goods and services. Their costs are financed from taxes paid to the government from the incomes and wealth of private individuals and businesses. Reducing the size of the public sector can therefore allow the government to reduce taxes. ➤ **1.1.1**

➤ Many public sector organizations are not required to make a profit so they can be inefficient and wasteful. Private sector firms make better use of resources in order to reduce their costs and increase their output and revenues because they aim to make profits.

- Public sector enterprises are usually not in competition with other firms. However, private sector firms do compete with each other for customers and sales. To do so each firm will try to offer better-quality products and lower prices compared to rival businesses.

- Growth in the public sector requires more government spending funded from taxes. In contrast, private sector firms are funded privately and can be more entrepreneurial. They can respond to new business opportunities and will create more jobs, incomes and output to benefit the economy.
   ➤ **6.1.1**

However, because private firms want to make profits they may employ fewer workers than public sector organizations in order to cut their costs. This means more people will be unemployed.

In addition, some private firms may charge higher prices for important services such as electricity supplies, rail and bus services to maximize their profits and because consumers have few alternatives they can use instead. ➤ **3.3.2**

ACTIVITY 1.6

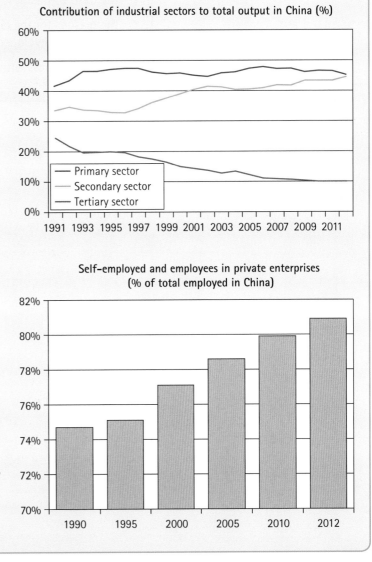

China to work on developing private sector

The Chinese government has set development of the non-public sector as one of its main tasks in the year ahead. Experts say that a bigger private sector will bring entrepreneurial vitality and more economic growth.

For example, the government has introduced policies to attract private capital to sectors such as railways, energy and telecommunications.

Li Yong of the China Association of International Trade said, "It's a good opportunity for private enterprises. Their participation in the economy will help boost efficiency due to competition."

The private sector has grown significantly over the last two decades. It now contributes 60% of China's national output compared to 29% in 1995, pays 50% of taxes and has created more than 70% of new jobs.

Contribution of industrial sectors to total output in China (%)

- Primary sector
- Secondary sector
- Tertiary sector

Self-employed and employees in private enterprises (% of total employed in China)

- ▶ What evidence is there in the charts and article that:
  - the Chinese economy has been developing rapidly
  - the Chinese government has been encouraging growth of the private sector and reducing the contribution of the public sector to the economy?

- ▶ From the article, identify and explain two reasons why the Chinese government wants to encourage growth of the private sector in the Chinese economy.

Country Y has a mixed economy: 48% of the 30 million people employed work in the secondary sector.

a   Define "secondary sector".   [2]

b   Calculate the number of people employed in the secondary sector.   [2]

c   Explain the term "mixed economy".   [4]

d   Explain **one** advantage and **one** disadvantage of reducing the size
    of the public sector.   [6]

e   Outline **three** possible reasons why the public sector produces
    good and services.   [6]

Learning CHECKLIST

Before you continue make sure you are able to

Identify and explain business activity in terms of **primary**, **secondary** and **tertiary sectors**:

✓   the basis of **business classification**

✓   the reasons for the changing importance of business classification, for example in **developed and developing economies**

✓   classify business enterprises as **private sector** or **public sector** in a **mixed economy**.

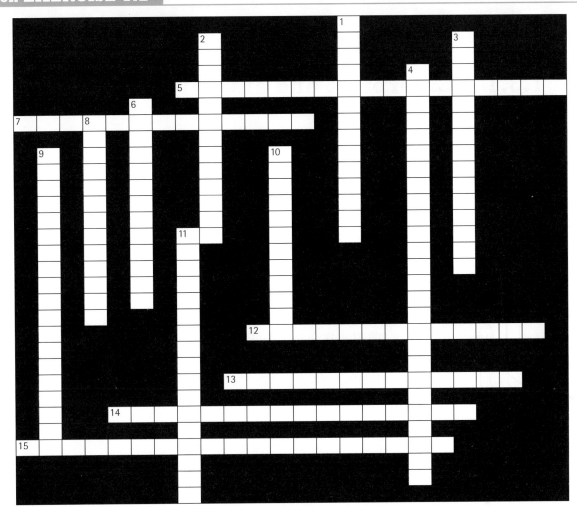

Clues down

1   All those industries in an economy providing services (8, 6)
2   A national economy that combines a private sector with public sector ownership and organization of resources for the purpose of productive activity (6, 7)
3   All manufacturing and construction industries in an economy (9, 6)
4   Another term used to describe a developing economy that has rapidly expanded its industrial base through growth in its manufacturing industries (5, 14, 7)
6   Public sector enterprises that earn revenue from the sale of goods or services direct to consumers (7, 6)
8   The process of turning unprocessed natural resources and other unfinished products into other, more desirable or useful goods (13)
9   A term that describes the proportion of total output and employment in a national economy resulting from the activities of different productive sectors, notably primary, secondary and tertiary (10, 9)
10 That part of a mixed economy owned and controlled by government (6, 6)
11 A collective term used to classify any group of firms in an economy specializing in the production of similar goods and services or using similar production processes (10, 7)

Clues across

5   A less-developed economy that is now experiencing rapid structural change, notably growth in the size and importance of its secondary and tertiary sectors (10, 7)
7   All extractive industries or those producing natural resources in an economy. Alternatively, it refers to all firms involved in the first stage of a chain of productive activity (7, 6)
12 The sale or transfer of public sector enterprises and activities to private sector firms (13)
13 That part of a mixed economy owned and controlled by private individuals and privately owned enterprises (7, 6)
14 Term used to describe any country that has a high level of economic development, including high average incomes, modern infrastructure and a wide range of secondary and tertiary industries (9, 7)
15 The observed decline in the size and importance of the manufacturing sector in many developed economies in terms of its contribution to total output and employment (19)

1.3.1 Enterprise and entrepreneurship

- Business know-how, and the ability and willingness to organize and manage the production of goods and services, is known as enterprise. People who are enterprising and use their skills to start and run businesses are entrepreneurs.

- Not everybody is suited to organizing and running a business. An entrepreneur must be prepared to take financial and other risks and work long hours.

- The most successful entrepreneurs are those who are self-motivated, confident, ambitious, able to learn from their own mistakes and from others, innovative and good communicators.

- Entrepreneurship is therefore the process of identifying a business opportunity, organizing the resources needed to start and run a business and taking both the risks and the rewards it involves.

- Starting a business requires careful research and planning. A business plan helps an entrepreneur to turn a business idea into a business, to set objectives for the business and to identify the resources and actions needed to achieve them.

- The contents of a good business plan should include details of the proposed ownership, location and objectives of the business, a plan for production, an assessment of the market for the product, its resource requirements and financial projections.

- Governments often provide financial and other support to help entrepreneurs start new businesses, especially in areas of high unemployment, because they create jobs for people, and increase output and competition. For example, governments may provide non-repayable grants and low-cost loans to help pay towards machinery and equipment, and offer free advice and training in business skills.

Business BUZZWORDS

Enterprise – business know-how, skills and qualities including the willingness to take considered financial and other business risks.

Entrepreneur – an enterprising person who is willing and able to take the risks and decisions necessary to organize resources to produce goods and services.

Entrepreneurship – the process of identifying a business opportunity, organizing the resources needed to start and run a business and taking both the risks and the rewards it involves.

Business plan – a written statement about a business idea: how it will be organized, what the owners want to achieve with it and how they will do so.

Government grant – a non-repayable sum of money given by a local, state or central government to another person or organization for a particular purpose; for example, to fund business start-up including the purchase of equipment and/or training.

What is enterprise?

Starting your own business can be risky but may be more rewarding than working for another organization

Business know-how, or the ability to organize and manage the production of goods and services, is known as **enterprise**. People who have enterprise and use their skills to organize resources into firms are **entrepreneurs**. They are the people who take the risks and decisions necessary to make businesses run successfully.

Not everybody is suited to organizing and running a business. It means being able to manage yourself and others, to prioritize and organize your own time, and make all the decisions. Not everyone wants to be responsible for their own hours of work, their own earnings and their own success or failure. Some people therefore prefer working for someone else because paid employment involves less risk and provides a steady income.

Starting and running your own business therefore has a number of advantages and disadvantages any would-be entrepreneur should consider before deciding to do so.

Advantages of being an entrepreneur	Disadvantages of being an entrepreneur
✓ **Making best use of your skills and interests**: running and owning your own business can be more satisfying than working in a job that is dull and repetitive.	✗ **Increased risk**: many new businesses fail within their first few years resulting in their owners losing the capital they invested in them.
✓ **Being independent**: being able to take decisions, for example about the hours you work and who you want to work with, rather than being told what to do by an employer.	✗ **Increased responsibility**: for taking all the decisions necessary to run and manage a business and possibly also for managing employees.
✓ **Increased motivation**: from being able to put your own ideas into practice, taking big decisions that will affect your future and being rewarded with profit if your business venture is successful.	✗ **Long hours**: business owners often have to work very long hours and if there is no one else to help them they will lose revenues and profits if they take time off for holidays or when they are ill.
✓ **The potential to earn more income**: by working hard to make your business successful and profitable.	✗ **High opportunity cost**: the loss of a steady income from regular paid employment.

> You need:
> - a burning wish to succeed
> - a pride in being different
> - a desire to be your own boss
> - a realization that success is 90% hard work and determination and only 10% talent.

Leah Hertz,

Successful author and businesswoman

> An entrepreneur is someone who has a vision for something and a want to create.

David Karp,

Tumblr founder and CEO

Characteristics of successful entrepreneurs

A successful entrepreneur works hard, is well organized and willing to take business risks.

Entrepreneurship refers to the process of identifying a business opportunity, organizing the resources needed to start and run a business and taking both the risks and the rewards it involves. Entrepreneurship can therefore result in entirely new businesses or in turning around failing businesses into successful ones.

Here are some photographs of well-known people who have been successful at doing both.

Lakshmi Mittal (1950–)
Born in a village without electricity in India, Lakshmi Mittal started his working life as a steel worker. He went on to buy his own steel mills and turn loss-making steel companies into profitable ones.

Anita Roddick (1942–2007)
Anita Roddick was the founder of The Body Shop, a cosmetic firm, with strong ethical principles against testing cosmetics on animals. Roddick showed how entrepreneurs could maintain ethical standards and still succeed in business.

Elon Musk (1971–)
Elon Musk was the co-founder of PayPal, which eBay bought for $1.5 billion in 2002. Musk then founded or co-founded five other companies including SpaceX and Tesla to help further his vision to change the world by reducing global warming and establishing a colony on Mars.

What personal qualities or characteristics do you think helped these entrepreneurs to become so successful?

ACTIVITY 1.7

Try to identify five characteristics the entrepreneurs in the articles below have in common.

Green fingers

Ged Ennis co-founded Ensign Energy two years ago to install green energy solutions including low energy technologies, solar panels and wind turbines. The company now has sales just short of £1 million.

Where did you get the idea?

"I was discussing the possibility of starting a recycling company with my friend Richard when we hit on the idea. Richard's background is environmental management and mine's in construction and building, so our separate skills complement the business."

How did you finance your company?

"We decided to risk our joint savings but we also had assistance from some of the local government grants available in our area. To begin with we didn't pay ourselves very much, and worked very long hours."

Was it difficult to start-up?

"Yes, because it was at the start of an economic downturn, but we felt confident in what we were doing. We worked hard to understand exactly what our customers wanted and researched the market in detail to find the best equipment and opportunities available."

A snack on track

Michelle Daniells launched children's nutrition company Benjoy five years ago and is expecting sales of £1 million for the next year of trading.

What is your idea and how did you come up with it?

"We are a food company that develops 100% natural and nutritious children's snacks in the first anti-spill, 'less mess' packaging of its kind anywhere in the world. I came up with the idea when I realized lots of snack foods I was feeding my son weren't nutritious at all."

How did you finance Benjoy?

"I used my savings, borrowed money from family and took out a mortgage on my house. I managed to get £200 000 together before we were ready to launch."

How have you marketed your products?

"This was a big challenge. I have spent a lot of time and effort, working very long hours and travelling up and down the country trying to persuade major supermarket chains to stock our products. Some now do and we have had some brilliant online customer product reviews since. However, we still don't have mass distribution yet which is holding back our sales."

Although there is no such thing as a typical entrepreneur the people who become successful entrepreneurs appear to share very similar characteristics. Key to their success is their ability to understand and see business opportunities and having the passion and drive to turn their business ideas into reality.

▼ Some common characteristics of successful entrepreneurs

Characteristic	Why it is important
Risk-taker	Entrepreneurs' willingness to take considered risks, including risking their own money and possessions, is vital in business. An entrepreneur is someone who is not afraid of failure.
Self-motivated	Entrepreneurs need to be able to work independently and have the perseverance to overcome obstacles and see things through.
Confident	The most successful entrepreneurs will have a clear belief in their own abilities and ideas. An entrepreneur who lacks self-confidence will be unable to convince investors, banks, suppliers and customers that they are able to run a successful business.
Ambitious	Once an entrepreneur has spotted a business opportunity, having a strong desire to succeed is vital.
Able to learn from others	Good entrepreneurs will learn from and build on the ideas and achievements of others, and also learn from their own mistakes.
Analytical abilities	It is important to have the capability of researching and assessing each aspect of the business including the best sources of finance, consumer preferences and buying patterns, the most effective places to advertise, suppliers who offer the best value, etc.
Hard-working	Many entrepreneurs have to work long hours, at weekends and during holidays to run their businesses.
Innovative	Being able to generate ideas, either for new goods or services or new applications for existing products or new ways of making them or selling them, is vital if the business is to stay ahead of the competition.
A good communicator	Entrepreneurs must be clear and confident communicators when sharing their ideas with investors and when advertising and promoting their businesses.

Producing a business plan

"A business that fails to plan is a business that plans to fail"

Starting a new business is not easy because there are so many factors an entrepreneur and owner cannot control, for example falling consumer demand, worsening economic conditions, increasing competition from other firms and changes in taxes and laws. Around one in four new businesses fail in its first few years of trading. Starting a new business therefore needs careful research and planning in advance.

Before going into business would-be entrepreneurs should produce a detailed **business plan**. This is a written statement about their business proposal: how it will be organized, what they want to achieve with it and how they will do so.

The contents of a business plan

There is no set format for a business plan. It will vary from business to business depending on the size of the business, the product it will make or sell, how it will be organized and financed and many other factors. However, all good business plans should cover in detail:

- the aims or objectives of the business ➤ **1.5.1**
- a description of the goods or services it will offer
- an assessment of the market potential for the goods or services ➤ **3.2.1**
- a plan for how and where production will be organized ➤ **4.1.2**
- the resources the business will require
- a financial plan and projections
- sources of finance and how much capital the business will need. ➤ **5.1.2**

How business plans assist entrepreneurs

A business plan helps an entrepreneur to turn a business idea into a working business capable of earning revenue and returning a profit.

A well-thought-through business plan is important for a number of reasons.

- **To assess whether it is possible to turn a business idea into a successful business**

    There is a lot more to a good business than a good idea. A business plan helps turn a business idea into a business capable of producing and selling a good or service that customers want and are willing to pay for. For example, to produce a business plan entrepreneurs need to identify what resources they will need, how much these will cost and how much they will need to sell to cover their costs. All this will take a few weeks to research and to write down if it is done properly.

- **To set out what needs to be done, how it needs to be done and when, to achieve the objectives of the business**

    Developing a business plan allows an entrepreneur to work out how to make his or her business a success and to reduce the risks of failure. It should be used to identify some challenging objectives for the business over time and the actions that will have to be taken to achieve them. It also identifies things that could go wrong, for example if competition from other businesses increases or if costs rise unexpectedly, the effect they could have on the business and what can be done to avoid or reduce their impact.

- **To support an application for financial help**

    Without a detailed plan and financial projections an entrepreneur will be unable to persuade other people or organizations to invest in or lend money to the business. They will need to know the owner has taken the time to investigate the business opportunity thoroughly and thought seriously about future potential. To inform their decision they will want detailed information on how the owner plans to operate the business successfully and earn enough revenue to repay their loans or return to them a share of its profits.

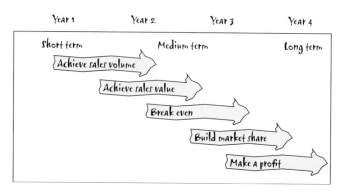

▲ Business objectives may change over time

- **To monitor how well the business is performing against its plan**

If the business is not achieving its objectives then the entrepreneur can investigate why and take actions that will get the business back on track. For example, if actual sales are lower than originally forecast then prices could be reduced or spending on advertising increased to attract more customers. Similarly, if costs are higher and profits lower than forecast then the entrepreneur will need to reduce costs, for example by reducing waste, the number of employees and/or finding cheaper suppliers.

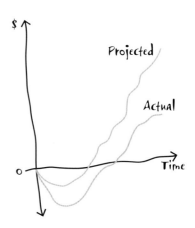

ACTIVITY 1.8

You have been approached to invest $60 000 in the business venture proposed in the business plan below. Identify and explain why the following information will be important to your decision:

▶ the experience of the entrepreneurs

▶ their market and competitor assessments

▶ their financial projections.

Business plan: U–Rock Health and Fitness Club	
Business details	U-Rock is a private limited company. Bethany Basalt and Carlos Kimberlite currently share equal ownership. Bethany has five years of experience in the fitness sector and will manage the club. Carlos has experience in design and construction and plans to train as a gym instructor.
Objectives	1 To become the primary centre for indoor climbing and fitness in the area.
	2 To achieve sales in the first 12 months of over $250 000.
	3 To ensure annual sales growth of at least 15% in years 2–5 of operation.
	4 To reach a profit margin from year 3 of 20% of sales.
Product and production plan	U-Rock Health and Fitness Club will offer all new, combined fitness and climbing facilities unique to the Boulder City location. Nationally, gyms offering indoor climbing have reported average revenue growth of over 15% per year for the last five years.
Market assessment	**Market size:** the local fitness market has expanded at an average of 10% per year over the last ten years. Current annual spending by local consumers on gym membership is over $1.2 million.
	Main target customer groups: children, college students and adults 18–45 years represent the greatest potential for revenue and profit.
	Competitor assessment: there are currently three other gyms in the Boulder City region but one is old and likely to close in the next few months due to declining membership.
	Pricing strategy: prices for day passes and monthly or annual membership will be set at least 10% below competitors, with additional discounts offered to children and groups of students.
Resource requirements	**Machinery and equipment:** fitness and climbing equipment ($65 000); fixtures and fittings ($25 000); computers ($10 000); vehicles ($120 000).
	Employees: one receptionist/office administrator ($25 000 per year plus bonus); two gym instructors ($45 000 per year each plus bonuses).
Financial plan *See financial appendices for further details*	**Sources of finance:** $60 000 invested by each of the owners plus a 15-year bank loan of $150 000.
	Projected income statement: the gym is projected to run at a loss of $40 000 in year 1; break-even costs and revenues of $290 000 are projected for year 2; projected profit from year 3 is $60 000+.
	Projected balance sheet: at the end of year 1 the business will have total assets including premises of $310 000 and total liabilities of $170 000.

Government support for business start-ups

Many governments offer financial and other supports to encourage business start-ups in their economies

Read the articles and in groups discuss why and how governments provide assistance to new businesses.

Government launches start-up loans for young entrepreneurs

The £82.5m start-up loans scheme, which was proposed by Sir Richard Branson last year and confirmed in this year's Budget, will offer finance and support to entrepreneurs aged 18–24, in a bid to kickstart more businesses and tackle youth unemployment in the UK.

Applicants will receive advice and guidance, with the most promising going on to receive formal mentoring and training, including help with developing a business plan. Those with approved plans will be eligible for low-cost loans of around £2500.

Government dishes out $5000 broadband grants to small businesses

The government has announced that small businesses in 10 cities are now able to apply for non-repayable grants of up to $5000 to cover the costs of installing better quality, high-speed broadband.

New enterprise zones announced

The location of five new Enterprise Zones were announced today by the government. "Across the country, they will help to increase local competition, create 20 000 new jobs by 2016 and develop new products to grow our domestic and export markets," said the finance minister.

New businesses located in the Zones will be eligible for grants towards the cost of equipment and training, rent-free premises and generous tax incentives. For example, a business that creates a new job for a local resident will be returned a tax credit of between 20–30% of the cost of their employment.

Nice and cheesy does it

When Selda arrived in the UK in 2012 as a refugee from Syria she was unable to find a job to help support her family. So after spotting a gap in the market, she decided to start up her own business making flavoured cheeses.

To help she applied for government support in the form of a New Enterprise Allowance (NEA) which provides practical and financial support to unemployed people who wish to start their own businesses. Her application for help was accepted and she we assigned a business mentor to help prepare a business plan. Once this was approved she received a start-up loan and a weekly income allowance during her first year of trading while she set-up her business.

Selda has now been in business for over 5 years, employs 5 other people and has won a number of awards for her cheeses.

Many governments around the world provide help to entrepreneurs setting up new businesses. This is because new business formation can achieve the following.

- **It can reduce unemployment**. New businesses can create additional employment opportunities for people who are out of work and teach them new skills. For example, around 90% of all businesses in India are small and provide jobs for about 50% of the workforce.

- **It can encourage social enterprise**. Some entrepreneurs may create not-for-profit enterprises that aim to protect the environment or help support disadvantaged groups of people in society. ➤ **1.5.1**

- **It can increase competition**. New businesses provide consumers with more choice and can help reduce prices as an increasing number of firms have to compete with each other for sales in an area. ➤ **3.3.2**

- **It can boost economic growth**. The output of goods and services in an economy will expand as more new businesses are created and grow. This will increase incomes and spending in the economy as the additional output is sold off. New businesses also tend to be more innovative than older, established businesses and may develop new advanced products that create new markets at home and overseas. ➤ **6.1.1**

Government support for business start-ups can take a number of forms.

Type of support	How is the support delivered?	How does this benefit business?
Grants	These are non-repayable sums of money from a local, state or central government to help fund business start-ups and investments.	Grants can be used to offset the cost of equipment, training, product development and employing workers.
Low-cost loans	These are loans of money repayable at a low rate of interest, for example to finance the purchase of new machinery, equipment and vehicles, or to buy business premises.	Because banks may be unwilling to lend to inexperienced entrepreneurs and new business ventures. If they do, they may charge very high interest rates. This will increase business costs and the risk of financial failure.
Tax incentives	Tax incentives are gained from reductions in taxes on the prices of goods and services, or reductions in taxes on business profits. Alternatively, a proportion of tax paid can be refunded for a particular purpose, such as to reduce the cost of employment.	Tax incentives help to reduce business costs and to boost profitability. Reductions in taxes on the profits of small businesses increase returns on investments in these businesses. This can encourage more people to start new enterprises.
Low-cost or rent-free premises	These include office and factory units, clustered together in an industrial park or zone, paid for by the government and made available to new businesses for a low or zero rent for a time-limited period.	Suitable and inexpensive business premises may be difficult to find in an area. Sales and revenues take time to grow. Access to rent-free premises during the first few months or years of business can significantly reduce the costs and risks of financial failure.
Free or low-cost advice and training	A government can organize classes and the provision of expert advice from experienced entrepreneurs and business mentors. Or, it may provide vouchers that new entrepreneurs can use to pay towards the cost of training.	Advice and training enable entrepreneurs to learn relevant skills for business, including finance and accounting, and to have access to expert business knowledge on all aspects of starting and running a business.
Training schemes	A government will pay towards the costs of training a new employee. An example of this is the National Apprenticeship Training Scheme in the UK. Apprentices combine on-the-job training with some study.	Apprentices work for the business whilst training which can free up some of the time of other employees. The training is relevant to the skills required by the business and is an inexpensive way of recruiting skilled workers for the future.

However, government support may not be available to all new and small businesses or in every area of an economy. Financial support can also be conditional. For example, it may depend on how many jobs a business creates or how much of their own money the business owners invest in the development of new advanced products. This is because governments often target their support at new businesses and investments in particular technologies, industrial sectors and areas. ➤ **4.4.1**

- Government support may be targeted at particular types of business in selected industrial sectors, for example manufacturing firms and those planning to develop new, high-tech products with the potential to create more added value and jobs in the economy in the future. In contrast, far less support, if any, may be available to retail and other service sector businesses.

- Business support may only be available to specific areas, such as **enterprise zones** in areas of industrial decline. This is because governments want to attract new businesses to locate in areas with the highest rates of unemployment.

- Some grants and other financial supports are only approved for specific uses, for example for the purchase of machinery, for the research and development of advanced products, for the installation of solar panels and other "green energy" technologies, or for training employees.

- Some grants may require "matched funding". For example, a $5000 grant may only be approved if the business owner invests the same amount of money from his or her own funds.

- Entrepreneurs in receipt of a grant or financial help from government may be required to complete regular reports on how they have spent the money and how their business is performing.

- An entrepreneur with a poor business plan is likely to be refused financial support.

Learning CHECKLIST

Before you continue make sure you are able to

Understand and explain the concepts of **enterprise** and **entrepreneurship**:

✓ the characteristics of successful **entrepreneurs**

✓ the contents of a **business plan** and how business plans assist entrepreneurs

✓ why and how governments **support business start-ups**, including through **grants** and training schemes.

1.3.2   The methods and problems of measuring business size

1.3.3   Why some businesses grow and others remain small

- ▶ It is useful to compare the size of different firms. Measures of size include:
  - • how many workers they employ
  - • how much capital they employ
  - • the volume or value of their output or sales
  - • their market share.

- ▶ Different measures of the size of firms may give different results. Some large firms may be capital-intensive but employ very few workers. In contrast, some firms may be labour-intensive but have very little capital employed.

- ▶ A firm can expand its scale of production internally or by external growth through the takeover of another business or a merger with another.

- ▶ Business growth can help a firm increase its sales and market share, reduce its production costs and increase profits.

- ▶ Some firms may experience problems with growth. These are called diseconomies of scale. Some large firms may be difficult to manage and may not be able to obtain all the materials and workers they need. Production costs may rise and profits may fall as a result.

- ▶ The most efficient size for a firm is closely related to the size of its market.

Capital-intensive – a firm or production process that requires more capital equipment than labour.

Labour-intensive – a firm or production process that uses more labour than capital equipment.

Market size – the total sales revenue or turnover for a particular product over a given period of time.

Market share – the proportion of total sales of a product achieved by one firm.

Internal growth – or organic growth, involves an increase in the scale of production within a firm through the employment of additional factors of production.

External growth – an increase in the size of a firm through the takeover of, or merger with, other enterprises.

Horizontal integration – the formation of a larger enterprise through merger or takeover between two or more firms in the same industry and at the same stage of production.

Vertical integration – the formation of a larger enterprise through merger or takeover between two or more firms at different stages of production of the same product.

Lateral integration – or conglomerate merger, involves merger or takeover between two or more firms in different industries to form a single, larger enterprise.

Merger – combining two or more firms with the agreement of the owners to form a larger enterprise.

Takeover – the acquisition of one firm by another with or without the agreement of its owners.

Diversification – a business strategy that involves producing a variety of different products and/or expanding into different markets to expand total sales and reduce the risk to the business from a fall in demand for any one product or in any one market.

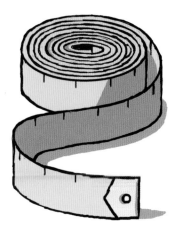

Methods of measuring business size

There are firms of different sizes at different stages of growth in all industries

Retailer Walmart Stores is one of the world's largest business organizations. It employs some 2.2 million people worldwide and has over $200 billion invested in buildings, computers, vehicles (including forklift trucks) and other capital assets.

Oil and gas producer PetroChina also ranks as one of the world's largest businesses. It employs around 550 000 people but has capital assets worth nearly $350 billion. So does this make PetroChina a smaller or larger business than Walmart?

Of course both these giant organizations are huge compared to the many millions of other business organizations worldwide that serve small local markets, employ very few workers and have few capital assets.

It is useful therefore to group firms together according to whether they are large enterprises or small and medium-sized enterprises (SMEs).

The size of firms can be measured in a number of ways. The most common are:
- **how many workers they employ**
- **how much capital they employ**
- **the volume or value of their output or sales**
- **their market share.**

The same measures can be used to determine the size of individual business units within a firm. Some firms operate more than one factory, shop, office or other business unit. For example, a firm may own and operate a chain of supermarkets located in different towns while **multinational enterprises** own and operate different business units located in many different countries. ➤ **6.3.2**

A firm's size is difficult to measure and judge. Different measures may give very different results. That is, according to some measures a firm may appear to be large, while on some other measures the same firm may appear to be small. It is therefore useful to use a range of different measures of firm size.

Why is it useful to measure the size of firms?

The following **stakeholders** (groups of people and organizations with an interest in businesses) may want to compare the size of different firms and monitor whether they are growing or shrinking in size over time.

- **Business owners** may want to know the size of rival firms they compete with.
- **Investors** will want to make a good return on the money they invest in different businesses.
- **Banks** will want to know whether a firm is big enough to take out a loan and make repayments.

- **Trade unions** and other organizations representing workers will want to know how many workers firms employ.
- **Consumers** or consumer representatives may be concerned about the power some large firms have over prices and the quality of goods and services.
- **Government officials** may want to encourage the creation and growth of small firms to compete with large firms and may set different tax rates on the profits of large and small businesses.

Measure 1: number of employees

This is a straightforward measure. Firms with fewer than 50 employees are often considered to be small. However, not all large firms employ many hundreds or thousands of workers.

Limitations

Some large firms are **capital-intensive** and employ relatively few workers. Instead they use a lot of machinery and computer-controlled equipment to automate their production processes in order to mass produce large quantities of output.

Measure 2: capital employed

Capital employed is money invested in the productive assets of a business by its owners from their own funds and from long-term loans. ➤ **5.4.1**

Assets used in the production of goods and services include machinery, factory and office buildings, stocks of materials and components and cash held by a business to pay wages and other costs.

The more capital employed in a firm the more it can produce and therefore the greater its size or scale of production.

Limitations

However, some large firms may be **labour-intensive**. This means their production process requires the employment of many workers but relative little capital. Labour costs are a significant proportion of the total costs of production in a firm that is labour-intensive.

Measure 3: output or sales

It is useful to compare firms in the same industry according to how much output they produce or how much they sell.

Output and sales can be measured in terms of **volume**, for example how many mobile phones are produced or sold per month or per year, or in terms of their **value** measured by how much revenue they earn per period of time from the sale of their products.

Limitations

It is not very sensible to compare the volume of output or sales of firms in different industries. For example, a major shipbuilding company may produce only one large warship or cruise liner each year, while a small local bakery may produce and sell many thousands of bread and cake products each year.

Measure 4: market share

The **market** for any good or service consists of all those consumers willing and able to buy it no matter where they might be located. ➤ **4.4.1**

The size of the market for a good or service is measured by the total amount spent by consumers on that product per week, month or year. The **market share** of a particular firm is therefore the proportion of total sales revenue or **turnover** that is attributable to the sales of that firm.

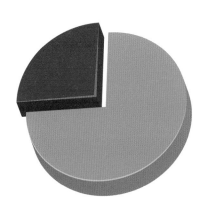

For example, the global market for carbonated soft drinks was worth an estimated $342 billion in 2015. The market is dominated by the Coca-Cola Company. Its share of the global market was 48.6%. In comparison, its major rival PepsiCo captured only 20.5% of the total market.

Limitations

However, not all markets are big. For example, a local hairdressing salon may be a very small business in terms of the number of people and amount of capital equipment it employs but it may have a very large share of the local market it serves because it is the only salon in a town, so many local people go there to have their hair cut and styled.

ACTIVITY 1.10

The table below contains information on four different business organizations.

▶ Which firm is the largest?

▶ Is it sensible to use only one measure of a firm's size?

▶ What are the problems with the individual measures used to determine a firm's size?

Name	Sector	Total employees	Capital employed ($ million)	Total output ($ million)	Global market share (% of revenues)
Google	Software and computers	20 222	21 795	31 768	67
ExxonMobil	Oil and gas production	79 900	228 052	459 579	10
GlaxoSmithKline	Pharmaceuticals	35 637	57 647	101 133	6
Toyota Motors	Automobiles and parts	358 304	112 196	261 837	13

Why the owners of a business may want to expand the business

Business owners may expand their firms to gain cost advantages and to increase their sales, profits and market shares

The Reliance Group is India's largest private sector enterprise. It began as a small textile maker in the 1960s using imported polyester to make a range of garments under the brand name "Vimal" which is now a household name in India. It soon began to manufacture its own polyester yarn and fibres and is now the world's largest producer of these synthetic materials. It went on to develop or merge with businesses involved in oil and gas exploration, petroleum refining, petrochemicals and also retail stores. In this way the business successfully controls its supply chain from the production of natural oils and gases that are used in the manufacture of petrochemicals needed to make polyester fibres for textile production to retail outlets that sell its brand of clothing. The business has a saying: "growth is life".

Through this growth in size the Reliance Group, like many other large businesses, enjoys a number of advantages over small firms.

✦ Banks may be willing to lend more money to large businesses and at lower rates of interest.

✦ Suppliers of materials, component parts, computers and other equipment and services may give price discounts to large businesses buying these items from them in bulk.

- A large firm may have the financial resources to invest more in the latest machinery and equipment.
- Business managers can increase their responsibility and salaries.
- Workers may benefit from more secure jobs and higher wages in large firms.
- Business owners may earn more profits.
- A large business can increase sales and its market share.
- A large firm may be able to produce a wide range of products for different markets at home and overseas and in this way it can protect the business from a fall in consumer demand in any one of them. Producing a varied range of products and expanding into different consumer markets to reduce risk is called **diversification**.
- Increasing the volume of output or **scale of production** of a product can reduce the average cost of producing each item or unit of output. These cost savings are called **economies of scale**. ➤ **4.2.3**

Different ways in which businesses can grow

The Reliance Group in India was able to grow its business using its own resources but also by combining with other new or established businesses.

- **Internal growth** involves a firm expanding its scale of production through the purchase of additional equipment, increasing the size of its premises and hiring more labour if needed.

  To finance this growth the owners will need to use the profits of the firm, borrow money from banks and other lenders or sell shares in the ownership of their business to other investors. To sell shares a firm must become a **joint stock company**. The new investors will become owners or **shareholders** in the company and this will entitle them to a share of any profits. ➤ **2.1.2**

  For example, Tiger Airways of Singapore raised $248 million from the sale of shares in January 2010 to help fund the purchase of 49 new aircraft to expand flights in Australia and South East Asia. In the same year, the Agricultural Bank of China, known as AgBank, sold over $22 billion of shares. It remains the world's largest issue of shares ever recorded.

- **External growth** is more common. It involves one or more firms joining together to form a larger enterprise. This is known as **integration** through merger or takeover.

- A **merger** occurs when the owners of one or more firms agree to join together to form a new, larger enterprise.

- A **takeover** or **acquisition** occurs when one company buys enough shares in the ownership of another so it can take overall control. This may happen with or without the agreement of the owners of the other company.

▲ Tiger Airways sold shares to finance the expansion of its business.

Integration between firms through mergers or takeovers can take a number of forms.

Horizontal integration involves a merger or takeover of firms engaged in the production of the same type of good or service. Most integration between firms is horizontal integration.

Horizontal integration may benefit a business in the following ways.

✓ The combined businesses will have a more substantial share of the market.

✓ The integration will reduce the number of competing firms in the industry.

✓ The integrated businesses may gain a number of cost advantages due to their combined size, for example by merging their finance, purchasing and other administrative functions to reduce staff and other costs, or from price discounts offered by suppliers for the bulk-buying of their goods.

▼ Horizontal integration

Vertical integration occurs between firms at different stages of production. For example, a car manufacturer may combine with a car retailer with multiple sales outlets or showrooms. The car manufacturer can benefit in the following ways.

✓ It can be certain it has a retailer through which it is able to promote and sell its cars and other products.

✓ The retailer can refuse to stock other makes of car from rival manufacturers.

✓ It can absorb the profit made by the retailer on each sale. The profit of the manufacturer from each car produced and sold will therefore increase.

✓ It will have direct access through the retailer to the final consumers of its products. This will allow the manufacturer to assess their characteristics and preferences in order to design promotions that will appeal to similar consumers and expand sales.

Alternatively, consider a cheese maker that combines with a dairy farm so that it is guaranteed supplies of milk and can benefit in the following ways.

✓ It can be assured regular and exclusive supplies from the farm.

✓ It can control the costs of supplies from the farm.

✓ It can absorb the profit of the farm.

▲ Vertical integration

Lateral integration occurs between firms in different industries in the same stage or different stages of production. It is also called **conglomerate merger** and creates firms called **conglomerates** because they produce a wide range of different products.

▲ Lateral integration

For example, Samsung is a major global business group well known for its televisions, mobile phones and other electronic products, but it also has business interests in shipbuilding, construction, chemicals, financial services and entertainment. This benefits the Samsung Corporation in the following ways.

✓ Producing and selling a wide range of goods and services reduces the risk of falling consumer demand for any one of its products having a major impact on its business.

✓ The different businesses can share ideas and innovations. For example, the development of touch-sensitive screens and voice-operated controls have been used on televisions, computer monitors and mobile phones.

▼ Some well-known business mergers and takeovers

ExxonMobil was formed in 1999 following an agreement by US companies Exxon and Mobil to merge their operations. The combined company is now one of the largest in the world and benefits from a bigger market share and significant economies of scale in oil and gas exploration, production and sales.

In October 2016, Anheuser-Busch InBev completed a $79 billion takeover of UK-based SABMiller to produce the world's largest brewer. By merging their operations the combined company will sell almost 3 in 10 beers worldwide and is estimated to yield annual costs savings of $1.4 billion.

1 Which of the following mergers or takeovers in the table involve horizontal, vertical or lateral integrations?

Merger or takeover	Horizontal	Vertical	Lateral
A chocolate maker takes over a cocoa plantation		✓	
A travel insurer merges with an online holiday company			
A clothing retailer takes over a clothes manufacturer			
A bus manufacturer merges with a car maker			
An investment bank takes over an electronics producer			
An aircraft maker merges with an aero-engine company			

Going bananas: two rivals merge to form world's largest banana company

US banana firm Chiquita will merge with its Irish competitor, Fyffes, in a deal that will create a banana industry giant: ChiquitaFyffes.

The world's largest banana company will have combined assets of $1 billion and could sell bananas at a rate of 160 million boxes a year.

The Chief Executive of Chiquita said the merger was "a milestone transaction for Chiquita and Fyffes that brings together the best of both companies". The company expects the merger to reduce costs from crop growers and other firms in the supply chain, and extend its global reach and market share.

2 What type of integration was involved in the merger of the two companies in the article?

3 From the article identify and explain two reasons for the merger.

Problems linked to business growth and how these might be overcome

Businesses can grow too much. This is exactly what happened when Mozambique's Mozal aluminium smelter wanted to expand its operations and increase output but was unable to do so because of a shortage of electricity in the country.

Similarly, the global US coffee shop chain Starbucks had to sell off 600 stores in the US in 2008 because coffee sales and the value of the properties the business owned were falling. The business expanded significantly in the 1990s and had invested a lot of money in business properties. The fall in property prices and consumer spending during the economic downturn in 2008 had a big impact on the business. Starbucks also closed 61 of its 85 shops in Australia due to weak sales. The business had failed to attract consumers away from established cafés and coffee bars in Australia's main cities.

Many firms may experience similar problems if they try to expand the size and scale of their production too quickly and by too much. These problems are **diseconomies of scale** because they can result in production problems, higher costs and lower profits. Below are some examples of problems caused by business growth and strategies that could be used to overcome them.

Potential problems caused by business growth	Possible business strategies to overcome growth problems
✘ Some very large firms may need vast quantities of materials and components for production. They may experience shortages and this may hold up production.	✔ Expand more slowly and/or integrate with a major supplier. ✔ Stockpile supplies and buy in bulk from several different suppliers.
✘ Managing a large firm can be difficult especially if the firm has factories or offices spread over many different locations.	✔ Improve communications with local managers using video conferencing facilities. ✔ Allow local managers at each business location to have more day-to-day control and decision-making authority.
✘ Some large firms may be unable to attract enough workers with the right skills. These firms may have to spend more money on training their workers and increasing wages to ensure that their workers do not leave to take jobs in other firms.	✔ Expand more slowly or adopt more capital-intensive production methods.
✘ Large firms may automate many production processes. Workers operating the machines may become bored, demotivated and less co-operative. Disputes and strikes may occur if workers feel poorly treated.	✔ Allow workers to swap or "rotate" their jobs regularly so they have more interesting and varied tasks. ✔ Offer employees performance-related pay or bonuses.
✘ Large firms may also find it difficult to continually attract new customers because their products are too standardized and they saturated their market.	✔ Expand more slowly and/or promote and sell products to new and expanding consumer markets overseas.
✘ To raise finance for business expansion the original owners of a firm may need to sell part of their ownership stake to other investors. The new owners may not always agree with the original owners or among themselves on how best to run the business. Disputes can occur which may harm the business.	✔ Expand more slowly and only when profits are sufficient to finance further growth.

Why some businesses remain small

Not all firms can or should grow into much larger enterprises

Most firms in any economy are small. Most firms start small. Some may grow over time into large national or even multinational organizations but the vast majority remain small for the following good reasons.

- **The size of their market is small**

  We know from section 1.1.1 that Lilliana's laundromat is located on a small island in the Caribbean. The island has a population of just 3000 people. Not all of them will want to use a laundromat. Lilliana estimated that just 30% of the population, or 900 mainly young people or people on low incomes, will use her laundromat at least once every month. Unless the population expands rapidly or fewer people buy their own washing and drying machines there is little reason for Lilliana to expand her laundry business.

▲ Many small businesses survive and prosper in small, localized markets.

The most efficient size for a firm is therefore closely related to the size of its market. If there are only a relatively small number of consumers willing and able to buy a product there is no point in a firm supplying that market growing to a large size.

There are many examples of sectors in which small firms thrive because the markets they serve tend to be small and localized. For example, hairdressers, restaurants and cafés, window cleaners, decorators and many hotels, taxi services and shops only supply the villages and towns they are located in. They are also able to offer their customers a more personalized service compared to many large firms that mass produce goods or provide standardized services across all their business locations. For example, local tailors can make made-to-measure suits and carpenters can make furniture to order, unlike many large clothing and furniture manufacturers.

Similarly, firms that produce luxury items may have relatively small markets. Only consumers with very high incomes may be willing and able to pay high prices for "exclusive" products like designer clothing and jewellery, sports cars and luxury holidays.

- **Access to capital is limited.**

Lilliana had to use up all her own savings to start her laundromat business. Banks would not lend money to her or would only lend her part of the money she needed and at a high rate of interest. This is because the bank managers she spoke to thought her business idea was too risky and may not be able to make enough revenue each month to repay a loan.

Because the size of her market is small Lilliana would like to invest in dry cleaning, pressing and ironing equipment to offer additional services to expand her business, but without any savings of her own or a bank loan she will be unable to do so.

Many small firms are in a similar position. They may be unable to raise enough money to rent or buy larger premises and the equipment they need to increase the scale of their production. Owners of small firms may not have enough personal savings to invest in these assets. Borrowed money from a bank can also be expensive to repay with interest.

- **New technology has reduced the scale of production needed.**

The size and cost of new technologies have fallen significantly over time. Most small businesses now have access to computers and other modern equipment. Many years ago they would not have been able to afford this equipment. Also, through the internet many small businesses can now reach suppliers and consumers all over the world.

- **Some business owners may simply choose to stay small.**

Some entrepreneurs may simply decide they do not want to increase the size of their firm as long as they continue to make a reasonable profit. Taxes on profits may also be lower for small firms than for large firms earning much bigger profits.

Running a large enterprise can be very time-consuming and stressful. Some entrepreneurs may also lack the skills they need to manage and run large firms employing many more people and much more capital.

Most firms are small and remain small. Make a list of all the reasons given in the quotes below from owners of small businesses against expanding their business.

> I can't be bothered to run a larger business. It would be too stressful and take up too much of my time. I am happy being small. I make enough profit and I get to keep it all! My business taxes are also low because I run a small business.

> I own and run a small restaurant serving a small, local market. There is no point growing larger. I know all my customers and can offer them a good personalized service. Large restaurant chains can't provide this.

> We make exclusive and luxury designer knitwear.
> All our garments are handmade and sell for between $500 and $1000 each. Our market is therefore quite limited.
> Most of our customers are high net worth individuals including film, TV and music industry celebrities.

> My bank wouldn't lend me enough money to finance the purchase of the new premises and equipment I need.

> I work from my home, designing and building websites for major business customers all over the world. I don't need to be big. I only need a computer and high-speed internet access.

Learning CHECKLIST

Before you continue make sure you are able to

Identify and understand methods and problems of **measuring business size**:

✓ different **methods of measuring business size**, for example by number of people employed, value of output and **capital employed**

✓ limitations of the methods of measuring business size.

Give reasons why some businesses grow and others remain small:

✓ why the owners of a business may want to expand the business

✓ different ways in which businesses can grow

✓ problems linked to **business growth** and how these might be overcome

✓ why some businesses remain small.

1.3.4 Why some (new or established) businesses fail

▶ Business "births" from new start-ups and "deaths" from business failures are common. The business environment is constantly changing, threatening the survival of some businesses and creating new opportunities for others.

▶ Business survival may be threatened by economic recessions, changes in consumer tastes and preferences, the failure of a major customer, an increase in competition, the introduction of new technologies and many other external factors.

▶ More new and small businesses fail each year compared to large and more established businesses. This is because many new business owners lack business skills and experience, fail to research and plan their business ideas and subsequently make poor business decisions.

▶ Poor financial management is a major cause of business failure. A business will be insolvent if it runs out of cash and is unable to pay its debts.

▶ Even a profitable business can suffer from liquidity problems. It can run out of cash and be unable to pay its debts. Unless it can borrow more or sell off some assets quickly to raise cash it will be declared bankrupt and be liquidated. Any remaining assets owned by the business will be sold off to pay its debts.

▶ A loss-making business need not be a failing business. Many businesses operate at a loss immediately after start-up or a major expansion, or during an economic recession. Businesses with good managers and strong financial control are best able to survive these periods and return to profit.

Business BUZZWORDS

Overstocking – or holding excess inventory, means a business has purchased and stored far more goods than necessary or desirable.

Overtrading – this happens when a business expands too quickly and takes on more work than it is able to finance and complete.

Insolvency – the inability of a business to pay its debts because it has run out of cash, i.e. because it has become illiquid.

Creditors – people, suppliers and other organizations to whom a business owes money.

Bankruptcy – a term used for a business that is declared in law as unable to pay its debt.

Liquidation – a legal procedure to close a bankrupt business involving the sale of its remaining assets to pay off its debts.

Going concern – a business that has sufficient financial and other resources to continue operating indefinitely. A business that is no longer a going concern is a business that is bankrupt.

Liquidity – a measure of the ability of an organization to raise enough cash to pay off its short-term debts as they fall due, either from its holdings of cash or by selling off some of its assets for cash.

What is business failure?

A good business plan identifies business risks and actions that the business can take to reduce their impact

Each year many businesses are born and many die. This is because business conditions are always changing, threatening the survival of some businesses and creating new opportunities for others. A failed business is no longer a **going concern**. This means it no longer has enough financial or other resources to continue production or trading into the future.

For example, around 10% of all private sector enterprises fail each year in the UK and around 14% are newly formed. This means the total number of active businesses in the UK tends to expand each year. However, between 2008 and 2010 the business death rate exceeded the business birth rate and the total number of active businesses fell in the UK. This was the result of a deep **economic recession** in the UK and many other developed countries. ➤ **6.1.1**

The survival of a business may also be threatened by wars, increases in interest rates, changes in laws, an increase in competition, changes in consumer tastes and preferences, the introduction of new technologies and many other external factors. A business cannot control these events but it can try to plan ahead in case they happen. For example, an increase in interest rates will increase the cost of repaying bank loans. Paying off any loans early or taking out a bank loan that has a fixed rate of interest will therefore protect a business from an increase in interest rates. ➤ **5.1.2**

A business that fails to identify how changes in business conditions may affect it and fails to make plans to deal with them is at a greater risk of failing than one that does.

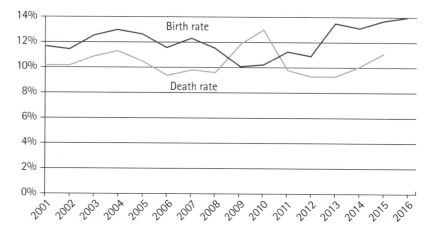

▼ Business birth and death rates in the UK
(i.e. new businesses as a % of active businesses vs. businesses that ceased trading as a % of active businesses)

More new and small businesses fail each year compared to large, more established businesses

New businesses are more likely to fail than large, established businesses for the following reasons.

✗ **Lack of skills and experience**: many people who start-up a business have never owned or run a business before and lack the skills they need to do so successfully. Many are inexperienced managers and make bad business decisions.

✗ **Failure to research and plan**: an entrepreneur who lacks experience and has failed to research his or her business idea fully may choose to make and sell a good or service for which there is little demand.

Small business failures

According to the US Small Business Administration 30% of new businesses in the US fail within their first two years but that rises to 50% by the five-year mark. Only around one in four US businesses survives more than ten years.

Similarly, around one in every three new businesses fails within three years of start-up in the UK, many within their first year of operation. The same is true in many other countries. For example, in Kenya an estimated 60% of small businesses fail in their first year.

- ✗ **Lack of finance**: business start-up can be expensive and banks are often unwilling to loan new businesses money. As a result many small businesses lack the funds they need to invest in good-quality premises, in sufficient promotional activities to advertise their products and in the latest production equipment and technologies to keep pace with rival firms. ➤ **3.3.5**

- ✗ **Wrong location**: lack of experience, market research and finance can all result in a entrepreneur choosing the cheapest location for his or her new business premises rather than the best location for attracting customers and sales. ➤ **4.4.1**

Causes of business failure

Poor management, weak financial control and changes in the external business environment are some of the main causes of business failures

Not all businesses can be successful. Even some large, well-established businesses can fail for one or more of the following reasons.

- ✗ **Lack of management skills:** this is a very common cause of business failure even in established businesses. Poor managers may take over from good ones as they move on or retire and even some experienced managers can make poor business decisions at times. For example, in 1999 the owners of the Excite Internet search engine declined an offer from the creators of Google to buy their new search engine for $750 000. Today, Excite no longer exists but Google is a global company worth $180 billion.

- ✗ **Changes in the business environment:** these can result in the failure of a business especially one that is unable to adapt to changes, including the following.
  - Economic recession. ➤ **6.1.1**
  - Changes in consumer preferences. ➤ **3.1.2**
  - The failure of a major customer.
  - Increasing competition from new start-ups or established firms. ➤ **3.1.2**
  - Technological change causing products or production processes to become outdated. ➤ **4.1.3**
  - Rising interest rates increase the cost of borrowing. ➤ **6.1.1**
  - Changes in laws and regulations. ➤ **6.2.1**

- ✗ **Liquidity problems:** poor financial control can cause liquidity issues which occur when a business runs out of cash and is unable to pay its employees, supplier and other running costs. Unless it is able to take out a bank loan or sell off some of its assets to raise the cash it needs the business will become **insolvent** and have to cease trading. Liquidity problems can be avoided if cash flows into the business from sales and out of the business to pay bills are managed sensibly. ➤ **5.2.1**

Effects of poor financial management

Overtrading: this happens when a business takes on more work than it is able to finance. Cash often leaves a business to buy supplies and pay wages before any cash comes in from sales. A business could therefore run out of cash to pay for the supplies and employees it needs before it is able to complete the work and earn revenue.

Insolvency: this is the inability of a business to pay its debts because it has run out of cash and is a major cause of failure in businesses of all sizes. It is therefore important for any business to forecast how much cash it will need each period to pay its bills as well as how much cash it can expect to earn.

Bankruptcy: creditors owed money by a business can have it declared bankrupt by a law court so it is forced into **liquidation**. This means the business must close down and sell all its assets to raise cash to pay off its debts.

From the news articles identify and explain at least three reasons why businesses fail.

Demolition company collapses

Denning Demolition has ceased trading after rescue efforts failed to save the company, with all employees made redundant.

Accountants for the company said "a series of poor financial decisions, declining turnover and an inability to pay its debts" prevented the business from being saved.

Business failures predicted to surge as recession deepens

Yesterday brought fresh gloom about the state of the economy with news of increasing unemployment claims and the first rise in business failures for six years.

Experts warn there is worse to come with many businesses showing signs of financial distress as unemployment rises and consumer spending continues to fall across the economy.

Taking Flight

Competition and rising costs are pushing airlines to the brink

Monarch is the third airline to collapse in Europe this year after Alitalia and Air Berlin due to intense competition for the skies which has seen fares slashed and profits tumble at a time when industry wages and fuel costs have been rising.

World's biggest music store to close

The world's biggest CD music store – HMV at 150 Oxford Street – is closing its doors for the final time this weekend after 30 years.

HMV was the biggest casualty of a tough Christmas for the high street. It had been struggling for years against competition from supermarkets and the rise of digital download services such as iTunes.

Net loss: the decline of UK fishing

Britain's fishing industry employed around 47 000 fishermen in the 1930s. Today there are around 13 000.

And fishermen's leaders are predicting further decline after the European Union announced deep cuts in the volume of fish fleets. Many thousands of jobs will not only be lost on the fishing boats, but also in the supply chain – in the fish processors, net makers, equipment suppliers and transport companies.

Icetech melts away as Comet fails

Icetech, a company manufacturing freezers in Castletown, Scotland, has been forced to close. It had been a major supplier to Comet, the electrical goods retailer, which collapsed owing the business £0.9 million. It was unable to recover from this blow and the loss of half its business.

▼ Changing consumer preferences and fashions can cause business failures

An unprofitable business need not be a failing business

Many people assume that a loss-making business is a failing business. However, it is common for businesses to operate at a loss immediately after start-up or a major expansion. Start-up and growth can be expensive and during these periods business costs often exceed revenues.

The most immediate aim of a new or expanding business is to increase sales. This may require increased spending on advertising and lowering prices to attract customers. However, as sales rise a business may be able to raise its prices and cut back its advertising and begin to earn profits. This means many businesses have short-term objectives to boost their sales in order to achieve their objective of increasing profits in the long term. ➤ **1.5.1**

Similarly, many businesses also make losses during an economic recession as consumer spending on many goods and services falls. Businesses with good managers and access to sufficient funds to continue production are best able to survive these periods and return to profit. ➤ **5.3.1**

Before a loss-making business is judged as failing it is important to consider the questions below.

> Are the factors that have resulted in a loss *internal or external* to the business?

Internal factors such as poor cost control and cash management can often be put right. A new management team can also be brought in to turn around a loss-making company. However, external factors, such as a fall in consumer demand for the product can be more difficult to change.

> Are the factors that have resulted in a loss *temporary or permanent?*

Losses during a start-up phase, business expansion or economic recession may be only temporary. However, a business may not be able to recover from a fall in demand for its product or products if it is permanent because consumer tastes and technologies have changed.

> Is the business objective *short-run or long-run profit maximization?*

Business costs may increase and exceed revenues for a time as a business attempts to expand and increase sales. If it achieves these aims this should help it become more profitable in the future.

Learning CHECKLIST

Before you continue make sure you are able to

Identify and explain why some (new or established) businesses fail:

✓ causes of **business failure**, including **lack of management skills** and **changes in the business environment**

✓ why new businesses are at a greater risk of failing.

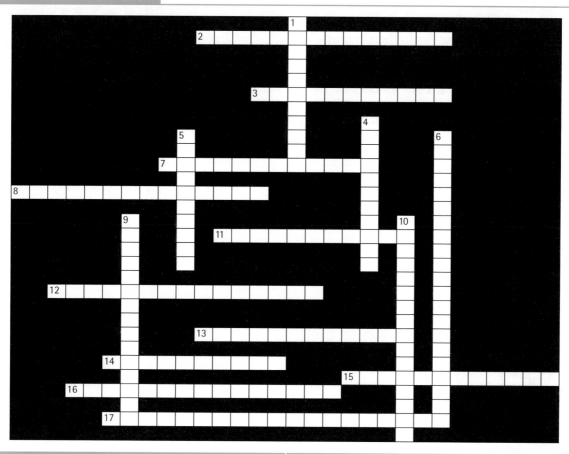

Clues down

1 The business know-how and skills required to combine and organize other factors of production into firms for the purpose of providing goods and services (9)

4 A business is described as doing this when it expands too quickly and takes on more work than it is able to finance and complete (11)

5 A legal term used to describe the inability of a business to pay its debts (10)

6 The formation of a larger enterprise through merger or takeover between two or more firms in the same industry and at the same stage of production, such as the merger of two car manufacturers (10, 11)

9 A term that describes a production process that requires more human effort than capital equipment to complete it (6, 9)

10 The process of identifying a business opportunity, organizing the resources needed to start and run a business and taking both the risks and rewards it involves (16)

Clues across

2 An increase in the size of a firm through the acquisition of another business or businesses (8, 6)

3 The proportion of total sales of a product achieved by one firm (6, 5)

7 An enterprising person who is willing and able to take the risks and decisions necessary to organize resources into firms for production (12)

8 Another term for an organic expansion in the size of a firm through the employment of additional factors of production (8, 6)

11 Selling off the remaining assets of a bankrupt business to pay off its creditors (11)

12 A business strategy that involves expanding into new markets or products to reduce the risk of a fall in consumer demand for any one product or in any one region or country (15)

13 A written statement about a business proposal covering its objectives, production plan, financial projections, resource requirements and how it will be organized and financed (8, 4)

14 When a business has insufficient cash to pay its debts (10)

15 A term used to describe the holding of excess inventory assets a business because it has purchased far more goods than is necessary or desirable (12)

16 The amount of money invested in a business in productive assets by the owners from their own funds and long-term loans (7, 8)

17 The formation of a larger enterprise through merger or takeover between two or more firms at different stages of production of the same product, for example the takeover of a food processor by a food retailer (8, 11)

1.4 | Types of business organization

1.4.1 The main features of different forms of business organization

- There are different types of private sector business organization. They vary according to how they are owned, controlled and financed, and the liability of the owners to repay their debts.

- Entrepreneurs consider how to finance and manage their business, and how much risk they are willing to take before choosing the most appropriate type of business organization to set up.

- Most business organizations are sole traders. They have an unlimited liability to repay the debts of their business in the event it fails. This is because a sole trader does not have a separate legal identity.

- Partnerships are popular business organizations among professions such as solicitors, doctors and accountants. Most are general partnerships in which partners have unlimited liability but some partners may have limited liability.

- Limited companies are incorporated businesses. They are also known as joint-stock companies or corporations. This is because they sell stocks (also known as shares) to raise capital.

- A public limited company is able to sell its shares publicly on the stock market. A private limited company can only sell its shares privately.

- The risks of starting and running a new business can be reduced by entering into a joint venture or a franchise with an established business organization.

Business BUZZWORDS

Unlimited liability – the owners of a business are legally responsible for the full amount of its debts.

Limited liability – the legal responsibility of the owners of a business to repay its debts is limited to the amount of capital they invest in the business.

Separate legal identity – a business organization considered to be legally separate from its owners.

Sole trader – a business organization owned and controlled by one person.

Partnership – a legal agreement between two or more people, usually up to 20, to jointly own, finance and run a business, and to share its profits.

General partner – a partner with unlimited liability.

Limited partner – a partner with limited liability.

Joint-stock companies – limited companies or corporations – are jointly owned by their shareholders.

Incorporated business – a business organization with a separate legal identity from its owners.

Stock market – the global market for the purchase and sale of new or existing shares (or stocks) in public limited companies.

Flotation – when shares in a public limited company are made available for sale to the general public for the first time through a stock exchange.

Franchise – an agreement by one company with another business organization to permit the distribution of its goods or services using its trademark or brand name.

Public corporation – a government-owned enterprise created to carry out a governmental function or public service.

Starting a business

Businesses are organized according to how they are owned, controlled and financed

An entrepreneur combines and organizes resources in a firm for the purpose of carrying out productive activity or business. Firms are therefore also known as business organizations. ➤ **1.1.1**

In a modern, mixed economy a firm may take a number of legal forms according to how it is owned, controlled and financed. For example, a small firm with just one owner will be very different in the way it is controlled and financed from a large firm which may have many thousands of owners who play little or no role in the day-to-day management of the organization.

The legal forms and characteristics of different types of business organization are very similar across the world although precise requirements and rules governing their ownership, finance and the distribution of profits can differ from one country to another and may change over time.

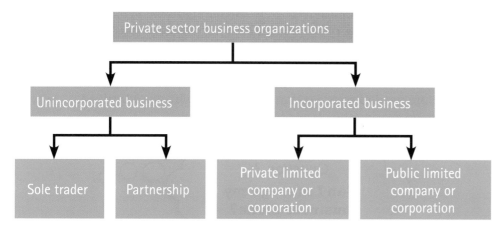

▲ Main types of private sector business organization

An entrepreneur should consider how to finance and manage the new business, and how much risk he or she is willing to take

Before starting a new business or expanding an existing one an entrepreneur needs to consider what type of organization he or she wants. This will largely depend on how much money the entrepreneur will need to start or grow the business, whether the entrepreneur wants to continue managing it alone, how much risk he or she is willing to take, and whether or not the entrepreneur wants to share the ownership and therefore the profits with others.

In the following sections we will follow the fortunes of a young entrepreneur called Saabira and look at the decisions she makes starting and running her own business.

Saabira is an unemployed school-leaver. She has identified a gap in the market for the delivery of freshly made sandwiches, snacks and cakes to nearby office workers. She therefore decides to start her own business. She is good at cooking, likes meeting people and wants to earn enough money from her business to help her save for a deposit on a house.

> ### Incorporated and unincorporated
>
> **Incorporated business:** A limited company with its own legal identity, separate from the identity of the owners who are shareholders. Can be a private limited company (Ltd) or a public limited company (PLC). The owners/shareholders have limited liability.
>
> **Unincorporated business:** Does not have a separate legal identity from the owners. Could be a sole trader or partnership. The owners have unlimited liability.

Like every entrepreneur, Saabira must first consider four key questions. The answers to these questions will help her decide what type of business organization is best for her.

Question 1:
Do I have enough money?

To start a business an entrepreneur needs **capital**. This is money used to finance a business.

Money invested in long-lived productive assets such as premises, machinery and other equipment is called **fixed capital**. Money used to pay running costs including wages and bills for electricity, telephones and purchases of materials is called **working capital**. ➤ **5.2.2**

Some business organizations need more capital than others. If Saabira does not have enough savings of her own to start her business, or is unable to raise the money she needs from friends and family or from a bank loan, then she may need to find investors who are willing to provide additional capital in return for a say in how the business is run and a share of any profits. Saabira may therefore need to consider starting a **partnership** or a **limited company** and sharing the ownership of her business.

Question 2:
Can I manage my business alone?

All promising entrepreneurs, including Saabira, must decide whether or not they can manage their business alone. Running a business can often mean trying to do everything yourself, working very long hours and going without holidays.

For example, to manage her business Saabira will need to organize the production of sandwiches and cakes, negotiate with suppliers of ingredients, ensure that her premises comply with food hygiene laws, make payments, keep accounts, develop a marketing strategy and, if necessary, recruit and manage staff. This means she will also need to be familiar with employment, minimum wage and health and safety laws, and much more.

Starting a business with others can therefore spread this heavy workload and also bring people with different skills into the business, for example skills in business law, accounting, purchasing, production, marketing and human resources management.

Question 3:
Do I want to share ownership of my business and any profits?

If Saabira's answer to this question is no then she must start her business alone and be a sole trader. However, if she does not have enough money to start her business and does not have the skills, time or energy to manage it alone then she will need to find other investors to help start her business. This means Saabira cannot make all the business decisions. She will first need to consult other owners who have a share in her business. She will also need to share any profits her business makes with them.

Question 4:
Am I prepared to risk everything I own?

Saabira needs to consider what type of business organization is most suitable for her enterprise. Different types of business organization carry different levels of risk for the entrepreneur. If Saabira goes it alone she could end up having to repay all her business debts if the business fails. Her liability for business debts would be unlimited. She may have to use up all her savings or sell her possessions to pay off her business debts.

Having **unlimited liability** means Saabira can be taken to court and declared bankrupt if bills are unpaid. This is because she does not have a **separate legal identity** from her business. The business and Saabira are considered to be legally the same under the law.

However, if Saabira does not want to risk losing everything she owns she will need to consider other types of organizations that will limit her liability to repay business debts. In a limited partnership or limited company most, if not all, of the owners have **limited liability** and their businesses are considered to be legally separate from them. This means in the event of business failure they will only lose the amount of money or capital they invested in the business. They cannot personally be held responsible for any business debts.

Understanding private sector business organizations

We will now compare different types of business organization in the private sector of an economy according to:

who owns the business

how it is controlled

how it is financed

the owners' liability to repay business debts

The sole trader

The sole trader is the oldest and most popular type of business organization

A **sole trader** or sole proprietorship is a business organization owned and controlled by one person. A sole trader may employ other people to work in the business, but it will only ever have one owner.

Most businesses are sole traders. It is the oldest and most common form of business organization in the world. Many small businesses run local shops or provide personal services such as hairdressing, plumbing, building and vehicle repairs. Many of today's largest corporations started out as sole traders many years ago.

 Most sole traders finance their business from their personal savings, borrowing from friends and family or from a bank loan. However, banks are often unwilling to lend to sole traders because they are considered risky enterprises. They can face considerable competition from large businesses and other small businesses, and many close down within their first few years of operation.

 Modern technology has reduced the cost of starting up a new small business. Many sole traders can operate their businesses from home thanks to the internet and mobile communications which allows them to keep in contact with customers and suppliers. However, in the event of business failure the sole trader is liable for all the business debts. That is, a sole trader has an unlimited liability.

ACTIVITY 1.14

From the article identify and list the main features, advantages and disadvantages of a sole trader business.

Pop in for something Bitesize

Customers of Bitesize, the new sandwich and coffee bar in the town, can look forward to good food and a personal, friendly service, according to owner Saabira Rahman. She was busy preparing fresh sandwiches, snacks and lots of delicious pastries for local shoppers and office workers when we popped in to sample her menu. We asked her why she had decided to open her own business.

"I ENJOY cooking but had been unemployed for some time," Saabira explained.

"By running my own business I am assured a job but I get to be my own boss and keep all the profits I make. Not that I have made any yet," she laughed. "I have to work every hour I can to run the business, whether it is buying ingredients, cooking and preparing food, serving, cleaning and even keeping the accounts. If I had the time and money I would hire some employees to help me!"

Starting your own business can be an expensive and risky business, as Saabira found out. "Banks wouldn't lend me any money. They said there was too much competition and my business could be at risk."

Instead Saabira had to use all her savings to buy equipment and pay the deposit on her shop premises.

"Monthly bills for ingredients, electricity and my mobile phone are also high," she said. "I must earn at least $400 in revenue each month just to break even. I'd love to take a few days off but I wouldn't make any money."

"Then of course, if the business fails I will have to repay any business debts even if it means selling my possessions to do so! But I plan to make the business a success and so far, so good!"

Bitesize can also provide sandwiches and pastries for business functions and parties.

Advantages of a sole trader	Disadvantages of a sole trader
+ They are easy to set up. There are few legal requirements needed for business registration.	− The owner has full responsibility for running the day-to-day business. This may mean working very long hours and going without holidays.
+ These businesses can often be set up with little capital.	− The business may lose revenues and profits if the owner is off sick or on holiday and cannot manage the business.
+ The owner is his or her own boss and has full control over the business.	
+ The owner receives all profits after tax and therefore has an incentive to work hard.	− The owner has unlimited liability to repay any business debts.
+ Personal contact with customers can increase customer loyalty.	− Sole traders often lack capital to buy new equipment or to expand.
+ Separate financial accounts are not required for the business.	− Sole traders often lack all the skills they need to run their businesses successfully.
+ The owner is able to keep financial details about his or her business private.	

Partnerships

Partnerships can inject additional capital and skills into a small business

A sole trader may find that more capital is needed to expand the business and additional owners are needed to help run it. The sole trader can do this by forming a partnership.

A **partnership** is a legal agreement between two or more people, usually no more than 20, to own, finance and run a business jointly and to share any profits. Most are small, local businesses. Partnerships are popular business organizations among professionals including solicitors, doctors, accountants and veterinary surgeons.

Most partners are **general partners** who share unlimited liability. However, it is also possible to have some **limited partners** with limited liability. A **silent partner** or **sleeping partner** will provide money to the partnership in return for a share of the profits, but will not be involved in the management of the organization.

In a **limited liability partnership (LLP)** some or all the partners can have limited liability, although laws governing this vary between different countries and often different regions within large countries. LLPs in which all partners have limited liability are therefore very similar to limited companies except that partners retain an automatic right to manage their business directly. Shareholders in limited companies do not.

From the article identify and list the main advantages and disadvantages of forming a partnership.

A bigger bite at Bitesize

TODAY Saabira Rahman, owner of Bitesize, celebrates over one year's successful trading with the opening of another bar near the main business district. So what is the secret ingredient in her success?

"Good, competitively priced food," she explained. "Our customers like the friendly atmosphere and personalized service. You tell us what sandwich you would like and we can make it!"

But the banks are not yet convinced. They have been unwilling to lend the business money to expand, suggesting the market is too competitive.

"Sure it is," Saabira agreed, "but it just means you have to work harder to be the best! We have proved the banks wrong and that's exactly what attracted my new partners to the business."

Bashir Chawd and Joanne Hicks have joined Saabira to form the Bitesize partnership. They have invested enough money in the business to open two bars and develop a modern facility to pre-prepare some food for the new bars.

"Not only that, they have brought some key skills into Bitesize and will help me manage the business from day to day. Bashir is a qualified chef and Joanne is an accountant."

"I may have to share the profits with my partners but at least I can take some time off at last!" Saabira joked.

So why did Joanne want to risk putting her savings into Bitesize?

"It's a good business model," she explained. "Of course, if it fails I will lose my investment and have to repay the debts, but we have exciting plans for Bitesize."

"These plans include more outlets and food preparation facilities across the country but raising the money we need for this may take some time."

We asked Bashir if the new partners foresee any other problems.

"Only when Saabira takes that time off!" he laughed. "And we all disagreed about the layout of the new bar but we eventually reached a good compromise."

Advantages of partnerships	Disadvantages of partnerships
+ Partnerships are relatively easy to set up. There are few legal requirements involved in drawing up a partnership agreement or deed of partnership.	− Discussion between partners can slow down decision-making and they may disagree on important business decisions.
+ Partners invest new capital into the business to finance expansion.	− Problems can arise if one or more partners are lazy, inefficient or even dishonest. There may be arguments, the business may lose money and other partners will have to work harder.
+ Partners bring new skills and ideas into a business.	
+ Partners share responsibilities for decision-making and managing the business.	− General partners have an unlimited liability to repay any business debts.
+ Partners share any profits and are therefore motivated to work hard.	− Raising additional capital to finance further business expansion can be difficult because many countries place a limit on the number of partners allowed in each partnership.
+ Partners share business and financial risks, but limited partners have limited liability.	

Limited companies or corporations

Limited companies sell shares to raise capital

Limited companies are also known as **joint-stock companies** or **corporations** in many countries. This is because they sell stocks (also known as **shares**) to raise capital. ➤ **5.1.2**

The people and organizations who invest in these shares become the owners or **shareholders** of joint-stock companies, so called because a company is jointly owned by the investors who have bought its stock.

Each share purchased in a company receives a share of its profit after any taxes on those profits have been paid. This payment is called a **dividend**. Therefore, the more shares a shareholder holds the greater the share of the company they own and the more dividends they will receive from any profits.

Shareholders elect a **board of directors** with valuable financial and business skills to manage their company from day to day. In small companies the directors are often the most important or largest shareholders in the company. However, company directors need not be shareholders.

Some large limited companies have many thousands of shareholders and these companies must each hold an **annual general meeting (AGM)** that their shareholders can attend if they choose. An AGM allows the shareholders of a company to be kept informed about its performance and important business decisions. At an AGM shareholders are usually asked to accept the financial statements of the company, elect directors to manage the business and vote on major decisions.

The two main types of joint-stock company are:

- a **private limited company** or "closed" stock company, so called because it can only sell shares privately to investors known to the existing shareholders

- a **public limited company** or "open" stock company which is able to sell its shares publicly through a stock exchange or bourse.

The number of shareholders allowed in each type of company varies between countries as do other rules. For example, in Saudi Arabia a company must have at least five shareholders while in some other countries it is possible for a private limited company to have just one shareholder and a public limited company to have a minimum of two shareholders. There is usually no upper limit on the number of shareholders a company can have.

Company abbreviations around the world

Country	Public limited company	Private limited company or equivalent
France	SA	SARL
Germany	AG	Gmbh
Greece	AE	epe
India	LTD	Pvt Ltd
Malaysia	Bhd	Sdn Bhd
Spain	SA	SL; SLNE; SRL
South Africa	Plc	Pty Ltd
UK	plc	Ltd
US	Corp.; Inc.	LLC; LC; Ltd Co.

You can often tell where a company is registered from the letters used after its name.

For example, the letters SA after a company name, for example Telefónica SA, means anonymous company or share company in many languages.

However, different abbreviations are used around the world to denote corporate status. The legal status of corporations can also vary between different countries.

People and other business organizations buy shares because they hope to earn good dividends from company profits. Demand for shares in companies expected to make a good profit therefore tend to be high and push up the market prices of their shares on the stock market. Share prices may fall in companies thought to be at risk of losing money or failing. The price of shares in many companies therefore tends to fall more generally during economic recessions. ➤ **5.2.6**

Limited companies are incorporated businesses

Limited companies offer a number of advantages over unincorporated businesses such as sole traders and partnerships. This is because in most countries limited companies are incorporated businesses or corporations.

An **incorporated business** has a **separate legal identity** from its owners, which means the following.

- All business owners (shareholders) have **limited liability**.

- The business can own assets and borrow money in its own right.

- The business can be taken to court and held responsible for any harm or injury suffered by an employee, customer or anyone else as a result of the activities of the business.

- The business can be taxed and must produce separate financial statements. ➤ **5.3.2**

From the article below find and make a note of the answers to the following questions.

► How do private limited companies raise capital?

► What does the term "limited" denote in "limited company"?

► Who decides who will manage the company?

► What are the main advantages of a private limited company?

► What are the main disadvantages of a private limited company?

Bitesize develops taste for incorporation

Bitesize, the chain of food and snack bars, is to become a private limited company following a private issue of shares in the ownership of the business. The sale of the shares will raise capital to finance a new expansion programme.

Founding owner Saabira Rahman, who is now managing director of Bitesize Ltd, explained her plans to expand the business into other major cities across the country, and to open their first restaurant.

"This all requires significant new capital" she said, "and we did not want to take on an expensive bank loan. So we decided to incorporate and to invite friends, family, our employees and our suppliers to buy shares in the company".

Head of catering, Bashir Chawd, explained the attraction. "We are a growing and profitable business. The more profit we make the more dividends our shareholders will receive. The only downside is they could lose their investment if the business fails, but they have no responsibility for business debts".

Saabira will hold a controlling 51% of the shares in Bitesize and will continue as managing director, but all shareholders will be able to vote on major company decisions and the election of other members of the board of directors to run the company at annual general meetings.

Finance director Joanne Hicks has been busy preparing all the legal documents required to form a limited company.

"It has been a difficult process at times," she explained. "We have spent a lot of time and money getting the legal and financial advice we need to incorporate and sell shares."

Limited companies are also required to keep and publish detailed annual accounts of their revenues and profits, capital, business loans and directors'

salaries.

"Yes, quite a list," she sighed.

Advantages of private limited companies	Disadvantages of private limited companies
+ Shareholders can elect directors to manage the business on their behalf. + Shareholders receive dividends from profits. + Limited companies have a separate legal identity from their owners. + Shareholders have limited liability. + The sale of shares can raise significant capital. + Private limited companies are a popular form of organization for family businesses or partnerships looking to raise additional capital to expand their businesses.	− Private limited companies are legally required to keep detailed financial statements of their income, profits, assets, loans and other liabilities, shareholdings, dividend payments and directors' salaries. In some countries they also are required to publish these details. − Large shareholders can outvote others on decisions that affect the company. − Directors may run a company in their own interests rather than in the best interests of the company's shareholders. − Shares can only be sold privately and only with the agreement of all other shareholders. This may make new investors unwilling to buy shares as they may be unable to sell them quickly if they want their money back.

From the article below, find and make a note of the answers to the following questions.

▸ Why is it likely to be easier for a public limited company to raise capital compared to a private limited company?

▸ How much share capital does Bitesize plan to raise from the sale of new shares?

▸ Why are the original owners of Bitesize now more at risk of losing overall control of their company?

▸ What are the main advantages and disadvantages of a public limited company?

4 THE CITY TIMES

Crunch time for Bitesize on the stock market

Bitesize has gone from strength to strength since owner Saabira Rahman started the catering chain just four years ago. But today's announcement that it has received the green light to issue shares for sale to the public will test the appetite among investors for further expansion plans.

"We plan to expand into all major cities nationwide and open our first restaurants and food preparation plants in New York, Mumbai and Cape Town," explained founding owner Saabira Rahman. "This of course requires a significant injection of new capital, but our projections for future growth and profitability are very healthy. We have already received a lot of interest from new investors."

The new issue of 500 000 shares with a face value of $5 each will raise $2.5 million for the business.

Obtaining a listing on a stock exchange to sell shares publicly can be a very involved and expensive business.

"We have worked closely with the

governing body of the stock exchange to ensure we have a sound business model and sufficient financial strength to attract new investors," said finance director Joanne Hicks. "Full information about the company and how to apply for shares is contained in a detailed prospectus."

"We plan to issue this next week

along with our annual accounts, and also publish it in all major national newspapers."

However, Joanne's position could be at risk if powerful new shareholders want to elect new board members to key positions such as finance.

"That doesn't worry me," said Joanne. "All shareholders including me will want the most highly skilled, motivated and honest people in key Board roles. I have a strong record of achievement with the company but if there is someone better then so be it."

Much of course will depend on who Saabira Rahman wants on her Board. She will remain the majority shareholder in Bitesize plc. Combined with the shareholdings of the original owner, Joanne Hicks and Bashir Chawd, the original shareholders, will retain the controlling interest in the company along with Saabira Rahman.

Public limited companies must obtain a public listing to sell shares on the stock market

In most countries a public limited company needs a minimum of two shareholders. Shares are issued for sale to the general public on the **stock market**. This is the global market for buying and selling new and existing shares in public limited companies.

A company that intends to "go public" must obtain a **public listing** to sell shares on a stock exchange or bourse. There are many stock exchanges around the world. Some of the largest and most well known are the New York Stock Exchange (NYSE) in the US, the London Stock Exchange in the UK, the

Tokyo Stock Exchange in Japan and the Deutsche Börse in Germany. Stock exchanges are business organizations, usually public limited companies, which specialize in providing facilities for other companies and investors to issue, buy and sell shares.

Before a limited company can sell shares through a stock exchange, the governing body of the exchange will investigate the company to ensure that it is trustworthy and financially sound. A company that meets these requirements will be allowed to sell its shares through the exchange. The public listing and issue of new shares for sale in a company is called a **flotation**.

Advantages of public limited companies	Disadvantages of public limited companies
+ A public limited company can advertise new issues of shares for sale using a prospectus.	− It can be expensive to form a public limited company. Many legal documents and company investigations are needed before a company can be listed on a stock exchange to sell shares.
+ The public sale of shares through the stock market can raise significant capital.	− Public limited companies are required by law to publish detailed annual reports and accounts and to hold AGMs with shareholders.
+ Shareholders can elect directors with key business skills to manage the business on their behalf.	
+ Shareholders receive dividends from profits.	− The original owners can lose overall control of their company unless they keep a controlling interest of at least 51% of all shares in the company. In this way they can outvote all other shareholders on major company decisions.
+ Limited companies have a separate legal identity from their owners.	
+ Shareholders have limited liability.	− The original owners may also lose control of their company if it is taken over by another. A takeover or acquisition occurs when one company buys enough shares in the ownership of another firm so it can outvote the owners of that company and take overall control.
	− Directors may run a company in their own interests rather than in the best interests of the company's shareholders.

Public limited companies are some of the largest and most successful business organizations in the world

There are more private limited companies in the world but they tend to be much smaller in size than most public limited companies. This is because a public limited company is able to raise far more capital for business expansion than a private limited company because it can sell shares to many more investors on the stock market.

Public limited companies are some of the largest and most successful business organizations in the world. For example, in 2017 WalMart Stores was the world's biggest company with an annual revenue of almost $486 billion. Other large public corporations include such **multinational** giants as Apple, Royal Dutch Shell, ExxonMobil and Toyota Motors. ➤ **6.3.2**

Other forms of business organization

Joint ventures

A **joint venture** is a contractual agreement between two or more organizations to share the expertise, investment, management, costs, profits and risks of running a new business project.

Large or small business organizations seeking to expand into new markets overseas or to develop new advanced products and technologies often seek to form joint ventures with other organizations with experience in these areas. In this way joint ventures help to spread and reduce business risks.
➤ **3.4.3**

For example, BP plc and General Electric Inc. formed a joint venture in 2006 to develop new hydrogen power projects to reduce greenhouse gas emissions from electricity generation. Similarly, the Sikorsky Aircraft Corporation and Tata Advanced Systems Limited (TASL) created a joint venture in 2009 to manufacture aerospace components for Sikorsky in India. Neither of these companies had sufficient finance or expertise to undertake these projects alone.

Joint ventures can be partnerships or limited companies and may be dissolved once their objectives have been achieved.

Advantages of joint ventures	Disadvantages of joint ventures
+ Costs and risks can be shared. + Each business in the joint venture gains access to the knowledge, technologies, superior management and customers of the other. + A joint venture may enjoy size advantages, increased market share and power, and economies of large-scale production.	− The businesses involved in the joint venture may disagree on important decisions. − Profits are shared. Ideas which could give one of the businesses a future competitive advantage also have to be shared. − The joint venture partners may have very different ways of running their businesses and their cultures may clash.

Franchises

The franchise business organization was first introduced in the US but is now popular the world over.

McDonald's is one of the largest and most well-known franchising companies in the world. It has more than 35 000 fast food restaurants worldwide in over 100 countries. Around 75% of its restaurants are owned and operated by independent local business owners who have bought the right to advertise, produce and sell McDonald's food products such as the Big Mac, Quarter Pounder, Chicken McNuggets and Egg McMuffin.

Franchising has allowed McDonald's to achieve rapid global growth in its brand and sales. A new owner pays up to around $45 000 for a franchise depending on the location, and then pays a monthly service fee and rent as a percentage of its sales to McDonald's.

In return McDonald's provides owner and staff training, restaurant equipment, supplies, promotional materials and if necessary help with finding suitable premises. It also monitors the performance of each restaurant. It is important for McDonald's that each restaurant provides good-quality food and service otherwise poor quality could damage the brand image and reputation of the entire business operation.

In addition to McDonald's there are many well-known examples of successful franchises, many in the fast food retailing industry including Subway, Pizza Hut and Burger King. Franchises are also popular in business sectors such as carpet cleaning, travel, fitness centres, personalized printing, car rental and pest control.

A **franchise** involves an agreement by one company to another business organization to permit the distribution of its goods or services using its trademark or brand name.

- The **franchisor** is an existing, usually well-known company with an established identity, market and brand name for its product.
- The **franchisee** is a sole trader, partnership or limited company that buys the right to use the business name, brand name, production methods and promotional materials of the franchisor.

To buy a franchise a franchisee has to pay an initial fee to the franchisor and a monthly or annual percentage from revenues or profits. The bigger and better known the franchise, the higher these fees are likely to be.

> There are lots of measures to show you how you're performing regionally and nationally – as well as your own figures for last week and last year. I just like to beat sales targets. It gives me a buzz.

Owner–operator of five McDonald's franchises

▲ McDonald's and Subway are two of the world's largest franchise operations

Advantages of franchises	Disadvantages of franchises
To the franchisee	**To the franchisee**
+ Selling or making an established product reduces the risk of business failure.	− Fees and ongoing payments can be expensive.
+ Banks are often more willing to lend to businesses looking to purchase a franchise because risks are lower.	− The role of business owners is reduced to being branch managers. Most business decisions are taken by the franchisor.
+ Training for staff, supplies and promotional materials are provided by the franchisor.	− There may be regular monitoring of performance by the franchisor.
To the franchisor	**To the franchisor**
+ Offering a franchise is a relatively quick and easy way to expand the business, sales and market share.	− The franchisees of each business unit keep most of the profits they make.
+ Fees and regular payments are received from franchisees.	− A franchisee that fails to maintain a good-quality product and level of service could damage the reputation of the entire business.
+ Franchisees are required to buy products and supplies from the franchisor.	
+ Management costs are minimized as franchisees manage their own business units.	

Antonio and Don own three successful coffee shops in a large city. They have been pleased with the profits over the past 5 years from the three shops. Good customer ratings on social media have raised awareness of their brand 'AD Coffee'. The partners would now like to expand the business and are considering whether to form a limited company or franchise the brand.

You are a business consultant advising Antonio and Don as to which form of organization they should choose. You should:

▶ give them as much information as is possible on the benefits and limitations of forming a limited company or offering a franchise

▶ make sure that they are fully aware of the risks involved

▶ recommend which option they should choose

▶ justify your recommendation.

Business organizations in the public sector

Public corporations carry out governmental functions or provide public services

The public sector in a mixed economy includes all organizations owned and controlled by national, state or local government authorities. Many of these organizations are the administrative departments, ministries or offices of government authorities responsible for developing, implementing or administering government policies, including the collection of taxes and the payment of social security or welfare benefits. ▶ **1.1.1**

However, some public sector organizations are **public corporations**. These are business-like organizations created by the national or central government to:

▼ The Saudi Arabian Oil Company (Saudi Aramco) is an example of a state-owned enterprise

- carry out particular government functions, such as a central bank or public broadcasting corporation

- provide essential public services, such as a public hospital or public sanitation

- carry out commercial activities on behalf of the government, such as a state-owned rail company or airline.

Public corporations that carry out commercial activities are also called state-owned enterprises or **trading bodies**. This means they produce and sell goods and services to earn revenues. Many state-owned enterprises were once private sector organizations that have been **nationalized**. This means they were taken into public ownership and control by the government. ▶ **1.2.2**

There are many different examples from around the world.

Some trading bodies are subsidized by their governments. This means they receive money from taxes or other government revenues to cover any losses they make from providing some or all of their services at prices below their costs of production. This is because they provide essential or economically beneficial services such as water supplies, postal services or electricity that should be available and affordable to all people and businesses regardless of their incomes.

However, some trading bodies are able to operate at a profit. Their profits can be reinvested to improve their services or used by the government to pay for other public expenditures. **> 6.1.1**

▼ Some examples of public corporations from different countries in 2014

Australia	India	UK
Australian Broadcasting Corporation	Air India	British Broadcasting Corporation
Australia Post	Cotton Corporation of India	Channel 4 Television
Australian Rail Track Corporation	Indian Oil Corporation	National Air Traffic Services
Reserve Bank of Australia	Indian Telephone Industries	National Nuclear Laboratory
	State Bank of India	Network Rail
	State Road Transport Corporation	Scottish Water

France	Thailand	US
La Poste	Airports of Thailand	Amtrak (national rail corporation)
France Télévisions	Electricity Generating Authority	Corporation for Public Broadcasting
Radio France	Metropolitan Waterworks Authority	Federal Crop Insurance Corporation
Électricité de France	Port Authority of Thailand	Federal Prison Industries
Aéroports de Paris	Provincial Waterworks Authority	Legal Services Corporation
	Thai Airways International	National Park Foundation

Many nationalized or state-owned enterprises have since been privatized in many countries. This means they have been returned to private sector ownership and control. **> 1.2.2**

Local government authorities may also organize and operate trading activities

In addition to the national or central government in a country, local government authorities may also operate public sector enterprises selling services directly to consumers. These may include local theatres, libraries, children's nurseries and swimming pools. Many of these services may be run at a loss or will at least be expected to cover their costs with their revenues. However, some may be able to set their prices or charges at a level that will earn a profit.

Advantages of public corporations	Disadvantages of public corporations
+ They can safeguard the supply of essential services such as water and electricity supplies.	− They may be managed and run inefficiently because, in many cases, they are not required to make a profit.
+ They can safeguard nationally important industries, such as nuclear energy for security and safety reasons, or industries that are major employers.	− They face little or no competition from other firms and may therefore provide poor levels of service.
+ They can provide socially or economically desirable services, such as public transport, broadcasting and health care, even if these activities make a loss.	− Governments may use them for political purposes, for example raising their prices to earn more public revenue rather than raising taxes, or to employ more workers in order to reduce unemployment prior to an election.

Key features of public corporations

- Government ministers set their objectives.
- They are managed by a board of directors appointed by government ministers.
- Government ministers are accountable to Parliament and the general public for the conduct of both public corporations and their boards of directors.
- Public corporations have a separate legal identity from their boards of directors and the government.

▲ Examples of local government enterprises

Exam **PREPARATION 1.3**

Susan set up her business as a sole trader running a kennels to look after dogs while their owners are away on holiday. The business is successful and has opened a number of new kennels since. Susan took on a business partner two years ago. Growth has continued and the business has 10 boarding kennels in different towns and villages.

Susan is now planning to expand further and wants to open more kennels. One option available to her is a merger with a business that owns and operates five kennels in another area of the country. Another option is to form a private limited company (Ltd).

a Explain the term "sole trader". [2]

b Dog boarding kennels are classified as a tertiary sector activity. Give **two** other examples of businesses that are also in the tertiary sector. [2]

c Identify and explain **two** advantages to Susan of having a business partner. [4]

d Identify and explain **three** potential problems to Susan's business of continuing to grow in the future. [6]

e Recommend whether Susan should merge with the other business or if she should form a private limited company as a way of expanding her business. Justify your answer. [6]

Learning **CHECKLIST**

Before you continue make sure you are able to

Identify the main features of different **forms of business organization:**

✓ the main features of **sole traders, partnerships, private and public limited companies, franchises** and **joint ventures**

✓ the differences between **unincorporated businesses** and **limited companies**

✓ the concepts of **risk, ownership** and **limited liability**

✓ recommend and justify a suitable form of business organization to owners or managers in a given situation

✓ the main features of business organizations in the **public sector**, including **public corporations**.

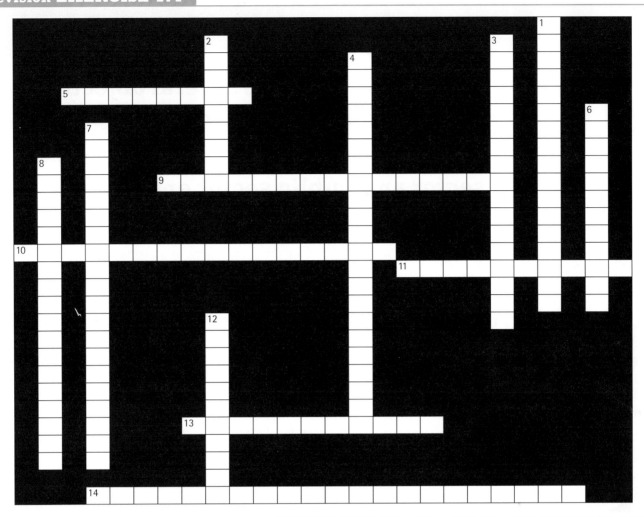

Clues down

1 A business organization jointly owned by its shareholders (5, 5, 7)
2 An agreement between a company and another business organization to permit the distribution of its goods or services using its trademark or brand name (9)
3 A government-owned enterprise created to carry out a governmental function or public service, for example a postal service or public broadcasting corporation (6, 11)
4 A business organization, either a sole trader or partnership, that is considered in law to be legally the same as its owners. This means the financial responsibility of the owners to pay off the debts of their business is without limit (14, 8)
6 The owners of an incorporated business (12)
7 A type of joint-stock company able to sell its shares publicly on the stock market without the prior agreement of its existing shareholders (6, 7, 7)
8 Sole traders and general partners have this. It means they are legally responsible for the repayment of the debts of their businesses even if they have to draw from their own personal financial resources to do so (9, 9)
12 The global market for the purchase and sale of new or "second hand" stocks (or shares) in public limited companies (5, 6)

Clues across

5 A share of the profit of a limited company received by a shareholder (8)
9 A person who invests in a partnership but plays no active role in its management and has a limited financial liability for any debts of the partnership (8, 7)
10 Limited partners and company shareholders have this. It means they not legally responsible for the debts of their business and in the event of its closure they will at most only lose the amount of capital they invested in the business (7, 9)
11 A type of business organization that is owned and controlled by one person and easy to set up. It is the most popular form of business organization in the world (4, 6)
13 A legal agreement between two or more people to jointly own, finance and run a business organization, and to share its profits. They are a popular form of business organization for doctors, accountants, lawyers and in other professions (11)
14 An incorporated business that can only sell its shares privately and with the prior agreement of its existing shareholders (7, 7, 7)

1.5.1 Businesses can have several objectives and the importance of them can change

1.5.2 Differences in the objectives of private sector and public sector enterprises

Key POINTS

▶ Business objectives are the goals or aims of business organizations.

▶ Many business objectives have clear and measurable business targets, for example to increase profits by 5% per year.

▶ A business organization makes production and other plans and undertakes practical actions to help it achieve its targets.

▶ Progress towards agreed targets can be measured and monitored over time.

▶ The most common objectives among private sector business organizations are profitability, growth and increasing market share.

▶ Business survival is a key objective for many new business organizations, but survival also becomes an important objective for large and established businesses during an economic recession.

▶ Business objectives may change over time as economic conditions, competition between firms or technology changes.

▶ Some private sector firms use business strategies to maximize improvements in social and environmental well-being rather than trying to maximize profits for their owners or shareholders. They are called social enterprises.

▶ Relatively few organizations in the public sector operate for profit. Instead they are set targets for the cost and quality of the public services they provide. Many are also required to meet social and environmental objectives.

Business BUZZWORDS

Profitability – the ability of a business to continually generate revenues that exceed its costs.

Business objective – a goal or aim the owners, managers and employees in a business work towards.

Mission statement – a brief written statement of the purpose and objectives of a business organization.

Business target – an objective expressed as a value or volume to achieve by a given date.

Profit maximization – choosing production methods, outputs and prices that will earn the business the greatest amount of profit possible from the resources it uses.

Social entrepreneur – a person who uses his or her business skills to set up and run organizations to maximize improvements in social and environmental well-being rather than profit.

Social enterprise – a private sector organization with social or environmental objectives that reinvests surplus revenues it makes towards meeting these objectives rather than paying them as profits to its owners.

The importance of business objectives

Business objectives are aims or targets businesses work towards

ACTIVITY 1.19

What are likely to be the main objectives of the private sector business organizations described below?

> Budget airlines including Spice Jet of India, Air Asia in Malaysia and Tiger Airways of Singapore are all planning to increase the number of routes they fly including new long-haul services to Europe and Australia.

> The automotive industry crisis of 2008–2010 was the result of the global financial downturn. European, North American and Asian automobile manufacturers all lost significant sales. For example, Spanish automobile manufacturer SEAT cut production by 5% in October 2008, due to falling sales. This affected 750 employees and continued until July 2009. In a similar move, Fiat of Italy announced temporary closures of its factories.

> Carmela has just opened a beauty salon in her hometown on the island of Panay in the Philippines. She is offering her first 20 customers a free makeover and will also serve free iced teas.

A **business objective** is a goal or aim a business wants to achieve.

A business cannot exist without knowing its purpose. It is important for owners, managers and other employees to understand the objectives of the business. Without this understanding, no one in the business would know what to do or how to plan for the future. Objectives are also important for monitoring and measuring the performance of a business.

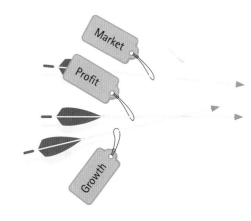

For example, in activity 1.19 Spice Jet and other budget airlines operating in South East Asia are pursuing aggressive expansion plans to grow their market share of international air travel on different routes in order to increase their sales and profits. To do so they will have to compete for passengers with many larger and established airlines already operating flights to the destinations they are targeting.

Similarly, Carmela hopes her business will be able to attract enough customers away from rival beauty salons in Panay to establish her business and make it profitable. In contrast, many car manufacturers were simply hoping to survive during the deep economic recession between 2008 and 2010 until car sales increased again; they did this by cutting their production and costs.

Many business organizations publish **mission statements** which summarize their main aims and objectives. A mission statement enables employees, managers, customers and suppliers to understand the ambitions and actions of a business.

Many business objectives involve clear and measurable **targets** that guide decision-making at all levels in a business. For example, a target might be to increase profitability by 5% per year or to achieve a 20% market share within five years.

A business organization makes production and other plans and undertakes practical actions to help it achieve its targets. Similarly, employees can be set personal objectives to achieve the organization's targets and be rewarded financially for doing so. Without objectives or targets to work towards nobody in a business would know what to do or aim for. Progress towards agreed targets can be measured and monitored over time so an organization will know if and when it has achieved its objectives.

▼ What business objectives provide

A clear set of goals for owners, managers and employees to work together to achieve

A focus for planning what the business needs to do to achieve these goals

A way of measuring business performance over time by assessing how close or far the business is from achieving them

Different business objectives

Profitability, growth and market share

Different businesses often have different objectives. The most common business objectives among **private sector organizations** are:

- **profitability**
- **to grow in size**
- **to increase market share**
- **survival**.

 Profitability is the ability of a business to continually generate revenues from the sale of its goods or services that exceed the costs of their production. Profit motivates entrepreneurs to set up and run business organizations. ➤ **5.3.1**

Many business owners in the private sector aim to maximize their profits. Profit maximization involves choosing production methods, outputs and prices that will earn the business the greatest amount of profit possible from the resources it uses. However, profit maximization can be difficult and often takes some time.

Before a business can increase its profits it may first need to increase its total sales and capture a sizeable share of the market for the product it supplies. It may only be able to do this by spending a large amount of money on developing and advertising its product. It may also have to sell its product at low prices to attract customers. All of these actions will initially reduce business profits. The business may even have to operate at a loss for a time. Many businesses therefore have an objective to achieve **long-run profit maximization**: after a period of growth, to earn a significant and sustained profit each year thereafter from its resources.

In contrast, some business owners may simply aim for a satisfactory level of profit that provides them with enough income to buy and enjoy the goods and services they want without having to work long hours or pay too much in tax.

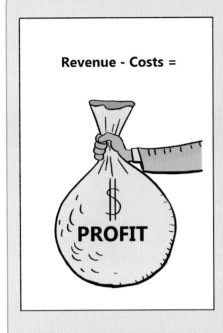

Revenue - Costs = PROFIT

Why is profit important?

- **Profit is a necessary reward for risk-taking in business**: without it people would not invest their money in businesses to produce the goods and services we need and want. **➤ 1.3.1**

  Shareholders buy shares in companies to earn dividends and also to gain from increases in the value of their shareholdings. The more profitable a public limited company is expected to be, the more demand there is likely to be for its shares on the stock market and this will increase the prices at which its shares can be sold. **➤ 1.4.1**

- **Profit provides a source of finance for a business**: profit can be retained or saved by a business and then reinvested in new productive assets to expand the business, in the development of new products and/or in the training of employees. Using profit to finance business activity is cheaper than using bank loans or selling shares. **➤ 5.1.2**

- **Profit is a measure of business success and financial stability**: this can be used to secure low-cost bank loans or to attract new investors or shareholders to provide capital for business expansion. **➤ 5.5.3**

 Growth is a key objective for many private sector business organizations.

Business owners and managers may want to increase the size of their business to increase sales, market share and profits. A large business can have cost advantages, called **economies of scale**, and reduce trading risks by producing a range of products for home and overseas markets. **➤ 4.2.3**

Growth is easier if demand for the goods or services of a business is rising. If consumer demand is not growing then a business may only be able to expand if it attracts customers away from rival firms.

The benefits of growth

- Compared to small firms, a large business may enjoy many cost advantages. For example, suppliers offer price discounts to large business customers who buy items from them in bulk.

- Large businesses produce more output and can offer lower prices due to their cost advantages to capture a larger market share.

- Large businesses can diversify into new products and markets, including overseas. Not only does this help to increase sales it also reduces the risk to the business of a fall in consumer demand for any one product or in any one country.

- Managers of large businesses are often paid higher salaries and feel more important because they have more responsibility.

Increasing market share is an important objective for many businesses. Rival firms will compete for a larger share of total consumer spending on a product.

A new firm entering a market for the first time may initially price its product very low and spend a lot of money on advertising to attract consumers to buy the product. Established rival firms may respond by cutting their prices and also increasing advertising. All of these actions will raise costs and reduce profits. However, a business that is successful in increasing its market share will achieve higher sales and may in future be able to raise its prices to increase its profits.

The **market share** of a business is measured by the proportion of the total sales of a product it achieves in a given period. For example, imagine that the value of total global sales of pencils last year was $100 million of which business A was responsible for producing and selling $30 million of those pencils. It therefore captured a 30% share of the market for pencils that year:

% market share of business A

$$= \frac{\text{sales revenue earned by A (\$)} \times 100}{\text{value of total market sales (\$)}}$$

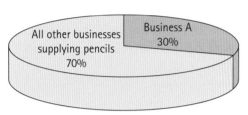

The benefits of increasing market share

- **Increased market power**: for example, shops are more likely to stock a popular, well-known product and the business can use this to ensure the product is placed in prominent positions with attractive displays within stores.
- **Increased influence over suppliers**: suppliers may offer a business with a large market share more generous price discounts and may also be prepared to deal exclusively with that business and not supply its competitors.
- **Reduced threat of competition**: a business that is able to dominate the market supply of a product by capturing a share of the market that is far larger than all of its competitors combined may be able to reduce the competitive threat they pose to its sales and profits.

Business objectives may change over time

Business objectives can change, over time, for many reasons. Some of the main reasons are: starting and running a business can be difficult, business costs can be high, consumer tastes and spending patterns can change quickly and competition from large businesses can be fierce. Many new businesses close within their first year in operation.

Survival is often the most important objective for newly created business organizations. Survival also becomes an important objective even for large and established businesses during an economic recession when unemployment rises and consumer spending falls for many goods and services. Many businesses are forced to close down during economic recessions. ➤ **6.1.1**

Technological change can mean that products and production processes need to be re-designed. Production, sales, growth and profit targets may need to change as a result.

Similarly, new sources of competition, for example from new start-ups or from businesses overseas, can cause an established business to rethink its objectives. For example, it may have to cut its prices and earn less profit in order to compete for sales and maintain its market share.

What is likely to be the main objective of the private sector business organizations described below?

> A large car manufacturer suffering a significant downturn in sales during an economic recession

> An established low-cost airline wanting to introduce flights to new overseas destinations

> A new small business offering window cleaning services to local homeowners

> A leading supermarket chain based in the north of the country seeking to develop superstores in the south

Some private sector enterprises aim to maximize social and environmental welfare rather than profit

Social entrepreneurs are people who set up and run businesses activities primarily to help solve social and environmental issues rather than to maximize profit. They usually reinvest any profits their activities make in their businesses to achieve their social and environmental goals.

The business organizations created by social entrepreneurs are known as social enterprises. Examples can be found in many countries and industrial sectors, including health care and social care, retailing, renewable energy, recycling, sport, housing and education.

Unlike many other private sector enterprises a **social enterprise** uses business strategies to maximize improvements in social and environmental well-being rather than to maximize profits for its owners or shareholders. A social enterprise can therefore be organized and financed as a sole trader, partnership or limited company, or may be a charitable organization. Here are some examples.

> **Social enterprise objectives**
>
> - **Social objectives:** to support the most disadvantaged people in society, including the poor, the sick and disabled.
> - **Environmental objectives:** to protect the natural environment, our oceans and wildlife.
> - **Financial objectives:** to earn profits to reinvest back into the business to improve or expand its social or environmental work.

The Big Issue Company is one of the UK's leading social enterprises. It publishes a street newspaper called *The Big Issue* that is produced and sold in many different countries including Australia, South Korea, South Africa, Kenya, Malawi and Taiwan.

It is written by professional journalists and sold by people who are homeless. They buy copies of the newspaper from the company then sell them at a higher, fixed price to earn a profit which they are able to keep. This provides them with a regular income from sales of the newspaper and teaches them valuable financial and business skills.

Waste Concern (WC) was set up in Dhaka in Bangladesh in 1995 with the motto "Waste is a resource". Each day people and businesses in the city create over 4000 tons of waste but less than half this amount used to be collected, leaving the remainder on roadsides, in open drains and in low-lying areas.

WC's aims include increased recycling and renewable energy use to reduce harmful greenhouse gases, environmental improvement and poverty reduction through job creation and teaching business skills. It achieves these aims by collecting household waste and taking it to community-run composting plants to be turned into organic fertilizer for farming and biogas to produce cheap, green electricity for local people. Local communities earn revenue from selling some of the fertilizer products to fertilizer companies.

Most public sector organizations are non-trading, non-profit making

Public sector enterprises that earn revenues from the services they provide, for example those running a national airline or operating rail services, may be set revenue or possibly profit targets by the government. ➤ **1.4.1**

However, the vast majority of public sector organizations in most countries are not trading bodies and earn no revenues from the provision of their services.

They are therefore set a combination of non-profit objectives and targets covering the cost and quality of the public services they provide and for their impact on different groups of people and the environment. Here are some example objectives.

 Achieve financial targets: because many public sector organizations are funded from taxes, including the administrative departments and ministries of national government, they are often set strict financial targets to achieve to control or reduce their running costs.

 Provide good-quality public services: to people and families including public health care, education, libraries, policing, public rail and bus services, and other socially and economically desirable services funded or organized by the government.

 Achieve social objectives: in addition to meeting financial targets, many public sector organizations have social objectives, including protecting or increasing employment and supporting people who are out of work, sick, disabled or on low incomes.

 Achieve environmental objectives: increasingly public sector organizations are being required to meet several targets related to environmental protection including reducing their water, paper and energy use. However, some public sector organizations have been set up specifically to deliver environmental objectives. For example, the Ministry for the Environment and Forests in India aims to conserve the flora and fauna of India, its forests and other wilderness areas and to prevent and control pollution and deforestation. ➤ **6.2.1**

▼ Public sector organizations are often set a variety of different objectives and targets

Example: public hospital

Reduce costs and increase efficiency by 4% per year

No person to wait more than 12 weeks for an operation after seeing a consultant

Reduce incidence of hospital-acquired infections in patients to less than two cases per year

Maintain patient survey score for hospital quality and service at 70% or above

Reduce water, paper and energy use to reduce environmental impact

Learning CHECKLIST

Before you continue make sure you are able to

Understand why businesses can have several objectives – and that the importance of these can change:

✓ the need for other **business objectives** and the importance of them

✓ different business objectives, including **survival**, **growth**, **profit** and **market share**

✓ the objectives of **social enterprises**

Demonstrate an awareness of the differences in the aims and objectives of **private sector** and **public sector enterprises**.

1.5.3 The role of stakeholder groups involved in business activity

Key POINTS

- ▶ Most businesses have a wide range of business stakeholders. They have an interest in what a business does and how it performs.

- ▶ Different stakeholders have different aims and objectives and a business may find it difficult to satisfy them all.

- ▶ The following are internal stakeholders.
  - Owners and shareholders who aim to increase the value of their investments in their businesses and to earn a profit.
  - Business managers who take important decisions to run a business and may aim for business growth and higher salaries before profit.
  - Employees who help to manage business organizations, operate equipment and produce goods and services. They are motivated by their pay and conditions. Better pay and working conditions can be costly and reduce profits.

- ▶ Important external stakeholders include the following.
  - Banks and other providers of finance to a business who are interested in its ability to repay its debts.
  - Suppliers who sell goods and services to a business on credit terms and want to know it will be able to pay for them when the credit period ends.
  - Consumers who want good-quality and reasonably priced products that offer value for money. A business will fail to make a profit if it does not attract enough customers.
  - Government authorities that raise taxes from businesses and regulate their activities.
  - The wider community or society that depends on the wealth created by business activity but will also be affected by the noise and pollution it can create.

Business BUZZWORDS

Business stakeholders – people and organizations with a direct or indirect interest in business activities and performance.

Trade credit – deferred payment terms offered by suppliers for goods and services they supply to a business.

Trade union – an organization of employees who have joined together to negotiate improved pay and working conditions with their employers.

Shareholders – owners of limited companies or corporations.

Main internal and external stakeholder groups

Stakeholders can affect business objectives, plans and actions

> I have invested my savings in the shares of a major company. I want the company directors to increase sales, keep wages and other costs down and make a good return on my investment.

> I work for a small company. I want the managers to increase my wages and improve my working conditions.

> The bank I manage lends a large amount of money to different businesses each year. I need to be sure these businesses are well run, financially secure and able to repay their loans.

Business stakeholders are individuals, organized groups of people or other organizations that have a direct or indirect interest in the activities and performance of a business.

Stakeholders are not only be affected by the objectives, plans and actions of a business but also help to determine what they are. For example, employees have a direct interest in the future prosperity of the organization they work for but also affect decisions taken on wages, recruitment and health and safety.

Objectives of different stakeholders may conflict with each other

When Swiss company Nestlé SA, the world's largest food company, raised its product prices and cut 645 jobs at one of its factories a few years ago it was in an effort to cut costs and to increase profits. Managers were under pressure from company shareholders to improve the financial performance of the company. However, clearly customers and some of the employees of the company were unhappy about these actions.

Like Nestlé SA most businesses have a wide range of different stakeholders with an interest in what a business does and how it performs. Different stakeholders will have very different aims and objectives and a business may find it difficult to satisfy them all at the same time.

Stakeholders' objectives can often conflict. Business owners and managers may therefore have to compromise when they decide the best objectives and targets for their business. For example, increasing wages can motivate employees to work harder but will increase costs and reduce profits. Cutting wages may boost profits but demotivate employees.

Stakeholders	Who are they?
Owners and shareholders	are people or other organizations that own a business organization. A **shareholder** is a person or organization owning a share of a limited company or corporation.
Managers	are people employed in senior positions in a business to run it from day to day.
Employees	are people who work for a business. Their interests may be represented by a **trade union** or labour union. A trade union is an organization of employees who have joined together to negotiate improved pay and working conditions with their employers.

▼ External business stakeholders

Creditors	are people and organizations that help to finance business activity. They include **banks** that provide loans and credit cards, and **suppliers** that accept payment at a later date for the parts and services they provide to a business. This form of deferred payment is called **trade credit**.
Employees	are people who work for a business. Their interests may be represented by a **trade union** or labour union. A trade union is an organization of employees who have joined together to negotiate improved pay and working conditions with their employers.
Government	comprises local, regional and central government authorities and elected officials. Overseas governments may also be interested in the activities of a business if it buys and sells products internationally.
Wider community or society	comprises people and all other organizations that may be directly affected by the activities of a business, for example people living in homes near the business premises who suffer industrial noise and traffic congestion; or people indirectly affected through the impact the activities of the business have on other people, animals and the natural environment. ➤ 6.2.1

ACTIVITY 1.21

Identify each of the stakeholders in the articles below.

▶ What are their interests in business activity?

▶ What are their key objectives?

▶ How might their objectives conflict with other stakeholders'?

Business leaders warn government plans to increase taxes on profits could damage the economy and increase unemployment

Lapping it up: fat cats cream the profits

A survey today showed top company directors' pay packages have soared over the past year. Their pay rises have far outstripped those of their employees and also the returns enjoyed by the shareholders of the companies they manage.

The average pay for a Chief Executive at one of the country's biggest companies is now over $3 million per year. This is almost 100 times the average earnings of an employee.

World Bank calls in loan from cattle giant

The International Finance Corporation (IFC) has withdrawn a $90 million loan to Bertin, the Brazilian beef producer. The loan from the IFC, the private lending arm of the World Bank, was being used by the cattle giant to expand into the Amazon region, causing destruction of the rainforest.

Consumer fury as bank charges and profits rise

Hewlett-Packard's profits meet expectations

Shareholders in Hewlett-Packard Co., the world's largest personal computer maker, welcomed the news that third-quarter profits had met their expectations after job cuts and other cost reductions helped make up for low demand.

Spanish postal workers union threatens strike action over job losses and pay

Mail bosses condemned the action, saying it would damage customer confidence and undermine the future of postal services.

Environment should come before profits argues Alliance Party

Stakeholders	Why are they important?	Their main objectives are:
Owners and shareholders 	• They invest money in starting and expanding a business. • They lose the money they have invested if the business fails. • They share any profits.	• to earn a good profit on their investments in businesses • to grow the business to increase the value of their investment.
Managers 	• They take important decisions to run a business successfully. • The business could fail if they make bad decisions.	• growing the business – which can give them more power, more status and a higher salary, but this may be at the expense of profits.
Employees 	• They are employed by a business to develop, test, make and sell goods and services. • They are paid wages or salaries by the business. • Unions may organize strikes to secure better wages and working conditions for employees. This can increase business costs and disrupt production. ➤ **2.2.4**	• good wages, salaries and working conditions • job satisfaction • job security. ➤ **2.1.2**
Creditors 	• They lend money to a business or sell it goods and services on credit. • If the business fails they will not be repaid. ➤ **5.1.2**	• to be involved with a well-run business that is able to repay it debts • business growth, which can increase the demand for their goods and services.
Consumers 	• Consumers are willing and able to buy products from businesses. • A business must attract customers to earn revenues. • A business will fail to make a profit if it does not attract enough customers. • Consumer wants are important. A business can carry out market research to identify these. ➤ **3.2.1**	• good-quality and reasonably priced products that offer value for money • good customer service and after-sales care, including refunds and replacements • a growing number of consumers are concerned that business activity should not damage the environment.
Government officials 	• Government officials control the economy and influence the overall level of demand for goods and services. • They raise taxes on businesses and incomes. • They pass laws and regulations to protect employees, consumers and the environment. These can increase business costs. ➤ **2.3.4**	• to encourage successful businesses that employ people, provide incomes and pay taxes • to support new and growing businesses to increase national output and incomes.
Wider community or society 	• People benefit from goods and services produced by business activity, from televisions to medicines, and from the jobs and incomes it creates. • People are affected by noise, air and water pollution created by business activity. • They may object to the damage a business activity causes to the environment, and may form lobby groups or pressure groups to stop the activity. ➤ **6.2.1**	• to improve their living standards • for business activity to provide jobs and incomes • for business activity to produce safe and worthwhile products that do not cause harm or damage the environment • for business activity to treat employees fairly and safeguard the natural environment.

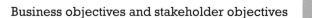

Segurex is a company that sells a range of insurance policies to businesses and the general public. The market for insurance is very competitive and Segurex is always looking for ways to reduce its costs and increase profits. The organization is relatively labour-intensive and so it has recently invested heavily in new computer technology to automate transactions with consumers.

a Segurex has many stakeholders. Explain what is meant by a "stakeholder". [2]

b Segurex is described as a large company. State **two** ways of measuring the size of a business. [2]

c What is profit? Explain **two** reasons why profit is important to businesses such as Segurex. [4]

d The management of Segurex should consider the needs of other stakeholders when making business decisions. Do you agree? Justify your answer with reference to **two** different stakeholders. [6]

e How do the objectives of public sector activities differ from those of Segurex and other organizations in the private sector? [6]

Learning CHECKLIST

Before you continue make sure you are able to

Describe the role of **stakeholder groups** involved in business activity:

✓ the main **internal and external stakeholder groups**

✓ the objectives of different stakeholder groups

✓ use examples to illustrate these objectives and how they might **conflict**.

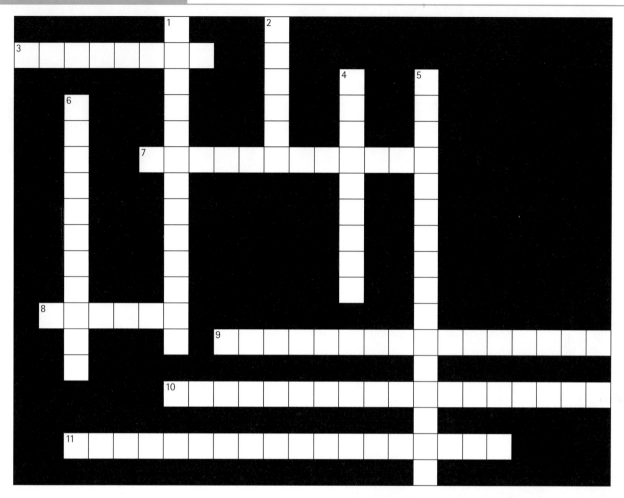

Clues down

1. A business objective of many private sector organizations to consistently generate revenues that exceed their costs (13)
2. This business objective aims to increase the size and value of a business organization (6)
4. These stakeholders help to finance the activities of a business. They include banks that provide loans and suppliers willing to accept deferred payment for the goods and services they supply to the business (9)
5. A short summary of the main aims and objectives of a business organization. They enable stakeholders interested in the business to understand its ambitions and actions (7, 9)
6. This is a measure of the proportion of total sales of a product over a period of time captured by a given business (6, 5)

Clues across

3. These stakeholders are employed in senior positions within organizations to take important business decisions. However, they may sometimes aim for business growth rather than additional profit for shareholders because of the increased status, salaries and power they can enjoy in larger organizations (8)
7. Different groups of individuals and organizations that have a direct or indirect interest in the activities and performance of a business. Their different interests and objectives may conflict with each other (12)
8. A measurable and time-limited business objective, for example to increase profits by 10% per year for the next three years (6)
9. A business with a primary objective that is not profit maximization for its owners or shareholders. Instead it will aim to reinvest any profits in expanding its services to achieve social and environmental objectives (6, 10)
10. The process of selecting a production method, level of output and selling prices that will earn a business the greatest amount of profit possible from the resources it uses (5, 12)
11. A person who uses their business skills and risks money to set up and run enterprises to help disadvantaged people or to protect the environment rather than aiming to maximize profit (6, 12)

2 People in business

2.1 Motivating employees	2.1.1 The importance of a well-motivated workforce
	2.1.2 Methods of motivation
2.2 Organization and management	2.2.1 Draw, interpret and understand simple organizational charts
	2.2.2 The role of management
	2.2.3 Leadership styles
	2.2.4 Trade unions
2.3 Recruitment, selection and training of employees	2.3.1 Recruiting and selecting employees
	2.3.2 The importance of training and the methods of training
	2.3.3 Why reducing the size of the workforce might be necessary
	2.3.4 Legal controls over employment issues and their impact on employers and employees
2.4 Internal and external communication	2.4.1 Why effective communication is important and the methods used to achieve it
	2.4.2 Demonstrate an awareness of communication barriers

2.1.1 The importance of a well-motivated workforce

- In addition to a need for money, working satisfies many different human wants and needs.

- A combination of different factors, both financial and non-financial, motivate people to seek work and be productive.

- Knowing what motivates people in work is vital in business. A key role for management is to ensure that the employees they supervise and support maximize their productivity and contribute fully to the goals of the organization.

- Employee behaviour has been studied many times and there are many theories about what motivates employees.

- If employees are primarily motivated by money they will be more productive if they are paid more. Wages and salaries provide money to buy food, shelter and clothing to satisfy their physiological needs.

- Employees are also motivated by the satisfaction of other needs, such as the need for job security and a safe working environment, and social needs to work as part of a team and gain the respect of their colleagues.

- Some employees may be motivated by money but dislike working. They may only be productive if they are supervised closely and rewarded with higher wages.

- Other employees may be self-motivated. They want to do a good job and realize their full potential. Instead of simply supervising these employees, managers should be supportive, give them opportunities to develop and encourage them with positive feedback.

Motivation – a desire to work hard and the satisfaction obtained from doing so.

Job satisfaction – how content an employee is with his or her job.

Motivational theories – ideas about what motivates people at work.

Physiological needs – basic human needs for food, clothing and shelter in order to survive.

Social needs – human desires to communicate and interact with other people.

Why people work and what motivation means

A combination of financial and non-financial rewards motivate people to work

Siemens employs over 400 000 people in its factories and offices worldwide. The engineering company designs and manufactures many of the products that improve our everyday lives, including domestic appliances such as kettles and refrigerators, magnets for medical scanners, wind generators and traffic lights.

The company knows it must attract the best engineers with the best ideas and motivate them to work hard and stay with the organization if it is to be the best engineering company in the world. Although it offers its employees attractive levels of pay, it knows this alone will not achieve these objectives.

The company recruits engineers at all levels in the company by offering apprenticeships to school leavers and professional training for university graduates, as well as recruiting experienced engineers directly into managerial positions.

As well as opportunities for further education and training, employees at Siemens can also enjoy different career paths by working in different areas such as research, manufacturing, sales and marketing, finance or project management. Skilled engineers place great importance on long-term progression in their careers.

Motivation is the desire an employee has to work hard and do a good job. Knowing what motivates people in work is therefore vital in a business such as Siemens. A key role for managers is to ensure that the employees they supervise and support maximize their productivity and contribute fully to the goals of the organization. ➤ 2.2.2

Most people go to work so they can earn money to buy the goods and services they need and want. That is, people exchange their labour for money.

> Siemens gives me the opportunity to progress and to learn new things. This makes me feel valued by the company.

> I like my work because the company encourages me to think creatively and suggest ways of improving products and processes. Managers recognize my achievements and the best ideas and projects are even rewarded financially.

What makes a job motivating?

Factors include:

- good wages and other benefits, pension, company car, etc.
- reasonable hours of work
- generous holiday entitlement
- a safe and clean working environment
- challenging and interesting tasks
- training opportunities
- working as part of a team
- being consulted on management decisions
- opportunities for promotion
- job security
- being trusted to take on new responsibilities
- regular feedback on performance
- bonus payments in recognition of good work
- job status
- good social relationships inside and outside of the workplace with work colleagues.

However, some people provide their labour for free, for example by undertaking voluntary work to assist charities, so money may not be the only reason people go to work.

In addition to a need for money, working satisfies many more of our different wants and needs. For example, working makes us feel useful, it provides the opportunity to meet new people and make new friends and it teaches us new skills and ideas.

A combination of different factors, both financial and non-financial, therefore motivates people to seek work and to work hard when they find a job they enjoy. ➤ **2.1.2**

These and other factors give an employee **job satisfaction**. A satisfied employee is likely to be more productive and more committed to achieving the business objectives of his or her employer. ➤ **2.4.2**

The benefits of a well-motivated workforce include:

- increased productivity – if workers are satisfied with their work and feel loyalty to the business, they are more willing to work efficiently and in the interests of the business, which will increase the amount of output and revenue they produce as well as improving the quality of their work.

- reduced absenteeism – workers who dislike their work or feel they are not rewarded well enough will tend to take more days off than well-motivated employees. Increasing job satisfaction can therefore lower absenteeism. This in turn means less output is lost and there is less need to arrange for other employees to cover the work of absent colleagues. Costs are therefore lower and profits will be higher as a result means that there is less need for cover which, in turn, results in lower costs and increased profit

- reduced labour turnover – motivated employees are more likely to stay with an organization, which lowers the need to recruit so less time is taken in the recruitment, selection and training process and training and recruitment costs fall.

There are many theories about employees' motivation and behaviour

What motivates people to go to work and to work hard has been the subject of many studies. These have helped many organizations and managers understand what motivates their employees and to improve their job satisfaction to the benefit of their businesses.

The concept of human needs

Maslow's hierarchy of needs

In 1968 the US psychologist Abraham Maslow proposed his hierarchy of human needs. He claimed people initially work in return for wages that will provide enough money to satisfy their **physiological needs** for food, clothing, warmth and shelter.

Once these needs are satisfied, people are motivated by the satisfaction of other needs, such as the need for job security and personal safety, and

Human needs		Employee needs
Developing your full potential A sense of achievement	Self-actualization	Taking on more responsibility Promotion and development
To feel valued Status and recognition	Esteem needs	Promotion opportunities Positive feedback from managers
Friendship A sense of belonging To gain respect	Social needs	Supportive work colleagues Working as a team Good working relationships
Personal safety Security	Safety and security needs	Job security Safe working environment
Food Clothing Shelter	Physiological needs	Reasonable wage or salary

▲ Maslow's hierarchy of human needs

social needs for communication, friendships, a sense of belonging to a team and the respect of others.

To maximize labour productivity, businesses must ensure that their employees are able to satisfy needs higher up in their hierarchy than physiological needs. For example, after satisfying their physiological, security and social needs, people will only be motivated further if they feel valued and trusted by others (esteem needs) and are able to use their creativity and develop to their full potential (need for self-actualization).

Siemens provides its employees with the opportunity to fulfil their higher-order needs. The company recognizes that skilled and creative workers like engineers want to be able to develop, test and implement new ideas. Allowing them the freedom to do so and recognizing their achievements will also help them to meet their esteem needs. For example, Siemens rewards the best ideas through team or individual bonuses or staff celebrations.

Staff training and development opportunities allow their engineers to meet their needs for self-actualization by extending their skills and capabilities and giving them the opportunity to progress to more senior positions. Training also helps to improve labour productivity and their ability to adopt new working practices and technologies that will allow the company to compete more effectively as global market conditions change.

However, not all employees are motivated by the same needs. For example, some people may only be motivated by money and status. High pay can be a status symbol. Others, for example older people who take a part-time job following early retirement, may not need much money but instead work to keep themselves occupied and to meet other people.

Key motivational theories

Taylor's principles of scientific management

Frederick Taylor (1856–1915) was a US engineer who pioneered work studies and spent many years researching ways of increasing labour productivity in factories by making work tasks easier for employees to perform.

Pardip is all *time* and no *motion!*

Zzzzzzz...

Taylor developed time and motion studies that divided up each job into a series of simple but repetitive tasks. He then calculated how many times an employee should be able to perform each task in each day and how much output employees could produce. These were then set as production targets.

According to Taylor, labour productivity would be improved if each employee specialized in a particular task and was rewarded with more pay if he or she achieved production targets. He argued employees are motivated by money and would therefore be more productive if they were paid more. The extra output they produced more than offset the extra pay they received, so average costs would be lower and profits higher. ➤ **4.2.3**

Many manufacturing businesses adopted Taylor's ideas and were successful at increasing productivity. However, Taylor's studies overlooked other factors that motivate employees. Undertaking repetitive tasks can demotivate employees through boredom. It is also difficult to measure the productivity of many employees in office jobs and many services. ➤ **4.1.1**

As a result, many modern organizations no longer follow Taylor's principles. For example, although Siemens has a performance-related pay system that rewards high-performing employees, the company also places great importance on encouraging employees to become more involved in decision-making and empowering them to suggest and implement improvements.

Herzberg's motivators and hygiene factors

Frederick Herzberg studied engineers and accountants at work during the late 1950s and early 1960s. He argued that people have two sets of needs they need to satisfy in work.

Hygiene factors are our basic needs for income, job security and status, among others. These do not motivate people but they must be satisfied, otherwise they will reduce job satisfaction and labour productivity. For example, a difficult relationship with a manager or poor working conditions will dissatisfy employees.

Motivators are our needs for achievement, recognition and personal development. If these needs are satisfied they will increase employees' motivation and boost productivity.

Hygiene factors include:	Motivators include:
▸ job security ▸ job status ▸ wages, salaries and other rewards ▸ working conditions and environment ▸ relationships with managers ▸ rules and regulations in the organization.	▸ a sense of achievement ▸ recognition for good work ▸ opportunities for promotion ▸ interesting and varied work ▸ being trusted with more responsibility ▸ personal development.

Which, if any, of the theories of employee motivation considered above can you identify from these articles about work?

Flexible working "benefits" small firms

Two-thirds of businesses believe flexible working practices improve productivity and efficiency, new research suggests.

Increased flexibility of working practices can partly be attributed to the development of mobile technology, such as laptops and smartphones, which means that employees no longer have to be tied to the office.

Mobile telecom company EE reports that responding to employees' needs by introducing less-rigid working practices is highly beneficial as it means that employers are more likely to keep their staff, so it reduces staff recruitment costs.

At a recent event, several small business managers reported that the ability to choose their locations and hours of work, and access emails offsite, improved their work–life balance and enabled them to go on holidays.

The board of Thai Airways International yesterday agreed to reward employees with bonuses and a pay increase for helping the flag carrier pull out of its financial woes.

When quality is a way of life

Tata Motors (formerly TELCO–Tata Engineering and Locomotive Company) of India introduced its "human relations at work" training programme in 1982. The aim was to empower the workforce to take responsibility.

The result has been the development of shop-floor quality circles, voluntary groups of up to 12 employees involving most of the workforce. They meet for around an hour each week to iron out problems – and discuss how to tackle alcoholism, family debt and communal tensions in their townships.

One group bailed out a colleague who became heavily in debt after personal problems. Another group repaired a fault on a metal press which had baffled German engineers.

Each year, employees make some 100 000 suggestions for improvements, saving Tata Motors nearly $3 million. The company is now making 16 000 more trucks with 6000 fewer workers and has enjoyed a strike-free industrial record over the last 21 years.

Teamwork can boost manufacturing productivity

People who work in the most complex manufacturing environments have the most to gain from teamwork, according to a recently published study.

Using data from steel minimills, the study shows that teams had the greatest impact if they tackled complex tasks together in these environments, enjoyed meaningful incentives and knew that management listened to them.

Learning CHECKLIST

Before you continue make sure you are able to

Understand the importance of a well-motivated workforce:

✓ why people work and what **motivation** means

✓ the benefits of a well-motivated workforce

✓ the concept of human needs in **Maslow's hierarchy**

✓ key **motivational theories** from Taylor and Herzberg.

2.1.2   Methods of motivation

- ▶ Managers and human resources departments in businesses have devised different methods of rewarding work to motivate their employees.

- ▶ The earnings of an employee each week or month may be made up of different financial rewards, including a basic wage or salary, overtime and performance-related pay.

- ▶ The wage rate for a particular job may consist of a basic wage for a given number of hours each week plus a time rate for any overtime hours worked and/or a piece rate for any additional output produced above an agreed target.

- ▶ An annual salary is normally paid to managers, office staff and other non-manual employees in 12 equal monthly payments.

- ▶ Performance-related pay can reward increased effort and productivity. For example, commission may often be paid in addition to a basic wage or salary to retail employees and others involved in sales. High-achieving employees may also receive bonus payments and a share of profits.

- ▶ In addition to financial rewards, business organizations may attempt to motivate their employees using non-financial methods such as job enrichment, job rotation, teamworking, training and opportunities for promotion.

- ▶ Employees may be more motivated, more productive and contribute more to the objectives of their organization if they have interesting and satisfying jobs to do. Labour productivity will increase, absenteeism and labour turnover will fall, leading to lower costs for the business.

Business BUZZWORDS

Net earnings – the take-home pay of an employee after any payroll and income taxes, pension contributions and/or trade union subscriptions have been deducted from gross earnings.

Wages – weekly or monthly payments in exchange for labour supplied to a particular occupation.

Time rate – a wage rate per hour worked by an employee.

Piece rate – a wage rate per unit of output produced by an employee.

Profit sharing – rewarding employees with a percentage of the profits of the business organization they work for.

Performance-related pay – financial rewards given to an employee or group of employees in recognition of high achievement and productivity.

Employee share ownership – rewarding employees with shares in the ownership of the company they work for.

Fringe benefits – non-financial rewards or "perks".

Teamworking – dividing the workforce into small groups of employees and giving them the responsibility for planning and organizing their own areas of work.

Job rotation – enabling employees within a team to swap tasks with each other.

Job enrichment – increasing the degree of challenge in a job by adding tasks that require more skill and responsibility.

Pay Slip	
Employee number:	H/537
Employee name: Hassan Mannippulu	
Wage (40 hours × $12 per hour)	**$480**
Overtime (6 hours × $18 per hour)	**$108**
Productivity bonus	**$100**
Total weekly earnings	**$688**

Financial rewards

Businesses have devised different methods of rewarding work to motivate their employees

Financial rewards are any payments of money made by an employer to employees in exchange for their labour. Methods of payment include wages, salaries and various performance-related payments.

The total or **gross earnings** of an employee each week or month may be made up of many different payments, including a basic wage or salary, overtime pay and a performance-related reward. An employer normally deducts any payroll and income taxes, pension contributions and/or trade union subscriptions from the gross earnings of employees before they are paid their **net earnings** or final take-home pay.

Wages

Wages are usually paid to employees per week or per month either in cash or directly into their bank accounts.

The **wage rate** for a particular job often consists of a **basic wage** for a given number of hours each week plus a **time rate** for any overtime hours worked and/or a **piece rate** for any additional output produced over and above a target level per week.

- **Time rate** is based on hours worked, so the more hours employees work the more they will earn. For example, if an employee is paid $20 per hour and works 35 hours each week his or her **gross weekly wage** will be $700.

In some countries there is a legal minimum wage rate per hour. Employers cannot pay any employees less than the legal minimum. ➤ **2.3.4**

Employees who work additional hours over and above their agreed number of hours each week may qualify for an **overtime rate**. This may be 1.5 or 2 times the normal time rate per hour.

Wages based on time rates are easy to calculate. All that is required is a record of the number of hours each employee has worked and at what time.

The main problem with time rates is that they take no account of how productive each employee is during the time he or she spends at work. Good employees and bad employees paid the same time rates will receive the same wages at the end of each week if they work the same number of hours.

- **Piece rate** is based on unit of output produced, so the more output an employee makes or contributes to the more he or she will earn. For example, if employees are paid $5 for every unit of output they produce, an employee who produces 100 units in a week will receive $500 in earnings.

The advantage of piece rates is that they encourage workers to work harder and produce more. However, this system may also encourage workers to rush and ignore the quality of their work. Power cuts or equipment failures also result in employees earning less and because this is not very fair, employees are often paid a guaranteed minimum amount of money.

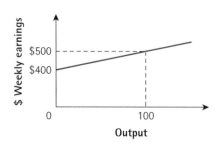

▲ Piece rate only

▲ Basic weekly wage plus piece rate

Piece rates cannot be used when it is difficult to measure the output of some jobs, for example those of a nurse, an office worker or a shop assistant. Time rates or other payments may be more appropriate for these and other service sector occupations.

Salaries

Salaries are normally paid to managers, office staff and other non-manual employees on a monthly basis. The **annual salary** for a job is divided into 12 equal monthly payments, often regardless of the number of hours worked by the job holder each month over and above an agreed amount of time, often between 35 and 40 hours per week. The monthly payment is only likely to change if an employee receives a pay rise, performance bonus or higher salary on promotion.

Performance-related pay

Piece rates are one way of rewarding performance. However, **performance-related pay** can take various forms to reward individual, team or organizational achievement.

- **Commission** is often paid in addition to a basic wage or salary to retail employees and others involved in sales, such as financial advisers and travel agents. The more sales they make or revenue they earn for the organization they work for the more they will earn, usually as a percentage of their sales. Commission is good way of motivating employees to increase sales and revenues.

- **Bonus payments** are normally one-off lump sums paid to employees who have performed well. Bonuses are usually paid at the end of each year. Sometimes they may be linked to the amount of profit a business has made.

- **Profit sharing** involves employees receiving a small percentage of the profits of the business they work for in addition to their basic wage or salary. This can motivate employees to increase their productivity and reduce costs.

- **Employee share ownership** may improve employees' commitment to the company they work for and the achievement of its goals. It involves giving employees some shares in the ownership of their company. As shareholders they become entitled to receive dividend payments from company profits. As profits rise, the more dividend payments they could receive. Also, if their company is doing well, the value of their shares could rise on the stock market. ➤ **1.4.1**

Non-monetary rewards can also be used to motivate employees and may be more cost-effective than increasing wages

In addition to financial rewards, business organizations may attempt to motivate their employees by awarding them **non-monetary rewards**.

Giving employees non-monetary rewards in addition to financial rewards can make a job more attractive and help retain and motivate employees. Some fringe benefits, such as a company car and the provision of a house, are also considered a status symbol and may only be made available to high-performing senior managers.

Non-monetary rewards may include:

- free medical insurance
- use of a company car
- price discounts on purchases of business products
- pension contributions paid by the business
- performance-related gifts, such as free holidays and large-screen televisions
- free accommodation
- free membership and use of a gym and spa.

The provision of non-monetary rewards may be more cost-effective for a business than giving large pay awards to workers. This is because a business with a large number of employees may be able to secure discounts on the purchase or hire of vehicles to provide company cars, or on corporate membership of medical schemes and gyms.

ACTIVITY 2.2

Look at the jobs advertised below. First decide how easy it will be to measure the output or effort of an employee doing each job. Then suggest methods you would use to motivate and reward each one and why. In addition to financial and non-monetary rewards these can include non-financial motivational methods as discussed on the next page.

Experienced window cleaner wanted

Must be happy to work outside in all weather conditions.

Senior Manager

Large banking group seeks experienced senior manager to run human resources department at head office.

Interested in a career in sales?

We are looking for enthusiastic staff to join our new main street fashion store.

Nursing assistant needed

40 hours per week at health care centre. May involve overtime and working at weekends.

Nanjing Bearings Ltd requires a machine operator to produce ball bearings. Good rates of pay but must be willing to work shifts.

Non-financial methods of motivation

Non-financial methods can help make a job more attractive, motivate employees and can be more cost-effective than awarding pay rises

Business organizations may also attempt to motivate their employees using **non-financial methods**, such as job enrichment, job rotation, teamworking, training and opportunities for promotion.

▼ Non-financial methods used to increase employee job satisfaction

Job enlargement	Job rotation
Employees working on flow production lines or operating tills in a large supermarket may become bored repeating the same tasks over and over again. Job enlargement involves adding extra and more varied tasks that require the same level of skill to an employee's job description. For example, instead of an employee bolting bumpers on to new cars he or she may also be asked to assemble the doors and fix on exhaust systems. Job enlargement is often criticized for simply adding more dull tasks to others.	Employees can be organized into small groups or teams and trained to carry out all the different tasks the group has to perform. Employees can then swap tasks with each other. This makes jobs more varied and employees can also cover for each other when one of the group is ill or on leave. However, if the tasks are all equally boring, motivation is unlikely to improve. Getting to know all the different tasks within an area of work or department is especially important in the training of managers and supervisors.
Job enrichment	**Teamworking**
This increases the degree of challenge in a job by adding tasks that require more skill and responsibility. However, some employees may resent being given additional responsibilities especially if it involves no extra pay. Some may find it difficult to cope with additional demands and work pressures. Managers may need to provide them with additional training and support.	This involves dividing up the workforce in an organization into small teams of employees and giving them the responsibility for planning and organizing their areas of work. It encourages greater co-operation and gives employees more responsibility for their own work. They become more involved in problem-solving and decision-making. This can motivate employees because they have more control over their work and feel a greater sense of ownership.
Training	**Opportunities for promotion**
Employees contribute to an organization's objectives. Employees with limited tasks may feel bored and unappreciated. Training can help employees understand how their work fits in with the aims of the business. If they see the importance of their work to the success of the organization, they will feel better about the tasks given to them. However, not all workers are willing to undertake training and may see it as interfering with their ability to get on with their jobs.	The possibility of promotion can motivate employees who want to progress in their careers. Promotion often means more security and higher financial rewards, which can mean the employee can have a more comfortable lifestyle. Employees who see opportunities to get promoted will want to prove that they are good workers. Not all employees are ambitious and some are happier staying in a job they know. Promotion often means more responsibilities and challenges which some workers do not want.

However, not all methods of motivation are appropriate for all employees. For example, flow production workers can easily become bored with routine, dull tasks. In this case, job rotation or job enlargement may help reduce the boredom for these workers.

Look at the three cartoons below showing three employees at work at different times during their working day. Which of the diagrams demonstrates job enlargement, job rotation or job enrichment?

Chris Kaur owns a plastic recycling business. Production is capital intensive and there are 50 employees who operate the machines. The machine operators are paid a weekly wage. Chris is considering introducing a bonus system to reward the most productive workers. Managers are paid by a monthly salary which is five times higher than the wages paid to the machine operators.

a   Define "capital intensive".   [2]

b   Define "bonus system".   [2]

c   Give **two** reasons why managers earn "five times higher than
    the wages paid to the machine operators".   [4]

d   Explain **one** advantage and **one** disadvantage of using a
    bonus system to motivate employees.   [6]

e   Outline **two** non-financial methods of motivation that Chris
    could use to motivate the machine operators.   [6]

Before you continue make sure you are able to

Identify and explain different methods of **motivation**:

✓   **financial rewards** including wages, salaries, bonus payments, commission
    and profit sharing

✓   **non-financial methods** such as job enrichment, job rotation, teamworking,
    training and opportunities for promotion

✓   recommend and justify appropriate methods of **motivation** in given
    circumstances.

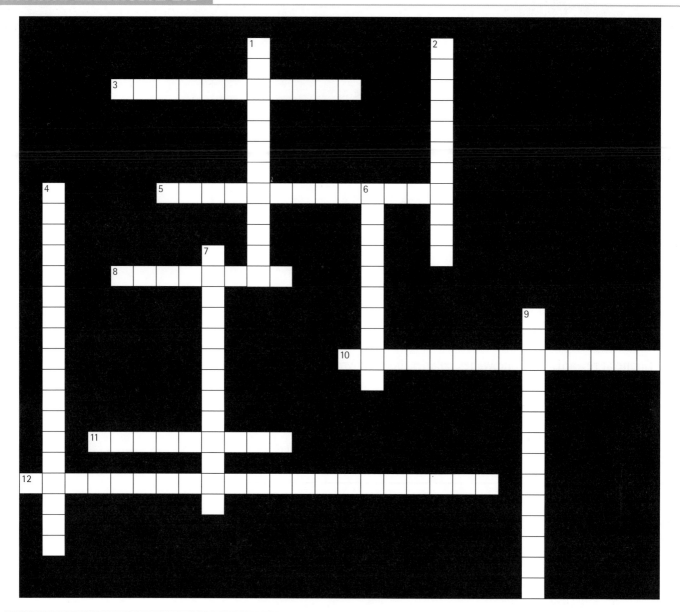

Clues down

1 Methods of motivation which do not involve payments to employees (3, 9)
2 A motivational method that enables employees within a team to swap tasks with each other to vary their work and make their jobs more interesting (3, 8)
4 The term used by Maslow in his motivational theory to describe basic human requirements for food, clothing and shelter in order to survive (13, 5)
6 The desire of an employee to work hard to achieve personal and organizational goals (10)
7 Rewarding employees with a percentage of the profits of the business organization they work for to encourage higher levels of productivity (6, 7)
9 Term used by Herzberg in his motivational theory to describe basic human needs for income, job security and status (7, 7)

Clues across

3 The term used to describe human desires to communicate and interact with other people in Maslow's theory of motivation (6, 5)
5 A motivational method that involves increasing the degree of challenge in a job by adding tasks that require more skill and responsibility (3, 10)
8 A wage payment per hour worked per employee (4, 4)
10 A method used to increase job satisfaction that involves adding extra tasks to a job without increasing the responsibility of the job holder (3, 11)
11 A wage payment per task completed or unit of output per employee (5, 4)
12 Financial rewards given to an employee or group of employees in recognition of high achievement and productivity (11, 7, 3)

2.2.1 Draw, interpret and understand simple organizational structures

▸ Organizational structure determines the roles, responsibilities and authority of managers and employees within a business.

▸ Most businesses are organized into divisions or departments that specialize in performing particular tasks such as production, sales, marketing and finance.

▸ Organizational charts are diagrams that provide a useful way of showing roles, responsibilities and relationships within an organization. A chart can show:

- the hierarchy of different layers of management within an organization; more layers may be added as an organization grows

- the chain of command each manager has in terms of how many other layers of management a manager has authority or control over

- the span of control each manager has in terms of the number of employees the person manages

- how tasks and responsibilities are delegated from managers to their staff.

▸ A hierarchical organization with a tall structure has a long chain of command and a relatively narrow span of control compared with organizations with flat structures.

▸ An increasing number of modern business organizations have chosen to widen their structure to cut out layers of management to reduce costs and increase the speed at which important decisions are taken and implemented.

Organizational structure – how roles, responsibilities and management authority are allocated within an organization.

Organizational chart – a diagram of an organizational structure.

Department – subdivision of a business organization that specializes in performing a particular job or function.

Hierarchy – the layers of management and command in an organization.

Chain of command – the line of management authority in a hierarchical organization.

Span of control – the number of subordinate staff a manager supervises.

Delegation – assigning tasks to other employees in a chain of command.

Managing director – the most senior manager in a company (also called the chief executive officer or CEO in some companies).

Tall structure – an organization with a long chain of command and in which managers have a relatively narrow span of control.

Flat structure – an organization with a short chain of command and in which managers have a relatively wide span of control.

Centralized organization – an organization in which authority, responsibility and decision-making is concentrated at the top of the chain of command.

Decentralized organization – an organization in which a lot of authority, responsibility and decision-making is delegated to lower levels of management.

Organizational structure

An organizational structure determines the roles, responsibilities and authority of managers and employees within a business

When Peter Voser became the chief executive officer (CEO) of multinational oil and gas giant Royal Dutch Shell, he took over a company that many investors and business analysts thought was too slow to grow, too big and too bureaucratic (i.e. too many procedures, rules and paperwork). It was failing to compete against other oil and gas companies such as ExxonMobil and was losing market share.

In response, Voser immediately began reorganizing the company, initially cutting 5000 managerial posts as part of a global programme to de-layer the organizational structure, cut costs by $2 billion and reduce bureaucracy. The number of employees remained over 100 000, which meant each manager now had a wider span of control.

Soon after, Voser announced he was cutting another 1000 managerial jobs to speed up decision-making and to save a further $1 billion. The exploration and production, gas and power and oil sands divisions were also merged to form two new streamlined divisions: upstream and downstream (the extraction and refining of oil and gas), and projects and technology (project management, technical services and the research and development of new technologies and products).

A spokesman for Shell said that the shake-up was about creating "a simpler, flatter company structure, more accountability and faster communication and implementation of decisions and strategy".

Voser explained his motives for the reorganization: "When I became chief executive I did think the organization of the company was working against us. Shell had become too complicated, and slower than I'd like, and working on too many areas and options at the same time."

It is interesting that he suggests "the company was working against us" because it was "too complicated". This means he thought the organizational structure of the company was too complex, had too many layers of management and, as a result, this was slowing down decision-making, making the company less competitive and therefore hindering its growth in sales and profits. Clearly then, how an organization is structured and how decisions are made within it can be important factors in how successful a business is.

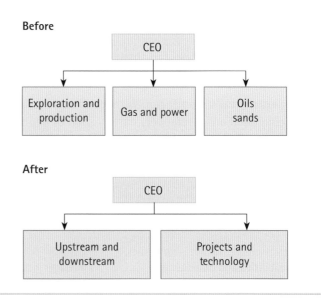

Organizational structure refers to the way in which a business allocates roles, responsibilities and management authority within its organization to best achieve its objectives. ➤ **1.5.1**

Every private sector or public sector organization needs a clear organizational structure so all managers and employees not only know exactly what their own roles and responsibilities are but also are aware of the roles and responsibilities of everyone else in the organization they work with.

Voser thought decision-making was slow in Shell because the original structure was too complicated. As a result, employees did not know which managers were responsible for making what decisions or whom to turn to when they needed help, for example to order materials, recruit new employees, pay wages, organize training, deal with customer complaints or manage financial accounts. Worse still, if an individual employee cannot find the right division or people within the organization to perform a particular task, the person may try to do something he or she is not qualified to do and may do it badly. This could increase business costs, damage the reputation of the business or even cause injury to the employee and others.

An organizational structure therefore sets out:

- who specializes in which tasks
- who is in charge of whom
- who is responsible for making different decisions
- who is responsible for carrying out those decisions
- how decisions and other information are communicated. **> 2.4.1**

Organizational charts show roles, responsibilities and relationships within a business

A simple way of showing how activities and individuals are organized within a business is to use an **organizational chart**.

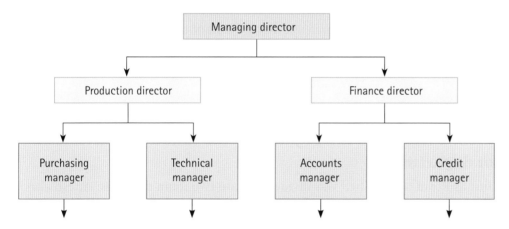

Lines and arrows are used to show relationships between different managers and other employees. Positions towards the top of an organizational chart have more authority and responsibility than those below.

An organizational chart can therefore show:

- the **hierarchy** of different layers of management within an organization
- the **chain of command** of each manager in terms of how many other layers of management that person has authority or control over
- the **span of control** each manager has in terms of the number of employees and job roles he or she is responsible for
- the **delegation** of tasks and responsibilities from senior managers to more junior managers and other employees in their chains of command.

A manager will not have time to make every decision about the day-to-day work of more junior managers or employees in their chain of command. It is therefore important for managers to empower people below them to make decisions about how to organize their work. However, for delegation to be successful the manager must be willing to give up control over those decisions and more junior managers and employees must also be willing and able to accept that responsibility and make sensible decisions. **> 2.2.2**

ACTIVITY 2.4

Before	After
Anesh owns and runs a small business selling seeds, pots and plants in a local market. He used to do everything himself from purchasing and marketing to managing the accounts. It proved too much for him so he hired a number of employees to help.	**Anesh** eventually opened a shop on a plot of land to grow plants for sale. He formed a small private limited company and became the **managing director**. His friend **Dimas** bought some shares in the business and became the **finance director** to manage the business accounts and cash flow. **Guntur** continued as **book-keeper** and filing clerk reporting to Dimas.
Guntur was hired to be his **book-keeper** and filing clerk. **Kersen** was hired to be his **assistant**. This allowed Anesh more time to look after the market stall and tend to his stock of plants.	**Bethari** was hired as **director of operations**, responsible for the management of the shop, marketing and purchasing. **Kersen** was promoted to **store manager** and employed a new **sales assistant** called **Iman**, to help her.
Business was booming so Anesh was very glad of his new business structure and agreed to extend his trading hours. He also expanded his stock of items for sale to include garden ornaments, tools and equipment and as a result he became busier and busier once more.	Bethari also created the positions of **marketing manager** and **stock manager** to report to her and hired **Gus** and **Mulia** to fill these roles.
Anesh, Kersen and Guntur agreed they would all need more help if the business was to grow and survive.	Anesh agreed his young nephew **Lemah** should be employed as a **stock assistant** reporting to **Mulia**.

Draw a simple organizational chart for Anesh's business before and after expansion.
Use boxes to denote people and their job titles, and lines and arrows to show who manages whom in their chain of command.

ACTIVITY 2.5

Investigate organizational structures, departments and management layers in:

▸ a bank

▸ a local hospital

▸ a school or college

▸ a hotel

▸ a major department store

▸ another business organization of your choosing.

Draw a simple organization chart for each one based on your research.

Most businesses are organized into functional divisions or departments

Just as Royal Dutch Shell was divided up into two main divisions, Anesh also divided up his business activities into two main groups. These divisions were finance and operations, and he delegated the responsibility for the day-to-day management of these activities to Dimas and Bethari. Operations were further divided into store management, marketing and stock control, each with their own manager in charge. In this way responsibility for specialist tasks was delegated by Anesh to managers in his chain of command, allowing him more time to focus on major business decisions.

Organizing roles and responsibilities within a business by division or department is common. A **department** is a subdivision of an organization that specializes in performing a major function such as production, sales, marketing, finance or human resources management.

Grouping together employees into departments according to the skills they have and jobs they do makes it easier for them to communicate with each other about their work, agree and monitor objectives and solve work-related problems.

Departments within an organization are functionally interdependent. This means each one relies on the work of the other departments to help fulfil its objectives. For example, sales will rely on the work of the marketing and production departments, and all departments need human resources and finance to operate effectively.

Departments can be organized in a number of different ways and as a business expands, more departments may be added. For example, consider the different ways a major consumer electronics manufacturer could be organized.

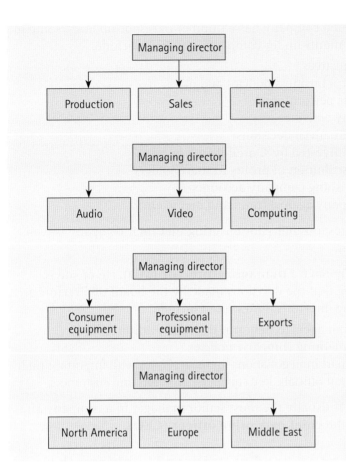

By key functions

Departments may specialize in particular tasks such as production, sales, human resources, research and development (R&D) and finance. This is a common structure for many medium-sized to large organizations.

By main product groups

A multi-product organization may create departments for each of its main product groups.

By main customer groups

Departments can be organized for different categories of customers. For example, many banks have departments for personal banking, small businesses and corporate banking.

By major region

Departments can be organized according to the region in which work is carried out or by main markets. Multinational organizations are often organized in this way. ➤ **6.3.2**

Roles and relationships in organizations

All business organizations need skilled people to run them

Many different activities and tasks need to be performed regularly to run a business successfully, from taking major decisions on business expansion to dealing with customers or operating machinery and computers.

In most businesses, these activities and tasks are divided up between different employees with different levels of authority.

Some employees have responsibility for organizing and managing the work of other employees, providing them with training and guidance and monitoring their performance. In some large organizations there can be many different levels of management, each with management responsibility for the level below.

Directors have overall responsibility for running a company

In a limited company the **board of directors** is the most senior management team. ➤ **1.4.1**

Directors are elected by company shareholders. Each director is normally responsible for managing the work of a main department in the organization structure, for example the director of finance or director of sales and marketing.

The board of directors of a company has a number of responsibilities, some of which are legal requirements under company law. They include:

- setting business objectives
- developing long-term business policies and plans
- monitoring business performance
- controlling company activities
- making important financial decisions
- safeguarding funds invested by shareholders
- determining the distribution of profits to shareholders
- preparing and publishing company accounts
- protecting the company against fraud and inefficiency.

Directors have overall responsibility for ensuring that their company is well managed and successful.

Large companies usually have a **managing director (MD)**. He or she is responsible for ensuring that the decisions made by the board of directors are carried out. A managing director's duties often include:

- appointing senior managers to help run the organization
- devising and implementing company policies
- meeting and taking part in negotiations on major issues with important trade union and government officials, key suppliers, investors and customers.

The managing director is usually the most senior manager in a company and may also be known as the **chief executive officer (CEO)**.

All organizations need good managers to achieve their objectives

Managers supervise or manage activities, people and other resources in business. The quality of management in an organization is very important in a competitive business environment. Managers influence all aspects of modern organizations. Production managers run manufacturing operations to produce goods and services to satisfy consumers. Sales managers organize sales teams to sell goods and services. Human resources managers select and recruit the best available staff and manage employment laws. Finance managers raise capital and ensure that money is well spent in an organization. **➤ 5.1.2**

In large organizations **senior managers** may be heads of departments, supported by **middle managers** and **junior managers** who have responsibility for running individual sections within a department.

Managers may have responsibility for:

- carrying out the instructions of their directors
- setting objectives and allocating tasks to their staff
- motivating staff to increase their productivity
- monitoring employees' performance and undertaking staff appraisals
- identifying the training needs of their staff
- holding regular staff meetings to discuss work issues
- managing budgets allocated to them by the finance department
- writing reports and making presentations to directors.

Supervisors are the first tier or layer of management in an organization

A **supervisor** is usually regarded as the first managerial grade in an organization structure. Many are junior managers.

Unlike some more senior managers, supervisors are usually recruited from employees within the organization. They are identified and promoted because of their initiative and leadership qualities.

A supervisor normally works alongside the small group of employees he or she supervises, closely managing their work on a daily basis and providing them with the training and guidance they need.

The supervisor is also the first in line to deal with routine problems and disputes as they arise, for example organizing the repair of broken equipment, arranging overtime work and disciplining employees if they are late for work or cause trouble.

Most employees are support staff, assistants and operatives

Most employees in an organization are supervised or managed by someone else. They can be skilled, semi-skilled or unskilled workers, specializing in particular tasks or providing general support to others, such as managing facilities, filing, cleaning, data entry, typing, serving customers or operating production machinery.

Operatives are "factory floor" workers who operate machinery or undertake essential tasks related directly to the production, packaging and distribution of goods and services. In an office environment these workers are administrative or office assistants. In a shop or retail outlet they are sales assistants and till operators.

Hierarchical structures

A hierarchy shows the chain of command in an organization

Different organizations are structured in different ways depending on their size, their objectives and, in many cases, what their managers feel is the best way of achieving those objectives. There is no single correct way for organizing a business. Some senior managers may like to have more direct control over the day-to-day operations of their businesses while others may prefer to delegate decision-making authority to more junior managers.

The **organizational hierarchy** refers to the different layers of management and authority within an organization. In a small business there are unlikely to be many layers of management or departments.

The structure of a hierarchical organization looks like a pyramid. It is narrow at the top because most organizations have only a few senior managers or directors. It then gets wider in the middle because there are a larger number of middle managers in charge of departments and divisions within departments and it is widest at its base where those employees with few if any management responsibilities are represented.

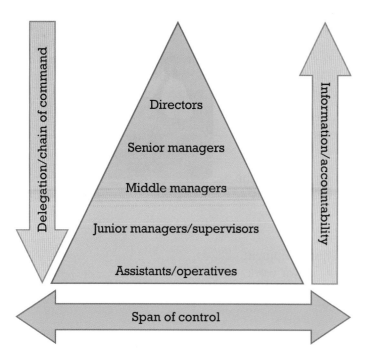

A hierarchy has a clear **chain of command** or line of authority, from the top layers of management down through the managers of each department or division and eventually to all other employees. The higher up the hierarchy, the more authority and responsibility a manager has.

- Key business objectives, major decisions and actions agreed by senior managers are communicated down their chain of command.
- Responsibility for day-to-day decision-making and management is delegated down the chain of command to lower levels of management. **➤ 2.2.2**
- Managers and employees are accountable to their more senior managers.
- Information which helps managers and directors make decisions, such as information relating to sales, customer feedback, costs and performance, is passed up the chain of command.

Organizational hierarchies can be tall or flat

McGraw-Hill Education Group is a publisher of educational books and materials based in the US. It is committed to empowering its staff and so senior managers decided a hierarchical structure was not suitable for the organization. It uses a much flatter structure where teams and their leaders are free to manage their own tasks and projects on a day-to-day basis.

Advantages of a hierarchical business structure	Disadvantages of a hierarchical business structure
+ There is a clear management structure. + Individual roles and responsibilities are clear to everyone inside the organization. + Senior managers and directors are able to make all major decisions and control the organization.	− Communications up and down the hierarchy can take time and slow down decision-making. − Managers recruited to senior positions may have limited experience and understanding of all the other functions performed in the organization. − If senior managers take all major decisions it can discourage junior managers and employees from developing new ideas and using their own initiative to solve business problems.

However, not all businesses have such flat structures. For example, consider two business organizations A and B which have similar numbers of employees.

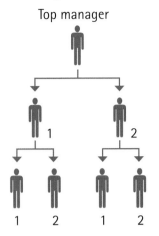

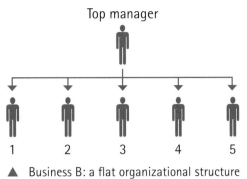

▲ Business B: a flat organizational structure

▲ Business A: a tall organizational structure

- Business A has decided to have many layers of management and a **long chain of command**. It has a **tall structure**.

- Managers in business A have relatively few subordinates reporting to them. That is, each manager has a **narrow span of control**.

- In contrast, business B chose to have fewer layers of management and a **short chain of command** compared with business A. It has a **flat structure**.

- Managers in business B have many subordinates reporting to them. That is, each manager has a **wide span of control**.

As a business expands in size it may grow taller or wider. There is no perfect structure and much will depend on what senior managers think will work the best. There are advantages and disadvantages to having a tall or flat organization.

Tall organizational structures	Flat organizational structures
Advantages	**Advantages**
+ Managers have fewer subordinates and are therefore able to communicate with them and supervise them more easily.	+ Communications are quicker and problems can be solved faster because there are fewer layers of management to go through.
+ Managers and employees are able to specialize in those tasks they are best able to do because they have fewer responsibilities.	+ Management costs are lower because there are fewer managers.
	+ Senior managers are less remote from their employees and the issues faced by the business.
Disadvantages	+ Managers and employees have greater freedom to make decisions and may be more motivated.
− Management costs are high because there are more managers.	**Disadvantages**
− Senior managers may find it difficult to manage and communicate with large numbers of junior managers.	− Senior managers may have less direct control over their organization and subordinates.
− Decision-making may be slow as there are many layers of management to consult and possibly many procedures to follow.	− Managers have more subordinates reporting to them making it more difficult to communicate with them and to supervise them personally. More mistakes may be made.

An increasing number of businesses are becoming flatter and decentralized

Peter Voser as CEO of Royal Dutch Shell thought the company structure was "too complicated" and this made the organization too slow and bureaucratic. By cutting many managerial posts he made the organization flatter so that it became easier and quicker to make and communicate business decisions.

Like Shell, an increasing number of modern business organizations are also choosing to widen their structure by cutting down their layers of management and bureaucracy.

This helps make their organizations more efficient and more responsive to changes in consumer demand. This is especially important in an increasingly competitive business environment where decisions on new prices, products and promotions need to be taken and implemented quickly. ➤ **3.1.2**

In a **centralized organization** authority, responsibility and decision-making are concentrated at the top of the chain of command. Managers and other employees lower down the chain of command have very little say in how the business is run.

In contrast, in a **decentralized organization**, a lot of authority, responsibility and decision-making is delegated down the chain of command.

This means decisions can be made quickly by managers and other employees who deal directly with customers or suppliers and understand the issues that concern them. Local knowledge and understanding will be especially important in an organization which has business units in different locations and, in the case of multinational organizations, in other countries. ➤ **6.3.2**

Flat, decentralized organizations may also be more creative ones because managers and employees may be "empowered" or authorized to use their initiative more. This means more authority and responsibility have been delegated to them by senior management.

However, major decisions that affect the entire organization will continue to be taken at the centre by senior managers and directors. These decisions will include the overall business strategy, its key objectives, methods of raising finance, budget allocations to different units and departments, new investments and mergers.

Soudoit PLC is a large firm with 2000 do-it-yourself stores across the world. The firm gets 40% of its sales revenue from selling products to the general public and 60% from sales to tradespeople such as joiners and plumbers. Over the past two years' sales have fallen from $680 million in 2017 to $578 million in 2018. The percentages of sales revenue from each segment has not changed in that time.

The directors think that the company's tall hierarchical structure is inefficient and costly. Too many managers with a narrow span of control has led to a bureaucratic organization. They plan to move to a flatter structure.

a   Calculate the percentage fall in sales revenue from 2017 to 2018.   [2]

b   Calculate the value of the sales revenue, in 2018, from the
    general public.   [2]

c   Explain the term "narrow span of control".   [4]

d   Explain **one** advantage and **one** disadvantage of a
    "tall hierarchical structure".   [6]

e   Consider whether Soudoit PLC should change to a "flatter structure".
    Justify your answer.   [6]

Before you continue make sure you are able to

Draw, interpret and understand simple **organizational charts**:

✓   simple **hierarchical structures** in terms of their **span of control, levels of hierarchy** and **chain of command**

✓   **roles and responsibilities** of directors, managers, supervisors, other employees in an organization and inter-relationships between them.

Learning CHECKLIST

2.2.2 The role of management
2.2.3 Leadership styles

▸ All organizations, public or private sector, need good managers if they are to achieve their objectives. Good managers make other employees more effective.

▸ Management involves a set of functions that help organizations make the best use of their financial, human, natural and man-made resources.

● Planning involves setting objectives and deciding on business strategies and actions needed to achieve them. Managers cannot do everything themselves.

● Organizing employees and other resources to achieve organizational objectives is one of their responsibilities.

● Co-ordinating involves bringing together employees and other resources in the organization to achieve organizational objectives.

● Commanding involves giving instructions to employees to carry out tasks.

● Controlling involves measuring and assessing the performance of employees to make sure their work is satisfactory and on target, and putting corrective actions in place if not.

▸ Managers may adopt different leadership styles depending on the situation or employees they are required to manage and the outcome they hope to achieve.

▸ Managers may become autocratic when decisions need to be taken quickly, democratic when problems need to be solved in consultation with employees and "hands-off" or laissez-faire when they trust employees to organize their own work.

▸ The delegation of tasks, authority and responsibilities from senior managers to more junior managers and employees in their chains of command becomes increasingly necessary as an organization expands and employs more people.

Management – the organization and co-ordination of people and activities in order to achieve agreed aims and objectives.

Management functions – the roles and responsibilities of managers, including planning, organizing, co-ordinating, commanding and controlling how labour and other resources are used in an organization.

Autocratic leadership – telling employees what to do without consultation.

Democratic leadership – consulting employees before making decisions.

Laissez-faire leadership – allowing employees the freedom to organize their work and make their own decisions about how best to achieve business objectives.

The role of management
Management involves achieving business objectives through people

Calendar	A day in the life of a sales manager
	Monday ▲
08 00	8.00 a.m. Weekly meeting with sales team to review performance and objectives. Yash reports sales 10% up on last quarter. Star performer is Anais who exceeded her personal target by 30%. We agree new objectives and sales targets for the next quarter and plan actions to achieve them. *Note to self : award Anais $500 bonus payment*
09 00	*Read papers for next meeting*
10 00	Teleconference with regional sales director. Head office wants to reduce admin costs by 20% over next 12 months. HQ wants options for cuts presented by Friday. Need to keep work confidential for now.
11 00	11.30 a.m. I ask Yash to meet me in my office. I explain we need to find cuts of 20% and ask him and his team to work up some options. Will need these to review by close of Wednesday. *Ask Megane to arrange meeting with Yash's team on Thursday to review and finalize options*
12 00	12.30 a.m. **Table booked at Clouds Café** *Meet Nilesh (HR manager) and Olivia (marketing) for working lunch to discuss new marketing strategy and associated staff training needs*
13 00	Lunch
14 00	2.30 p.m. until 4.30 p.m. Interviews for new commercial sales team leader. Three good candidates but Roshan Macall's application stands out. *Megane to arrange interview room, refreshments and to make sure interview panel has relevant papers*
15 00	3.45 p.m. An important customer shows up for a meeting – not in diary – was meant to be tomorrow?!! Third interview due so have to ask head of consumer sales to handle meeting until I can arrive.
16 00	
17 00	5.00 p.m. Interviews and customer meeting over. I write up interview records and agree decision with HR to offer Natasha Dardy the position. Roshan Macall failed to perform well in interview but we may be able to offer him a trainee position.
18 00	6.00 p.m. Meet David Patrice: second verbal warning due to his continual lateness and underperformance. *Pick up suit from dry cleaners* ▼

A day in the life of a manager in a business organization can be long and varied. Just look at all the tasks and responsibilities the sales manager in the diary above had to fulfil in a typical working day: reviewing staff and business performance, planning and setting objectives, delegating tasks to other managers and employees, recruiting new employees and reprimanding others, meeting and co-ordinating activities with other managers, and much more.

All organizations, public or private sector, need good managers. Good managers make other employees more effective than they would have been without them. A poorly managed business will not meet its aims and objectives.

Management therefore involves the organization and co-ordination of people and activities in order to achieve agreed aims and objectives.

Not all managers are called managers. They may be company directors, team leaders, supervisors, heads of departments or a chief surgeon or matron in a hospital, a head chef in a restaurant or a major in an army. Whatever their titles, all managers need to perform similar functions.

ACTIVITY 2.6

Use the job advertisements for different managers below to identify and list as many tasks or functions managers must perform and the skills and qualities they need to perform them successfully. You may also draw on your own experience of being managed or observing a manager in your school, college or place of work.

HOTEL GENERAL MANAGER

We are looking for a highly motivated professional who possesses a keen interest in hospitality with the ability to manage a well-established luxury five-star resort effectively.

The successful candidate will be responsible for:

- effective running of the day-to-day operation of the resort while ensuring all cost-effective measures are enforced
- maintaining a positive and professional work attitude towards all employees and guests
- developing and enforcing new objectives and policies
- analysing and preparing operating and capital budgets
- maintaining confidentiality at all times with a view to protecting the resort and its customers
- organizing staff recruitment and training.

The successful candidate should have:

- extensive experience at a senior managerial level in the hospitality industry
- at least a Master's Degree in hospitality or hotel management
- the ability to function effectively in a multicultural environment
- excellent communication, organizational and decision-making skills
- excellent computer skills
- the ability to motivate employees, control costs and maximize profit.

The jobholder must live on the property and be willing to work long hours including public holidays and weekends.

Please forward your CV via post to: Jenny Capili, Human Resources Department, Turtle Cay Resort, PO Box 193, or via email to: jcapili@turtlecay.com by 14 June.

The Lakeside Restaurant

seeks a suitably qualified individual with the requirements below for the position of

Restaurant Manager

The individual:

- must be able to plan and manage all aspects of the business
- must be able to oversee, motivate and co-ordinate staff for the effective running of the business to achieve industry standards, including customer service, food quality, cleanliness, sales, costs and staff training
- must have a minimum of three years' proven managerial experience in a full service restaurant with clear problem-resolution skills
- must have experience of developing and managing budgets and inventories, and preparing profit and loss accounts.

Remuneration will be based on qualifications and experience.

Please submit your letter of application and CV to Blaze Group Ltd, Town Centre Mall by 18 January.

Management functions involve planning, organizing, co-ordinating, commanding and controlling activities and people

Business management involves a set of functions that help organizations make the best use of their financial, human, natural and man-made resources. Here are the main **management functions**.

Planning

This involves setting aims and objectives for an organization, for example to increase profits by 5% per year or increase market share from 30% to 40% within three years. Business strategies and actions that will help achieve these aims must then be agreed, such as launching a new product or marketing campaign. This also includes identifying and meeting the training needs of employees to ensure that they have the right skills to fulfil the business objectives.

Organizing

Managers cannot do everything themselves. They must organize employees and other resources to achieve organizational objectives. To do so they must first determine what roles and skills are needed, identify employees to fulfil these roles and then delegate tasks and responsibilities to them.

Co-ordinating

This involves bringing together employees and other resources in the organization to achieve organizational objectives. Not all employees will share the same objectives as the organization they work for. There is also a risk of individual departments in the structure pursuing their own objectives. For example, there is no point in the production department planning a new product if it does not consult with the finance, marketing and sales departments to ensure that this product can be funded and promoted and meets the needs of customers.

Commanding

This involves giving instructions to employees to carry out tasks. Managers have the authority to make decisions and the responsibility to see they are carried out. To do so successfully, managers must be good leaders and be able to guide and motivate employees to fulfil their tasks and objectives.

Controlling

All managers need to measure and assess the performance of employees on a regular basis to make sure their work is satisfactory and on target to achieve organizational objectives. If this is not the case, managers must put in place corrective actions depending on the cause. For example, there may be a hold up in supplies or a breakdown in machinery, a pay dispute with workers or a need for training if employees lack the right skills.

On some occasions an employee or group of employees may not be working as intended and may be disruptive to others. This may require a manager disciplining those employees for their poor performance and if it continues they may need to be dismissed. A manager may have the power to hire or fire employees, or to promote them. However, in large companies, a manager may only recommend such actions to the next level of management or to the head of the human resources department.

Good managers are able to communicate with and motivate others

To fulfil management functions successfully a manager must be good at managing other people and resources. But what makes a good manager?

At least some of the skills and qualities good managers should possess are:

- **effective communication skills** so they can clearly explain and present their ideas and objectives to their staff, tell them what tasks they need to do and give them useful feedback on their performance ➤ **2.4.1**

- **drive, enthusiasm, the initiative to get the job done** and to demonstrate good standards of work and behaviour to others

- **good analytical skills** so they can understand complex problems and work out solutions

- **strong leadership and influencing skills** so they are able to motivate others to achieve organizational objectives. ➤ **2.1.1**

Managers with good leadership skills can inspire and motivate others to achieve more than they would without their guidance and encouragement. Good leaders can be found in sports teams, politics, local communities and business organizations. A good leader in business is someone who can motivate employees and help them achieve their full potential. However, not all managers make good leaders.

Business organization	Who owns the business?	Who controls the business?
Sole trader	A single owner	The owner
Partnership	Partners	Senior partners have more control than other partners
Limited company	Shareholders	The board of directors and senior managers
Franchise	The franchisee	The franchisor controls many aspects of the business

The importance of delegation

As an organization grows, business owners tend to delegate more decisions and control to managers

The owners of a business are the people who have invested money and organized resources into a firm and are entitled to share its profits.

However, the controllers of a business are those people who take the day-to-day management decisions.

In many small organizations, the owners and controllers are the same people. However, as a business grows control tends to pass from the owners to the managers they employ to run their business. In a limited company, the owners or shareholders elect a board of directors to run their company and take important business decisions. By doing so, the owners agree to give up day-to-day control of their business. ➤ **1.4.1**

Hendrick has been a shareholder in the MMH Corporation for many years. He used to own 25% of the company but since it expanded following a new issue of shares he now owns only 14%. He is worried this means he now has less control over how the business is managed.

Look at the cartoon strip below and describe what is happening. Do you think Hendrick is right to worry about how much control he has over how the company is managed?

This "divorce of ownership from control" in a large company can cause conflict. ➤ **1.5.1**

- Directors in a large company may award themselves and their senior managers large pay rises and annual bonuses even if the performance and profitability of the company has been poor. Large pay awards can reduce profits available to shareholders.

- Directors may spend a lot of money purchasing luxury company cars and having their offices lavishly decorated. This can also reduce company profits.

- Directors may also agree to expansion plans which may be considered too big and risky by the shareholders. Running a large company can increase the status of its directors and justify an increase in their salaries.

- Directors may take more financial risks than shareholders if they have not invested their own money in the company.

If directors pay themselves large sums of money, spend wildly or take too many risks, shareholders may be able to vote to replace them at an AGM. Shareholders can also try to influence important company decisions taken by the directors, for example on whether or not to merge with another business organization. ➤ **1.4.1**

As a business continues to grow, senior managers need to delegate more decisions and control to junior managers and employees lower down their chain of command

It is impossible for any one manager in all but the smallest business organization to control all day-to-day tasks and make every decision. Managers must therefore delegate some of the functions they perform and

Disney's Eisner rebuked in shareholder vote

Despite a shareholder revolt that led him to lose the chairmanship of The Walt Disney Co., Michael Eisner vows that he will stay on as CEO through to the end of his term.

Earlier today, 43% of shareholders who voted at the company's annual meeting withheld their support for Eisner. The number of shareholders who withheld their support was higher than many had been expecting.

Shareholders blast Qantas over payouts

Shareholders at Wednesday's annual general meeting for Qantas Airlines again expressed their anger over big payouts to executives.

The central issue was the final payment to chief executive Geoff Dixon, who left last year. Mr Dixon pocketed nearly $11 million despite lower share value, employee lay-offs and mid-air incidents.

▲ Some examples of how the objectives of business managers and owners can conflict

decisions they must make to others in their chain of command. The delegation of tasks, authority and responsibilities to more junior members of staff in the organizational hierarchy becomes even more important as the business expands and employs more people. ➤ **2.1.1**

Successful delegation requires a manager to trust the junior employee. This can be difficult for some managers who feel that they may lose control of the tasks for which they are responsible. If a manager tries to control a task given to a junior employee, then the junior employee will feel that they are not trusted. This can demotivate the junior employee and may even result in that person taking time off or leaving the organization.

I hate to fire people, so I'm ordering you two to fire each other.

For example, Matthias Bichsel is the Global Director of Projects and Technology for the oil and gas giant, Royal Dutch Shell. He is ultimately responsible for around 8000 employees worldwide but he cannot possibly manage all of these staff on a day-to-day basis. He must therefore delegate some of his management functions and authority to make decisions to others. For example, his Director of Projects and Technology in Malaysia has his delegated authority to manage the operations of the local business and its 700 employees. However, even this director cannot be expected to take every decision required to manage the work of all 700 Malaysian employees. He must also delegate some management responsibilities to more junior managers in his chain of command.

Authority, accountability and responsibility in a chain of command

- ▶ A manager has **authority** over more junior managers and employees.
- ▶ A manager can **delegate** tasks and authority to make some decisions to more junior managers and employees.
- ▶ Those junior managers and employees with delegated authority are **accountable** for their decisions to their manager.
- ▶ The manager is **responsible** for the work and decisions of junior managers and employees in their chain of command. If a poor decision has been made or a task is done badly, the manager may reprimand more junior managers and employees but must still accept responsibility for their poor work or decisions.

In turn, more junior managers can delegate tasks to employees who report to them in their chain of command. They will, however, remain accountable for the successful completion of those tasks to the Director of Projects and Technology in Malaysia who in turn is accountable for their decisions to Matthias Bichsel as Global Director of Projects and Technology at the company.

For this delegation of decision-making authority to work successfully in Shell and other organizations, the following are required.

- Tasks and authority should only be given to more junior managers and employees with the right skills and motivations to complete them.

- More junior managers and employees who do not have the right skills should be given the training and guidance they need before they are given delegated authority.

- Senior managers should make sure everyone in their chain of command understands their individual objectives and what their tasks involve.

- Managers should monitor the performance of all their employees and provide them with regular feedback.

Successful delegation down the chain of command in an organization should provide a number of benefits.

Benefits of delegation for managers	Potential problems of delegation for managers
+ They can spend more time on more important business decisions and tasks.	✗ They fear losing control over some tasks and decisions.
+ They can make best use of the skills and experience of different employees in their chain of command to improve the employees' motivation and productivity.	✗ They may not explain clearly enough to junior managers and employees what they are required to do, what decisions they should be responsible for and why.
+ They can monitor the performance of their employees more easily against agreed tasks and objectives.	✗ Their junior managers and employees may lack the required skills meaning there is a high risk they will make poor decisions and tasks will be poorly completed.
+ They can train their employees to become future managers in the organization.	✗ They remain responsible for any poor decisions taken by managers or employees down their chain of command.

Benefits of delegation for employees	Potential problems of delegation for employees
+ Their work may become more interesting.	✗ They may lack the skills and training they need.
+ They can specialize in those tasks they are best able to perform.	✗ They remain accountable for their actions and decisions to their manager.
+ They can learn new skills.	✗ They may suffer stress from taking on more responsibilities.
+ It prepares them for more senior positions within the organization.	

Leadership styles

Managers may adopt different leadership styles depending on the situation or employees they are required to manage

The method or **leadership style** a manager uses often reflects his or her personality and personal objectives. These styles affect how managers communicate with employees and how much authority they delegate down their chains of command. For example, Enterprise Rent-A-Car has over 75 000 employees worldwide. It encourages managers to operate an "open door" policy. This enables everybody in the organization to have direct contact with senior managers, whether through meetings or having lunch in the same dining area.

Good managers may change the way they lead a group of employees or manage a particular situation depending on what style will best achieve the outcome they want and depending on what motivates their employees.

There are three main leadership styles.

▲ Autocratic manager

▲ Democratic manager

Autocratic management	Democratic management	Laissez-faire management
An autocratic manager tells employees what to do and expects his or her orders to be followed without question. This is a good style to adopt in emergencies and other situations when decisions need to be made and actions taken quickly. However, if a manager is always autocratic, employees may become dissatisfied because they are unable to contribute ideas or challenge decisions they think are wrong.	A democratic manager consults employees and involves them in problem-solving and decision-making. Communication is two-way. Information and ideas about work and the future of the business are discussed openly before the manager makes an informed decision on what actions should be taken. Democratic management helps employees feel valued but it can slow down decision-making.	A laissez-faire manager is "hands-off". He or she communicates business objectives to employees and then leaves them to organize their work and make their own decisions about how best to achieve those objectives. This encourages employee creativity and decision-making but some employees may need more support and direction. Workers may fail to co-ordinate their activities if the lack of leadership fails to provide the direction they need and creates confusion.

ACTIVITY 2.8

Which style of management is being used by the manager in each situation below?
What style would you adopt if you were the manager and why?

The manager of a large fashion store informs employees the store will now remain open every week day until 9 p.m. It currently closes at 5.30 p.m.

The manager explains the shop needs to be more competitive and earn more revenue, otherwise jobs will need to be cut. Employees understand the need to increase opening hours but do not think it is sensible for all of them to work late every night. Some have family commitments and some do not want to travel on public transport late at night.

The manager tells them the changes will have to take place and they will either have to comply or leave.

The captain of a cruise ship has received news of a storm that could prevent the ship docking at a major port. The storm may worsen and place his crew, passengers and ship in danger. However, it will take three days to sail to the next port.

He consults his crew and passengers. They want him to take the risk and continue into port. The crew argue they are required under employment law to take some time off and they want to do so on shore. Many of the passengers are due to leave the cruise at the port to return home. If they have to sail to the next port the cruise company will have to meet the extra costs of their accommodation and travel.

Val Singh has spent 15 years building up her business in construction. Val enjoys good relationships with all her employees who appreciate her laissez-faire style of leadership. The business has grown so much that Val has decided to convert her business to a private limited company and employ to managers to whom she can delegate some tasks. Unfortunately, one of the managers has upset some of the employees who find his autocratic style of leadership demotivating.

a   Define "private limited company".   [2]

b   Explain the term "delegation".   [2]

c   Outline **two** management functions.   [4]

d   Explain **one** advantage and **one** disadvantage of an "autocratic
    style of leadership".   [4]

e   Consider whether it is important for a manager to have a
    good relationship with other employees. Justify your answer.   [6]

Learning CHECKLIST

Before you continue make sure you are able to

Understand the role of **management** in an organization:

✓   functions of management – **planning, organizing, co-ordinating,
    commanding** and **controlling**

✓   the importance of **delegation** and the trade-off between trust and control

Explain different **leadership styles**:

✓   the features of the main leadership styles – **autocratic, democratic** and
    laissez-faire

✓   recommend and justify an appropriate leadership style in given circumstances.

2.2.4 Trade unions

- The trade union movement worldwide has helped to secure significant improvements in the safety of working environments, increased wages for both union and non-unionized workers, reduced hours of work and improved education and other benefits for many poor and working families.

- A trade union is in a strong bargaining position to negotiate improved wages and working conditions if it represents all workers in a workplace producing vital products for which there are few alternatives for consumers to use.

- Trade union members may take disruptive industrial action if they fail to reach agreement with employers through collective bargaining. Affected businesses may suffer higher costs and lost output, revenues and profits during industrial action.

Business BUZZWORDS

Trade union (or labour union) – an association representing employees in a particular workplace or industry, the aim of which is to negotiate improved pay and working conditions with employers.

Closed shop – trade union membership in a firm is made a compulsory condition of employment within that firm.

Collective bargaining – negotiation between organized workers, usually through a trade union, and their employer or employers to agree wages and working conditions.

Single union agreement – an agreement between an employer and a trade union that the union can represent all workers in the organization.

Industrial action – organized disruptive actions, such as a strike or work to rule, that workers may take to increase their bargaining power over wage or other demands or to address their grievances.

Arbitration – a process involving the judgement of an independent person or body to help resolve industrial disputes between workers and employers.

AngloGold Ashanti remains of the opinion that a strong, well-organized trade union is an essential component of its approach to collective bargaining and to the way we do business.

What is a trade union?

Trade unions aim to protect and improve the wages and welfare of employees

There have been many strikes by workers in gold mines in South Africa over time. However, while many in the past had lasted several weeks and involved violent clashes between striking workers and the police, a strike by the National Union of Mineworkers (NUM) and Solidarity trade unions a few years ago, affecting all gold mining companies in South Africa, was peaceful and lasted just four days.

The unions asked their members to stop working and to go on strike, because their negotiations over wages and working conditions with the gold mining companies failed to reach an agreement. Before the strike, the unions were demanding a 12% increase in miners wages compared to an offer of 5% by their employers. In addition, the unions were demanding the companies to allow employees to take breaks at Christmas, to improve their accommodation subsidies and to increase contributions to their retirement fund.

The closure of the mines halted production and so the gold companies increased their offer to a 7% increase in wages. They also agreed the other demands. The unions accepted this new offer and called off their strike.

Abe Bardin was Head of Labour Relations at the AngloGold Ashanti mining company at the time and was pleased the dispute had been resolved quickly and in an orderly way through negotiation. He said this was because the unions were well organized and essential to the business.

Many workers belong to labour unions or **trade unions** all over the world. Trade unions promote and protect the interests of their members with the purpose of improving their wages and working conditions. In return, members often pay a small fee to belong to a union.

Trade unions first developed in European countries during the industrial revolution in the 18th and 19th centuries following the development of factories and mass production. During this time the structure of these Western economies changed rapidly, from ones based on farming and craft industries to industrialized economies in which manufacturing industries produced most of the total output and provided most of the jobs. Work in factories was often poorly paid and undertaken in appalling conditions. Workers therefore began to organize themselves into unions to challenge the owners of factories to improve their conditions. The trade union movement worldwide has helped fight and bring to an end child labour in many countries, improved workers' safety, increased wages for both union and non-unionized workers, reduced hours of work, and improved education and other benefits for many poor and working-class families.

Trade union functions include:
- negotiating wages and other non-wage benefits with employers
- defending employees' rights and jobs
- improving working conditions, such as hours of work or health and safety
- improving pay and other benefits, including holiday entitlement, sick pay and pensions
- encouraging firms to increase workers' participation in business decision-making
- supporting and advising members who have been dismissed or who are taking industrial action
- developing the skills of union members by providing training and education courses
- providing social and recreational amenities for members
- influencing government policy and employment legislation.

Before trade unions existed, a worker had to negotiate on his or her own for increased pay and better working conditions with his or her employer. With few rights, a worker could face being sacked for asking for improvements. Trade unions, however, can negotiate with and put pressure on employers on behalf of all their members to secure these aims. Trade unions therefore helped to reduce the power employers had over their workforces.

However, trade unions do not have the legal right to represent workers in some countries. Trade unions are even outlawed in some countries and union officials can be jailed.

In other countries, however, trade unions work closely with, and even fund, political parties. They can also use their power to influence government policies and employment laws to be more favourable to their members or to workers in general. In addition, many trade unions offer their members education and training to improve their skills and provide their members with recreational amenities including social clubs.

The effect of employees being members of a trade union

Employees who join trade unions can often achieve positive effects through collective bargaining:

- Equality through negotiating better working conditions and higher pay.

- Increased training in the workplace by organizing training or negotiating better training from employers.

- Improved health and safety of workplaces by working with employers to ensure high standards. Trade unions will also monitor conditions to ensure that high standards are maintained.

- Reduced labour turnover as workers feel more secure in an organization if they see that they are supported by a trade union. A trade union gives the employees representation in any issues that arise.

- Reduced absenteeism as by improving working conditions employees are less likely to take time off because of stress-related illness.

A trade union is in a strong bargaining position if it represents all employees in a workplace producing essential products

Public sector electricity workers in Nigeria launch an indefinite strike over wages

Nigeria's National Union of Electricity Employees (NUEE) called off its nationwide strike today after reaching an agreement with the federal government

How long do you think it took for the second headline to be published in a Nigerian newspaper after the first one appeared announcing a strike by electricity workers? The answer is, it took just one day!

An indefinite strike by all 40 000 employees of the government-owned Power Holding Company in Nigeria would have left many people and businesses in the country without power causing hardship and halting production. As a result the government of Nigeria held urgent talks overnight with union representatives and together an agreement on wages was reached.

In contrast, when 1500 cleaners at Dutch Railways went on strike to highlight the poor wages and working conditions of all 150 000 cleaners employed in the Netherlands, it took nine weeks to resolve with employers. So why did reaching an agreement take so long in this case? Much depends on the bargaining strength of the trade union.

The process of negotiating wages and other working conditions between trade unions and employers is called **collective bargaining**.

Trade unions often argue for improved wages and other working conditions if:

- price inflation is high and rising

- other groups of workers have received pay rises

- new machinery or working practices have been introduced in the workplace

> A trade union is in a strong bargaining position when:
>
> - the union represents most or all of the workers in that firm or industry
> - union members provide products consumers need and for which there are few alternatives, such as electricity, public transport, health care and education.

- the labour productivity of their members has increased
- the profits of the employing organization have increased.

The National Union of Electricity Employees in Nigeria was in a strong bargaining position to negotiate higher wages because their strike was supported by all of Nigeria's electricity workers and because they were responsible for providing an essential service to a great many people and businesses. In contrast, only 1% of cleaners in the Netherlands went on strike over improved pay and conditions. Most cleaners continued providing useful but non-essential cleaning services to different businesses in the Dutch economy. Other Dutch Railway employees were also able to help clean railway stations and trains when their cleaners took strike action.

Unions and employers may also negotiate over employment levels and other benefits such as pension rights, holiday entitlement, training and the introduction of new technology and working practices.

However, sometimes trade unions and employers may be unable to reach a collective agreement, for example if the pay rise wanted by union members is too high or the employer wants to cut more jobs than the union is willing to agree to. If negotiations break down, trade union members may take industrial action in an attempt to force employers to agree to their demands.

Industrial disputes can disrupt production and damage businesses

Industrial disputes occur when negotiations between employers and unions fail to end in agreement. Workers may take disruptive **industrial action** to put pressure on their employers to address their demands or grievances. **Official action** has the backing of the trade union, and other unions may also take action in support. **Unofficial action** means workers taking the industrial action do not have the support of their union.

Forms of industrial action	
Overtime ban	Workers refuse to work more than their normal hours.
Work to rule	Workers deliberately slow down production by complying rigidly with every rule and regulation.
Go-slow	Work is carried out deliberately slowly to reduce production.
Strike	Workers refuse to work and may also protest, or **picket** outside their workplace to stop deliveries and prevent non-unionized workers from entering.

Industrial action can increase the bargaining strength of workers to force employers to agree to their wage and other demands. However, union action can also have significantly detrimental effects on businesses, employees and consumers.

- **Businesses** suffer higher costs and lose output, revenues and profits during industrial action. If the action goes on for a long time a business may also lose important customers to rival firms.

- **Union members** are not paid their wages or salaries during a strike, although some may receive income support from their union's strike fund.

Some workers may also lose their jobs if employers cut back their demand for labour because the industrial action has lost them customers and profits.

- **Consumers** may be unable to obtain the goods and services they need and may also have to pay higher prices if firms pass on their increased costs.

- The reputation of **an economy** as a good place for business may also be damaged by frequent and widespread industrial action. Firms may decide to invest and set up businesses elsewhere. This will affect many more businesses, employees and consumers by increasing unemployment and reducing incomes.

Arbitration may be necessary to settle industrial disputes. This involves employers and unions agreeing to let an independent referee, often a senior government official or lawyer, help them reach agreement. This normally means both sides in the dispute accepting a compromise – something that is satisfactory to both parties but rather less than what they had initially wanted.

Laws and no-strike agreements may be used to limit and control industrial action

Because industrial action can be so damaging, some businesses and unions have reached "no strike" agreements. In return, for not taking disruptive actions, businesses often agree to pay their employees more generous wages and to improve other working conditions.

Laws have also been introduced in many countries relating to the power of trade unions to take industrial action. For example, an employer in the UK can seek legal damages from a union for lost profits if industrial action is taken without first balloting its members. Mass picketing is also unlawful. Only a handful of strikers are allowed to picket outside their workplaces.

Learning CHECKLIST

Before you continue make sure you are able to

Describe the work of **trade unions**:

✓ explain what a **trade union** is

✓ identify the effects of employees being union members.

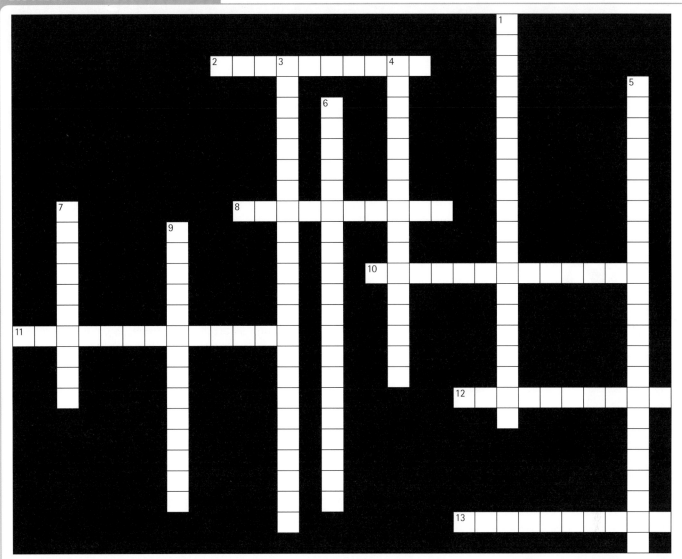

Clues down

1 The process of negotiating pay and working conditions between trade union representatives and employers (10, 10)
3 How roles, responsibilities and management authority are allocated within an organization (14, 9)
4 Disruptive actions, such as a strike or work to rule, that workers may take in an attempt to force their employer to agree their wage or other demands or address their grievances (10, 6)
5 A business in which authority and decision making is concentrated at the top of the chain of command (11, 12)
6 An agreement between an employer and a trade union that the union can represent all the employees at the workplace of the employer. This helps to speed up negotiations and improve relations between the employer and the union (5, 5, 9)
7 A style of leadership that involves telling employees what to do without consultation (10)
9 The line of management authority in an organization down which tasks and responsibilities are communicated and delegated to more junior managers and employees (5, 2, 7)

Clues across

2 A leadership style that involves consulting employees before making decisions (10)
8 An association representing employees in a particular workplace or industry whose aim is to negotiate with employers over pay and working conditions (5, 5)
10 An organization that has a long chain of command and relatively narrow span of control is said to have this (4, 9)
11 This refers to the number of subordinate employees a manager supervises and is responsible for (4, 2, 7)
12 The term used to describe the people within an organization with the authority to plan, organize, co-ordinate, command and control other employees and resources to achieve agreed aims and objectives (10)
13 Assigning tasks and decision-making authority to more junior managers and employees in a chain of command (10)

2.3.1 Recruitment and selecting employees

Key POINTS

- The most valuable resource in any business organization is its employees, or human resources. The success of a business depends on the quality of its workforce.

- Recruitment and selection involves attracting and choosing the most suitable employees for an organization.

- Every job vacancy will have a job description of its main tasks and responsibilities and a person specification listing the skills and qualities an employee needs.

- A job vacancy can be filled through internal recruitment, by advertising the vacancy externally in newspapers and magazines or using recruitment agencies and government employment centres.

- Most vacancies are filled through external recruitment. It can be more time-consuming and expensive than internal recruitment but enables a business to attract employees with new and perhaps more advanced skills.

- Most people recruited to work in an organization work full-time. A person who is in full-time employment will usually work 35 hours or more each week but an increasing number of employees are being recruited for part-time employment to extend hours of business operation and meet peaks in consumer demand.

Business BUZZWORDS

Recruitment – the process of attracting job applicants, for example using job advertisements.

Job analysis – identifying a job vacancy and the tasks and responsibilities of that job.

Job description – a document describing the tasks and responsibilities required to do a job.

Person specification – or job specification – is a document listing the skills, qualifications, experience and personal qualities a person needs to do a specific job.

Internal recruitment – filling a job vacancy from the existing workforce within an organization.

External recruitment – attracting job applicants from outside an organization to fill job vacancies.

Selection – assessing the suitability of applicants for a job and choosing the most suitable candidate.

Sifting – comparing and marking job applications against the requirements of a person specification.

Shortlisting – selecting the most promising candidates for a job from a set of job applications.

Full-time employment – a job that usually requires 35 or more hours of work each week.

Part-time employment – a job that usually requires less than 35 hours of work each week.

Human resources management

There is a direct relationship between the quality and motivation of a workforce and the success of a business organization

The most valuable resource in any business organization is its people, or human resources. For example, US fast food restaurant franchise company McDonald's is a firm believer that the success of its business depends crucially on the quality and motivation of its workforce in its headquarters and restuarants owned by the company and franchisees all over the world. This is because the senior management of McDonald's recognize that the satisfaction of over 60 million customers each day in over 100 countries depends on the attitudes and abilities of the employees who serve them. Good workers are therefore key to the company's sales growth and success.

Recruiting and training new staff is expensive so choosing wisely and keeping employees motivated in work helps to keep staff turnover and business costs down. In order to recruit the right people, McDonald's has identified the essential skills and behaviours that applicants must be able to demonstrate. For each job there is a **job description** outlining the duties and responsibilities of the employee and a **person specification** listing the skills and abilities they should have. It is then a matter of choosing the right place to advertise the jobs, and then selecting and interviewing applicants who appear to have the right experience, attitudes and skills.

Employee recruitment and selection is a key task for human resource managers in an organization. The purpose of **human resource management** is to ensure employees are selected, used and developed in the best and most effective ways possible so their organization can achieve the highest levels of productivity and quality of work.

Within a small business, the owner is likely to be responsible for planning, organizing and managing human resources. In contrast, most medium and large businesses are likely to have a human resources department (or personnel department) employing staff with skills in human resource management.

All other departments within an organization rely on the human resources department to carry out a number of important functions. ➤ **2.2.1**

Recruitment and selection involves attracting and choosing the most suitable employees for an organization

Recruitment involves identifying and advertising a job vacancy. **Selection** involves choosing the right candidate to fill the vacancy. This involves attracting and sifting job applications, holding interviews and then offering the best candidate the job.

> Our commitment to our customers is to be better, not just bigger. That includes a major effort to remodel and modernize McDonald's restaurants, revitalize the menu with more choice and variety, and increase investment in staff training and personal development.

McDonald's Executive Vice President

The functions of a human resources department are:

- planning the future manpower requirements (employee numbers and skills) for the organization
- advertising job vacancies
- the recruitment and selection of new employees to fill vacant posts
- providing terms and conditions of employment to new employees
- identifying training needs and appropriate courses for employees
- managing staff promotions and transfers
- devising and implementing financial and non-financial rewards systems
- ensuring that the organization follows all employment laws and health and safety regulations
- managing communications and industrial relations between employees and senior management
- resolving employee grievances and industrial disputes
- managing employee redundancies, dismissals and disciplinary matters.

▼ The stages involved in recruitment and selection

Identify the job vacancy

What does the job entail (job analysis)?
Write a job description

What type of person is needed to fill the job?
Write a person specification

Advertise the job and send out details and
application forms on request

Compare job applications with the person
specification to select a shortlist of the
best applicants to interview

Send invitations to attend interviews to
job applicants who were shortlisted

If the applicant is not shortlisted,
send a letter of regret

Prepare and conduct job interviews

Select the best applicant and make a
formal job offer in writing

Draw up a contract of employment

Recruitment

Every job vacancy has a job description of its main tasks and responsibilities and a person specification listing the skills and qualities the employee needs

The first stage in the process of recruitment and selection involves identifying a job vacancy in the organization, deciding what the job will involve and the skills and competencies the job holder will need to do it effectively. This is called **job analysis**.

Job vacancies may arise in a business for any of these reasons.

- Key staff have left for other jobs, retired or been dismissed and need to be replaced.

- Some employees have been promoted to more senior positions within the organization, leaving their previous posts vacant.

- The business is expanding and needs more employees.

- The business has introduced new advanced equipment and processes and needs employees with the skills to use them.

- The business has changed its organizational structure and identified new roles that need to be filled or new skills needed in the business.

Once a business has identified a job vacancy and decided what the job involves, it is necessary to prepare a **job description**. Every job in a business will have a job description describing the role, responsibilities and tasks required in that job. People applying for a job vacancy can use the job description to identify what will be expected of them and whether or not they have the right experience to be a suitable applicant. Once employees are in post, their performance can be judged against how well they carry out the tasks listed in their job description.

ACTIVITY 2.9

Look at the people in the photographs.

For each one discuss and write down:

▶ the job you think the person has

▶ the key tasks and activities you think the person will perform

▶ the skills and qualities the person doing the job should have.

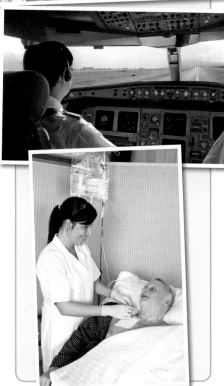

What's in a job description?

It sets out:

- the job title
- the main purpose of the job, for example to manage a restaurant or to drive a bus
- position in the organizational structure, for example director, manager, supervisor
- the department the job is in, such as the finance department or the production department
- who the job holder will be responsible to; that is, the job holder's manager

- who the job holder will be responsible for (if appropriate) and how many subordinates the job holder will manage
- main tasks and responsibilities
- working conditions, hours and wages or salary
- the name and location of the business organization.

Job title: Closing Crew

Reports to: Front of Restaurant Manager

Hours of work
- 4 p.m. until midnight or 1 a.m.
- Flexible schedule for full or part-time working

Main duties and responsibilities
- Serving customers
- Taking closing payments and operating till until closure
- Reconciling till receipts
- Cleaning and dish washing

Training
Full till training provided. We are recognized by the National Council on Education for our restaurant management curriculum. Your participation in our training programmes can earn you up to 46 college credits towards two-year or four-year degree programmes.

Job title: Personal Assistant

Responsible to: Human Resources Director

Hours of work: 0830–1700 Mon–Fri

Significant working relationships
- All managers and secretaries
- All staff division

Overall purpose
- To provide an administrative and secretarial function to the Human Resources Director and her department

Principal responsibilities
- Managing the Human Resource Director's office and diary
- Typing and filing business correspondence
- Organizing and arranging meetings
- Receiving visitors and providing the hospitality required
- Making travel arrangements as necessary
- Sending outgoing faxes
- Distributing mail
- Ordering and controlling stationery
- Other support tasks necessary to ensure the smooth running of the office and department

Training
- Word processing package
- Graphics package

Qualifications and personal skills
- Good office management and communications skills
- Typing and shorthand
- Word processing
- An ability to speak French is desirable

Job title: Business Assistant

Responsible to: Group Financial Director

Main responsibilities and activities
- Gather and record financial information
- Keep a computer database of financial data
- Prepare monthly cash flow forecasts
- Assist in preparing annual accounts

Specific responsibilities
Planning
- Plan and manage own time to achieve mutually agreed delivery schedules
- Provide advice and input into the financial reporting process

Confidential information
- Access to customer information database
- Access to group financial information of a confidential nature

Working conditions
- Based at the group head office in Buenos Aires
- Occasional foreign travel
- Salary approx $30 000 p.a.
- 37.5 hours per week
  (flexitime: core hours 1000–1600 Mon–Fri)

▲ Some examples of job descriptions

The next stage is to use the job description to produce a **person specification** listing the skills, qualifications, experience and personal qualities a person will need to do the job effectively. Some of these may be essential, for example a driving licence to be a bus driver, while others may be desirable, such as language skills for an assistant in a bank in case the employee needs to deal with people visiting from other countries.

People applying for a job vacancy can use the person specification to decide whether or not they have the right skills and attributes required to do the job effectively.

What's in a person specification?

It sets out:

- the job title and the main purpose of the job
- position in the organizational structure, for example director, manager, supervisor
- skills and evidence of training and past experience required
- educational qualifications required
- personal qualities and motivation required, for example whether the person should be a self-starter, ambitious, good at reaching specific, short-term targets

- professional and other qualifications required, for example a driving licence for a heavy goods vehicle, appropriate professional qualification for a chartered accountant's job
- special aptitudes, for example whether the person can work under pressure, speak a foreign language
- special circumstances, for example will the person need to travel or does the person want to work flexible hours.

▼ Some examples of person specifications

Job title: Closing Crew

Qualities
- Neat and tidy appearance
- Friendly and outgoing
- Reliable and trustworthy
- Enthusiastic and self-motivated
- Ability to work independently under pressure
- Age 16 years +

Skills and experience
- Good communication and numeracy skills
- Previous experience of cash till operation and working in customer service

Benefits
Got what it takes? Then join the team! We offer a long list of good things like flexible schedules, training and development programmes, advancement opportunities, uniforms and much more! See Restaurant Manager for details.

Job title: Business Assistant

Physical attributes
Minimum
- Good health record. Few absences from work. Tidy appearance.

Desirable
- Smart appearance, creates good impression on others

Mental attributes
- Above average intelligence, good communication skills

Qualifications
Minimum
- Higher education in a business discipline, preferably business administration

Desirable
- Further education in public relations and marketing

Experience, training and skill
Minimum
- Experience from positions involving similar duties
- Experience using PCs as part of daily work, for example word processing, spreadsheets

Desirable
- Conversational ability in German and French

> Choose a job you would like to do when you complete your studies.

| Business studies teacher | Human resources manager | Motor vehicle mechanic |

> Find out as much as you can about your chosen job using the Internet, careers advisory services, looking at job advertisements in newspapers and/or from someone you know who does the job or did so in the past. Use this information to develop a job description and a person specification for the job.

A job vacancy can be filled through internal recruitment or by advertising the vacancy externally

Once a job vacancy has been identified and details of the role specified, the next task is to decide how the vacancy should be filled.

For managerial postions in its restaurants and offices, McDonald's first tries to fill them through internal recruitment. More than half of all its management positions are filled by hourly paid employees on promotion. Providing employees with opportunities to advance their careers not only motivates them in work but also allows the company to reward and retain its best employees and capitalize on the investment it made in their training, including at McDonald's own Hamburger University.

Vacancies filled by suitable candidates already employed within a business involves **internal recruitment**. Job vacancies can be advertised internally on a notice board, via email or in an organization's newsletter or newspaper.

Advantages of internal recruitment	Disadvantages of internal recruitment
+ It can save time and money over external recruitment.	− It creates other vacancies elsewhere in the organization.
+ It allows the business to reward and retain high-performing employees.	− It prevents recruiting people with new ideas and skills into the business from other organizations that may have more efficient methods.
+ Existing employees already know the business and working practices.	− It may create jealousy among competing employees for the job vacancy.
+ Opportunities for new jobs and promotions help motivate employees.	

If there are no suitable candidates internally the human resources department in an organization may advertise the vacancy externally. **External recruitment** involves recruiting employees who are either seeking work for the first time, are unemployed or are working for another organization. Most vacancies are filled through external recruitment because it can be used to attract employees with new and more advanced skills, but it can be more time-consuming and expensive than internal recruitment.

Advertising job vacancies

A job advertisement must attract the right people, quickly and cost-effectively.

- Advertisements should be clear, accurate and legal. They should contain enough information from the job description and person specification for people to know what the job involves and whether or not they would make suitable candidates. Key information includes:
  - › job title, purpose and main tasks
  - › experience, skills and qualification required
  - › pay and working conditions
  - › brief details of the organization and location
  - › how to apply.

- Choose the right place to advertise. This will depend on the type of job vacancy, how many vacancies there are and the cost of advertising. Where a large number of vacancies exist, for example for nurses or teachers, a recruitment campaign on television or in national newspapers may be appropriate. National business newspapers and specialist websites, such as LinkedIn, may also be used to recruit very senior managers if there are few people with the relevant skills locally.

- Examine how good or bad the response was to the advertisement. Did the advertisement reach its target audience? How many people applied? Were the applicants suitable? Answers to these questions will help a business to plan and design better job advertisements in the future.

McDonald's advertises most of its vacancies on its websites and encourages applicants to apply for them online. People who do not have access to the internet can call their Recruitment Hotline instead or pick up a pre-paid Business Reply Card from a McDonald's restaurant. However, choosing the best method of attracting external job applicants often depends on the organization, the job available and the type of employee required.

- Some businesses may contact **educational institutions** to recruit high-performing students direct from schools, colleges or universities on completing their studies. McDonald's often recruits university graduates to fill many of its trainee manager positions in its corporate headquarters.

- A business may use **professional associations** and websites to advertise jobs with highly specialized skills. For example, there are many professional associations around the world for doctors, engineers, librarians, accountants and lawyers.

- Some firms may use **recruitment agencies**: these are business organizations specializing in helping other businesses recruit the staff they need. These agencies advertise and interview people for different jobs. They also keep records of people looking for work that they can use to find suitable candidates for jobs. This can be especially useful for hiring employees for temporary vacancies that need to be filled quickly.

  Some agencies specialize in the recruitment and selection of professional and managerial staff, and often complete the entire recruitment and selection process for a business including job analysis, writing job and person specifications, reviewing and sifting application forms and interviewing shortlisted candidates.

  Using these agencies' services can be expensive. They often charge a fee for finding a suitable candidate based on the salary for the job vacancy.

- Very senior managers or people with specialist skills are sometimes **headhunted** from other organizations. People identified as having the right experience and skills are approached discreetly by a recruitment agency to find out if they are interested in moving to another employer, often for more pay.

- Some businesses may use **government employment agencies**. Many central and local government authorities run employment agencies or job centres to advertise local job vacancies and provide advice to unemployed people looking for work. These organizations pass details of vacancies to interested people or those people thought to have relevant experience. Most of the vacancies advertised are for manual, unskilled or semi-skilled jobs.

ACTIVITY 2.11

You are head of human resources at Flinchem plc, a major manufacturer of kitchen appliances that are sold all over the world. You have asked a professional recruitment agency to help you find a new finance director for the company. The agency has produced two advertisements for the job. One is good. One is not.

▶ Identify the good advertisement and use it to produce a checklist of information a job advertisement should contain.

▶ Compare your list to the bad advertisement. What is wrong with this advertisement? How could it be improved? Use a word processing programme on a computer to redesign the advertisement to make it better and more attractive.

▶ Suggest how you would advertise the job vacancy and why.

Finance Director   c$100 000

Dynamic kitchen appliance maker seeks an experienced finance director. She will be a key member of the board and work closely with the chief executive.

To apply you must be a graduate and qualified accountant with a minimum of two years' experience of finance and marketing, and the ability to work under stress. You will be required to manage the financial reporting process, establish internal controls and procedures, co-ordinate planning and company administration, and assess the potential for e-commerce.

If you are interested in this exciting opportunity contact

High Profile Search Associates

Finance Director

Singapore   **c$100K + benefits**

An outstanding opportunity for an entrepreneurial, commercially biased person to join a dynamic listed white goods company. The company, established three years ago, has an innovative new product due for market launch next year in Singapore, and thereafter across Asia and the Middle East. The successful candidate will be a key member of the board of directors and work closely with the chief executive to create a company that will generate growth over the next five years of trading.

The Role
- Manage monthly financial reporting against agreed budgets
- Establish internal controls and procedures
- Define the IT framework
- Co-ordinate planning against an agreed basis
- Monitor and summarize product variable costs
- Manage cash planning against an agreed basis
- Establish company book-keeping procedures and ensure that key issues such as banking, payment of payroll, etc. have back-up processes
- Co-ordinate the activities of all company administration procedures to ensure a smooth flow of key business data
- Address the opportunity for e-commerce

The Person
- A graduate, qualified accountant
- A minimum of two years' experience as the finance director of a company with a turnover of at least $40M
- A background in consumer goods or where retail product marketing is strategically important
- Conversant with statutory and tax legislation
- Demonstrate a proven ability to work under pressure, often with limited resources
- Possess an optimistic outlook and demonstrate a "can do" attitude
- Have an ability to build strong relationships across all levels, both internally and externally

Apply for an application pack at www.HPS.com

- Businesses may **advertise in newspapers, magazines and online**. Local newspapers may often be used to fill more junior and unskilled positions in a business. In contrast, national newspapers may be used to fill more senior and specialist positions which may require skills that are in short supply and cannot be found locally.

- Specialist magazines, journals and websites may also be used to recruit people with highly specialized skills, such as surgeons and scientists. They are read by highly technical and qualified people all over the world.

To apply for an advertised vacancy, job applicants may be required to complete an application form, a letter of application or a CV

A job advertisement must contain information about how people should apply for the job and by when.

There are a number of ways people can respond to a job advertisement. They can:

- complete an **application form**, online or in writing
- write a **letter of application**
- prepare and send a **curriculum vitae** (CV) or resumé.

A business may sometimes ask for all three documents depending on how important the job is and how much information the recruiter requires from each candidate.

Once the closing date for applications has passed, the human resources department and the managers of the department advertising the vacancy will review applications received. Information provided by applicants will be matched against the requirements listed in the person specification for the vacant job. Applicants who do not match these requirements will be rejected.

Any personal information about applicants should be treated confidentially.

Application form	CV	Letter of application
An application form will normally require some or all of the following information to be provided by a job applicant: - personal details including name, address, telephone numbers, email address, date of birth, nationality - title of job applied for - schools, colleges and universities attended with dates - educational qualifications, for example examination grades and dates taken - work experience, including previous jobs, former employers, main tasks and responsibilities - interests and hobbies - names and addresses of referees who can provide a reference (that is, give their opinion on the character and suitability of the applicant for the job).	A CV should be no more than one or two pages in length and will contain very similar information to an application form: - personal details including name, address, telephone numbers, email address, date of birth, nationality - schools, colleges and universities attended with dates - educational qualifications, examination grades and dates taken - work experience, including previous jobs, former employers, main tasks and responsibilities - names and addresses of referees to provide personal and employment references if required - interests and hobbies - any other relevant experience, for example the ability to speak a foreign language, possession of a clean driving licence, ability to use IT equipment and software packages.	Sometimes applicants will be asked to write and submit a letter of application containing all the same information as an application form or CV would. However, more usually an applicant will send a short covering letter to accompany a CV. Writing a letter of application often requires more skills than completing an application form or CV. A human resources department will look for letters which are well written and presented and contain: - reasons for applying for the job - the skills, experience and qualities the applicant has and why he or she is well suited to the advertised job - details of relevant work and other experience if not already provided in a CV - any dates the applicant could not attend an interview if required.

Job applicants will be shortlisted for interview before the most suitable candidate for a job is selected

The fifth stage is the selection of suitable candidates. There may be many applicants for an advertised job vacancy.

Applicants who fail to match the criteria will be **sifted** out and rejected. Rejected applicants will be sent a letter informing them they have not been successful but thanking them for their application. Applicants who are a close match to the person specification in terms of their skills, experience and other qualities will be shortlisted for interview.

Shortlisting involves selecting the most promising candidates for a job. The referees provided by an applicant may also be asked to provide a reference at this time to confirm the personal qualities, skills and suitability of the applicant for the job. References are normally confidential and will usually be from a former teacher, employer or other person in a position of authority who knows the applicant well.

Candidates selected for the final shortlist will then be invited to attend an interview at a given date, time and place. They will also normally be told the names and job titles of the people who will interview them.

The final stage in the recruitment and selection process is the interview of shortlisted candidates

The purpose of sifting is to find applicants who appear to be suitable candidates for the advertised job. They will normally be invited to attend an interview. At McDonald's a shortlisted candidate attends an initial interview and, if successful, is then offered "on-the-job experience". This is normally a two-day trial in a restaurant. Successful completion of the trial then leads to a final interview, after which managers decide whether or not to hire the applicant.

Interviews at McDonald's and other organizations are used to:

- confirm factual information provided by each candidate in his or her application
- assess the communication and interpersonal skills of each candidate
- identify any particular strengths or weaknesses that may be a problem
- assess whether or not the candidate will fit into the organization well
- select the most suitable candidate for the job.

There are three main types of selection interview.

- A **one-to-one interview** takes place between an interviewee (the job candidate) and an interviewer (usually the manager of the advertised post or someone from the human resources department).

- A **panel interview** involves several interviewers, for example a senior manager, the manager of the employee who will be doing the advertised job and a human resources manager. Panel interviews can reduce the risk of personal bias in interviews or unsuccessful candidates claiming their interview was unfair.

- A **board interview** may involve a much larger panel of senior and other managers. A board interview will often be used to select other very senior managers and can be used to judge how they perform in group discussions and when they are under stress.

The types of question often asked at interview include the following.

- Why have you applied for the advertised job?
- Why do you think you are suitable for the job?
- What are your key skills and qualities?
- What do you know about the organization?

Some candidates may also be asked to take written and practical tests to demonstrate the skills they have, for example their typing speed, driving skills or specialist knowledge.

▲ One-to-one interview

▲ Panel interview

▲ 'Bored' interview! An uninterested candidate will not be successful

Ethical and legal obligations in recruitment and selection

The recruitment and selection of employees by an organization relies on both the job applicant and the employer being fair and honest. For example, if a job involves weekend working then the job description should say so. Similarly, information supplied by an applicant on an application form, CV or during an interview should be truthful. Failing to disclose relevant information or giving false information, such as lying about qualifications or previous experience, will invalidate a contract of employment if it is discovered and will probably result in dismissal.

A business needs to comply with any employment laws and regulations that govern the conduct of recruitment and selection. For example, it is an offence in many countries to discriminate against any job applicant because of the person's sex, race, religion, disability, age and/or trade union membership.

Job advertisements, application forms and interviews must be carefully worded to avoid being discriminatory.

For example, in some countries it would be an offence to ask whether an applicant was married or to advertise for young women only to undertake secretarial work.

However, it is possible for an employer to express a preference for one type of person over another in a job advertisement if there is a genuine need to do so for the job concerned.

For example, it is legal to advertise for a male attendant for male toilets, a female housemistress for a girl's boarding school, an Asian actor to play an Asian character in a television show or only for male applicants in countries which have laws or customs that prevent females doing some types of work.

What methods would you use to advertise and recruit for the following job vacancies and why? What questions would you ask candidates at interview? What other methods could you use to test their skills and qualities?

| International airline pilot | Care assistant in a home for severely disabled people | Farm labourers to pick fruit during summer | Manager of a major department store |

Once a new employee is selected and appointed he or she requires a contract of employment and his or her performance should be monitored

Once interviews have been completed and a decision made, the advertised job can be offered to the successful candidate.

- The successful candidate will normally be informed by telephone or in writing that he or she passed the interview and is being offered the job.

- A letter of appointment will confirm the job offer and contain details of wages or salary, hours of work and a start date and time. Interviewed candidates who were unsuccessful will be sent a letter thanking them for their attendance at interview. They may also be offered the chance to discuss their interview performance with the human resources department or interviewer.

- Once a new employee has been appointed he or she must be given an **employment contract** to sign. This is a legal statement of the person's terms of employment, such as wages, hours of work and holiday entitlement, and lists the rights and responsibilities of the employee and the employer. ➤ **2.3.4**

- Once the new employee is in post, his or her progress and performance should be monitored over time. This will help to confirm whether or not the right choice was made and whether the employee needs additional support and training. For example, newly recruited staff at McDonald's are assessed over a three-week probationary period Following that, employees are rated on their performance and after which they are either kept on or their employment is terminated.

Hours of work

An organization may recruit employees to work full-time or part-time

A person who is in **full-time employment** will usually work 35 hours or more each week and usually for seven hours each day for five days per week. However, hours of work vary greatly in different countries. For example, the full-time working week in France is 35 hours while full-time employees in Chile usually work 45 hours each week.

▼ **Full-time employment has the following benefits and limitations**

Benefits to employers	Benefits to employees
+ Full-time employees work fixed, predictable hours. + Full-time employees are more likely to develop loyalty and be more committed to their employer. + The employees usually only hold one job, making it easier to control their time and productive efforts. + They can continue to run a business in the owner's or senior manager's absence.	+ Full-time employees have fixed, predictable hours of employment. + Wages per hour are usually higher than those paid to part-time employees doing the same or similar jobs. + Annual leave, sick leave, health insurance and other benefits may be more generous than those offered to part-time employees. + Full-time jobs are often considered to be part of a career, with more chance of receiving training and promotions to reach more senior positions.
Limitations to employers	**Limitations to employees**
× Full-time employees may not want to work extended hours. × Those who agree to work evenings and weekends will have to be paid premium or overtime wage rates. × Annual leave and other benefits given to full-time employees are costly.	× Less time is available for leisure activities or spending with family and friends. × Full-time employees may also be required to work overtime on top of normal hours. × The work may be boring and lack variety.

An increasing number of employees are being recruited to work part-time. People who are in **part-time employment** work fewer hours than people in full-time employment, usually less than 35 hours each week.

Some part-time employees may have set hours to work each day while others may work different hours or "shifts" each day they work. For example, a person employed to work 15 hours a week may work five hours a day for three days, or may be required to work three hours per day for five days each week.

Many organizations have replaced full-time employees with part-time employees because its allows them to use labour more flexibly to extend their hours of opening or operation, for example, by employing more people to work evenings and weekends without the need to pay overtime rates. ➤ **2.2.2**

There are many reasons why people want to work part-time, including being unable to find a full-time job, and why many businesses and other organizations want part-time employees.

▼ **Part-time employment has the following benefits and limitations**

Benefits to employers	Benefits to employees
+ Part-time employees can be an excellent staffing option for new and small businesses, due to the flexibility they offer and their relatively low cost. **+** A business can vary the number of hours each part-time employee works based on the amount of work available, for example requiring them to work more hours at busy times. **+** Part-time employees may not qualify for all the same benefits as full-time employees and are therefore cheaper to employ.	**+** Part-time employment offers people more flexibility, for example to look after family members, continue in education or pursue their other interests. **+** Some part-time employees may have more than one job, providing them with more variety in their work and teaching them more skills. **+** There may be more and a greater variety of part-time jobs open to an employee than full-time employment opportunities.
Limitations to employers	Limitations to employees
✗ Some part-time employees may hold more than one job which may make them less loyal than full-time employees to their employer. **✗** Turnover is often higher. This means recruitment and selection costs may be higher because part-time employees tend to change their jobs more often than full-time employees. **✗** Part-time employees may not be as skilled or as productive as full-time employees and may require more training. **✗** It can be difficult to communicate with part-time employees during periods when they are not in work. For example, they may miss important business meetings.	**✗** The wages rates may be lower than that in an equivalent or similar full-time job. These employees may have to take another part-time job to boost their earnings. **✗** They may not qualify for the same benefits full-time employees receive from their employers, such as health insurance. **✗** They may receive less training than full-time employees because their employers think they are less likely to stay with them in the same job for as long or want promotion. **✗** They may be less likely to be promoted to more senior positions because they do not work full-time. **✗** They may miss important business meetings.

Kausik owns a café in a large city. He employs eight members of staff as follows:

Task	Number of full-time employees	Number of part-time employees
Preparing and cooking food	2	1
Making hot drinks	1	0
Serving tables	2	1
Cash desk	1	0

Kausik has a democratic style of leadership. He pays all members of staff to come in one hour early once a week for a staff meeting.

a   Define "democratic style of leadership".   [2]

b   Outline **one** advantage and **one** disadvantage of employing part-time staff.   [4]

c   Kausik needs to employ another member of staff to make hot drinks. Advise Kausik on the difference between a job description and a person specification.   [6]

d   Advise Kausik on what method of selection he should use to select the right person for the job. Justify your answer.   [6]

Before you continue make sure you are able to

Explain methods of recruiting and selecting workers:

✓   **recruitment and selection methods**

✓   the difference between **internal and external recruitment**

✓   the main stages in recruitment and selection of employees

✓   recommend and justify who to employ in given circumstances

✓   the benefits and limitations of **part-time employees** and **full-time employees**.

Learning CHECKLIST

2.3.2 The importance of training and the methods of training

Key POINTS

▶ Training employees can increase their job satisfaction and motivation and increase the amount and quality of the work they do.

▶ Training employees to improve their existing skills and to learn new ones can help a business introduce new equipment and technologies, reduce supervision and improve health and safety at work.

▶ A multi-skilled workforce can adapt quickly to organizational changes and changes in working practices.

▶ Training methods used by an organization vary depending on the objective, for example the induction of new employees or teaching professional qualifications.

▶ Induction training involves teaching new employees about the organization they work for and their responsibilities.

▶ On-the-job training has the advantage of work continuing while employees train.

▶ Off-the-job training involves employees attending training and educational courses away from their normal place of work.

▶ Off-the-job training can be more expensive than on-the-job training. Fees and charges for training courses and venues can be very high and employees on training courses will not be available for work.

Business BUZZWORDS

Induction training – teaching new employees about the organization they work for.

Multi-skilling – training employees in a variety of skills so they are more flexible in the work they can do.

On-the-job training – training employees while they carry out their normal duties.

Off-the job training – training employees away from their normal workplace.

The importance of training

Training can improve employees' skills and motivation, resulting in higher levels of labour productivity

It is not difficult to see why training new pilots is so important for major international airline companies such as Lufthansa of Germany, Emirates Airline and Singapore Airlines, to name a few. Accidents can cost lives and many millions of dollars.

Successful candidates for cadet pilot positions therefore spend up to 18 months training on simulators and small aircraft to acquire a pilot's licence. It may then take them many more years of flying and management training before a pilot can become a captain.

But training employees is equally important to many other organizations. As we learnt in the previous section, fast food retail company McDonald's even has its own university to teach its management trainees using a combination of classroom instruction, role play simulations and e-learning on a computer. The company sets challenging targets for quality, customer service and cleanliness in each of its restaurants. Without well-trained and motivated employees and managers they would be unable to meet these standards and would therefore risk losing customers to other restaurants.

Training employees can increase their job satisfaction and motivation and increase the amount and quality of the work they do.

Skilled workers are also able to change their jobs more easily, be promoted more quickly and earn more money than less-skilled workers.

However, training can be expensive and reduce profits, so there must be a clear need for the training and substantial benefits to the business, including greater efficiency and increased profitability. The human resources department in an organization can help identify and monitor employees' training needs and evaluate the outcomes of their training.

Training can benefit a business in a number of ways.
- New equipment and technologies can be introduced.
- Employees' motivation and productivity can increase.
- Staff turnover can be reduced.
- Employees may need less supervision.
- It prepares key employees for promotion.
- Health and safety at work can improve.
- It can create a **multi-skilled** workforce that can adapt quickly to organizational changes and changes in working practices.
- Managers can improve their skills in leading, managing and motivating others.

Training methods vary depending on the objectives, for example the induction of new employees or teaching professional qualifications

The three main types of training are:
- **induction training**
- **on-the-job training**
- **off-the-job training.**

Induction training involves teaching new employees about the organization they work for and their responsibilities. It is also an opportunity to meet other new employees and people they will be working with closely in their jobs.

An induction programme may last a day, a week or sometimes longer and can include information about the aims and objectives of the organization, how it is structured, the different roles in the organization, rules and safety procedures and basic information about on-site facilities, such as where the toilets and the canteen are located.

Without induction training new employees may make mistakes, fail to understand what the aims of the organization are and take much longer to become effective in their jobs. They could even become demotivated very quickly and decide to leave, which means the entire recruitment and selection process will have been wasted.

- **On-the-job training** takes place in the workplace as employees carry out their normal tasks. It usually involves an unskilled or semi-skilled employee working with a more experienced worker and watching the person carry out different tasks. This is sometimes called **shadowing**.

  This method of training has the advantage of work continuing while employees train. However, more experienced workers may be less productive than normal because of the time it takes them to coach trainees in different tasks. The choice of trainer is important. For example, the trainer will need to be patient with the trainees and have good communication skills to explain what is being done and why. If the trainer has any bad habits he or she may pass these on to the trainees.

- **Off-the-job training** involves employees attending training and educational courses away from their normal place of work. A wide range of skills can be taught in off-the-job training through lectures and using techniques such as role plays and simulations. For example, leadership and management training courses often use role plays to demonstrate how different management styles can be used in different situations.

  - **In-house courses** are organized and run on the premises of the employing organization. Some large organizations, such as major banks, supermarket chains and government departments, have their own residential training centres or colleges used to teach and train their employees.

  - **External courses** are provided by other organizations, for example specialist training centres or a supplier of new equipment who is willing to train workers how to use it.

  - **Vocational and professional educational courses** are provided by schools, colleges and universities as a means of supporting on-the-job learning. Vocational courses provide training in job-related skills. Professional courses, for example in accountancy and law, are normally completed by university graduates entering these professions in order to further their skills and careers.

Off-the-job training can be more expensive than on-the-job training. Fees and charges for training courses and venues can be high and employees on training courses will not be available for work. This means output will be lower while employees are attending training courses. However, this can be avoided if employees attend courses outside working hours, at evenings and weekends.

Welcome meetings
Company objectives
Standards and expectations

Development Programme
On-the-job training
Mentoring by experienced crew
All aspects of restaurant operation
Management training

Data–based learning
Restaurant operation
Cleanliness
Customer service

▲ McDonald's training programme for new restaurant employees

Type of training	Benefits	Limitations
Induction	• Helps new employees to understand the expectations, aims and objectives of the organization. • Helps new employees to avoid making mistakes. • New employees have an opportunity to meet other new employees. • The organization will have a more effective worker. • The employee will feel more of a sense of belonging and is likely to stay with the organization for longer.	• Only training specific to the organization. • If badly designed, can leave new employees feeling confused. • Confused employees are more likely to make mistakes and take a long time to become efficient in the job. • Often involves existing employees explaining things to the new recruits so they have to take time away from their work. • Time spent on induction activities is time away from doing the job and can affect productivity.
On-the-job	• Work can continue whilst the new employees trains. • Relatively cheap and easy to arrange. • New employees can see how the job can be done. • The experienced employee can offer help and advice so that the new recruit settles in quicker. • New employee gets to know some of their co-workers.	• Reduces the productivity of the trainer because of the time taken to train the new employee. • The trainer may be impatient and alienate the new recruit. • Some skilled employees resent having to train new recruits; they don't feel that is part of their job. • If the more experienced worker has bad habits, then the new recruit may pick up these. • Not all experienced workers are good communicators so may confuse the new employee.
Off-the-job	• Training carried out by experienced teachers with good communication skills. • Employees can focus on the training without worrying about getting a job done. • Allows a wide range of teaching methods to be used. • A wider range of skills can be taught. • Can provide the employee with qualifications.	• Expensive. • Takes time out of work if provided during working hours. • Employees can find it difficult to fit in training, especially if it requires attendance in "out-of-work" hours. • Employees may get a better job elsewhere because of the training so the organization does not get the benefits.

Look at the pictures below. For each one suggest:

▶ what knowledge or skills are being taught

▶ what training methods are being used

▶ what types of business you would expect to use these methods

▶ what other types of training could be used to teach the same skills.

Investigate the training available to two employees you know, preferably in different occupations.

▶ What methods are used to train them?

▶ How often do they receive training?

▶ What skills have they learnt or improved?

▶ What do they think are the benefits?

So how would you apply this technique in your usual jobs?

One of the main functions of management is to *communicate*.

I'll show you where the canteen is before I introduce you to your work colleagues.

Show me how you did that again, Raul.

Exam PREPARATION 2.5

Wheelace PLC sell new and used cars. They also provide garage services for car repairs. They have recently expanded their operations by opening a new car showroom and garage in a neighbouring city. This required them to recruit 50 new employees to staff all departments. The managers are considering whether they should offer any training to the new recruits.

a   Identify **two** benefits to Wheelace PLC of having a more highly trained staff.   [2]

b   Explain **two** different types of training that could be used by the company.   [4]

c   Explain **one** benefit and **one** limitation of each training method you explained in b above.   [6]

d   Discuss whether all staff should be trained by the same method. Justify your answer.   [6]

Learning CHECKLIST

Before you continue make sure you are able to

Identify and explain different **training methods**:

✓ the importance of training to a business and to employees

✓ the benefits and limitations of **induction training, on-the-job training** and **off-the-job training**.

2.3.3   Why reducing the size of the workforce might be necessary

▶ A business may reduce or downsize its workforce following the automation of its production processes, due to falling demand for its products or following a merger with another organization in order to reduce its costs.

▶ Downsizing can be achieved in some cases without job losses, for example, by not replacing workers who retire due to old age or ill health.

▶ Cutting jobs involves making employees redundant. Some employees may choose to voluntary redundancy, for example, older employees who want to retire early or those who can easily get jobs elsewhere.

▶ Compulsory redundancy may be necessary if an organization needs to make a large number of employees redundant. Closure of an organization or its relocation to another country will result in compulsory redundancy for the entire workforce.

▶ In addition to redundancy, employees may also be dismissed from an organization for incompetence or gross misconduct; for example, for stealing or sexually harassing colleagues at work.

▶ An organization can follow a disciplinary procedure to discipline and eventually dismiss an employee who continues to perform or behave badly.

▶ A disciplinary procedure normally involves giving verbal and written warnings to an employee about his or her poor performance or behaviour.

Workforce planning – determining the right size, skills and composition of a workforce a business will require to fulfil its future needs and objectives.

Downsizing – reducing the size of the workforce in an organization.

Compulsory redundancy – when a job is cut and the employee is forced to leave employment in return for monetary compensation.

Voluntary redundancy – when an employee chooses to leave employment in return for monetary compensation.

Disciplinary procedure – formal rules and actions followed in an organization when an employee breaches his or her contract of employment.

Dismissal – terminating the employment of an employee.

"Rightsizing" a workforce

Changes to the size of a workforce may be needed following changes in production processes and consumer demand or due to relocation

The total number of people employed by a business at any given time, whether they are temporary, part-time or full-time employees, is its workforce. Changes in the size and composition of a workforce are common due to many factors, for example future sales forecasts and business expansion plans, the introduction of new technologies and products or changes in the cost of employing people.

Deciding how many people a business needs to employ, what skills they will need and what hours they will work requires **workforce planning**. As a business grows, for instance, it may need to permanently increase the size of its workforce. It may also need to take on extra staff on a temporary basis at certain times of the year to meet peaks in consumer demand for its products. For example, a hotel in a popular holiday destination may require more staff during summer months when more people are on vacation. Similarly, retail outlets may hire more staff during their spring and winter sales periods.

Finding the number and type of employees to meet the future needs and objectives of a business is often referred to as "rightsizing": the process of reorganizing or restructuring an organization through changes in production processes, layers of management and the size and composition of its workforce, for example by recruiting more part-time workers. ➤ **2.3.1**

Rightsizing a workforce may, however, involve cutting the total number of jobs and therefore employees within an organization to reduce costs and improve efficiency. This is called **downsizing**.

ACTIVITY 2.14

From the articles identify as many reasons as you can as to why organizations downsize their workforces.

Airbus-parent EADS to downsize defence and space business

EADS, the maker of Airbus, is set to announce a major restructuring plan tomorrow that is likely to include thousands of job cuts.

The focus of the plan will be on the company's defence and space operations. Both have suffered a significant drop in orders from customers over the last few years.

Job cuts follow the merger of two leading supermarkets

800 jobs lost as Dyson relocates manufacturing to Far East

47% of all jobs to be automated by 2034, argues new report

Staples to close stores, focus on online sales

Office supplies retailer, Staples, announced yesterday that it would be expanding its online business, funding the expansion by cutting $250 million in costs over the next two years. The savings will come from the closure of 30 of its US stores and 45 stores in Europe.

Staples is the latest example of office supplies retailers struggling to survive as more shoppers buy products like computers, pens, paper and paper clips online.

Downsizing a workforce may be required for the following reasons.

- New technologies and equipment have been introduced to automate many of the tasks carried out by employees. This is called **labour substitution**. ➤ **4.1.3**

- There is falling demand for the goods or services of the business due to increased competition from other firms or because consumer tastes have changed. ➤ **3.1.2**

- The business premises are closing, due to relocation or a change in the way the business distributes its products to its customers, for example because of an increase in online shopping. ➤ **3.3.3**

- Two businesses have integrated following a merger or takeover resulting in a number of jobs becoming surplus to the requirements of the new combined enterprise. For example, it will not require two human resources departments or two finance or sales departments. ➤ **1.3.3**

- The business is closing following its financial failure or because its owners want to pursue other, more profitable business opportunities. ➤ **1.3.4**

- The business is relocating its operations to another country. ➤ **4.4.1**

Workers no longer required by an organization are usually made redundant and some may qualify for redundancy payments

Reductions in the size of a workforce may be achieved:

- by not replacing workers who retire due to age or ill health

- by not replacing workers who leave to take jobs with other employers

- through the dismissal of workers because of their poor performance or behaviour

- by making one or more employees redundant because their jobs are no longer required due to changes in the structure, work or size of the organization.

Redundancy involves terminating the employment contracts of those employees who are no longer needed by an organization.

An employee who is made redundant is usually given a sum of money to compensate for the loss of his or her job. For example, this could be one week's wages for every year the employee has worked for the organization. In some countries, minimum redundancy payments are set out in law.

Some employees may choose to take **voluntary redundancy**, for example those employees who can easily get jobs elsewhere or older employees who want to retire early. In contrast, forcing employees to take redundancy – known as **compulsory redundancy** – may be necessary if an organization needs to make a large reduction in the size of its workforce.

Unless a business closes down completely with the loss of all jobs, often difficult decisions need to be made about which employees to make redundant. How skilled and productive the employee is, the length of time the employee has been with the organization and the person's employment history are important factors.

An organization will retain:	An organization will make redundant:
✓ the most skilled and productive workers or those with skills that can be transferred to other departments within the organization	✗ workers whose jobs are no longer required, for example because their work has been automated or the department they worked in has been closed
✓ workers who have been with the employer the longest because they are the most experienced	✗ the least skilled and least productive workers
✓ workers who have been with the employer the longest because they will also be the most expensive to make redundant if redundancy payments are made and linked to length of time employed.	✗ workers with poor punctuality and attendance records
	✗ workers who have not been with the employer very long because their redundancy payments will be low; this policy is often referred to as "last in, first out".

ACTIVITY 2.15

Sparkle and Shine Cleaning Services is a partnership providing cleaners to homes and offices. Due to falling demand for their services, the partners have to cut costs if the business is to survive. The partners estimate that they need to make cost savings of $6000 over the next 12 months. As the organization is labour-intensive, the cost savings will have to come from redundancies.

In groups of 3-4, study Tables A and B and decide who to make redundant. Justify your recommendations.

Table A:

Employee category	Redundancy payment due
Worked less than 2 years	0
Under 22 years old	Half a week's pay for each year worked whilst under the age of 22
22–41 years old	One week's pay for each full year worked between the ages of 22 and 41
Over 41 years old	One-and-a-half week's pay for each year worked at the age of 41 and older

Table B:

Name	Age	Role	Weekly pay	Time in the job	Employment notes
Lee-Ann	40	Supervisor	$480	18 years	Recently other employees have complained about her laziness and that she is too bossy. In the last 6 months has been late for work 8 times.
Mohsin	35	Team leader	$390	14 years	Always punctual and polite. Positive feedback from customers and other employees.
Sheila	56	Cleaner	$360	15 years	Good worker. Helps train new employees. Gets on well with everybody.
Ying	29	Cleaner	$360	3 years	Punctual but some negative feedback from customers.
Kausik	20	Cleaner	$300	2 years and 6 months	Positive feedback from customers. Always willing to take on extra hours.
Jack	19	Cleaner	$280	18 months	Good worker. Punctual. Positive customer feedback.

Disciplinary procedures at work and the dismissal of employees

An employee may be disciplined or even dismissed from a job if his or her performance or behaviour is unacceptable

An employer is entitled to discipline employees if they do not fulfil their responsibilities or fail to follow rules and safety procedures. If the work and behaviour of an employee continues to be unacceptable he or she could be dismissed from the job.

An organization can follow a **disciplinary procedure** to take action against an employee who is performing or behaving badly. The first stage involves a manager giving a verbal warning to the employee that his or her work or behaviour is unsatisfactory and must improve. If there is no improvement the employee will receive a written warning. A final written warning will normally result in **dismissal**.

Alternatively, an employee may be demoted to a less senior position, suspended for a period of time with or without pay from their job or, in some cases, even dismissed instantly if he or she has been involved in a very serious breach of rules or safety procedures. Serious breaches can include stealing, being drunk at work or a deliberate violation of health and safety regulations that puts other employees and the business at risk.

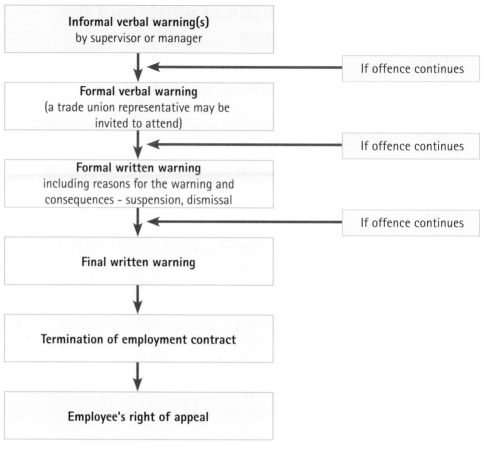

▲ A typical disciplinary and dismissal procedure

Reasons for the fair and legal dismissal of an employee include gross misconduct, incompetence and redundancy

Employment laws in many countries govern the ways in which employers can discipline and dismiss their employees. For example, it is an offence in most countries to dismiss an employee simply because of his or her sex, race or religion. Employees who are dismissed unfairly normally have the legal right to seek compensation from their former employer.

Reasons for the fair and legal dismissal of an employee can vary but normally include:

- **gross misconduct by the employee**, which includes drunkenness, drug intoxication, theft, fraud, disobedience, frequent lateness or absence, giving out confidential information, sexual harassment or negligence which involves a breach of the employment contract

- **incompetence**, which includes producing sub-standard work, underperformance and an inability to fulfil tasks satisfactorily

- circumstances **where an employee's continued employment breaks laws**, for example, if the driver of a heavy goods vehicle has been banned from driving

- cases **where the employee fails to accept reasonable working practices and procedures**

- **redundancy**, when the employment contract of an employee who is not required by the employer is terminated.

Discuss the following offences in small groups. In each case discuss whether or not the employee needs to be disciplined and, if so, which of the following actions you will take:

A informal verbal warning

B formal verbal warning

C a formal written warning

D a final written warning

E instant dismissal.

If you choose C or D then you must warn the employee that if the offence continues he or she will face one of the following punishments:

▸ suspension with pay pending investigation

▸ suspension without pay

▸ demotion to a less senior position

▸ dismissal.

Which punishment do you think is the most appropriate and why?

1
A production worker has been caught stealing a computer.

2
An employee is found asleep at work. His wife has recently died and he has a good record at work.

3
An office worker has left confidential papers on her desk overnight. They should have been locked away. A security officer has found them.

4
A supervisor who has already received a verbal and written warning for continued lateness is late again without reasonable cause.

5
A sales manager is accused of sexually harassing his secretary. She has reliable witnesses in the organization who are able to confirm the harassment.

6
The police inform the human resources department that they have detained one of the firm's van drivers for driving while drunk.

7
An employee who has been verbally warned for incompetence has recently failed again to meet her work targets.

8
A newly promoted manager is unable to cope with the increased demands of his new job and has lost the respect of his staff.

Before you continue make sure you are able to

Learning CHECKLIST

Understand why reducing the size of a workforce might be necessary:

✓ the difference between **dismissal** and **redundancy** and use examples to illustrate the difference

✓ understand situations in which downsizing the workforce might be necessary, for example due to automation or reduced demand for products

✓ recommend and justify which workers to recruit or make **redundant** in given circumstances.

2.3.4 Legal controls over employment issues and their impact on employers and employees

▸ Some employers may exploit their employees or treat them unfairly, for example by making them work long hours for very low wages in order to keep their costs as low as possible and boost their profits.

▸ Many governments have therefore introduced legal controls to protect the rights and responsibilities of employees and also those of their employers.

▸ Employment laws regulate the relationship between employers and the people they employ to ensure they treat each other fairly.

▸ The amount of protection different laws give to workers in different countries varies but usually covers their right to:

  ● an employment contract specifying the terms and conditions of their employment, including hours of work, holiday entitlement, wage or salary

  ● protection from unfair dismissal

  ● protection from discrimination

  ● receive wages free from unlawful deductions made by their employers.

▸ Health and safety laws and regulations have also been introduced in many countries to ensure that employers provide safe and healthy working environments. Employees must also observe these laws and regulations so that they do not put other employees or their employers at risk.

▸ Some governments have also introduced a legal minimum wage to prevent employers from paying some groups of workers very low wages.

Business BUZZWORDS

Employment laws – legislation that governs the rights and responsibilities of employees and their employers.

Indirect discrimination – when a group of people is disadvantaged by their sex, race, religion or other characteristics because they fail to meet an unjustified requirement for a job.

Direct discrimination – the unequal treatment of job applicants or employees because of differences in their race, religion, sex, disability, age or other characteristics.

Legal minimum wage – the minimum amount of money workers must be paid for their employment per period of time.

Employment contract – a formal legal agreement between an employer and an employee that details the workplace duties and responsibilities the employee will perform in return for an agreed wage or salary.

Health and safety laws – legal controls designed to set minimum standards of safety and cleanliness to reduce the risk of injury and ill health resulting from working.

Employment tribunal (or industrial tribunal) – a court of law that determines a dispute over employment rights between an employer and an employee.

Rights and responsibilities of employees and employers

Employment legislation determines many of the rights and obligations of employees and employers

Some employers may seek to exploit their employees or treat them unfairly in order to keep the costs of the business as low as possible and boost profits.

For example, Global Fashion in Honduras used to make clothes for export to Walmart stores in the US. The plant made a substantial profit from these exports but when the National Labor Committee, a US pressure group on human rights, visited the Global Fashion plant, it found a "sweatshop" in which many young women, some as young as 13, worked in appalling conditions. They were not allowed to take breaks or have a drink of water if they were thirsty. They regularly worked shifts of up to 12 hours each day for just 31 cents each per hour and used poorly maintained and often hazardous machines.

Employees also had to raise their hands to go to the toilet and were not allowed to talk to each other during work. They would be searched as they entered the plant and any sweets or foods they had was confiscated. The workers at Global Fashion could also be sacked from their job without notice or compensation, especially if they were injured or became ill or pregnant.

Treating employees in these ways is considered unethical in many societies and employment laws have been introduced to protect them. **Employment laws** are used by governments to regulate the relationship between employers and the people they employ to ensure they are all treated fairly. However, sweatshops like Global Fashion are workplaces that ignore employment laws. They are therefore illegal in most countries, but still tolerated in some. The amount of protection given to workers by employment laws varies by country but often includes their right to:

- a written statement of employment terms and conditions
- protection from unfair dismissal
- protection from discrimination
- a safe and healthy working environment
- wage protection, including in some cases a minimum wage.

Legal controls over employment contracts

The female workers at the Global Fashion sweatshop in Honduras were prevented from learning about and exercising their employment rights by their managers. Had they been able to, they would have known the way they were being treated at the clothing plant was illegal. This is why employment laws in most countries require employers to give their employees an employment contract on or soon after the day they start work.

An **employment contract** is a legal document that lists the main terms and conditions of employment of an employee in an organization. These can vary widely depending on the type of job, experience of the employee, location and business organization.

Terms and conditions of employment

A contract of employment is drawn up by an employer and signed by the employee.

It is a legally binding agreement and can be enforced in law.

A contract may contain many different details but commonly include:

▸ name of the employee and employer

▸ date on which employment began

▸ date on which employment will end if it is a fixed-term contract

▸ job title

▸ wage rate or salary, payment intervals and method of payment and any deductions

▸ normal hours of work and rest periods

▸ holiday entitlement, holiday pay and public holidays

▸ conditions relating to sickness, injury and maternity pay

▸ pension entitlement if relevant

▸ length of notice required to quit the job

▸ disciplinary rules and procedures

▸ arrangements for handling grievances

▸ trade union membership

▸ dress code

▸ work location or locations.

Terms of employment agreed in a contract of employment are **expressed terms**. There can be many, so a contract may simply refer to other documents that set these out in full including company rules and guidance on disciplinary and grievance procedures. **➤ 2.3.4**

In addition, there are many unwritten **implied terms** that are assumed to form part of an employment contract between an employer and employee. For example, implied terms include expecting employees to achieve business objectives, follow orders from their managers and comply with health and safety procedures.

An employment contract therefore protects an employee against unfair treatment but also provides an employer with protection against an unsatisfactory employee. An employee that breaks the terms or conditions of his or her employment can be dismissed fairly.

The different types of employment contract are:

- **permanent full-time contracts** for employees who are employed to work for 35 or more hours each week for an indefinite period of time

- **permanent part-time contracts** for employees who work fewer than 35 hours each week for an indefinite period of time

- **fixed-term contracts** for full-time or part-time work but only for a specified period of time, usually between six months and two years.

Unless workers agree to work voluntarily they have a right to be rewarded for the work they do. An employment contract will therefore contain details of:

- the wage rate or salary an employee will receive

- how frequently payments will be made

- how and how often wages or salaries will be reviewed.

Legal controls over unfair dismissal

Once recruited into a job a worker may need protection from being dismissed unfairly. For example, rather than continue to pay an employee on sick or maternity leave a business might dismiss that person and hire someone else instead.

In many countries it is considered unfair for a business to dismiss workers because:

- of their race, religion, sex, age or disability

- they become pregnant or fall ill

- they join a trade union.

If a worker feels he or she has been dismissed unfairly, the employee may be able to take the case to an industrial tribunal or **employment tribunal**. These are special law courts that determine disputes between employers and employees over employment rights. A tribunal will listen to both sides of an argument and make a ruling. If it finds dismissal was unfair an employer may need to pay compensation to its former employee.

What is considered to be the fair and legal dismissal of an employee can vary but normally includes gross misconduct, including theft and being drunk at work, incompetence, the failure of an employee to accept reasonable working practices and procedures or redundancy due to downsizing. ➤ **2.3.3**

Legal controls over discrimination at work

Governments in many countries have equal opportunity policies and laws to protect workers from unfair discrimination at work.

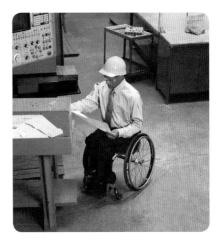

While it is perfectly legal to discriminate between people in work according to their experience, performance and ability it is unlawful in many countries to discriminate against people because of their sex, race, religion or disability and also their age in some countries. This means the recruitment and selection of employees, wages and salaries, holiday entitlement and the selection of employees for training courses, promotion or dismissal must all be free from unfair discrimination.

For example, the Equal Pay Act in the UK makes it unlawful for employers to discriminate between men and women in terms of their pay and conditions if they are doing the same or similar work of equal value.

Direct discrimination occurs when a person is treated less favourably than another because of their sex, race, religion, disability or another distinguishing characteristic. For example, this may occur if a pregnant woman is selected for redundancy or a black person is overlooked for promotion or paid less than others simply because of the colour of his or her skin.

Indirect discrimination occurs when a person or group of people is disadvantaged by their sex, race, religion or another characteristic because they failed to meet an unjustified requirement for a job. For example, this would occur if a business advertised for an accountant who was able to drive a pick-up truck. As this will prevent some people with disabilities from applying and as driving is not a core requirement for doing the job, the business is indirectly discriminating against this group of people.

Victimization occurs when a person is treated less favourably than others after claiming he or she has been discriminated against repeatedly. For example, a female worker might be made redundant or moved to a less well-paid job following complaints she made against a manager who was sexually harassing her.

Discrimination is usually only legal where it involves a genuine and justifiable occupational qualification. This means it is possible to advertise, recruit, train, promote, pay or dismiss employees because of their different skills, performance and behaviour at work. ➤ **2.3.1**

Legal controls over health and safety at work

Many years ago workers had little protection from injury or ill health caused by poor working conditions. Many workers were killed or disabled using hazardous machinery or from using and inhaling dangerous chemicals. Guards and safety cages were not fitted around machines and protective clothing was rarely provided. Conditions in factories were often very hot, noisy and unhealthy. Workers who fell ill or became disabled were usually dismissed without compensation because they could no longer work.

Thankfully, today health and safety in the workplace is of vital importance to most businesses, workers and governments. Businesses that fail to look after the health and safety of their employees will find it difficult to recruit, motivate or retain good workers and as a result they will fail to meet their business objectives for sales and profits. Only those businesses that demonstrate their commitment to the highest standards of health and safety at work will attract, motivate and retain the best workers. ➤ **2.1.1**

For example, St Regis plc takes health and safety issues very seriously because of the impact it can have on its business costs and revenues. St Regis manufactures and recycles paper and employs around 1400 staff. Managers had noticed that accidents and injuries at the plant were increasing and resulting in more staff being unable to attend work, increased medical insurance costs and reduced production. When two accidental deaths occurred it was clearly time to review its health and safety management systems. Working with employees, senior managers identified problems and developed an action plan including fitting improved guards on paper mills and cutting machines, health and safety training for employees and regular site inspections and meetings. The business benefits were significant. Injuries fell by 61%, days lost due to injury by 18% (saving around $150 000 each year) and claims for medical bills fell by 73%.

However, some businesses may continue to overlook or ignore health and safety measures because they may increase the costs of production and reduce profits. Laws have therefore been passed in many countries to ensure that business organizations provide safe and healthy working environments. Businesses failing to do so could face heavy fines or closure. Business owners and managers may also face manslaughter charges if workers suffer fatal injuries due to poor health and safety measures.

> By improving our health and safety management, we're protecting the health and safety of our employees, visitors to our sites, and also our shareholders' investments.

Minister commemorates workers injured or killed in work-related accidents

Today the Minister of Labour attended a ceremony to mark the National Day of Mourning, to commemorate workers killed, injured, disabled or suffering illness as a result of workplace tragedies.

Nearly one million work-related injuries and illnesses are reported each year in Canada, and many of these accidents are preventable.

Workers injured in blaze on Al Reem Island

Several workers were injured in the fire at a building under construction on Abu Dhabi's Al Reem Island.

Their colleagues managed to flee to the top floors of the building to escape the thick smoke and flames after the blaze started at about 3 p.m. on Sunday.

Measures that can make a workplace safer, healthier and more pleasant to work in include:

- providing protective clothing, ear defenders, goggles, breathing masks, etc.

- placing guards and signs on hazardous machines and substances

- providing and maintaining fire and safety equipment

- providing hygienic kitchen and washing facilities

- installing filters to reduce air pollutants

- controlling workplace temperatures

- providing first-aid kits and training in first aid

- allowing regular rest breaks so workers do not become tired and make mistakes

- training workers in health and safety procedures, for example how to operate machinery safely.

Many of these measures are required under **health and safety laws** and regulations. In addition, many countries require employers to provide health insurance for their employees and to pay compensation to injured workers. For example, the Lebanese workers' compensation law requires employers to provide workers injured at work with full medical care, 75% of their daily salary starting from the day of their injury and compensation for permanent disabilities and death.

Employees may also be required by law to take all reasonable care and precautions to avoid injury to themselves and others and to co-operate fully with employers on health and safety matters. Trade unions may also be given the right to inspect workplaces and to investigate the causes of any accidents or illnesses.

Sadly, not all countries enforce or even have sensible health and safety laws. Workers, including children in some countries, may still work very long hours for low wages with little or no protection from danger or disease.

However, not all businesses in these countries treat their employees in this way. Owners and managers of many businesses may believe it is unethical to ignore the safety and welfare of their employees. A business may also risk damaging its international reputation and losing sales if it is discovered to be exploiting workers in less-developed countries.

Legal control over wages

Wage protection laws in many countries make it illegal for employers to make deductions from the wages and salaries of an employee unless they are:

- statutory deductions required by law, such as the payment of personal income taxes and social security contributions

- voluntary deductions agreed in writing by the employee, for example union membership fees, pension contributions and subscriptions to clubs and societies.

Many countries have also introduced **minimum wage laws** to protect vulnerable and low-paid workers from exploitation by powerful employers.

The first **legal minimum wage** was introduced in New Zealand in 1896, followed by Australia in 1899 and the UK in 1902, and again in 1999. In 2016, the UK introduced a minimum wage called the National Living Wage. Apart from raising the pay of low-paid workers it is argued that favourable minimum wages will make them work harder and achieve higher levels of productivity. However, some employers argue a legal minimum wage set above what they would normally offer will simply raise their costs and result in them employing fewer workers.

Advantages of a legal minimum wage	Disadvantages of a legal minimum wage
+ It protects young and unskilled or semi-skilled workers from being paid very low wages by some employers.	− It increases business costs and reduces profits.
+ It can motivate workers to be more productive.	− Businesses may reduce their demand for labour.
+ It may encourage more people to seek employment.	− Higher-paid workers may want pay rises to maintain their pay relative to less-skilled workers.
	− Businesses may pass their increased costs on to consumers in higher prices for their products.

ACTIVITY 2.17

What types of legal protection do you think should apply in the following cases?

Turkey is well and truly stuffed

Carol Smith is not in a festive mood this Christmas. Bosses have told her and fellow workers there will be no bonus payments this year and have also deducted $30 from workers' wages to pay for the office party. "They never even asked our permission," said Carol. "So we want our money back and intend to party somewhere the bosses are not invited!"

Abusive child labour ring is exposed

China said on Wednesday that it had broken up a child labour ring that forced children from poor, inland areas to work in booming coastal cities. Officials took more than 100 children, many aged 13–15, who were forced to work in factories in the southern city of Dongguan, one of China's largest manufacturing centres for electronics and consumer goods sold globally.

Authorities in southern China's Guangdong Province said they had made several arrests.

Car firm guilty of "women only" bias

A firm that sacked its salesmen was found guilty of "blatant" discrimination. Swithland Motors denied discrimination, admitting that most of the sales staff at its 19 sites were women, but that they were selected purely on merit.

Muffling the sound of justice

A local government worker has won damages worth $100 000 for loss of hearing and stress caused by tinnitus. K. Misisck worked in road maintenance for five years, regularly using pneumatic drills and cutting equipment. He claimed the local authority had continually failed to provide adequate ear protection and information on the effects of exposure to high levels of noise. Local government officials claimed warning posters had been placed in all workplaces and workers only had to ask for ear defenders if they needed them.

Learning CHECKLIST

Before you continue make sure you are able to

Identify and explain **legal controls** over employment issues and their impact on employers and employees:

✓ legal controls over **employment contracts, unfair dismissal, discrimination, health and safety, legal minimum wage**.

Clues down

1 A set of formal rules and actions followed in an organization to reprimand or dismiss an employee who is in breach of his or her contract of employment (12, 9)

2 The unequal treatment of job applicants or employees because of differences in their race, religion, sex, disability, age or other characteristics. It is unfair and usually illegal (5, 14)

4 The process of filling job vacancies in an organization from its existing workforce (8, 11)

6 This type of employment normally requires the employee to work 35 hours or more per week and usually for a fixed number of hours between the same times each working day (4, 4)

8 A document used to prepare a job advert that describes the tasks and responsibilities of the position (3, 11)

11 This type of training teaches new employees about the objectives, structure and other important features of the organization they have just joined (9)

12 The process of determining the total number and type of employees a business will require in future to meet its needs and fulfil its objectives (9, 8)

13 This occurs when a job is cut and the worker is forced to leave employment in return for monetary compensation (10, 10)

15 This happens when the employment of a worker is terminated, for example due to poor performance or stealing (9)

Clues across

3 A document listing the skills, qualifications, experience and personal qualities an organization wants an employee to have in order to perform a specific job role (6, 13)

5 The process of choosing the job applicant to fill an advertised vacancy (9)

7 This type of employment normally requires the employee to work less than 35 hours each week. Many of these employees will work weekends or flexible hours at different times each working day or week (4, 4)

9 A formal written statement agreed between an employer and an employee detailing the duties, responsibilities and hours of work of that employee and the wage, annual leave and other benefits he or she will receive in return (10, 7)

10 This type of training requires an employee to stop his or her normal duties to attend in-house or external courses (8)

14 This type of training involves developing the skills and knowledge of employees while they continue to carry out their normal working duties (2, 3, 3)

16 Selecting the most promising candidates for an advertised job for interview from a set of job applications (12)

17 The process of attracting job applicants from outside an organization to fill job vacancies (8, 11)

18 The process of attracting people with the right skills and qualities to apply for job vacancies (11)

19 Cutting the number of employees in an organization, for example due to automation or a fall in demand for the products they make (10)

2.4.1 Why effective communication is important and the methods used to achieve it

2.4.2 Demonstrate an awareness of communication barriers

▸ Businesses need to communicate with their customers, other organizations and employees on a daily basis. A business that fails to communicate the right information at the right time to the right people or organizations will not be successful.

▸ Good internal communications are vital to ensure that everyone in an organization knows what their objectives and responsibilities are.

▸ Good external communications are needed, especially with customers to encourage them to continue buying the goods or services of the business and with suppliers to ensure that goods and services required by the business are delivered on time and are of the required quality.

▸ Information and messages can be spoken, written or visual and many can be transmitted electronically using information technology (IT).

- Verbal communications include meetings, telephone calls and conferences.
- Written communications include letters, memos, emails, notices and press releases.
- Visual communications include pictures, charts and diagrams.

▸ The cost, speed and size of the intended audience are important considerations in choosing methods of communication.

▸ Communication breakdowns occur when messages are misunderstood, wrongly targeted or just ineffective, for example when the people trying to communicate do not have the same language skills or because the message is too technical for the intended audience.

Internal communications – messages and information passed between people within an organization.

External communications – sending or receiving information and messages to or from individuals or organizations outside of a business.

Vertical communications – messages and information passed up and down a chain of command.

Horizontal communications – messages and information passed between different departments in an organization.

Two-way communications – these involve direct feedback from the receiver to the sender of a message or information.

Open communications – can be read or listened to by anyone.

Restricted communications – messages or information intended only to be received by an identified person or group of people.

Verbal communications – spoken messages.

Written communications – handwritten or electronically typed messages.

Communication barriers - obstacles and problems that prevent effective communication.

Communication breakdowns - a failure to communicate accurately and effectively.

Effective communication in business

What is effective communication and why is it important?

How do you communicate with your family and friends, your teachers or with assistants in shops and other people? Do you talk to them face-to-face or over the telephone, write them letters or emails or simply text them on your mobile phone? You probably use all these methods of communication at one time or another depending on who you want to communicate with and why.

Communication is part of everyday life but to be effective it must be clear and easy to understand. Imagine if you sent a message to your friends to meet them at a local park but forgot to tell them which park, which day and at what time. It would not be very effective.

Imagine now if a business did something similar when organizing deliveries of their products to other organizations. This could have very serious implications for the future success of that business.

ACTIVITY 2.18

The following situations occur every day in business. All of them involve communication.
Imagine you are a manager in the company in the situations below. In each case identify and write down:

▸ who the communication is with

▸ why you need to communicate with them

▸ what information you need to communicate

▸ what is the best way of communicating the information to them.

4
A customer has written a letter to you complaining about late delivery of goods she ordered from your company. How would you reply?

1
A customer has sent an email to your company asking for information about your range of products. How would you reply?

5
An employee is always late for work and has ignored your verbal warnings. How would you inform the employee that, if he does not start on time in future, he will be dismissed?

2
You take an important phone call for a work colleague who has gone out for lunch. You need to leave shortly for a meeting and it is unlikely your colleague will return before you go. How would you make sure your colleague gets the message?

6
Some new fire-fighting equipment has been installed in the company. How would you make sure other managers and employees know how to use it in case of an emergency?

3
The purchasing department has taken delivery of the office equipment you have ordered. How should the head of the department notify you?

7
You have to cancel a meeting at short notice with another organization. How would you communicate this information and be sure the organization had received it?

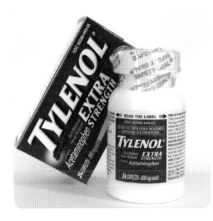

The importance of effective communications in business is clearly illustrated by the following incident.

Johnson & Johnson is a well-known US multinational producer of pharmaceuticals, medical devices and packaged consumer goods, with famous brands such as Band-Aid, Johnson's Baby Powder and the Neutrogena skin and beauty range.

It also makes and sells Tylenol, one of the most successful over-the-counter painkillers in the US. However, some years ago, before the internet was available, there was a major incident when seven people in Chicago died after taking the painkillers. For reasons unknown to this day, someone had tampered with packages of Tylenol on sale in pharmacies and food stores and replaced the painkillers with cyanide poison capsules.

As a result, suddenly and without warning the company faced a major outcry and had to try to explain to the world why its well-known product was killing people. Clear communication was vital, firstly to protect customers and secondly to save the product.

The company's first actions were to warn consumers using TV, radio and newspaper messages that someone had been tampering with the product in the Chicago area and that they should not buy or consume any more. The company also established a free telephone hotline that concerned consumers could ring for advice or to report a suspect packet.

It then communicated with its retail business customers and wholesalers in Chicago to withdraw all packets of Tylenol capsules from their shelves.

At the same time it also had to communicate internally with employees to investigate whether there had been any tampering with the product during the production and shipping process and, following the withdrawal of the product from retailers and wholesalers, to check through all the packages to find any that had been tampered with. Two more were found, so the company then ordered a national withdrawal of the product. Although this cost the company many millions of dollars it also demonstrated to consumers that the company was not willing to risk public safety.

Each day during the crisis the company would also update the news media with press releases and at press conferences.

Johnson & Johnson also communicated their new tamper-proof, triple-safety-sealed packaging for Tylenol capsules a few months later at a press conference at the manufacturer's headquarters. Widespread external communications including advertisements, new conferences and appearances of top executives on TV chat shows also helped reassure consumers and restore sales of Tylenol.

The handling of the incident by Johnson & Johnson clearly demonstrates the benefits of open and effective communications with consumers, employees and other business stakeholders. Had the communications instead been more limited and slow to inform concerned consumers and news organizations the result may have been more panic and an irreversible loss of confidence by consumers in the product and the company. Worse still, more people may have died.

External communications

Communication is the process by which a message or information is passed from one person or organization to another.

External communications involve sending or receiving information and messages to or from individuals or organizations outside a business, for example communications with its customers and suppliers.

Communicating with customers

Business organizations aim to sell goods and services to customers. A business that fails to communicate effectively with existing and potential customers is in danger of losing them to rival firms.

It is especially important for the first communication between a customer and a member of a business organization to make a good impression on the customer. First impressions last and the organization will hope that these customers will communicate their good experience to other potential customers.

Communications with customers can involve:

- advertising products and prices on posters, in magazines, on the radio or television

- providing product information in person or in brochures or catalogues

- taking orders and making sales over the counter, telephone or internet

- arranging a delivery date over the telephone or via email

- responding to customers' enquiries and complaints, face-to-face or in writing.

Just one chance to make a good impression

The retail business of a well-known US film and entertainment company provides guidelines to employees on acceptable greetings and goodbyes to use with customers. In addition, staff are encouraged to provide product information in their sales conversations, highlight in-store promotions and say something nice about their customers.

"Good morning and welcome"
"Hi, how are you?"
"Hello"
"Hi, is this your first visit to the store?"
"Have fun"
"Don't hesitate to ask if you need any help"
"Hello, how are you today?"

"Goodbye"
"Goodbye, please call again"
"Goodbye, have a great day"
"Bye, safe journey"
"Goodbye, hope to see you soon"
"Goodbye and take care"

> ## Communicating with other organizations

To be successful a business needs to communicate effectively with many other organizations. These include business customers, suppliers including electricity and telephone companies, providers of finance and insurance, advertising and recruitment agencies, and government tax, customs, employment and other authorities.

Imagine if a business was unable to communicate accurately how it has complied with the payment of taxes or laws on employment and health and safety. This may result in the business being fined or, worse still, forced to close by government authorities due to inaccurate or unconvincing communications. ➤ **2.3.4**

Similarly, ineffective communications with suppliers could result in a business being sent the wrong materials, perhaps even to the wrong location. This will hold up production, increase business costs and lose the business revenue.

Internal communications

> ## Communicating with employees

Information and messages passed between people who own or work in the same organization involve internal communications.

These can include vertical communications up and down an organizational hierarchy, between different layers of managers and their staff, or horizontal communications between managers and employees at the same level but in different departments.

For example, senior managers will communicate business strategy and objectives down their organization hierarchy. Employees and middle managers may communicate sales figures, production levels and financial performance up the organization to senior managers. In contrast, meetings and other communications between managers in the production, finance and marketing departments in an organization may take place to discuss developing and promoting a new product.

IMPORTANT NOTICE

RECYCLING BINS FOR ALL CANS AND TINS

All staff please use the recycling bins provided for the disposal of cans and tins only.
The bins should not be used for general waste.

Should you have any queries on this or any other energy or environmental issues, please contact Jatan Singh (Extension 4337)

Facilities Management Team

MEMO

To: All senior managers

From: A Torres CEO

Meeting on 28 April

Meeting has been cancelled and rescheduled to 14 May. Venue and time are unchanged.

Please phone my secretary Maria Pérez (x6744) to confirm attendance.

With apologies.

AT

▲ Business meetings, memos and notices are good ways to communicate internally

Everyone in an organization must work together as a team. Good **internal communications** between people in an organization are therefore vital to ensure that everyone knows what their objectives and responsibilities are and how their work contributes to the work of others.

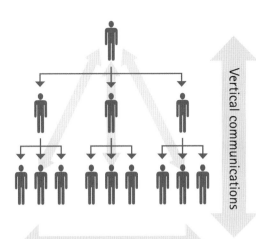

Communications within a business can take many forms. Just a few examples are:

- senior management meetings to discuss business strategy
- a manager providing feedback on an employee's performance
- negotiations with trade union representatives about wages
- internal job advertisements and notifications
- notices about health and safety in the workplace
- written warnings about an employee's workplace behaviour
- emailed memos (memorandums) about pay awards and bonuses
- telephone calls to major business customers and suppliers.

Communications can be one-way or two-way

To be effective, communications require:

a transmitter	the person who wants to send a message or information
a transmission	the message or information to be sent
a medium	the method used to communicate, for example a business letter
a receiver	the person to whom the message or information is to be sent
feedback	indication from the receiver to the transmitter that the message or information has reached the right person and has been understood.

Two-way communications involve direct feedback from the receiver of some information or a message. They are a useful way of checking whether others have understood the information or message received. For example, customer surveys, telephone conversations and business meetings all involve two-way communications.

Two-way communications are especially important within an organization so that employees feel included in discussions and feel able to contribute ideas. This can help motivate employees and increase their productivity.

Similarly, two-way communications between a company and its shareholders at AGMs are also important to discuss and agree the company's policy and its financial accounts. Directors can inform shareholders about the company's performance and the AGM gives the opportunity for the directors to be answerable for their actions. ➤ 12.1.2

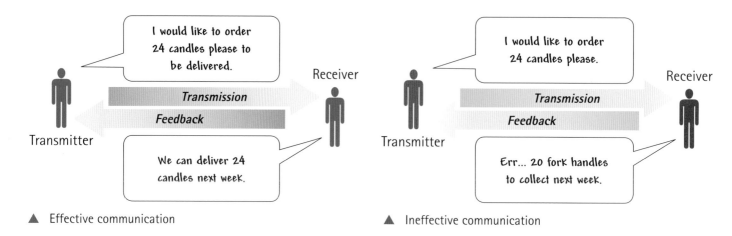

▲ Effective communication   ▲ Ineffective communication

However, not all good communications require feedback. **One-way communications** send people and organizations information or messages that require no direct feedback from their receivers.

For example, one-way communications include bus timetables, news announcements, advertisements or simple instructions passed vertically down an organizational hierarchy from managers to their staff. However, to be effective they must still be clear and easy to understand.

Official or **formal communications** involve structured messages and information necessary to ensure that a business operates effectively. For example, notices about health and safety in the workplace, letters to customers dealing with their complaints and a written record of actions agreed at a business meeting all involve formal communications.

However, many communications are informal. For example, **informal communications** involve conversations between work colleagues over lunch or sending each other text messages. They can involve communications about business issues as well as covering many other topics.

Informal communications can sometimes spread gossip and rumour which may be unhelpful in a business.

Communications can be open or restricted

Open communications can be read or listened to by anyone. Public notices, television advertisements, restaurant menus and bus timetables are all examples of open communications.

However, many communications in business need to be **restricted**. This means a sender only intends his or her message or information to be received by a limited number of people or organizations. This is because the communication may be personal, for example between a doctor and a patient, or commercially confidential such as information internal to a business on its development of new products, its pricing strategies or financial performance. It will be important to restrict this information from competing business organizations.

Methods of communication

Information and messages can be spoken, written or visual, and many can be transmitted electronically

There are many different ways of sending or transmitting communications.

- **Verbal communications** involve the sender speaking direct to a receiver.
- **Written communications** involve the sender writing to a receiver.
- **Visual communications** include sending pictures, charts and diagrams.

All three methods may be combined in some situations and in modern businesses many now involve **electronic communications** using IT. For example, live video conversations and videoconferences are now possible using mobile phone apps or programs such as Skype.

Verbal communications involve meetings and telephone conversations

One-to-one meetings	These are direct, usually two-way, verbal communications between a sender and a receiver. For example, they may be between a manager and an employee to discuss the person's performance, a sales assistant and a customer in a shop or between two work colleagues.
Business meetings	Formal meetings are a common means of discussing ideas or resolving problems in a business. A well-run meeting will involve the right people, a good chairperson, an agenda issued in advance setting out what the meeting will cover and a written record of key points and actions produced after the meeting has ended. This record is called the "minutes".
	Meetings can involve a few or many people. Meetings can also be external, for example meetings to discuss contracts with suppliers or finance with a bank. Meetings can also be informal, between work colleagues during a lunch break or after work.
Telephone conversations	The fixed telephone, mobile telephone and also tablets and computers are vital pieces of equipment in a modern business. They allow managers and employees within an organization to talk to each other, their customers, suppliers and other organizations, almost anywhere in the world at any time of the day. The cost of equipment and calls can be expensive but they save time and money on other forms of communication.
Video-conferencing	The internet and modern telephone systems can be used to send live video pictures as well as sound over very long distances. This means business meetings can be held between people located in different places in the world without the need to travel to meet face-to-face.

Advantages of verbal communications	Disadvantages of verbal communications
✛ Information and messages can be communicated instantly and to many people at the same time if business meetings are used. ✛ Messages in face-to-face meetings can be reinforced using facial expressions and body language. ✛ Written and visual materials can also be used to reinforce spoken messages. ✛ Feedback from the receiver or receivers can be immediate.	‒ It can be difficult to determine whether receivers are listening and understanding messages or information transmitted, especially on a telephone or in a big business meeting. ‒ Internet speeds and telephone line quality can vary. This can make telephone calls and videoconferencing difficult. ‒ Verbal communications rely on the sender and receiver being able to speak the same language well enough to understand each other. ‒ Verbal communications do not provide a record of discussions for later reference.

Written communications include letters, reports, memos and notices

Business letters	This is by far the most used and important method of sending restricted information or messages to customers and other business organizations. Business letters are used for a great many purposes, including: • arranging and confirming meetings • making complaints to suppliers about poor service • writing to government officials on matters of concern • notifying employees they are no longer required • responding to customers' complaints • awarding contracts of work to suppliers • providing terms and conditions of employment to a new employee.
Reports	A report is a detailed document, usually produced by experts, on a specific business issue, for example financial performance and forecasts, business strategy, organizational restructuring, the effectiveness of a recent promotional campaign or trading conditions in global markets. The main findings and recommendations of a report are often discussed by managers at a business meeting. Limited companies are required by law in many countries to publish their final accounts. ➤ 1.4.1
Memos	A memo is used to record and transmit short but important messages within an organization, for example dates and times of meetings, to make a special request or to notify staff of holiday arrangements and cover.
Minutes	Minutes form a record of key points and actions agreed at business meetings.
Notices	A notice is normally used to display factual information which is open to anyone to read, such as health and safety regulations or notices in public bathrooms about hygiene and not wasting water. Notices are normally displayed in prominent places.
Faxes	A fax or facsimile is a reproduction of a written communication transmitted from one fax machine to another connected via the telephone network. The fax machine receiving the fax reproduces a copy of the original document. Reproduction quality can sometimes be poor so sending information by fax is best suited for short messages and letters.
Press releases	A business uses a press release to make a written public announcement or statement that is newsworthy, for example about its profitability or expansion plans, or in reaction to public and media criticism, for example about its environmental record or treatment of employees. Press releases are targeted at newspapers, magazines and television and radio broadcasters. ➤ 3.3.4
Emails and text messages	Emails are a fast and cost-effective method of sending messages and information to one or many receivers at the same time using the internet. Copies can then be printed on paper if required. Many memos, minutes, faxes and press releases are now written and sent as emails. All the above written communications can also be attached and sent as electronic documents in emails. Mobile phones can also be used to send short text messages and memos.

Which methods would you use to communicate the following messages and why?

▸ The customer services department responds to a letter of complaint from a customer.

▸ The head of the human resources department wants to invite a job applicant to an interview.

▸ Employees need to be told that safety goggles must be worn at all times in the paint-spraying area.

▸ The chief executive officer wishes to announce her retirement to all employees.

▸ The marketing department wants to inform the board of directors of the results of a recent survey of customers.

▸ The finance director is to inform shareholders of the financial performance of the company over the last year.

▸ The director of purchasing personally wishes to apologize to a major supplier for late payment.

▸ A supervisor must warn an employee about the person's poor time-keeping for the first time.

▸ The managing director who is currently away overseas on business wants to see the latest sales projections.

▸ A manager wants to tell his colleague he will be ten minutes late meeting him for lunch.

▸ Senior managers want to discuss expanding business operations into new markets.

Identify, note and/or ask permission to collect examples of different written and visual communications used in your school or college. For example, these may include notices, posters, letters, charts and reports. For each one, identify what it is communicating and why you think the method used was chosen.

Communication barriers

What causes communication barriers and breakdowns?

Communication barriers occur when messages are misunderstood, wrongly targeted or just ineffective.

For example, Professional Business Communications is a company that helps other businesses and their employees improve their communications. A French company executive approached them for help because he was having problems making presentations to the company board. They would often fail to listen, would interrupt to ask many questions and usually failed to support his recommendations.

His English was excellent, but because he spoke quickly and with a heavy French accent, board members often misunderstood what he was saying. He also used a lot of hand and arm gestures which distracted his audience. The board would also spend too much time trying to read the slides he had prepared for his presentations rather than listening to what he was saying because his slides contained too many tables and lists of bullet points.

When Professional Business Communications filmed and played back one of his presentations, the company executive immediately knew he had to slow down his speech, move around much less and prepare fewer slides which contained only his key points. At his next presentation to the company board the directors were much more attentive and agreed his recommendations for cost-cutting measures.

Blah blah blah blah blah blah blah blah blah blah blah blah blah blah blah blah...

For years, the Parker Pen Company has advertised reliable fountain pens that will not leak in your pocket and cause embarrassment.

The slogan was "Avoid embarrassment – use Parker Pens". Unfortunately, when the company entered the Mexican market it translated the slogan into Spanish as "Avoid pregnancy" apparently using the verb "embarazar" by mistake!

This example highlights some of the many **barriers** to effective communications that can lead to communication breakdowns in business.

- The people sending and receiving a message may not speak the same language or have the same understanding.

- Confusion can be caused by the use of technical terms.

- Some communications may be too long so people fail to listen to them or read to the end of a message.

- Messages get lost, for example, a letter may not arrive in the post or an email may be blocked.

- Accessibility to the message can be difficult for different audiences or receivers with special needs, for example, for deaf, blind or visually impaired people.

- Electronic communications may stop working due to power loss, hackers or breakdowns.

- Wrong perceptions happen when the people trying to communicate with each other may not like each other or will only hear what they want to hear because of their own prejudices.

- Rumour, gossip and fake news can distort communications.

How communication barriers can be reduced or removed

In the example above, Professional Business Communications was able to demonstrate how many of communication barriers can be relatively easy to overcome.

- Employees should receive training in effective communications.

- Communications should be short, to the point and jargon-free.

- Understand your target audience, their language skills and any hearing or visual impairments.

- Choose the right method based on your target audience and urgency of the message. For example, do not send letters if the communication is urgent and needs to be received by many people at the same time.

- Ask receivers for feedback to check whether communications have been understood.

- Keep records so messages can be re-sent if necessary if they have been lost or if communication equipment has failed.

- Use an alternative if one commuciation method fails; for example, use a mobile telephone to send a text if electronic communications have failed.

The managers of Tech-Med Pharmaceuticals know that good internal communications within a business are important. They also know that sometimes communications break down.

The company currently has factories in six different countries and the managers are thinking of expanding into another. Two alternative methods are being considered, namely to set up a franchise or to operate a joint venture.

a   What is meant by a "franchise"?   [2]

b   Identify **two** reasons why good internal communications are important
    to a business.   [2]

c   Identify and explain **two** reasons why internal communications at
    Tech-Med Pharmaceuticals might break down.   [4]

d   Identify and explain **three** advantages that a joint venture might
    offer Tech-Med Pharmaceuticals.   [6]

e   Identify **two** stakeholders who may be interested in the expansion plans
    of Tech-Med Pharmaceuticals. Do you think that these two stakeholder
    groups would benefit from the company's expansion? Justify your answer. [6]

Before you continue make sure you are able to

Understand why **effective communication** is important in business and the methods used to achieve it:

✓   effective communication and its importance to business

✓   the benefits and limitations of different **communication methods** including those based on **IT**

✓   recommend and justify which communication method to use in given circumstances.

Demonstrate an awareness of **communication barriers**:

✓   how communication barriers arise and the **problems of ineffective communication**

✓   how communication barriers can be reduced or removed.

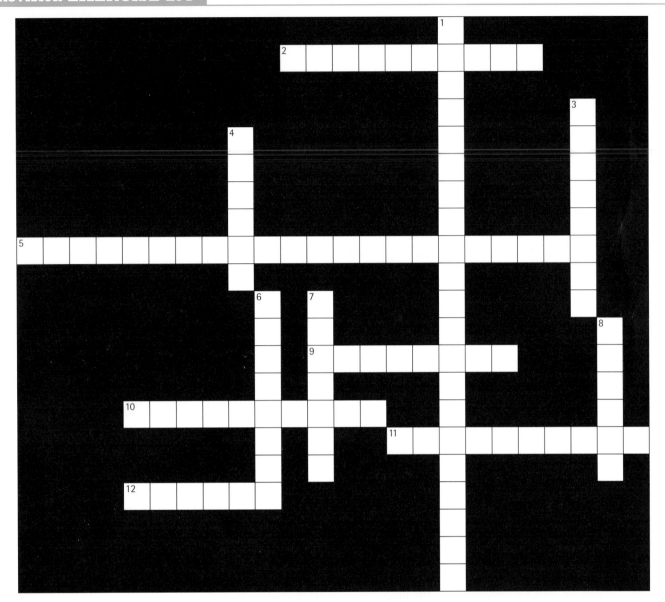

Clues down

1 These will stop transmitted messages or information from achieving their objective and being effective (13, 8)

3 The type of communications that take place between a business and its consumers, suppliers and other organizations (8)

4 These communications involve feedback from the receiver of a message to its sender (3, 3)

6 Communications up and down the chain of command in a organization are described as this (8)

7 Business letters, memos and emails are examples of this type of communication (7)

8 These communications include notices and other important official messages transmitted to people within an organization to ensure that it operates effectively (6)

Clues across

2 Communications produced, sent or received using computers, mobile phones or other information technologies (10)

5 This will occur when an important message or information is not sent or not received, or is received but by the wrong person or organization, or is received as intended but not understood, or is received too late to be effective (13, 9)

9 The type of communications that take place between different people and departments within the same organization (8)

10 Communications containing sensitive information that are intended for a named receiver should be classified as this (10)

11 Communications across an organization between managers or employees at the same level but in different departments are of this type (10)

12 Telephone conversations, videoconferences and face-to-face meetings are examples of this type of communication (6)

3 Marketing

3.1	Marketing, competition and the customer	3.1.1	The role of marketing
		3.1.2	Market changes
		3.1.3	Concepts of niche marketing and mass marketing
		3.1.4	How and why market segmentation is undertaken
3.2	Market research	3.2.1	The role of market research and methods used
		3.2.2	Presentation and use of market research results
3.3	Marketing mix	3.3.1	Product
		3.3.2	Price
		3.3.3	Place – distribution channels
		3.3.4	Promotion
		3.3.5	Technology and the marketing mix
3.4	Marketing strategy	3.4.1	Justify marketing strategies appropriate to a given situation
		3.4.2	The nature and impact of legal controls related to marketing
		3.4.3	The opportunities and problems of entering new foreign markets

3.1.1 The role of marketing

▶ **Marketing** involves anticipating, identifying and satisfying consumer needs and wants.

▶ Most businesses, unless they are small, have a marketing department responsible for marketing activities including the research and development of new products and the sale, promotion and distribution of products.

▶ **Marketing objectives** include raising consumer awareness and improving the image of a product or organization, developing new or improved products, increasing or maintaining market share, creating and maintaining **customer loyalty** and, ultimately, increasing and sustaining sales and profits.

▶ The **marketing mix** combines strategies concerning **product** design, **price**, **place** of sale and **promotions**. Each part of the mix must be effective and complement the others.

Market – all the producers and consumers of a given product.

Marketing – the anticipation, identification, creation and satisfaction of consumer needs and wants.

Product-oriented firm – a business that focuses on production processes and products.

Market-oriented firm – a business that focuses on identifying consumer needs and wants using market research.

Marketing mix – the combined elements of a marketing strategy focused on the design, price, promotion and place of sale of a product.

The role of marketing

The market for a particular good or service consists of all the consumers and producers of that product

In business, a market is not a physical place where goods and services are sold. The **market** for any given product, whether a good or a service, consists of all those consumers willing and able to buy the product and all those producers willing and able to supply it, wherever they are located. So, for example, the market for computers consists of all those people and firms worldwide who want to buy, make or sell computers. Similarly, there is a market for every type of food, clothing, television, car, holiday, insurance and every other good or service. Some markets may be small and local while others are worth many billions of dollars each year and involve sales all over the world.

▼ Markets can be local, national or international

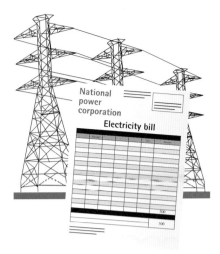

For any market to work, buyers and sellers simply need a way to exchange products for money. This can be in a shop or other retail outlet, ordering a product from a catalogue or over the internet using e-commerce. ➤ 3.3.5

The market size for a product is therefore measured by the total amount spent by consumers on the product per week, month or year. ➤ 1.3.2

Changes in consumer demand over time and the amount of competition between producers can affect the volume and value of different goods and services sold. As a result, market prices and the profits firms can make from their products can also change over time. Changes in technology and government policy can also affect markets. Businesses need to be aware of how these changes can affect them and how to adapt their products, prices and promotional strategies in order to stay successful. This is the objective of marketing.

Marketing involves anticipating, identifying and satisfying consumer needs and wants

Marketing is not just about advertising and selling products. To be successful it must include the following.

Identifying consumer needs and wants

Identifying consumer needs and wants means finding out what kind of products different groups of consumers need and want, the quality they want and the prices they are willing to pay, where and how they want to buy these products, how their needs are influenced by different promotions and the after-sales services they require. Businesses also need to identify any gaps in the market and any changes in consumer demand so they can provide the wanted product or adapt their existing products to consumer needs. This means that high-quality market research is essential.

Satisfying consumer needs and wants

Consumers expect the right product to be available in the right place at the right time and at the right price. Businesses compete with each other to satisfy their requirements. A business that prices its products above what consumers are willing to pay, or fails to make its products available to buy online, will not satisfy consumers who have these wants. As a result, the business will be unable to sell its products. Part of satisfying customer needs and wants is to make sure that consumers know the product is available and that it is convenient for consumers to purchase. Consumers want high-quality and reliable products so quality assurance is part of satisfying consumer needs and wants.

Maintaining customer loyalty

Many businesses rely on repeat sales to existing customers. To encourage repeat sales, they may offer these customers more generous price discounts, loyalty bonuses or other exclusive offers. Regular communication with existing customers is important in maintaining customer loyalty. Building and maintaining a good relationship with customers is usually cheaper than attracting new ones away from rival businesses. Great customer service will result in customers returning. An important part of achieving all this is making sure all employees are trained in customer care.

Building customer relationships

Building customer relationships requires that the business ensures that the customer has a great experience when they buy a product and also afterwards if they need to return it or have it repaired. There should be sufficient well-trained employees able to communicate effectively with customers and find out what they want. Businesses should ask for customer feedback so that they can continue to improve customer service. Complaints should be dealt with promptly and offer to make things right.

Marketing therefore affects every activity carried out by an organization and the success of that organization depends on how good its marketing is.

Most businesses, unless they are small, have a marketing department responsible for marketing activities including the research and development of new products and the sale, promotion and distribution of products.

Product-oriented firms	Market-oriented firms
This type of firm focuses on product development and production processes. These firms develop products and then try to find or create a market for them.	A **market-oriented firm** first investigates whether or not there will be enough consumer demand for its products.
This can be a risky strategy if ultimately consumers do not want their products. As such, few firms today are so product-oriented in their approach to marketing.	Businesses that spend millions on developing products and mass produce for national and global markets cannot afford to risk producing a good or service in the hope it will sell. They need enough confidence in the future market for their product to invest in its development and production.
Product-oriented firms tend to produce basic items including foodstuffs and materials, such as corn, cotton and steel. These products do not require fancy packaging and differ very little regardless of which business has produced them. As such, advertising and other promotions are unlikely to be very cost-effective. The producer, retailer and consumer are likely to be more concerned about the products' price, quality and availability.	Market-oriented firms continually review and analyse market trends and modify their product design, pricing strategies and other marketing activities to ensure that they continue to satisfy consumer wants. In doing so, they are also able to identify when new market opportunities arise and be the first to take advantage of them.
Businesses introducing advanced technologies for the first time may also be product-oriented. This is because until the technology has been tried and tested there will be no market for it.	These firms are likely to have a well-resourced marketing department and marketing budget to spend on market research and other marketing activities.

The objectives of marketing include growth, increasing or maintaining market share and making a profit

The goals of marketing reflect the objectives of the organization. For example, a private sector business will aim to make a profit. A charity will aim to generate enough donations and other income to fund its services to people or animals in need.

Good marketing increases the value added to resources used in the production of goods and services. ➤ **1.1.1**

Look at the newspaper articles below. What do you think is the main marketing objective of the organization in each one?

NLTB works to improve public image

Board management say they are determined to change the National Land Trust Board's image with its customers to that of an efficient, effective and modern organization.

General Manager Operations Solomon Nata said NLTB management will be holding workshops with staff to discuss ways they can improve their service.

Nata said they are asking staff to be honest and diligent, and adhere to basic employment policies such as coming to work on time.

PepsiCo. to invest in healthier products

PepsiCo. has announced that it is to capitalize on the expanding health food and drinks market with the launch of several new products. The company plans to treble revenues from its healthier ranges.

Dutch brewer Heineken is seeking to increase its market share in the growing Chinese market through premium brands and aggresssive marketing after taking a 40% stake in CRH Beer, China's largest brewing company.

Eurostar introduces on-board magazine to boost customer loyalty

The new magazine is part of the European train service operator's strategy to repair its broken reputation after a series of major breakdowns in services. It will be used to publicize its green credentials and build customer loyalty. This will be especially important as it faces possible competition in the cross-Channel rail market.

Eurostar hopes the magazine will refocus customer attention to its environmental credentials, including a commitment by the company to reduce CO_2 emissions by 35% per passenger this year.

Jamaica International Insurance Company (JIIC) looks outside of Jamaica to grow its business

"Growth is very important for us. Over the last couple of years we have started growing outside of Jamaica. We have gone to the Turks and Caicos Islands, we have gone to Dominica and we would like to continue that expansion," said managing director, Andrew Levy.

But the company, which lays claim to 17.2% of the local general insurance market, is also seeking growth through new products.

JIIC has joined the ranks of insurance companies offering products exclusively to women with the launch last week of "Premier Lady", comprehensive motor insurance cover designed to recognize good driving habits of females.

Marketing objectives therefore vary but are likely to include some or all of these aims to:

- raise consumer awareness of a product of the organization
- improve the image of a product or the organization
- improve the design and quality of existing products
- develop and introduce new products
- maintain or increase market share
- enter new markets at home or overseas
- encourage repeat purchases and maintain customer loyalty
- increase and sustain higher levels of sales and profits.

The marketing mix

Product, price, place of sale and promotion

The marketing mix refers to the combination of all the activities involved in an organization's marketing strategy for a product.

To demonstrate, consider the example of Zara, one of the world's leading fashion retail chains. It was formed in 1975 as part of the Spanish company Inditex, which is now the biggest fashion group in the world, with brands including Massimo Dutti, Bershka, Oysho, Pull and Bear and Stradivarius, among others.

Zara has changed the way the clothing industry works where design, production and delivery to retailers often takes up to six months. Zara's unique sales strategy is to create or imitate the latest trends within a two-week period. The new styles are available on sales floors for no longer than four weeks. This encourages consumers to visit their stores more regularly than other high street stores to pick up the latest designs. If a product does not sell, it is withdrawn immediately and discontinued after one week. This approach is central to the marketing mix of the company.

Product: The company has its own team of designers who design clothes based on emerging trends in fashion shows, trade shows and from observing people in nightclubs. Store assistants also talk to their customers and pass on their ideas and desires to headquarters.

Price: Zara's marketing is effective because of its high-quality clothes at affordable prices and unique response to market demands. As items move so quickly through Zara stores, customers feel the pressure to buy an item in fear that it may no longer be available the next time they visit. Also because of the rapid turnover of clothes in stores, customers tend to visit Zara stores up to six times more on average than they do other retail outlets.

Place of sale: Zara has over 1700 retail outlets across the globe but since most of the production still takes place in Spain and some other European countries, the company maintains its own efficient supply chain and distribution system. A fleet of 40 trucks distributes clothes to stores twice a week, sometimes up to three times, from Zara's main manufacturing plant in La Coruña in Spain, to each place or point of sale.

> The showcase is the best marketing strategy for Zara: the store location and price are their weapons. Word of mouth does the rest.

Promotion: The company has an aggressive growth objective but from the outset has funded this mostly from its revenues rather than from borrowing money from banks. It does not carry out publicity campaigns, which is an unusual marketing strategy in a fashion industry that often advertises widely on television and in fashion magazines. It prefers instead to invest revenues in opening new stores in the busiest commercial areas in each city. The locations, design and image of their stores are therefore key to the promotion of the Zara brand.

Zara demonstrates how the marketing mix of any business is made up of four main elements.

Product	Price	Place	Promotion
The design and quality of the product and its packaging, and how it compares to rival products. ➤ **3.3.1**	The price at which the product is sold. What competitive and other pricing strategies are used? ➤ **3.3.2**	The channels of distribution to final consumers; where and how the product is sold. ➤ **3.3.3**	Brand name and product image; advertising and other promotions to raise consumer awareness. ➤ **3.3.4**

▲ The marketing mix

▲ Product design, price, place of sale and promotions are all important aspects of marketing

Product, price, place and promotion form the "four Ps" of the marketing mix. It is the role of the marketing department to co-ordinate the planning, organization and implementation of the marketing mix across the entire company.

It is vital that each part of the marketing mix in the marketing strategy for a product is effective and complements the others. For example, there would be no point selling expensive, handmade jewellery in cheap-looking packaging for display and sale in supermarkets.

Learning CHECKLIST

Before you continue make sure you are able to

Describe the role of **marketing**:

✓ identifying **customer needs**

✓ satisfying **customer needs**

✓ maintaining **customer loyalty**

✓ building **customer relationships**.

3.1.2 Market changes

- Every market has two sides: a demand side, affected by changes in consumer spending habits and preferences, and a supply side, affected by changes in the number, price and quality of rival products and producers. It is important for businesses to monitor and respond to changes in these market conditions.

- Consumer spending patterns are always changing. A good business will try to predict the products and product features consumers will want in the future and supply them before rival firms do.

- To analyse market trends it is important to know what is causing them and what factors may cause them to change in the future.

- Changes in income, populations, technologies, social and cultural factors, tastes and fashions, seasonal factors and laws can all affect consumer demand and spending patterns.

- Competition to supply the markets for many goods and services is growing. Business growth in newly industrialized economies, such as China and India, and technological change are driving this trend.

- Increasing price competition and non-price competition can lower prices and improve the quality of products and choice for consumers.

- Competition forces businesses to innovate, increase their productivity and reduce their costs, but not all businesses may survive.

Business BUZZWORDS

Market conditions – features or characteristics of a given market, including the degree of competition between producers and the numbers, types and spending levels of different groups of consumers.

Expanding market – a market in which consumer demand and sales revenues are rising over time; there is an upward trend in sales.

Contracting market – a market in which consumer demand and sales revenues are falling over time; there is a downward trend in sales.

Disposable income – personal income that is available to spend or save after the deduction of personal income or payroll taxes.

Competition – rivalry between businesses trying to win consumers' acceptance, sales and loyalty.

Price competition – rivalry between similar businesses over the selling prices of their products.

Non-price competition – rivalry between businesses over different features of their products, such as quality, image, and packaging, and their customer services, after-sales care and advertisements.

Analysing market trends

Market conditions are continually changing

Sales of different products by different businesses can change from day to day and more significantly from year to year. Similarly, product designs, prices and promotions can also change over time. New firms can enter a market and increase the degree of competition between rival producers for sales. As a result, some firms may fail and exit the market. These and other market characteristics or **market conditions** are continually changing.

Some markets change rapidly, for example markets for modern consumer technologies including tablet computers and mobile phones. Other markets change less rapidly, such as markets for basic foods like bread and vegetables. Nevertheless, it is important for all businesses in every market to be aware of how their market conditions are changing over time so they can determine how to respond in order to remain competitive and be able to satisfy customer needs and wants.

Businesses can monitor changes in market conditions according to whether they are the result of:

- demand side factors – changes in consumer preferences and spending
- supply side factors – changes in the number, prices and quality of rival products and the type and amount of competition between rival producers.

A business that fails to monitor and respond to changes in consumer demand is a business at risk of failing

Consumer demand in Europe for healthier foods is likely to grow steadily over the next few years as the population continues to grow heavier and more out of shape, according to a new report.

African Farmers Growing Organic Foods for European Markets

African farmers are making more money producing organically grown crops for European markets, where demand for healthier food is growing.

Nearly 5000 farmers in Burkina Faso, Cameroon, Ghana, Senegal and Sierra Leone are now exporting organically grown produce to Europe.

Global sales of compact discs continue to decline. Physical sales of music such as CDs fell by 12.7% globally last year, while sales of online music downloads rose by over 9%.

CD player production ends at Linn

Some are saying this is the beginning of the end for the compact disc player.

Linn Products has become the first manufacturer to announce it will give up on CDs from the start of next year. The company will instead focus on producing digital streaming equipment.

The news articles on the previous page show how changes in consumer demand influence business decisions. Farms in Africa have responded to increasing consumer demand for healthier foods in Europe by increasing their production and exports.

In contrast, declining sales of compact discs are causing many manufacturers to cease production of compact disc players and focus their resources instead on the production of personal music players capable of downloading music from the Internet.

Consumer demand, spending patterns and how people shop are always changing. Today's consumers may no longer want products that were popular five or ten years ago. A good business will try to predict the products and product features consumers will want in the future and supply them before rival business organizations do. A firm that fails to produce what consumers want, or produces it too late, will not be successful.

A **market trend** in consumer demand or spending refers to the general direction of change or growth in sales over time. For example, sales of sun protection lotions may go up every summer and down every winter but if year after year summer and winter sales are higher than in previous years, the long-term trend in sales is clearly upwards.

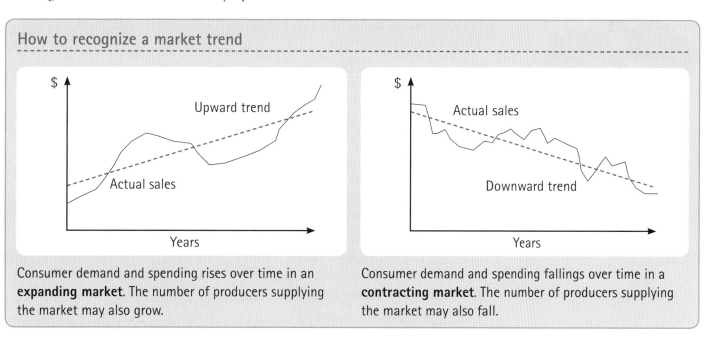

How to recognize a market trend

Consumer demand and spending rises over time in an **expanding market**. The number of producers supplying the market may also grow.

Consumer demand and spending fallings over time in a **contracting market**. The number of producers supplying the market may also fall.

Businesses examine short-term and long-term trends in consumer spending

Some trends in consumer demand can be short-lived, perhaps lasting only a few days or even hours. For example, tickets for concerts by major music groups or for big sporting events can sell out in a matter of hours or days. Other upward trends in consumer demand may last a year or two but then fall away as fashions, tastes or technologies change. Short-term trends are often due to fads or crazes.

In contrast, some trends in consumer demand and spending have been observed over many years. For example, global car ownership has been rising

▼ Global sales of the Rubik's Cube puzzle soared briefly in the 1980s

steadily since cars were first mass-produced in the 1920s. In 2002 there were around 600 million cars in the world. There are now more than 800 million cars in the world and demand continues to grow, especially in expanding markets in Asia, the Middle East and Latin America.

A downward trend in demand and sales of a product, whether short-lived or long-term, can spell trouble for the firms producing it. They may eventually be forced to close down unless they switch to the production of goods and services for which demand is rising over time.

Changes in prices, income, tastes, social attitudes, population, advertising and the availability of different products can affect consumer spending patterns

It is important to identify and understand the causes of change in consumer spending patterns. We can group causes according to whether they are **price factors** or **non-price factors**.

Price factors

When Sony cut the price of its Play Station 3 computer games console by $100 weekly sales rose by 30%. In contrast, when US company Apple increased the price of popular music downloads from its iTunes online store from $0.99 to $1.29 sales fell sharply.

Most consumers buy fewer goods and services, or buy them less often, as their prices rise. Unless their incomes rise as well, consumers will simply not be able to afford to buy as many goods or services if prices are higher than before. Many consumers may also switch their spending towards cheaper alternatives.

It follows that as the price of a good or service falls, consumer demand for it tends to rise. Increased competition between business organizations to supply a good or service often force prices down as each business tries to attract customers away from rival suppliers.

Technological advances can also reduce the prices of modern products over time. For example, modern technology has reduced the cost of producing many electronic goods such as large flat-screen televisions, computers, mobile phones and microwave ovens.

Falling production costs have allowed manufacturers to lower their prices over time without reducing their profits. As prices have fallen, consumer demand for these items has expanded.

Non-price factors

Many of the reasons why consumer demand for different goods and services changes over time are unrelated to changes in their prices.

- **Changes in incomes**

   The more **disposable income** consumers have, the more they can afford to spend on different goods and services. Disposable income is the amount of income individuals have available to spend or save after any personal income or payroll taxes have been deducted from their wages or salaries. ➤ **2.1.2**

Rising disposable incomes in many developed and developing economies have greatly increased opportunities for existing and new businesses to expand their sales and outputs and to develop and market entirely new products to satisfy growing customer needs and wants.

- **Changes in the population**

Global population growth has increased the demand for many goods and services and has expanded business opportunities. The global population is expected to expand by another two billion people between now and 2050, but the population of some countries is growing rapidly while for others it is declining. This means markets for some goods and services are expanding in particular countries and shrinking in others. Some businesses may respond to these trends by moving their operations to different countries overseas. ➤ **3.4.3**

For example, the population of India has risen rapidly over time and is forecast to grow to around 1.7 billion people by 2050. In contrast, there is very little or no population growth in many European and other Western countries. Birth and death rates are low and the average age of these countries' populations is therefore rising. Indeed, it is estimated that 22% of the world's population will be over 60 years of age by 2050.

"Ageing" populations are affecting consumer spending patterns in many countries. Older people tend to spend more on health care, home furnishings, pets, holidays and leisure activities. This is creating new opportunities for businesses targeting older consumers in these markets.

- **Changes in tastes, habits and fashions**

Spending patterns reflect people's tastes, habits and fashions. As these change, so does the pattern of consumer spending in an economy. This creates opportunities for new businesses and products. In contrast, some existing businesses may need to adapt their products and reduce their prices if they are to survive.

For example, a growing number of people are concerned about the impact of their diets on their health and are now spending more on healthy foods, such as rice, fruits and vegetables, while spending on fatty foods and meat products is falling.

Growing concern for the natural environment is also causing a shift in spending towards products that cause less damage to plant, marine and animal life. Opportunities for more environmentally friendly products have expanded rapidly around the world. For example, global demand for low-energy light bulbs is growing at the expense of standard light bulbs which burn up to 80% more electricity. Many governments have also passed laws requiring producers and consumers to phase out the production and use of traditional light bulbs over the next few years.

▲ Contracting

▲ Expanding

▼ Markets for Islamic finance, Islamic fashions and Halal foods are growing

- **Social and cultural factors**

  Spending patterns can differ greatly between different regions and countries. This is due to different social, cultural and religious factors in different areas. For example, consumers in Greece eat more cheese on average than consumers anywhere else in the world, while more rice is consumed per person each year in Burma than in any other country.

- **Seasonal and other factors**

  A great many other factors can affect consumer demand and spending patterns. The weather is one example. Spending on sun lotions, cold drinks and ices tends to rise during the summer. A cold winter increases spending on fuel and warm clothing.

  Changes in laws can also affect the demand for some products. For example, it is illegal in many countries to ride a motorbike without a crash helmet, and an increasing number of countries are outlawing smoking in public places. Laws and regulations can therefore expand some business opportunities and restrict others. ➤ **6.2.1**

- **Technological change**

  Rapid advances in technology have created many new products, including 3D televisions, tablet computers and in-car satellite navigators. As new products are introduced demand for older products declines. Consumer spending therefore shifts from firms producing older products to those producing new, more advanced ones. To compete, firms must develop new and better technologies and adapt their production lines in order to meet the changing tastes and expectations of consumers.

  Technology has also changed the way people shop. More and more people are now ordering the goods they want from cheaper, online retailers using the internet and spending much less time and money in shops. In response, many retailers have "moved" online and closed many of their shops to save costs. ➤ **3.3.5**

> Five of the fastest-growing industries in 2018 related to emerging forms of technology were green technologies, including solar panels, cryptocurrencies such as bitcoin, cybersecurity, virtual reality applications and 3D printing.

Responding to change

Vritika Herbotech in India is a manufacturer and exporter of herbal drinks and other natural products. The global demand for herbal teas and drinks has been expanding in recent years. So, how has this affected the company?

- Sales and profits have been rising.
- Stocks of herbal drinks have sold out more quickly.
- To meet rising demand it has expanded output using existing machinery. The company has also had to buy more herbs and other ingredients, plus more cans, bottles and labels. Employees have been asked to work longer hours.
- Suppliers of herbs and other products used in the production of herbal drinks have experienced rising orders. At first they supplied these orders from their inventories, but as their inventories ran out they expanded their output.

- If demand continues to rise, Vritika Herbotech and other businesses producing herbal drinks may need to buy more machinery, hire more workers and move into larger premises to expand output further.
- The increasing profitability of herbal drinks may encourage new businesses to start up to supply the market.

Why markets become competitive

Why do businesses compete?

Competition for a market involves rivalry between two or more businesses producing the same or similar products in an effort to achieve the following objectives.

- **To increase their customer base.** Businesses compete with each other on price, product quality, customer services, after-sales care and promotional strategies to increase the number of consumers buying their products.

- **To increase sales revenues.** Businesses not only seek to increase numbers of customers but also try to persuade existing customers to buy more. Cutting prices can increase sales revenues if customers buy more as a result. Advertising and other promotions, such as offering free gifts or loyalty bonuses, can also help retain customers and attract new ones without cutting prices.

- **To expand market share.** Businesses compete to increase their share of total market sales. The larger an organization's share of a market and the more widely established its product is, the more able it will be to withstand new sources of competition from new products and businesses. **➤ 1.3.2**

- **To enhance their image.** Businesses also compete on image. Consumers' perceptions of an organization tend to be reflected in sales. A poor image, for example because a business is known to pollute the environment or exploit employees, can reduce sales. A good image on the other hand can help expand sales and market share. **➤ 3.3.4**

- **To maximize their profits.** Ultimately, businesses that can achieve the above objectives should enjoy increased profits. **➤ 1.5.1**

Firms compete on prices and quality

Competition in a market can take many forms.

Price competition

This involves competing against rival businesses to offer consumers the best price for a product. For example, it may involve cutting prices, offering a discount, free delivery for online purchases or other special offers such as "buy one, get one free". **➤ 3.3.2**

Non-price competition

Firms also compete with each other on distinctive product features other than price, such as the quality of the good or service, product image, packaging, customer services, after-sales care and advertising. Many of these features are just as important to consumers as the price they must pay. **➤ 3.3.4**

Changes in prices, products, promotions and market shares are features of highly competitive markets

Price and non-price competition between rival businesses is usually good for consumers. In a competitive market, business organizations compete with each other to reduce their production costs so they can lower their prices and attract customers away from competitors without reducing their profits.

Competition for customers and sales also encourages businesses to provide more information to customers about their products and activities, to be more socially and environmentally responsible and spend more on researching and developing new products and processes so they can stay ahead of rival firms.

One or more of the following features are therefore a sign that a market is competitive compared to markets where there is less rivalry between firms.

- A number of similar firms produce similar but differentiated products.

- Expenditures on product development and marketing are often significant.

- New firms may enter the market causing others to fail.

- There is more innovation in product design and production.

- Firms may be more innovative in product design and production to out-compete rivals.

- Prices and product features tend to change more frequently.

- Price cutting, discounting and price "wars" may happen more often.

- The market shares of different firms change over time.

Why competition in many markets is increasing

Competition between business organizations is increasing in many markets due to the following factors.

- The rapid growth of some developing economies, such as India, China, Malaysia and Brazil, has created many new businesses able to produce at lower costs than many businesses in more developed economies. Wages in these "emerging" economies are relatively low at present. ➤ **1.2.2**

- Rising incomes around the globe and advances in transportation have created more opportunities for international trade. Increasingly, rival businesses located in one country compete not only with each other but also with goods and services imported from overseas producers. ➤ **1.3.2**

- New technologies have reduced the costs of modern machinery and equipment and, therefore, the cost of starting up and running new businesses. ➤ **4.1.3**

- E-commerce allows consumers to shop easily over the internet and search for the best products and prices from different suppliers anywhere in the world. ➤ **3.3.5**

- Consumers are becoming more intelligent or "savvy". This means they are shopping around more for the best deals and demanding more information on products and businesses before they choose what to buy and how much to spend. Businesses therefore need to compete more for their custom.

Businesses must respond to increasing competition by becoming more innovative and efficient

Businesses must become more innovative and efficient in response to increasing competition.

What evidence is there in the article that the market for tablet computers is becoming increasingly competitive? Consider your answers in terms of changes in:

▸ prices

▸ product innovations and quality

▸ consumer choice

▸ the number and market shares of different producers.

Keep taking the tablets: the future of competition for portable devices

The tablet market will still be dominated by Apple in 2020, according to market analysts.

Apple defined the tablet market with the release of its first iPad in 2010 and has since captured around 60% of the market despite increasing competition. This has been forcing down prices and forcing manufacturers to invest in new designs, sizes and power upgrades.

Apple's main competitors are more likely to steal market share from one another than from the iPAD, said one analyst pointing to disappointing sales of Motorola's Android-based Xoom, RIM's QNX-based PlayBook and HP's webOS-powered TouchPad.

Apple's costs "are materially lower than those of competing tablets," according to the analyst. This has enabled it to price the iPAD competitively without cutting into its profit margin. The iPAD also continues to dominate in terms of apps, which makes it a more versatile device than other tablets.

However, the growing trend for detachable tablets has opened up a new front in the battle for market share. Demand for detachable tablets, which include Apple's iPAD Pro and Microsoft's Surface Pro, more than doubled last year and could quadruple by 2020. By then the devices, which have the option of being used in conjunction with a keyboard, would represent a sizable chunk of the wider tablet market according to forecasters.

Microsoft holds the upper hand in this growing market segment. Its Windows 10 operating system has been specifically designed to recognise when the user of a mobile device is using a keyboard and mouse or using a touchscreen and to react accordingly for 'seemless' operation. By 2020 its predicted that more than half of detachable tablets will be powered by Microsoft's Windows 10 operating system. In contrast, less than a quarter will be iPAD Pros and the remaining portion will be powered by Google's Android operating system.

Global giant Samsung has recently launched its answer to the iPad Pro, the Galaxy TabPro S. Previously, Samsung had used Android for all of its tablet devices but its new detachable TabPro S runs on Microsoft's Windows 10.

Businesses must respond to increasing competition by becoming more innovative and efficient

A business that is able to out-compete all other rivals will be able to enjoy a commanding market share and significant market power. Competition therefore involves a continual battle for market domination and survival. Organizations that lack the skills or finance to compete effectively may be forced out of business. ➤ **1.3.4**

For example, the Lille region in France was once the second-largest textile manufacturing region in the world. However, in the 1970s competition with producers in other countries increased and one by one, the textile mills in Lille shut down as cheaper imports of clothes flooded European and other markets. Textile manufacturers in countries such as China, Bangladesh, Vietnam and Morocco all enjoyed wage costs that were a fraction of those in France.

Competition involves a continual battle for market domination and survival. A business that is able to out-compete all other rivals will be able to enjoy a commanding market share and significant market power. Organizations need

ACTIVITY 3.3

Choose a business organization you are familiar with. This could be a local shop where you buy your food or clothes or a major multinational business that produces and sells products all over the world. Gather information on how the business competes with rival organizations.

▶ Why does it compete with other business organizations?

▶ What is its market share?

▶ Who are its main competitors?

▶ Is there evidence that competition is increasing or decreasing between it and other business organizations?

▶ How do their prices compare?

▶ What forms of non-price competition do the organizations use?

the skills or finance to compete effectively. Production should be efficient to ensure the lowest costs possible. Low cost means the business can charge lower prices than competitors. Products should have a unique selling point (USP) and should be appropriately marketed to target the right product at the right consumer.

For example, IBM was once the dominant supplier of computer technology to business. They enjoyed this competitive advantage for nearly 30 years, until the mid-1980s. Apple now dominates the computing market. Apple's development of personal computers helped revolutionize computing products and IBM failed to keep up. By the early 1990s IBM reported the largest annual loss in American corporate history – $4.96 billion. Apple produced cheaper and better alternatives to IBM's machines. In the long-run, IBM stopped producing computer hardware and moved into producing software and services.

Competition therefore forces business organizations to become more efficient, to cut their costs and increase their productivity in order to survive and grow.

To compete effectively, a business organization needs to:

● be innovative to find better ways to cut its costs, lower its prices, improve its products and attract more customers

● research new consumer trends and wants and develop products to satisfy them

● improve its image and become more socially and environmentally responsible

● develop better advertising campaigns and other promotions

● employ the latest technologies and production methods

● attract and retain the best workers and managers

● find low-cost sources of finance to fund all the above activities

● co-operate with other organizations, for example through joint ventures or joint marketing campaigns, that are able to help it with the above activities. For example, food producers in an economy often jointly develop and pay for campaigns to promote the drinking of milk and the consumption of home-produced meat.

Flying into trouble

Airfix is a UK manufacturer of plastic scale model kits of aircraft, ships, cars and other objects. It was formed in 1939 and sold its products all over the world.

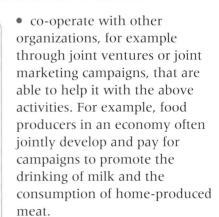

However, in the 1980s, the plastic kit-modelling hobby went into a rapid decline due to the rise of video games, advances in other toy technologies and also declining birth rates in many developed countries resulting in declining numbers of potential kit consumers. The rise in global oil prices also greatly increased the cost of plastics used to produce Airfix kits.

Airfix was slow to respond to these changing market conditions. Its market share and financial health deteriorated sharply and the company was declared bankrupt in 1981. Since then the brand has been owned by a number of different companies. Although kits are still produced and sold worldwide, the Airfix factory in the UK was demolished in 2008 and the plastic kit-modelling market is now considered a niche market.

Wild Adventures is a small company that specializes in overseas tours for people with interests in wildlife photography. The company is the current market leader in this type of tour and has a good reputation for quality. Demand for wildlife and other adventure holidays is growing but, as a result, the market is becoming increasingly competitive.

a   What is meant by the term "demand"?   [2]

b   Identify **two** features of an "increasingly competitive market".   [2]

c   Identify and explain **two** possible reasons why consumer demand for
     adventure holidays has been rising.   [4]

d   Identify and explain **two** advantages to companies such as
     Wild Adventures of segmenting the market for holidays.   [6]

e   The managers of Wild Adventures are thinking about starting a
     new range of family beach holidays, aimed at the mass market.
     Do you think this is a good idea? Justify your answer.   [6]

Before you continue make sure you are able to

Show understanding of **market changes** and how businesses might respond to them:

✓   why customer or **consumer spending patterns** may change

✓   the importance of changing customer needs

✓   why some markets have become more competitive

✓   how businesses can respond to changing spending patterns and increased **competition**.

3.1.3 Concepts of niche marketing and mass marketing

Key POINTS

▶ **Mass marketing** strategies are developed to mass produce, price, promote and sell products in large national or international markets.

▶ **Niche marketing** strategies are used for small, specialized consumer markets. Technology, design and quality of products and the reputation of the producer are more important considerations than price and promotions.

Business BUZZWORDS

Niche marketing – a marketing strategy aimed at a small, specialized market.

Niche market – a small part or segment of a large market consisting of consumers with specialized tastes or preferences.

Mass or niche marketing?

A marketing strategy is designed to appeal to a particular target market

If the market for a product is a very large national or international market, **mass marketing** strategies will be developed to mass produce, price, promote and sell the product.

For example, relatively low-priced items that most people buy and use on a regular basis, such as washing powders, toothpastes, newspapers and fizzy drinks, are mass-produced using automated production methods and mass-marketed including through advertisements on national television and in national newspapers. ➤ **3.3.4**

▲ Niche market

▲ Mass market

Mass marketing strategies are therefore used for products that have mass appeal and are designed to reach mass audiences.

Benefits of mass marketing	Limitations of mass marketing
+ Mass marketing can create opportunities for business expansion.	− Mass markets attract many different firms that compete vigorously with each other on product quality and price and through advertising, for sales.
+ The return, in terms of increased sales and profits from investments in mass marketing, can be significant.	− Mass marketing can be very expensive and losses can be significant if the strategy fails to appeal to consumers and therefore fails to generate sales.
+ The business can benefit from marketing economies of scale: the cost of advertising a product on television may be high but the advertising cost per item sold will be low due to mass sales.	− Some customers do not like to buy mass-produced products and prefer items that are less standardized.
+ By making and selling several variants of the same product a business can reduce the impact of a fall in demand for any one of the variants on its total sales and profits. For example, washing powder manufacturers often produce and advertise several variants of their products, with different names, aromas and packaging, for hot washes and cold washes, for coloured clothing and white garments, etc.	

If the market for a product is small and specialized then **niche marketing** strategies will be more appropriate. A **niche market** consists of a group of consumers who prefer more specialized and exclusive products and who form a small part or segment of a large product market. For example, niche markets exist for high-end sports cars, designer clothes and luxury yachts. Many of these products are designed and made to order, usually by small, specialized firms, because they do not sell in sufficient volumes to make mass production by large firms cost-effective.

Benefits of niche marketing	Limitations of niche marketing
+ There is usually less competition due to the small market size and specialized or exclusive nature of niche products.	− Opportunities for sales and growth are more limited than for other producers.
+ Product quality is more important to customers than promotions; therefore, advertising costs tend to be lower.	− Many niche producers specialize in making and selling just one product: a fall in demand for the product may cause the business to fail.
+ Customers are usually willing to pay a much higher price for niche products.	
+ Over time, a niche producer can develop a reputation for its specialism.	

Niche markets also exist for highly specialized items such as books on astrophysics and other very technical subjects, and for highly specialized machines used in production processes. In niche markets, the technology, design and quality of the product and the reputation of the producer is often far more important to customers than price and promotions.

For each of the products listed in the table below, indicate by ticking the relevant column whether you would recommend using a mass marketing or niche marketing strategy to promote consumer awareness and sales.

Product	Mass marketing	Niche marketing
Private jets		
A national newspaper		
A technical engineering consultancy		
Exercise equipment		
A new big-budget, action film release		
Yoga mats		
A magazine for coin collectors		
Holidays to the Galapagos islands		
A firm of legal advisers		
Breakfast cereals		
A shop selling antique jewellery		
Electric hybrid vehicles		
Cartons of milk		
Medical instruments		
Ready-made meals		

Learning CHECKLIST

Before you continue make sure you are able to

Describe the concepts of **niche marketing** and **mass marketing**:

✓ the benefits and limitations of both approaches to marketing.

3.1.4   How and why market segmentation is undertaken

▸ Market segmentation involves dividing up a market into different groups of consumers with similar characteristics, preferences and buying habits in order to identify the target market for a product and promotions.

▸ Market segmentation recognizes that all potential users of a product are not alike, and that what appeals to one group of consumers may not appeal to others.

▸ Consumer characteristics, preferences and buying habits differ between market segments but are broadly similar within the same market segment.

▸ Market research can be used to find out the preferences and buying habits of consumers in different market segments. Businesses can use this information to design different products, pricing strategies and promotions that will appeal to consumers in different market segments.

▸ Consumer preferences and buying habits depend on such factors as consumers' age, gender, income and lifestyle. Consumer preferences can also depend on their religion, culture and where they live.

▸ Lifestyle, income and education are often closely linked to a socio-economic group. For example, people in managerial and professional occupations tend to have more educational qualifications and earn more income than people in semi-skilled and unskilled occupations.

Business **BUZZWORDS**

Market segmentation – grouping together consumers who have similar characteristics, preferences and buying habits.

Market segment – an identifiable group of individual or business consumers sharing similar characteristics or preferences.

Target market – a group of consumers (or market segment) that a business will design its products and marketing strategies to appeal to.

Lifestyle segmentation – dividing up consumers into groups according to their hobbies, interests and opinions.

Socio-economic group – a group of consumers with similar social, economic and/or educational status.

How markets can be segmented

Market segmentation involves dividing up consumers in a market into different groups with similar characteristics, preferences and buying habits

Before a market-oriented firm can design a product and its promotion, it will want to know who they will appeal to. Information about the preferences and buying habits of different types of consumers is therefore extremely valuable to a business. It means it is able to identify the **target market** of consumers with particular characteristics at which to aim a product and marketing strategy.

ACTIVITY 3.5

The consumers below all buy a brand of luxury handmade sweets. These consumers form part of the market for the product yet they all have very different characteristics. Each consumer is representative of a different segment in this market.

Use the table below to identify their main characteristics. How could you use this information to determine where to sell chocolates to the different market segments the consumers represent, how to design different packaging that will attract them and what advertisements and other promotions to target at them?

"I just love the taste of sweets. I save up and treat myself and my other half every now and then."

"We are retired but we are fortunate enough to afford luxuries occasionally."

"I buy these when I go and visit my friends and family for dinner."

"The children love them but we can only afford to buy them for religious festivals. I'm also concerned about the amount of packaging they use."

Characteristic	Consumer 1	Consumer 2	Consumer 3	Consumer 4
Male				
Female				
Young				
Middle-aged				
Old				
Single				
Married with children				
Health conscious				
Regular buyer				
Infrequent buyer				
Care for environment				
Low income				
High income				

Market segmentation is the first important step in developing a marketing strategy. In order to plan their product development, pricing strategies and promotions, businesses will divide up the consumers who are likely to buy a product into different **market segments**. Market segmentation recognizes that all potential users of a product are not alike, and that what appeals to one group may not interest other consumers. For example, the types of clothes and cars purchased by young people will be very different from those bought by older adults with families.

For example, the market for mobile telecommunications is segmented in a number of ways in order to develop call tariffs, product features and promotions that will appeal to different customer groups. The simplest way to divide up the market is between residential customers and business customers and then according to how they pay for their mobile services.

Mobile phone service providers such as Vodafone then further segment their residential user market according to income, age, pattern of usage (emergency only, peak or off-peak), value of customer usage (high, medium or low revenue), customer lifestyles and attitudes and their geographic location. For example, Vodafone identified a youth market segment in many countries consisting of consumers between 12 and 24 years of age. Key features of this customer group are that most still live at home, have limited income, are very social and image-conscious and share many common interests in movies, sports and music.

The youth market was then further divided up by Vodafone into early teens (12–15 years), late teens (16–19 years) and young adults (20–24 years). The needs of each of these segments were further analysed in order to design product features and price plans that are best able to satisfy them.

Youth market segment needs	Mobile service requirements
Communication	
▸ to share	▸ calls and video calls
▸ catch up with friends	▸ SMS texts
▸ to show affection	▸ sending a song
▸ to chat	
Entertainment	
▸ to have fun	▸ playing a game
▸ to "escape"	▸ taking and sending photos and videos
▸ to address their different moods	▸ listening to music
	▸ downloading new ring tones
Information	
▸ to receive news	▸ finding and sending information
▸ to organize	▸ internet access
▸ to learn	▸ receiving alerts

Vodafone, like many business organizations, knows that consumer preferences and spending habits vary widely depending on such factors as age, gender, income and lifestyle. Consumer preferences can also depend on consumers' religion, culture and where they live. For example, people in India and Morocco drink more tea per person per year than any other population. ➤ **3.1.2**

The table below shows some of the main ways markets can be segmented.

Income	Age
In general, the more money we have the more we spend and the greater the variety of goods and services we buy. However, some people may prefer to save more of their income than others. As income rises, consumers tend to increase spending on housing, transportation, electronics, travel, health care, education and other services.	Our needs, wants and buying habits change as we grow older. Younger people may spend more of their income on fashionable clothes, music and computer games compared to older people who may spend more income on furnishing their homes, travel and their children or grandchildren. The average age of many populations is rising and there is increasing demand for health care, leisure facilities and financial services.
Lifestyle	**Gender**
Lifestyle segmentation involves identifying how different people choose to express their personality and their beliefs, including their hobbies, how health conscious they are, their political views, how they spend their free time, how much they care for the environment, what value they attach to having money and status, their educational background and so on. Lifestyle, income and status are often closely linked.	Men and women have different preferences and buying habits. For example, according to the Global Youth Survey, 40% of young women spend the majority of their money on clothing compared with just 12% of men. Video surveillance in Canada also found men generally shop alone and seldom compare prices. In contrast, women prefer to shop with friends and compare prices and quality in detail.
Location	**Socio-economic group**
Incomes, occupations and lifestyles can vary greatly within a country and globally. Incomes are generally higher and lifestyles more hectic in urban areas than in rural areas. The way people talk may also differ according to their regional accents. Television broadcasting regions may be used as a way of targeting regional market segments. Television advertisements can be designed to appeal to people in different regions. Marketing may also target particular features of different regions such as beach and ski resorts.	**Socio-economic groups** segment consumers by their social, economic or educational status usually by using their main occupation, for example: • higher managerial and professional occupations • lower managerial and professional occupations • small employers and the self-employed • skilled routine occupations • routine semi-skilled or unskilled occupations • casual workers and the unemployed. Definitions may vary. Sometimes groups are referred to as upper, middle and lower social classes.

Potential benefits of segmentation to business

Segmenting a market in one or more of the above has the following advantages.

✓ Marketing is more effective. A business can adapt its products, pricing strategies and promotions to appeal to the preferences of consumers in different market segments, for example, producing value brand foods to appeal to low-income groups and more luxury brands at premium prices targeted at high-income groups.

✓ Gaps in a market can be identified more easily. Some groups of consumers may have needs or wants that are currently unmet. A business that can quickly adapt its existing products and promotions, or design new ones to appeal to these consumers, can create additional sales and establish a leading position in the market segment. For example, a number of companies have produced software and apps for mobile phones so they can be used easily by people who are blind or have other disabilities.

✓ Sales and profits are increased because marketing is more effective.

The products are similar in each pair of photographs but they are designed to appeal to different market segments. How do you think the market in each case has been segmented? What is the key characteristic of each market segment?

Learning CHECKLIST

Before you continue make sure you are able to

Understand how and why **market segmentation** is undertaken:

✓ how markets can be segmented, for example according to age, **socio-economic grouping**, location and gender

✓ potential benefits of segmentation to business

✓ recommend and justify an appropriate **method of segmentation** in given circumstances.

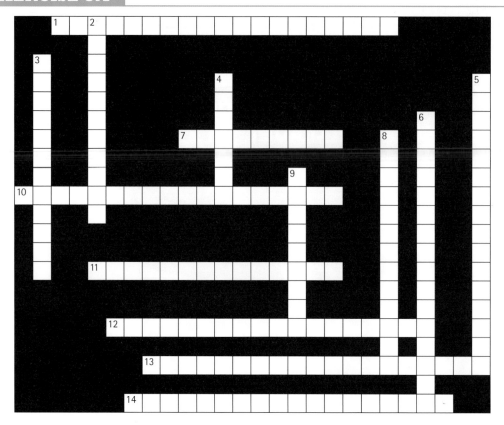

Clues down

2 A small part or segment of a larger market consisting of consumers with specialized tastes or preferences (5, 6)

3 What does the following describe? The market segment which a firm will design its products and marketing strategies to appeal to (6, 6)

4 What does the following statement describe? Every product has one. Each one involves the exchange of a particular good or service between its producers and consumers. The size of each one is measured by the total amount spent on the particular good or service by its consumers each week, month or year (1, 6)

5 The distinctive characteristics of any given market, including the degree of competition between its producers and the numbers, types, preferences and spending levels of different groups of consumers. A business will need to anticipate and respond to changes in these if it is to survive (6, 10)

6 What must have increased if consumers are able to both spend more on goods and services and also save more? (10, 6)

8 A marketing strategy for mass-produced goods with mass appeal (4, 9)

9 Which method of market segmentation does the following describe? Segmenting consumers according to their opinions and beliefs, what newspapers they read and how they like to spend their free time (9)

Clues across

1 Rivalry between businesses over different features of their products, such as quality, image, packaging and their customer services, after-sales care and advertisements (3-5, 11)

7 An important business function that involves the anticipation, identification and satisfaction of consumer needs and wants in order to generate sales, encourage customer loyalty and earn profit (9)

10 A business that will research what consumers need and want before it develops products and promotions that will appeal to them (6-8, 4)

11 This type of marketing strategy is used by firms producing the same product in a competitive market in an attempt to make their products appear different from those of their rivals, for example by adding product features, using different packaging and offering different sizes (14)

12 The process of identifying and classifying different consumers of a product according to their characteristics, preferences and buying habits (6, 12)

13 Which method of market segmentation does the following describe? Identifying and classifying consumers according to their education and occupational status (5-8, 6)

14 What has the following features? A number of similar firms producing similar but differentiated products; firms tend to be more innovative and efficient than others and their prices, product features, promotions and market shares tend to change more frequently (1, 11, 6)

3.2.1 The role of market research and methods used

3.2.2 Presentation and use of market research results

- ▶ Market research is used to identify customer preferences and spending patterns, competitive threats from rival producers, and how they are changing.

- ▶ A market-oriented business will always use market research before it designs its products and marketing strategies. Investments in products and marketing strategies can be wasted and sales lost if they do not appeal to the consumers they have been designed for.

- ▶ Market research can collect quantitative data, such as sales and price information, and qualitative data, including consumers' opinions.

- ▶ New or primary data is collected to meet specific business requirements but can be expensive. It can be collected from interviews, surveys, panels of consumers or by observing consumer behaviour.

- ▶ Sampling is used in primary data collection because it is impractical to interview or survey all consumers in a target population or market.

- ▶ The accuracy of market research data can be affected by bias in the way it is collected. For example, sampling bias will occur if the sample chosen is not representative of consumers in the target population, and questionnaire bias will occur if questions are misleading or badly designed.

- ▶ Secondary data is often cheaper and less time-consuming to obtain than primary research data, and can be collected from existing internal sources, such as sales records, or external sources, including published reports and statistics, many of which are now available quickly and cheaply online.

Business BUZZWORDS

Market research – the collection and analysis of data about consumers' preferences, spending patterns and other market conditions.

Quantitative data – numerical information.

Qualitative data – written or verbal information.

Primary research – new data collection from "field research".

Secondary research – desk-based research using data from existing sources.

Test marketing – a limited field trial of a new product or promotion to test consumer reaction.

Random sampling – choosing consumers to interview or survey at random.

Quota sampling – choosing consumers to interview according to pre-specified characteristics, such as age or sex.

Sampling bias – choosing consumers to interview or survey who are not fully representative of those in the target population in terms of their characteristics, buying behaviour, tastes or opinions.

Market leader – the firm with the largest share of a market or market segment measured by its share of the total number of units sold or total value of sales per period.

Uses and types of market research

Market research involves the identification of consumer wants and market features. A business will only be successful if it can produce something consumers are willing and able to buy now and in the future. Good **market research** can reduce the risk of developing and producing products that do not appeal to consumers by finding out what they want and what rival businesses are offering them.

A **market-oriented business** will always use market research before it designs its products and marketing strategies. Investments in new or improved products and marketing strategies can be wasted if they do not appeal to the consumers they have been designed for and as a result sales, profits and market shares can be lost to rival firms. ➤ **3.1.1**

Market research therefore involves the gathering and analysis of information or data about the preferences and spending patterns of different groups of consumers and about other market conditions, such as prices and competition.

It can help to identify the type of consumers likely to buy a product, for example the consumers' age range, sex, income level and lifestyle, the prices consumers are willing to pay, how they react to different promotions and where they like to buy products. Accurate market research is therefore vital to the development of an effective marketing mix.

Types of market research

Information gathered from market research are in two main forms.

- **Quantitative data** are statistics, for example about the quantity of consumer demand, prices, values and market shares.

- **Qualitative data** are written or verbal responses to questions that express consumers' opinions, judgments or reactions, for example questions such as "What do you like about the product?"

Quantitative and qualitative data can be collected in two ways.

Primary research involves field research by gathering data directly from existing or potential customers and from observing their buying behaviour.

Market research information

Product

What products do consumers want?

What product features do they like most?

What is the consumer reaction to new products?

Price

How much are consumers willing to pay?

What methods do they prefer to use to make a payment?

Place and method of sale

Where do consumers prefer to shop?

What is the reaction of retailers to new products?

Are consumers satisfied with customer service?

Promotions

How effective have promotional campaigns been?

How do consumers react to different promotional ideas?

Market

What is the size of the market?

Is the market expanding or contracting?

What are the main characteristics (age, sex, lifestyle, etc.) of existing and potential customers?

Competition

Who are the main business competitors?

What are their strengths and weaknesses?

What are their market shares?

How do they promote their products?

What are their pricing strategies?

- **Secondary research** involves desk-based research using market information that is already available from internal business records or from data collected by other organizations, including the government's statistical publications or specialist market research organizations.

▼ The stages of market research

Stage 1
What is the purpose of the market research? What information is needed? What action will be taken as a result of the research findings, for example change product design or alter the pricing strategy.

Stage 2
Decide on the most appropriate research methods, depending on the amount of time and budget available to spend.

Stage 3
Design a questionnaire. Determine how consumers should be asked questions. Decide what characteristics (age, sex, income, lifestyle, etc.) those people asked should have. Identify secondary sources of relevant market research data.

Stage 4
Undertake the research.

Stage 5
Analyse the results, draw conclusions and produce a report of the findings. Make recommendations and decisions on the future marketing strategy.

Methods of primary research

Primary research involves observing consumer behaviour and gathering new data directly from existing and potential customers

Primary data is information that is newly created from "field research". That is, it involves market researchers going out and about collecting new and original data on consumer behaviour, spending patterns and opinions as well as monitoring the behaviour of competing businesses.

As primary data is new data it can be expensive to collect. However, primary research data has some clear advantages.

✓ It is collected to meet the specific requirements of a business, for example to test reaction to its new product or advertising campaign.

✓ It is more up to date and exclusive to a business than existing and published sources of data.

Methods of primary data collection include the following.

- **Face-to-face interviews** using a carefully designed questionnaire allow the interviewer to target a particular type of consumer either individually or in groups. However, some people may not be willing to participate.

- **Telephone and online surveys** can be targeted at different groups of consumers. Telephone surveys can be expensive and it is important that a researcher is able to speak to people who make the spending decisions in their families or households. Online surveys are quicker and cheaper and can be sent to people via email or programmed to "pop up" on screen at the end of an online purchase. However, not everyone is willing to talk on the telephone or answer surveys, and not everyone has access to a telephone or the Internet.

- **Postal surveys** involve sending out questionnaires for people to complete and return by post. However, many people simply throw them away. Prize draws may be used to give people the incentive to return their completed surveys.

Advantages of interviews and surveys	Disadvantages of interviews and surveys
+ They can be a cost-effective way of gathering data, including opinions from a large number of consumers. + Different types of consumers with different characteristics can be targeted for information gathering. + Questions can be explained in face-to-face and telephone interviews to people who may have difficulty hearing or understanding them.	− Many consumers may be unwilling to take part. − Telephone and postal surveys can be expensive, especially if response rates are poor. − They can be time-consuming. − Poorly designed questions may be misunderstood and answers may be misleading. − Interviewers must be careful not to mislead respondents or influence their answers. Interviewers' bias will give inaccurate results.

- **Consumer panels** involve asking a group of consumers, or "focus group", to test or give their opinions on new products and/or promotions and to discuss ways they could be improved. Panels may also be used to record their weekly spending decisions to monitor how they change over time in response to changes in prices and promotional campaigns.

Advantages of consumer panels	Disadvantages of consumer panels
+ They are a good way of gathering a range of different consumers' opinions in one place at the same time. + Monitoring the spending decisions of members of a consumer panel provides information on how purchasing behaviours change over time.	− They can be time-consuming and expensive to set up. Members of consumer panels often receive a fee or free gifts for their participation. − Some members may be easily influenced by how other members react or by what they say rather than giving their own true opinion.

- **Observation** can be used to monitor the behaviour of consumers over time. For example, observers could count the number of shoppers visiting a shopping mall at different times of the day to identify peak shopping periods, record television and radio audiences for different programmes using viewing meters or gather sales information from electronic tills in supermarkets. Observation can also be used by visiting rival shops or businesses to find out about the prices and services they offer.

- **Test marketing** is a good way of testing market reaction to a new product or promotion on a limited group of consumers or in a particular region before it is released more widely. If consumer reaction and sales are poor the products or promotions can be withdrawn or modified before they are launched on to a national or international market. These experiments are also known as field trials.

Advantages of observation and field trials	Disadvantages of observation and field trials
+ They are cost-effective ways of gathering a large amount of quantitative data on consumer behaviour and spending patterns over time. + Field trials reduce the risk of a new product or promotional launch failing by first testing consumer reaction.	− Observation and field trials can be time-consuming. − Observation cannot provide reasons for observed consumer behaviour. − Consumer behaviour observed in one region may not reflect how consumers will react in others.

Good questionnaire design is vital for gathering accurate primary research data

Questionnaires are a useful way of collecting information from consumers about their buying behaviours, tastes and opinions through individual and panel interviews and through surveys. However, a poorly designed questionnaire will gather poor or inaccurate information.

ACTIVITY 3.7

▶ Do you think the questionnaire opposite is a good one or poorly designed?

▶ Would you be able or even willing to answer these questions?

▶ What do you think is wrong with each question?

▶ How would you redesign the questionnaire to improve the questions and improve the usefulness of the responses they are designed to gather?

1 Do you ever take a bath? Yes / No
2 How often do you bathe?
   A More than once each day
   B Once each day
   C Less than once each day
   D Never
3 What is the chemical composition of your favourite brand of soap?
4 How much water do you use in your bath?
   A Less than 50 litres
   B 50–100 litres
   C More than 100 litres
   D Don't know
5 Where do you buy soap?
6 How much would you pay for a new soap?
   A Less than $1
   B $1–$1.50
   C $1.50–$3
   D More than $5
7 Do you think the price and the colour of soap are its most important features? Yes / No
8 You do like this soap don't you?

The questions in activity 3.7 are very poor and unlikely to gather useful or accurate information.

- Questions 1 and 2 could embarrass people and they may refuse to answer.
- Questions 3 and 4 are too technical.
- Question 5 is too open-ended and will produce too many different answers.
- In question 6 consumers cannot choose a price between $3 and $5.
- Question 7 should either ask whether price or colour is more important.
- Question 8 may force people to answer "yes".

A number of useful rules can guide questionnaire design.

✚ Questions should be asked in a logical order.
✚ Questions should not be offensive or embarrassing.
✚ Questions should be short, easy to understand and easy to answer.
✚ Questions should not trick or force people into giving a particular answer.
✚ Questions should limit the number of possible responses.
✚ Do not ask for names and confidential details.
✚ Avoid asking too many questions.

Two main types of question can be used in a questionnaire. An **open question** allows people to give a wide variety of different answers and can therefore provide a good deal of useful and detailed market research information.

In contrast, a **closed question** limits the number of possible answers a person can give, for example to a simple "yes" or "no" or to a limited range of multiple choice options such as different price or age ranges. Ranges may be useful when people find it difficult or embarrassing to give a precise answer, such as the price they would be willing to pay for a product or their age!

Closed questions result in a narrower range of responses and prevent people from giving their opinions, but they make the analysis of gathered data much easier.

1 How satisfied are you with the purchase of your product?

Very satisfied ☐   Satisfied ☐
Not very satisfied ☐   Very dissatisfied ☐

2 Would you consider using personal banking on the Internet?

Yes ☐   No ☐

3 How often do you eat out at a restaurant?

More than once every week ☐   Once a month ☐
Once a week ☐   Less than once a month ☐
More than once every month ☐   Never ☐

▲ An example of some well-designed market research questions

Before a questionnaire is used in interviews it is useful to test it on a few people first to judge how easy it is to understand and answer the questions and to make sure it will provide accurate information. Once it is ready to use, a market researcher then needs to think whom to ask and where the best place is to ask the questions. For example, there may be lots of people to approach at a busy train station but few may be willing to stop to answer questions because they may be in a hurry.

Sampling involves choosing whom to interview, survey or observe from a target population of consumers

Products and their promotions are targeted at different groups of consumers. The **target population** or **target market** for a particular product or marketing strategy consists of all the potential consumers of that product. ➤ **3.1.1**

However, it would be very expensive and impractical to interview, survey or observe everyone in a target population. Instead market researchers gather primary data from a small number of consumers called a **sample population**. Choosing whom to interview, survey, have on a consumer panel or observe is therefore known as **sampling**.

As long as the sample of consumers chosen for research includes people with similar buying habits, tastes and opinions to all the other consumers in the target population, the sample will give a good indication of what most of the other consumers will want. Using large samples reduces the risk of choosing the wrong types of consumer but can make research more expensive to conduct.

Random sampling and **quota sampling** are the two most commonly used sampling methods.

Random sampling involves picking consumers at random. Every business or member of the population therefore has an equal chance of being selected for interview or survey.

People or businesses can be selected at random in the street or by a computer from telephone or address records.

Random sampling reduces the chance of biased samples. However, random sampling often gathers unnecessary information from consumers who are not part of the target market for a particular product.

Quota sampling involves choosing consumers according to their particular characteristics, such as their age, sex or income. This involves market segmentation. ➤ **3.1.4**

For example, quota sampling may require interviews with 50 people between 20 and 44 years of age, 30 people aged between 45 and 64 and 20 people over the age of 65.

Quota sampling avoids gathering information from consumers other than those in the target market for a product. The risk is that people chosen for interview may not be representative of most other consumers in the same market.

You are the head of a major market research agency. A number of business organizations have asked your organization to conduct primary research on various products for them. You must advise them, giving reasons, about what is the best method of primary research and method sampling to use for each one. The products are:

▶ a new luxury make-up range for women

▶ a proposal for a new sports, leisure, swimming pool and spa complex

▶ a range of existing household cleaning products, for which there is going to be a new advertising campaign

▶ a change in the timetable for rail services between two major towns

▶ a new company set up to offer property, car, life and medical insurance to people over 50 years.

Methods of secondary research

There are many useful existing sources of secondary data including sales records, statistical publications and market research reports

Secondary market research is desk-based research using existing sources of market-relevant information. Some may be from internal sources in a business, others from external sources produced by other organizations.

Many businesses have useful files and records containing valuable secondary research data about the performance of products and promotions and the impact price changes in the past have had on customer spending. For example, the sales department in a business will keep data on sales of different products over time and by region, and the finance department will have records on production costs and payments received from customers. Internal sources of secondary data may include:

● accounting records of revenues and costs

● stock records

● records of customer orders, payments and deliveries

● sales records showing variations in sales over time, by season and by area

● a database of customer complaints received by customer services

● opinions of retailers.

There are also many different external sources of secondary data a business can obtain and use; their cost and usefulness may vary. Here are some examples of external sources of secondary data.

● **Government reports and statistical publications.** Central governments often collect and publish detailed statistics over time on population characteristics, industrial sectors, production, numbers and sizes of businesses, household income and expenditure patterns, prices, exchange rates and much more. Many government statistics and reports are available for free online.

● **Market reports published by specialist market research organizations.** Market research agencies are specialist organizations that design and carry out market research on behalf of other businesses. They also conduct and publish their own research into different markets. These contain very comprehensive and detailed information but can be expensive to buy.

- **Newspapers, magazines and journals** contain useful articles on different markets. They also sometimes commission and publish their own market research.

- **Trade associations.** A trade association represents the interests of their member organizations in a particular industrial sector, such as an aerospace manufacturers association, bank association, farming association or even a small business association. They often produce reports on market trends in their industries.

- **Publications from competing organizations.** The annual reports and business accounts published by competing companies are available to download from their websites and are usually free. They contain useful information on their sales, profits, market shares and objectives.

- **The internet.** Many of the above publications, articles and statistical databases plus many more sources can now be searched for and accessed quickly online, and are often available to download for free.

ACTIVITY 3.9

Suggest research methods, sampling methods and/or secondary sources you could use to gather market-relevant information on:

▶ consumers' opinions on a new range of bank savings schemes

▶ statistics on average household income and spending patterns in overseas countries

▶ the number of customers visiting a supermarket at different times of the day

▶ the likely success of a new fizzy drink

▶ consumers' reaction to a new movie prior to its release

▶ what prices to charge in a new coffee shop

▶ the sales, market shares and profitability of rival companies in an industry

▶ recent trends in the automotive industry.

Which of the following sources of market research information will provide primary data and which will contain secondary data? The sources are:

▶ an analysis of common customer complaints

▶ an article on technological advances made by a rival company in a specialist journal

▶ a head count at the entrance to a sports ground of football fans arriving for a match

▶ a market research agency's report on the retailing industry

▶ a consumer panel to test new cosmetic products

▶ weekly sales information from the sales department

▶ government statistics on international trade and exchange rates

▶ responses to an online survey on social and environmental issues of most concern to people.

The accuracy of market research data

Factors affecting the accuracy of primary market research data

Despite organizations spending a lot of money and time on gathering market research information, many products and marketing strategies still fail after they have been launched. Sometimes, consumer wants and markets change more quickly than businesses anticipate. However, in some cases, this may be due to poorly designed market research.

Inaccurate primary data occurs due to bias. For example,

- **Sampling bias** occurs when the people or businesses chosen for interview or survey are not representative of the target market of consumers at which a product or promotion is aimed. This produces inaccurate data.

- **Questionnaire bias** results from misleading or badly worded questions which may cause the people being interviewed to give answers that do not reflect their true buying habits or opinions.

- **Response bias** occurs because some people may make up answers to interview questions because they cannot remember their last purchase or other relevant information, such as the price they paid or how frequently they buy or use an item. They may even make up some of their answers thinking it will improve their image, for example by overstating their income or giving a false age.

Factors affecting accuracy of secondary market research data

Some secondary market research data may also be inaccurate or inappropriate.

- Data collected by other organizations may also have suffered from sampling errors and other forms of bias.

- Biased results may have been presented on purpose, for example some newspapers and political parties may intentionally emphasize or overlook some results so that their comments are more sensational.

- Statistics date quickly and may not reflect the latest market trends.

Market research data must therefore be gathered, used and analysed carefully. Investment decisions based on misleading data can result in very costly business mistakes. The usefulness of market research data crucially depends on its accuracy and reliability, and this in turn depends on the methods used to collect it.

When market research goes wrong

One of the biggest blunders in market research is attributed to Coca-Cola. Following the Second World War it had a global market share of cola flavoured drinks of over 60% but by 1983 it had shrunk to just 24% due to intense competition from Pepsi-Cola, a sweeter tasting cola drink. Pepsi was also outselling Coca-Cola in supermarkets.

In response, Coca-Cola launched New Coke in 1985 to replace its existing "classic" cola drink. This followed extensive market research trials involving consumer panels. New Coke was introduced because in blindfolded taste tests panel members preferred sweeter tasting Pepsi to Coca-Cola.

But New Coke failed miserably. Why? Because the research results were misleading and because Coca-Cola did not understand their customers. In blind taste tests, people usually only take a small sip of cola, whereas in real life, they will drink a full can or glass of cola. People usually only prefer sweetness in moderation so when it came to drinking a can of cola, consumers continued to prefer Coca-Cola's less sweet formula to Pepsi's sweetness.

Within three months Coca-Cola had relaunched its classic cola.

ByteSize is a market-oriented company. It produces customizable USB computer flash drives targeted at large business customers. Five years ago it was the market leader but more recently its market share has fallen and profits have been squeezed. As a result the amount the business spends on market research each year has been cut to reduce costs.

a   What is meant by "market-oriented company"?   [2]

b   What is meant by "market research"?   [2]

c   Identify and explain **two** methods that ByteSize may use to gather primary market research data.   [4]

d   Identify and explain **three** possible reasons why the market share of ByteSize has fallen.   [6]

e   Do you think that ByteSize would benefit from spending more on market research? Justify your answer.   [6]

Analysing market research data

To inform marketing decisions, raw market research data must be converted into a form that is easy to understand, analyse and present

A great deal of data gathered from market research will be in a raw form, from interviews, surveys and other sources. To be of use for making business decisions it will need to be converted into a form that is easy to understand and analyse. For example, in response to questions on important product features it will be important to be able to assess which one received the most responses from consumers and which one the least. Similarly, if people on consumer panels have recorded data on their shopping patterns over time it will be important to use this data to identify any trends and the impact changes in prices or promotions may have had on their past spending decisions.

Raw data from market research can be added up and summarized in tables, charts or graphs for the purpose of presenting results and analysis.

Tables are one of the easiest ways of presenting data on different market variables such as sales, prices and costs. They are especially useful for showing data on different things at the same time or where numbers are needed to make calculations.

Tables can contain descriptions and lists in addition to quantitative values. For example, the table below shows average weekly household expenditure on different categories of goods and services in New Zealand in 2007, 2010 and 2013. In the final row, total average weekly expenditure per household for each year is calculated by adding up the values in each column.

All tables, charts and graphs should have clear, easy-to-understand titles

Average weekly expenditure per household on goods and services, New Zealand ($)

Main product groups	2007	2010	2013
Food and drink	162.90	177.50	192.50
Clothing and footwear	33.90	30.30	31.60
Housing and household utilities	209.00	251.60	272.90
Household contents and services	50.00	45.10	27.10
Health	24.00	24.20	48.80
Transport	141.20	131.00	158.30
Communication	30.70	33.60	35.80
Recreation and culture	100.30	98.20	107.20
Education	12.50	16.60	18.40
Other	173.70	210.60	218.80
Total	938.20	1018.70	1111.40

Source: Household Economic Survey, Statistics New Zealand

Always show the source of your data

Charts and graphs are a good way of presenting quantitative data visually. Totals, relative amounts and changes or trends over time in different variables can be easily identified using them. Computer spreadsheets can be used easily and quickly to produce attractive charts and graphs from raw data.

Charts and graphs include the following.

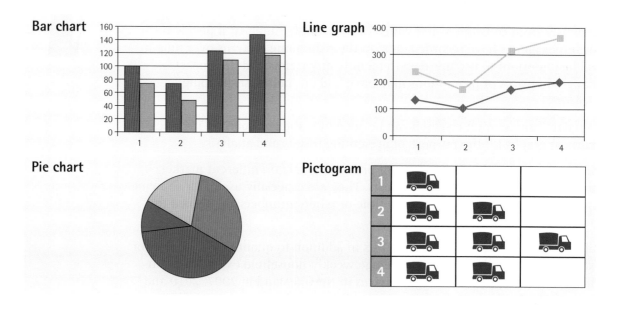

Bar chart

Line graph

Pie chart

Pictogram

How to draw a bar chart

Bar charts are one of the best ways of presenting data graphically. The height of each bar is proportional to the value it represents so different totals can be compared easily. Bars can represent whole numbers or percentages. A bar representing 40% will therefore be twice the height of a bar representing 20%.

For example, the bar chart below displays information on how much more willing US consumers would be to pay for a range of environmentally friendly products. The bar chart clearly shows that around half the number of consumers interviewed said they would pay up to 15% more for detergents and automobiles if they were eco-friendly, but less than half said they would pay more for environmentally friendly computer paper or wooden furniture. This information can help businesses producing these products determine whether or not they will be able to raise prices to cover the costs of developing more eco-friendly goods.

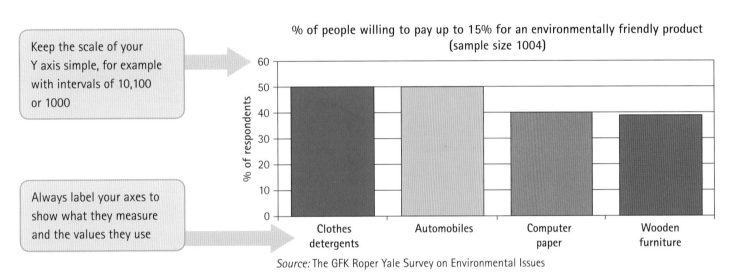

Keep the scale of your Y axis simple, for example with intervals of 10, 100 or 1000

Always label your axes to show what they measure and the values they use

% of people willing to pay up to 15% for an environmentally friendly product (sample size 1004)

Source: The GFK Roper Yale Survey on Environmental Issues

How to draw a bar chart

- Tabulate the variables and values you will use in your bar chart.
- Draw a vertical (Y) axis. The highest number on the axis should be the highest value in your table.
- Draw a horizontal (X) axis. This should be divided up into the number of different values in your table, for example number of years or the number of different variables.
- Plot the data from your table in the chart area formed by your Y and X axes.
- Label your Y and X axes with the variables they measure and how they are measured, for example years, dollars, percentage of consumers.
- Decide on a title for your bar chart describing briefly what it shows.

How to draw a line chart

Line charts are a great way of showing changes or trends in data over time, and the relationship between two or more variables. Lines may be straight or linear, curved or curvilinear or very irregular, for example if the value of a variable changes rapidly up and down over time.

For example, the line chart below shows there is a very strong relationship between national income (measured by GDP) and household spending on consumer goods and services in Turkey. Total household spending has been rising over time and with income rises in the country. However, in 2008 Turkey and many other countries experienced falling income and spending during the global economic recession, but many have since recovered. Information on growth in total income and spending will be useful to overseas businesses planning to export their products to Turkey or those seeking to relocate their operations to Turkey.

Keep the scale of your Y axis simple, for example with intervals of 10, 100 or 1000

Always label your X axes to show what they measure and the values they use
Keep the scale of your Y axis simple, for example with intervals of 10, 100 or 1000

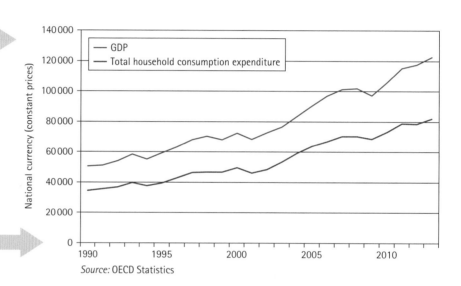

Source: OECD Statistics

How to draw a line chart

- Tabulate the categories and values you will use in your line chart.
- Draw a vertical (Y) axis. The highest number on the axis should be the highest value in your table.
- Draw a horizontal (X) axis. This should be divided up into the number of time periods in your table.
- Plot the data from your table in the chart area formed by your Y and X axes.
- Label your Y and X axes with the categories they measure and how they are measured, for example hours, weeks, years.
- Decide on a title for your line chart describing briefly what it shows.

You have gathered and tabulated the following market research data for the company you work for. Your manager has asked you to develop a presentation of no more than four slides summarizing the data using bar graphs and line charts.

For each table decide whether to use a bar graph or a line chart and give reasons for your choice. Then draw these by hand or using a computer spreadsheet. Do not forget to label your axes and to provide titles.

On the fourth slide you must summarize in words the main trends and patterns in your charts and graphs.

Consumer survey: most important product features

Product feature	% of respondents indicating importance	
	Product A	**Product B**
Price	90	80
Quality	75	88
Packaging	35	24
Eco-friendly	53	67

(Sample size = 1000)

Production cost data: average cost per unit

	Product A	**Product B**
Materials	$5	$2
Labour	$20	$12
Marketing	$3	$4
Overheads	$16	$14

Year	Sales revenues $000	
	Product A	Product B
1	100	–
2	105	–
3	113	–
4	107	–
5	105	–
6	110	70
7	117	89
8	121	110
9	125	125
10	131	137
11	127	146
12	125	154
13	121	157
14	115	161
15	112	170

How to draw a pie chart

A pie chart is simply a circle divided up into different segments. The size of the pie represents a total value and each segment or slice therefore represents a proportion of that value. The bigger the slice, the bigger the proportion of the total value it represents.

The pie chart here shows the market shares of mobile telephone operators in India in 2013. Market size was measured by the number of mobile subscribers rather than by total revenue. ➤ **1.3.3**

GSM market shares in India, 2013
(total subscribers 657 million)

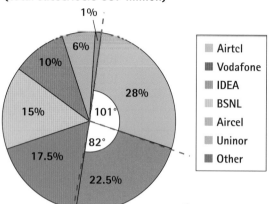

▨	Airtel
▨	Vodafone
▨	IDEA
▨	BSNL
▨	Aircel
▨	Uninor
▨	Other

Airtel was the **market leader**. This meant it had by far the largest share of the total market with 184 million subscribers out of a total of 657 million Indian mobile phone users – a leading market share of 28%. Next was Vodafone with 148 million subscribers – a market share of 22.5%.

As a pie chart is a circle it can be divided up into 360 degrees. Half the pie or 50% of the total represents 180 degrees, one quarter or 25% is 90 degrees, 10% is 36 degrees and so on. In this way, the size or angle of each segment from the centre of the circle can be calculated from data.

In the pie chart, Airtel has a market share of 28%. The size of this share in the pie chart was calculated as:

$$\frac{\text{Subscribers to Airtel}}{\text{Total number of subscribers in India}} = \frac{84 \text{ million}}{657 \text{ million}} = 0.28 \times 360 = 101 \text{ degrees}$$

Similarly, the market share and pie chart segment of Vodafone was calculated as:

$$\frac{\text{Subscribers to Vodafone}}{\text{Total number of subscribers in India}} = \frac{148 \text{ million}}{657 \text{ million}} = 0.225 \times 360 = 82 \text{ degrees}$$

How to draw a pie chart

- Add up all the values you will use to find the total value.
- Divide each value by the total value to calculate proportions.
- Take each proportion and multiply by 360 to obtain numbers of degrees.
- The number of degrees for each proportion represents the size of each segment in the circle.
- Check that the total number of degrees you have calculated adds up to 360.
- Draw a circle and use a protractor to measure and draw each segment.
- Label each segment or use a key.
- Decide on a title for your pie chart describing briefly what it shows.

ACTIVITY 3.11

The following table shows the annual sales of a company making and selling different sizes of T-shirts. Complete the table and produce a pie chart using the number of degrees you have calculated for each size of T-shirt. The first segment has been completed for you.

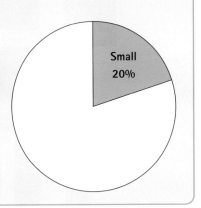

Size of T-shirt	Total volume sold	Proportion of total volume	Number of degrees in pie chart
Small	4000	20%	72
Medium	8000		
Large	5000		
Extra large	3000		
Total	**20 000**	**100%**	**360**

Before you continue make sure you are able to

Appreciate the role of **market research** and the different methods used:

✓ **market-oriented businesses** (uses of market research information to a business)

✓ **primary research** and **secondary research** (benefits and limitations of each)

✓ methods of primary research, for example, postal questionnaire, online survey, interviews, focus groups; and the need for **sampling**

✓ methods of secondary research, for example, online access to government sources, paying for commercial market research reports

✓ factors influencing the accuracy of market research data

Present and analyse simple market research results:

✓ analyse **market research data** shown in the form of graphs, charts and diagrams

✓ draw simple conclusions from such data.

Learning CHECKLIST

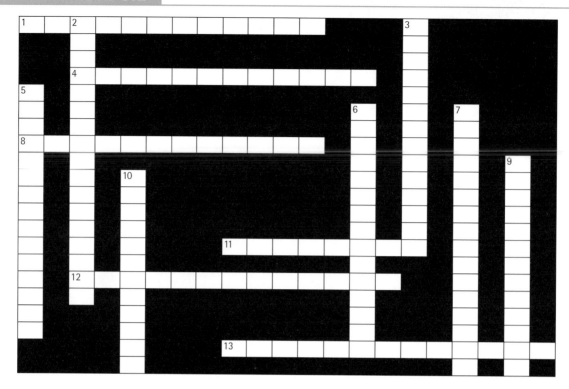

Clues down

2 The process of investigating and gathering market information from existing sources including sales and customer records of the business and articles, databases and reports compiled by other organizations. It may be cheaper and easier to collect than primary research data but it can date quickly and may not reflect the latest trends (9, 8)

3 Choosing consumers to interview or observe as part of a market research survey without discrimination so that each one has an equal chance of being selected (6, 8)

5 Gathering new or original market research data to address the specific information requirements a business has, for example through telephone, postal or online surveys of its customers. The research can be expensive but the data collected will be more up to date and relevant for the business (7, 8)

6 The term used to describe all non-numeric market research information that captures consumers' views and preferences in written or verbal form (11, 4)

7 Market research information in numerical form, such as sales figures and numbers of consumers willing to pay different prices. It can be tabulated or presented in graphical formats for ease of comparison and analysis (12, 4)

9 This method of sampling involves selecting a given number of consumers from each age group, income group or with other pre-defined characteristics, to interview or observe as part of a market research project (5, 8)

10 The term used to describe any inaccuracy in market research data that results from choosing a small group of consumers to interview or survey that is unrepresentative of all other consumers in the target population or market (8, 4)

Clues across

1 This occurs when consumers give false answers to market research questions or if the consumers who complete surveys have views or preferences which are not representative of all other consumers being targeted by the product or marketing strategy of the business (8, 4)

4 A set of questions used for primary market research that consumers are invited to answer via email or immediately following purchases they have made from an online retailer using a "pop up" survey on the retailer's website (6, 6)

8 That business with the largest or dominant share of a given market. It is called this because of its commanding market position (6, 6)

11 It would be impossible or far too costly to interview or survey every consumer from the population of consumers or market targeted by a product or promotion. Instead, a business will select a small group of consumers to research who have views and preferences that are representative of all the others. What is this process called? (8)

12 Another term used to describe a "focus group" of consumers selected to test, compare, discuss and give their opinions on different products, product features and promotions (8, 5)

13 Trying out a product or promotion in one area to examine the impact it has on consumers before it is introduced more widely to other areas (4, 9)

3.3 Marketing mix

3.3.1 Product

- Producing the right product at the right price is vital. A product must meet customer requirements and be sold at a price that consumers are willing and able to pay.

- A poorly designed or unreliable product can damage the reputation of an entire product range and business.

- Good packaging designs not only protect products but can also increase their appeal.

- Creating and advertising a strong brand name and image helps develop brand awareness – the ability of consumers to recall and recognize the brand.

- A brand image can create the impression that a product has particular qualities or characteristics that make it special or unique. In this way, consumers may be persuaded to pay a higher price for the branded product.

- Product life cycle analysis helps a business to plan its marketing strategies. A product's life cycle can be divided into several stages: product development, launch, growth, maturity and, eventually, decline.

- Changes in the marketing mix will usually be required over the life cycle of a product. Extension strategies may be used to boost sales and the profitable life of a mature or declining product, for example by selling it into new markets, adding product variants or developing a new advertising campaign.

- Many product life cycles are becoming shorter due to rapid advances in technology and increasing global market competition. A business will need to manage its product portfolio by introducing new products as old ones mature and decline.

Product benchmarking – comparing rival products so that a firm is able to match or improve on them.

Reverse engineering – taking apart competing products to discover their strengths and weaknesses and how they were made.

Branding – the process of creating distinctive and durable perceptions of a product in the minds of consumers.

Brand name – a name used to identify and distinguish specific goods, services or businesses from others.

Product life cycle – the profile of sales and profitability of a product over its commercial lifespan. It is characterized by a number of different stages starting with product development and launch and ending with maturity and eventual decline.

Extension strategies – marketing methods used to extend sales and the profitable life of a mature product.

Product portfolio – the range of different products produced and marketed by a business at any given point in time.

Products in the marketing mix

Producing the right product at the right price is key

When consumers buy a product, they are attempting to satisfy a wide range of requirements or desires. For example, people buy a new car because they need it for transport but they may also want it to look stylish, incorporate all the latest engine, entertainment and satellite navigation technologies, have low exhaust emissions, be guaranteed against faults and be easy to repair. It is therefore the job of the marketing mix of the car manufacturer to persuade consumers that their car will satisfy all these needs and wants in order to secure their custom.

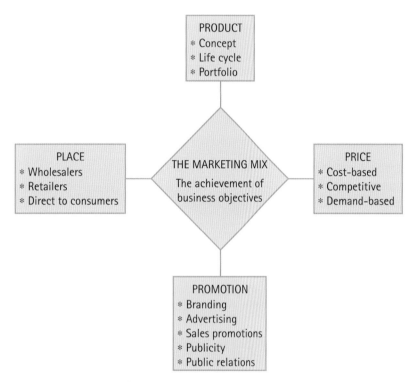

▲ What's in the mix?

The **marketing mix** refers to the combination of different elements that make up the marketing strategy of a business designed to meet or create a consumer want for its product; and it is the role of the marketing department in that business to plan and implement the marketing mix across the whole organization. ➤ **1.3.2**

The key elements of any marketing mix are:

- the product
- the price of the product
- the place or places the product is sold
- the promotions used to make consumers aware of, and want, the product.

A good marketing mix will create sales and customer loyalty but each element must be right if it is to be successful. ➤ **3.1.1**

For any firm, producing the right product at the right price is the first and probably the most important part of its marketing mix.

- The product has to satisfy consumer needs and wants. Price, place of sale and promotions will not be effective if consumers dislike the product or prefer rival products.

- The product needs to be "fit for purpose". This means it must fulfil the role or function intended, perform to the standard required and have features consumers expect. A poorly designed or unreliable product can damage the reputation of an entire product range and organization.

- The cost of producing each item or unit of the product must be below the price consumers are willing and able to pay. If not the business will be unable to make a profit. ➤ **4.2.1**

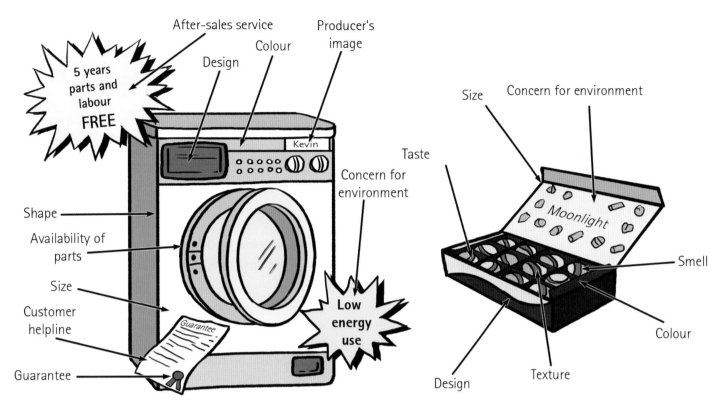

▲ Products are designed with features that will maximize their appeal to consumers

Good packaging not only protects a product but can also increase its appeal

For physical products, good packaging design is also an important part of the marketing mix. Packaging is used to fulfil the following functions.

- It protects the product during transportation and storage. It must therefore be tough enough to withstand knocks and allow products to be stacked one on top of another.

- It has to keep perishable items, such as meat and vegetables, fresh.

- It has to be easy to open and use. For example, a carton or bottle will be ideal for storing and pouring liquids but not toothpastes which are too thick to pour and are therefore packaged in easy-to-squeeze tubes.

- It has to be easy to remove and dispose of. Increasingly firms must design packaging that is biodegradable and keeps waste to a minimum so that it does not create litter and harm the natural environment.

- It can provide important product information including instructions, "use by" dates and lists of ingredients so that consumers can be aware of any substances contained in the product that may be hazardous to them.

- Its design, colour and shape can help to create and reinforce a brand image. For example, an expensive or luxury brand will need attractive and luxurious packaging. In contrast, consumers will only expect plain and simple packaging on low-price, lower-quality products.

- It must comply with relevant laws and regulations, for example giving information on the storage of hazardous materials and chemicals, and must display information about contents and country of manufacture.

Developing a new or improved product can be a source of competitive advantage and boost sales

The development and production of a new or improved product needs careful planning and testing. Once a business has used market research to identify the needs and wants of consumers it can start the process of designing and developing products and product features that will appeal to them. However, it also needs to take account of competing products – how they are designed and what features they offer.

▼ A typical product development flow chart

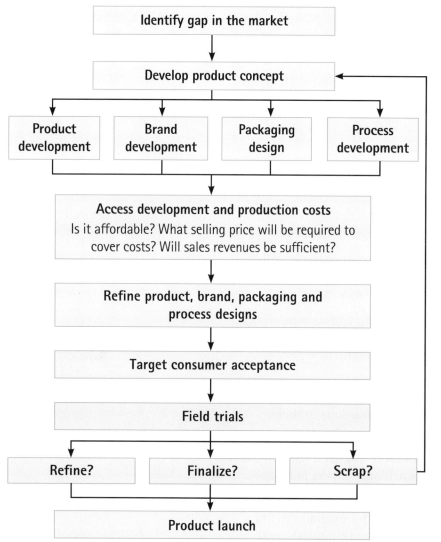

A new or improved product should address a gap in the market and be able to compete with rival products on cost, price and quality. **Product benchmarking** involves comparing rival products so that a firm is able to design a product that matches or improves on them. This process can sometimes involve **reverse engineering**, the taking apart of competing products to discover their strengths and weaknesses and how they were made.

Field trials can be used to test sales potential and consumer reaction before a product is finalized and launched on to a national or international market.

✘ Product development can therefore be a very long and expensive process for some firms and products.

✘ Time, money and effort will be wasted if the product design has to be scrapped because it performs poorly in trials.

✘ Sales and reputation can be lost if the final product fails to meet customer requirements.

However, the product development process has some clear benefits.

✚ Careful planning and testing can reduce the risks of developing a product consumers will not want or need and therefore will not buy.

✚ A new or improved product that addresses a gap in the market will give the firm a competitive advantage over its business rivals.

✚ It can help the business to increase its market share in existing markets or even expand into new markets at home or overseas.

✚ It may extend the product range of the business, thereby increasing its total sales while reducing the impact a fall in demand for any one of its products may have on its performance.

The same stages in the product development process are followed by many firms, regardless of the types of goods or services they produce. However, the amount of time, money and effort spent on each stage will vary. The larger the firm, the larger the target market and the more technically complex the product is, the more involved and costly the development process is likely to be because the risks of getting things wrong are much greater.

Firms produce and sell many different types of product to many different types of consumer. Some, such as machinery and other capital equipment, are made for business customers while others, including different food products, televisions and beauty treatments, are for individuals and households – or the final consumers – to purchase and use.

▼ Different types of products aimed at different groups of consumers

Consumer goods	Services	Capital goods
Durable goods, such as washing machines, DVD players and cars, tend to last a long time. **Non-durable goods** are used up quickly or are perishable, such as many foods and drinks, cosmetics and soaps.	**Consumer services** are personal services such as health care, personal banking, beauty treatment, service in cafés and restaurants. **Producer services** are services for business customers, such as business banking, management consultancy and marketing research.	These are produced for other businesses and include capital equipment such as machinery, ships and lorries. **Semi-finished goods** are materials and component parts used to produce other goods.

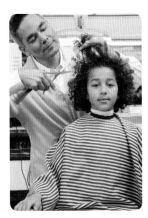

1	Amazon	Retail and consumer electronics
2	Apple	Computing and consumer electronics
3	Google	Internet search engine services
4	Samsung	Conglomerate including consumer electronics
5	Facebook	Online social media and networking services
6	AT&T	Conglomerate including telecommunication services
7	Microsoft	Computer software
8	Verizon	Telecommunication services
9	Walmart	Retail corporation
10	ICBC	Banking service

Brand image and its impact on sales and customer loyalty

Branding is the process of creating distinctive and durable perceptions of a product in the minds of consumers

Few businesses sell direct to consumers. Instead they use intermediaries – other businesses and retailers. So how do they make sure that they get across the right message about the features and benefits of their products? Creating a powerful brand can help do so.

A **brand** is a name used to identify and distinguish a specific good, service or business from others. A successful brand makes the consumers in the target market remember a product when they shop. A brand name can be reinforced with a product slogan, image, packaging, design, logo and significant advertising of key product features such as its energy efficiency or care for the environment.

Essential features of a brand therefore include the following.

- A **brand name** needs to be easily remembered by consumers.
- A **brand image** has to create the impression that the product has particular qualities or characteristics that make it special or unique. In this way, consumers can be persuaded to pay a higher price for the branded product.
- A brand should be able to build and maintain **brand loyalty**. Consumers can be persuaded to continue buying the same brand instead of trying other very similar products because the brand symbolizes quality, status or other desirable aspects they want. ▶ **3.3.4**

Creating and advertising a good brand name and image helps develop **brand awareness** – consumers' ability to recall and recognize the brand. A brand that becomes widely known achieves **brand recognition,** like the ten examples listed here. Some brand names have become so well established they are used to describe a whole range of products regardless of who makes them. For example, the brand name Sellotape is often used to describe all types of semi-transparent adhesive tape from different manufacturers.

Some brands are global. A global brand, like Coca-Cola or Intel, is one that is perceived to reflect the same set of values around the world. Global brands have strong, enduring relationships with consumers across countries and cultures.

ACTIVITY 3.12

For each of these product ranges investigate:

▶ brand names

▶ the images created for each brand

▶ how they are promoted

▶ the types of consumers likely to buy them.

Clothes detergents	Teenage magazines
Canned soft drinks	Petroleum

The product life cycle

Knowledge of a product's life cycle can help businesses plan their marketing strategies to enhance sales and profitability

Each product has its own life cycle. A product is "born", matures and will eventually die out. Many of the products we use today may not be around in five or ten years' time, at least not in their current form. Consumer tastes and technologies are constantly changing and products must change to keep up with them.

Product life cycle analysis helps a business to plan its marketing strategies for the future. A product's life cycle is divided into several stages characterized by the sales revenue and/or profit generated by the product over time.

▼ A typical product life cycle

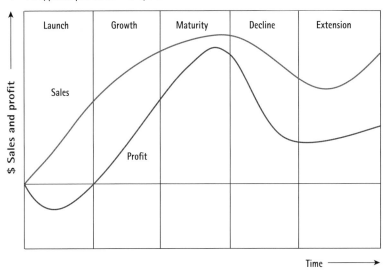

Stage 1: Launch (or Introduction)

The product is introduced to a market. Prices may be set low and significant informative advertising used to encourage consumer acceptance. As a result, the product may make a loss initially. However, it may be possible to price at a premium to recover development costs if the product is novel and there are few competitors. This is called **price skimming**.

Stage 2: Growth

Sales increase. Persuasive advertising is used to boost sales and encourage brand loyalty. Price competition may increase as new businesses enter the market attracted by growing demand and profits.

Stage 3: Maturity

The product becomes established. Growth in sales and profits slows down. Competition with rival products on price and advertising may become intense. At **saturation**, sales and profits peak and no new firms enter the market.

Stage 4: Decline

Changes in tastes and the introduction of new products cause sales and profits to decline. Some businesses may close or leave the market. The product may be withdrawn from some outlets and production may eventually stop.

Stage 5: Extension

The product, pricing and promotional strategies may be redesigned and relaunched to persuade consumers to continue buying the product because it has been improved. Successful extension strategies start well before sales of a product decline.

▼ Marketing objectives and strategies over a product life cycle

	Launch	Growth	Maturity	Decline
Sales	*Low*	*Rising*	*At a peak*	*Falling*
Objective	Increase product awareness	Build brand loyalty and compete effectively	Maintain brand loyalty	Product or business survival
Product	Offer one version	Add new versions	Offer a full product range	Keep best-sellers, scrap the rest
Price and competition	Price low to create sales	Price competitively to build market share as competition increases	Defend market share and profits from competitors	Adjust prices to stay profitable
Place	Use limited outlets	Increase places to buy	Expand methods and places of sale to their maximum	Reduction in number of retailers willing to sell the product
Promotion	Use informative advertising to build awareness	Use persuasive advertising to build brand loyalty	Remind consumers of product qualities	Reduce to a minimum or introduce an extension strategy

The lengths of product life cycles vary. Products with very short-lived life cycles are "fads". Sales of fads rise quickly and then fall away just as rapidly. Past examples have included novelty products such as the Rubik's cube, Tamagotchi and ZhuZhu Pets. In contrast, other products such as the petrol engine car and refrigerator have been around for more than a century in one form or another. They have exhibited a very long and stable maturity phase.

Extension strategies can prolong the profitable life of a product

As a product progresses through its life cycle, changes in the marketing mix will usually be required in order to adjust to different challenges and opportunities.

Product features, prices and promotions can be modified to extend the sales and profitable life of a product, sometimes again and again. Brands such as Coca-Cola, Ford and Kellogg's have successfully done this for more than a century to retain their market positions.

Extension strategies are designed to boost sales and the profitable life of a product. Possible extension strategies might include:

- introducing product line extensions, for example new flavours of ice cream
- using a new advertising campaign
- selling the product into new markets, possibly overseas
- introducing a new, improved version of the product
- selling the product through additional retail outlets and online
- adding services such as longer warranty periods and free delivery.

Look at the two line graphs below.

▸ What evidence is there that products have life cycles?

▸ Which products are in their growth phase and which are in decline in the graphs?

▸ What impact do you think the introduction of mobile phones and Skype will have had on the sales trends in the first graph?

▸ How do you think the second graph will look in another ten years from now?

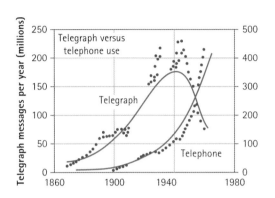

Source: *New Scientist*, 6 February 1983

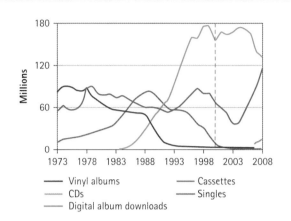

Source: *UK Social Trends*, 2010

Businesses can manage their product portfolio to ensure that new product developments replace mature and declining products

Product life cycles are, on average, becoming shorter. For example, in consumer electronics, new models of flat-screen televisions, high-definition camcorders and Blu-ray disc players are being launched every six months or so. They have rapidly replaced conventional televisions, digital tape video recorders and DVD players. Shortening product life cycles are due to rapid advances in technology and increasing global market competition. In turn, these are fuelling more rapid changes in consumer preferences.

Since product life cycles are shortening, many modern organizations produce more than one product and operate in more than one market. **Diversification** into other products and markets helps reduce the risk of business failure caused by falling consumer demand for any one product. A business can do this by introducing new products as old ones mature and decline. The **product portfolio** of a business includes the range of products, sizes, brands and types of packaging it offers.

However, there are many examples of brand or line extension strategies that have not worked because businesses have failed to take account of consumer preferences and the impact the introduction of new products could have on their brand image. For example, when Colgate, best known for its range of toothpastes, tried to extend its brand to a range of food products called Colgate's Kitchen Entrees, not only did the move fail to attract customer attention it also reduced sales of its core toothpaste products. Because of the strength of the Colgate toothpaste brand consumers found it difficult to associate something used to clean their teeth with something tasty they could eat.

Dabur, one of the largest consumer goods companies in India, is very aware that getting the right product to the right consumers is the difference between business success and failure. It has business units in health care, personal use and food products and over time has developed five powerful product ranges and brand names that are now recognized in over 50 countries.

▼ Dabur's brands

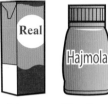

| Juices | Digestive supplements | Health care | Personal use | Hair care |

Dabur has recently extended its product line for juices following market research, segmentation and consumer trend analyses. The extension strategy consists of the following new products.

- Coolers (low fruit content)
- Real (high fruit pulp content)
- Real ACTIV (health-conscious market)
- Real Juniors (for children less than 6 years of age)
- Real Schoolpacks (for schoolchildren)

A range of new flavours, cartons and bottle sizes were also introduced to widen product appeal. Dabur products originally appealed primarily to older groups of consumers and sales growth was slowing down. The objectives of its extension strategy were therefore to expand sales by targeting new market segments (notably the expanding youth and health-conscious consumer markets, plus schoolchildren and young mothers), renew interest in the brand and increase market share.

The extension strategy was reinforced with a price-cutting strategy to boost demand, a growth strategy that extended the sale and distribution of Dabur products to overseas markets and a promotional strategy that used the growing popularity of Indian films at home and overseas and product endorsements by a well-known Indian cricketer and his wife.

ACTIVITY 3.14

Draw a product life cycle chart and place the following products at the appropriate stage. Give reasons for your answers.

- Cinemas
- Electric cars
- Virtual reality headsets
- 3D Smart TVs with internet connection
- Film streaming services
- Diesel cars

Learning CHECKLIST

Before you continue make sure you are able to

Demonstrate an understanding of **brands** and the **product life cycle**:

✓ the costs and benefits of developing new products

✓ **brand image** – impact on sales and **customer loyalty**

✓ the role of **packaging**

✓ the **product life cycle** – main stages and **extension strategies**

✓ draw and interpret a product life cycle diagram

✓ how stages of the product life cycle can influence marketing decisions, for example promotion and pricing decisions.

3.3.2 Price

- The costs of production, degree of competition and strength of consumer demand must be taken into account by a business in its pricing decisions.

- The objective of cost-plus pricing is to cover production costs and earn a good profit margin. However, this does not take into account what consumers may or may not be willing to pay or how much competition there is to supply the market.

- Competitive pricing strategies are used to deter new competition, defend market share or help a business to survive. Destruction pricing involves deep cuts in prices, often below costs, in order to "destroy" the sales of a new or existing competitor.

- Demand-based pricing strategies take account of what consumers are willing to pay in order to build sales and market share.

- A high price skimming strategy may be used for a new advanced or novel product that faces little or no competition following product launch. Alternatively, a low penetration pricing strategy may be used to build sales of a new product in a highly competitive market.

- Knowledge of the price elasticity of demand for different products can help a business predict what is likely to happen to consumer demand and total sales revenue following a change in the price of its goods or services.

- Cutting prices when demand is price inelastic reduces revenue, while cutting the prices of products for which demand is price elastic increases revenue.

Business BUZZWORDS

Cost-plus pricing – adding a mark-up for profit over the average cost of producing a product.

Destruction pricing – cutting price, sometimes below costs, to force a rival out of business.

Price war – intense price competition between rival businesses.

Price skimming – setting the initial price high at product launch in order maximize profits in the short run when there is little or no competition.

Penetration pricing – setting price low at product launch to encourage sales and consumer acceptance of the new product.

Promotional pricing – reducing the price of a product for a short period of time to boost sales, for example to sell off old and unwanted inventory.

Psychological pricing – using prices to influence consumer perceptions of a product.

Price elasticity of demand – the responsiveness of consumer demand to a change in price.

Price elastic demand – when a small change in price causes a significant change in demand.

Price inelastic demand – when a change in price causes only a modest change in demand.

The pricing decision

The strength of consumer demand, the degree of competition and the costs of production must be taken into account when setting prices

Setting the price of a good or service is a difficult decision. For example, when Apple announced a steep price cut for its new iPhone just 10 weeks after it was launched it angered many of the early adopters who had bought their handsets at a premium price shortly after it came on the market. This anger could mean future new product launches may not attract so many consumers who may instead wait for prices to be cut.

If a business sets the price of a product too high consumers may be unwilling to buy the product. If on the other hand the price is set too low, it may not cover its costs of production. Setting the right price for a product is therefore an important element of the marketing mix.

A business must also be careful to choose a price that complements other parts of its marketing mix. If a business creates a high-quality, luxury product and brand image but sets the price too low, consumers may not believe the product is as good as it is supposed to be and may be unwilling to buy it. Similarly, a brand associated with value for money should have a low price.

The amount of competition in a market is also a major factor in price setting. If there is a lot of competition, prices need to be low enough to compete with rival products. If there are no or very few alternative products to buy, the business may be able to charge consumers a higher price without losing sales.

The three major factors that therefore influence the pricing decisions of different firms are:

- the costs of production and level of profit required
- the amount of competition from rival producers to supply a market
- the level and strength of consumer demand.

▼ Influences on the pricing decision

What price?

Bargain! $1.50 Only $10 $99.95 $275

Constraints on the pricing decision

Market conditions
What are consumers willing to pay?
Can advertising be used to increase product image and price?
Is the product sold into a mass market or niche market?

Taxes and subsidies
Value added tax (VAT) and customs and excise duties raise product prices
Government subsidies will allow producers to lower prices

Production costs
Price must cover costs
In the short run, price must cover variable costs
In the long run, price must also cover fixed costs otherwise the firm will close

Business objectives
Maximize profits or maximize sales?
Increase market share?

Marketing structure
How fierce is competition from rival firms?
What prices are rival firms charging?

Marketing mix
What stage is the product at in its life cycle?
How is the product being promoted?
Where is the product to be sold? For example, supermarkets sell low-price items to mass market

Costs, sales and the degree of competition vary over a product's life cycle, so pricing strategies also need to change over time. In the early stages of product launch and growth, prices may have to be set low to build sales and fight off competition, but this can cause a business to lose money. In the longer term, a business must be able to recover its costs if it is to make a profit and survive.

Governments can also affect the prices consumers finally pay for different products in shops and online. Any duties or taxes added to the prices of goods or services raise their final retail prices. In contrast, any subsidies paid to producers to offset their total costs allow them to lower the prices they charge for their products. ➤ **6.1.1**

Pricing methods

Cost-plus pricing involves adding a margin for profit to the cost of producing each item

If a business is to survive in the long run it must be able to cover its costs of production and earn a profit. If revenues fail to match costs a business will make a loss.

The objective of **cost-based pricing** strategies is to cover production costs and earn a good profit margin. It involves calculating the average cost of producing each item or unit of output, and then adding a mark-up for profit. ➤ **4.2.1**

For example, if a firm produces 10 000 packets of biscuits at a total cost of $10 000, the average cost per packet is $1. A 40% mark-up for profit will mean each packet is priced for sale at $1.40.

The calculation is as follows:

$$\text{Selling price per unit} = \left[\frac{\text{Total cost}}{\text{Total output}}\right] + \% \text{ mark-up for profit}$$

The difference between the price at which an item is sold and its cost of production is called its **profit margin**.

The main problem with cost-plus pricing is that it is does not take into account what price consumers may or may not be willing to pay or how much competition there is.

In the example above, if consumers are only willing to pay $1.20 for a packet of biscuits or if competing brands of biscuits are all priced at less than $1.20 then a 40% mark-up would not be very sensible.

Competitive pricing methods can be used to protect a business from new competition and defend market share

In markets where there is fierce competition between rival businesses for sales and market share, firms often adopt competitive pricing strategies. Competitive pricing strategies can be used to deter new competition, defend market share or protect a business from closure. These strategies usually involve setting prices the same as or just below the prices of rival products.

Price war heats up in New Zealand telecoms

2degrees launched an aggressive calling plan yesterday that will challenge the prices of Vodafone and Telecom.

The mobile carrier has dropped the cost of calls between networks by nearly a third, in a bid to increase its market share.

Indian telecom market crowded by new entrants

Uninor, controlled by Norwegian telecom company Telenor, is the 14th player to enter India's cellular market.

But after soaring growth in customer numbers to almost 17 million, industry revenues are flattening as rivals slug it out in a savage price battle.

For example, when existing electricity supplier Airtricity in Ireland announced it would also start supplying gas, it said it would undercut the prices of the established gas supplier, Bord Gáis, by 10%, saving the average family up to €200 a year. There are many other similar examples of destruction pricing strategies, especially in mobile telecommunications markets around the world, that have seen both consumer demand and the number of competing suppliers expand rapidly.

- **Destruction pricing** involves deep cuts in prices, often below costs, in order to "destroy" the sales of a new or existing competitor and force it to make losses. If a business is successful at removing the competition it can then raise its prices again and recover its losses.

- **Price wars** may develop in markets that are very competitive if one or more businesses cut their prices or if the market shares of established businesses are threatened by a new entrant. Prices may be cut drastically to force the new business out of the market.

Price wars involve competing firms continually trying to undercut each others' prices. They occur frequently but are not popular because all businesses usually end up losing money by trying to out-compete each other on price. Therefore, to avoid price wars, competing firms often set their prices to be the same and instead focus on product design, promotions and other forms of non-price competition to compete for sales and market share.

▲ Competitive pricing strategies

ACTIVITY 3.15

Read the article below then answer these questions.

- What is a price war?

- What motives do you think P&G had for cutting its prices?

- What impact has the price war had on the profits of the two companies?

- What is a "product portfolio"?

- Explain why Hindustan Unilever's "much larger size, market share and product portfolio should enable it to continue aggressive pricing strategies more than the smaller P&G".

- What other pricing strategies could the two companies have used to avoid a price war?

Will Hindustan Unilever tide over price war?

Shares in Hindustan Unilever have fallen in price amid concerns about a renewed price war emerging in the detergents category.

The previous such turf war in 2004 had led to profit margins for both main players taking a substantial hit, though Hindustan Unilever (HUL) did manage to hold on to its market share by matching Procter & Gamble's (P&G) moves.

The renewed concerns about a price war with HUL's arch rival P&G have been triggered by a series of events. Selling prices of detergents in the mass market category have been heading down for several months now but the battle for market share entered a fresh chapter recently with aggressive television advertisements pitting HUL's Rin brand against P&G's Tide Naturals.

Reports now suggest that P&G has increased volumes for its Tide Naturals by 25%, without changing prices. This translates into a 20% reduction in effective prices for the brand.

HUL's much larger size, market share and product portfolio should enable it to continue aggressive pricing strategies more than the smaller P&G. This suggests that the company may be able to eventually ward off this new threat to its market share. However, for investors in HUL this could mean lower prices and profits in one of HUL's key product categories for some time to come.

Demand-based pricing methods set prices to promote products and penetrate new markets

A market-oriented business uses market research to find out what consumers are willing and able to pay for a product. Demand-based pricing strategies therefore involve setting prices at "what the market will bear". This means setting prices according to how much consumers are willing to pay. Producers therefore tend to price high when consumer demand is high and price low when consumer demand is weak.

- **Price skimming** is a pricing strategy that is often used when there is little competition in a market for a new or improved product. It involves charging a high price to recover development costs and to yield a high initial profit from those consumers who are willing to pay more because the product is new or unique. As rival products are introduced, prices are lowered to increase sales and to protect market share.

Price skimming is a strategy often observed in the market for new technologically advanced products such as computers, televisions and music and video disc players. For example, the first large flat-screen televisions, DVD players and more recently high-definition Blu-ray disc players launched on to the consumer electronics market were priced very high. Some consumers were willing to pay these high prices because they wanted to be the first to purchase the new advanced products. These consumers are known as early adopters.

- **Penetration pricing** involves setting prices low to encourage consumers to try a new product in order to build sales and product loyalty. In this way, a new product is able to "penetrate" a market. It is an important strategy if the product and the business organization are new and if there are already well-established rival products in the market.

However, penetration pricing can also be used to boost sales of existing products that have so far failed to attract much consumer attention. For example, World of Goo was a computer game that had already been available in retail outlets and online for over a year at a price of $20. The producers of the game, Ron Carmel and Kyle Gabler, were looking for a way to promote the one-year anniversary of their World of Goo game and decided to allow consumers one week to download the game online and pay whatever they wanted to.

The strategy was an extreme version of penetration pricing and Gabler was cautious about its likely success. However, he need not have worried. At the start of the experiment "there were many one cent payments and it was really discouraging watching them come in, but then some people actually paid more and it made up for the people who got the game almost for free," Gabler said.

In the first week, World of Goo made $100 000 with roughly 50 000 purchases, at an average payment of about $2 per purchase. The pricing strategy was such a success, the duo decided to extend the sale a second week, during which they sold an additional 33 000 copies.

However, penetration pricing can be a high-risk strategy and only large businesses may be able to afford to do it. It may involve setting a price below the average cost of producing each product so a business makes a loss. If sales do not increase rapidly the business may not be able to survive.

Further, in markets that are very competitive, penetration pricing by a new business could start a **price war** with rival firms.

- **Psychological pricing** strategies recognize that consumers use price as an indicator of product value and quality. Prices can therefore influence consumer perceptions of different products.

  For example, charging a very high price for an attractive product such as a sports car, expensive jewellery or a designer handbag may appeal to consumers who are "ego-sensitive" and want to purchase the product because it is a symbol of wealth and status.

  In contrast, supermarkets may mark up products that are bought on a regular basis and then offer them at a significant discount so that consumers think they are getting good value for money.

  Another use of psychological pricing is in price-ending numbers. For example, research has shown that consumers will prefer to pay $9.99 for a product rather than $10 because $9.99 appears to be cheaper than it clearly is.

- **Promotional pricing** involves setting prices low for a short period of time in order to boost sales. The strategy is often used to renew consumer interest in a product if sales are declining and to sell off old and unwanted items to reduce inventories and free up storage space for new product lines.

  For example, summer clothes are often sold off cheaply towards the end of summer to make way for new winter clothing. Similarly, as manufacturers release new and more advanced televisions, mobile phones and tablet computers, the prices of the older models they will replace are often discounted heavily to sell them off, even if they are sold at a loss. This is because the loss would be even greater if they were not sold and had to be scrapped or given away instead.

  Price discounts offered during sales and "buy one, get one free" (BOGOF) offers are examples of promotional pricing strategies.

▲ Promotional pricing

- **Dynamic pricing** is a pricing strategy in which businesses charge different and highly flexible prices for their goods or services to different market segments depending on current demand conditions. It is a common practice in the travel, sports and entertainment industries where it is used to make sure all seats on flights, or at football matches and concerts, are filled. For example, tickets for a flight or concert may be priced high initially and then, if they fail to sell quickly, their prices are reduced gradually to encourage the rest to sell. This is why some flights, holidays and theatre tickets can be bought for very low "bargain" prices just hours or days before they are due to take place.

▲ Dynamic pricing is often used by airlines to ensure as many seats as possible are sold on each flight

Some flight destinations and times are also more popular than others and so prices also differ by route and by time of day, week or year. Flights during summer holidays and at weekends therefore tend to be priced at a premium compared to flights at other times. In some cases, prices may start relatively low and then rise quickly if seats prove popular and sell out rapidly.

However, charging very different prices for similar products and changing them too frequently can be expensive for a firm and may aggravate consumers who spend a lot of time searching for the best prices.

Pricing strategy	Benefits	Limitations
Cost-plus	✓ Ensures all costs are covered and a profit made ✓ Easy to calculate ✓ Easy to see if costs rise and to take action to keep costs down	✗ Does not take into account the price that customers are willing to pay ✗ Does not take account of competitor prices ✗ Can result in overpricing when adding a percentage for desired profit
Competitive	✓ Ensures that the business can compete on price ✓ Price comparison websites show that consumers can be price sensitive so this pricing strategy will help increase sales ✓ Business can make sure that the price is not too low as well as too high for the market	✗ Price may not cover all the costs of production ✗ Some consumers are not price sensitive e.g. luxury goods. They often take price as a signal of quality. So may lose some loyal customers ✗ Competitors may not have priced their products correctly ✗ Can start a price war where some businesses will be forced out of the business
Penetration	✓ Can quickly build up a customer base ✓ Fast growth in sales for new products ✓ Can take market share from competitors ✓ Forces the business to keep costs low to sustain a low price ✓ May force other firms out of the market	✗ Business is sacrificing profit in the initial launch stage of the product ✗ If the product goes into decline too quickly the business cannot increase price later ✗ May only attract customers looking for cheap products rather than building a customer base

Skimming	✓ Ensures a high profit yield	✗ May not be successful in a very competitive market
	✓ The business is able to recover research and development costs	✗ Some countries have strict regulations regarding consumer rights. This may be seen as exploiting the consumer
	✓ Will attract customers who equate a high price with quality	✗ If a business regularly introduces new products using this pricing method, then consumers will become used to it. Many will wait for the price to fall
	✓ Takes advantage of the higher prices early adopters are willing to pay	
Promotional	✓ Increases sales of the product	✗ Business sacrifices profit in order to boost sales
	✓ Helps expand the customer base by attracting new customers	✗ Business may even make a loss if price does not cover costs
	✓ Gets the buyer to "buy now" rather than wait	✗ Competitors might also launch a promotional pricing strategy and start a price war
	✓ Can take market share away from competitors	✗ May only attract customers who look for bargains rather than those who might continue to buy

ACTIVITY 3.16

What pricing methods would you advise using for the products in the following market conditions? Give reasons for your choice in each case.

A new consumer hi-tech 3D camera, the first of its kind, has been launched

An established mobile phone company with the largest share of the Chinese market faces competition from a new smaller rival offering an exciting new range of phones and call charges

A major supermarket chain has introduced a new value brand range covering food, cosmetics and cleaning products

A new eco-friendly washing-up liquid is launched in a highly competitive market in which many brands compete for market share

A Paris fashion house has introduced a new designer watch collection aimed at the "rich, famous and glamorous"

The significance of price elasticity

Firms want to know how responsive consumer demand and sales revenue are to changes in price

When Sony announced it was cutting the price of its PlayStation 3 computer games console by 25% to $299 it expected sales of the console to increase by between 40% and 60%.

However, when Tesco Ireland announced its annual sales revenues fell by 7.5% to just under €2.9 billion, the supermarket giant said competitive price cuts of up to 20% were the main reason. Lower prices had, however, led to an increase in the volume of sales and the number of people in its stores.

Firms want to predict what is likely to happen to consumer demand and their total sales revenue when they change the price of their goods or services. How demand and revenue respond to a change in price depends on the price elasticity of demand for a product.

Price elasticity of demand is the responsiveness of consumer demand to a change in price.

In the example below, a passenger train company has increased its peak and off-peak rail fares for travel to and from the city. Consumer demand for rail travel is high during peak periods at the start and end of each working day because people want to travel to and from their places of work in the city. This is because there are few alternatives or substitutes. Journeys by bus or car into the city take too long and car parking charges are high. As a result, passenger numbers fall only slightly following the increase in the peak rail fare from $4 per journey to $5 and total fare revenues rise from $400 to $475 per day.

In contrast, the rise in off-peak fares from $2 to $2.50 per journey has caused a significant drop in passenger numbers and total fare revenue has fallen from $120 to $100. This is because off-peak passengers may decide to spend their leisure time doing something else or will travel into the city by car or bus instead because the roads are not so busy at off-peak times.

> The $299 price point is important to get to a point where the next segment of price-conscious consumers can jump into the market and it will most certainly re-energize sales of the platform.

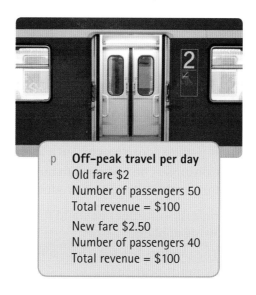

p **Peak travel per day**
Old fare $4
Number of passengers 100
Total revenue = $400

New fare $5
Number of passengers 95
Total revenue = $475

p **Off-peak travel per day**
Old fare $2
Number of passengers 50
Total revenue = $100

New fare $2.50
Number of passengers 40
Total revenue = $100

In this example, passenger demand for off-peak travel is price elastic while demand for peak travel is price inelastic.

- If a small increase in the price of a product causes demand and total sales revenue to fall significantly then consumer demand for that product is **price elastic**. That is, demand is very sensitive, or responsive, to changes in price.

  Similarly, demand and sales revenue will increase significantly following a cut in price if demand for the product is price elastic.

- In contrast, if a small increase in the price of a product causes only a minor decrease in consumer demand for that product then consumer demand is **price inelastic**. As a result, total sales revenue will increase.

  It follows that if consumer demand is price inelastic there will only be a relatively small increase in demand for a product following a cut in its price so, as a result, total sales revenue will fall.

Knowledge about the price elasticity of demand for its products therefore helps a business determine the right pricing strategies. Cutting prices of products for which demand is price inelastic will lose revenue, while cutting the prices of products for which demand is price elastic will boost total sales and increase revenue.

ACTIVITY 3.17

Here is a problem to stretch you. Assume the prices of the following products all increase by 10%. Copy and complete the following table by stating whether or not you think there will be a large or small fall in consumer demand for each product as a result of the price rise, what is likely to happen to sales revenue, whether consumer demand is price elastic or inelastic, and why.

Product	Will the change in demand be large or small?	Will sales revenue rise or fall?	Is demand price elastic or inelastic?	Reasons for the price elasticity of demand
Bread A washing detergent Newspapers Large flat-screen televisions Boxes of matches Luxury holidays Electric power				

Consumer demand for a product tends to be **price elastic** if the following applies.

- The product has many close substitutes consumers can buy instead if price rises, for example different types of washing detergents.
- It is an expensive item, such as many luxury goods.
- Consumers do not need to buy it frequently, so they have time to search for suitable alternative products if price rises.

In contrast, consumer demand for a product tends to be **price inelastic** if the following applies.

- The product has few close substitutes, for example travel into city centres by rail at peak times.
- It is a low-cost item, such as a box of matches or a newspaper.
- It is a necessity that consumers need to purchase regularly, such as many basic food items and electricity.

Modest rise in sales of *Daily Star* after price cut

The decision to slash the price of the *Daily Star* newspaper by 50% helped to boost month on month sales of the tabloid newspaper by 0.27% to 864 315 copies.

A study by health economists in Japan found that the price elasticity of demand for influenza vaccinations was highly inelastic nationally.

In contrast, a study of Australian livestock grazing industries found demand for beef, lamb and pork was highly price elastic.

Toyota sales surge after slashing prices

The world's biggest car maker saw US sales of its vehicles rise by 41% in March from a year earlier, having fallen 16% year on year in January and 9% in February.

Toyota attributed this increase in sales to providing buyers with discounts of up to $2250 a vehicle last month. The price incentives, including interest-free loans and discount leases, were worth an average of 10% on each new vehicle.

1   What is meant by "price elasticity of demand"?

2   Why do you think demand for influenza vaccinations was "highly price inelastic" and demand for meats was "highly price elastic"?

3   From the articles, what types of pricing strategy do you think the *Daily Star* newspaper and Toyota cars have used? For which product do you think consumer demand is more price elastic and why?

PRoCam manufactures professional cameras. Some of its products are in the maturity stage of their product life cycle. The market for professional cameras is becoming very competitive. The management team know that sales depend on the right marketing mix decisions. The marketing manager believes that the demand for professional cameras is price elastic. The table below gives some data about PRoCam.

PRoCam sales data (last financial year)	
Sales volume (units)	500
Sales revenues ($000)	4 000

The total market value of camera sales in the last financial year was $20 million.

a   Calculate for PRoCam:
  (i)   the unit selling price   [2]
  (ii) its market share.   [2]

b   Draw and label the stages of a typical product life cycle.   [4]

c   Identify and explain how **two** elements of a marketing mix, other than price, might help the sales of PRoCam products.   [6]

d   Do you think that the marketing manager should increase the price of the company's cameras? Justify your answer.   [6]

Before you continue make sure you are able to

Understand how pricing decisions are made:

✓   **pricing methods – cost-plus, competitive, penetration, skimming** and **promotional**; their benefits and limitations

✓   recommend and justify an appropriate pricing method in given circumstances

✓   understand the significance of **price elasticity** – the difference between **price elastic demand** and **price inelastic demand**; the importance of the concept in pricing decisions.

Learning CHECKLIST

3.3.3 Place–distribution channels

▶ **Distribution** involves getting the right product to the right consumers, in the right place, in the right quantities and at the right time, as quickly and as cheaply as possible.

▶ Some producers sell their products direct to their final customers. This can be done in a number of ways, for example through retail outlets owned by the producer, via mail order or telesales. E-commerce using the internet has increased direct selling.

▶ Alternatively, producers can distribute their products through intermediaries such as retailers, wholesalers or agents. Intermediaries can also help promote goods at their point of sale.

▶ Without intermediaries, manufacturers will need to sell their products direct to customers. This will increase their costs of administration and employing sales staff.

▶ Wholesalers buy in bulk and break up the bulk to sell small quantities to retailers. Many small retailers may be unable or unwilling to buy in bulk because they do not have enough storage space. Also, many food items will perish if they cannot be sold quickly.

▶ Many manufacturers and large retailers have developed their own warehousing and distribution systems in order to speed up delivery times and capture the extra profit that would otherwise be earned by a wholesaler.

▶ There is increasing competition between producers to reduce delivery lead times. Businesses therefore need to balance the cost and speed of different methods of transporting goods in their distribution decisions.

Business BUZZWORDS

Logistics – the science of moving things, including managing inventories, transportation and distribution systems.

Distribution channel – the people and organizations involved in the physical movement and the transfer of goods and services from producers to consumers.

Retailer – a business organization specializing in the sale of products to consumers.

Wholesaler – an intermediary that buys and stores products in bulk from producers and sells small quantities to retailers.

Delivery lead time – the time lag between placing an order for a product and its delivery.

Distribution channels

Getting the right products to the right place of sale and at the right time needs careful planning

After developing a product and deciding on the right pricing and promotional strategies a business must then get the product to the consumer. An organization can spend a great deal of time and money on developing and promoting a product, but if it is not in the right place at the right time for consumers to buy, all this money and effort will have been wasted. For example, if fresh vegetables are not delivered to shops and consumers quickly they may perish and cannot be sold. The objective of distribution is to make sure this, and similar problems, do not happen.

Global fashion company Zara manufactures, distributes and sells all its own clothes using its own fleet of vehicles and through its own retail outlets across the globe. A key part of Zara's overall marketing strategy is to rapidly introduce new clothing lines and have them on sale within its stores for only four weeks until they are replaced. To do this the company controls all aspects of its distribution channel from its manufacturing plants through to the final consumer. This enables the company to distribute its new clothes to its retail stores quickly and cheaply to meet its marketing objectives.

In contrast, the Danone Group, owner of the Evian brand, a bottled mineral water from France, uses the services of other companies to manage the marketing, bottling, sales and distribution of its water all over the world. Evian is marketed as a luxury and expensive bottled water that is sold through a wide range of different food retailers, hotels, health clubs and spas, restaurants and many other points of sale all over the world. For example, Coca-Cola, which already has a huge bottling and distribution network of its own, distributes Evian in the US and Canada while marketing, sales and distribution of the brand is handled by specialist drinks distributor Narangs Hospitality Services Pvt Ltd in India.

Using established local distribution companies means Danone does not have to deal direct with retailers and other sellers in different countries or invest in local distribution networks, warehouses and vehicle fleets of its own.

Distribution is often considered to be the final part of the marketing mix. It can be very expensive so it requires careful business planning and management. Firms need to consider physical storage and transportation methods, the places consumers want to buy products and the ways in which they want to buy and receive their products.

The method of distribution and the image and quality of the place of sale can all affect consumers' buying behaviour. For example, consumers may be unwilling to buy an expensive bed online direct from a manufacturer without first being able to test how comfortable it is. Similarly, a clothes shop in a run-down area of a town is unlikely to attract consumers who want to buy luxury designer clothes.

Consumers may also be persuaded to buy a rival product if the product they really want is difficult to obtain, either because it is out of stock at many shops and online stores or if it is only sold through a handful of outlets many miles away which do not offer home delivery.

Effective logistics

Logistics is the science of moving things. Effective logistics in business is therefore about managing the process of distribution so that the right product gets to the right consumers, in the right place, in the right quantities and at the right time as quickly and as cheaply as possible.

Logistics therefore involves:

- managing inventories
- controlling the availability of goods and services
- improving the speed and lowering the cost of deliveries
- identifying the best channels of distribution to consumers.

There are many distribution channels to consumers; a producer may sell direct or through intermediaries including wholesalers and retailers

Businesses must decide how to get their products to consumers. A **distribution channel** includes all the people and organizations involved in the physical movement of a good or service from producer to consumer. The main channels of distribution are shown in the diagram below.

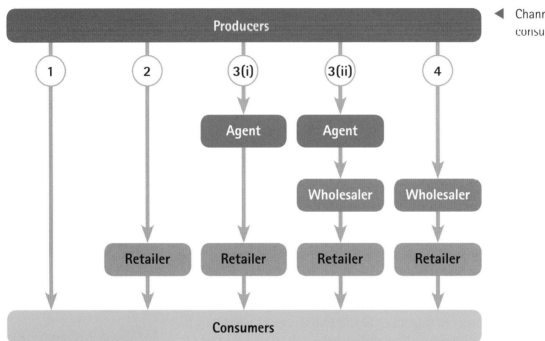

◀ Channels of distribution to consumers

Distribution 1: direct from the producer to the customer

Like Zara, some producers sell their products direct to their final consumers. This can be done in a number of ways, for example through retail outlets owned by the producer, via mail order or telesales direct from the producer or over the internet using the producer's website. The increase in e-commerce has allowed many more producers today to sell direct to consumers, thereby cutting out the cost of distribution through wholesalers and retailers.

To guarantee that shops stock their products some producers own their own retail outlets. For example, many car manufacturers own their own car showrooms to sell their cars. Similarly, many farms have farm shops. If farmers are unable to get their produce quickly to consumers it may perish.

Personal services are usually sold and delivered direct to people, such as hairdressing, restaurant meals and made-to-measure suits.

Firms selling specialized capital equipment and component parts to other businesses also often use this channel of distribution.

Advantages of selling direct to the customer	Disadvantages of selling direct to the customer
+ The business retains full control of the distribution channel. + The business can build a close relationship with its customers. This is especially useful when designing and selling highly specialized equipment and other products to business customers. + Distribution costs are lower than if a wholesaler or retailer had been used, because these businesses add an additional mark-up to the price to cover their own costs and earn a profit. + A business can advertise and sell its products online or via mail order. + This is an effective way of selling and delivering services.	✗ Bulk products will be expensive to transport if customers are located far away from the factory, farm or centre of distribution. ✗ The investment required to own and operate a distribution system, including warehouses and vehicles, is high and may only be suitable for very large businesses. ✗ While online and mail order methods can be used to sell small products to large numbers of customers in different locations, the costs of sending them by post or courier can be high.

Distribution channel 2: indirect through a retailer

A retailer is a business organization that specializes in selling products to consumers. Most retailers own shops or retail outlets and buy products from a variety of different producers. For example, high street clothes shops stock a range of different clothing brands from different manufacturers. Similarly, large supermarkets stock a wide variety of food and drink products from farms and food processing plants all over the world.

However, some small shops may only stock the products of one manufacturer. For example, they may have the exclusive right to stock expensive designer furniture, artworks or jewellery for sale to niche markets. ➤ **3.1.3**

Retailers may buy products direct from a producer or from a wholesaler or an agent. They can also help promote goods at their points of sale. However, they can add their own mark-up to the prices they will charge their customers to cover their running costs and earn a profit.

Advantages of selling through a retailer	Disadvantages of selling through a retailer
+ A business can sell large quantities to major retailers. + Some large retailers with stores in multiple locations can operate their own distribution systems saving the business significant distribution costs. + Retailers can help promote goods at their point of sale.	✗ The business has no control over the final sale of the product to customers. ✗ The business has no relationship with the final consumers of its product. ✗ The final selling price of the product may be higher because the retailer will want to sell it at a price that covers its costs. As a result, sales of the product may be lower than they might otherwise have been.

Place of sale: types of retail outlet

Supermarket	A large self-service grocery store that sells food and household goods. Some large supermarkets are multiples and offer their own brands in addition to others.
Hypermarket	A large self-service superstore, often outside of a town, that combines a supermarket and department store to sell a huge range of different products.
Discount store	A low-price store that tends to buy up the unsold stock of other organizations and sell it at a substantial discount.
Department store	A large city centre shop, generally multi-storey, offering a wide range of products including cosmetics, clothes, furniture and electronics.
Boutique	A small, single outlet offering a specialist range of clothing or other merchandise serving niche markets.
Multiples	Retail outlets owned by the same organization that specialize in the sale of a narrow range of products, such as clothes, footwear, books or stationery.
Independent store	A specialist such as a greengrocer, baker, fish shop or delicatessen, or a large family-owned general grocery store which typically operates as a sole trader.
Factory outlet	A farm or factory shop selling the farm or factory products direct to consumers. Factory outlets often sell mass-produced clothing and footwear at discount prices.
Non-store retail	This includes online selling, telephone selling, catalogue mail order, door-to-door sales, television shopping and vending machines.

Distribution channel 3: indirect through an agent

Sometimes a producer may use the services of an agent to sell its products. For example, travel agents sell holidays on behalf of tour operators. They earn a commission on every holiday they sell.

Manufacturers often use an agent when they are selling goods overseas. Agents based in other countries have local knowledge and language skills they can use to sell the products of the manufacturer in return for sales commission or even a share of profits. ➤ **3.4.3**

Using an agent reduces the need for a business to employ its own specialist sales staff.

Advantages of using an agent	Disadvantages of using an agent
+ Agents based in other regions or overseas have more detailed knowledge of local conditions, customs, consumer preferences and legal controls. They can advise on and select the best ways to distribute and sell a product in a given location.	✗ The business has far less control over the distribution and sale of its product. ✗ Product distribution costs and final selling prices will be higher because the agent will receive commission or charge a mark-up to cover its owns costs and earn a profit.

Distribution channel 4: indirect through a wholesaler

A **wholesaler** is a business organization that buys in bulk from food processing plants and other manufacturers or their agents, and then breaks up the bulk into small quantities for retailers to buy. In this way, a wholesaler offers significant advantages to both the manufacturer and the retailer.

▼ The function of a wholesaler

Without a wholesaler	With a wholesaler

Firm A   Firm B   Firm C   Firm A   Firm B   Firm C

                                            Wholesaler

Retailer X   Retailer Y   Retailer Z   Retailer X   Retailer Y   Retailer Z

The advantages of using a wholesaler are as follows.

Advantages to a manufacturer	Advantages to a retailer
A wholesaler will:	A wholesaler will:
+ buy in bulk and pay for storage	+ break up the bulk to sell small quantities to retailers, often allowing payment at a later date
+ use its own transport and cover costs of transportation to retailers	+ offer a wide range of products
+ reduce the manufacturer's costs of making and handling sales	+ deliver products when they are needed, thereby reducing transport and storage costs
+ provide market research data on what is or what is not selling well from its contacts with retailers.	+ pass on some bulk purchase discounts from manufacturers to retailers
	+ provide information on new products and their availability.

The great advantage of a wholesaler is that it will buy in bulk, which saves a manufacturer dealing with many small orders from retailers. Instead retailers can buy small quantities from a wholesaler. Many small retailers cannot afford to buy in bulk because they do not have enough storage space. Holding less inventory saves working capital being used to pay for purchases and also saves on storage costs. Many food retailers may also be reluctant to buy in bulk because many food products have only a limited shelf life before they perish.

However, there are also a number of disadvantages to using a wholesaler.

Disadvantages to a manufacturer	Disadvantages to a retailer
✗ A manufacturer has less control over the distribution and sale of its product to retailers and the final consumer.	✗ Products may be more expensive than if they had been bought direct from the manufacturer.
✗ A wholesaler will add a mark-up for profit. If the manufacturer has its own distribution system it can earn this additional profit for itself.	✗ A single wholesaler may not stock the full range of products the retailer requires so the retailer will have to place orders and take deliveries from others.
✗ Perishable products take longer to reach the final customer.	✗ Wholesalers may not sell and/or transport goods to very small retailers.

As a result of these factors, wholesaling has declined in recent years as major retailers and manufacturers have set up their own warehousing and distribution systems instead.

The most appropriate choice of distribution channel and place of sale depends on the type of customer, the type of product and how frequently it is required

Every business must decide the most effective way to get its products to the final customer. Distribution direct to the customer is usually the only channel businesses providing services can use. For example, banks and insurance companies deliver their services through their own outlets or online, while window cleaners and decorators deliver their services to the home or premises of the customer.

However, for farms, food processors and manufacturers the choice of distribution channel is more complex, depending on the type of product and customer.

- If the products are bulky materials and component parts are required by manufacturers for "just-in-time" processing or production, then distribution direct to those customers is likely to be the most effective method.

- If the products are specialized machines, vehicles and equipment produced for sale to business customers, then direct distribution is appropriate. This is because customers will require technical experts from the manufacturers to explain how the products work. For example, aircraft maker Airbus trains pilots from its airline customers how to fly its planes.

- If customers are located overseas then distribution through an agent may be sensible unless the products can be sold online and delivered via a postal service or courier.

- If the products are mass-market consumer goods then final distribution through retailers is likely to be the most effective channel. The larger the size of the market and the more dispersed the customers are geographically, the more sensible it will be to distribute through a wide range of retailers serving different locations.

- Items that are perishable, such as fresh milk and fruit, and items that are purchased frequently, including daily newspapers, need to be easily and quickly available to customers and therefore should be sold through a wide variety of different outlets, including newsagents, supermarkets and even at garages selling petrol.

- In contrast, luxury items such as designer clothes and expensive jewellery should only be sold in a limited number of exclusive shops. Distributing them through a supermarket chain will not create the right image or reach the intended target market of wealthy customers.

Recommend the most appropriate channels of distribution for the following products? Justify your choice.

▸ Washing machines

▸ Mobile phones

▸ Car insurance

▸ Fresh blueberries

▸ Business textbook

Now make a list of five other goods you or your family have bought over the last month or so. Where did you buy these products? Try to find out what channel of distribution the manufacturer of each product used to distribute the product to you.

Physical distribution involves choosing the most effective method of transport

Whatever the channel of distribution used to sell a product to the final consumer, most require the movement of goods or people providing services from one place to another. Firms need to consider both the cost and speed of different methods of transport in their distribution decisions. For example, transport by air is very expensive for bulky items but it is a fast way of delivering small, expensive items over long distances, especially overseas.

Risk of damage during transport can be reduced using suitable packaging materials, while refrigeration units on planes, trains or lorries can be used to transport perishable items such as flowers, meats and vegetables. Similarly, pipelines are used to transport liquids in bulk such as oil or liquefied gases over very long distances rather than pumping them into tankers.

The time taken between a customer placing an order with a business and when it is delivered is the **delivery lead time**. There is increasing pressure from customers and competition between producers to reduce lead times. A business that is able to deliver an order faster than others is likely to gain more customers and sales. For example, "just-in-time" production methods rely on suppliers delivering materials and component parts to manufacturers just in time for them to be processed; otherwise there are production delays. ➤ **4.1.2**

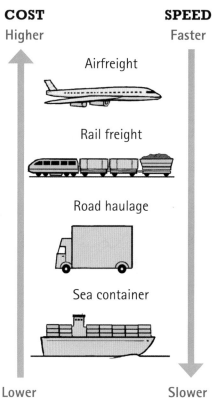

COST — Higher / SPEED — Faster

Airfreight

Rail freight

Road haulage

Sea container

Lower / Slower

Before you continue make sure you are able to

Appreciate the importance of **distribution channels** and the factors that determine their selection:

✓ advantages and disadvantages of different channels

✓ recommend and justify an appropriate distribution channel in given circumstances.

Learning **CHECKLIST**

3.3.4　Promotion

▶ Promotions are marketing communications designed to influence consumer behaviour and spending decisions. They make consumers aware of a product, its brand name and features, where it is sold and the price it sells for.

▶ Advertising involves above-the-line promotions in newspapers and magazines, on television, via the internet and other advertising media. Persuasive advertising is designed to create a consumer want and boost sales of a product.

▶ The most suitable choice of advertising media depends on the target audience or market segment intended for the advertisement. National newspapers and television have large audiences but can be expensive. They are more suitable for mass advertising.

▶ Creating a powerful brand image and spending a large amount of money on advertising can create a barrier to new competition.

▶ Below-the-line promotions are used to support and reinforce above-the-line promotions. They are normally short-lived, such as free gifts or money-off coupons or product placements in new films and television programmes.

▶ Point-of-sale promotions include attractive stands and product displays, posters near checkouts and friendly sales representatives who can offer customers free samples to try or demonstrate how a product can be used.

▶ Promotions are often the most expensive activities to fund in a marketing strategy and will need to be carefully planned and controlled.

▶ A marketing budget is a managerial tool that helps balance what a business needs to spend on promotions against what it can afford. The budget can then be used to monitor actual spending on marketing communications and whether they are meeting their objectives.

Business **BUZZWORDS**

Above-the-line promotions – marketing communications using mass advertising media.

Below-the-line promotions – marketing promotions that do not use mass media.

Informative advertising – advertising that provides factual information about goods, services or organizations.

Persuasive advertising – advertising designed to influence consumer preferences, encourage brand switching and increase sales.

Public relations – actions to establish and maintain a good company and product image with the general public.

Point-of-sale promotions – promotions targeted at the customer at places where a product is displayed and sold.

Personal selling – face-to-face marketing communications with a customer.

Marketing budget – a financial plan for the marketing of a product.

Promoting the product and the organization

Promotions are designed to create consumer wants for products, inform customers where to buy them and retain their loyalty

The main aims of promotions are to:

- raise consumer awareness about a new or existing product

- create a demand for the product

- expand the customer base

- create brand loyalty

- build customer loyalty

- increase sales, market share and profit.

For example, LPI Consumer Products makes and distributes patented ShaveMate all-in-one razors that feature shaving cream dispensed from the handle. The company has been developing its line of razors since 1997.

After years of market and product research and development, the company took its razors to the US military because it had heard many soldiers posted overseas had no other option than to dry shave without the use of foams, gels or even water. The company's first razor featured just two blades with shaving cream that could be squeezed from the handle. The military became a repeat customer.

However, to grow the business further the company needed to enter and compete for a share in the $2.6 billion per year razor and blade market in the US, dominated by razor producers Gillette and Schick. US retailers were at first reluctant to stock ShaveMate razors instead of razors from Gillette and Schick. Store managers encouraged LPI to improve its product by adding more blades. In response the company developed the Titan 6 for men and Diva 6 for women. Both razors offered six blades, one more than its competitors' products at the time, and were the only all-in-one razor with shaving cream in the handle.

When Titan 6 and Diva 6 were in prototype, LPI promoted the razors at trade shows, but while retailers were interested in the products most thought the ShaveMate razors lacked brand awareness.

To raise consumer awareness and create demand for the razors, the company had to develop an effective promotional campaign. It considered three options.

Option 1: match the marketing communications of its much larger rivals Gillette and Schick with a national newspaper, television and radio advertising campaign, plus in-store promotions and money-off coupons. However, this would cost the company $150 million. With annual revenues of just $2 million, the option was unaffordable.

Option 2: promote ShaveMate on the company shavemate.com website and through speciality retailers like hotels, airport stores and cruise ships, using their slogan "The future of shaving is here". This was the most affordable option costing an estimated $100 000 to produce samples, displays and other promotions. However, it was the least likely to build widespread consumer awareness and sales quickly.

Option 3: a two-pronged promotional strategy for about $1 million. The first part would use low-cost public relations, press releases and samples to bring

ShaveMate to the attention of newspaper editors and TV producers who may be tempted to publish a story about the product or the company. The second part of the strategy was a national "as-seen-on-TV" advertising campaign on cable television channels using two-minute commercials, possibly using a well-known celebrity, to demonstrate how using ShaveMate razors could simplify shaving.

The company opted for option 3, believing it was likely to be the most cost-effective solution for raising awareness and creating sales quickly. Sending out samples and promotional material had immediate results. ShaveMate products were featured in magazines and tested on air by local news stations. The owners of the company were also invited to feature on a TV programme on the Discovery Channel about the use of marketing by business.

As a result of the media attention and product exposure a number of major retail chain stores decided to sell ShaveMate products in their stores nationally.

The experience of LPI and its ShaveMate razors demonstrates how carefully designed and budgeted-for promotions can make a product a financial success.

Promotions such as newspaper and TV adverts, in-store displays, money-off coupons and trade shows all involve communicating with consumers about a product or organization in an attempt to influence their buying behaviour. Promotion therefore involves much more than just advertising.

Promotion makes consumers aware of a product, its brand name and features, where it is sold and the price it sells for. It therefore covers all aspects of the marketing mix.

LPI used both above- and below-the-line promotions for ShaveMate.

- **Above-the-line promotion** involves marketing communications using mass advertising media, such as television, radio, newspapers and mobile phones, to increase sales.

- **Below-the-line promotions** are all other forms, including product placement and endorsements by famous celebrities, public relations (PR), direct mail, personal selling and sales incentives such as free gifts and competitions.

A promotional plan can have a wide range of objectives, including creating a consumer want, providing product information, gaining consumer acceptance for a new product, creating a brand image, increasing sales and market share, competing for the market and/or improving corporate image.

Advertising

Each year many billions of dollars are spent by organizations on advertising. This is because good advertising can create a consumer want for a product and increase sales. If sales revenues increase enough this will not only cover the costs of advertising but also increase business profits.

There are two main types of advertising.

- **Informative advertising** provides information about a product to a consumer. Some examples include bus and train timetables, restaurant menus, technical specifications for computers and the ingredients of foodstuffs. Informative advertisements can also help to increase product credibility and generate a good reputation for a business. Government organizations and agencies often use informative advertising to tell people about new regulations or to increase awareness of personal health and safety issues.

- **Persuasive advertising** is designed to create a consumer want and boost sales of a particular product, often at the expense of rival products. This is known as brand switching. Persuasive advertising is targeted at particular market segments and provides attractive messages and images to grab the attention of consumers and create a demand for the advertised product.

The main objective of persuasive advertising is to create and reinforce a brand image that will in turn create a consumer want for, and loyalty to, that product brand.

Most product brands are very similar to others they compete with but are differentiated by their brand name, attractive design or features, a slogan, eye-catching packaging and an easily recognizable logo. Advertising can make a consumer aware of all these and create the right **brand image** to go with them.

Of course, it does not really matter whether or not the product is very different from rival products as long as consumers end up thinking it is. For example, most washing detergents are very similar yet individual manufacturers of detergents often spend vast amounts of money attempting to persuade consumers that their brand is more powerful, is better quality, smells better, makes clothes softer or whiter and is kinder to the environment than other detergents. This non-price competition is designed to boost sales and create brand loyalty so consumers continue to keep buying the same brand. ➤ **3.1.1**

Brand loyalty has the following benefits for a business.

- Repeat purchases from loyal customers provide a steady stream of revenue.

- Customers continue to buy the brand even if the prices of rival products fall.

- It helps to protect market share from competition.

- Customers may pay a higher price for the brand.

In these ways, brand loyalty helps to reduce the price elasticity of consumer demand for the product. As a result, increasing the price of the brand will have little effect on sales and will increase revenue.

Creating a brand image can be a successful strategy because firms have realized that consumers not only buy a product but also try to buy into the images and lifestyles associated with them. For example, car manufacturer Volkswagen used to advertise the typical VW driver as an affluent, carefree, attractive, professional type of person. The advertising slogan referred to "VW people". The campaign was successful as a large market segment identified with or wanted to be like the type of people portrayed as "VW people". Sales of VW cars rose and VW was also able to price its vehicles at a premium to reinforce the affluent brand image.

Choosing the wrong method of advertising can "make or break" a product regardless of how good it is, how competitively it is priced, where it is sold and how attractive the advertisement is. The most suitable choice of advertising media depends on the target audience or market segment intended for the advertisement. For example, it would not be cost-effective to advertise products intended for elderly people in pop music magazines or during children's television programmes. Similarly, it would not be sensible to launch a mass advertising campaign on television for a product aimed at mountaineering enthusiasts. It would be more cost-effective to advertise that product in specialist mountaineering magazines.

▲ Informative?

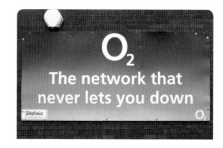

▲ Persuasive?

▼ Types of advertising media

Advertising media	Advantages	Disadvantages
National newspapers 	+ Newspapers are bought by a large number of people. + A lot of product information can be provided in an advertisement. + Readers can keep the newspaper and refer back to an advertisement. + It is reasonably inexpensive to advertise.	− Most newspapers are only in black and white. − Small advertisements tend to get "lost" among others. − Readers often ignore advertising sections. − Sales are falling due to more online news.
Regional and local newspapers 	+ Advertisements can be linked to local products, features and events. + Advertisements can be used to test market promotions before national launch.	− Most of these are only in black and white and reproduction can be poor. − The average cost per reader is relatively high due to limited circulation.
Magazines 	+ Advertisements can be linked to featured articles. + Advertisements can be targeted at specific magazines and the consumers who read them, for example gardening, travel, sports and car magazines.	− Advertisements often have to be submitted a long time before publication. − Magazines may only be published weekly or monthly. − Advertising in magazines is more expensive than in newspapers. − Competitors' products are often displayed on the same page.
Radio 	+ Creative use can be made of sound, including music. + Advertisements are relatively cheap to produce and broadcast. + There are a growing number of digital stations. + Advertisements can be targeted at different stations and audiences, for example younger people listening to pop music stations.	− Visual messages cannot be broadcast. − The advertisement is often short-lived. − Consumers may not listen to advertisements. − Radio has more limited audiences than national newspapers and television.
Television 	+ Creative use can be made of moving images, colour, music and sound. + There are large audiences. + Repeats can reinforce messages. + Advertisements can be targeted at different audiences by type of programme, for example for insurance and security systems during police dramas.	− Production and broadcast costs are high, especially at peak times. − Advertising messages are usually short-lived. − Television audiences may use advertising breaks in programmes for other activities, for example to make a drink or go to the toilet.
Movies (including new releases at cinemas, on disc and online) 	+ Creative use can be made of moving images, colour, music and other sound. + Advertisements can be targeted at different audiences by type of movie, for example advertising toys, fizzy drinks and sweets during cartoon movies.	− These have more limited audiences than television and some other media. − Messages cannot be reinforced by repeat showings.

| **Posters and billboards** | + These offer cheap and permanent displays.
+ They can be placed in areas where many people drive or walk by or where people have to wait, such as platforms at train stations. | − Messages can be missed as people often ignore them or pass by very quickly.
− Posters and billboards can only provide limited information.
− They are susceptible to vandalism and adverse weather conditions. |

| **The internet** | + It is easy and relatively cheap to develop a website and sell products online.
+ Websites can deliver information in an attractive way to large numbers of potential consumers all over the world.
+ Up-to-date and personalized promotional messages and product offers can be targeted at different groups of consumers using emails and via social media, including Facebook and Twitter. | − Internet access is limited in some countries.
− There are many competing websites.
− Search engines and comparison sites may not highlight a website.
− Online credit card fraud may discourage customers from buying online. |

| **Leaflets** | + This is a cheap form of advertising, especially for small, local businesses such as restaurants and repair shops.
+ Leaflets can be handed out to a wide range of potential customers near the business.
+ Leaflets can contain discount codes or money-off coupons to encourage people to keep and use them to make purchases. | − Many leaflets can be wasted: people may not read them or may throw them away in the street creating litter and a poor reputation for the business.
− Leaflets delivered door to door may be considered "junk mail", annoying customers and thereby putting them off using the business or buying the product advertised. |

| **Other** | + Other methods include inexpensive forms of advertising, for example logos and messages on carrier bags, T-shirts or other products. | − Advertisements may not be seen by consumers in target markets.
− It is possible to send a negative message, for example if lots of carrier bags bearing a logo or message are discarded. |

ACTIVITY 3.20

Copy out the table headings below and add at least 20 rows. Now put your feet up in front of the television and watch at least 20 advertisements at different times of the day. Complete a row in the table for each advertisement and tick any description that you think applies in each case. An example has been completed for you. Are the advertisements mostly persuasive or informative? How many use slogans and brand images, and who are they aimed at?

Product advertised	Target audience?	Prime time?	Off-peak?	Mostly informative?	Mostly persuasive?	Brand image used?	Is a slogan used?	Is humour used?
Bathing gel	Females in professional occupations	✓			✓	Luxury; eco-friendly		

Now look through some national and local newspapers. Select at least five advertisements that grab your attention. For each one note answers to these questions.

- ▸ What is it advertising?
- ▸ Why did it grab your attention?
- ▸ What messages does it contain?
- ▸ What images does it use or try to create?
- ▸ Which market segment or segments is it aimed at?

Below-the-line promotions

Below-the-line promotions reinforce advertising messages and aim to "pull" customers into retail outlets to buy products

Below-the-line promotions are used to support and reinforce above-the-line advertising promotions. They are normally relatively short-lived, such as offering free gifts or money-off coupons for a short period of time, or product placements in new films and television programmes.

Below-the-line promotions are often directed at the final customer of a product and involve a "pull" strategy. That is, they attempt to "pull" consumers into shops and other retail outlets to buy products.

✳ Publicity

There are a number of ways a business can advertise its organization and its products relatively cheaply and easily. It can use:

- **sales literature**, including promotional booklets and leaflets, handed out to people in busy shopping centres or delivered door to door, often used for sale promotions

- **signage** on the business premises to advertise the business name and products

- **vehicle livery** on the side of delivery and other vehicles, advertising the company's or products' names and logos

- **product endorsements** from well-known sports, film and other personalities who are paid by a business to wear or use its products in public

- **product placements** on television and film sets so audiences see a product being used in the programme or movie

- **trade shows** which attract many potential business and individual buyers to look at new or existing products of different businesses – a stand or stall at a trade show can be used to publicize the product range of a business.

✳ Public relations

Public relations (PR) is a form of promotion that involves efforts to establish and maintain a good image for a company and its products with the general public. This can be especially important if the company's image and reputation has been damaged in some way, for example following food poisoning at a restaurant or a disastrous oil spill from a tanker that belongs to a major international oil company.

▼ Sponsoring a sporting event can help improve PR

PR can take many forms, for example:

- **sponsorship**, such as the funding of football and rugby matches, art shows, fetes or other public events

- **donations** to charities or relief programmes following natural disasters

- business owners, managers and employees taking part in **fundraising events**

- **press releases** – published statements released to the media to publicize new initiatives, such as the introduction of new environmental practices or free day care for the young children of the organization's employees.

❋ Point-of-sale promotions

The point of sale of a product is the place where it is displayed and sold, for example, on a supermarket shelf and at the checkout. **Point-of-sale promotions** therefore include attractive stands and displays, posters near checkouts and friendly sales representatives who offer customers free samples to try or to demonstrate how a product can be used. These promotional methods are also sometimes referred to as in-store merchandising.

The design and layout of retail outlets can also encourage sales. For example, sometimes checkouts are intentionally hard to find so customers have to look around a store to find them. In doing so, they may be tempted to buy many more products. Similarly, sweets and magazines are often displayed at checkouts in supermarkets to encourage children to pressure their parents into buying them while they wait in the queue.

❋ Sales incentives

These promotions are often aimed at creating customer loyalty by providing extra incentives for them to continue purchasing the same product, and include the following.

- **Money-off coupons** may be printed in magazines or on product packaging. Customers sometimes have to collect a number of coupons before they qualify for money off their next purchase. Coupons may also entitle a customer to a free gift.

- **Competitions** or prize draws offering an expensive prize or large sum of money to a person who has purchased a product are good ways of encouraging repeat sales, especially if customers are required to collect a number of tokens printed on product packaging before they can enter.

- **Loyalty cards** and **bonuses** are used by many retailers to encourage customer loyalty. Usually, the more customers spend in a store the more points they accumulate on their loyalty card and the more discounts they will be entitled to next time they shop at the same store.

❋ Direct mail

Direct mail is letters and emails containing promotional messages, discounts and other offers that are delivered to target groups of consumers. This can be used for both advertising and sales promotion. Although the letters and emails are often mass-produced and delivered, modern computer technology allows them to be personalized with names and addresses from customer records and publicly available databases. However, a lot of direct mail is viewed as "junk mail" or "spam" by many recipients.

❋ Personal selling

The final sale of financial products, hi-tech electronics equipment, expensive products such as cars or a personalized item that is made and delivered to order normally involves personal selling. This is because consumers often want to discuss product features, specifications and prices face-to-face with a sales representative in a shop before they finally decide what to buy.

Sometimes customers also want advice and information on other matters relating to a potential purchase, such as whether the product can be delivered, if it is guaranteed against breakdown and for how long, the method of payment they can use, whether credit terms are available and where to obtain a refund if necessary. These are all important features of providing good customer service. A decision on whether or not to buy a particular product from a particular business organization will in part be based on the customer receiving satisfactory help and advice on these issues.

Many businesses therefore spend a significant amount of time and money on teaching their sales representatives product and organizational information, and training them how to serve customers effectively. For example, staff can receive training in how to deal with customer complaints, their telephone manner and their sales techniques, including how best to greet customers.

▲ Too pushy?

▲ Too abrupt?

▲ Just right?

Personal selling therefore involves verbal marketing communications with a potential customer. Sales staff can deliver informative and persuasive messages to a customer necessary to "close the sale".

ACTIVITY 3.21

For each of the following products, decide the best methods of above-the-line and below-the-line promotions to use. You can choose more than one method for each one but you will need to give reasons for your choice.

A new pop music magazine for young girls	New personal 3D television glasses you can wear to watch films, instead of watching a television screen	A brand of furniture polish, the sales of which have reached maturity and are starting to decline

A new pizza restaurant near a housing and shopping development

A major national sporting event

After-sales care

After-sales care is a product feature as well as a promotional device. After-sales care encourages sales of more expensive products, such as cars and many consumer electronic products, by reassuring customers that if the product goes wrong they can have it replaced or repaired easily. Customers need to be given confidence that they can find help if anything goes wrong with their purchase. Organizations that fail to offer a good after-sales service will lose custom to those that do, regardless of any other promotions that encourage sales and customer loyalty.

The need for cost-effectiveness in spending the marketing budget

Marketing communications are expensive and need careful budgeting

Promotions can be expensive. In addition to product development they are often the most significant cost within an overall marketing strategy. Spending on promotions therefore needs to be carefully planned and controlled to make sure they are **cost-effective**. This means identifying and spending only the minimum amount necessary to achieve agreed marketing objectives for consumer awareness, sales, customer loyalty and market share. Being cost-effective does not mean doing everything "on the cheap"; it means investing in only those promotional activities that will deliver the best returns.

A **marketing budget** is therefore a financial plan for the marketing of a product over a given period based on an estimate of all the likely future costs involved in developing, releasing and monitoring advertisements and other marketing communications for that product or for the organization as a whole.

The starting point is a well-thought-out promotional strategy with clear objectives and plans on how to achieve them. These plans and actions can then be costed to see whether they are affordable.

A typical marketing budget will therefore take into account the costs of market research, website development, marketing communications, the wages and salaries of marketing staff and their travel, and office costs.

Marketing budget

Market research costs include:
- design, preparation and analysis
- conducting interviews and surveys
- test marketing
- subscriptions to secondary sources.

General marketing expenses include:
- advertising agency commissions
- salaries for marketing managers
- salaries for marketing assistants
- office space
- fixtures and fittings
- travel costs.

Marketing communications costs include:
- printing and mailing
- development of a brand's logo
- developing and hosting a website
- designing a brochure
- radio, television and cinema advertising
- direct marketing
- newspaper advertising
- attending events
- personal selling
- PR
- sponsorships and donations
- sales incentives, including competitions.

A marketing budget is therefore a managerial tool that helps a business balance what needs to be spent on marketing against what it can afford. Clearly, if the business cannot afford a large budget then this will place a limit on what it can spend on promotions. For example, a small budget will rule out spending on expensive advertisements on national television, so cheaper ways of advertising will have to be identified and used instead.

Actual spending on marketing is regularly monitored by managers against the set budget, in order to control costs and make sure the budget is not exceeded.

Managers also monitor how effective spending is and whether marketing objectives are being met. They will want to know whether consumer awareness of the business and its products has risen sufficiently and whether sales have increased enough to justify continuing to spend money on advertising and other promotions.

ACTIVITY 3.22

What are the main objectives of Joe's marketing strategy in the article below?

What evidence is there from the article that new, small businesses may have to spend more on marketing to establish a market share?

How has Joe decided how big his marketing budget should be?

What evidence is there that Joe is concerned with the cost-effectiveness of his marketing budget?

Barking up the right tree?

Joe's Redhots, a hot-dog cart selling to office workers, wanted to use popular media such as television, radio and newspapers to advertise, along with promotional free product samples and coupons. Joe learnt from his suppliers that his competitors in the downtown office area were spending little or no money to promote and advertise their cart luncheon businesses.

He estimated that the most successful hot-dog cart spent 5% of net sales revenue for promotion and advertising. Joe decided to spend at least 10% of his net sales during the first year to develop consumer awareness and to boost his sales and market share.

Joe ranked all his possibilities in order of probable effectiveness, with estimated costs.

Advertising
• Television ($500 for a 30-second

advertisement per station)
• Radio ($50–$100 for a 60-second advertisement per station)
• Newspaper advertisements ($500 per advertisement)
• Cart signage ($100)
• Leaflets ($100 @ $0.10 each).

Below-the-line promotion
• Free samples ($25/day @ $0.25 each)
• Coupons ($5/day @ $.025 each)
• Loyalty card ($15/day).

Joe found that any broadcast advertisement required additional production costs that were at least as much as the cost of a single advertisement. In addition, he needed to run at least four or five advertisements per station to be effective. Break-even cost coverage would be too expensive, with over a year's estimated sales needed just to pay for a small television

and radio campaign. And it's difficult to advertise with available media just to his target group of office workers within a radius of six city blocks.

Joe decided to have his cart painted ($100) with a clever message ("The best place to have a quick lunch"), hand out 1000 leaflets ($100) over three months to offices and try to get a free mention in local newspapers and downtown television and radio stations by sending free samples to editorial staff before lunch. He figured he could afford to hand out leaflets and samples all year long and stay within his 10% budget limit.

For example, it may be better value for money spending $2 million developing a website than it is spending $2 million on a national television advertising campaign if the website generates more brand awareness, sales and an improved corporate image than television advertisements would.

Similarly, paying an advertising agency to develop an advertising campaign may be more cost-effective for a small business than the business trying to do this itself with limited skills and experience.

Exam PREPARATION 3.4

Kozmetika is a business that manufactures cosmetics. Kozmetika's marketing director wants to increase marketing expenditure next year. Members of the board of directors of the company want to see a detailed marketing budget as they do not think past expenditure, mainly on advertising, has been very cost-effective. The table below shows data on its sales, market share and marketing expenditure over the last two years.

Year	Kozmetika sales ($m)	Kozmetika market share (%)	Advertising expenditure ($m)
1	300	10	25
2	350	8	35

a   Calculate the value of the **total** market sales for cosmetics in year 1. [2]

b   What is meant by a "marketing budget"? [2]

c   Identify and explain why Kozmetika's market share has fallen in year 2 even though the value of its sales has increased. [4]

d   Identify and explain **three** ways in which Kozmetika could increase its market share, other than spending more on advertising. [6]

e   Do you think that Kozmetika's marketing expenditure was cost-effective in year 2? Justify your answer. [6]

3.3.5　Technology and the marketing mix

- ▶ New technological developments are affecting every element of the marketing mix. The internet is now a powerful sales and marketing tool in business.

- ▶ Many businesses now sell their products direct to their customers and take payment for their purchases over the internet. Websites provide "shop windows" for the products of businesses that are "open" every hour of every day to consumers the world over.

- ▶ E-commerce over the internet allows businesses to reach more potential customers and expand sales while reducing their sales and marketing costs. However, businesses using e-commerce must also offer a good product, delivery service and after-sales help to ensure that their individual and business customers get good all-round service.

- ▶ E-commerce has increased consumer choice and competition between businesses, but online fraud is increasing and firms are having to invest heavily in new electronic security features in response.

- ▶ Internet-based applications known as social media are transforming the way businesses promote their products and brands. Posting promotional messages on social networking sites, such as Facebook and Google+, is a cost-effective way of reaching a large number of potential customers around the world.

- ▶ Many forms of social media are free and allow businesses to target their promotional messages at specific customer groups in particular locations. These messages can also be updated quickly and easily as market conditions change.

Business BUZZWORDS

Internet – the shared global computing network that enables electronic communications between all connected computing devices.

E-commerce – promoting, buying and selling goods and services using electronic systems connected to the internet. This can be business-to-business (B2B) or business-to-consumer (B2C).

Search engine – an internet application or website that hunts for, gathers and reports information available on the internet.

Social media – internet applications that enable users to create and share content or to participate in social networking.

Technology in marketing

Advances in computer and other technologies are affecting every aspect of the marketing mix

New technological developments are transforming the way businesses plan and implement their marketing strategies. They are affecting every element of the marketing mix.

PRODUCT

Technological change has created new consumer wants and products to satisfy them, including smartphones and satellite navigators. Many product life cycles are becoming shorter. ➤ **3.3.1**

A new product can now be designed using 3D software and manufactured by computer-controlled machines. ➤ **4.3.1**

PRICE

Prices of items sold online can be adjusted quickly as market conditions change using dynamic pricing. For example, the price of holidays on specific dates can be reduced if they fail to sell out in time. ➤ **3.3.2**

Price discounts can be targeted at different consumers to encourage their purchases using email and coupon websites.

$25

PLACE

Many businesses now sell their products direct to their customers and take payment for their purchases over the internet.

Service providers, such as banks and insurance companies, are also able to offer their services direct to customers online. ➤ **3.3.3**

PROMOTIONS

Websites provide "shop windows" for the products of businesses that are "open" every hour of every day to consumers all over the world.

Businesses can also promote their products through "pop-up" adverts on the websites of online retailers, for example Amazon, or on social networking sites such as Facebook.

This section looks specifically at how the internet has changed the way businesses sell and promote their products.

▲ Amazon and Alibaba are the world's largest online retailers

How the internet and e-commerce is changing business

The internet is a powerful sales and marketing tool in business

The article on Amway below reveals how businesses can dramatically reduce their marketing costs and increase their sales using the internet. **E-commerce** involves the use of **internet** websites and electronic mail (**email**) to promote, sell and buy goods and services. The internet has grown in use considerably since the end of the last century.

E-commerce between businesses, for example to buy or sell component parts or to hire skilled workers using the services of specialist recruitment organizations, is often referred to as business-to-business (**B2B**) commerce. Similarly, e-commerce involving sales and marketing to non-business consumers is known as business-to-consumer (**B2C**) commerce.

A business will normally have an attractive website on the internet to provide relevant business and product information for consumers. To make a purchase a customer must enter credit card and address details. These details can be protected by password. Many websites also offer encryption to change personal information into secret codes to prevent other internet users from accessing another person's details.

A link from the website to a computer in the credit card organization allows personal payment details to be checked. Once these are accepted the website automatically sends the purchase order for any goods and the customer's address details to a warehouse so that delivery can be arranged.

Amway is a direct-selling company based in the US that manufactures a variety of products, primarily in the health, beauty and home care markets. It sells around $9 billion worth of products through small independent business owners each year in more than 80 countries and territories in Asia, Africa, Europe and the Americas. The independent business owners are able to buy, market and deliver those Amway products that meet the different needs and wants of their individual customers without the consumer having to visit a shop.

Amway was aware that most of its sole traders worked from home and many had other jobs. They therefore wanted a flexible working relationship that allowed them to work at a time that was most convenient for them during the day or night. Making greater use of the internet to communicate with the business owners was therefore a good way of doing this and it would offer the 24-hour service its business customers were wanting.

To do this Amway developed attractive and easy-to-use websites for its customers. Website brand names and logos were developed to appeal to different countries and territories. For example, in Europe Amway launched its Amivo website, which combined well-known Spanish and Italian words for friendship and life.

The purpose of its Amivo and other websites was to provide e-commerce support for the small business owners that would help them manage their businesses. The site was available 24 hours a day and 7 days a week and was developed to help users find products, place orders, repeat previous orders and check all of the information about their businesses. All users needed was a computer and access to the internet. To encourage the independent business owners to go online they were offered a number of launch promotions and other bonuses.

Using the internet not only helped the small business owners reduce their costs, it also helped Amway attract new business customers and sales. There were also clear cost savings for Amway in being able to communicate with its customers through the internet, rather than by using postal or telephone services.

Computer programs called **search engines**, including Google, Bing and Baidu, and shopping comparison websites, such as moneysupermarket.com, Gocompare.com and shopping.com, enable consumers to search quickly through millions of websites to find suppliers offering the best prices for the products they want. The businesses that have developed these programs and websites earn significant revenues from advertising the products of other firms.

ACTIVITY 3.23

You are a small business owner. You are considering opening a shop to sell the goods you produce but before you make this decision you want to investigate the possibility of creating a website and only selling goods online. You have searched the internet to find the articles below to help you decide. Use these, and any others you can find online, to make a list of the possible advantages and disadvantages of e-commerce to your business.

The real cost of e-business

One of the more significant roadblocks to e-business is that managers and business leaders have continually underestimated the costs of e-business systems.

The implementation of new systems usually costs more than expected. In addition, ongoing maintenance, operation and staff training costs can typically be 40–60% of the implementation costs per year.

Internet "increases competition" for businesses according to a new study

Small and medium-sized enterprises (SMEs) will find it harder to attract customers via the internet, due to more people using the internet, creating a more competitive marketplace.

46% of SMEs said that the internet has made business more complicated.

A further 62% of the 422 SMEs surveyed said that the international nature of the internet had increased competition from foreign traders.

Online fraud soars

US citizens reported losing more than $550 million last year in internet fraud, falling prey to a variety of increasingly sophisticated scams, according to a report by the Internet Crime Complaint Centre.

Experts blamed the rise on fraudsters using increasingly clever methods including malware scams, where customers' computers are infected with a virus which records the keys they press, including their passwords and personal data.

Unless more concerted action is taken, consumers' confidence in the internet is likely to be damaged with significant implications for business.

Amazon drones to deliver in an hour!

Until now the quickest way to get a product was to go to a shop. Now Amazon are trialling the use of drones to deliver orders to customers. This will make online shopping the quickest and most convenient way to get your goods.

Many businesses can reduce their costs, increase sales and improve competitiveness through the use of e-commerce

E-commerce is changing the way people shop and how firms conduct business. Firms that fail to provide online services are likely to lose custom and revenue to those that do.

Businesses can therefore cut their costs, improve their productivity and become more competitive through the use of e-commerce compared with businesses that have not adopted the new technology. However, e-commerce cannot do this alone. A business using e-commerce must also offer a good product, delivery service and after-sales help to ensure individual and business customers get good all-round service.

Advantages of e-commerce to businesses	Disadvantages of e-commerce to businesses
+ Websites are a cheap way of marketing and selling to consumers all over the world. + A business can attract more customers through a website than through using other methods. + It saves money buying or renting retail outlets and on the employment of retail staff. + Businesses can search for low-cost providers of the goods and services they need. + Information about customers and their purchasing histories can be recorded easily and used to target email promotions about product offers and discounts to different customers.	− It increases competition between businesses, including with firms located overseas. Domestic firms may lose custom and revenue. − Increased competition may force some shops and shopping chains to close down. − Staff will need to be trained to maintain and update websites and to deal with online ordering, payments and distribution. − Businesses must protect themselves from online fraud and credit card scams. If they do not it may stop customers from shopping online. − Website design and maintenance costs can be high.

E-commerce offers consumers increased choice and stimulates competition between businesses, but online fraud is increasing

E-commerce offers consumers substantial benefits in terms of a greater choice of products and suppliers, and potentially lower prices due to increased competition between online businesses, but there are downsides too.

Personal information provided over the internet by customers is sometimes passed on to other businesses without their agreement and in some cases stolen and misused by internet hackers. This makes consumers reluctant to provide their credit card and bank details despite protections offered both by businesses and credit card companies.

Advantages of e-commerce to consumers	Disadvantages of e-commerce to consumers
+ Consumers can choose to buy from a wider variety of goods and services and from a greater number of suppliers based in different countries. + Increased competition between businesses using e-commerce can help to reduce prices and improve product quality and customer services. + Consumers need not spend so much time and money travelling to shops. This can also help reduce road congestion and pollution.	− Increasing online shopping may force local shops to close. Consumers without internet access will have less choice and may have to travel further to shops. − Consumers may have to take time off work to accept deliveries of goods purchased online. − It may be more difficult to return damaged or faulty goods than to simply take them back to a shop. − Despite security measures, online fraud is rising. Consumers' personal credit card and bank details are being stolen and misused by online criminal hackers. − Consumers may receive irritating and unwanted email promotions and spam emails.

With increasing reliance on e-commerce there is a risk that local shops and markets may close, causing the loss of jobs and also the loss of communities.

Spam, also known as junk email, involves sending almost identical electronic promotional messages to many thousands of people at the same time. They are often targeted at children to buy toys and games, and other vulnerable groups such as people on low incomes to encourage them to take out "easy payment" loans that have very high, but hidden, interest charges.

This form of direct marketing communication has grown rapidly and now exceeds several billion messages a day. Many people and businesses consider them a nuisance and use filters on their email accounts to control them.

Spam is also used by criminals to trick people into entering personal information on fake websites using forged emails designed to look as if they are from a bank or another organization such as PayPal. This is known as **phishing**. Businesses affected by these must often spend a lot of money protecting their websites and their reputations from spammers. If they do not, customers will stop buying from them online.

Social networking sites are an effective way to target promotional messages at different consumer groups

The internet, or more specifically internet-based applications known as **social media**, is transforming the way businesses promote their products and brands. This is because it provides a fast and cost-effective way of communicating with potential customers. For example, market-leading social networking sites Facebook and Google+ each have over 1 billion users and are still growing. Although many users are young, the number of older users is growing rapidly.

As a result, advertising using social media is fast overtaking television and other ways of advertising. Advancements in smartphones and mobile internet technologies are helping to fuel this growth.

A growing number of applications can be used for business promotions including the following.

- **Social networking sites**, such as Facebook and Google+, allow a business to have conversations with large numbers of customers, post photos and videos and promote special offers. A business can have its own page on one or more of these sites and can also pay for pop-up adverts to appear on them.

- **Micro-blogging services**, such as Twitter and Instagram, allow businesses to send and receive short messages to and from existing customers and potential customers.

- **Online video-hosting services**, such as YouTube, enable users to upload and share their videos including promotional videos for products.

- **Online blog** sites contain a series of entries or "posts" about topics of interest to the author, much like an online "diary".

- **Coupon websites** offer discount coupons for goods, services and events.

- **Location-based marketing websites** deliver targeted marketing messages to customers in particular locations, through mobile devices such as smartphones and tablets.

Domino's credits social media for sales growth

Domino's Pizza has attributed strong growth in online sales to its use of promotions on location-based mobile application Foursquare and social media after revealing a 29% surge in pre-tax profits to £17.5 million.

For each of the following businesses, identify three possible ways they could promote their goods or services over the internet. Which one would you recommend in each case and why?

A new café is opening in your nearest town	A television station wants to promote a new weekly music, fashion and news programme aimed at teenagers	A publisher has just released a new business studies textbook	A manufacturer of expensive shoes and boots wants to increase its market share

Advantages of using social media	Disadvantages of using social media
+ It is a cost-effective way of reaching a large number of potential customers around the world.	✗ Some consumers may find pop-ups and constant messaging from many different businesses annoying and may ignore them.
+ Many forms of social media allow businesses to target specific groups, often in particular locations.	✗ Pop-up advertisements need to be paid for and can be expensive. Businesses also have less control over how their advertisements are displayed by the host site.
+ Many forms of social media are free.	
+ Promotional messages can be updated quickly and easily as market conditions change.	✗ Some promotional messages may be changed by social media users and forwarded on to others with the intention of ridiculing a business and damaging its reputation.
+ Consumers in the target market will see the marketing messages and advertisements as soon as they enter social networking sites.	✗ The governments of some countries restrict the use of social media.
+ Messages can be personalized and two-way, allowing customers to correspond directly with the business thereby creating good customer relationships and loyalty.	

Sales of even the most successful products reach maturity. Companies often introduce extension strategies to prolong the life of such products. The figure below shows the product life cycle for a computer game.

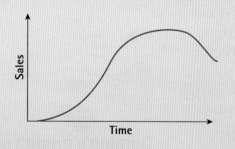

a   What is meant by the term "product life cycle"?   [2]

b   Identify **one** feature that characterizes "maturity" in a product life cycle.   [2]

c   Identify and explain **one** possible extension strategy that the computer game manufacturer could use.   [4]

d   Identify and explain **three** advantages to the game manufacturer of using a website to promote its services.   [6]

e   How important are low prices in determining the long-term success of the game manufacturer? Justify your answer.   [6]

Before you continue make sure you are able to

Understand the impact **technology** has had on marketing:

✓   define and explain the concept of **e-commerce**

✓   the opportunities and threats of e-commerce to business and consumers

✓   use of the **internet** and **social networks** for promotion.

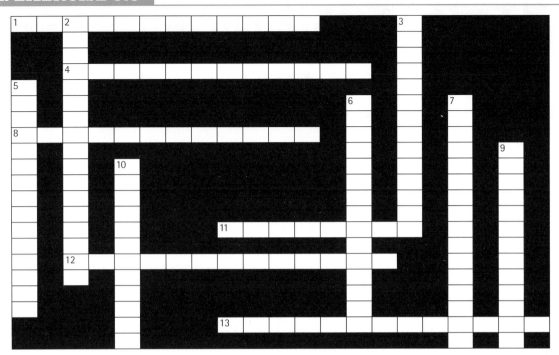

1   The different stages a product passes through over time characterized by the value or volume of sales generated during each stage (7, 4, 5)

3   This measures the responsiveness of demand for a product to a change in its price (5, 10, 2, 6)

5   The type of advertising designed to create a consumer want for a product, encourage brand switching and increase sales (10)

6   Marketing actions used to extend sales and the profitable life of a mature product including, for example, new promotions, price reductions and product modifications (9, 10)

7   Term used to describe customer demand for a product if it falls significantly following a small rise in its price (5, 7)

11 The combination of all the different elements – often referred to as the four Ps – that make up the marketing strategy of a business designed to meet or create a consumer want for its product (9, 3)

12 A pricing method that involves adding a mark-up for profit to the cost of an item to determine its selling price (4-4, 7)

13 These types of promotions include using product placements and endorsements by famous celebrities, public relations, direct mail, personal selling and sales incentives such as free gifts and competitions (5-3-4)

14 At this stage of the life cycle of a new product a business will spend heavily on promotions to raise consumer awareness and price low to encourage sales. As a result, the business may trade at a loss during this stage (6)

16 Promotions targeted at customers in places where the product is displayed and sold (5, 2, 4)

17 That stage of a product life cycle when sales of the product have peaked (8)

2   An intermediary in a distribution channel that will buy and store products in bulk from different producers and sell them in smaller quantities to retailers (10)

4   The promotion, purchase and sale of products using electronic systems connected to the internet (9)

8   A business will often launch new products as others reach maturity and decline to maintain its total sales. This is the term used to describe the range of products at different stages of their life cycles produced and marketed by such a business (7, 9)

9   Internet applications that enable users to create and share content or to participate in social networking. They are a cost-effective way of targeting promotional messages at specific customer groups and updating them quickly as market conditions change (6, 5)

10 A financial plan for managing spending on advertising and other promotions, also including the costs of market research and marketing staff (9, 6)

15 These promotions involve mass marketing communications using media such as national television and newspapers (5-3-4)

16 A pricing strategy that involves setting price high initially for a newly launched product to maximize profits in the short run when there is little or no competition (5, 8)

18 An established business may use this pricing strategy if its sales and market share are threatened by a new competitor. It involves cutting price dramatically to force the new competitor to make losses and to withdraw from the market (11, 7)

19 A business will often spend a significant amount of time and money creating a memorable name, design, logo and consumer perception for its product so that it appears to be desirably different from rival products and encourages customer loyalty (5, 5)

3.4.1 Justify marketing strategies appropriate to a given situation

▸ A marketing strategy determines the target market of a business and the most appropriate choice of marketing mix. It therefore combines product development and design, pricing, promotion and distribution.

▸ Marketing objectives include growing the sales of a new or existing product, increasing or maintaining market share, seeking a commanding position in a niche market or, in some cases, exiting a market if sales have declined significantly.

▸ Most marketing strategies aim to influence consumer wants and buying behaviour. They require careful planning based on good market research and analysis. Marketing strategies should be flexible and adapt as consumer preferences change, competition increases and products mature.

Marketing strategy – a plan detailing the marketing objectives of a business and the actions and resources needed to achieve them.

Developing a marketing strategy

A marketing strategy identifies the marketing objectives of a business and the actions and resources needed to achieve them

A **marketing strategy** combines product development and design, pricing, promotion and distribution; that is, all the main elements of the marketing mix. It identifies the target market and marketing objectives of a business and all the actions and resources needed to achieve them. ➤ **3.1.1**

Marketing strategies differ depending on the different market conditions faced by each individual business, including the amount of competition from other businesses and the strength of consumer demand for their product. However, many have similar objectives.

- **Grow sales of an existing product**. This objective seeks to increase the overall sales of products a business currently markets. This can be done by:
  - ▸ getting existing customers to buy more
  - ▸ getting potential customers to buy; that is, those who have yet to buy
  - ▸ selling existing products to new markets, for example overseas.

- **Grow sales with new products**. This can be accomplished by:

  ▶ introducing updated versions or refinements to existing products

  ▶ introducing products that are extensions of current products

  ▶ introducing new and innovative products not previously marketed.

- **Grow market share**. This strategy aims to increase the overall percentage or share of market sales of the business. In most cases this can only be achieved by taking away sales from competitors. As such, this strategy often relies on aggressive marketing tactics.

- **Gain sales in a niche market**. This strategy seeks to obtain a commanding position within a segment of an overall market. The niche market is much smaller in terms of total customers and sales than the overall market. Ideally, this strategy aims to differentiate the product of the business from all others in the market, either by creating more exclusive product features and/or by creating a brand image consumers view as being different from that of companies targeting the larger market.

- **Maintain the status quo**. This strategy aims to maintain the current market position of a business, such as maintaining the same level of sales or market share. This is especially important if competition is increasing and/or the product is reaching maturity.

- **Exit a market**. Sometimes it may be necessary to withdraw a product from a market, for example if sales have declined significantly as new models become available. Alternatively, a business could sell the rights to make and market its product to another business, for example if that business wishes to expand into other markets and wants to raise finance.

Above all, a marketing strategy must be cost-effective. This means choosing the best marketing mix and methods that will achieve agreed marketing objectives and the highest possible return in terms of revenue or profit for the lowest possible total cost. ➤ **3.3.4**

Different elements of the marketing mix can influence consumer purchasing decisions in different ways

- Price can persuade some consumers to make a purchase if it is a low, competitive price and can increase sales. Businesses might use a pricing strategy such as competitive or penetration pricing when launching a new product or when entering a new market. For other consumers, price is an indicator of quality, so a high price is more likely to persuade such customers to buy. The Apple iPhone is a premium brand which does not compete on price. Price is an important consideration for most consumers.

- Promotion can persuade customers to buy a product by informing them about the product or using persuasive techniques such as paying celebrities to advertise or blog about products. This can be the best way of creating and building brand loyalty. Car firms rely heavily on different promotion techniques to attract new customers and maintain existing customers.

- Place should ensure that the product is convenient and easily accessible by consumers. Amazon realise that the way to attract more customers is to make internet shopping as convenient and quick as going to a local store. Many insurance providers will go through an intermediary, such as a price comparison site, to attract customers. Fresh fruit is best provided by a local shop which buys from farmers or wholesalers.

- Product design, quality and reliability are important for many consumers, especially in the consumer electronics industry. This is the main way in which Apple competes. Apple regularly updates models and offers new features to maintain customer loyalty and attract new consumers. Apple's latest iPhone incorporates facial recognition technology. Tesla are trialling self-driving electric cars.

Marketing strategies should be carefully planned and based on good market research and analysis

A marketing strategy needs careful planning and its development should be informed by good market research and analysis into what consumers want, where and how often they buy, the prices they are willing to pay and what promotions they respond to most. ▶ **3.3.4**

Pre-marketing strategy research should also involve benchmarking and a SWOT analysis to assess the strengths and weaknesses of competing businesses or products and the market opportunities or threats they face.

Below is a simple SWOT analysis of a major sportswear company. A rival sportswear company could use this to develop a marketing strategy to exploit weaknesses and market opportunities. For example, it could introduce a new fashionable sports footwear and clothing brand aimed at the market segment of 12–24 year olds, especially for consumers in China and for sale exclusively online.

STRENGTHS
▶ The company is able to source products from lowest-cost manufacturers anywhere in the world.
▶ It has a global brand.

WEAKNESSES
▶ Revenue is heavily dependent upon sales to retailers and its share of the sports footwear market.
▶ Retail sales are highly price sensitive.

OPPORTUNITIES
▶ Young consumers buy sportswear as fashion items.
▶ There are opportunities to expand the product range with higher-value items such as bags and sunglasses.
▶ The company could expand into new emerging consumer markets such as China and India.

THREATS
▶ Competitors are developing alternative brands and could reduce the company's market share.
▶ Consumer demand for sportswear is very price elastic.
▶ Trading internationally exposes the company's costs and sales revenues to risks related to exchange rates.

Marketing strategies should be flexible and adapt as market conditions change and products mature

Markets are dynamic. This means they are always changing. Consumer tastes and spending habits change over time, new technologies and products are created and new businesses may enter a market increasing the amount of competition while others may exit. The more mature a product is the more likely these changes are. ➤ **3.3.1**

A marketing strategy must therefore try to predict how market conditions could change over time and put in place plans to deal with the changes. For example, a business may increase spending on product differentiation and persuasive advertising and use a destruction pricing strategy if competition increases significantly.

Even if market changes are unforeseen, a marketing strategy may still need to change. For example, if competition becomes too intense in its home market a business may be forced to rebrand its product and enter markets overseas to create new sales. ➤ **3.4.3**

Once a product matures and sales and profits stop growing, a business will need to look at a range of extension strategies, including releasing new versions of its product, cutting prices, relaunching the brand image and other promotions to attract old and new customers to the product. If, however, sales and profitability start to fall then market exit may be the most cost-effective strategy.

▲ Successful products and brands can be repeatedly redesigned and relaunched to extend their profitable lives

A marketing strategy therefore needs to be flexible. Over time, the marketing mix within an overall marketing strategy will need to change in response to changes in consumer demand, competition and other market conditions. It is therefore the job of the marketing department in an organization to keep its marketing strategy under review, make sure the organization has up-to-date information on the latest market developments, analyse their implications on the business, recommend appropriate changes and then, once these are agreed, implement them. A business that continually fails to adapt or is too slow to adapt its strategy to changes in market conditions will fail.

Look at the case studies below.

▶ At what stage in their life cycle are the products?

▶ What were the marketing objectives of the producers of each product?

▶ Briefly describe the main elements of the marketing strategy each producer was following.

▶ Do you think the marketing objectives and strategies used in each case reflect the stage at which each product was in its life cycle? Explain your answer.

▶ Were the marketing strategies cost-effective? Use evidence from the case studies to justify your answers.

▶ Suggest alternative product differentiation, pricing and promotional strategies the producers could have considered using instead to achieve their marketing objectives. Give reasons to support your views.

NIVEA VISAGE YOUNG

Introduction

Beiersdorf is a global company producing skin and beauty care. NIVEA is one of its major brands. Market research demonstrated that there was a gap in the market for a beauty range aimed at young women aged 13–19 years. This was to help them get into a proper skin care routine. Having identified the gap, NIVEA VISAGE Young was launched using all elements of the marketing mix.

Product

To understand what the product should look like, Beiersdorf researched key market segments using focus groups, talking directly to consumers and testing products. It found that teenagers wanted face care that offered a "beautifying" benefit, not medicated care for skin problems. The new product provides a unique bridge between the teenage and adult market. The research led to improvements in both the product itself and the packaging for the range. The company:

▶ reduced packaging and waste by using larger pack sizes
▶ used more natural products such as minerals and sea salts
▶ made the product containers more recyclable.

Price

Prices for the new range were set slightly higher than previously, due to the improvements to the range.

Place

Beiersdorf uses a central distribution point in the UK. Distribution of NIVEA products is mainly through retailers. High street stores provide 65% of sales. The other 35% of sales come from large supermarket chains. Many purchasers are mums, buying for teenagers while out grocery shopping.

Promotion

NIVEA decided not to use above-the-line routes, but to talk to the target market directly through modern channels that help teenagers identify with the product.

▶ It gave away a million product samples at events and through the website.
▶ It set up an online magazine called *FYI (Fun, Young and Independent)*, as well as pages on social networking sites MySpace, Facebook and Bebo.

HOW SRI LANKA WENT NUTS FOR DONUTS ON FACEBOOK

Background

Lalin Jinasena has always loved donuts, especially those that come in unusual shapes and sizes. Being a donut fanatic, it was only natural that when he opened the first donut shop in his hometown of Colombo, Sri Lanka, that he called it "Gonuts with Donuts". His café features a wide variety of donuts, ranging from Cappuccino Cream and Strawberry Cream to Butterscotch and Cookies.

Objective

Drive brand awareness for the café, Gonuts with Donuts, and increase its sales.

Strategy and implementation

Lalin was drawn to the idea of being able to target ads directly at different consumer groups. People in Colombo, the country's largest city, spend a lot of time on Facebook these days, according to Lalin. As a result, he believed that advertising on Facebook would be an effective way to directly create brand awareness for Gonuts with Donuts. He decided to build a presence on Facebook for his café to establish a lasting relationship with his customers. He created a Facebook page and targeted Facebook ads at potential consumers, with the objective of getting them to connect and post comments.

Results

Within a few months, more than 10 000 people interested in learning more about Gonuts with Donuts had connected to his Facebook page. "It proved to be a very cost-effective marketing tool that can be geared exactly to the market segments I needed," said Lalin. The company has since successfully opened seven additional stores with the help of Facebook advertising.

ACTIVITY 3.26

You are the marketing director of a company that manufactures consumer electronic products. The company is the first to develop an entirely new robotic toy car that is able to drive and steer itself around obstacles or follow lines drawn on the ground and is capable of being controlled by voice or smartphone.

Your marketing team has produced the following diagram showing the likely sales and profits of the new product over its forecast life cycle.

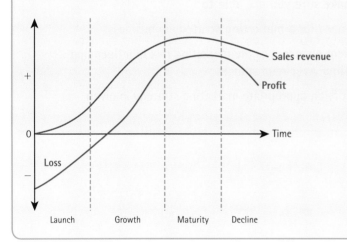

▸ For each stage of the product life cycle identify and explain what is forecast to happen to (i) sales and (ii) profits (or losses), and why.

▸ During which stage will market forecast become saturated? That is, identify on the chart where sales and profits are forecast to reach their maximum and should stabilize for a while. Competition will be fierce at this stage but no new competitors are likely to enter the market after saturation.

▸ You decide to distribute your product direct to retailers.

   (i) What are the advantages and disadvantages of using this method of distribution?

   (ii) Suggest what is likely to happen to the number of retailers who want to purchase your product for sale and the number of places they will offer it for sale at each stage of its life cycle.

- From the options provided below select a pricing strategy and a promotional strategy you would recommend using at each stage of the product life cycle following the product development phase. Justify your choices.

- Suggest a possible extension strategy for the product once it has matured and begun to decline. This can involve aspects of product, price, place and promotions.

Possible pricing strategies	Possible promotional strategies
• Promotional pricing: significant price discounts are made to boost sales and to sell off unwanted inventory. • Competitive pricing: strategies are used including, if necessary, destruction pricing to protect sales and market share from new competitors attracted to the market due to rising sales and profits. • Price skimming: a premium price is charged while competition is low. • Penetration pricing: the product is priced relatively low to attract more customers, generate sales and grow market share.	• Informative advertising spend is cut as spending on persuasive advertising and above-the-line promotions increases significantly to boost sales, deter new competitors and encourage customer loyalty. • Promotional spending is reduced in total and is focused on below-the-line promotions at places of sale. • There is significant spending on informative advertising, publicity, free samples and competitions to generate consumer awareness. • There is a high but reasonably stable level of spend on above- and below-the-line promotions to defend sales and market share against established competitors.

Learning CHECKLIST

Before you continue make sure you are able to

Show awareness of the need for a **marketing strategy** in business:

✓ importance of different elements of the marketing mix in influencing consumer decisions in given circumstances

✓ recommend and justify an appropriate marketing strategy in given circumstances.

3.4.2 The nature and impact of legal controls related to marketing

Key POINTS

▶ Some businesses may use their marketing activities to make misleading or inaccurate claims about their products and prices in order to boost their sales and profits.

▶ To protect consumers from exploitation many governments have introduced consumer protection laws to control marketing activities to ensure they are fair and accurate.

▶ Consumers may be protected from misleading product descriptions and price claims, the sale of unsatisfactory or poor-quality products, failure to disclose hidden fees and charges and the sale of underweight items or the use of inaccurate weighing equipment.

▶ Businesses found to be breaking consumer protection laws may be fined heavily, regulated or even forced to cease trading.

▶ The governments of many countries have also banned the production and sale of many products and substances that are considered harmful or dangerous to people and the environment.

Consumer protection laws – legal controls on businesses designed to protect consumers from misleading or inaccurate marketing claims, unfair trading practices and the production and sale of damaged, faulty or dangerous goods and services.

Business BUZZWORDS

Protecting consumers from misleading promotion

Some business organizations may use their marketing strategies to mislead and exploit consumers to boost their sales and profits

Alima lives in the United Arab Emirates (UAE). She received a leaflet advertising a new garage in her town offering a "full engine service including emissions test" for only 499 dirhams (around $130). This seemed a very good offer but her friend had already warned her about some garages overcharging their customers and undertaking unnecessary repairs to boost their revenues. He therefore advised her to check everything thoroughly before and after the service and not to agree to any additional work before getting a second opinion on whether it was necessary and how much it should cost.

So, Alima took her car to the new garage but when her service was completed Alima was presented with a bill for 950 dirhams (around $240). This included charges for changing the engine oil, oil filter and spark plugs and for repairing the engine radiator.

Alima complained to the garage manager that the leaflet she had received was misleading because it claimed to provide a "full engine service" which should normally include changing the oil, oil filter and spark plugs, and that she had not agreed to the repair of the engine radiator and did not think it necessary.

The manager disagreed with Alima but said he was prepared to reduce her bill by 100 dirhams. However, Alima was not satisfied with this and decided to complain to the consumer protection department in the Ministry of Economy. It investigated her complaint and found the garage guilty of making false claims. The garage was fined and ordered to repay Alima in full and to print new leaflets making it completely clear what engine parts and labour were included in the price of 499 dirhams and what the service excluded.

Alima's story is a common one in many countries and many different business sectors.

Businesses may take advantage of consumers' lack of knowledge about many products, for example how they work, what their ingredients are and what prices customers can expect to pay for them. This is because consumers rarely get the chance to try products before they buy them. For example, the quality of a restaurant will not be known to customers before they eat there. Similarly, many modern products are technically complex and have many different features so it is difficult for consumers to make comparisons or know exactly how they are meant to work.

If goods prove to be dangerous or faulty, the manufacturer may be forced to ask customers to return the product to rectify the fault or offer a full refund, known as a product recall. When Samsung launched a new phone in 2017, the Galaxy Note 7, customers reported exploding phones that were catching fire. Samsung had to recall 2.5 million phones at a cost of $5 billion in losses and lost sales.

To prevent businesses from using their marketing activities to mislead or exploit consumers many governments have introduced legal controls to protect consumers. Businesses found to be breaking these **consumer protection laws** may be fined heavily or even forced to cease trading.

Consumer protection laws vary by country but many outlaw:

- supplying a good or service which is unsafe or not fit for the purpose intended, such as a waterproof jacket that leaks or glue that fails to stick anything

- supplying a good or service that is in an unsatisfactory condition or of poor quality

- giving false verbal or written product descriptions or misleading product claims, such as claiming a pair of shoes are made of leather when they are made from man-made materials

- selling underweight items or using inaccurate weighing equipment

- misleading consumers about the true price they will pay for a good or service, by failing to explain any hidden fees, interest charges and/or sales taxes

- making false claims about price reductions, for example, by suggesting the sale price of a product is 50% less than the recommended retail price when it is not

- demanding payment for products delivered to customers who did not order them

- preparing and selling food in unhygienic conditions or with harmful ingredients

- failing to offer customers refunds for goods returned with a proof of purchase

- offensive or indecent advertising.

BUSINESS ORGANIZATIONS NEED CUSTOMERS BECAUSE THEY:
1 PROVIDE INCOME
2 PROVIDE REPEAT BUSINESS
3 CONTRIBUTE TO PROFIT
4 ARE AN IMPORTANT SOURCE OF INFORMATION
5 ENSURE THE SURVIVAL OF THE BUSINESS

ACTIVITY 3.27

These cartoons all illustrate real-life examples of complaints by consumers about possible misleading claims or the sale of potentially harmful products by businesses.

In each case, do you think the business involved has acted in the best interests of consumers or not? Do you think consumers need some legal protection from the actions of the business in each case? Give reasons for your answers.

Protecting consumers from faulty and dangerous goods

In addition to consumer protection laws, some products are banned from sale because they are considered harmful or dangerous to people and the environment. Guns, explosives and dangerous drugs are illegal in many countries. The production and sale of alcohol, many chemicals and pesticides are also outlawed in some countries.

Complying with consumer protection laws may increase costs but expand sales

Business owners and managers must make sure their businesses comply with consumer protection laws. However, this can increase business costs in the following ways.

- Goods and services may need to be redesigned and new equipment purchased to ensure minimum safety and quality standards are met.
- Advertising claims and product brochures might have to be altered.
- Some leaflets, posters and other printed materials may need to be thrown away if they do not conform to legal requirements.
- Labels may need to be changed to provide information on the ingredients, safety and country of manufacture of a product as required by law.
- More staff may need to be employed to manage customer complaints and refunds effectively.
- Some prices may be controlled, leading to a reduction in some prices and charges, and price lists may need to be altered and reprinted.

Complying with consumer protection laws can increase a business's costs, but it will improve the reputation of a business and consumer confidence. However, governments must be careful not to introduce too many complicated laws and regulations that could significantly increase the cost of doing business and restrict lawful activities. For example, legal controls should not be required to protect consumers from paying higher prices in a competitive market if they have failed to shop around for the best bargains, or if they buy products on impulse due to persuasive but not misleading advertising and later regret their purchases.

Exam PREPARATION 3.6

Desayuno plc is a company that manufactures breakfast cereals and snacks. Figures 1 and 2 show the product life cycles of two of its brands of breakfast cereal, identified as A and B.

Figure 1: Product A

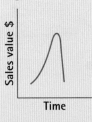

Figure 2: Product B

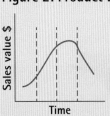

a   Identify **two** stages, aside from maturity, of the product life cycle.   [2]

b   Identify the **four** stages of the product life cycle of product B.   [2]

c   Identify and explain **two** main differences in the life cycles of the two products shown in Figure 1 and Figure 2.   [4]

d   The government is introducing new consumer protection laws. Identify and explain **three** ways in which the business could be affected by these new laws.   [6]

e   Consider the advantages and disadvantages of **two** channels of distribution that Desayuno could use for a new range of breakfast cereals. Recommend which of these channels Desayuno should use. Justify your answer.   [6]

Learning CHECKLIST

Before you continue make sure you are able to

Show awareness of the impact of **legal controls** on marketing strategy:

✓   for example, controls on misleading promotion, faulty and dangerous goods.

3.4.3 The opportunities and problems of entering new foreign markets

▸ Population growth and rising incomes are expanding consumer markets in many developing countries, creating opportunities for new and existing businesses in those countries and overseas.

▸ A business can enter an overseas market in a number of ways, by:

- selling exports directly to overseas buyers

- setting up a business unit in the target country

- using a local expert or contact in the target country.

▸ Market entry overseas can be costly and risky. A business seeking to do so will need good market knowledge and language skills to make contacts, generate sales and avoid failure.

▸ Customs, cultures, tastes, laws, regulations and tax systems can vary widely. A foreign business will need to be aware of these and make sure it acts appropriately or complies.

▸ Operating in overseas markets also exposes a business to exchange rate risks and possible non-payment by overseas buyers. A rise in the value of its national currency against other currencies will make products exported by a business more expensive to buy overseas but will reduce the cost of business location overseas.

▸ A business may overcome some of the problems of entering markets overseas through the use of local contacts, or through joint ventures or mergers with established businesses in the target countries.

Business BUZZWORDS

Market entry – targeting promotion and sales of a new or existing product at a group of consumers, often overseas, that has not previously been targeted by the producer.

Joint venture – a contractual agreement between two or more organizations to share the expertise, investment, management, costs, profits and risks of forming a new business. The new business may produce and sell an existing product to a new market or develop an entirely new product.

Entering new markets in other countries

International markets offer significant growth potential

An increasing number of businesses are producing and selling their goods and services to customers in different countries. The reasons for this are as follows.

- Markets are expanding rapidly in many countries as their populations and incomes grow. The future growth potential of many developing economies is creating opportunities for new and existing businesses to expand their sales and profits overseas. **➤ 1.2.1**

- International trade across national borders is becoming easier due to advances in shipping, e-commerce and the removal or lowering of trade barriers used by governments in some countries to protect domestic firms from competition from rival products and businesses overseas. **➤ 6.3.1**

- Markets in other countries provide an opportunity for established businesses to extend sales of products that are mature or in decline in their home markets. **➤ 3.3.1**

- Businesses can increase their scale of production if sales of their products are expanding overseas and will be able to take advantage of cost advantages (economies of scale) associated with business growth. **➤ 4.2.3**

- Some countries have lower wages costs, fewer regulations and lower taxes than others, making them attractive places in which to set up business activities. Government grants and other incentives may also be available to new or established businesses relocating to these countries. **➤ 4.4.1**

Businesses may face significant problems entering foreign markets

A business can enter an overseas market in a number of ways, by:

- selling goods and services directly to residents of the target country

- setting up a business unit in the target country

- using a local expert or contact in the target country such as an agent or a distributor.

Deciding on the best way to enter an overseas market is a crucial part of any business export strategy. All of these ways can have problems, just like the ones experienced by the young entrepreneur in activity 3.28 below.

ACTIVITY 3.28

Look at the series of cartoons below about a young Swedish entrepreneur trying to set up a global business.
What problems do you think the cartoons illustrate?

When sales in US and European markets of Kellogg's breakfast cereals peaked in the 1990s and then began to decline due to increasing competition from other brands, US company Kellogg's targeted Indian consumers. The Indian market was potentially huge with a population of 950 million people and the incomes of people in cities were growing rapidly.

In 1994 Kellogg's invested $65 million launching its famous Corn Flakes breakfast cereal brand in India. This was followed by the launch of its other brands including Frosties, Special K and Honey Crunch. Sales were good at first as many Indians tried the new product but then sales fell away rapidly. Kellogg's attempt to produce more Indian style cereals, including mango and coconut flavoured cereals, also failed to attract many consumers.

Attracted by the size of India's population, Kellogg's had overlooked the many different cultures there. Traditional breakfasts in India consist of stuffed breads and hot vegetables. The prices of Kellogg's cereals were also much higher than competing breakfast food products.

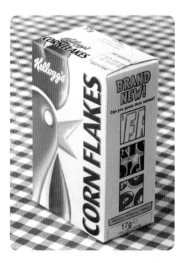

Kellogg's is not alone in experiencing problems launching its products in the rapidly expanding Indian market. Many businesses have faced similar and other problems entering new markets overseas, including the following.

- **There may be language barriers.**
  This should be an obvious problem for many business ventures seeking to enter overseas markets. Although most global business activity is conducted in English, it may not apply to businesses in all countries, especially small businesses. Clearly, English is not the first language of many people involved in business around the world. Terminology and everyday sayings also differ widely by region and country, even in the same language whether it is English, Spanish, Hindi, Arabic or any other major global language.

- **Different cultures, customs and tastes need to be understood.**
  What may be acceptable in one country may be unacceptable or disliked in another. Businesses will need to take account of different cultures, local traditions, practices and tastes in their conduct, product designs and marketing. For example, it is considered rude to point with your index finger in many cultures of the Far and Middle East. Similarly, not every culture celebrates Christmas, nodding as if in agreement means "no" in Greece and Bulgaria, and shoes should be removed before entering a person's home in Thailand and Japan.

- **The business must comply with different legal controls and taxes.**
  Countries may have very different laws and regulations, often reflecting their different cultures. Any business entering a foreign market needs to be aware of these and make sure it complies. For example, the importation and use of some chemicals is illegal in some countries and not others and limits on working ages and hours differ. It is therefore useful for a business to have local contacts who understand these laws and customs.

- **The business must manage exchange rate risks.**
  A business selling exports to consumers in other countries or investing in business operations in another country with a different currency will need to be aware of how changes in exchange rates can affect its costs and revenues, and plan accordingly. A business exporting to foreign markets may find demand for its products falls as the value of its national currency rises. This is because the increase in the value of the currency will make its products more expensive overseas. However, a business paying for wages and materials to run a business unit in another country will enjoy lower costs as the currency of its home country rises in value. **➤ 6.3.3**

- **There are increased risks of non-payment.**
  Care should be taken selling products internationally. A business should first investigate the reputation of foreign firms and their ability to pay before allowing them to import its products. Some buyers may not pay on time, if at all, and it may be difficult to find and force them to pay.

Overcoming the problems of entering foreign markets

A business can reduce the risks of entering markets overseas through the use of local contacts or joint ventures with local businesses.

- **A business can use local contacts.**

  To overcome many of the above problems a business may rely on the help of an expert, agent or business in a target country with detailed local knowledge and language skills. For example, the local organization can distribute and sell the products of the business, provide legal and tax advice, prepare appropriate marketing materials and negotiate with local suppliers, government authorities and worker representatives.

- **A business can set up assembly or sales-only business units abroad.**

  If a manufacturing business wants to set up a factory in another country but is worried about the quality of foreign work, it may set up an assembly-only operation. This can be used to assemble or put together finished products from parts made by the business in its home country. Alternatively, it may simply set up retail outlets in other countries through which to sell its finished products. Multinational companies such as Toyota (cars), Vodafone (telecommunications) and Procter & Gamble (detergents, beauty products and other consumer goods) operate factories and retail outlets in many different countries, producing and selling products that appeal to local consumers, using local labour and suppliers of components or business services. ➤ **6.3.2**

- **A business can license or franchise foreign firms.**

  Risks associated with entering a new foreign market can be reduced for a business if it authorizes or "licenses" one or more good-quality firms located in the target country to produce and sell its branded products. In return the business will usually provide support and expertise and receive a share in the profits.

  Alternatively, a business can franchise the production and sale of its products to foreign firms. Franchising involves a business selling the right to use its successful product, brand or business idea to other firms. For example, McDonald's has successfully franchised its fast food restaurant concept and brand in more than 100 countries. More than 80% of its restaurants worldwide are owned and operated by local franchisees. ➤ **1.4.1**

- **It can enter into a joint venture with a foreign business.**

  A **joint venture** is a contractual agreement between two or more organizations to share the expertise, investment, management, costs, profits and risks of running a business. Many Western companies have set up joint ventures with companies in countries such as China, India and Malaysia. A local partner in these countries will have the local knowledge and contacts with local suppliers and government departments a business will need to gain market access. For example, the Indus Motor Company is a joint venture between the House of Habib and Toyota Motor Corporation for the assembling, manufacture and sales of Toyota cars in Pakistan. ➤ **1.4.1**

- **A business can merge with or take over an existing business located in another country.**
  Rather than set up an entirely new business unit in another country a business organization could simply merge with or acquire an established business in a target country. An established business will already have a customer base and trained workers. ➤ **1.3.3**

- **A business must undertake proper and prior market research.**
  Above all, before a business attempts to enter a new foreign market it should carry out detailed market research into the preferences and spending patterns of consumers in the target country, its customs, laws and traditions, and its workforce skills and wage levels. It should also research rival businesses already located there or selling into the same market. This will help identify if and where `there is a gap in the overseas market and what type of product and product features consumers want. New products and promotions can then be designed or existing ones adapted to satisfy local tastes, cultures, customs and laws. Adapting an existing brand can often be more cost-effective because it means the modified product will retain many of the same features and marketing mix that made the established one successful.

▲ Adapting an existing brand to consumer's tastes, cultures and laws in different countries can be cost-effective

Methods of overcoming problems entering foreign markets	Benefits	Limitations
Local contacts	✓ Provides detailed local knowledge ✓ Language skills ✓ Less cost than recruiting and training own employee	✗ May be difficult to provide an after-sales service through an intermediary ✗ Business may lose control of brand image ✗ Not all local contacts are reliable
Set up own operation	✓ Keep control of quality and brand image ✓ Easier to provide an after-sales service ✓ Reduces transport costs ✓ Can tailor products to the local market	✗ Can be very expensive ✗ Requires recruitment, training and selection of local employees which adds to costs ✗ May be difficult to control an operation in a foreign country

License or franchise a foreign business	✓ Reduces the risk of entering overseas market	✗ Less control over output and profit
	✓ Inexpensive way of achieving brand recognition	✗ Requires formal paperwork and incurs high legal costs
	✓ Business can receive a fee and a share of the revenue/profits	✗ Requires investment of time and money to recruit licensees/franchisees and to develop the business
		✗ Unreliable licensees/franchisees could damage the brand reputation
Joint-venture with a foreign business	✓ Experience, costs and risks are shared	✗ Partner business may focus on own business so the joint venture suffers
	✓ Local business will have detailed local knowledge and language skills	✗ Conflicts and disagreements can arise if objectives and responsibilities are not clear
	✓ Can make use of local suppliers	✗ Could be a clash of cultures and management styles
		✗ May be hard to exit if unsuccessful
Take over or merge with a foreign business	✓ Established local business	✗ Communication and coordination difficulties might lead to diseconomies of scale
	✓ Customer base already exists	✗ High costs involved
	✓ Trained local employees already in place	✗ Integration may be difficult due to language and cultural difficulties
	✓ Economies of scale can result in lower costs	✗ Some employees may feel insecure and resent the takeover

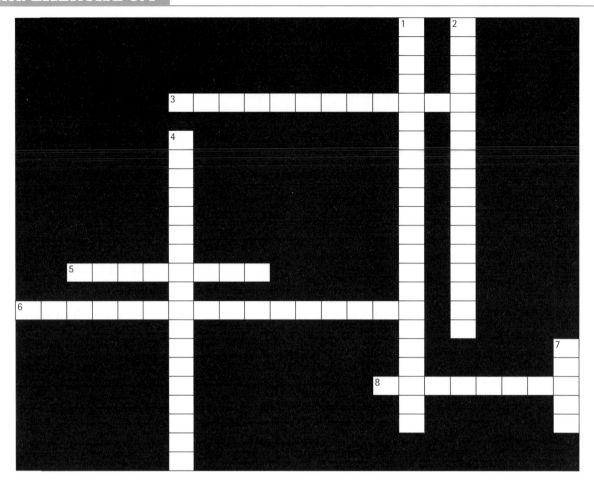

Clues down

1   Another term for legal controls on businesses that outlaw misleading or inaccurate marketing claims, unfair trading practices and the production and sale of damaged, faulty or dangerous goods and services (8, 10, 4)

2   A plan detailing the marketing objectives of a business and the actions and resources it will need to achieve them. The plan must be flexible as it will need to change over time in response to changes in consumer demand, competition and other market conditions (9, 8)

4   A pricing strategy a business may use involving heavy discounting to renew consumer interest in its product if sales are in decline and to sell off inventory to free up storage space for new product lines (12, 7)

7   A person or business with local knowledge and language skills who specializes in representing or acting on behalf of another business in order to distribute its products to customers in an overseas market (5)

Clues across

3   This is one way a business can reduce the risks associated with entering a new market overseas. It involves entering into an agreement with an established business in the overseas market to share the expertise, investment, management, costs, profits and risks of forming a new business enterprise. The new business may produce and sell an existing product in that market or develop an entirely new product for it (5, 7)

5   This is another way a business can reduce the risks associated with entering a market overseas. It involves the acquisition of an established business located in the target market (8)

6   A pricing strategy a business may use as it enters a new market and attempts to grow its sales and market share at the expense of new or existing competitors (11, 7)

8   Lack of knowledge of this will be a barrier to entering a new market overseas because it will result in communication breakdowns (8)

4 Operations management

4.1 Production of goods and services	4.1.1 The meaning of production
	4.1.2 The main methods of production
	4.1.3 How technology has changed production methods
4.2 Costs, scale of production and break-even analysis	4.2.1 Identify and classify costs
	4.2.2 Economies and diseconomies of scale
	4.2.3 Break-even analysis
4.3 Achieving quality production	4.3.1 Why quality is important and how quality production might be achieved
4.4 Location decisions	4.4.1 The main factors influencing the location and relocation decisions of a business

4.1.1 The meaning of production

- ▶ **Production** is a process that involves using resources to make goods and services to satisfy consumer needs and wants.

- ▶ Resources are the **inputs** to productive activity while **products** are the **outputs** of productive activity.

- ▶ **Productivity** measures the amount of output that can be produced from a given amount of input. Productivity increases if more output or revenue is produced from the same amount of resources, or the same output or revenue can be produced using fewer resources.

- ▶ **Labour productivity** is the most common measure of productivity in business. It measures how efficient workers are at using other resources.

- ▶ The aim of any business is to combine its resources in the most **efficient** way. That is, it will aim to produce as much output as it can with the least amount of resources it can, and therefore for the lowest cost it possibly can.

- ▶ Teaching new labour skills, reducing waste, introducing new processes and working practices or replacing labour with advanced equipment and machinery to automate production can all help to increase efficiency.

- ▶ **Lean production** methods seek to eliminate waste and create more value added.

- ▶ Lean initiatives include keeping **inventories** (stocks) to a minimum using **just-in-time inventory control** and "continuous improvement" in production, or **Kaizen**, including through the reorganization of production processes, the repositioning of equipment and stocks so they are located closer together and the constant monitoring of production targets.

Production – using resources to provide goods and services to satisfy consumer needs and wants.

Productivity – a measure of the efficiency of use of resources in a business by comparing the volume or value of output with the resource inputs used in production.

Labour productivity – average output or revenue per employee.

Lean production – improving efficiency and eliminating waste in a production process so that products can be made better, cheaper and faster.

Inventories – stocks of materials, work-in-progress and finished goods stored by a business to ensure uninterrupted production and to meet peaks in consumer demand.

Just-in-time inventory control – keeping inventories of materials and work-in-progress to a minimum by taking delivery of new parts and materials only when they are needed for production.

Kaizen – the continuous improvement of production processes to remove waste and increase efficiency.

The meaning of production

Production involves managing resources effectively to make goods and services to satisfy consumer wants

The role of the operations director or manager in a firm is to combine and manage resources in the most efficient way to produce goods or services able to satisfy consumer needs and wants.

Production is therefore a process that is not complete until those goods or services reach the people and businesses who need or want them. To do this, the operations director must work with his or her colleagues in the purchasing, human resources, sales and finance departments to identify and select the best resources, methods and locations to use in the production process.

Resources are the **inputs** to productive activity. **Products** are the **outputs** of productive activity. ➤ **1.1.1**

Production adds value to the resources it uses by turning them into products consumers want and are willing to pay for. For example, a business that produces 500 000 chocolate bars with a market value of $1 million but which cost only $700 000 to produce will have added $300 000 to the resources it has used in their production – labour, cocoa powder, milk, machinery, vehicles, foil, paper, electric power, etc.

The total output of a business organization is measured by the volume or value of all the goods or services it produces each week, month or year.

Productivity measures how efficient production is

Productivity measures the amount of output that can be produced from a given amount of input, meaning that it measures how efficient production is. For example, a business that uses 10 units of resources to produce 40 units of output per week is twice as productive as a business that uses 10 units of the same resources to produce just 20 units of output per week.

The aim of any business is to combine its resources in the most efficient way. That is, it will aim to produce as much output as it can with the least amount of resources it can, and therefore at the lowest cost possible.

For example, Pakistan obtains 33 million tonnes of milk from 20 million milking animals, compared with over 37 million tonnes obtained by China from 15 million animals and 84 million tonnes of milk produced in the USA by 9.1 million cows.

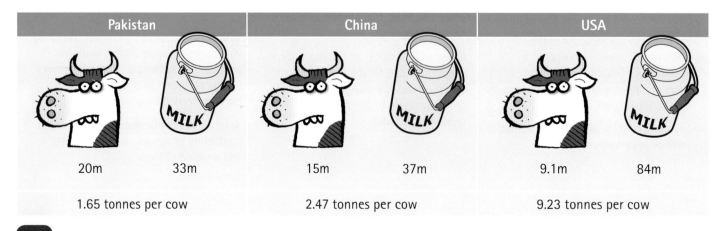

Pakistan		China		USA	
20m	33m	15m	37m	9.1m	84m
1.65 tonnes per cow		2.47 tonnes per cow		9.23 tonnes per cow	

Although Pakistan is the fourth largest producer of milk in the world after India, the USA and China, the productivity of milking animals in Pakistan is clearly much lower than that in these countries.

Low milk yields increase the cost of production of milk. For example, US farmers feed 1 cow to obtain the same quantity of milk that a Pakistani farmer obtains by feeding 4.5 cows.

According to livestock experts, milk yields of dairy herds in Pakistan could be increased by around 600 litres per animal by providing cows with adequate clean drinking water. Another 600 litres of milk production per animal could be gained by feeding cows a balanced diet and improving hygiene.

Productivity therefore measures how efficiently resources are being used in production. Accordingly, **improving efficiency** in production means improving the way resources are combined and used to increase their productivity.

In general, productivity in a business will have increased if more output or revenue is produced from the same amount of resources, or the same output or revenue can be produced using fewer resources.

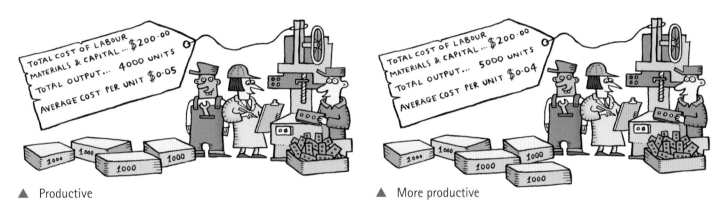

▲ Productive   ▲ More productive

Resources cost money to buy or hire. For example, materials must be purchased from suppliers, wages must be paid to hire labour, machinery and equipment must be purchased outright or leased and premises must be bought or rented. Therefore, if the same amount of labour, land and capital can produce more output for the same total cost, then the cost of producing each unit of output will have fallen.

Increasing the productivity of resources can therefore reduce production costs, make a business more competitive and increase profits. A firm that fails to increase productivity at the same or a faster pace than rival firms will have higher production costs and therefore lower profits than its competitors.

In summary, therefore, increasing productivity or the efficiency of resource use can benefit a business in several ways. It can:

✓ increase output and revenues

✓ reduce the (average) cost of each item produced and/or sold

✓ reduce the total amount and total cost of resources required by the business

✓ increase the ability of the business to compete with rivals on costs and prices

✓ increase wages received by employees as their total output increases

✓ increase profitability.

Labour productivity is the most common measure of productivity in a business

Labour productivity is calculated by dividing total output over a given period of time, for example each day, week or month, by the number of workers employed. This gives a measure of the average productivity per worker per period.

$$\text{Average productivity of labour} = \frac{\text{Total output}}{\text{Number of employees}}$$

The average productivity of labour is a useful measure of how efficient workers are and how efficiently they use other resources. For example, if a company employs 10 workers who produce 200 plant pots each day, the average product per employee per day is 20 pots. If daily output is able to rise to 220 pots per day without employing additional workers, then productivity will have increased to 22 pots per worker per day.

Productivity in business organizations producing services can be more difficult to measure. For example, a hair salon could measure the number of customers or hair treatments per day per employee, but not all employees in the salon will be hairdressers. Some may be office staff or cleaners, so how can we measure their productivity?

A better measure of overall productivity is the average revenue per worker per period.

$$\text{Average revenue productivity of labour} = \frac{\text{Total revenue}}{\text{Number of employees}}$$

Productivity is also difficult to measure in organizations that do not produce a physical output or earn revenue, for example in free hospitals or schools, government departments or a police force. Other performance measures, such as time spent waiting for an operation, meeting deadlines, numbers of students passing qualifications and numbers of arrests are often used instead.

Another problem with productivity measures is that they take no account of the quality of work. Increasing productivity is also about improving a product's quality because consumers demand, and are often willing to pay a premium for, better quality goods and services.

Manteau Designs Ltd is a small private limited company that manufactures luxury passport holders. The company started four years ago with just five production workers. Since then it has successfully expanded its sales, output and workforce.

Productivity at the factory has also increased over time as workers have become more experienced in the production of passport holders. The increase in workforce to 20 full-time production workers has also meant that the machinery and equipment installed at the factory is now fully employed throughout each working day.

With sales continuing to grow, the company's owners are thinking of expanding output further over the next year. They are considering two possible options.

Option 1: Employ five more workers, costing the business an additional $100 000 in wages each year to be funded from revenues.

Option 2: Use retained profits to finance the purchase and installation of new, more advanced machinery costing $300 000. The new machinery should remain productive for 10 years.

Year	Total output achieved (* forecast)	No. of workers	Average annual labour productivity
1	100 000	5	
2	210 000	10	
3	330 000	15	
4	460 000	20	
5	570 000 *	25 (Option 1)	
5	540 000 *	20 (Option 2 using new machinery)	

▸ Calculate the average output of each worker each year to complete the table.

▸ Do you think the company is right to consider increasing the workforce by employing five more workers?

▸ Should the company install new machinery instead of employing five more workers? Justify your answer.

▸ Suggest other ways the company may be able to improve the productivity of its workforce.

Increasing efficiency

Increasing the productivity of resources reduces costs of production but may require the replacement or retraining of labour

Take the example of Mercadona, a leading supermarket chain in Spain. According to a study it has managed to increase its productivity over time to such an extent that it now offers consumers the lowest prices in Spain and its operational performance exceeds that of comparable Spanish and foreign supermarkets.

Sales per employee at Mercadona were 18% higher than those of other Spanish supermarkets and more than 50% higher than those of US supermarkets.

So why is Mercadona so much more productive than other supermarkets? The study argues it is because Mercadona has focused on continuous improvement in its processes and products.

For Mercadona, investment in employees is a key part of process and product improvement. Each new employee spends up to four weeks training compared to just seven hours on average in the US.

Mercadona also trains its employees in a wide variety of tasks so they can rotate their jobs to make them more interesting, and so that cleaners can work the cash registers during busy periods and cashiers can shelve products during quiet periods. In addition, departmental specialists can assist customers during busy periods and order merchandise and arrange their sections during "slack" periods when there are far fewer customers in their stores. The result is that customers receive a much better service.

Many other supermarket chains employ many part-time workers to fill different shift patterns and pay them according to the numbers of hours worked which can vary significantly from week to week. In contrast, over 85% of Mercadona's store employees are full-timers and they have fixed salaries with a variable bonus linked to their productivity performance. This also helps to motivate employees.

Another feature of Mercadona's productivity performance is its focus on selling a narrower range of products. Mercadona believes it has a responsibility to select the highest-quality, most affordable products for its customers. This enables the company to buy more products in bigger bulk consignments usually at a much more favourable discount. This also means fewer products go to waste beyond their sell-by date.

The case of Mercadona illustrates how all businesses can attempt to increase the productivity of their resources by:

- training employees to improve their skills and to use new technologies

- rewarding employees who increase their productivity with performance-related pay

- improving the working environment to increase employees' job satisfaction

- introducing new production processes and working practices to reduce waste.

In addition, productivity can be increased by:

- managing **inventories** (stocks of materials, semi-finished and finished goods) effectively

- introducing **lean production** through new processes and ways of working to continually reduce waste and inefficiency

- replacing old equipment and machinery with **new technologies** and automating production processes. ➤ **4.1.3**

Why businesses hold inventories

Inventory is one of the most important assets of a business. Holding too much or too little can reduce productivity

Imagine the impact on a business if it ran out of materials to continue production or the impact on a shop that ran out of goods to sell to its customers.

A business that had no materials from which to manufacture its goods would still have to pay its workforce and other running costs despite not been able to continue production. It may also miss deadlines for supplying goods ordered by its customers, thereby losing sales and possibly their repeat orders in future.

Similarly, a shop that cannot serve customers the items they want will lose sales and possibly also its customers to rival retailers that have enough items in stock to satisfy customer demands.

Therefore, to help maintain production or sales at efficient levels all businesses will hold some goods in stock on their premises. These stocks are called **inventories**. They include raw materials and parts to be used in manufacturing processes, stocks of semi-processed or manufactured goods, called **work-in-progress**, and finished goods ready for sale to customers. In addition, a business may also hold some office supplies, including pens, paper and computer discs, plus other consumable items, such as packaging materials, in stock.

▼ Different types of items held in inventories

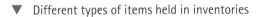

A manufacturing business will hold:	A service business will hold:
<ul><li>raw materials</li><li>component parts and chemicals</li><li>work-in-progress (semi-finished goods)</li><li>finished goods for sale</li><li>office supplies and other consumables, including packaging materials.</li></ul>	<ul><li>finished goods for sale in a shop</li><li>consumable items used to provide the service, such as carrier bags in a shop, cleaning fluids in a dry-cleaner, dyes and threads in a tailor, medicines and bandages in a veterinary practice.</li></ul>

Inventories are therefore items of value – or **current assets** – the business has invested money in which it will use up over the next few months to help it earn revenue. ➤ **5.4.1**

However, because inventories cost money to purchase and take up storage space on the business premises or in a warehouse, it is clearly not sensible to hold too much stock. Any business must therefore monitor its inventories to make sure they do not run out, for example due to an expected increase in customer demand, or become excessive.

▼ Too much inventory – too little cash

▼ Less inventory – more cash

As items are used up in production, or sold off if they are finished goods, a business will reorder replacement stock from its suppliers as its inventories reach a critical level. If inventories fall below this level then the business may run out of items to continue production or to sell to its customers. The business must allow enough time for items to be delivered before its inventories fall too low.

The time taken to deliver an item after an order has been placed is called the delivery **lead time**. The longer delivery lead times are, the more items a business will need to hold as a "buffer" in its inventories to allow production to continue without interruption.

Effective management of inventories is therefore vital in many businesses to control costs, manage cash flows and ensure production is efficient.

Overstocking	The rate of inventory turnover
Holding **excess inventory** has the following disadvantages. ✗ More cash is used up purchasing inventories leaving the business with less to pay other commitments. ✗ More storage space must be used or rented by the business. ✗ Work-in-progress and finished goods held in storage for a long time will lose value if they perish or go out of fashion: they may have to be sold at a loss or written off.	This measures how quickly inventory is used up in a business and therefore how quickly the item needs to be reordered and replaced. It will vary by the type of product and at different times each year.   Expensive consumer durable items tend to have low rates of inventory turnover. / Sweets have a very high rate of turnover during the Islamic festival of Eid due to increased demand.

The concept of lean production

A lean production process is one that eliminates waste and inefficiency

Production processes can always be improved and made more efficient. Time can be saved, waste and mistakes can be reduced, new and cheaper materials introduced, and so on. Doing all these things can reduce costs, increase output and improve quality, so a business can attract more customers, boost revenue and increase profits.

Lean manufacturing or lean production involves just this: "doing more with less". That is, creating more value from fewer resources and less effort. Lean production focuses on eliminating any time or resources wasted in a production process so that products can be made better, cheaper and faster.

For example, consider the introduction of lean manufacturing principles at Gold Seal Engineering Products (Pvt Ltd) in India. Gold Seal employs 160 workers to manufacture rubber and PVC profiles, seals and body trimmings for automobiles.

Until recently the company was a typical batch production company, where machinery required to complete each stage of the process, including moulding, cutting and packaging, was located in different areas of the plant.

Gold Seal engineers and support personnel from scheduling, supervision, engineering and maintenance came together to look at processes and break them down into their components. The team then measured and mapped the manufacturing processes to identify where time and space could be saved.

By rearranging the machines and reorganizing the floor space, including levelling and repainting, the company increased usable production space by 45% with the additional benefit of improved safety and material flow on the shop floor. Machinery downtime was also cut by 60% resulting in increased output.

Gold Seal engineers also participated in a training programme which focused on standardizing and streamlining working procedures. Through training, workers were also able to develop additional skills which led to an increase in workforce flexibility. Altogether this led to a reduction in the lead time between the start of a batch production and the completion of goods by 25% and a reduction in the volume of scrap by 75%.

The experience of Gold Seal illustrates the main lean production principles of:

- making continuous improvements in production processes

- speeding up the flow of production through the various stages of the process

- making the flow of production as continuous as possible

- reducing waste and improving work quality at all stages.

Lean production ideas were first developed by the Japanese manufacturing industry, notably in car production.

Removing waste from production

Lean production recognizes seven types of waste that can occur in production. They involve:

- transportation: moving products around unnecessarily

- stocks: storing too many components, semi-finished and finished products

- motion: people or equipment moving or walking more than is required to perform a task

- waiting time: time wasted between each stage of the production process

- overproduction: producing more than is needed to meet customer demand

- over-processing: creating unnecessary activities due to poor equipment or product design

- defects: the effort involved in inspecting and fixing product defects.

Just-in-time inventory control

This involves suppliers delivering components or materials to production lines "just in time" for them to be processed. **Just-in-time inventory control** is therefore called "stockless production" or **just-in-time production**.

It is based on the principle that products should be produced when customers need them, and in quantities customers want, in order to keep stocks of materials, components, work-in-progress and finished goods as low as possible.

Just-in-time production can therefore benefit a business in the following ways.

✓ Costs of holding and storing inventories are reduced, which in turn means the business will have more money available for other uses.

✓ Space used for storage can be used for production instead or rented out to another business to earn income – or the business can move to smaller, cheaper premises.

✓ Turnover increases as finished goods are sold off quickly, which in turn brings cash back into the business more quickly and regularly to pay for new supplies and its running costs.

However, just-in-time production can be riskier than holding stocks on the premises. A hold-up in supplies or the failure of a major supplier can seriously affect production and therefore sales.

The following requirements are therefore necessary for just-in-time production to be effective.

- The quality of materials and parts must be high. Poor materials and defective parts can hold up production on an assembly line.

- The supplier must be dependable and deliver on time. Just-in-time production requires that lead times between placing orders for more supplies and getting them delivered are as short as possible.

- It helps if suppliers are located near the company, but quality of materials and components and reliability of deliveries are more important.

Daily News

Earthquake halts car production

Toyota expects to make 9.34 million vehicles worldwide this year despite a temporary production shutdown due to earthquake damage at a key supplier of car parts in Japan.

Toyota's president, Katsuaki Watanabe, said the earthquake shutdown will result in delivery delays of 55 000 vehicles, but it wouldn't change the company's just-in-time system of production. "We've been implementing this strategy for decades … and we'll keep on with it."

Kaizen

Kaizen means "continuous improvement" in Japanese.

All workers can participate in Kaizen in a business by identifying problems and making suggestions to improve production and remove waste. An employee is expected to stop production machinery if a problem occurs and agree a solution. The solution, once agreed, then becomes standard production practice. This is called **autonomation**.

Autonomation prevents the production of defective products, eliminates overproduction and focuses attention on understanding the problem and ensuring it never occurs again. It is therefore a good method of quality control in production.

Kaizen also involves reorganizing production processes and patterns of work, repositioning equipment and stocks so they are located closer together to eliminate unnecessary lifting and carrying, and constantly checking production times and outputs against targets.

Kaizen therefore works best in a business when there is good teamwork and where workers are skilled, motivated and take pride in their work.

Kaizen can therefore deliver the business benefits of:

✓ reduced waste and improved quality in production

✓ reduced inventories of works-in-progress, saving storage space and cash

✓ reduced amount of space required for a production process, allowing the business either to reuse the space for other productive activities such as the research and development of new products or to move to smaller and cheaper premises

✓ more efficient use of labour if, as a result of all the changes, some jobs can be combined or cut allowing affected employees to carry out other tasks or jobs in the business

✓ improved employee motivation through teamwork, job enrichment and greater involvement in decision-making

✓ increased labour productivity and overall resource efficiency.

ACTIVITY 4.2

Using the article explain:

▸ the main principles of lean production and Kaizen

▸ how Kaizen has been used successfully in the Paddy Hopkirk Car Accessory factory.

Back to basics on the factory floor

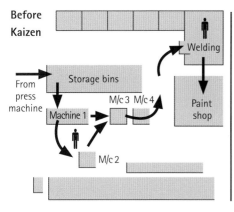

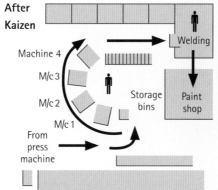

It takes a brave man to allow consultants to tear up his factory and rearrange it overnight.

At the Paddy Hopkirk Car Accessory factory in Bedfordshire, just before Christmas, consultants inspired by the Japanese concept of continuous improvement - or Kaizen - did just that.

One morning the factory was an untidy sprawl of production lines surrounded by piles of crates holding semi-finished components. Two days later, when the 180-strong workforce came to work, the machines had been brought together in tightly grouped "cells". The piles of components had disappeared, and the newly cleared floor space was neatly marked with colour-coded lines mapping out the flow of materials.

Overnight, there were dramatic differences. In the first full day, productivity on some lines increased by up to 30%, the space needed for some processes had been halved, and work-in-progress had been cut considerably. The improved layout had allowed some jobs to be combined, freeing up operators for deployment elsewhere in the factory.

One of many Japanese management practices which have been adopted in the west, Kaizen is most frequently applied in large companies. But it is equally valid in small factories. Paddy Hopkirk has sales of £6 million a year, but with the help of continuous improvement thinks this can reach £9 million.

A central part of Kaizen is the elimination of waste. It not only exists in obvious piles of excess inventory. It is also wasteful when an operator makes more movements than is necessary to complete a task because his or her machine is badly positioned.

To reduce one of the biggest sources of waste, Kaizen favours one-piece production, involving as many processes as possible being carried out on a single part consecutively rather than one process being done in a big batch. Parts are only delivered to the next stage of the production or assembly process when they are needed.

Another central theme is the drive to reduce the time wasted in processes that do not add value, like carrying pans or moving from one machine to another.

Before you continue make sure you are able to

Understand the meaning of **production:**

- ✓ managing resources effectively to produce goods and services

- ✓ the difference between **production** and **productivity**

- ✓ the benefits of increasing **efficiency** and how to increase it, for example increasing productivity by automation and technology, and through improved labour skills

- ✓ why businesses hold **inventories**

- ✓ the concept of **lean production**, and how to achieve it, for example using **just-in-time inventory control** and **Kaizen,** and the benefits of lean production.

4.1.2 The main methods of production
4.1.3 How technology has changed production methods

▸ Production methods can vary from the production of individual custom-made products (job production) to the continuous production of identical items on a mass scale (flow production).

▸ A business will choose a method of production that best meets the demands of its customers in terms of the type of product and the size of the market.

▸ The increasing pace of technological change has changed, and continues to change, many production methods.

▸ New technologies can save labour, reduce costs, increase quality and make production more efficient. However, costs of buying or hiring new technologically advanced machines, such as robots and other advanced equipment, can be high. Workers may also need retraining.

▸ New technologies have replaced many tasks originally undertaken by labour but have also created a demand for new skills, for example in computer software engineering, computer-aided design (CAD) and computer-aided manufacturing (CAM) and in "green" technologies.

Business **BUZZWORDS**

Job production – the production of a single item or items made to order, usually involving labour-intensive techniques.

Flow production – mass production of a large number of identical items in a continuous, usually automated, process.

Batch production – production of a limited number of identical products to meet a specific requirement or customer order. Each new batch may be slightly different from the last one produced.

Computer-aided design (CAD) – the use of computer systems to create, modify and optimize the design of a product.

Computer-aided manufacturing (CAM) – the use of computers to control and monitor the use of machinery and equipment in a manufacturing process.

Research and development – improving existing products and the discovery, testing and development of new products, materials or production processes, to gain a competitive advantage or to increase social welfare.

Disruptive technologies – new products, materials or processes that completely change the way businesses produce and operate or completely change what consumers want and buy.

Technological spillovers – the application of a new technology developed in one sector to the products and production processes of other industrial sectors.

Factor substitution – replacing one factor of production with another in a production process. For example, advanced capital equipment has replaced labour in many modern production processes.

The features, benefits and limitations of different production methods

Production methods can vary from the production of individual custom-made products to the continuous production of identical items on a mass scale

Production can be organized in a business in a number of different ways. There are three main methods of production.

Job production

This method is used to provide goods or services that are made or delivered to order, such as hand-crafted jewellery, custom-made furniture, garden design or home decoration.

There are many other examples where **job production** is used, including made-to-measure suits and wedding dresses, cosmetic surgery, the construction of a new cruise ship and highly specialized machinery built to perform a particular task, such as the burrowing machine used to dig the Channel Tunnel that connects the UK with France.

▲ An example of job production

> ### Advantages of job production
> + Products meet the precise requirements of their customers.
> + Businesses can often include a premium in the price they charge their customers to reflect increased quality.
> + Workers have varied jobs and many can make a finished product from start to finish. This can motivate workers and create a sense of pride in their work.
>
> ### Disadvantages of job production
> − It is labour-intensive and often takes a long time.
> − Wage costs can be high.
> − As products are produced to order any mistakes can be expensive.

Flow production

In contrast to the job production of custom-made and delivered goods and services, **flow production** involves the mass production of identical or standardized products in a continuously moving process.

It is called flow production because products are assembled, finished and packed as they move or "flow" along a production line. Many modern production lines are automated and involve very little labour.

Flow production is very cost-effective for large-scale production and many food products, liquids and household goods, including televisions, microwaves, computers and even cars, are made in this way.

Advantages of flow production

+ Goods can be produced quickly and cheaply. Average costs per unit are lower due to economies of scale.
+ Lower production costs can be passed on to consumers as lower prices helping to boost demand and revenues.
+ Automating production lines can reduce the number of workers needed and cut labour costs.
+ Automated production can be continuous for 24 hours each day.
+ It allows workers to specialize in specific, repeated tasks.

Disadvantages of flow production

- The costs of equipment and machinery required to automate production lines can be high.
- Storage requirements and the costs of stocks of materials, components and finished products can be substantial.
- Machinery breakdowns, power cuts or supply problems with components will hold up production.
- Workers undertaking repetitive tasks may become bored.

▲ An example of flow production

Batch production

This method is used for producing a limited number of identical products to meet a specific requirement or customer order. Within each stage of the production process, work is completed for a whole batch before the next stage is begun. This helps to provide greater economies of scale compared with job production, but fewer economies of scale compared with flow production. ➤ **4.2.3**

Bread and cakes are often baked in batches. Similarly, clothing and wallpapers are often produced using batch production, with different batches allowing for changes in colours and designs. Newspapers are also produced in batches each day.

Advantages of batch production

+ It is a good way of adding variety to otherwise identical products to give consumers a wider choice, for example producing a car with a choice of different colours and engine sizes.
+ Workers' tasks are more varied than in flow production, reducing the risk of boredom.

Disadvantages of batch production

- It needs careful planning to minimize the amount of unproductive time between different batches.
- Costs will be higher than for production on a mass scale.

▲ An example of batch production

Choosing a method of production

A business will choose a method of production that best meets the demands of its customers in terms of the type of product and quantity they want

The method of production chosen by a business will depend on a number of factors.

- **What is the nature of the product?** For example, is it a personalized good or service? If so, job production may be the most appropriate method. Alternatively, can the product be mass-produced on an automated production line with little labour input?

- **What is the size of the market?** This will determine how much output a business can produce and supply. Small businesses tend to serve small, local markets or nationwide niche markets. Large organizations generally sell into large international markets and can therefore justify mass production.

- **What is the nature of demand?** Will consumers purchase the product in large quantities on a regular basis, as with products such as food, petrol and washing powders? Or will consumers only want to buy the product infrequently, as with many items of furniture and electrical goods?

- **What is the productive capacity of the business?** If required, does the business have enough resources to produce on a large scale? Further, can the business afford to invest a large amount of money in new plant and technology? Can the business afford new technologies? If not, flow production on a mass scale will not be possible.

ACTIVITY 4.3

Suggest appropriate production methods for the products shown below. Give reasons for your suggestions.

A

PINK PAINT

▲ Production target: 1000 units per week

B

▲ Production target: 5 units per month

C

▲ Production target: 500 000 units per week

D

▲ Production target: 15 customers per day

E

▲ Production target: 200 units per day

F

▲ Production target: 1 unit per year

How technology has changed production methods

Technological advance has created new materials, products and processes

▲ Old technologies   ▲ New technologies

"Out with the old and in with the new" is a well-known saying in some regions of the world. Today, old materials, products and production processes are rapidly being replaced with new ones as the pace of technological change increases.

Many years ago most goods were produced by hand using hand-held or hand-operated machinery and tools. Today, many more millions of goods are produced each year by machines and equipment with very little human effort required. The development of sophisticated machinery and equipment has allowed the production of many goods, first to be mechanized, then integrated into continually flowing production or assembly lines and finally automated.

Many production processes are now controlled by computers programmed by people. The first computers, in use around 60 years ago, had far less power and capabilities, filled huge rooms and cost many millions of dollars compared with the small desktop and tablet computers many people and firms own and use today.

- **Computer-aided design (CAD)** allows detailed component parts and finished products to be drawn and redrawn easily and accurately using computer software which also allows the drawn images to be rotated so they can be viewed from every angle.

Mechanization
Production carried out by machines operated by people

↓

Integration
Each stage of a production process is combined into an assembly line to form a continuous flow

↓

Automation
Each stage of an integrated production process is carried out by computer-controlled machinery and equipment

---

- **Computer-aided manufacturing (CAM)** relies on computers to control industrial robots and other advanced machines designed to complete many different tasks in an integrated production process. CAM is used to create a faster and more accurate production process. The use of CAM therefore increases output, reduces waste and improves quality in production.

- **Computer-integrated manufacturing (CIM)** combines CAD and CAM into one continuous flow. Once the detailed design of a component or finished product has been finalized it can be sent directly over the internet to computer-controlled equipment for manufacturing.

Technologies invented and used in one sector often "spill over" into other uses

Technological advances made in one industrial sector can often "spill over" into other sectors. For example, fibreglass was originally invented for use as insulation material but is now used in the production of bows and crossbows, roofing panels, automobile and aircraft wings, surfboards, artificial limbs and many more products.

Similarly, the internet is based on a system first developed in 1973 by the US Defense Advanced Research Projects Agency to enable communications between military computers to withstand nuclear attack. The internet is now used extensively in business for communications, marketing, taking orders and payments from customers and placing orders with suppliers. ➤ **3.3.5**

Technological spillovers are therefore examples of external benefits, whereby the actions of one producer benefit another producer or production process. As a result, governments are often willing to provide financial help to businesses investing in the research and development of new technologies because of the employment and other benefits they can create across many industrial sectors. ➤ **6.2.1**

New technologies can reduce costs, improve quality and increase efficiency

Firms are continually looking for ways to use their resources more efficiently in order to reduce their costs, increase their profits and make products that will attract consumers away from rival businesses. A new product or way of making something can give a firm a competitive advantage. However, the **research and development** of new products, processes and materials can be very expensive and not all will succeed.

Every now and then, though, new technologies are developed which completely change production, marketing and other business activities. These new technologies are known as **disruptive technologies** and examples include the introduction of telephones, electricity, the motor car and more recently the internet, mobile communications and robotics.

▼ Major advances in technology have revolutionized production and the way businesses operate

Timeline	
1785	Water power Textiles Iron
1845	Steam power Railways Steel Telephones
1900	Refrigeration Plastics Electricity Chemicals Internal combustion engine
1950	Petrochemicals Jet engines and aviation Electronics
1990	Digital cameras Mobile phones Computer software Biotechnology
2000	Wind, wave and solar power Electric cars MySpace and YouTube
2010	3D cameras and televisions iPad
2015	Apple pay Drones Virtual reality goggles
2020 +	?

Disruptive technologies also include many new processes and products that destroy the demand for others. For example, digital cameras have replaced cameras that used film; biotechnology has created cleaning products, weedkillers and fertilizers from harmless living bacteria and organisms that have replaced more harmful chemicals; and nanotechnology has produced tiny computer circuits no bigger than a red blood cell and other nanomaterials that are used in many different products and processes the world over, from making solar panels to making medicines.

So what is next? Many experts predict 3D printing will soon replace many existing manufacturing processes and revolutionize the way we receive and repair goods in the future, simply by printing them out.

New technology has replaced many tasks originally undertaken by labour

Factor substitution has taken place in many production processes in many countries over time. Tasks once carried out by employees are now increasingly completed by advanced machines and other production equipment. That is, labour input has been replaced or substituted with capital or man-made resources. ➤ **1.1.1**

This substitution has occurred as technological advance has continually reduced the cost of advanced machinery, computers and other equipment while increasing their productivity relative to labour. For example, the work of once skilled typesetters and compositors in the printing industry has been replaced by desktop publishing software on computers operated by writers and journalists. Intelligent robots controlled by computers have also taken over many human tasks in manufacturing processes from car assembly to food processing.

However, labour and capital are not always perfect substitutes. The ability of a firm to substitute capital for labour very much depends on the type of product and the production process used and their relative costs. Consider the following issues.

- Machines cannot replicate the work of a doctor, solicitor, hairdresser or other workers providing personalized care and services.

- Buying and installing new and more productive equipment can be expensive.

- Workers may need to be retrained to operate new equipment.

- Workers may strike if they fear they could lose their jobs.

- Not all products can or should be mass-produced using automated production processes. For example, some consumers want personalized and handmade products.

India steps up to robotics

With the Indian manufacturing sector booming, the robotics industry is gearing up for sharp growth. At India's biggest auto manufacturer, Tata Motors, the workforce has been reduced by 20%, while the company's turnover has increased 2.5 times. Its Pune plant alone has invested in 100 robots.

At the same time the country's top government scientists are at work on robot and artificial intelligence (AI) technologies for use in everything from border patrols to the deployment of "robot armies" to replace human soldiers.

"The use of robots is growing extremely fast in India," say industry analysts. "Robotics can be expensive to buy and implement but robots save labour and help companies raise their productivity and quality, to meet the demands of international competition. Customers in India are also beginning to understand how useful robots are in production: they not only save costs, but are a safer and a healthier option."

Scotland plans to use greener technology to create thousands of new jobs

Tens of thousands of new jobs could be created in Scotland in the next five years under plans to invest in greener technology. The jobs would be created from a major expansion in the number of companies developing state-of-the-art ways to tackle pollution, manage waste and reduce carbon.

ACTIVITY 4.4

Look at the article "India steps up to robotics" above.

▸ What do you think are some of the advantages of employing robots in business?

▸ Why do you think industrial robots are described as labour-saving technology?

▸ How can the use of robots in business affect workers and consumers?

▸ What do you think may be some of the main obstacles to employing more robots in businesses in your economy and other national economies?

Advantages of new technology to business	Disadvantages of new technology to business
• Firms can increase productivity and efficiency.	• Research and development of new products and processes can be expensive and not all will succeed.
• Labour costs can be reduced. Hi-tech businesses can recruit, train and manage fewer workers.	• The initial costs of buying or hiring new technologically advanced machines, like robots and other advanced equipment, can be high.
• Machines can be kept working all day, every day.	
• Product quality can be controlled and improved, resulting in less waste.	• Firms unwilling or unable to afford to invest in new technologies will lose custom to firms that do.
• The development of a new desirable product gives a firm a competitive advantage over others.	• Product life cycles are becoming shorter. This means businesses may earn less profit from each product and have to spend more money and time developing new ones.
• Consumers are replacing products and buying new ones more often to get the latest features.	
• Many modern technologies, such as computers, are affordable to even the smallest of firms.	• Workers may need to be retrained to use new materials, production processes and equipment.
• The internet and electronic communications allow information and payments to be exchanged easily, quickly and cheaply.	• Workers and trade unions may be reluctant to learn new skills, may resist changes in working practices and may even take strike action if the introduction of new technology threatens their jobs.
• Governments may offer tax and subsidy incentives to encourage investments in research and development and new technologies to boost economic growth.	

Emma Sorrel is a sole trader manufacturing plates for hospital cafeterias. The flow production she uses is capital intensive. She employs six people in the factory and two delivery drivers. Each machine requires two people to operate and can produce 1200 plates per 8-hour day. Currently 800 plates are being produced daily. Emma would like to increase the output of plates per day and thinks she could do this if the employees worked harder. The inventory consists of 5000 plates.

a Explain the term "capital intensive".   [2]

b Calculate the average labour productivity per hour.   [2]

c Explain **one** advantage and **one** disadvantage, to Emma, of being
   a sole trader.   [4]

d Advise Emma on ways in which she could increase the output of
   plates per day.   [6]

e Consider whether flow production is the most efficient way for Emma to
   produce plates. Justify your answer.   [6]

Learning CHECKLIST

Before you continue make sure you are able to

Describe the main **methods of production**:

✓ the features, benefits and limitations of **job, batch** and **flow production**

✓ recommend and justify an appropriate production method for a given situation

Understand how **technology** has changed production methods:

✓ for example, through the use of computers in manufacturing and design.

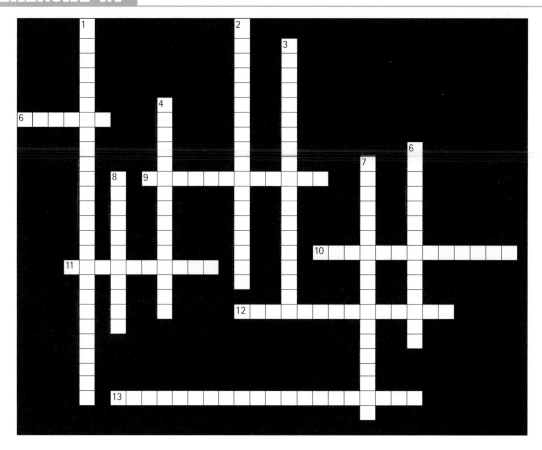

Clues down

1 The use of computers to control and monitor the use of machinery and equipment in a production process (8, 5, 13)

2 Replacing one factor of production with another in a production process, for example replacing labour with capital equipment because it is cheaper, more accurate and more productive (6, 12)

3 The use of computer systems to create, modify and optimize the design of a product (8, 5, 6)

4 This method of production involves producing a limited number of identical products to meet a specific requirement or customer order, for example for 100 tins of pink paint followed by 100 tins of blue paint (5, 10)

6 Mass production of a large number of identical items in a continuous, automated process (4, 10)

7 A measure of the average output or revenue per employee per period and, therefore, a measure of how efficiently employees use other productive resources (6, 12)

8 To maintain production or sales at efficient levels, all businesses will hold some items they need in stock, for example in case additional supplies are late being delivered. They will include stocks of materials and works-in-progress to supply their production processes and stocks of finished goods to satisfy customer demands. This term is used to describe all the different items held in stock in a business (11)

Clues across

5 A business seeking to continually improve the efficiency with which it uses resources has reorganized its production line by repositioning its machinery and stocks of components so they are located closer together. The aim is to reduce unnecessary lifting, carrying and movement. What principle has the business applied? (6)

9 A measure of how efficiently a business is using its resources by comparing the volume or value of output with the resource inputs used in their production (12)

10 This production method is used to make a single item or items to order, usually involving labour-intensive techniques (3, 10)

11 The use of machines and technology to make production processes run on their own without the need for workers to complete each of the various tasks involved (10)

12 The collective term used to describe various techniques and initiatives designed to reduce or eliminate waste from a production process so that products can be made better, cheaper and faster (4, 10)

13 Holding too many items in stock is costly and uses up too much cash in a business. Instead many firms only order and take delivery of items from suppliers as they are required for production or for sale to their customers. This form of inventory control is often called "stockless production". How else it is described? (4-2-4, 10)

4.2.1 Identify and classify costs
4.2.2 Economies and diseconomies of scale
4.2.3 Break-even analysis

▶ Controlling costs is important to any business. Some costs will be fixed while others, such as the cost of materials and components, will increase as more is produced. A business will need to cover its fixed costs regardless of how much output it produces.

▶ The total cost of producing a given level of output will be equal to the total fixed costs of the business and the total variable costs of producing that level of output.

▶ Increasing the scale of production can benefit from economies of scale that reduce the average cost of producing each unit of output. If price is unchanged then the profit margin on each unit will be increased.

▶ Many large firms have cost advantages over small rival firms because they receive discounts for buying supplies in bulk and they can access cheaper sources of finance and invest in specialized equipment, highly skilled workers, and new products and processes to increase efficiency.

▶ If the price at which each unit is sold exceeds the cost of producing each unit, or average cost, the business will make a profit on each unit.

▶ To break even, a business must earn enough revenue to equal its costs. At the break-even level of output profit or loss is zero.

▶ Total revenue and total cost can be plotted on a break-even chart to identify levels of output that will make a loss, break even or yield a profit.

Fixed costs – costs that do not vary with output (also known as overheads).

Variable costs – costs that vary directly with output (also known as direct costs).

Direct costs – costs that can be attributed to a specific activity or the production of a particular product.

Overheads – or indirect costs, are the day-to-day running costs of an organization.

Average cost – the cost of producing each unit of output.

Profit margin – the difference between the selling price per unit and the average cost per unit.

Break-even level of output – the minimum level of output a business will need to produce and sell to cover its costs.

Break-even analysis – using cost and revenue data to calculate the break-even level of output.

Economies of scale – a fall in the average cost of producing each unit due to an increase in the scale of production.

Diseconomies of scale – rising average costs due to a business being too big to operate efficiently.

Classifying costs

Profit is the difference between revenues and costs

Geoff Watt has had a bright idea. He is about to launch a new business venture, producing and selling low-energy light bulbs. He has spent $2000 of his own savings on market research to find out what consumers want in terms of the product's quality, design and colours, and what they are willing to pay. He decides to call his business Bright Lights.

Geoff knows that running a successful business means taking decisions about how best to organize resources in order to maximize their productivity and make a profit, where:

Profit = Total revenue – Total costs

Geoff can therefore increase his profits by reducing the costs and/or raising the revenues of his business.

Every business decision, whether to launch a new product, to change advertising methods or to expand production, has an impact on costs. As the main objective of most private sector firms is to make a **profit** it is therefore essential that businesses are able to keep a tight control on their costs. ➤ **1.5.1**

Cost control is equally important in public sector organizations and charities that do not seek to make a profit. They will still want to keep the costs of their operations as low as possible.

In order to control his costs, Geoff must therefore be able to identify what they are, calculate how much they are and then set targets for future cost levels.

Costs can be fixed or variable with output

Before a business can start production and make goods and services for sale, it will need to buy or hire many items. A business may need premises, vehicles, computers and other equipment, and may need to buy stationery and undertake market research. These are **start-up costs**. Starting a business or developing a new product can be expensive and there will be no revenue to cover these start-up costs until production begins and products are sold.

Even when a business is up and running it will still need to pay many costs whether it is producing and selling few or many goods or services. **Fixed costs** do not vary with the amount of goods or services produced. They include the costs of buying or hiring machinery and equipment, advertising, loan repayments, insurance premiums, rent for premises, the wages of office staff and telephone charges. Fixed costs are also referred to as **overheads**. ➤ **5.4.1**

In contrast, **variable costs** vary directly with the amount of goods or services produced. These are the **direct costs** of purchasing or producing items for sale. They include payments for materials and components, the wages of production workers, and the direct costs of electricity to operate machinery and other production equipment. The more a business produces the more its total variable costs will be.

The sum of all fixed and variable costs gives the **total cost** of all the activities of a business. It is important to know total cost in order to be able to work out total profit.

1 The Comfy Coffee Bar had the following costs last year.
   Which costs would you classify as fixed costs and which costs are variable?

Purchases of coffee, teas, milk and sugars	$8500	Hire charges for equipment	$2300
Supplies of soft drinks	$9300	Office stationery	$500
Telephone charges	$1200	Advertising costs	$1200
Consumables (paper cups, cleaning fluids, etc.)	$3700	Computer maintenance contract	$400
Wages (piece rates) of serving staff	$45000	Deliveries of cakes, biscuits and pastries	$16000
Electricity charges	$5000	Basic wages of office staff	$20000
Insurance premiums	$1500	Bank loan repayment	$6000

2 How much were the total fixed costs and total variable costs of The Comfy Coffee Bar?

3 Investigate the costs of a small business of your choice. Try to arrange a short interview with the business owners or managers. Ask them what their main business costs are and then classify them according to whether they are fixed costs or variable costs.

Direct and indirect costs

Business owners and managers may also classify and monitor costs in other ways.

Direct costs are those costs that can be attributed directly to a specific business activity or function, or the production of a particular product. They include the materials and labour costs of employees directly involved in making a product. Direct costs are therefore very similar to variable costs.

Indirect costs or **overheads** are the day-to-day running costs of a business organization, including insurance charges, loan repayments, cleaning and office costs. Indirect costs are therefore very similar to fixed costs.

Calculating and presenting total costs of production

Like other business owners and managers, Geoff will want to know what the fixed, variable and total costs of his business will be at different levels of output.

- **Fixed costs:** Geoff has calculated these will be $3000 per month regardless of whether he produces 1, 1000 or 6000 light bulbs. The costs include the rent of a factory unit, hire charges for machinery and many administrative costs. Therefore:

  Total fixed costs = Sum of all fixed costs

- **Variable costs:** Geoff has estimated the cost of materials, labour and power needed to produce each light bulb is $2. So, if Geoff produces 1000 light bulbs each month his total variable costs will be $2000 and if he produces 6000 light bulbs his total variable costs will be $12000 each month. That is:

  Total variable costs = Variable cost per unit × Total output

- **Total costs:** by adding together total fixed costs and total variable costs, Geoff can calculate the total cost of producing any given number of light bulbs per period:

Total costs = Total fixed costs + Total variable costs

As output rises total costs will rise because total variable costs will increase. So, for example, if Bright Lights produces 6000 light bulbs each month its total costs will be $15 000. That is, $3000 of fixed costs and $12 000 of variable costs.

Using this information, Geoff is able to produce the following table showing the fixed, variable and total costs of producing different amounts of light bulbs each month.

Output (units per month)	Total fixed costs	Total variable costs	Total costs	Average cost per unit
0	$3000	0	$3000	–
1000	$3000	$2000	$5000	$5.00
2000	$3000	$4000	$7000	$3.50
3000	$3000	$6000	$9000	$3.00
4000	$3000	$8000	$11 000	$2.75
5000	$3000	$10 000	$13 000	$2.60
6000	$3000	$12 000	$15 000	$2.50

▲ Total and average costs of production at different levels of output for Bright Lights

Better still, Geoff can see the impact different levels of output has on costs by plotting this data on a chart. First, he plots his total fixed costs against different levels of output per month as follows.

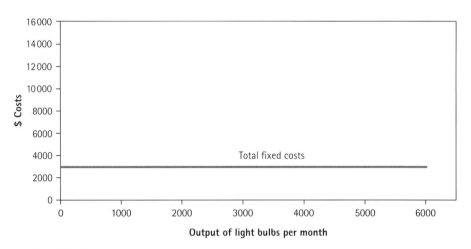

▲ Total fixed costs

The plot of total fixed costs is a flat line. This is because fixed costs do not vary with the amount of output.

Second, Geoff plots his variable costs of producing different levels of output each month. The plot is an upward sloping line because total variable costs increase as output rises.

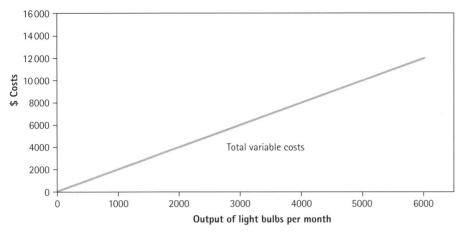

▲ Total variable costs

Finally, Geoff can combine these plots into one chart and, adding total fixed costs to total variable costs, can show the total cost of producing each level of output as follows.

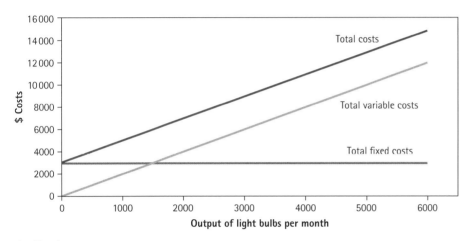

▲ Total costs

Like Geoff's table of cost information, the chart shows that when output is zero the total cost of production will be exactly equal to the total fixed costs he will have to continue paying to remain in business. If, however, output is 6000 light bulbs per month, then total costs will be $15 000 per month.

Calculating the average cost of producing each unit of output

It is also useful to calculate the average cost of producing each unit of output using the following equation:

Average cost per unit = Total cost / Total output

You will have noticed that the table of cost information on page 310 that Geoff produced for his business Bright Lights also contains his calculations of how much it will cost to produce each light bulb.

If Bright Lights produces just 1000 light bulbs each month at a total cost of $5000 (fixed costs of $3000 plus total variable costs of $2000) then the average cost of producing each light bulb – or cost per unit – will be $5.

Average cost per light bulb = $5000 / 1000 = $5
(when output is 1000 per month)

However, if Bright Lights produces 6000 light bulbs each month at a total cost of $15 000 (fixed costs of $3000 plus total variable costs of $12 000) then the average cost of producing each light bulb – or cost per unit – will be $2.50.

Average cost per light bulb = $15 000 / 6000 = $2.50
(when output is 6000 per month)

As the table and these calculations show, the average cost of producing each light bulb or unit of output falls as the total number produced is increased. This is because fixed costs remain unchanged as output is increased.

The same holds for all businesses in all industrial sectors: the average cost of producing each unit of output will fall as output is increased if fixed costs and the variable cost per unit remain unchanged. Many large businesses therefore have a significant unit cost advantage over small, rival businesses with lower levels of output.

Cost data is used to make important decisions

Knowledge of total and average costs is essential to inform important production and pricing decisions. Now that Geoff knows his fixed, variable, total and average costs of producing different levels of output he can use this knowledge to make a number of important business decisions.

- What selling price does the business set to earn a profit on each item sold?
- What level of output does the business need to produce and sell to cover its costs?
- What level of output does the business need to produce and sell to earn a satisfactory level of total profit, or to maximize total profit?
- If demand for the product falls, at what level of output should production stop in order to avoid high losses?

Geoff knows that the total cost of producing 1000 light bulbs each month will be $5000 per month. In turn, this means that the average cost of producing each light bulb will be $5. Geoff will therefore need to sell these light bulbs at a price greater than $5 each to earn a profit on each one sold.

However, Geoff's market research suggests that consumers are not willing to pay more than $3 for each low-energy light bulb.

If Geoff only produces 1000 each month at an average cost of $5 each he will make a loss of $2 per light bulb sold at a selling price of $3 where:

Profit (or loss) per unit = Selling price per unit – Average cost per unit

It follows that if Geoff makes a loss of $2 per unit sold then if he sells all 1000 light bulbs each month his total loss will be $2000 per month.

Geoff must now decide whether he should stop or continue production. If he stops production, he would still have to pay fixed costs of $3000 per month, in the short run. The $3 price of the light bulbs would cover his total fixed costs but not his total variable costs. Geoff should continue to produce light bulbs in the short run as the loss of $2000 per month is less than the fixed costs of $3000 per month. Continuing production means he can pay his fixed costs.

When output = 6000 units per month

When output = 1000 units per month

Total cost = $5000
So, average cost = $5 ($5000/1000)
If selling price per unit = $3
Then loss per unit = $2

Total cost = $15 000
So, average cost = $2.50 ($15 000/6000)
If selling price per unit = $3
Then profit per unit = $0.50

The maximum amount of light bulbs Geoff can produce each month in his existing premises and without having to hire or buy additional machinery is 6000. The total cost of producing 6000 light bulbs per month is $15 000 per month. Therefore, the average cost per light bulb produced will be $2.50. If each light bulb or unit is sold for $3 then the profit per unit will be:

$0.50 (Profit per unit) = $3 (Selling price per unit) − $2.50 (Average cost per unit)

The **profit margin** in his selling price per unit is therefore $0.50. If Geoff sells all 6000 light bulbs each month then his total profit each month from sales will be $3000.

Total profit = $3000 = $0.50 (Profit margin per unit) × 6000 (Units sold)

If Geoff sells 6000 light bulbs per month, then he should continue to produce in the long run as he is covering both fixed and variable costs (total costs) and making a profit of $3000 per month.

Economies of scale

A business may benefit from cost advantages as it increases its scale of production

Geoff can only produce so many light bulbs with the premises, machinery and equipment his Bright Lights business has. We know that as he expands total output and therefore makes more use of these resources, the average cost of producing each light bulb falls. However, once these resources are fully employed, Geoff will only be able to increase output and therefore reduce his average costs of production further if he invests in additional machines and equipment, and possibly even larger premises to expand the scale of production at his business. Although this will increase fixed costs, the larger his business becomes the more cost advantages it may be able to enjoy over small businesses. These cost advantages are called **economies of scale**.

From the articles below try to identify different cost advantages large businesses may have over small organizations.

Chamber of Commerce complains of banks overcharging small businesses

Banking groups are restricting loans to small businesses, charging them high interest rates and forcing them to pay costly fees for bank services according to the Chamber of Commerce.

"Small businesses cannot survive without low-cost sources of capital," said a Chamber of Commerce spokesperson. "Interest charges on loans for small businesses are much higher than those charged on loans to much larger business customers."

The Banking Association said it had a fair lending policy that reflected the relative risks of lending to small and large businesses.

Tech Group signs major contract to supply Hinshu

Tech Group, a leading supplier of engine cooling systems, has signed a $1.5 billion contract to supply Hinshu Motors over the next three years.

Hinshu Motors is scaling up production of its successful range of automobiles. Delton Williams, Marketing Director at Hinshu, said the deal was a good one for both companies because "Tech Group offers high-quality components, fast delivery times and substantial discounts for bulk orders to its largest business customers. It is cheaper for them to make one large delivery each week than several smaller deliveries over the same period."

Government sets up information technology advice centre and website to help small businesses

Investing in IT can greatly improve business efficiency and lower costs but unlike their larger rivals, small businesses cannot afford to employ the specialists they need to advise them on their IT needs and how best to use and maintain their IT systems. The new government scheme will employ IT specialists to provide free help and advice to small businesses.

Large businesses fare better than small ones during recession

According to a new report large businesses continue to enjoy many cost advantages over small businesses that have allowed them to discount their prices more heavily in the recession to maintain customer demand. Large businesses also benefit from serving more than one market, many overseas, which has reduced their risk of falling demand at home.

Economies of scale reduce the average cost of producing each unit of output as the scale of production is expanded in a business. There are five main types of economies of scale.

Purchasing economies. Large firms are often able to buy the materials, components and other supplies they need in bulk because of the large scale of their production. Suppliers usually offer price discounts for bulk purchases because it is cheaper for them to make one large delivery than to make several small deliveries.

Marketing economies. Large businesses may buy or hire their own vehicles to distribute their goods and services rather than rely on other firms to do so. In this way, a large firm can reduce its costs because it does not have to pay the profit margin of a wholesaler or distribution company. It may also be able to increase the reliability and efficiency of its distribution. Similarly, the fixed costs of advertising in a newspaper or on television will be spread over a much larger output in a large firm than in a small firm.

Risk-bearing economies. A large firm may have more customers, sell into more markets at home and overseas and offer a larger range of products than a small business. In this way, a large firm is able to reduce the risk to its business of losing a major customer, or a fall in demand for one of its products in one of its markets.

Technical economies. Large businesses often have the financial resources available to invest in specialized machinery and equipment, to train and recruit highly skilled workers and to research and develop new products and processes to increase the efficiency of their production. Small firms may not be able to afford to do so.

Financial economies. Large businesses can often borrow more money and at lower interest rates than small businesses. Bank managers and other lenders often consider lending to big organizations as less risky than lending to small ones. Large public companies are also able to sell shares to raise permanent capital that never has to be repaid. **➤ 1.4.1**

Managerial economies. Large businesses can employ specialist managers for each function e.g. finance, human resources, operations and marketing. This can increase productivity and efficiency as each manager will have expertise in that function. This will help reduce costs and increase output. Small firms do not usually have the resources to employ specialist managers and may just have a general manager who is responsible for all the functions.

Diseconomies of scale can occur if a business grows too large

Sometimes a business organization may grow so large that it becomes less and less efficient as it expands. As a result, its average costs of production may start to rise. These problems are caused by **diseconomies of scale**.

Management diseconomies. A large firm may have too many departments and layers of management. This can cause communication problems and disagreements between different managers in different parts of the organization. Poor communication will slow down decision-making and it may take longer for decisions to be acted on by workers at the bottom of the organization's hierarchy. If managers do not communicate effectively with each other, there will be weak coordination, which can lead to an inability to solve problems properly. **➤ 1.3.3**

Labour diseconomies. Large firms often use specialized machinery and flow production to produce on a mass scale. Workers who carry out repetitive tasks may become bored, demotivated and feel they are not valued. This causes a lack of commitment from employees which can lead to an increase in absenteeism and labour turnover. As a result, productivity may fall and labour disputes may also occur which can disrupt production. **➤ 2.2.4**

Break-even analysis

To break-even a business must earn enough revenue to cover its costs

To break even a business must earn enough revenue to cover its costs. Geoff has a production and sales target for Bright Lights of 6000 light bulbs per month. He knows that if he is able to sell all 6000 each month at a price of $3 each he will make a profit of $3000 per month.

But what if Geoff is unable to sell 6000 light bulbs each and every month? He would also like to know therefore the minimum number of light bulbs he must make and sell each month in order to cover his costs of production and stay in business. To find this out he can use break-even analysis.

Break-even analysis is used to calculate the minimum level of output a business needs to produce and sell to cover its costs.

The **break-even level of output** is that level of output which, if sold, will generate a total revenue that will exactly equal the total cost of producing that level of output. At the break-even level of output a business will make neither a profit nor a loss. That is, breakeven occurs where:

Total revenue = Total cost

Or,

Profit (or loss) = 0 = Total revenue – Total costs

Geoff has decided to set a price of $3 per light bulb based on his market research of consumer preferences. It is also a price that is competitive with those charged for light bulbs manufactured by other firms.

Now that his selling price has been set, Geoff is able to extend his table of cost information on page 310 at different levels of output to include total revenues from sales of light bulbs at $3 per unit.

Output (units per month)	Fixed costs	Variable costs ($2 per unit)	Total costs	Total revenue ($3 per unit)	Profit or loss
0	$3000	0	$3000	0	-$3000
1000	$3000	$2000	$5000	$3000	-$2000
2000	$3000	$4000	$7000	$6000	-$1000
3000	$3000	$6000	$9000	$9000	0
4000	$3000	$8000	$11 000	$12 000	$1000
5000	$3000	$10 000	$13 000	$15 000	$2000
6000	$3000	$12 000	$15 000	$18 000	$3000

From this table Geoff is able to identify his break-even level of output as 3000 lights bulbs per month. If all 3000 light bulbs are sold each month at a price of $3, then his total revenue will be $9000 per month ($3 × 3000 units sold) and exactly equal the total cost of their production of $9000 (fixed costs of $3000 plus total variable costs of $6000).

In addition to costs, Geoff can also use this table to plot a chart showing total revenues per month at different levels of output. He can use this to identify his break-even level of output.

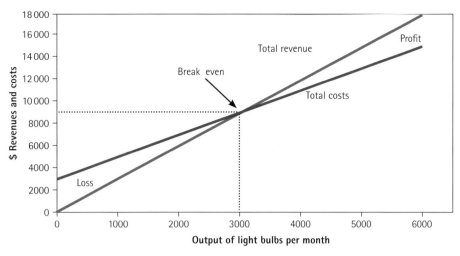

A break-even chart for Bright Lights

The chart is called a **break-even chart** because it shows the total revenues, costs and therefore total profit or loss of the business at different levels of output. In the chart, the minimum level of output Bright Lights must produce and sell each month is found at the point where its total revenue line crosses its total cost line. It shows that the business will break even if it produces and sells 3000 light bulbs each month.

At every level of output below 3000 light bulbs per month, the business will make a **loss**. In the chart then the total revenue line will be below the total cost line. The area between them is the area of loss.

In contrast, at every level of output above 3000 light bulbs per month the business will make a **profit**. In the chart then the total revenue line will be above the total cost line and the area between them is therefore profit.

ACTIVITY 4.7

InkPot Ltd is a small company that makes and sells printer cartridges for a popular brand of inkjet computer printers. It has fixed costs of $50 000 per year and variable costs of $2.50 per cartridge. Each cartridge sells for $5.

1 Use a computer spreadsheet to complete the following table of costs and revenues for different levels of output.

Output (cartridges per year)	Fixed costs	Total variable costs	Total costs	Total revenue	Profit/Loss
0	$50 000				
10 000					-$25 000
20 000			$100 000		
30 000					
40 000		$100 000			
50 000					
60 000				$300 000	

2 Use the table to plot a break-even chart.

3 What is the break-even level of output?

4 What will be the break-even level of output if the variable costs per cartridge increased to $4? Use your spreadsheet to recalculate total variable costs, total costs and the profit or loss at each level of output.

5 What will be the break-even level of output if the price of each cartridge increased to $7.50? Use your original spreadsheet to recalculate total variable costs, total costs and the profit or loss at each level of output.

Costs, scale of production and break-even analysis

A business should plan to have a margin of safety by producing and selling more than its needs to break-even

All businesses aim to make a profit by producing and selling products above the break-even output. Geoff forecasts sales of 6000 light bulbs per month. If he sells 3000 light bulbs per month, he breaks even. Sales of 6000 light bulbs per month would give him a **margin of safety** of 3000 light bulbs per month. The margin of safety is the difference between the actual level of output and the break-even level of output. It can be calculated as follows:

Margin of safety = Actual output 6000 – Break-even output 3000 = 3000 light bulbs per month margin of safety

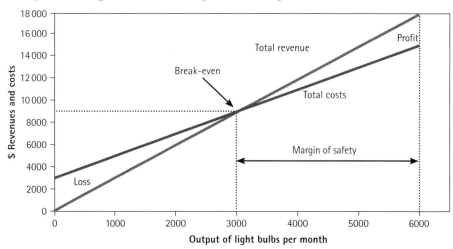

▲ Margin of safety chart for Bright Lights

Break-even analysis is used to make important production and pricing decisions

A break-even chart is a useful business planning tool. Business owners and managers can use break-even charts to examine what might happen to their break-even level of output and profits if costs or selling prices change.

For example, if costs rise, the amount of output a business must produce and sell each month or year to break even also have to rise.

Geoff uses his break-even chart to look at the effect of a rise in his variable costs of production from $2 per light bulb to $2.40. This has the effect of moving the total cost line from TC1 to TC2. From the chart Geoff realizes he will have to produce and sell 5000 light bulbs each month just to break even if his costs rise in this way.

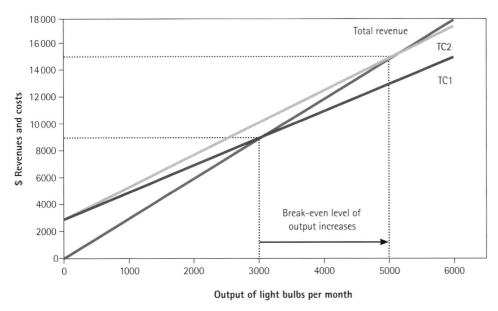

▲ The break-even chart for Bright Lights following an increase in variable costs

Geoff also considers what would happen instead if he was only able to sell each light bulb at a price of $2.75. This would have the effect of reducing the profit margin on each unit sold from $0.50 to $0.25. Total revenue and therefore profit would be lower each month. In the chart below, the total revenue line moves from TR1 to TR2. As a result, Geoff will need to make and sell at least 4000 light bulbs each month to break even.

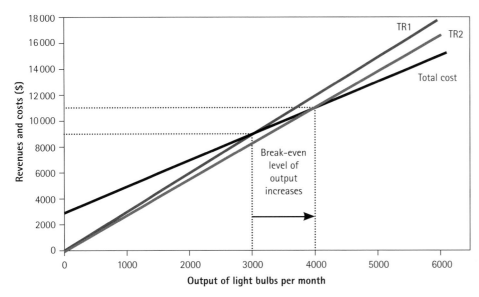

▲ The break-even chart for Bright Lights following a decrease in revenue

Because Geoff intends to produce 6000 light bulbs each month, the two charts show he will still be able to make a profit from their sale even if his variable costs increase to $2.40 per unit or he has to cut his selling price to $2.75 per unit. Producing and selling 6000 light bulbs each month therefore provides Bright Lights with a "safety margin" over and above a break-even level of output and sales of either 3000 light bulbs each month (if price is $3 per unit), 4000 per month (if variable costs rise by $0.40 per unit) or 5000 per month (if price is cut to $2.75).

Only a rise in price and/or a fall in costs will allow the business to increase its safety margin and break even at a lower level of output.

An increase in price ...

Or a fall in costs ...

... will make it easier for a business to break even.

ACTIVITY 4.8

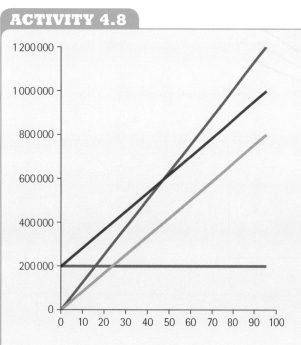

1 Copy the break-even chart opposite and add the following labels.
   ▸ Revenues and costs ($)
   ▸ Output (thousands of units per year)
   ▸ Total fixed costs
   ▸ Total variable costs
   ▸ Total costs
   ▸ Total revenue.

2 From the chart:
   ▸ identify the break-even level of output
   ▸ calculate the variable cost per unit
   ▸ calculate the selling price per unit.

3 Use the chart to show what would happen to total revenue and the break-even level of output if the firm raised its price to $13 per unit.

4 Identify and explain two reasons why the firm may be unable to raise its price to $13 per unit.

The limitations of break-even analysis

Break-even analysis is a useful decision tool in business but it has limitations. Business owners and managers need to be aware of these before making pricing and production decisions.

- Break-even charts assume the total output of a business will always be sold off, so there will be no unsold products left over. However, in reality most businesses build up stocks or inventories of their products in order to meet any unforeseen increase in consumer demand. This means a business may sometimes produce more than it sells. Similarly, a business may hold more materials and components than it needs just in case it has to increase production quickly to respond to a rise in consumer demand. **➤ 4.1.1**

- Break-even analysis assumes fixed costs do not change. However, to expand output significantly a business may need to invest in additional machinery, equipment and larger premises.

- Break-even analysis assumes selling prices are the same at all possible levels of output. In reality as a business increases its output, it may have to reduce its selling prices and therefore cut its profit margin, in order to persuade customers to buy the additional output.

- Market conditions are always changing. This affects the prices at which a business can sell its products. For example, Geoff may have to offer discounts to large business customers to persuade them to buy his light bulbs. He may also need to cut his prices if competition to supply low-energy light bulbs increases as more businesses enter the market. As market conditions change it becomes more difficult to predict the break-even level of output.

- Break-even analysis needs accurate data on costs. A business producing a wide range of different goods or services may find it difficult to allocate different overheads and other costs to individual products, especially if their production shares the same premises, machinery, equipment and labour.

Nazim is the managing director of a company that makes batteries for cars. Nazim wants the business to grow so that it can benefit from economies of scale. He thinks the business needs to become more efficient.

a   What is meant by "to become more efficient"?   [2]

b   Nazim gathered data concerning the productivity of his workforce.

Year	Total labour-hours worked per week	Output per week (units)	Output per employee per week (units)
1	80 000	240 000	?
2	100 000	270 000	108

The factory employees each worked 40 hours per week in both years.

Calculate the output per employee per week in year 1.   [2]

c   State and explain **two** possible reasons why the productivity of the workforce changed in year 2.   [4]

d   Identify and explain **two** economies of scale that could benefit Nazim's company if it expands the scale of its production.   [6]

e   Nazim has heard recently of a production method known as lean production.

Do you think lean production methods would help improve efficiency in the factory? Explain your answer.   [6]

Learning CHECKLIST

Before you continue make sure you are able to

Identify and classify **costs**:

✓   classify costs as **fixed, variable, average** and **total**, and use examples to illustrate them

✓   use cost data to help make simple cost-based decisions, for example whether to stop or to continue production.

Understand the concepts of **economies of scale** and **diseconomies of scale** and give examples of both.

Explain, interpret and use a simple **break-even chart**:

✓   understand the concept of **breaking even**

✓   construct, complete or amend a simple break-even chart

✓   interpret a given chart and use it to analyse a situation

✓   use a chart to help make simple business decisions, for example to examine the impact of higher price

✓   understand the limitations of break-even charts.

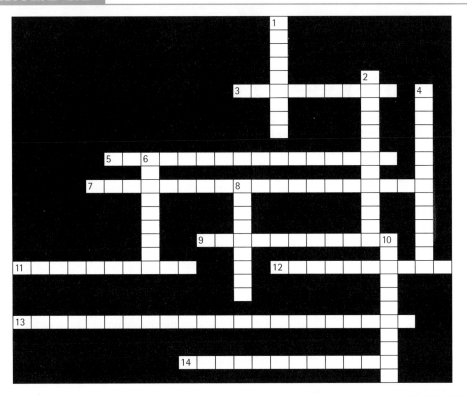

Clues down

1 What type of economy of scale does the following describe? Banks will often loan more money and at lower rates of interest to large firms than they would to smaller, less financially stable firms (9)

2 These costs vary directly with the amount of output produced. They will include the costs of materials, components and electricity used to power the machinery used for production (8, 5)

4 A graph used to plot costs and revenues to show the minimum amount of output a business must make and sell to cover its costs (5, 4, 5)

6 Another term used to describe the indirect costs or day-to-day running costs of an organization including insurance premiums, heating and lighting, telephone and other office costs (9)

8 What type of economy of scale does the following describe? Large businesses may buy or hire their own vehicles to distribute their goods and services rather than rely on other firms to do so. In this way, a large firm can reduce its costs because it does not have to pay the profit margin of a wholesaler or distribution company. Similarly, a large firm can spread the fixed costs of advertising in a newspaper or on television over a much larger output in a large firm than a small firm (9)

10 A firm has the following costs: total fixed costs of $10,000 per month and variable costs of $10 per unit. If the firm is able to sell all the units it produces at a price of $15 each how many will it need to produce and sell each month to break-even (in words)? (3, 8)

Clues across

3 What type of economy of scale does the following describe? Larger firms can afford to invest in specialized machinery, equipment and labour to reduce their average costs of production further below those of smaller firms producing the same items (9)

5 Cost savings associated with increasing the scale of production. For example, larger firms often receive substantial price discounts from their suppliers because they will buy items in bulk (9, 2, 5)

7 A rise in the average cost of producing each unit of output because a firm has expanded too much and is no longer being run or operated efficiently because of, for example, internal communication problems and labour disputes (12, 2, 5)

9 A measure of the cost per unit of output found by dividing the total cost of producing a given level of output by the amount of units produced (6, 4)

11 These costs do not vary with the amount of output produced. They include costs such as rent, loan repayments, insurance premiums, telephone bills and machine hire charges (6, 5)

12 The sum of all fixed costs and total variable costs at a given level of output (5, 5)

13 That level of output per week, month or year which, if sold in full, will generate a total revenue exactly equal to the total cost of its production. That is, there is no profit or loss at this level of output (5, 4, 5, 2, 6)

14 The difference between the selling price of a product and the average cost of producing that product (5, 6)

4.3.1 Why quality is important and how quality production might be achieved

▸ Achieving quality in business means being able to supply a good or service that is fit for purpose. That is, the good or service will fulfil the purpose, role or function intended or as described by the firm supplying it.

▸ Improving the quality of products and processes reduces costs, increases consumer satisfaction and boosts sales. A business that has a reputation for supplying poor-quality goods and services will fail to attract and retain customers, high-quality managers and other employees.

▸ Quality control is focused on removing faulty or defective products from the end of a production line to stop them from being shipped to retailers or direct to customers, but it will not stop defects or errors from happening.

▸ Quality assurance ensures that quality is considered at every stage of production. It involves the setting and monitoring of quality standards across all departments or processes within an organization in order to stop as many defects or errors as possible from occurring.

▸ Many modern organizations are now focused on total quality management (TQM) and the continuous improvement of quality and customer satisfaction. TQM aims for "zero defects" so that every part of a production process is "right first time".

Quality – producing a good or service that is fit for the purpose intended and meets customer expectations.

Quality control – checking the quality of a good or service for any defects or errors at the end of its production process.

Quality assurance – the setting and monitoring of quality standards across an organization and ensuring that they are met.

Total quality management (TQM) – continuous improvement in products and every business process at every stage of production.

What quality means and why it is important

Achieving quality means providing goods and services that are "fit for purpose"

What would happen if you bought a pair of shoes, wore them once and the heels came off? You would not be a satisfied customer. You would return them to the retailer to exchange them for another pair or to get a refund. Now imagine if the retailer refused to do either of these things. You would be very angry and would probably tell all your friends never to buy from that retailer. You should also contact a consumer helpline to find out what your rights are because consumer protection laws exist in many countries, which force retailers to replace or refund the purchase of faulty items. ➤ **3.4.2**

A business can avoid getting a bad reputation for supplying faulty goods or poor service if it produces and sells products that are free from defects and if it offers good customer services and after-sales care. These are all aspects of quality that are important to customers and should therefore also be important to a business. Achieving quality in business means being able to supply a good or service that is **fit for purpose**. That is, the good or service will fulfil the purpose, role or function intended or as described by the firm supplying it. A shoe with a broken heel, a tablet computer that fails to work properly and the failure to deliver an item ordered by a customer within a reasonable period of time are not therefore fit for purpose.

However, the level of quality required to be fit for purpose can be different depending on the types of customers a business deals with. This is because what is important to one set of customers may be less important to another set. Some customers may be willing and able to spend a lot of money on a product to ensure it is of the highest possible quality, while others may be less concerned about quality and will prefer to pay a low price as long as the product meets certain minimum standards. For example, if you paid $100 for a ticket to fly with a low-cost, no-frills airline would you expect the same standard of comfort and service before, during and after your flight as you would had you paid $2000 to enjoy a premium, first-class service in an exclusive cabin? Your answer is probably "no" but you would still expect the low-cost airline to be safe and get you to your destination on time.

▲ Customer markets can be segmented by their expectations of quality and willingness to pay

Improving the quality of products and processes helps to reduce costs, increase consumer satisfaction and boost sales

In a competitive business environment a business has to compete with rival suppliers on both the price and quality of its goods or services. This is because quality is one way a business can differentiate its product from those of rivals and gain a competitive advantage. Offering a superior product that meets or exceeds customer expectations will help to increase sales and expand market share. Customers may also be willing to pay more for a better quality product and this will increase profit margins in selling prices.

A business with a good reputation for quality is also likely to attract and retain more high-quality and highly skilled managers and other employees compared to a business with a poor reputation.

Investing more time, effort and money into improving the quality of production processes and products can therefore deliver significant business benefits.

Benefits of investing in and improving quality	Costs of failing to invest in or maintain quality
+ It helps to create or maintain a good reputation for the business.	✗ The business will develop a reputation for poor quality goods or services.
+ It helps to create or reinforce a strong brand image.	✗ Customers will tell their friends and family members not to use the business.
+ Customers will share their positive experiences with friends and family, or with other consumers via social media or on internet sites such as Trip Advisor for hotels and holidays and Zagat for restaurant reviews.	✗ Sales and market share will be lost to rival firms able to supply better quality goods and services.
+ It helps the business gain a competitive advantage over rival firms which in turn will increase its sales and market share.	✗ Costs will increase because the business needs to devote more staff to handling refunds and responding to complaints.
+ It helps to build and maintain customer loyalty and repeat custom.	✗ Profits and the value of the business are likely to fall.
+ Long-term profitability is likely to increase.	✗ Staff turnover is likely to be higher and the business will not be able to attract high-quality managers and employees because of its poor reputation.
+ The business can attract and retain skilled staff because of its good reputation and increasing profitability.	

Managing and improving quality

There are a number of ways businesses can manage and improve the quality of the goods they produce or services they provide to customers. These are:

- **quality control** of finished goods or services
- **quality assurance** at every stage of production
- **total quality management (TQM).**

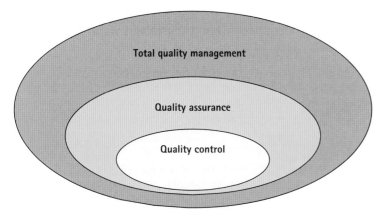

▲ Different levels of quality management

ACTIVITY 4.9

From the articles, identify how and why the two companies have improved the quality of their products and processes.

Japanese company **Toyota** was originally a truck manufacturer. It began producing passenger cars during the 1960s and is now one of the largest and most profitable car manufacturers in the world.

Initially, each car that rolled off its production lines was inspected and if any defects were found they were corrected or the car was scrapped. This was wasteful, so engineers at Toyota set about finding out what was causing defects to occur. They found that the biggest cause was wear in the machines that made the parts stop working, due to the build-up of dirt and metal shavings. The number of defective parts produced would increase as machines wore down, but it was only when a machine finally broke down that it was ever cleaned, repaired or replaced.

Another complication was that workers tended to move from machine to machine, often resulting in confusion.

To solve these problems Toyota completely changed the way it operated its plants. First, it stopped moving workers around so much, reduced clutter and assigned workers to have responsibility over individual machines. Parts and materials were then only delivered to their work stations as and when they were needed – or just in time for production.

The next step was to tackle the dirt responsible for creating defects. Production workers started with regular sweeping and cleaning of their work station areas and then regularly taking apart their own machines to clean them. Finally, they designed special guards and covers to keep dirt and metal chips out of their machines permanently.

Today, all Toyota employees have two roles: their own job and quality assurance. On each vehicle production line, a cord runs along the length of the line. If a line worker notices anything unusual, such as a defect, the worker pulls this cord and the line stops. The team members then concentrate all of their effort on correcting the defect before the line starts up again.

Zurich Insurance Group provides insurance and other financial services to individuals and businesses. The group has more than 130 years' experience and is one of the world's largest insurance groups. It has more than 60 000 employees and operates in over 170 countries.

In the financial services industry, products and prices can appear very similar to customers; therefore, quality is one way in which Zurich can differentiate its services from those of its competitors. Customers that have a positive experience are much more likely to renew their policies, buy other products and services and recommend the company to others.

Zurich recognizes that quality is not a "one-off" process. Its commitment to providing world-class service requires that it continuously listens to its customers' changing needs and expectations. Therefore, to ensure customers have a positive experience, Zurich focuses on:

- clearly identifying what its customers want
- effective planning and processes
- putting in place the right resources (people and systems) to do the job well
- providing in-depth employee training to ensure all staff are focused on satisfying customers
- setting appropriate and achievable targets, and ensuring continuous measuring and monitoring of progress against these targets, including regular checking of levels of customer satisfaction.

The concept of quality control

Product inspections can remove items with faults or defects from a production line but will not stop errors from happening

Some firms employ people specifically to inspect or test the quality of their goods or services. These people are **quality control** specialists or inspectors. Their role is to identify and stop any faulty or defective products from being shipped to retailers or direct to customers.

They also monitor the quality of services delivered to customers. For example, they will check how well a hotel room has been cleaned or the level of food hygiene and speed of service in a restaurant kitchen.

However, because inspections only take place once a good has been produced or a service has been delivered they cannot stop defects or errors from happening.

Scrapping defective products, carrying out a service again or offering a refund is costly. In a manufacturing environment, extra items must be made to replace the faulty products. There will also be costs in terms of staff time and other resources needed to put things right.

Advantages of quality control	Disadvantages of quality control
+ It ensures faulty items are removed from sale before they are sold or delivered to customers. + Production workers do not require additional training. + If possible, materials and component parts from faulty items can be recovered and reused.	× It does not fix the reason why product defects or errors occur during production. × Materials and component parts may be wasted if it is not possible to recover them from faulty items. × Additional items may be required to be made to replace the faulty ones. × Additional resources, including materials, staff time, equipment use and power, will be used up making the additional items. × It is not an effective way of controlling the quality of services: a poor service will only be discovered after it has been delivered to a customer and a complaint has been received.

Quality assurance

Setting and monitoring quality standards at every stage in a production process can reduce defects and errors

Quality assurance ensures that quality is not simply considered at the end of a process but at every stage. It involves the setting and monitoring of quality standards across every department or process within an organization and ensuring they are met. Quality assurance is therefore applied to materials and component parts as well as to finished products, to production, management and inspection processes and to customer services.

In this way quality assurance attempts to improve every aspect of production and stop as many defects or errors as possible before they happen. Good quality assurance processes within a business will also help to assure its customers that the goods or services they receive from it will be of good quality.

Quality assurance requires **total quality management** (TQM). TQM aims to achieve "zero defects" and long-term success through continuous improvements in customer satisfaction.

While quality assurance can still result in some defective products or poor services, TQM is an approach that seeks to ensure all parts of a production process are "right first time". That is, it aims to identify and remove any source of defect or error from production. In doing so, TQM increases the efficiency with which resources are used and reduces production lead times, waste and costs.

Many large, modern organizations combine TQM and Kaizen to deliver continuous improvements in products and production processes. This requires every employee, every function and every process within an organization to be focused on satisfying customers to achieve sales and long-term profitability.

Nestlé SA, founded in 1866, is a multinational food and drink company with headquarters in Switzerland. It manufactures a range of products from baby food to pet food. Quality assurance and product safety is one of Nestlé's 10 corporate principles. Its quality policy requires commitment, from all employees, to a "zero-defect, no waste" attitude. This makes quality assurance everybody's responsibility. The quality assurance system it has implemented, to guarantee compliance with food safety regulations and quality requirements, includes the following:

- Regular quality checks by external, independent inspectors.
- Suppliers agree to a quality code set out, by Nestlé, in an eight-page document.
- Regular, no notice, inspection of suppliers.
- A control and monitoring system to prevent any hazards that are significant for food safety.
- Raw food ingredients are kept separate from prepared foods.
- Each ingredient has its own area, equipment and utensils. This is to prevent cross-contamination.
- All employees are trained in the principles of good hygiene.
- Food and drink recipes have a scientific formula to ensure uniform products that conform to quality standards.
- Every batch of products is tested before leaving the factory – Nestlé carry out over one million tests per year.
- Packaging informs the customer about preparation, storage and use of the products.
- Information on any allergens, such as nuts, are also put on the packaging.
- Batch codes are on all packaging so the batch can be traced back to when and where it was manufactured.
- Chilled transport of products.

Despite these extensive measures, mistakes can still happen. Nestlé had to recall a batch of KITKAT Original Milk Chocolate Bites. The bags contained KITKAT Peanut Butter Bites, a health risk to someone with a nut allergy.

Quality marks and standards can signal product quality to customers

A business that is able to demonstrate high levels of quality in its products and processes may be given permission to display quality marks awarded by independent bodies. These independent approvals help to increase consumer confidence in a business and its products, and are therefore a source of competitive advantage that help to attract customers away from rival products.

For example, the International Organization for Standardization (ISO) is a body that sets international standards. It is composed of representatives from many national standards organizations and sets standards for many products and processes. A business or organization that has been independently audited and certified to have met the conditions of a particular ISO standard may publicly advertise that it is ISO certified or ISO registered.

▲ Some examples of quality marks and standards

Exam PREPARATION 4.3

Rishi is a sole trader who owns a carpet cleaning business. In the past, he cleaned carpets and rugs himself, but now he is the manager and employs other people to do the cleaning.

Table 1 shows data for a typical week for Rishi's business.

Table 1	
Average price per customer $10	Weekly overheads $400
Variable cost per customer $2	Number of customers 60

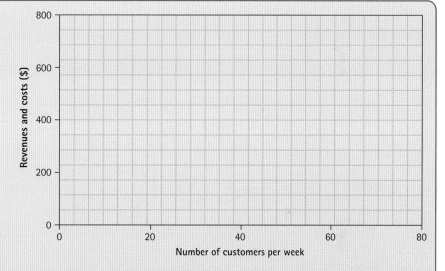

a What is meant by the term "variable cost"? [2]

b Identify **two** examples of overhead costs that Rishi might incur in business. [2]

c Using the data given in Table 1, draw a break-even chart for Rishi's business in the area provided. [4]

d Identify and explain **three** management functions that Rishi performs. [6]

e Do you think Rishi should monitor and manage the quality of the cleaning service his employees provide to customers? Justify your answer. [6]

Advantages of quality assurance	Disadvantages of quality assurance
+ The risk of defects and errors occurring is reduced.	✗ It is more difficult to implement across an organization than quality control inspections because it relies on all employees observing and meeting quality standards.
+ Waste is reduced as fewer items have to be scrapped or reworked.	✗ More employee training is required in how to identify and correct defects or errors.
+ Customer complaints are reduced.	✗ Some defects and errors may still occur.
+ Long-term profitability is likely to increase.	✗ The costs of monitoring quality are higher because it is done for every function or part of a production process.

Before you continue make sure you are able to

Explain why **quality** is important and how quality production might be achieved:

✓ what quality means and why it is important for all businesses

✓ the concept of **quality control** and how businesses implement quality control

✓ the concept of **quality assurance** and how it can be implemented.

Clues down

1   One of two key aims of total quality management within an organization for the quality of its products and processes, and levels of customer satisfaction (10, 11)

2   The process of setting and monitoring quality standards at each stage of a production process and ensuring they are met. The aim is to prevent as many defects or errors occurring in production as possible and to give customers confidence that products are of good quality (7, 9)

4   These are groups of employees who work for the same supervisor or manager and carry out similar tasks. They identify and solve problems together to improve their part of a production process (7, 7)

6   Delegating decision-making authority to less senior managers and employees (11)

Clues across

3   A term used to describe the combined characteristics of a particular good or service that are required to make it fit for the purpose for which it was intended and to meet customer expectations (7)

5   The process of checking the quality of a good or service for any defects or errors at the end of its production process. The main drawback is that it will not stop further defects or errors from happening (7, 7)

7   A good or service will be described as this if it can perform the function, role or use for which it is intended (3, 3, 7)

8   The process of checking or observing standards in products and processes attained in rival businesses in order to improve on them to produce superior goods or services (12)

9   The second of two key aims for total quality management within an organization to ensure every part of its production process is "right first time" (4, 7)

4.4.1 The main factors influencing the location and relocation decisions of a business

▶ Businesses choose locations that minimize their costs of production and maximize other advantages, such as being able to attract skilled labour.

▶ Two major considerations in business location decisions are ease of access to customers and access to sources of materials and other supplies.

▶ Locations near to sources of raw materials or suppliers of component parts may be important for a manufacturing business especially if they are heavy or bulky and if they need to be delivered quickly for just-in-time processing.

▶ Improvements in transport and communications have reduced the need for many businesses to locate near to materials or customers.

▶ Businesses that cluster together in the same location with ancillary firms can benefit from external economies of scale. Shops also tend to locate together to attract passing trade from greater numbers of customers visiting the area.

▶ The government may offer government grants and subsidies to encourage business start-up or relocation in underdeveloped areas and areas of high unemployment to provide jobs and incomes.

▶ Some businesses may locate operations in other countries in order to expand sales, reduce wages and other costs, reduce the taxes they pay and avoid trade barriers.

▶ Planning laws and building regulations may restrict the type of business activity and the design of business premises allowed in certain areas to protect local residents and the natural environment.

Business BUZZWORDS

Footloose industries – industries that have no need to locate near their markets or sources of materials.

Ancillary firms – firms that supply business support services to other organizations, such as transportation, marketing and equipment maintenance services.

External economies of scale – cost advantages arising from locating near to other similar businesses. This is because areas where similar businesses cluster together attract ancillary firms.

Planning controls – laws and regulations that restrict the type and scale of development in certain areas to protect local residents and the natural environment.

Building regulations – rules governing how buildings, including factories, shops and offices, should be constructed.

Factors that influence location decisions

Businesses choose locations that minimize their costs of production

You have been hired as a consultant to advise on the best locations for:

▶ a major supermarket selling foods, confectionery, cosmetics, electrical goods and many other household items

▶ a large manufacturing plant which assembles wind energy turbines, many of the parts for which are imported.

Work in groups and use the map to identify a good location for each business. For each business location, write down the reasons for your choice and present these to your class.

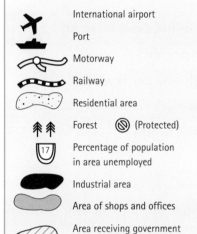

- International airport
- Port
- Motorway
- Railway
- Residential area
- Forest   (Protected)
- 17 Percentage of population in area unemployed
- Industrial area
- Area of shops and offices
- Area receiving government aid (i.e. grants of money for building new buildings and machinery, low rent rates on buildings and land). The total population of the surveyed area is 6 349 000

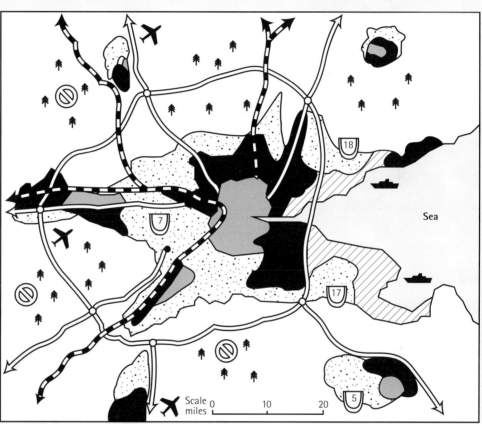

Most business organizations choose a location that minimizes their costs of production and maximizes other advantages. There may be many trade-offs.

Consider the example of Bruce Nave in the US who was deciding where to locate a biodiesel production facility. Biodiesel is a "greener" alternative to diesel oils used to power vehicles and generators. It can be made from waste vegetable oils or from oils from crops such as rapeseed, palm or soybean.

Bruce had been using biodiesel in his construction business for over a year but with petrol prices rising he saw an opportunity to start producing biodiesel on a commercial scale. He knew that the success of his planned enterprise would depend in part on location, as each location would have different start-up costs, costs of living, local laws, costs of doing business and costs of shipping raw materials and the finished product. Even relatively small differences in these costs could mean the difference between a profit margin and a loss.

Bruce knew he needed to locate in an area where he could easily grow the crops he needed for biodiesel production so he chose Northwest America, where

For each of the service providers shown below suggest at least two factors you think will be the most important in deciding where to locate.

GRAND SLAM FISHING CHARTERS

• MARLIN   • BONEFISH
• SAILFISH   • TARPON
• WAHOO   • GROUPER
• MAHI-MAHI   • SNAPPER

GWENDOLYN FISHING

agricultural land is readily available and relatively cheap. He and his wife also had an emotional attachment to the area because they had grown up there.

However, the Northwest covers a wide area so after considering a number of possible sites, he narrowed it down to three locations to assess in further detail: two were near major ports; the third was where the Yakima River joins the Columbia River. All were near major farming areas, towns and cities and therefore close to consumer markets for biodiesel, including farmers for their tractors and farm machinery, public bus companies in the towns and cities and even the ferry company operating on the Columbia River. The goal was to sell all the biodiesel he produced while minimizing his total transportation costs. Locations near to ports also meant finished biodiesel could be shipped to markets further away relatively quickly and cheaply.

Bruce made his final decision by comparing each location in terms of:

- likely growth in local demand for biodiesel
- monthly rents for suitable business premises
- waste disposal costs
- access to hospitals able to treat chemical burns in case of accidents
- numbers of local business and other permits needed
- price and availability of housing for his family and key workers
- availability of skilled labour and average wages
- number and quality of schools and universities nearby
- diversity of population
- access to an airport.

Two major considerations in most business location decisions are ease of access to customers and access to sources of materials and other supplies. Which factor is more important often depends on how bulky or heavy the materials are compared to the finished product.

If inputs of materials to a production process are bulkier or heavier than the final product, then transport costs can be minimized if the business locates near to the materials or parts it needs for production. If the materials are imported this could mean locating near a port.

In contrast if the final product is bulky and difficult to transport, then locations near to customer markets may be more cost-effective. An example is the production of footballs. Because they are round and filled with air footballs will take up more space than the rolls of vinyl or leather used in their production. As a result the cost of transporting the footballs will be more than the cost of transporting the materials.

Many services, such as high street shops, restaurants, cleaners and motor mechanics, have no product to transport and therefore locate in or near to their main customer markets.

Footloose industries are those that do not require locations near their main consumer markets or sources of materials. Other factors such as the ability to attract highly skilled labour or being near to international airports or high-technology firms will be more important to their location decisions.

Location factors	Manufacturing businesses	Businesses in the service sector
Scale of production	The greater the scale of production the larger the area a manufacturing business is likely to need for its factory and equipment, and for the storage of finished goods and works-in-progress.	The larger an organization and the more people it employs the more space it is likely to need, whether it is a large supermarket, a major legal or business consultancy or a government department.
Access to supplies of materials and components	Locations near to sources of raw materials or suppliers of component parts may be particularly important if they are heavy or bulky and if they need to be delivered quickly, for example for just-in-time processing. For example, food processors may locate near to farms so the produce they receive is fresh. If materials are imported a location near to a port may be beneficial.	This factor is less important for many service providers, although major retailers rely on regular deliveries of foods and other products from their suppliers. Improvements in transport and the ability to communicate and sell products quickly over the internet have reduced the need for many retailers to locate near to their major suppliers.
Access to markets	Locating near to major markets is important for businesses that produce bulky items and especially if products are perishable foodstuffs and need to be delivered quickly. For example, producers of dairy, bread and meat products may choose locations near to major retailers because they want these goods to be fresh on delivery. However, the use of preservatives in many foodstuffs has reduced this need.	Being close to customers is a particularly important factor in the location decisions of providers of personalized services. However, the widespread availability of the internet and internet banking services has greatly increased the amount and value of goods and services traded online. It has therefore reduced the need for many internet-based businesses to locate near to their markets.
Access to a supply of suitable labour	If the manufacturing process is labour-intensive a location in or near a densely populated area or an area of high unemployment may be suitable. Locations in such areas are much less important for capital-intensive businesses. Locating in a region or country where wage rates are low may also be more cost-effective.	The skills required by a service-based business depends on the services it supplies. For example, a local supermarket will recruit mainly unskilled workers locally. In contrast, a major law firm may recruit specialists skilled in legal matters from all over the world and may therefore choose locations in major cities near other major legal practices.
Availability and cost of suitable premises	Manufacturers need suitable factory units or land on which to construct purpose-built factories. If these are not available in an area or are too expensive to rent or buy, a manufacturing plant will be unable to locate in the area.	The more popular a location the more difficult it is to find suitable vacant office or retail space, and the higher rents and local taxes are likely to be. Sales revenue at these locations need to be high to pay these costs. Access for delivery vehicles and adequate car parking space for customers and employees may also be important factors.
Access to good transport and communications infrastructure	Improvements in transport and communications have reduced the need for businesses to locate so near to sources of materials or their main markets. For example, refrigerated ships and lorries can ensure that foodstuffs remain fresh during transport.	Safe and reliable transport is vital for modern business. Employees need to travel quickly to and from their places of work. Businesses want to reach more customers over a wider area and rely on efficient transport systems to deliver goods to them.

Other influences on location decisions

Being near other businesses

Most retailers want to locate their shops in areas visited regularly by shoppers. This usually means locating near other shops, in popular retail parks, shopping malls or town centres. New shops can attract passing trade from people who walk past them on their way to other shops. Although this means a new shop will be in competition with many others, a wide choice of shops can encourage more customers to visit the area and therefore increase combined sales.

Businesses often locate together in clusters served by suppliers of components and other business support services, such as transport providers, warehouses, marketing agencies and specialists in computer and machinery maintenance. These are known as **ancillary firms**.

Rival businesses that cluster together with ancillary firms can all benefit from the **external economies of scale** they provide. This is because it is usually cheaper for a group of businesses located together to share the services of ancillary firms than for each business to spend money on its own distribution system, warehousing facilities, marketing or technical specialists.

Climate

Climate is a major consideration for businesses involved in agriculture and tourism. However, climate may also be important in some manufacturing processes.

For example, mild and damp conditions were thought many years ago to be beneficial to clothing and textile manufacturing because moist threads were less likely to become brittle and break as they would in dry, hot conditions.

In contrast, Silicon Valley in the US state of California attracted many computer companies because the dry climate was thought to reduce the risk of damage during the production of computer memory chips. In both cases, climate concerns are no longer important due to advances in technology.

Heating costs are also lower in locations with a warm climate.

Security

High rates of crime, such as vandalism and theft, in an area increase security risks for a business and its employees.

Insurance costs will be higher and a business may also need to employ expensive security equipment and guards. This can deter location in such areas.

Personal preferences of the owners

The personal preferences of the business owners may influence their final location decision. For example, it may be a location they particularly like or grew up in.

Locations near to families and friends and to good schools for their young children may also be considerations.

Government influence

A government may offer grants or subsidies to business organizations to locate in a particular area of their country, for example to provide jobs and incomes to local people in areas of high unemployment.

In contrast, planning laws may restrict business activities in some areas, for example in national parks and land protected for agricultural use only.

Choosing a location in another country

Globalization has created more opportunities for businesses to relocate to other countries

The rapid growth in a number of developing economies, improvements in global transport and communications, and increasing international trade between different countries has created more business opportunities in other countries than ever before. As a result, an increasing number of businesses are locating some or all of their operations overseas. ➤ **6.3.1**

A number of factors influence a decision to relocate to another country and the choice of location.

Access to new and cheaper sources of materials

A business may be forced to seek new locations in other countries if its main source of raw material runs out or the cost of obtaining or extracting the raw material in its current location becomes too high. This is especially true of primary sector businesses such as oil and mining companies.

Access to new markets

New and growing markets in other countries may attract manufacturing and service-based businesses to relocate to them. The first business to relocate to a growing foreign market may gain a **first-mover advantage** and grab the largest market share of sales. ➤ **3.4.3**

Lower wage costs

It may be more profitable to relocate a labour-intensive business if wage costs are lower in other countries. Many manufacturing businesses have relocated from developed to less-developed countries to reduce their wage costs.

Lower business and personal taxes

High taxes on profits and personal incomes may cause a business to consider relocating to a country where these taxes are lower. ➤ **6.1.1**

Avoid trade barriers

A government may use tariffs and trade barriers to restrict the amount of goods entering its country. To avoid these restrictions an exporting business may relocate to that country. For example, many Japanese car manufacturers have located plants in European countries to avoid the common external tariffs EU member states impose on many imported goods. ➤ **6.3.1**

Limits on expansion at home

A business may want to grow in scale but may be limited by the capacity of its current premises, the size of its home market and planning restrictions, so it may therefore look at new, larger premises and foreign markets in which to expand. The lower costs of doing business in some other countries or their growing markets may make expansion within them cheaper and more profitable.

Availability of government grants and other incentives

Governments may offer grants and tax incentives to attract large modern business organizations to relocate to their countries because they will create jobs and incomes. These businesses will also import their technologies and teach local workers new skills.

You are a senior manager at Stone Works Ltd, a medium-sized company that makes and supplies a range of products made out of different natural stones, for example marble tiles and table tops, bricks, paving and garden ornaments. Export sales have been rising steadily and the company is seeking to increase the scale of its production but it cannot do so at its existing premises.

You have been asked by the board of directors to produce a report on the costs and benefits of relocating production overseas. You have identified two suitable but very different countries for the new factory. Information on the two countries is presented below. Select the best one to recommend to your board and set out the reasons for your choice in your report.

Country X	
GDP per head	$9500
Customer base	Small but growing
Industrial base	Underdeveloped. Lack of ancillary firms.
Sources of materials	Abundant and cheap source of raw materials nearby
Transport	New international port under construction. This will be needed to export products to markets overseas. Limited major road network.
Communications	Slow and expensive internet connections
Labour	Mainly unskilled
Wage rates	Low
Profit tax rates	Low
Trade barriers	High tariffs and quotas
Government help	Generous grants available
Regulations	Few planning, employment or business laws

Country Y	
GDP per head	$24 500
Customer base	Large home market
Industrial base	Significant business services sector and technology base
Sources of materials	Most materials will need to be imported
Transport	Good international ports and airports, road and rail connections
Communications	Well developed. Fast broadband speeds.
Labour	Good broad-based skills. Some in short supply.
Wage rates	High
Profit tax rates	High
Trade barriers	Few
Government help	No financial help available
Regulations	Many business, employment, consumer protection and environmental regulations

How legal controls influence location decisions

Legal controls can restrict business location in different areas

Business location decisions may sometimes conflict with government objectives for different areas in their economies.

For example, bicycle manufacturer BC Cal Ltd, in the case study on the next page, had its original plan for a factory design rejected by its local government authority on environmental grounds because it would have spoilt the views many people had over the landscape and destroyed many mature trees and wildlife habitat.

To achieve planning consent the company would have had to significantly alter the design of its new factory and this would have increased its construction costs by 14%. As a result the company decided to relocate to an area where there were fewer planning restrictions and also where financial assistance from the government was available.

BC Cal Ltd is a medium-sized company that manufactures bicycles. It exports many to markets overseas in Southern and South Eastern Asia.

Due to rising demand, it wanted to expand production. The board of directors agreed to invest around $25 million of their shareholders' capital in the construction of a new, purpose-built factory on open land just five miles from an international port and near an area where there was a good supply of skilled labour.

However, initial designs for the new bicycle factory were rejected by the planning authority of the regional government. It argued the planned facility was much taller than local commercial and residential buildings and would block views towards the coastline for many people living nearby.

It also stressed the need to retain mature trees on the construction site to provide nesting sites for bird populations as well as help to mask views of the factory building. Architects employed by the company estimated these changes would add $3 million to the construction costs.

The government's health and safety agency also reviewed the designs and advised that they fit additional air filtration and cooling systems to reduce dust particles and working temperatures in the factory. These would add an additional $1.5 million to the construction cost.

"As a result of these additional costs we decided to construct the new factory at another location 100 kilometres inland," a spokesman for BC Cal Ltd revealed. "The new location was in an area of high unemployment and the government was prepared to grant the company $6.5 million towards our construction costs. There were also fewer planning restrictions, including on the height of buildings which meant we could use our original design concept."

"Although our transportation costs would be more," she continued, "wages were cheaper because of the unemployment, but most people lacked the skills we needed. However, in addition to the capital grant towards construction costs, the government was also prepared to subsidize the training of locally hired workers. This made the new location more attractive."

National and local governments may seek to protect certain areas from uncontrolled business use while encouraging increased business activity in others to provide jobs and income and to improve social welfare.

- **Planning laws** and regulations can stop businesses locating premises in particular areas, for example in national parks or nature reserves, to protect the natural environment and wildlife.

  Restrictions may also be placed on the types of business activity allowed in some areas because they may conflict with other land uses and because of the noise and traffic levels they may create. For example, it would not be very pleasant for local residents if a large power station was allowed to be built and operated next to a housing development. Similarly, the building of a large out-of-town supermarket in a rural area near to a village may create too much traffic congestion on local roads.

- **Building regulations** or standards define how a new building or alteration is to be constructed so that it is structurally safe, protected from risk of fire and energy efficient. They can also restrict the height of business premises and ensure they blend in with other buildings nearby. Such regulations can add significantly to the cost of locating a business in some areas.

ACTIVITY 4.13

The following locations were chosen by businesses and planning applications made to government authorities. Evaluate the location decision made in each case by considering:

1. How appropriate the chosen location is for the type of business.

2. What factors should each business take into account when making a location decision?

Justify your answers.

Application	Comments made by government officials
To construct a new steel plant in the national park creating 160 new jobs	Reject. We have to make sure the plants, animals, wildlife, unique landscape and fascinating buildings in the national park are not lost to the next generation.
To convert a residential property into a night club and bar	Reject. The development is out of keeping with the residential nature of the area. Noise from music, customers and traffic levels late into the night would be undesirable.
To redevelop a historic building as a five-star hotel and golf complex	Defer decision. More information is required on safeguards to protect key features of the historic property and grounds and on the impact on local roads.
To construct a new out-of-town shopping complex	Reject. The proposal will have a negative impact on existing retail centres and retail employment in the area and will increase congestion on local roads. It will also mean the loss of a popular woodland area.
To construct a new 300-metre-high office and apartment building in Singapore	Reject. Any building above 280 metres could interfere with the safe and efficient operation of flights into and out of Singapore airport. The tower will also be visually intrusive.
Car manufacturing plant on an old industrial site	Approve. The new plant will bring new investment, jobs and skills into an area of industrial decline and high unemployment.

High-tech manufacturers flock to China's Suzhou region

The Yangtze River basin city of Suzhou has belonged totally to China for the past 2500 years, but today it looks like San Jose, California in the early 1990s. One-time fish farms and cropland on two sides of the city are mushrooming into high-tech industrial parks for foreign-financed companies because overseas business people have found over the past few years they like the region's modern infrastructure, tech-savvy population and local government support.

Suzhou, along with its better-known neighbour, Shanghai, and the east China coastal region as far south as Hangzhou, is attracting hundreds of electronics, software, mobile communications and pharmaceutical companies that want to research, manufacture or sell in Asia.

Company representatives say they like the Shanghai–Suzhou region because it's close to Shanghai's port, the local infrastructure approaches the level of Western countries and because local people have the right education but work for relatively low local wages. Local governments have also kept land prices lower than in other parts of Asia and have given companies material incentives to locate here. The region is in the geographic centre of Asia,

making it easy for companies to reach clients, partners or branch offices.

Moreover, the region has been one of China's wealthiest and most progressive since the 12th century and still leads China in talent and business amenities. Shanghai Jiaotong University and Fudan University teach technical skills that foreign IT firms want. Suzhou has cheaper land and a business park for high-tech factories, as well as nine universities that teach technical trades. Incentives to locate in Shanghai or Suzhou include tax exemptions, free use of office space, discounted land prices and fast-track business permitting, as Michelle Wu, chief executive officer of the California-based China Internet Group, has pointed out. "Generally, the local governments for both cities are well educated, run quite efficiently," Wu said. Foreigners in Shanghai say they get tax breaks for home ownership and find schools with international curricula for their children.

Many foreigners also enjoy the after-hours life in this area more than anywhere else in China. In Shanghai, they frequent bars, cafés and shops near the Bund, a Western-style banking district about 100 years old. In Suzhou, they linger at canals and gardens that

have prompted comparisons to Venice. "The lifestyle is quite close to Western cities, yet with a low crime rate and safe and clean environment," Wu said.

Nokia tells a typical story of a foreign IT firm in the region. In 1998, the Finnish mobile phone giant opened a $50 million, 400-employee factory in the Suzhou Industrial Park to make wireless base stations, because the park offered what the company needed in Asia, said the site's general manager Timo Lansilahti.

Suzhou has its own customs depot for the park, so most of Nokia's incoming supplies are duty-free. Local Nokia employees usually come from Suzhou itself or a nearby city, and 90% have stayed with Nokia since the plant opened. Half the management is also local. Foreign employees who prefer Shanghai can get there by expressway in less than an hour, and buses go directly from the Shanghai airport to Suzhou eight times a day.

▶ Imagine you are considering starting a business overseas. Suggest reasons why the Shanghai and the Suzhou region of China might provide an attractive location for your business venture.

▶ What evidence is there in the article that Chinese government authorities have a regional policy?

▶ What do you think are the main objectives of the Chinese government's regional policy?

▶ How could the location of foreign companies in Shanghai and the Suzhou region benefit other firms in these areas?

Antonio and Sylvie started an ice-cream making business called "@Flavours" 10 years ago with $4000 borrowed from family and friends. The product uses natural, high-quality ingredients. Using cost-plus pricing, the partners were able to charge a price that covered all costs and gave them a good profit. The business grew quickly and was able to take advantage of economies of scale. Five years ago, the partners converted the business into a private limited company. Antonio believes that the next phase of growth should be to open an overseas operation. Sylvie disagrees and thinks the next phase of growth should be to convert to a public limited company.

a   Define "private limited company".   [2]

b   Define "cost-plus pricing".   [2]

c   Outline how growth may have helped @Flavours achieve economies of scale.   [4]

d   Explain **one** advantage and **one** disadvantage of @Flavours converting to a public limited company.   [2]

e   Do you think @Flavours should open an overseas operation? Justify your answer.   [6]

Learning CHECKLIST

Before you continue make sure you are able to

Identify the main factors influencing the **location** and **relocation** decisions of a business:

✓ factors relevant to the location decision of **manufacturing businesses** and **service businesses**

✓ factors that a business could consider when deciding which country to locate operations in

✓ the role of **legal controls** on location decisions

✓ recommend and justify an appropriate location for a business in given circumstances.

Clues down

1 These laws and standards define how a new building or alteration should be designed and constructed so that it is structurally safe. They can also restrict the height of premises and ensure they blend in with other buildings nearby (8, 11)

2 A form of competitive advantage enjoyed by a firm over rival businesses because it is the first to develop and market a new product or to supply a new market (5, 6, 9)

3 The term used to describe firms in productive sectors of an economy that do not need to locate close to either their main markets or sources of materials. Other factors, such as access to skilled labour, international airports and high-tech firms will be more important considerations (9, 10)

5 Legal controls used to restrict business location to protect people and the environment from uncontrolled business development and associated congestion and pollution (8, 4)

7 A policy, adopted by a national government, that is aimed at attracting business activity to underdeveloped or declining areas in the national economy to create jobs and incomes (8, 6)

Clues across

4 These firms supply services that have been specifically adapted to meet the needs of their main business customers. Services may include the manufacture of specialist parts or machinery required by other firms, or the supply of specialized transportation, marketing and equipment maintenance services. They will often locate near to their main business customers, especially when they are clustered or co-located together in the same area (9, 5)

6 Close to what? Which location factor is likely to be the most important consideration for a firm that supplies finished goods that are smaller, lighter and cheaper to transport than the inputs it requires in bulk and just-in-time to make them? (9)

8 Cost advantages enjoyed by all firms in a major industry because of its size, especially those who locate together in the same area. Together they can benefit from specialized services, provided by ancillary firms with the scale and expertise to provide them at a lower cost (8, 9, 2, 5)

9 Close to what? Which location factor is likely to be the most important to a firm supplying perishable products or products that are more expensive to transport when they are finished than the inputs needed to make them? (6)

5 Financial information and decisions

5.1	Business finance: needs and sources	5.1.1	The need for business finance
		5.1.2	The main sources of finance
5.2	Cash-flow forecasting and working capital	5.2.1	The importance of cash and of cash-flow forecasting
		5.2.2	Working capital
5.3	Income statements	5.3.1	What profit is and why it is important
		5.3.2	Income statements
5.4	Statement of financial position	5.4.1	The main elements of a statement of financial position
		5.4.2	Interpret a simple statement of financial position and make deductions from it
5.5	Analysis of accounts	5.5.1	Profitability
		5.5.2	Liquidity
		5.5.3	How to interpret the financial performance of a business by calculating and analysing profitability ratios and liquidity ratios
		5.4.4	Why and how accounts are used

5.1 Business finance: needs and sources

5.1.1 The need for business finance

- All businesses need money or finance for business start-up, expansion and survival.

- Without sufficient finance, an enterprise cannot obtain all the goods and services it needs to begin or stay in business.

- Businesses need capital to fund capital expenditure and revenue expenditure.

- Capital refers to money used to purchase or acquire business assets including land, premises and equipment, and includes working capital to pay for day-to-day running costs such as the payment of wages, telephone services and insurance premiums.

- Non-current assets, such as buildings and machinery, can last a long time, so it is sensible to pay for them over a long period of time. To do so requires long-term finance.

- Businesses use short-term finance to pay for equipment that has a shorter productive life, such as telephones and laptop computers, and for major operating expenditures such as quarterly or annual electricity bills and bulk purchases of materials and other supplies.

Capital expenditure – money spent on the purchase or acquisition of non-current assets such as premises and machinery.

Revenue expenditure – money spent on day-to-day running costs.

Short-term finance – funds available to a business for up to a year or so, usually used to fund operating expenditures.

Long-term finance – funds available to a business over many years, usually for investments in non-current assets.

Venture capital – funding for business start-ups and small businesses with exceptional growth potential.

Fixed capital – money invested in non-current assets with long productive lives, including premises, machinery and vehicles.

Working capital – money available to a business (from its holdings of cash or other assets that can be sold off quickly for cash) to finance its day-to-day operations or running costs.

Reasons why businesses need finance

All businesses need money to finance their activities

When Suleman Sacranie decided to launch online discount store 99c Shopper, he already had dreams of growing his enterprise into a multi-million-dollar corporation.

It was the first discount shop online selling all goods for 99 cents. However, Suleman only had $750 of savings to spend on developing his website. It was not enough. Suleman went to 28 different web companies and was initially quoted a cost of $75 000 but eventually managed to get his website set up for just $7500. This was still more money than he had, so he approached many different companies to help him finance his business idea. It was initially rejected by many.

Suleman is now looking to sell franchises to set up 99c discount retail outlets in towns and cities across Europe.

Like Suleman, all business organizations need money or finance to start up and continue their activities. Without sufficient finance an enterprise can not obtain all the goods and services it needs to begin or stay in business.

ACTIVITY 5.1

Using the articles identify and list:

▶ reasons why businesses need money

▶ how businesses obtain money to finance their activities.

PTT Asahi Chemical borrows $400 million for new plant

PTT Asahi Chemical Co. Ltd (PTT Asahi) has signed loan agreements for $400 million to build a new hi-tech petrochemical plant in Hemaraj Eastern Industrial Estate (Map Ta Phut) in Rayong Province.

The loans will be provided by the Mizuho Corporate Bank Ltd, Bank of Tokyo Mitsubishi-UFJ Ltd, Sumitomo Trust & Banking Co. Ltd, HSBC and ING Bank among others.

MRCB sells RM566 million shares

Malaysian Resources Corp. Bhd (MRCB) will sell shares to raise up to RM566 million to fund future expansion of the business into property and infrastructure development.

MRCB said the share issue would allow the company to raise new funds without having to make loan repayments or incur interest charges.

Tanzanian government bails out TRL

The government has been forced once more to find money to pay workers of the troubled Tanzania Railway Limited (TRL).

The workers have been on strike since early this week over non-payment of their November salaries and have been demanding the company's management to be sacked.

The government has decided to look for the money after the TRL management said it could no longer afford to pay the workers' salaries due to the financial problems the company was trying to solve.

A gifted business

"I've always wanted to make personalized gift cards and start my own business," said Nasiya Hall, who has recently opened her first shop in the local shopping district.

"The main obstacle was raising sufficient funds to buy the equipment I needed, pay the deposit on the small shop I am renting and buy enough materials to get going."

To start her business, Nasiya used her savings and loans from friends and relatives. She also made some purchases using her bank credit card.

Capital refers to money used to invest in business assets including land, premises and equipment and to pay for day-to-day running costs such as the payment of wages, telephone bills and insurance premiums. ➤ **4.2.1**

Businesses need capital for three main reasons.

Business start-ups need capital for:
- the purchase or hire of fixed assets such as premises and equipment
- the purchase of materials
- the payment of any business fees and licences.

Business expansion needs capital to:
- fund the research and development of new products
- replace old equipment and machinery with new technology
- set up overseas operations
- take over another company.

Business survival requires capital to:
- cover any losses
- continue to pay short-term expenses such as wages, electricity and telephone bills, which are necessary to continue in business.

Businesses need capital to fund two main forms of expenditure.
- **Capital expenditure** is money spent on acquiring long-lived assets (or non-current assets) such as premises, vehicles and equipment.
- **Revenue expenditure** is money spent on running costs including wages, rent, telephone charges and other overheads.

Capital is often classified according to how it is used in business.
- **Venture capital** is often used to describe funds available for businesses to start up and for small businesses with exceptional growth and profit potential.
- **Fixed capital** is invested in long-lived, non-current assets.
- **Working capital** is used to finance day-to-day operations or running costs. ➤ **5.2.2**

Money or finance for these purposes may be found "inside" a business, for example from profits or the personal savings of the business owners, or from external sources, such as from banks and through the issue of shares to investors. ➤ **5.1.2**

The difference between short-term and long-term finance needs

Imagine you are about to start a new small business. You have identified suitable premises costing $125 000 to buy. You have calculated your business could make a profit of $25 000 per year in the first five years. However, if you now add in the cost of buying the premises your business will show a loss of $100 000 in the first year and this will take another four years to pay off before you could return to profit. It would be much more sensible to obtain a 20-year low-cost loan to buy the premises. The loan and any interest could then be paid off more slowly from revenues generated by your business each year. After deducting loan and interest payments of $6000 per year you calculate that your annual profits will be $19 000 over the next few years.

Most businesses cannot afford to pay for everything they need outright to start up or expand. They require finance.

Non-current assets, such as buildings and machinery, remain productive for many years, so it is sensible to finance them over similarly long periods of time. To do so requires **long-term finance** over more than one year. So, for example, a machine with an estimated productive life of ten years can be financed from a long-term bank loan that is repayable in instalments over ten years. In this way, the bank loan can be repaid from the revenues generated from the sale of items produced by the machine over its productive life.

In contrast, **short-term finance** over a few days or for up to a year is often needed by a business to pay for small items of equipment, such as telephones and tablet computers, that will be replaced more frequently because of wear or technological change. Short-term finance is also required from time to time to help pay for major revenue expenditures such as quarterly or annual electricity bills and bulk purchases of materials and parts.

ACTIVITY 5.2

Look at the photographs of different business assets and activities.
Which ones do you think may require:

▶ capital or revenue expenditure

▶ short-term or long-term finance?

Learning CHECKLIST

Before you continue make sure you are able to

Identify the main needs for **business finance**:

✓ the main reasons why businesses need finance, for example **start-up capital**, capital for expansion and additional **working capital**

✓ understand the difference between **short- and long-term finance** needs.

5.1.2　The main sources of finance

- A business can finance its capital requirements from its own internal sources including from retained profits, the savings of its owners and the sale of unwanted assets.

- Capital may also be available from external sources of finance including from banks, a government, leasing companies and suppliers.

- Banks are one of the most important external providers of debt finance in the form of repayable short-term or long-term loans.

- Limited companies can sell shares and debentures to raise finance. The sale of shares (equity finance) provides non-repayable permanent capital for a company.

- Choosing finance requires business owners and managers to assess the costs and benefits of different methods available. The assessment should consider why finance is needed and what it is needed for, how much capital is needed and how quickly it is needed, how much it will cost and how much risk it involves.

- It is important to match the type of finance to the use it will be put to. Long-term finance should be used to acquire long-lived assets such as premises and machinery. It should not be used to meet short-term running costs.

- A highly geared business will find it difficult to raise additional capital. Holding too much debt increases the risk of business failure.

- A business with a poor track record of financial performance and inexperienced managers is unlikely to attract many lenders or investors.

Internal sources of finance – capital that a business can raise from its own resources.

Retained profit – profit saved by a business for reinvestment that is not returned to the owners as dividends.

Mortgage – a long-term loan to buy property.

Trade credit – short-term finance provided by a supplier to a business customer. The customer will often have between 30 and 90 days in which to pay for each purchase from its supplier.

Hire purchase – paying for a non-current asset in instalments. The supplier continues to own the asset until it has received payment in full.

External sources of finance – money raised from organizations and individuals that are not part of the business.

Leasing – renting the use of a non-current asset, usually with the option to buy it at a later date.

Collateral – assets of value that a customer can offer as security against a loan. If the customer is unable to repay the loan the lender can sell off the assets instead.

Debenture – a loan certificate issued for sale by a company that can be bought and resold by investors. The final holder of the certificate at maturity is repaid in full plus interest.

Permanent capital – the non-repayable capital of a company, equal to the total of shareholder's funds invested in that company.

Equity finance – permanent capital raised by a company from the sale of its shares.

Debt finance – repayable long-term loans.

Micro-finance - small loans and other financial services provided by specialist organizations to people who are poor and unable to use traditional banks.

Default – failure to repay debt finance.

Gearing ratio – the proportion of total capital invested by a business in assets that has been financed by debt.

Highly geared – a term used to describe a business that has far more debt finance than equity finance.

Internal sources of finance for a business

Business organizations may be able to raise finance from internal or external sources, but some may have few options

If you wanted to buy a new personal computer or games console you could either use money from your savings or borrow the money from someone else. Businesses face a similar choice when they want to purchase equipment and other assets to start up or expand their operations.

A business could use its own **internal sources of finance**, such as the owners' savings or profits, or it may be able to borrow money or attract new investment from **external sources of finance** such as a bank loan or government grant.

For example, when Manik Thapar started Eco Wise Waste Management Pvt Ltd, in his own words "to clean up India", he and his father wanted to finance the new venture from their own money to keep their costs down. In fact, 90% of their business finance to buy vehicles, waste treatment equipment and premises came from their own savings and only 10% from a bank loan. The business collects, separates and treats different types of waste material from households and businesses to produce compost and other recycled materials that can be reused in the production of other products. Business is booming and the business continues to be self-financing with all profits being ploughed back into expanding the business.

This is because internal sources of finance tend to be cheaper than external sources because they do not require repayment with interest. However, both internal and external sources of finance may be limited. Unlike the owners of Eco Wise Waste some business owners may have few savings or profits to draw from. Banks and other external providers of finance may also be reluctant to lend to a business that has a poor record of profitability.

The amount of capital a business can raise internally will be limited to drawing on retained profits, the personal funds of owners or the sale of assets

Internal sources of finance are funds raised from within a business organization from its own resources. Most provide a one-off injection of funds into the business for either short-term or long-term use.

- **Retained profits** are profits not paid out to the business owners but instead kept by a business to invest in more assets. Many large organizations often "plough back" a significant amount of their profits into research and development, business expansion and new advanced equipment to remain competitive against rival firms.

Advantages of using retained profits	Disadvantages of using retained profits
+ Profits do not have to be repaid.	− New and small businesses may have very little or no profit to draw on.
+ There are no interest charges to pay.	− Retaining profits to buy assets reduces dividend payments to business owners.
+ Profits can be used to expand the business and increase future profitability.	

- **Personal savings of the business owners** are an important source of finance for many new and small businesses, especially sole traders and partnerships.

Advantages of using owners' savings	Disadvantages of using owners' savings
+ They do not have to be repaid.	- Small business owners may have few savings to draw on.
+ There are no interest charges to pay.	- Using their own savings increases the financial risk taken by owners.
+ They are available to use quickly.	

- **Selling off assets**, such as surplus and unwanted equipment, stocks of unsold products or unused materials and parts, can provide cash for a business. However, if these assets are needed to keep production going in the business it would not be sensible to sell them off.

Advantages of selling assets	Disadvantages of selling assets
+ It is an easy and cheap way to raise finance.	- Small businesses may have few or no surplus assets to sell.
+ Selling off stocks reduces storage requirements.	- It may take time to find willing buyers.

- **Sale and lease back** of non-current assets, such as land, premises and machinery, involves selling off these assets to other organizations then leasing or renting them back for a monthly fee from the new owners. Doing so allows a business to raise cash from their sale but to continue using the assets for production.

.Advantages of sale and lease back	Disadvantages of sale and lease back
+ It provides cash for investments in other productive assets.	- Monthly or annual lease payments can be expensive.
+ The seller retains control of the productive assets.	- The business needs to find a leasing company that will agree to buy the assets.

ACTIVITY 5.3

Valentina owns and runs a small coach hire business. She owns three coaches of different sizes which are hired out with a driver for wedding parties, sightseeing tours and other uses. The small 12-seat and large 52-seat coaches are heavily used and earn the most revenue.

Her business makes a very small annual profit and she has very little money of her own in savings.

She would like to raise some finance to refit the coaches and buy some new computer equipment. She does not want to borrow from external providers and has asked for your advice on the best way to extract the money she needs from her own business. What will you advise and why?

External sources of finance for a business

External sources can provide a range of short-term and long-term finance for business activities

External sources of finance refer to individual investors and organizations outside of a business that can provide it with capital in the form of either **debt** (repayable loans) or **equity** (non-repayable capital invested in limited companies by their shareholders).

Debt finance is normally repaid with interest. The **interest rate** is the cost of borrowing money and is charged as a percentage of the amount borrowed. ➤ **6.1.1**

An external provider of finance will therefore want to know if a business:

- has sensible long-term plans and good prospects

- is well managed and profitable

- can afford to repay any repayable loans provided plus interest charges

- owns sufficient assets of value that can be sold off to repay any repayable loans. These assets can be offered by the business as security or **collateral** to the provider for the repayment of a loan. This means that in the event the business is unable to repay the loan, or fails, the provider can sell the assets in order to recover the debt.

A business that is unable to demonstrate these features is unlikely to attract external finance.

Banks are one of the most important external providers of debt finance

Banks are a major source of debt finance for many businesses. Different banks may specialize in different types of business customer and finance.

- **Commercial banks** have retail branches in most modern shopping districts. Online banking also means many of their services can now be accessed via the internet.

  Commercial banks also include Islamic banks that provide finance on terms consistent with Sharia law. This means they do not provide loans or charge interest. Instead an Islamic bank buys goods directly for a customer to rent or lease and charges fees to cover its risks and costs. An Islamic bank may also invest funds in a business venture in return for a share of its profits instead of providing loans.

- **Credit unions** were originally set up to help people and small businesses with low incomes to borrow money. They now provide a range of commercial banking services.

- **Savings and loan associations** (mutual or building societies in some countries) specialize in long-term finance called mortgages to buy property but they also offer many commercial banking services.

- **Investment banks** specialize in helping large business organizations sell their shares and debentures on the stock market.

Banks provide finance that can be repaid over many years or for just a few days. Loans that are repayable within one year are a form of **short-term finance**. In contrast, loans that can be repaid over a period lasting more than one year are considered a source of **long-term finance**.

Short-term business finance available from banks

Short-term finance	Advantages	Disadvantages
An **overdraft** allows a business customer to "overdraw" their bank account by an agreed amount. It provides a convenient short-term loan, for example to pay a large electricity or wage bill.	+ This is a quick and easy method of borrowing a limited amount of money for a short period of time.	− Interest rates or charges can be high, often much higher than a bank loan and can vary over time. − An overdraft can be withdrawn at any time requiring the borrower to repay it in full.
A **credit card** can be used to make purchases of supplies, travel and equipment. Payment is not required until a month or so later. Interest is charged if the full balance is not paid off within this time.	+ Using a credit card is a quick and easy way of borrowing money for a short period of time. + There is an interest-free period, often up to 56 days.	− Interest rates or charges vary but can be very high. − The amount a business can borrow is limited.

Long-term finance available from banks

Long-term finance	Advantages	Disadvantages
A **commercial loan** is normally used to finance capital expenditures. Repayment periods can vary from 6–12 months to 15 or more years.	+ A commercial loan is relatively easy to arrange. + There is a choice of repayment periods. + Large profitable companies may get preferential interest rates on large loans.	− Monthly repayments must be made inclusive of interest or fees. − Interest rates or charges are normally fixed for the length of the loan and can be high. This helps reduce uncertainty. − Security or **collateral** is required.
A **mortgage** is a long-term loan, usually repayable over 25 or 30 years, for the purchase of property. Commercial mortgages are used to finance the purchase or construction of business premises.	+ There is a choice of repayment periods. + Large profitable companies may receive preferential interest rates on large loans.	− Interest rates or charges may be fixed or variable but can be high. − There may be an arrangement fee and a large deposit may be required. − The loan will be secured against the property. It will be sold if the business is unable to repay its loan.

Trade credit provided by suppliers is a valuable form of short-term finance

Trade credit is short-term finance available from suppliers of parts, materials and finished goods. Many suppliers allow their business customers to "buy now and pay later". This means payment can usually be made up to 30–90 days later. This allows a business to use the items to earn revenue before it has to make payment. It therefore helps a business manage its cash flows more effectively. ➤ **5.2.1**

Advantages of trade credit	Disadvantages of trade credit
+ Suppliers may give discounts for bulk purchases. + No interest is charged. + Supplied items can be used for production and to generate sales before payment is required. This improves cash flow.	− Discounts may be withdrawn if payments are late. − Suppliers may refuse to deliver more goods and services if payments are not met in time.

Hire purchase and leasing enable businesses to spread the cost of non-current assets

Banks and specialist finance houses also offer **hire purchase (HP)** agreements. HP is a common way of paying for major items, such as cars, furniture and computers. An HP contract allows a business to hire the goods for a monthly rent plus interest. A business will not own goods bought on HP until the end of the contract and once the full price of the goods has been repaid with interest.

HP is also known as close-ended leasing. In contrast, open-ended **leasing** involves paying a leasing company a monthly rent to hire an asset but without the need ever to purchase it. At the end of a leasing agreement a business may purchase the asset at a discount or return it to the leasing company.

Advantages of HP and leasing	Disadvantages of HP and leasing
+ They are good ways of spreading payments for productive assets, vehicles and office equipment. + Care and maintenance of equipment and machinery is often carried out by the leasing company.	− A cash deposit is normally required to buy an item on HP. − Leasing charges can be high, adding up over time to more than the total cost of buying the new equipment or machinery.

Venture capital funds provide finance for firms with high growth potential

Venture capital organizations use their funds to invest in new and innovative companies with exceptional growth and profit potential. Many are in advanced technology sectors. In return, venture capital organizations usually share in the ownership and management of these enterprises.

For example, in 2008 when Victoria Willis founded NuBeginnings, a luxury spa and weight loss retreat, she approached a business angel to buy the premises. Victoria did not have enough money to buy and fit out the premises herself and did not want to take out an expensive mortgage. She agreed to pay the business angel investor a monthly rent for the premises and a share of her profits.

A **business angel** is a single wealthy individual who provides venture capital for a business start-up, usually in exchange for a share in the business.

Victoria also used her savings and managed to get a $15 000 government grant to pay for marketing expenses and a bank loan to launch NuBeginnings at a cost of around $225 000.

Advantages of venture capital	Disadvantages of venture capital
+ The investments do not have to be repaid. + There are no interest charges to pay.	− Venture capital is provided in return for a share in the ownership and management of a company.

Limited companies can sell shares and debentures to raise long-term finance

A limited company can issue shares to sell to investors who then become **shareholders** in that company. This is called **equity finance**. It provides **permanent capital** for a company because shares never have to be repaid. If shareholders want their money back they must sell their shares to another investor.

Private limited companies can sell shares to friends, family and business contacts. In contrast, public limited companies can sell many more shares to the general public through a stock exchange. ➤ **1.4.1**

However, arranging a new share issue is complex and can be expensive. A company would also need to consider whether investors would be willing to buy the new shares and what price they would be willing to pay for them. If the company prices them too high they will not sell and the company will fail to raise enough capital.

If there is insufficient demand, a new issue of shares could reduce the price of existing shares on the stock market. If this happens the market value of shares held by existing shareholders will fall. They may also lose overall control of their company if their total shareholding falls below 51%. A **rights issue** of new shares can however avoid this problem. It gives existing shareholders the right to buy the new shares in the same proportion to their existing shareholding rather than selling shares to new investors.

Advantages of new share issues	Disadvantages of new share issues
+ Share issues can raise significant new capital. + They provide permanent capital because the capital never has to be repaid by the company.	− Issuing shares is complex and expensive. − Issuing more shares can reduce the market price of existing shares. − The original owners of a company may lose control as more shares are issued.

Limited companies can also issue debentures for sale to raise long-term finance. **Debentures** are long-term loan certificates issued for sale by limited companies.

Debentures can be issued for different time periods, from a few years to 25 or more years. Investors who buy debentures provide companies with capital and are repaid in full plus interest at the end of their term.

Advantages of issuing debentures	Disadvantages of issuing debentures
+ Debentures can be used to raise long-term finance to purchase major business assets and to fund expansion.	− Debentures must be repaid with interest at the end of their term.

Governments often provide financial support for business activity to create or safeguard employment

Governments often provide financial help to businesses in their national economies to help them start up, expand, research and develop new products or overcome financial difficulties which might otherwise force them to close down.

Supporting new and existing businesses can help create and safeguard employment and incomes.

Financial support from a government may be in the form of non-repayable grants, concessions against taxes or low-cost repayable loans. More help may be available to businesses located in areas of high unemployment. ➤ **4.4.1**

Advantages of government support	Disadvantages of government support
+ Grants and concessions are non-repayable. + Governments may provide finance and low-interest loans when banks refuse to do so.	− A government may insist on certain conditions, such as creating or maintaining an agreed number of jobs in a specified location.

Can too much borrowing be bad for business?

Limited companies have a choice between borrowing money (**debt**) or issuing shares (**equity**) to raise finance. Most carefully balance the two forms of finance but some do not.

For example, when the global investment bank and financial services company Lehman Brothers Holdings Ltd collapsed in 2008 during the global financial crisis and recession, it reportedly had just $25 billion of shareholders' capital supporting over $700 billion of liabilities – a very high debt to equity ratio of 28:1.

Lehman Bros had borrowed heavily to invest in property including many houses and upmarket resort developments. When the financial crisis struck in 2008, property prices fell rapidly in many countries which meant the property Lehman Bros owned was now worth much less than its total debt. The company suffered massive losses. Lenders demanded their loans back but Lehman Bros did not have enough money to pay them. As a result the company went bankrupt.

Lehman Bros is a good example of how too much debt can cause problems for a business.

- Loans must be repaid with interest. A business that does not have enough assets to sell or does not make enough revenue will be unable to meet repayments.
- Interest rates may rise over time making it more difficult for a business to meet loan repayments and interest charges.

- Banks and other lenders that may be worried about the future viability of a business may withdraw their loans early, requiring payment by the business of outstanding loan balances in full.
- Banks and other lenders usually insist business assets are used as security or collateral against loans. If a business **defaults** (i.e., if it does not repay the loan) lenders can insist these business assets are sold to recover their money.

A business that has a large amount of debt compared to equity is described as **highly geared**. Banks and other providers of finance will be reluctant to lend more money to a business that is highly geared.

Potential investors in the shares of a company may also be reluctant to become shareholders if the company is highly geared. This is because meeting loan repayments and interest charges reduces future profits and therefore dividend payments.

Unlike loans, **shareholders' funds** from the sales of shares do not have to be repaid. However, issuing more and more shares has two possible disadvantages.

- The original owners may lose control of their company as the number of shareholders increases.
- As the amount of shares available to buy in a company increases it may reduce their market price on the stock market. Existing shareholders will see the value of their shareholdings fall.

Alternative sources of finance

Micro-finance helps people on low incomes to create successful small businesses

Banks are unwilling to lend money to people who earn very little income and own very few assets of value to offer as collateral for loans. This is especially true in many low-income, developing economies where many people live in poverty, sometimes on less than $1 or $2 per day.

Some of the least developed economies have very little industry and therefore very few employment opportunities. So, in order to earn incomes and raise their living standards many people wish to create their own small businesses but lack the capital to do so. Although most only require a very small amount of money, small loans are not profitable for banks to provide so they do not offer them.

These people also lack access to banking services including deposit accounts and electronic payment services so, to help them, specialist providers of loans and other financial services for poor people and households have been set up in many developing countries.

One of the first and most famous providers is the Grameen Bank, set up in 1976 to provide small loans to the poorest people in rural Bangladesh without the need for collateral. Today 90% of the shares of the bank are owned by the people who have borrowed money from it, while the remaining 10% is owned by the government.

ACTIVITY 5.4

Lakshmi and her family arrived in Suryapet in India with very few possessions and no money. Her husband's business was not doing well enough for anyone to agree to a loan, and the couple were worried about the future and bringing up their three children.

However, Lakshmi was able to take out a loan for 10000 Indian rupees (around $200) from SKS Microfinance Ltd. It did not require any collateral from Lakshmi and she was able to use this money to buy ready-made clothes that she sold in the surrounding villages.

She began saving the money she earned and as her sales increased she took out a second loan for 12000 Indian rupees to expand her micro-business. Today, she has learnt valuable business skills and is earning revenue of around 30000 Indian rupees each month. This has allowed her to pay for her children to attend school.

1   Why do you think banks were unwilling to lend money to Lakshmi and her family?

2   Using the article, write a short statement to explain what micro-finance is and how it differs from other forms of debt finance.

3   Identify and explain the benefits of micro-finance to Lakshmi and her family and to the Indian economy.

Source: www.globalhand.org

Micro-finance therefore involves providing small loans and other financial services to people who are poor, to help them create or expand small ("micro") businesses so that they can earn incomes to improve their living standards.

Without it many of the world's poorest people would have no prospect of starting up their own small businesses, learning valuable business skills or improving their living standards. Critics of micro-finance argue however that it has burdened many poor people with debts that they cannot afford to repay.

Crowdfunding allows businesses to raise money to fund new ideas by asking large numbers of people to each make a small contribution

Banks and venture capitalists are not always willing to lend money to help an entrepreneur to start a business. Crowdfunding is a relatively new and growing way for entrepreneurs to source the finance for their business. Crowdfunding allows businesses to borrow from large numbers of people who each contribute a relatively small amount of money, usually accessed through the internet. To encourage donations, a business may offer to give people a share of its future profits, a non-financial reward or a product in return once their business idea is up and running or successful.

Advantages of crowdfunding	Disadvantages of crowdfunding
It is a quick way to raise finance.	The process can be quite complex as the entrepreneur has to apply to a crowdfunding website. Not all ideas are accepted.
It is a way of advertising your business/product.	Not all products/ideas are successful in getting finance.
It is a form of market research – if people like your product they will contribute finance.	The entrepreneur has to do a lot of work to build up interest and attract people to their idea/product. This will take time and, often, money.
It can build a customer base as people who contribute money may become loyal customers.	If the entrepreneur does not reach their funding target, any finance already received has to be returned, so they get nothing.
It is an alternative source of finance for entrepreneurs who could not get funding elsewhere.	If the business idea has not been protected with a patent or copyright, someone could steal the idea.
People who donate can track the progress of the business through the crowdfunding website. This can help promote the business through their social networks.	If the rewards or return to contributors is wrongly calculated then the entrepreneur can end up giving away too much.
There are no fees to pay at the start of the process.	Damage to the business/entrepreneur's reputation if the business idea fails.

Choosing a method of finance

The best method of finance will depend on what it is for, how much it will cost and its impact on financial risk

There are many different types and sources of business finance available in a modern economy. Before choosing a suitable method of finance, the owners or managers of a business must assess the costs and benefits of the different methods available to their business. Their assessment should consider the following questions.

What sources of finance are available to the business?

This will depend on the following.

The size and legal form of the business. Limited companies, especially public limited companies, may face fewer risks and be more financially secure than many small businesses. As a result, they have a wider choice of methods of finance available to them than many small businesses and often at lower cost. Selling shares and debentures are not options for sole traders and partnerships.

The track record and experience of the management team. A business with a poor track record of financial performance and inexperienced managers is unlikely to attract many lenders or new shareholders.

The growth prospects and profitability of the business. Investors are more likely to buy shares in a company if it has a good business plan and is expected to grow strongly over time and generate significant profits. Banks may also be more willing to lend to growing and profitable businesses.

Value of existing loans. Banks and other lenders will be reluctant to provide finance to highly geared businesses – those that already have a significant amount of debt finance. This is because they may struggle to repay any further loans.

Why is finance needed and what is it needed for?

For example, will the finance be used to buy expensive non-current assets that can remain productive for many years? Or is the purpose of the finance to buy materials or pay for electricity charges?

It is important to match the type of finance to the use it will be put to. The methods of finance to purchase non-current assets that last a long time should therefore be non-repayable, such as permanent capital from share issues or long-term loans or mortgages for business premises. If a business does not want the trouble of owning and maintaining these assets then it may consider leasing them instead.

In contrast, short-term finance such as trade credit or the use of a bank overdraft should be used to pay for running costs or to buy parts and materials.

How much capital is needed?

If a business requires a large amount of money to finance business expansion or the introduction of new advanced machinery then the choice of sources may be limited.

For example, a business may not have enough retained profit or assets to sell off to raise the funds needed from internal sources. Bank loans may be the only option available unless the business is a limited company and can sell enough shares or debentures to cover these capital requirements. However, banks and other lenders may be reluctant to provide large, long-term loans to small businesses.

How quickly is the capital needed?

If a business has internal sources of finance available these are usually quicker to draw on than external sources. Applying for a bank loan or arranging a new issue of shares can involve a lot of time and expense.

How much will it cost?

External finance normally requires repayments to include interest or other finance charges. Some providers may also require the payment of a finance arrangement fee.

The cheapest form of finance for a business is to use retained profits. Trade credit and government grants also offer finance at no extra cost to a business.

Length of time

If the finance is to purchase non-current assets that will be in the business for more than a year, then long-term finance should be used. Such purchases are usually relatively expensive and will need financing from e.g. a long-term loan or a share issue. If the finance is to pay for expenses such as wages or purchases, then a short-term source of finance should be used, such as an overdraft or trade credit.

How much risk is involved?

Too much borrowing can increase the risk of business failure. This risk is measured by the **gearing ratio** of a business. This is the proportion of total capital invested in a business that has been financed by long-term borrowing. If this is high, for example over 50%, then a business is said to be **highly geared** and could find it difficult to repay its long-term loans if its revenues fall or if finance costs rise.

Instead of increasing its debt further a company can issue shares to raise non-repayable permanent capital. Shareholders in a company have limited liability and will only lose their investment if the company collapses.

However, issuing more shares will increase the risk that the original owners will lose control of their business because other shareholders may be able to outvote them on important business decisions. Issuing too many shares could also reduce the value of new and existing shares on the stock market. The value of the company may fall. ➤ **1.4.1**

ACTIVITY 5.5

A small limited manufacturing company has identified the financial needs for its business below. The company currently has total capital of $50 million of which $10 million has been financed by long-term loans. What method of finance would you advise in each case? Justify your answer.

▲ A modern factory and office complex costing $30 million that will allow the business to double output

▲ A fleet of four new vans to replace older vehicles used to distribute finished products to customers

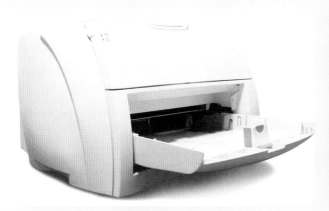

▲ Six new laser printers and three new laptop computers to use in the offices

▲ An increase in inventories of parts and materials to meet a large order from a customer

▲ The payment of a large electricity bill when the company has insufficient cash in its bank account to do this

▲ The takeover of another limited company that owns a chain of retail outlets in key locations

David is the managing director of a limited company that operates 20 bars and cafés. He wants to grow his business by another 10 outlets. He knows his company will need to raise capital to finance the expansion but his company already has a high level of debt.

a Define "limited liability". [2]

b Define "dividend". [2]

c Give **two** reasons why David might set growth as one of the objectives of the business. [4]

d Explain **three** sources of internal finance that David may use to finance expansion. [6]

e Do you think that David should increase the company's debt to finance its expansion? Justify your answer. [6]

Learning CHECKLIST

Before you continue make sure you are able to

Identify the main sources of **capital** available to different businesses:

✓ **internal sources** and **external sources** with examples

✓ short-term and long-term sources with examples, for example, an **overdraft** for short-term finance and **debt** or **equity** for long-term finance

✓ the importance of alternative sources of finance, for example, **micro-finance** and **crowdfunding**

✓ the main factors considered in making the financial choice, for example size and legal form of business, amount required, length of time, existing loans

✓ recommend and justify appropriate source(s) of finance in given circumstances.

Clues down

1   Term used to classify funds provided to a business by organizations and individuals who are not owners or employees of that business (7, 7)
2   Funds available to new and small businesses with exceptional growth potential from specialist investors, usually in return for a share in the ownership and profits of the business (7, 7)
4   Assets owned by a business that a lender can use as security against a loan. The lender can sell the assets to repay the loan in the event the business is unable to repay it (10)
5   Money raised from the sale of shares or from loans that are repayable over more than one year, to fund investments in non-current assets (4-4, 7)
6   Profit saved or held by a company for the purpose of reinvestment rather than being returned as dividends to shareholders (8, 5)
9   You need to finance the purchase of a new truck for your new business. You expect the truck to last 10 years. What source of finance will you use? (10,4)
10 The proportion of total capital invested in business assets that has been financed by long-term debt (7, 5)

Clues across

3   A time-limited loan certificate issued for sale by a company to raise debt finance. It is repaid with interest to the person or organization holding the certificate at its maturity (9)
7   You own a small business. In a few days you are expecting to receive payment from a business customer for goods it purchased on credit but before then you will need to borrow some money to pay a large electricity bill. What do you think is the most suitable source of finance to use? (4, 9)
8   An important source of finance for people on low incomes in developing economies. It involves the provision of small loans without the need for collateral to people who are poor and unable to use traditional banks (5-7)
11 Term used to describe funds raised from repayable loans and other forms of borrowing (4, 7)
12 Term used to describe long-term finance for companies that do not require repayment because it is raised from the sale of shares (9, 7)
13 Money available to a business for up to one year to finance revenue expenditures (5-4, 7)
14 Your company is successful and you are planning to expand into a new market overseas. To do this the company needs long-term finance. What source of finance is likely to be the most appropriate? (6, 7)
15 Your company intends to buy new premises using debt finance. What form of debt finance is likely to be the most suitable? (8)

5.2.1 The importance of cash and of cash flow forecasting

5.2.2 Working capital

▶ A business that runs out of cash has a cash flow problem and will need to find ways to increase the amount of cash it has available to make payments.

▶ A business that is unable to raise cash quickly has a liquidity problem. Cash is the most liquid asset a business can hold.

▶ A business will have a positive net cash flow when its cash inflows exceed its cash outflows.

▶ A cash flow forecast helps a business to manage its cash flows and cash reserve. It shows expected inflows, outflows and the balance of cash remaining or available to a business at the end and start of each month.

▶ All businesses can experience cash flow problems if they expand too quickly, invest too much in non-current assets and inventories, borrow heavily or give too much credit to customers.

▶ A business that maintains positive working capital will be in a good liquidity position because it will have more than enough cash and other liquid assets to pay off its short-term debts.

Cash – notes and coins available for immediate payment.

Liquid asset – an asset, such as money held in a bank account, that is easily converted into cash.

Liquidity problem – not having enough liquid assets to convert to cash quickly.

Insolvency – inability to pay short-term debts.

Cash inflow – cash received by a business.

Cash outflow – cash paid out by a business.

Cash flow cycle – the continuous flow of cash into and out of a business over time.

Cash reserve – a holding of cash over and above what is needed to meet immediate payments. The reserve is held on the business premises or in an easy-access bank account.

Net cash flow – total cash inflows less total cash outflows per period.

Cash flow forecast – a projection of anticipated monthly cash inflows and outflows to estimate future cash requirements.

Debtor – a customer that owes a business money for goods and services it purchased on trade credit.

Positive working capital – exists when a business has sufficient money left over after it has paid its short-term debts to continue paying its day-to-day running costs. That is, the cash and other liquid assets held by the business exceed its current liabilities.

The importance of cash in business

Cash is a liquid asset that can be used to make purchases and pay bills

What would happen if a business ran out of cash? The managers of that business would not be able to give customers change, pay any wages in cash or make purchases that need to be paid for immediately, such as a taxi ride to a business meeting.

This is exactly what happened to Ignacio and Maria Ruiz. The husband and wife team had set up a business installing and maintaining swimming pools. In their first summer in business the order book was full and revenues were good, but this soon reversed during the cold winter months that followed when outdoor pool construction and maintenance became difficult and demand also fell away.

"As a result we ran out of cash to pay our bills," explained Maria. "When revenue and profits were good during the summer we ploughed a lot of money back into the business, buying new machinery and stocks of chemicals. Then when winter came and business ground to a halt, we still had to pay rent, insurance, electricity and other costs for our business premises, but didn't have enough cash to do so."

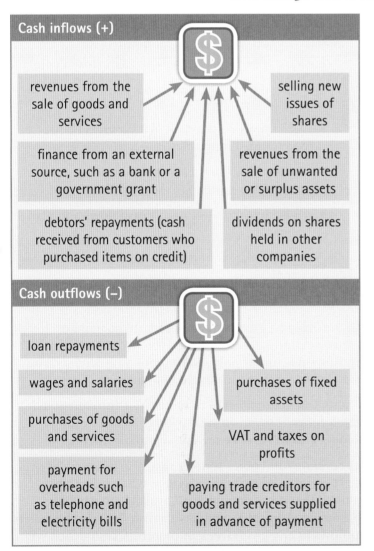

So how did the business survive through to the following summer? "We knew we had to do two things. Firstly, we had to find a way of generating some revenue during winter, and secondly we had to manage our cash better next summer and keep a reserve big enough to keep our business ticking over in winter. The first one was relatively simple. We had some spare pools so we installed these in our premises along with some sun beds and opened up a spa, tanning and massage business for people to enjoy during the winter."

Managing cash flow is a big challenge for all businesses, but especially seasonal businesses like Maria and Ignacio's pool business when sales might be condensed into a short period but staff, property costs and other running costs generally need paying all year round.

A business that runs out of cash has a **cash flow problem** and will need to find ways to increase the amount of cash it has available so it can continue to pay its bills. For example, a business may withdraw cash from its bank account or sell off some unwanted stocks of finished products and materials for cash. These and other assets which can be turned into cash quickly are known as **liquid assets**.

Cash is therefore the most liquid asset a business can hold. It consists of notes and coins held on the business premises or in a bank account with easy access, so that the cash can be used immediately to make payments.

A business that has tied up all its money in non-current assets such as premises and equipment may have few liquid assets it can draw on to provide cash at short notice.

A business that is unable to raise cash quickly has a **liquidity problem**. If it is unable to pay its bills because it cannot raise sufficient cash then suppliers of materials will stop supplying the business, its telephone and electricity supply may be cut off and a bank may repossess assets if the business fails to repay its loan. A business that is unable to pay its debts on time is **insolvent** and may be forced to close down if it cannot raise cash. ➤ **5.5.2**

All businesses should forecast their cash inflows and outflows

Knowing how much cash a business needs to hold and being able to forecast future cash requirements is one of the most important but difficult tasks faced by business managers.

Cash flows into and out of a business in a number of ways. **Cash inflows** are receipts. **Cash outflows** are payments made by the business.

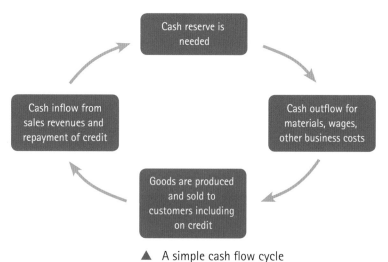

▲ A simple cash flow cycle

Major inflows and outflows of cash from a business occur at different times

The continuous flow of cash into and out of a business over time is called the **cash flow cycle**.

The cash flow cycle illustrates a number of important points.

- Cash tends to flow out of a business before it receives cash from sales.

- When cash flows back into a business it will be needed to buy more materials, pay wages, etc.

- It is important to forecast cash flows and plan ahead.

- Cash should be held in reserve in order to meet cash outflows.

- The longer the time between cash outflows and inflows the greater the reserve required.

Many cash outflows from a business involve regular monthly payments, for example the payment of wages and salaries, and repayments of loans. However, some cash outflows may occur only quarterly or annually, such as charges for telephones and electricity or the payment of taxes on profits.

A business must make sure it has enough cash to meet large, infrequent bills. This means being able to forecast how much cash will be needed in future to meet these bills and holding a **cash reserve** big enough to pay them.

Cash inflows from sales revenues and other sources may also be irregular over time. A business should therefore add to its cash reserve when it has a positive **net cash flow** or surplus so that it has enough cash available to pay bills when there is a net cash deficit. A business will have a cash flow surplus when cash inflows exceed outflows in any given week or month. A cash deficit will occur when outflows exceed inflows.

Cash flow forecasting

Forecasting cash flow helps a business to manage its cash flow

A business that fails to make a reasonable forecast of its future cash flows could run out of cash and be unable to pay its bills. It may be forced to raise cash quickly by selling off some assets that are important to the business. This could damage the future profitability of the business. Alternatively, the business may have to borrow money at a very high rate of interest and this will also reduce its profits. In the worst case, the business may have to close down if it is unable to pay its costs.

Business managers develop cash flow forecasts based on past experience of cash flows into and out of their business and what they expect to happen to trading conditions, output and costs in future.

A **cash flow forecast** is a financial budget for cash. It lists all expected monthly inflows and outflows over a given period of time – usually up to six months to one year ahead. It helps business managers to identify:

- periods when cash inflows are likely to exceed outflows, resulting in a cash surplus

- periods when cash outflows are likely to exceed inflows, resulting in a cash deficit

- how much cash the business will need to keep in reserve to pay future bills

- how much the business must borrow from a bank or other lenders to avoid insolvency.

Keeping too little cash in reserve may result in a business running out of cash. However, keeping too much cash in reserve can also be bad for a business. This is because the cash could be used more productively if it was invested in fixed assets or used to pay off bank loans. Holding too much cash can therefore mean the profitability of a business is less than it could be.

A cash flow forecast shows expected inflows, outflows and the balance of cash remaining or available to a business at the start and end of each month

The table on the next page provides an example of a cash flow forecast for a small business that is just about to start producing plug-in mosquito repellents.

At the start of the year the business owners have no cash in reserve but inject $10 500 into their business from a bank loan and using their own savings. They invest $5000 in equipment and spend a further $2500 on renting premises, charges for vehicle leases and an annual insurance premium. At the end of January they have $3000 in reserve in the business bank account. This closing balance at the end of January therefore becomes the opening balance at the bank for February.

Production is expected to start in February and the business expects to sell $10 000 worth of plug-in repellants to a big retail store on credit. The store does not pay for the devices until late March. This will be the first cash inflow the business receives following start-up in January.

The forecast predicts the business will have net cash deficit between February and April. During this period it will need to draw down its cash reserve in its bank account to pay for ongoing costs including wages, salaries and materials. However, the business will not have enough reserves to do so. It will need to overdraw its account.

The bank has already agreed to let the business have an overdraft facility up to $10 000 based on the cash flow forecast provided by the business owners, which shows the cash position of the business improving and going into surplus from April. The cash surplus will allow the business to pay off its overdraft and start to build up its cash reserves. By the end of June the business is forecast to have a cash reserve of $4000. ➤ **5.1.2**

▼ A cash flow forecast

$		January	February	March	April	May	June
Opening balance (A)		0	$3000	-$7000	-$10 000	-$5500	0
Cash inflows							
Cash sales					18 000	18 000	18 000
Credit sales				10 000			
New capital	Bank loan	6500					
	Savings	4000					
Total cash inflows (B)		$10 500	0	$10 000	$18 000	$18 000	$18 000
Cash outflows							
Wages and salaries			6500	7000	8000	8000	8000
Cash purchases	Equipment	5000					
	Materials		2000	3000	3000	3000	3000
Overheads	Loan repayments		1000	1000	1000	1000	1000
	Rent	500	500	500	500	500	500
	Electricity			1000			1200
	Lease charges	800			800		
	Insurance	1200					
	Telephone			400			300
	Maintenance						
	Other			100	200		
Total cash outflows (C)		$7500	$10 000	$13 000	$13 500	$12 500	$14 000
Net cash flow (D) (= B – C)		$3000	-$10 000	-$3000	$4500	$5500	$4000
Closing balance (= A + D)		$3000	-$7000	-$10 000	-$5500	0	$4000

Interpreting the cash flow forecast above.

- Cash is spent on productive activity before cash is received from sales. This is because the owners have set-up costs to pay before trading.
- There is **negative cash flow** in February (-$10 000) and March (-$3000). The business will need to arrange an overdraft to cover the shortfall in cash during this period.
- The bank account is overdrawn by the end of February by $7000. That is, negative cash flows have reduced the bank balance.

- The **closing bank balance** at the end of each month becomes the **opening bank balance** at the start of the next month.
- There is positive cash flow in April ($4500), May ($5500) and June ($4000).
- The cash surpluses pay off the bank overdraft by 1 June. That is, positive cash flows improve the bank balance.
- By the end of June the business has a closing bank balance of $4000. A positive cash flow.

Cash flow management

All businesses can experience cash flow problems if they expand too quickly, over-invest in assets, borrow heavily or sell too much on credit

Escada was once a leading fashion clothing company. It started as a small partnership in Munich in 1978, became a publicly traded company in 1986, and by 1990 it had grown into one of the world's best-known fashion brands, popular with many international film stars and celebrities.

However, in recent years the company struggled with internal management disputes, design flops and a shrinking market for luxury fashion items. The company had a string of retail outlets all over the world and a number of these had proved unpopular.

It had also invested heavily in developing new summer and winter collections that proved to be unpopular. Stocks of the clothes built up as sales fell sharply and the company plunged into loss. Unable to sell off its stocks of unwanted clothing, cash flows into the business were not sufficient to cover running costs and, importantly, were not enough to pay for the design, development and launch of a new clothing collection for the next year.

With no way to launch a new collection that may have helped boost sales and with losses mounting, investors lost confidence in the company and its share prices plummeted on the stock market. Creditors were unwilling to lend more to the company and so it became insolvent and was declared bankrupt.

Although Escada was once a very profitable business, it quickly ran out of cash because it had expanded too quickly, had tied up too much cash in stocks of clothing that proved unpopular with consumers and was unable to persuade creditors to lend it more money to help pays its bills.

Businesses, even highly profitable ones, can run short of cash because of the following problems.

- **Holding excess inventories of materials and finished goods.** The purchase of materials, components and finished items for sale use up cash. They may be difficult to sell off to raise cash, especially if there has been a fall in consumer demand for the products. ➤ **4.1.1**

- **Expanding too quickly.** Increasing production creates the need for more cash to pay for extra materials, parts, power and possibly overtime payments for workers. However, it may be some time before the business is ready to sell the extra output to raise additional cash. ➤ **1.3.3**

- **Investing too much money in non-current assets.** Buying new machinery, vehicles and other non-current assets uses up valuable cash reserves. It may be more sensible to lease assets or purchase them using long-term debt finance to spread their cost over their useful lives. ➤ **5.1.2**

- **Borrowing too much.** This means loan repayment and finance costs each month will be high. If interest rates or finance charges rise, monthly repayments will increase. These repayments are likely to be a severe drain on cash flow and profit. ➤ **5.1.2**

1. Copy the cash flow on page 380 into a computer spreadsheet program.

2. Enter formulae into the spreadsheet to calculate the total cash inflows, total cash outflows, net cash flow and closing balance for each month.

3. Copy the cells in the row containing the closing balance for each month to the row for the opening balance, remembering that the opening balance for each month is the closing balance from the previous month.

4. Use your spreadsheet to investigate the impact of the following changes on the cash flow forecast.

   ▸ The business sells an additional $1000 of its plug-in devices in April.

   ▸ The bill for electricity in June is $800 more than expected.

   ▸ Sales are $500 less than expected in May.

   ▸ The business ends the lease agreement on its vehicle and instead buys a new truck for $7000 in June.

- **Poor credit control.** Allowing customers to "buy now and pay later" is a good marketing strategy that can help a business to increase its sales. However, a business should only offer credit to business customers who are reliable and have enough financial resources to pay their bills on time. Customers who owe a business money are known as its credit customers or **debtors**. Some debts can turn bad, meaning the business will be unable recover them. This can happen if debtors fail or are unable to repay their debts.

- **Inflation.** Rising prices and wages increase costs and, as a result, cash outflows will increase. Firms often underestimate the impact of rising prices on costs in their cash flow forecasts.

- **Seasonal variations in sales.** These occur in the markets for some goods and services. For example, a producer of Christmas decorations will spend money throughout the year making decorations but its main source of cash inflow will be in the weeks leading up to Christmas. The business will therefore have to manage its cash flows carefully so that revenues in the period before the end of December are sufficient to pay for costs incurred throughout the following year. Similarly, many holiday resorts rely heavily on their cash inflows during the busy summer months to cover their fixed costs throughout the rest of the year.

Overcoming short-term cash flow problems

A business may be able to avoid running out of cash for short periods of time by taking some of the following measures.

- **Increase debt finance**, for example by arranging a bank overdraft or a short-term loan to make up for a shortfall of cash. However, loans will need to be repaid and will incur interest or other finance costs, all of which will increase cash outflows later.

- **Delay payments to suppliers** for goods purchased on credit. A business may have up to 90 days to settle its debts and so rather than pay them off early it could wait to do so until they fall due. However, a business will often receive additional cash discounts from a supplier if the business settles its debts promptly. Delaying payment until the last minute will therefore mean the total cost of items purchased by a business will be higher. A supplier may also refuse to sell further items to the business on trade credit if it is continually late paying off its debts.

- **Call in debtors early**. This means asking business customers who have purchased goods on credit to settle their debts earlier than usual. For example, instead of offering them 90 days to pay, a business can require them to pay within 30 days. This means the business will receive cash payments earlier than it would otherwise have done. However, as a result, some business customers may prefer to buy items from other suppliers offering longer repayment periods. The business may therefore lose customers and sales.

- **Improve credit control**. Good credit control involves taking actions to minimize the risk of loss from bad debts by restricting or denying trade credit to customers who are not a good credit risk. It means carrying out financial checks on all new customers before deciding whether or not to allow them to pay for their purchases at a later date, or insisting that they pay immediately in cash. Purchases on credit should only be allowed for those customers who are financially secure and have good bank references, or repayment histories in the case of existing credit customers.

The offer of additional cash discounts can also be used to encourage customers who have bought goods or services on credit to repay their debts early. This will help to advance cash inflows to the business.

The importance of working capital

A business must maintain a positive working capital if it is to pay off its debts and avoid running out of cash

If a business is to avoid continual short-term cash flow problems it must manage its working capital effectively. This means holding more than enough cash and other liquid assets that can be converted quickly to cash to pay off its short-term debts. This is so a business will still have enough money left over to purchase inventories and pay future running costs including any unforeseen costs such as an unexpected repair bill.

Working capital refers to the amount of capital a business has readily available to fund its day-to-day running costs. It is the difference between the value of its **current assets** (cash and other assets that can be quickly converted into cash) and its short-term debts (or **current liabilities**). A business that has more current assets than it has current liabilities has **positive working capital** and will be in a good liquidity position. ➤ 5.4.1

Current assets > Current liabilities

Having enough working capital is therefore a key measure used by external stakeholders to judge how well a business is being managed financially and its ability to pay off its debts and continue production. ➤ 5.5.1

A business with **negative working capital** risks failure. This is because its short-term debts exceed the value of its current assets: it will not be able to pay off all its debts and continue to buy inventories. External providers of finance may be unwilling to lend the business any more money and suppliers may refuse to provide it with any further deliveries of goods or services it needs on credit to continue production.

▼ How to improve the working capital position of a business

Increase current assets	Reduce current liabilities
✓ **Improve cash inflows**, for example by offering customers price discounts. This can help boost demand and sales revenues.	✓ **Pay off short-term debts**.
✓ **Cut costs and cash outflows**, for example by finding cheaper suppliers.	✓ **If they cannot be paid off, refinance short-term debts** with long-term loans. This will help lower the cost of monthly repayments by spreading them over a longer period of time.
✓ **Sell off unwanted assets** for cash.	✓ **Reduce purchases of goods on credit**, for example by running down excess inventories.
✓ **Get debtors to pay more quickly**.	

Deft Designs is a small business run by Precious Williams from a small rented art studio. She designs and makes hand-made greeting cards to sell in craft shops.

Precious would like help producing a cash flow forecast so that she can manage her business finances better and plan for unforeseen events that may have an impact on her business costs and revenues. She was sick a few months ago and was unable to meet some orders. As a result, her revenue was down and she had to use a bank overdraft to cover a large electricity bill. The overdraft has now been paid off but Precious does not want to run out of cash again.

Using a computer spreadsheet prepare a cash flow forecast for Precious for the 6-month period 1 January to 30 June December to show:

▶ the opening cash balance at the start of each month (starting with a cash balance of $1,500 on 1 January)

▶ total cash inflows of $2,000 each month from sales

▶ total cash outflows each month (regular cash outflows are shown in the table)

▶ the closing cash balance at the end of each month

Deft Designs		
Cash outflow	How much?	How often?
Rent for studio	$95	Each month
Materials and paints	$275	Each month
Loan repayments	$53	Each month
Wages	$800	Each month
Power, telephone and insurance	$290	At the end of each quarter (i.e. payments are due on 31 March and 30 June)

In addition to her regular cash outflows, Precious bought a new computer for $1,500 on 6 March. She will use the computer to keep accurate financial records for her business.

Before you continue make sure you are able to

Understand the importance of **cash** and **cash flow forecasting** in business:

✓ why cash is important to a business

✓ what a **cash flow forecast** is, how a simple one is constructed and its importance

✓ how to amend or complete a simple cash flow forecast

✓ how to interpret a simple cash flow forecast

✓ how a short-term cash flow problem might be overcome, for example by increasing loans, delaying payments, asking **debtors** to pay more quickly

Understand the concept and importance of **working capital**.

Clues down

2 Money available to a business from its holdings of cash and other liquid assets to meet its day-to-day running costs after it has paid all its short-term debts or current liabilities (7, 7)

3 Money spent or expended by a business on its day-to-day running costs (7, 11)

4 You own a shop selling sports shoes that you purchase regularly from JK Wholesalers Ltd. Sales have recently increased and you want to increase your inventory. You don't want to pay for the shoes until you have sold them all in a month or two. What form of short-term finance could your supplier provide to allow you to do this? (5, 6)

5 A collective term used to describe actions taken by a business to increase sales revenue by offering credit only to those customers who are financially secure and reliable while minimizing the risk of loss from bad debts by restricting or denying purchases on credit to customers who have poor bank references or repayment histories (6, 7)

6 An asset, such as money held in a bank account or an inventory of finished goods available for sale, that is easily converted into cash (6, 5)

7 Total cash inflows to a business less its total cash outflows over the same period. It will increase the bank balance of the business if it is positive (3, 4, 4)

9 Also known as the credit customers of a business to whom it has sold goods or services on deferred payment or trade credit terms. This means they owe the business money. Requesting that they settle their debts early can help the business overcome a short-term cash flow problem (7)

Clues across

1 A projection of the anticipated monthly cash inflows to, and outflows from a business, used to identify and manage its future cash needs (4, 4, 8)

8 Money spent to purchase or acquire non-current assets such as business premises and machinery (7, 11)

10 At the start of last month, a business had an opening bank balance of $3000. During the month cash inflows were $28 000 and total cash outflows were $21 000. In thousands of dollars, what was the net cash flow during the month? Write your answer in words. For example, if you think the answer is $3000 then write "three" (5)

11 For the business in clue 10, what was its closing bank balance at the end of the month? Write your answer in words. For example, if you think the answer is $2000 then write "two" (3)

12 A business is described as being in this financial state if it has run out of cash and is unable to pay off its short-term debts in full (9)

5.3.1 What profit is and why it is important
5.3.2 Income statements

Key POINTS

- ▶ Profit is a reward for enterprise and risk-taking in business. Without it people would be unwilling to start up and own businesses.

- ▶ Profit is also an important source of finance for many businesses and a measure of their success.

- ▶ An income statement is used to calculate and monitor the profit or loss made by a business over a 12-month accounting year. This can be compared with the previous period to examine whether profitability has improved or deteriorated.

- ▶ A business will make a gross profit if revenue from the sale of its goods or services exceeds the cost of those sales.

- ▶ A business will return a profit at the end of its accounting year if the total income it earned during that year exceeded the total costs it incurred earning it.

- ▶ If total costs exceed total income, a business will have made a loss from its activities.

- ▶ Profit remaining after any taxes on profit have been deducted can be distributed to the business owners or retained in the business for reinvestment.

- ▶ A profit is made on an item when it is sold and not necessarily when cash payment is received. This is because some items may be bought and sold on credit terms. Cash will not be exchanged for them until a later date. This means the amount of cash a business holds at the end of each week, month or accounting year is not a measure of the profit it has earned over the same period.

Business BUZZWORDS

Income statement – a financial statement used to record and report the income, expenses, profit or loss of a business.

Accounting year – the 12-month period for which a business prepares its income statement.

Gross profit – revenue from sales less the cost of the items sold.

Cost of sales – the cost of the items sold, for example the cost of purchasing the goods from suppliers or the variable costs of the materials and labour used to produce the goods or to provide the services sold.

Profit – gross profit less all other expenses.

Profit after tax – profit remaining after corporation tax or tax on profits has been deducted.

Distributed profit – profit after tax paid out to the business owners or as dividends to company shareholders.

Retained profit – profit after tax that has not been distributed to owners but is instead held by the business for reinvestment.

The importance of making a profit

Profit rewards, enterprise and risk-taking in business

Most entrepreneurs who invest their time and money starting and running private sector business organizations aim to make a profit. This means generating more income from a business than the total costs incurred earning that income. ➤ **1.5.1**

Profit is a reward for enterprise. Without it, people would be unwilling to start up and own businesses. People who invest money in business activities stand to lose their money if their businesses fail. Enterprise therefore involves risk-taking and high risk normally requires a high reward. Without such rewards for enterprise there would be far less business activity, fewer jobs, much less income and far fewer goods and services to buy.

In contrast, people who save their money in bank accounts will rarely lose their money. Although some banks may fail, as some did in 2008 and 2009 during the global financial crisis and economic recession, this is quite rare and some governments now offer savers protection by guaranteeing their deposits in bank savings accounts.

Consider Jalil and Mayra. They each have $100 000 to invest or save. Jalil chooses to save his money in a bank account that pays an annual rate of interest of 5% (or $5000). In contrast, Mayra chooses to invest her money starting a small retail company selling soft toys imported from a manufacturing company in China. This is far more risky than saving so she hopes to earn more than 5% a year on her investment; otherwise she should have just saved her money instead.

In its first year of trading the annual costs of running Mayra's business are $200 000. However, revenue from customer sales are $240 000. Her total profit is therefore $40 000 in the first year – a return of 40% on her investment of $100 000. This profit is Mayra's reward for risking her money starting and running a business, but it is not necessarily the final profit Mayra will receive.

Profit is also an important source of business finance and a key measure of success

Mayra's company has done well. It has made a healthy profit of $40 000 in its first year of operation. This will be important information for banks or investors should Mayra decide to apply for a loan or sell shares in her company to raise new capital. This is because profit is an important measure of business success and the capability of its managers.

Mayra's company must pay 20% of its profit (or $8000) in corporation tax to the government. This leaves a profit after tax of $32 000. Mayra now faces a choice whether to take all the profit remaining after tax out of her company for her own personal use or keep some of it in her business.

For example, some of the company profit after tax could be invested in a business savings account at a bank. Mayra could then draw on this to purchase additional inventory to sell or to invest in non-current assets, such as additional equipment, machinery or vehicles, to expand her company without the need to borrow money or sell shares.

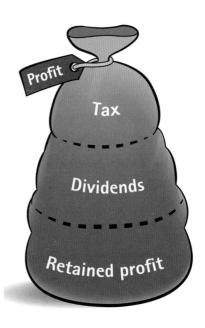

Profit after tax that is paid to the business owners is known as **distributed profit**. In a limited company it is distributed to the company's shareholders as dividends on their shares. ➤ **1.4.1**

Profit saved or held in reserve by a business or reinvested in assets is known as **retained profit**.

Accounting for profit

The amount of profit a business has made cannot be measured by the amount of cash it holds

Profit is important to many business owners. It is therefore important that the business owners are able to calculate and monitor how much profit their business is making. For each business this requires keeping accurate and up-to-date records or accounts of all the transactions made by the business each day, week or month – that is, all its costs and revenues. ➤ **4.2.1**

From these the owners of the business will be able to calculate its profit very simply as follows:

Profit = Total revenues – Total costs

Without accurate accounting records business owners will not know whether their business is making a profit or loss. For example, just because a business holds a large amount of cash at the end of each week, month or year does not mean it has made a profit in the same period. This is because a business may owe a lot of money to a number of suppliers for goods it has purchased on credit and for the use of electricity, telephone services and premises that it has yet to pay for. These are business costs that will reduce profit.

Similarly, the business may have sold a lot of goods or services on credit and has yet to receive cash payment for them. The business will have paid out for materials, wages and other costs to produce these goods and services and will have recorded their sales as revenue, which will have added to profit even if cash payment will not be received for them until a later date.

The difference between profit and cash

Earning a profit is not the same as having cash in a business. Mayra discovered this for her company after recording the following transactions during her first month's trading.

Soft toys sold for cash	$10 000
Soft toys sold on credit (payable in 90 days)	$10 000
Cost of soft toys sold	$12 500
Gross profit for month 1	**$7500**

Mayra was pleased to have sold soft toys with a retail value of $20 000. These cost $12 500 to buy from the manufacturer leaving her with a profit of $7500 from these sales.

However, despite recording a profit, the cash reserve of her business fell the same month. This was because $10 000 of these sales were on credit and Mayra did not receive cash payment for them until 90 days later.

Cash inflow (soft toys sold for cash)	$10 000
Cash outflow	$14 500
of which	
Cost of soft toys sold ($12 500)	
Additional purchases of soft toys ($2000)	
Net cash flow	**–$4500**

In addition, the business paid out $2000 in cash to import more soft toys in order to make further sales and profits. In total, therefore, Mayra's cash reserve fell by $4500 that month.

The net cash flow of a business is not, therefore, a measure of the amount of profit a business has made.

An income statement is used to calculate, report and monitor the revenues, costs and profit of a business

Mayra, like other good business owners, will need to prepare an **income statement** at the end of each accounting year to calculate and report the revenues, costs and profit of her company.

In future years, Mayra will be able to compare the amounts recorded in the income statement for her company to the amounts in previous income statements to see whether or not the company's performance and profitability has improved or deteriorated over time.

Mayra could also prepare income statements more regularly if, for example, she wanted to monitor how revenues, costs and profits vary each month.

> An **accounting year** is the 12-month period over which a business calculates its profit and prepare its income statement.
>
> Dates can vary. For example, one business may have an accounting year that runs from 1 January to 31 December each year while another may have an accounting year running from 1 June to 31 May each year.

Recording profit in an income statement

Revenue = receipts from trading activity, that is from the sale of items for cash and on credit.

Cost of sales = the costs of the items sold for revenue, for example the cost of purchasing the items from suppliers or the variable costs of the materials and labour used to produce the goods or to provide the services sold.

Gross profit = revenue from sales less the cost of those sales.

Profit = gross profit less all other business expenses (or **overheads**) such as rent, power, telephone, insurance bills and the depreciation of non-current assets.

Profit after tax = profit before tax less any corporation tax or tax on profits that is payable.

Distributed profit = the amount of profit after tax that is paid out to the owners.

Retained profit = the amount of profit after tax that has not been distributed to the owners.

If revenues from sales exceed the cost of the items sold a business will make a gross profit

The first part of an income statement is called the **trading account** because it is used to calculate and record:

- **total revenue** from sales during the accounting year

- the total cost of items sold (the **cost of sales**) during the accounting year

- the **gross profit** or **loss** from the items sold during the year.

It therefore records how good the business is at selling items at a price greater than their cost.

- If revenue from the sale of items exceeds the cost of the items sold the business will have made a **gross profit**.

- If the cost of the items sold is greater than the revenue earned from their sale, the business will have made a **gross loss**.

During its first year of trading, Mayra's company sold 15 000 soft toys at a price of $16 each, earning it a total revenue of $240 000. She had purchased the soft toys she was able to sell from a supplier in China at a total cost of $10 each. The cost of those sales was therefore $150 000. The gross profit of her company from those sales over the year was therefore $90 000.

Business or company name		

Mayra's Company

Income statement for the year ended 31 December 201X

	$
Revenue	240 000
Less cost of sales	150 000
Gross profit	**90 000**

Business or company name →

End of the accounting year or period covered by the income statement →

In a retailing business like Mayra's, the cost of items sold is simply the amount the business paid to its suppliers for the items. This will not necessarily be the same as the total amount it spends on purchases from suppliers of finished items for resale. This is because a business may purchase more items during an accounting year than it is able to sell. It will therefore have unsold inventory at the end of the year that it is able to carry over into the next year to sell. **➤ 4.1.1**

However, for a manufacturing business, the cost of the items it sells will be the costs it incurred making them: the costs of the materials and components used in their production and the wages paid to production workers for the time they spent manufacturing them; that is, the manufacturer's cost of sales will be its total variable costs of production. **➤ 4.2.1**

Profit is the surplus that remains after all other business costs have been deducted from its gross profit

Gross profit is not the final profit of a business for the following reasons.

- A business can earn income from other, non-trading activities including interest on its business savings or rent received from letting out surplus space in its premises to another business.

- A business costs money to run regardless of how much it produces and sells.
- A business may have to pay tax on its profits to the government.

The second part of an income statement is therefore called the **profit and loss account** because it is used to calculate and record:

- the **total expenses** incurred by the business during the accounting year
- the **profit** or **loss** of the business after all costs have been deducted from its total income.

It therefore shows how good a business has been at controlling its running costs or **overheads**.

- If the sum of gross profit plus non-trading income exceeds total expenses the business will have made a **profit**.
- If total expenses exceed the sum of gross profit plus non-trading income the business will have made a **loss**.

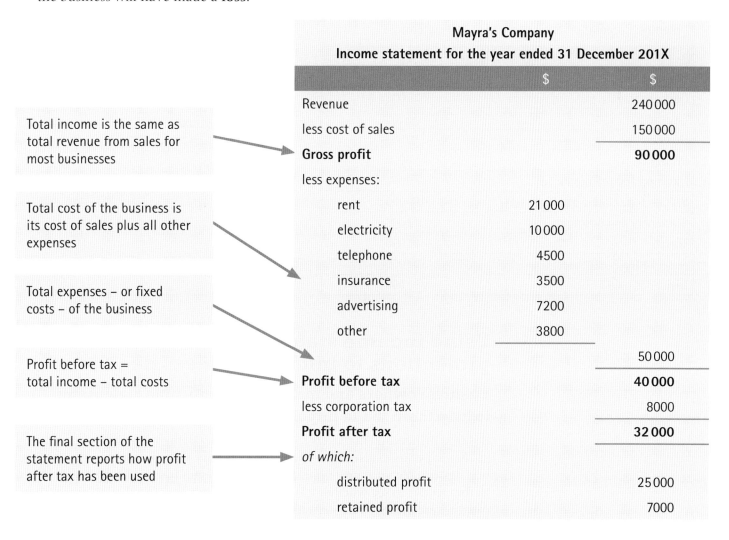

Mayra's Company			
Income statement for the year ended 31 December 201X			
		$	$
Revenue			240 000
less cost of sales			150 000
Gross profit			**90 000**
less expenses:			
	rent	21 000	
	electricity	10 000	
	telephone	4500	
	insurance	3500	
	advertising	7200	
	other	3800	
			50 000
Profit before tax			**40 000**
less corporation tax			8000
Profit after tax			**32 000**
of which:			
	distributed profit		25 000
	retained profit		7000

Total income is the same as total revenue from sales for most businesses

Total cost of the business is its cost of sales plus all other expenses

Total expenses – or fixed costs – of the business

Profit before tax = total income – total costs

The final section of the statement reports how profit after tax has been used

The completed income statement on the previous page shows Mayra's company made a gross profit of $90 000 in its first year of trading.

During the year the running costs of her company were $50 000. These included rent for the company premises, electricity and telephone bills plus all other fixed costs.

The total of these costs was deducted from the sum of its gross profit plus non-trading income to record company **profit for the year** of $40 000 (= $92 000 – $52 000).

However, even this profit figure was not the final profit Mayra could pay herself as a dividend or use to reinvest in her company. This is because her company had to pay **corporation tax** at 20% ($8000) of its profit to the government.
➤ **6.1.1**

ACTIVITY 5.8

The following information is available from the accounts kept by a small private limited company over the last 12 months. Corporation tax is charged at 20% of profit.

	Total at end of period ($)
Revenue	980 000
Cost of sales	525 000
Electricity	12 000
Depreciation	16 000
Insurance	8000
Cleaning and maintenance	9000
Wages and salaries of office staff	160 000
Stationery and postage	12 000
Travel	56 000
Miscellaneous expenses	32 000
Dividends paid	90 000

1 From the information provided calculate:
  ▸ gross profit
  ▸ profit for the year
  ▸ profit after tax
  ▸ the amount of profit after tax retained by the company.

2 Explain why retaining some profit will be important to the company.

Using income statements and profit projections to inform business decisions

Business owners and managers use income statements to help them make important business decisions

Business owners and managers compare income statements for different accounting years to determine whether profits have risen or fallen over time. They may also be able to compare how much profit the business is making compared to its competitors to see whether it is performing better or worse than they are. They can then use these comparisons to determine whether they need to take actions that will increase business revenues, control its costs and boost its profits. ➤ **5.5.1**

To increase gross profit	To increase profit (or reduce loss)
+ Increase total sales, for example by introducing a new product, expanding overseas or increasing advertising – but will this be cost-effective and raise revenue by more than it adds to total costs? + Raise the selling price to increase the revenue per item sold – but how competitive is the market for the product? If demand is price elastic total sales and revenue will fall. Cutting price instead may therefore increase total sales. + Reduce the cost of sales, for example purchase items from cheaper suppliers – but are these suppliers reliable and will the quality of the items be the same?	+ Increase gross profit. + Increase non-trading income, for example by subletting surplus space in the premises. + Cut the number of office and sales staff – but staff may object and cause disruption, there may be redundancy costs and if too many employees are cut it may reduce the ability of the business to function effectively and make sales. + Find cheaper premises – but will the location be as near to customers (or major suppliers) and as profitable as the previous one? + Find cheaper suppliers of electricity, insurance, maintenance and other expense items.

For example, business owners and managers can use projections of revenues and costs to choose between the most profitable location for new premises, whether or not to introduce a new product, to change prices or to enter a new market overseas.

ACTIVITY 5.9

Mayra is trying to decide whether or not to extend the product range of her company in its next accounting year by selling gift cards or children's clothes in addition to soft toys. She has undertaken some research and has produced the projections below. Which option will you recommend to her and why?

Projections for Year 2	Option 1 Gift cards	Option 2 Children's clothes
Revenue	60 000	75 000
Cost of sales	35 000	45 000
Increase in annual expenses		
Insurance	600	900
Advertising	1500	2000
Other	400	600

1   Calculate the projected gross profit and profit from each option.

2   Mayra has underestimated the amount of local competition from other retailers already selling children's clothes. What effect could this have on her projections?

3   Mayra has failed to include equipment maintenance costs her company will incur in both options. What effect will this have on her projections?

Hardcoat Paints plc manufactures specialist paints for industrial uses. It holds a substantial inventory of different chemicals and dyes so it is able to produce paints quickly to order from its major business customers who require 90 days to make payment. The table below shows Hardcoat's Paints income statement for the 12-month accounting year ending 31 December 2014. Some figures are missing.

Hardcoat Paints plc	
Income statement for year ended 31 December 2014	
	$ million
Revenue	?
Costs of sales	350
Gross profit	150
Overheads	110
Profit	40

a Define "gross profit".   [2]

b Calculate the value of company revenue from sales.   [2]

c Identify **four** costs likely to be included in the total overheads of the company on its income statement.   [4]

d Explain **two** reasons why it is important for Hardcoat Paints to manage its working capital.   [6]

e The directors of Hardcoat Paints plc believe the company's performance has improved. In 2014, sales of the company rose by $100 million and profit by $5 million compared with the previous accounting year. Do you agree with the directors? Justify your answer.   [6]

Learning CHECKLIST

Before you continue make sure you are able to

Explain what **profit** is and why it is important:

✓ how a **profit** is made

✓ the importance of profit to private sector businesses, for example as a reward for risk-taking/enterprise and a source of finance

✓ the difference between profit and **cash**

Understand the main features of an **income statement**:

✓ **revenue, cost of sales, gross profit, profit** and **retained profit**

✓ use simple income statements in decision-making based on profit calculations.

Clues down

1   The term used to describe the amount of money deducted from sales revenue to calculate the gross profit or loss of a business. It is the amount incurred by a business purchasing or producing the items it sold for revenue (4, 2, 5)

2   A key measure of business success. It is calculated in an income statement as gross profit less business overheads and before any taxes payable on profit have been deducted. Alternatively it can be calculated as total income less total costs (5)

7   Another term for the total operating or running costs of a business deducted from its gross profit to calculate its profit before tax (9)

Clues across

3   Revenue remaining from the sale of items after the cost of the items sold has been deducted (5, 5)

4   What impact would be the immediate effect a sale of goods on credit of $500 on the profit of a business? Use "noeffect", "increase" or "decrease" for your answer (8)

5   Kwesi and Sarah are sold traders. Last year Kwesi's business made a gross profit of $95 000 last year and incurred overheads of $35 000. In comparison, Sarah's business generated total income of $210 000 and incurred total costs of $165 000. Which trader - Kwesi or Sarah - made the most profit before tax last year? (5)

6   Term used to describe that amount of profit after tax that is held back by a business for reinvestment in assets and is therefore not distributed to business owners (8, 5)

8   What impact would be the immediate effect of a sale of goods on credit on the cash position of a business? Use noeffect, increase or decrease for your answer (8)

9   Profit after tax earned by a business that is paid out to its owners or shareholders (11, 5)

10 A financial statement used by a business to record, calculate and report its profit or loss, usually over the previous 12-month period (6, 9)

5.4.1 The main elements of a statement of financial position

5.4.2 How to interpret a simple statement of financial position

---

▶ The value of the assets, liabilities and capital of a business on a given date is recorded in its statement of financial position or balance sheet. It reveals how much the business may be worth after all it debts have been settled.

▶ Money is invested in non-current assets and current assets in a business for the purpose of carrying out productive activities. The money invested in these assets will have been financed from capital provided by the business owners and from loans and other liabilities.

▶ The liabilities of a business – or amounts it must repay to other people and organizations – include its current liabilities repayable within a year and its long-term or non-current liabilities.

▶ A balance sheet clearly shows the amount of working capital in a business. It is a vital indicator of the ability of the business to pay off its current liabilities and still have enough money remaining in cash and other current assets to fund its ongoing running costs.

▶ A balance sheet also records the amount of long-term capital employed in assets that will enable a business to continue production and generate revenue well into the future.

Statement of financial position or Balance sheet – a statement recording the value of assets, liabilities and capital of a business on a given date.

Non-current assets – (or fixed assets) are long-lived assets, including machinery and equipment. They remain productive for more than one year.

Current assets – cash, inventories and accounts receivable. They will be used up by a business within the next 12 months to make payments.

Accounts receivable – a balance sheet term for debtors. It is the total amount of money owed to the business by customers who have purchased items on credit terms payable within the next 12 months.

Accounts payable – a balance sheet term for creditors. It is the total amount of money owed by the business to suppliers who have sold items on credit terms that it must repay within the next 12 months.

Current liabilities – accounts receivable, bank overdrafts and any other amounts owed by a business to other people or organizations that will fall due for payment within the next 12 months.

Non-current liabilities – (long-term liabilities or loan capital) are loans and other amounts owed by a business to other people or organizations that will fall due for payment after one year.

Working capital – capital available to a business to pay its day-to-day running costs. It is calculated as current assets less current liabilities (or net current assets).

Shareholders' funds – the share capital and retained profits shareholders have invested in their company. Also called shareholders' equity or the owners' capital.

Capital employed – long-term capital from non-current liabilities and shareholders' funds invested in a business (therefore also equal to total assets – current liabilities).

Balancing assets and liabilities

A statement of financial position records how much a business owns and owes

An income statement is used to record and report the total revenue, costs and profit or loss of a business at the end of each 12-month accounting year. However, the amount of profit a business has made in any one year does not tell us very much about how much a business may be worth now or in the future if it was sold by its owners.

A business may be very profitable at present but if it was sold tomorrow it may raise very little money. For example, the business may have significant debts that the owners will need to repay. Or it may have old and worn-out machinery and equipment that the new owners will need to replace.

Alternatively, the sale of a loss-making business may raise a large amount of money because it has a lot of valuable assets that the new owners can use to create new products and to increase output and sales in order to be profitable in the future.

The financial health of a business and how much a business is worth therefore depends on the value of its assets and liabilities and not just how much profit it is currently making. Business assets and liabilities are recorded in a **statement of financial position** (also called a balance sheet).

A statement of financial position is used to record the value of the assets, liabilities and capital of a business on a given date.

ASSETS ● Items of value owned by the business

LIABILITIES ● Amount of money owed to external creditors

CAPITAL ● Amount of money invested in the business

These values can change from day to day and therefore a statement of financial position can be prepared at any time.

Total assets = Non-current assets + Current assets

Non-current assets (or fixed assets)

These include machinery, equipment, vehicles, land and premises owned by a business and used in productive activity.

They are physical assets that are usually kept and used by a business for more than one year. The value of non-current assets falls over time as they age and wear out through repeated use.

Current assets

These include cash, inventories of materials and finished products and money owed to the business by its credit customers (its **debtors** or **accounts receivable**).

They are used up by a business within the next 12-month accounting period to pay its immediate debts and running costs.

Total liabilities = Non-current liabilities + Current liabilities

Non-current liabilities (or long-term liabilities)

Money owed to external providers of long-term finance that are repayable over more than one year, for example a ten-year bank loan.

Bank loan

Mortgage

Debenture

Current liabilities

Money owed to external providers of short-term finance that will fall due for repayment within 12 months, for example a bank overdraft.

Trade credit

Overdraft

Credit card

Assets will always equal liabilities plus capital

Money invested in the non-current and current assets of a business can be funded in two ways, by:

- **owners' capital (or equity):** money provided by the business owners or shareholders
- **liabilities:** loans and all other amounts repayable.

Therefore, all of the money invested in business assets is owed to someone else, either to the business owners or to external providers of finance such as banks and credit card companies. This results in the following very important relationship on a statement of financial position.

Assets = liabilities + owner's capital

> *For a sole trader or another unincorporated business:*
>
> **Total assets = total liabilities + owners' capital**
>
> *For a limited company:*
>
> **Total assets = total liabilities + shareholders' funds**

A statement of financial position is therefore very important to the owners of a business. It enables them to:

- examine how much their business owes to other people or organizations
- examine how much money they have invested in their business
- monitor whether their investment increases in value over time.

Nice Creams is a small limited company producing high-quality, handmade ice creams. On 30 June last year the finance director listed the values of the company's assets and liabilities on that day. These are shown in the table below.

Item	Non-current asset	Current asset	Non-current liability	Current liability
$9000 payable to suppliers within 90 days for items bought on credit				*$9000*
Assorted machinery valued at $75 000				
Computers and other equipment valued at $30 000				
$14 000 owed by customers who have been sold goods on credit				
Outstanding bank loan of $60 000 repayable over five years				
Inventory of finished goods valued at $21 000				
Company vans and cars valued at $25 000				
$15 000 in cash held on the premises and in the company bank account				
Bank overdraft of $1000				
Total ($)				

1 Complete the table by:

▶ identifying what type of asset or liability each item is

▶ writing the value of each item in the appropriate column (as shown for the first item)

▶ adding up the column totals to find the total values of the different types of assets and liabilities.

2 Use the information from the completed table on the total assets and total liabilities of Nice Creams to calculate how much capital invested in the company belongs to its shareholders.

Interpreting a statement of financial position

A statement of financial position shows how capital has been invested in a business and how it has been financed

Using the values of the assets and liabilities in the table in activity 5.10, the finance director of Nice Creams prepared the following statement of financial position for the company. It shows that as of 30 June last year the business owned total assets valued at $180 000 financed by $70 000 of total liabilities and $110 000 of capital belonging to the company's shareholders.

What else does the statement of financial position tell us about the business?

▼ Statement of financial position (full format)

	Nice Creams Statement of Financial Position at 30 June last year		
		$	$
	Machinery	75 000	
	Equipment	30 000	
	Vehicles	25 000	
A	**Non-current assets**		**130 000**
	Cash	15 000	
	Inventories	21 000	
	Accounts receivable	14 000	
B	**Current assets**		**50 000**
C	**Total assets (A + B)**		**180 000**
	Accounts payable	9000	
	Bank overdraft	1000	
D	**Current liabilities**		**10 000**
	Bank loan	60 000	
E	**Non-current liabilities**		**60 000**
F	**Total assets less total liabilities (C – D – E)**		**110 000**
	Shareholders' funds		
G	Share capital	78 000	
H	Retained profits	32 000	
I	**Total shareholders' funds (G + H) = (F)**		**110 000**

Business or company name, plus date of statement of financial position

Final column is used to total the amounts entered in previous columns

1 The total value of the **non-current assets** of the company at the date given on the statement of financial position.

2 The total **current assets** of the company, including amounts owed to it by customers who have been sold goods on credit. They are its **debtors** or **accounts receivable**.

3 The **total assets** of the company:
Non-current assets + Current assets

4 The total **current liabilities** of the company: the short-term debts of the business which must be repaid within 12 months. They include bank overdrafts and amounts due to suppliers for items purchased by the business on credit. These suppliers are its **creditors** but in a statement of financial position they are recorded as **accounts payable**.

5 The long-term loan capital or **non-current liabilities** of the company. These are bank loans and other debts that the company will repay over more than one year. ➤ **5.1.2**

6 The value of **total assets – total liabilities**. This shows how much capital would remain invested in the company after it had paid off all its liabilities. The amount of capital remaining would belong to the shareholders.

7 The section is used to record the total funds or capital invested in the company by its shareholders. It consists of:

8
- **share capital**: the amount of capital originally invested by the shareholders when they purchased new shares issued by the company ➤ **5.1.2**
- **retained profits**: profits accumulated by the company from the current and previous years that were not distributed to the shareholders. ➤ **5.3.2**

The final section of a statement of financial position is therefore a very important section for the owners or shareholders of a business organization. This is because it shows how much their investment in the organization is worth.

In the case of a limited company such as Nice Creams, the money invested in the company that belongs to its shareholders is called the **shareholders' funds**. This represents their investment, their "stake" or **equity** in the company. It is the amount that would remain in the company if it repaid all its liabilities in full.

> Total assets = total liabilities + shareholders' funds
>
> Therefore:
>
> Shareholders' funds (or equity) = total assets – total liabilities

The statement of financial position below is a summary of the one on the previous page and more clearly shows how the assets of the company have been financed. Examination questions will often present statements of financial position in this format.

▶ Statement of financial position (summary format)

Nice Creams			
Summary of statement of financial position at 30 June last year			
		$	$
A	Non-current assets		130 000
B	Current assets	50 000	
D	Current liabilities	10 000	
WC	Working capital (B – D)		40 000
NA	Total assets – current liabilities (A + WC)		170 000
	Financed by		
E	Non-current liabilities	60 000	
I	Shareholders' funds	110 000	
CE	Capital employed (E + I) = (NA)		170 000

9 **Current assets – current liabilities = working capital.** This is capital available to the company to pay its ongoing running costs. It is positive because the value of its current assets is more than enough to pay off its current liabilities. ➤ **5.2.2**

No business could survive very long without sufficient working capital to pay its short-term debts. Suppliers of materials, electricity, telephone services and other creditors would stop supplying items if the business could not pay its bills.

Working capital is also known as **net current assets**.

10 **Total assets – current liabilities.** This is equal to the "fixed capital" invested in non-current assets plus the working capital of the company. It shows how much long-term capital has been invested or "employed" in assets that will allow the company to continue production and trading well into the future.

Total assets less current liabilities may also be described as **net assets** in some examination papers.

11 This section shows the sources of the long-term **capital employed** in the non-current assets and working capital of the company. It consists of:
- **non-current liabilities**: the long-term liabilities or loan capital of the company
- **shareholders' funds**: the permanent capital of the company raised from the sale of shares or financed from retained profits.

Capital employed is sometimes called **fixed and working capital employed**.

Cove Ltd is a construction company that specializes in the repair and renovation of small residential and office buildings. Its most recent statement of financial position is shown below.

Cove Ltd Statement of financial position at 31 December		
	$(000)	$(000)
Non-current assets		900
Current assets	500	
Current liabilities	600	
Total assets – current liabilities		**800**
Financed by		
Non-current liabilities	600	
Shareholders' funds	200	
Capital employed		**800**

1 Explain why (Total assets – current liabilities) = Capital employed.

2 Identify two non-current assets and two current assets the company is likely to own.

3 Identify two types of current liabilities the company is likely to owe to other organizations.

4 Define "working capital".

5 Do you think the business is in a good financial position? Use information from the statement of financial position to justify your answer.

Learning CHECKLIST

Before you continue make sure you are able to

Understand the main elements of a **statement of financial position**:

✓ the main classifications of **assets** and **liabilities**

✓ use examples to illustrate these classifications.

Understand how to interpret a simple statement of financial position and make deductions from it:

✓ for example how a business is financing its activities and what assets it owns, and sale of inventories to raise finance.

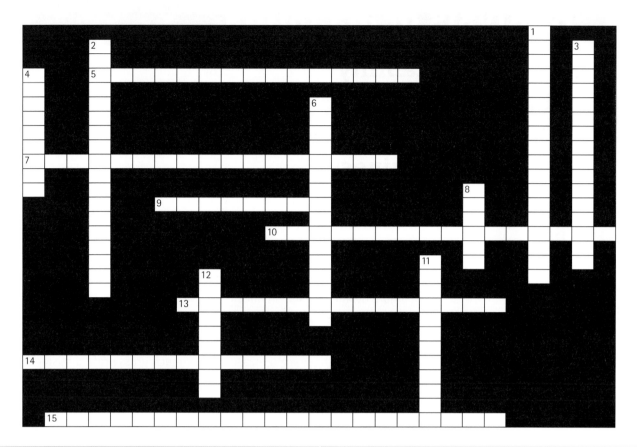

Clues down

1   Defined as the short-term debts of a business that are due for repayment within the next 12 months (7, 11)

2   Another term used to describe the amount owed to a business by its debtors – customers who have purchased items from the business on credit for payment at a later date (8, 10)

3   Another term used for working capital, or current assets less current liabilities (3-7, 6)

4   At the end its first accounting year a business had total assets of $10 million and current liabilities of $4 million. After 12 months the business recorded total assets of $13 million and current liabilities of $6 million. What happened to the amount of capital employed in the business over this period? Answer "unchanged", "increased" or "decreased" (9)

6   Premises, machinery, equipment, vehicles and other productive assets owned by a business that have useful lives of more than one year (3-7, 6)

8   Another term used to describe the investment or "stake" shareholders have in their company. It will increase if the amount of share capital and/or retained profits they hold in their company increases (6)

11 Another name for the statement of financial position (7, 5)

12 At the end of last year a company recorded a loss in its income statement. What impact would this have had on the value of the shareholders' funds in the company? Answer "unchanged", "increased" or "decreased" (9)

Clues across

5   The total amount of long-term loan or permanent capital invested in business assets that will enable it to continue production or trading into the future. It is calculated as total assets less current liabilities, or as the sum of the loan capital and the owners' or shareholders' funds invested in the business (7, 8)

7   The equity shareholders hold in their company. It is measured by the value of its total assets less total liabilities (12, 5)

9   If a business has $17 000 in cash and other current assets and owes $20 000 in current liabilities is its working capital positive or negative? (8)

10 The total amount of money owed to other people or organizations by a business (5, 11)

13 Another term used to describe the amount owed by a business to suppliers who have delivered goods or services to the business and will not require payment for them until a later date (8, 7)

14 Defined as the capital available to a business to finance its day-to-day running costs. It is calculated as the value of current assets minus current liabilities. If it is negative the business will be unable to pay off its short-term liabilities in full and will have no capital to continue paying its ongoing running costs (7, 7)

15 Long-term repayable loans and other amounts owed by a business to other people and organizations that will fall due for repayment in more than one year (3-7, 11)

5.5.1 Profitability

5.5.2 Liquidity

5.5.3 How to interpret the financial performance of a business

‣ Ratio analysis can be used to monitor the performance of a business over time and to compare the performance of different businesses.

‣ An accounting ratio or financial ratio involves comparing two figures in the financial statements of a business. A financial ratio is produced by dividing one figure by another and producing a value to measure performance.

‣ Performance ratios measure how well a business is using its assets to generate profits.

  ● The gross profit margin measures how much gross profit a business has earned as a proportion of its total revenue from sales.

  ● The profit margin is a measure of how much profit a business has earned as a proportion of its total revenue from sales.

  ● The return on capital employed (ROCE) expresses the profit of a business as a percentage of its long-term capital employed in assets.

‣ Liquidity ratios measure the ability of a business to pay its short-term debts – or current liabilities – from its holdings of cash and other current assets.

  ● A current ratio of less than one means a business has negative working capital and does not have enough current assets to meet its current or short-term liabilities.

  ● The acid test ratio measures whether or not a business is able to meet its short-term liabilities without having to sell off its inventories.

Ratio analysis – using accounting ratios to measure, monitor and compare the financial performance of a business over time and with other businesses.

Performance ratios – measures of how well a business is using its assets to earn profits.

Gross profit margin – gross profit as a percentage of revenue.

Profit margin – profit before tax as a percentage of revenue.

Return on capital employed (ROCE) – profit expressed as a percentage of the capital employed in a business.

Liquidity ratios – or solvency ratios, measure the ability of a business to settle its current liabilities from its cash and other current assets.

Liquidity – a measure of the ability of a business to raise cash from its current assets to meet its immediate and short-term debts.

Illiquid – term used to describe a business that has insufficient cash or other current assets it can convert quickly and easily to cash.

Current ratio – the value of current assets expressed as a ratio of the value of current liabilities.

Acid test ratio – current assets less inventories expressed as a ratio of current liabilities.

Interpreting financial performance

Ratio analysis involves comparing information in the financial statements of a business to measure its performance

If a business is to survive and grow it must make a profit and have enough cash to pay its bills. However, simply measuring how much profit a business makes each period and how much cash it has doesn't tell us very much about its financial strength or performance.

Most businesses aim to make a profit and calculate their profit as the difference between their revenues and costs each period using an income statement. However, some businesses are able to generate more profit from their resources than others. For example, compare the financial information on the two companies below.

Better Buy plc	year to June
	$m
profit	2
Capital employed	10
Cash	3
Liabilities falling due	4

Smart Buy plc	year to June
	$m
profit	2
Capital employed	4
Cash	1
Liabilities falling due	0.5

Both Better Buy plc and Smart Buy plc each made the same amount of profit last year. However, Better Buy plc is a much larger business organization than Smart Buy plc.

The owners of Better Buy have invested $10 million of capital in their business. A profit of $2 million therefore represents a return of 20% on their investment.

In contrast, the owner's capital invested in Smart Buy is just $4 million. A profit of $2 million therefore provides its owners with a 50% return on their investment. Smart Buy is therefore a more profitable business because it generates more profit from each $1 invested in its capital than Better Buy.

However, Better Buy held more cash than Smart Buy last year but it also had far bigger debts or liabilities to pay off than Smart Buy. In fact, Better Buy had a liquidity problem because it didn't have enough cash or other assets it could convert to cash to pay off all its debts in need of settlement that year.

Simply looking at the amount of profit each business makes and how much cash it holds therefore tells us nothing about their **profitability** or **liquidity**. Analysing financial information from business accounts by comparing two or more figures, such as profit as a percentage of capital employed or the ratio of cash to current liabilities, provides a much better picture of business performance and is called **ratio analysis**.

Ratio analysis can be used to monitor the performance of a business over time and to compare the performance of different businesses

Cash flow forecasts, income statements and statements of financial position contain important information that can be examined by stakeholders interested in how well or badly different businesses are performing.

An **accounting ratio** or **financial ratio** is simply the comparison of two figures in the financial statements of a business. A ratio is produced by dividing one key figure by another and in many cases taking a percentage. Accounting ratios are a good way to monitor how the performance of a business has changed over time and how it compares with other businesses. Many different accounting ratios can be calculated. The main ones used to analyse business accounts are:

- **Profitability ratios** which measure how well a business is using its assets to generate profits ➤ **5.3.2**

- **liquidity ratios**, which measure the ability of a business to pay its short-term debts (or current liabilities) as they fall due from its cash and other liquid assets including its inventories and debtors. ➤ **5.4.2**

Below are financial statements for Sunset Bay Ltd, a major hotel resort in a popular Caribbean holiday destination. The resort opened two years ago and business managers at Sunset Bay Ltd are confident that performance has improved over time following a major expansion in year 2 that added more rooms, pools and other leisure facilities. This was funded through a new issue of shares, which also helped the resort pay off some of its short- and long-term liabilities.

We will use the accounts of Sunset Bay Ltd to calculate and compare a number of key performance and liquidity ratios.

Sunset Bay Ltd Income statements	$ million	
	Year 1	Year 2
Revenue	150	200
less cost of sales	90	100
Gross profit	60	100
less overheads	15	20
Profit before tax	45	80
less corporation tax	9	16
Profit after tax	36	64
of which		
distributed profit	30	50
retained profit	6	14

Sunset Bay Ltd Statement of financial position	$ million			
	End Year 1		End Year 2	
Non-current assets		221		295
Cash	10		30	
Inventories	20		15	
Accounts payable	14		5	
Current assets		44		50
less current liabilities		40		25
Working capital		4		25
Total assets – current liabilities		225		320
Financed by				
Non-current liabilities	150		120	
Shareholders' funds	75		200	
Capital employed		225		320

Calculating and analysing profitability ratios

Profitability measures how well a business is using its resources to generate profit

Profit is a surplus of revenue over costs and is an absolute money amount. ➤ **1.5.1**

In contrast, **profitability** measures and compares profit relative to business size. In doing so, profitability measures how well or efficiently the business is using its resources to generate profit compared to other businesses.

Although a business may earn a profit it will not be considered profitable if

- its profit is less than rival businesses of a similar size selling the same or similar products; and/or

- the owners of the business could earn more profit if they invested their capital in another business venture or even in a bank savings account.

Increasing profitability is therefore one of the most important tasks of business owners and managers. Increasing profitability will increase the value of the business and will also make the business more attractive to new investors.

Profitability ratios measure how much profit has been made as a percentage of revenue or capital employed

A number of accounting ratios are used to measure and compare the profitability of different businesses. They are:

- **gross profit margin**
- **profit margin**
- **return on capital employed (ROCE).**

Analysing the gross profit margin

The gross profit margin measures the proportion of money left over in a business from its sales revenues after it has paid off the cost of the goods it has sold. A gross profit margin that is lower than the industry average could indicate that the business is under-pricing its products or its costs of goods sold are too high. Investors will be attracted to firms who have a gross profit margin that is above the industry average.

The **gross profit margin** is calculated as follows:

$$\text{Gross profit margin (\%)} = \frac{\text{Gross profit}}{\text{Revenue}} \times 100$$

	Year 1	Year 2
Gross profit ($ million)	$\underline{60} \times 100 = 40\%$	$\underline{100} \times 100 = 50\%$
Revenue ($ million)	150	200

Using the information on gross profits and sales revenue from the income statements of Sunset Bay Ltd on page 406 we can calculate and compare the gross profit margins over its first two accounting years in business.

These ratios show that:

• for every $10 of sales in year 1 Sunset Bay Ltd made a gross profit of $4

• in year 2 this had improved to $5 of gross profit from every $10 of revenue

• the company has become more successful at generating a gross profit from its sales because it has been able to reduce its cost of sales and/or raise the selling prices of its holidays. ➤ **5.3.2**

The gross profit margin will increase if:	The gross profit margin will decrease if:
• there is an increase in sales revenue • the selling price of each item can be increased without a significant loss of sales, for example because consumer demand is rising and there are few other businesses to compete with • early payment discounts given to credit customers (debtors) are reduced • the cost of sales falls, for example because the business purchases items from cheaper suppliers or buys more in bulk to take advantages of discounts offered by suppliers.	• there is a fall in sales revenue • the selling price of each item is reduced, for example because competitors have reduced their prices • the business offers more generous early payment discounts to credit customers in an attempt to boost credit sales and bring forward cash inflows • the costs of sales rises, for example because suppliers have increased their selling prices.

Analysing the profit margin

The profit margin is another key indicator of the financial health of the business. It shows the amount of money left after costs and expenses have been paid. The profit margin tells investors and lenders how efficiently a business can convert the sale of its products to income.

The **profit margin** is calculated as follows:

$$\text{Profit margin (\%)} = \frac{\text{Profit before tax}}{\text{Revenue}} \times 100$$

Profit is calculated by deducting overheads from gross profit. The difference between gross profit and profit therefore gives an indication of a firm's ability to control its overhead costs. The more total revenues exceed total costs, the higher the profit margin.

The profit margin and gross profit margin provide a useful means of judging the performance of a business when comparing performance across two or more years. If gross margins stay constant but profit margins decrease, this means that overheads must have increased during the year. With this information, management may wish to improve cost control measures.

The profit margins of Sunset Bay Ltd were as follows.

	Year 1	Year 2
Profit ($ million)	$\frac{45}{}$ × 100 = 30%	$\frac{80}{}$ × 100 = 40%
Revenue ($ million)	150	200

These profit margins are a very good outcome for the company. They show the following.

- After deducting overheads from gross profit the company was still able to generate profit before tax of $3 from every $10 of revenue in its first year.

- This improved in year 2 to $4 of profit before tax from every $10 of revenue.

- This was because gross profit had increased by $40 million compared to an increase in overhead costs of just $5 million.

- The company had become more successful at controlling its overheads or fixed costs for example because it was making more efficient use of its office employees and electricity and/or had found cheaper suppliers of cleaning and maintenance services.

- The profit margin of its main competitor in years 1 and 2 was 30%. This means that Sunset Bay Ltd has become more profitable than its rival. ➤ **5.3.2**

The profit margin will increase if:

- gross profit increases
- non-trading income increases
- overheads are reduced.

The profit margin will decrease if:

- gross profit falls
- non-trading income falls
- overheads increase.

Analysing the return on capital employed (ROCE)

The **ROCE** expresses the profit of a company as a percentage of the total value of its capital employed. The ROCE of a business should ideally be higher than the rate of interest its owners could earn by simply saving the same amount of money in a bank account. This is because business owners are taking more risk with their money than savers. If the ROCE is lower than the return on savings, the owners would be better off selling their business assets for cash and putting this money into a savings account earning interest.

In limited companies the business owners are its shareholders and they expect to be paid a dividend from company profits. They will clearly want to earn more from their money invested in shares than they could get from interest on a savings account or from investing their money in another business venture. The ROCE ratio allows them to compare all these alternatives.

The ROCE can be calculated as follows:

$$ROCE\ (\%) = \frac{\textbf{Profit before tax}}{\textbf{Capital employed}} \times 100$$

where

Capital employed = Non-current liabilities + Shareholders' funds
= Total assets – Current liabilities

	Year 1	Year 2
Profit ($ million)	$\underline{45} \times 100 = 20\%$	$\underline{80} \times 100 = 25\%$
Capital employed ($ million)	225	320

The ROCE will increase if:

- profit increases
- capital employed is reduced without any impact on profit
- capital employed is unchanged but is used more efficiently to increase profit.

The ROCE will decrease if:

- profit falls
- capital employed is increased but without any impact on profit
- capital employed is unchanged but is used less efficiently so profit falls.

The higher the ROCE of a company, the better it is for shareholders. This is because the more profit there is, the more dividends they will receive, or the more they can reinvest in their company to expand its ability to generate additional revenues and profits in the future.

The rate of return on the capital employed in Sunset Bay Ltd is calculated from profits recorded in its income statements and its total assets less current liabilities from its statement of financial position.

The ROCE recorded for Sunset Bay Ltd gives the following information.

- The amount of profit "returned" from each $10 of capital employed in the company was $2 in year 1.

- By year 2 this had increased to $2.5 of profit from every $10 of capital employed in the company.

- These returns were much more than the owners could have earned from interest payments had they simply saved their capital in a bank savings account instead.

- At 25% the ROCE of Sunset Bay was also much higher than the 18% return earned by its main competitor over the same period, thereby making the resort a more attractive investment for its owners.

- The operating efficiency or productivity of the company had increased. Although capital employed had increased from $225 million to $320 million it had become more successful at using its assets to generate profit. For example, the increase in the scale of the company had allowed it to benefit from substantial economies of scale. ➤ **4.2.3**

MT Agricultural Wholesalers is a limited company operating in Bangladesh. It has been operating successfully for over 11 years. Below are some key results from its financial statements for the last two years.

MT Agricultural Wholesalers Pvt Ltd Summarized results from financial statements		
	Year 10 $ (000)	Year 11 $ (000)
Revenue	400	420
Cost of sales	240	252
Gross profit	?	?
Overheads	130	147
Profit for the year	?	?
Capital employed	200	210

1   From the information presented calculate each year the company's:

   ▶ gross profit and gross profit margin

   ▶ profit for the year and profit margin

   ▶ ROCE.

2   Identify and explain for each accounting ratio:

   ▶ whether it has improved or deteriorated over time

   ▶ if it has improved or deteriorated, two possible reasons why it has changed.

Liquidity

Liquidity measures the money available to pay business debts

The liquidity of a business is measured by how quickly and easily it can raise cash to pay off its debts. A liquid asset is either cash or an asset that can quickly be converted into cash. Debtors and stock that will be sold quickly are examples of liquid assets.

A business will be in a good liquidity position if it holds enough cash and other current assets that it can easily convert to cash in order to meet its current liabilities. A business that is unable to pay its debts on time is **illiquid**. A business that is illiquid

● may have to obtain an expensive bank loan or sell off important assets, such as machinery, to raise cash. The loss of assets could reduce the amount of output the business could make and sell in future

● may be forced to close down if it cannot raise cash. The business would be bankrupt. ➤ **1.3.4**

In the short-term, liquidity is more important than profitability. However, all businesses need to make a profit so in the long term profitability is important.

Liquidity ratios, also known as **solvency ratios**, are useful as they can give an early warning of financial problems that might occur if there is an unexpected bill to pay and sudden need for cash in a business.

Analysing the current ratio

The **current ratio** measures the ability of a business to pay its immediate and short-term debts (current liabilities):

$$\text{Current ratio} = \frac{\text{Current assets}}{\text{Current liabilities}}$$

Using data from its statement of financial position, the current ratios for Sunset Bay Ltd were as follows.

	Year 1	Year 2
Current assets ($ million)	$\frac{44}{40}$ = 1.1	$\frac{50}{25}$ = 2
Current liabilities ($ million)		

The following is shown by these results.

- The current ratio at the end of year 1 was rather low. The company held $1.1 in cash and other current assets for every $1 it owed in current liabilities. Although the company could pay off its short-term debts from its current assets it had very little working capital (current assets – current liabilities) left over to meet any unexpected bills, for example a higher than anticipated electricity charge or equipment repair bill.

- By the end of year 2 the managers of Sunset Bay Ltd had reduced its current liabilities to $25 million and increased its current assets to $50 million. It did this by increasing its cash sales and holding more cash in reserve. This meant it now held $2 in current assets for every $1 it owed in current liabilities.

Many businesses adopt a rule that current assets should be around double current liabilities to give a current ratio of two. Any lower and a business could be in danger of running out of cash and other current assets to meet its short-term debts and have enough working capital left over to continue financing its day-to-day running costs.

A ratio of less than one means that the value of current liabilities exceeds the value of current assets so there is negative working capital. A business will not be able to pay its immediate debts. This means it is **insolvent**. It may have to sell off some of its non-current assets to raise cash and may even be forced to close.

The current ratio will increase if:	The current ratio will decrease if:
• the amount of cash the business holds on its premises or in its bank accounts is increased	• the amount of cash the business holds on its premises or in its bank accounts is reduced, for example due to falling cash sales
• current liabilities are reduced, for example because the business pays off its creditors and bank overdraft using a long-term loan	• current liabilities increase, for example because the business increases its purchases on credit or overdraws its bank account
• overheads are reduced so cash outflows decrease	• overheads increase so cash outflows from the business increase to pay the higher costs
• purchases of equipment and other non-current assets are delayed so that the business holds on to its cash for longer	• cash spending on equipment and other non-current assets is increased
• the amount of profits paid out to the business owners is reduced (or dividends to shareholders are reduced) so that the business retains more profit to hold as cash.	• retained profits are reduced and paid to the business owners instead.

Analysing the acid test ratio

The **acid test ratio** provides an alternative ratio for measuring liquidity:

$$\text{Acid test ratio} = \frac{\text{(Current assets} - \text{Inventories)}}{\text{Current liabilities}}$$

The acid test ratio excludes inventories of finished products and materials from the valuation of current assets; that is, the ratio measures whether or not a business is able to meet its short-term debts without having to sell off items it holds in stock.

Acid test ratios for Sunset Bay Ltd at the end of years 1 and 2 were as follows.

	Year 1	Year 2
Current assets – inventories ($ million)	$\frac{44 - 20}{} = 0.6$	$\frac{50 - 15}{} = 1.4$
Current liabilities ($ million)	40	25

These results show the following.

- Liquidity in the company at the end of year 1 was low. The company held only $0.6 in current assets other than inventories for every $1 it owed in current liabilities. This meant it would be unable to pay off its short-term debts in full without selling off its inventories of food, drink, bed linen, towels and other items. The company would have become insolvent if it was unable to raise enough cash quickly from their sale.

- Recognizing this danger, the managers of Sunset Bay Ltd increased its cash holdings and reduced its current liabilities. By the end of year 2 these actions had improved the acid test ratio of the company to $1.40 of current assets other than inventories for every $1 it owed in current liabilities.

In business, an acid test ratio of one – where the value of current assets less inventories is exactly equal to the value of current liabilities – is considered reasonably safe. This is because a business will be able to settle its short-term debts from cash and payments received from its debtors without the need to sell off items it holds in stock.

If the ratio falls below one a business may be forced to sell off its inventories to pay off its current liabilities. This may be difficult if for example there is insufficient consumer demand for its items.

Think back to MT Agricultural Wholesalers. Below are some key results from statements of financial position prepared for the company at the end of the last two years.

MT Agricultural Wholesalers Pvt Ltd Summarized results from financial statements at 31 December		
	Year 10 $ (000)	Year 11 $ (000)
Cash	20	30
Inventories	50	40
Accounts receivable (debtors)	60	50
Total current assets	**130**	**120**
Accounts payable (creditors)	80	70
Bank overdraft	20	10
Total current liabilities	**100**	**80**

1   From the information presented calculate for the company each year its:

▸ working capital

▸ current ratio

▸ acid test ratio.

2   Identify and explain for each measure in question 1:

▸ whether liquidity in the company has improved or deteriorated over time

▸ if liquidity has improved or deteriorated over time, two reasons why it has changed.

3   Do you think the managers of the company should be satisfied with the liquidity of the company at the end of year 11? Use your answers to questions 1 and 2 to justify your response.

Exam PREPARATION 5.3

Stepwell is a public limited company that makes and installs escalators, moving walkways and elevators. Table 1 gives selected information from its statement of financial position for the last two years.

Table 1: Stepwell statement of financial position at 30 June				
	$ million			
	Year 1		Year 2	
Non-current assets		400		450
Current assets	300		360	
Current liabilities	180		100	
Total assets – current liabilities		**520**		**610**
Financed by				
non-current liabilities	400		440	
shareholders' funds	120		170	
Capital employed		**520**		**610**

a Define "shareholders' funds". [2]

b Identify **two** examples of Stepwell's current assets. [2]

c Give **two** reasons why a business might have creditors. [4]

d Give **three** possible reasons why Stepwell's total assets less current liabilities have increased by the end of year 2. [6]

e Do you think the success of Stepwell's business activities can be assessed just by analysing its statement of financial position? Justify your answer. [6]

5.5.4   Why and how accounts are used

▸ The financial statements of a business are also called its final accounts. This is because a business usually prepares a full income statement and statement of financial position at the end of its accounting year or financial year.

▸ The final accounts of a business may be examined and used in decision-making by a wide range of business stakeholders.

▸ Business owners and managers will use the final accounts of their business to secure and maintain sources of short-term and long-term finance and, if relevant, to meet legal requirements.

▸ Business owners will also wish to monitor how much their investments are worth. New business investors will also use them to compare the returns of different companies in different business sectors before deciding where best to invest their capital.

▸ Banks and creditors will use the accounts of a business to judge whether or not a business can meet its short-term and long-term debts.

▸ Employees and trade unions will monitor the profitability of the businesses that employ them to determine whether or not those businesses can afford to increase wages.

▸ Competing businesses will use the accounts of rival businesses to assess their financial strength and efficiency, their ability to finance new product developments and to compete on prices and costs.

▸ Final accounts are required by government tax authorities to calculate business tax liabilities and limited companies are also legally required to publish their accounts.

▸ However, the use of accounts and accounting ratios has limitations. They show how a business performed in the past. Future financial performance may be very different.

▸ Different businesses may use different accounting years and accounting methods to value their assets. This makes comparisons difficult.

Business BUZZWORDS

Final accounts – the income statement and statement of financial position a business will produce at the end of its accounting year.

Accountant – a person who specializes in keeping and inspecting financial records and preparing financial statements.

Preparing and using financial statements

All businesses need to keep accurate financial records summarizing their financial position and performance

Units 5.3 and 5.4 introduced the income statement and statement of financial position. These are the financial statements or **final accounts** of a business.

INCOME STATEMENT	STATEMENT OF FINANCIAL POSITION
revenue	assets
gross profit	liabilities
overheads	capital
profit	

These final statements are called final accounts because a business normally produces them at the end of each of its accounting years. The very first accounting year of a business normally starts on the first day it started trading or, in the case of a limited company, the day it was incorporated. However, some very large companies may produce and publish their final accounts twice each year or even every quarter.

Business organizations produce accounts for a number of reasons.

- **To monitor business performance**. The final accounts of a business provide a record of how well it has performed over the accounting year in terms of sales, cost control, assets, liabilities and profits. These figures can be compared with those from earlier accounting years and actions to improve performance: action can be taken if business performance has deteriorated over time.

- **To secure and maintain short-term and long-term finance**. All businesses need capital to invest in assets and may need to raise this money from external providers of finance, such as banks and suppliers, or from the sale of shares if the business is incorporated. Any person or organization thinking of providing capital to a business, for example through the purchase of shares issued by a company, will wish to check whether it is profitable and has sufficient assets to repay its debts.

- **To meet legal requirements**. All businesses must produce accounts for government tax authorities so that any corporation tax or tax on profits can be calculated and applied. Liabilities to pay VAT and any sales taxes collected from customers will also need to be calculated and collected by the government. Limited companies are also required by law in many countries to publish their accounts.

The role of accountants

Most businesses use the services of an accountant to help them produce their accounts. Some large businesses can afford to employ their own accountants full time.

There are two main types of accountant a business can use or employ.

- A **financial accountant** keeps and inspects financial records and produces final accounts.
- A **management accountant** uses budgets and financial information to help control and manage a business.

Users of accounts and accounting ratios

A wide range of business stakeholders

Many different groups of people and organizations – or business stakeholders – will wish to see and use the final accounts and accounting ratios of a business. However, in many countries only the final accounts of limited companies need to be made public. The accounts of unincorporated businesses, such as sole traders and partnerships, will therefore only be seen by the business owners and managers and those stakeholders they choose to share them with. For example, these could include their suppliers and bank managers. ➤ **1.5.2**

▼ How different stakeholders will examine and question the accounts of a business

- Is my business profitable?
- Is profitability increasing?
- How do its profit margins and return on capital employed compare with those of competing businesses?
- If profits are falling should I withdraw my capital or sell my shares and invest the money in another more profitable enterprise?
- If profits are rising should I invest more to expand the business?
- How much is my investment worth now compared to last year?

Business owners

In addition to the final accounts we will require more regular financial reports and summaries because we need up-to-date figures to control and manage the business to:
- monitor costs, revenues and working capital
- identify any actions that need to be taken in the business to control its costs and/or boost sales
- compare business performance against competitors: are profit margins and returns on capital employed better or worse than those of competitors, and how can our business become more competitive?
- set new financial performance targets.

Business managers

- Should I invest my capital in the business (for example by joining a partnership or buying shares in a company) or invest elsewhere?
- Will the business provide a good return on my investment?
- How do its profitability ratios compare to those of other businesses? I am unlikely to invest in the business if they are lower and have no prospect of improving.
- Has the value of the business increased or decreased over time according to its statement of financial position? I am unlikely to invest in the business if its value is not growing or, worse, falling.
- Does the business hold enough current assets to settle its current liabilities? I will not invest in the business if it has a significant liquidity problem and will not be able to raise enough cash to continue operating.

A new investor

Employees and trade unions

- Is our employer profitable?
- Have profits been rising or falling over time?
- If profits have been falling, are our jobs secure?
- If profits have been rising, can our employer afford to increase our wages and salaries and improve our working conditions – and by how much?

A competing business

- How do the profitability ratios of the business compare to our results?
- If they are better, what actions should we take to improve our own ratios? For example, should we cut prices and increase marketing to boost sales? Can we improve efficiency to cut costs?
- How much is the business worth?
- Is the financial strength of the business, and therefore its ability to compete, improving?
- Should we try to take over the business?

Government authorities

- How well are all businesses performing?
- Are they creating more output, jobs and incomes?
- How much tax revenue do they owe?
- Should the government provide financial assistance to an individual business? Is it managed well and how much financial support does it really need?

Suppliers of goods and services on credit payment terms

- Should the business be allowed to buy more items on credit?
- Is the business a good credit risk?
- How much are its total current and other liabilities?
- Will it be able to settle its debts when payment is required?
- Does it have enough working capital to continue operating?

- Has the business applied for a bank overdraft or a long-term loan?
- How much is the application for and how will it be used?
- Is the business well managed financially?
- Does it have a good business plan and projections of future profits?
- Based on its statement of financial position, does the business hold enough liquid assets to pay its current liabilities as they fall due?
- Does the business have sufficient working capital to pay its running costs so it can continue to operate and earn revenues?
- Does the business already have significant long-term liabilities?
- If so, can it afford to take out and repay another loan?
- Does the business have enough assets to offer as collateral which can be sold to repay the loan if the business fails?

Banks and other lenders

Kingfisher's lenders plan to recall loans

India's Kingfisher Airlines Ltd was on the brink of collapse on Tuesday, with its banks saying that they plan to recall loans worth $1.5 billion because the company has not been able to come up with a viable revival plan.

The airline, which has made losses since its inception in May 2005, now owes more than $2.5 billion to its lenders, suppliers, leasing companies, airport operators, other airlines, employees and to the government in taxes. Many leasing companies have already taken away several of Kingfisher's planes.

Perform Group shareholders bail out of company after second profit warning

Shares in sports rights company Perform Group plunged almost 60% as it unleashed its second profit warning on the market.

The company, which buys the rights to sport and licences video clips or live content, said its profits will be "significantly below" previous expectations, having already cut forecasts by £4 million in November.

The news triggered a sale of the company's shares on the stock market resulting in a huge drop in the share price. The slump wiped more than £600 million off the value of the company.

▲ How the stakeholders of two companies used and reacted to their financial results and forecasts

The limitations of accounts and accounting ratios

Businesses may compile their final accounts in different ways: accounting years, methods and ratios may not be comparable and may not provide useful indicators of future performance

Every business organization is different. Businesses can be at different stages of their development, have different capital needs and use different accounting methods. Users of accounts therefore need to be aware of their following limitations.

- **Future performance may be different from past performance.**

    Just because a business has performed well in the past does not necessarily mean it will continue to do so in the future. Many things can change. For example, new technology and competitors may force an established business to lose sales.

- **Values recorded in accounts will be affected over time by inflation.**

  A business records any items or money it receives or pays out at their current prices or values on the day the transactions occur. However, prices or values can change over time. Inflation will reduce the real value of business assets and liabilities.

- **Different businesses use different accounting years and methods.**

  If different businesses use different accounting years and accounting methods, for example to value their vehicles and other non-current assets, then comparing their performance cannot be done on a "like for like" basis.

- **Not all indicators of business performance are financial.**

  Many businesses have non-financial objectives that represent important targets. For example, many businesses are now far more aware of environmental issues and have been set targets to clean up their production processes, reduce waste and repair environmental damage caused by their past activities. These actions may reduce profits in the short term but businesses that fail to improve their environmental performance over time may eventually lose customers, and therefore revenue, to businesses that do. ➤ **6.2.1**

Exam PREPARATION 5.4

Cooldown Ltd manufacture air conditioning units for sale to retailers. It is considering converting to a Public Limited Company (PLC). Below are some key performance indicators for Cooldown Ltd and the air conditioning manufacturing industry.

3-year comparison	Cooldown Ltd			Industry		
Year	1	2	3	1	2	3
Gross profit margin %	40	42	45	36	40	40
Profit margin %	15	19	18	12	15	20
Return on capital employed (ROCE) %	15	20	16	12	14	16
Current ratio	1.4	1.6	1.2	1.2	1.1	1.1
Acid test ratio	0.6	1.0	0.8	0.7	0.9	0.9

a Define "acid test ratio".   [2]
b Identify **two** potential users of Cooldown Ltd's accounts.   [2]
c Give **two** possible reasons why Cooldown Ltd might want to convert
   to a PLC.   [4]
d Outline why a new investor might use Cooldown Ltd's accounts.   [6]
e Consider whether a new investor should buy shares in Cooldown Ltd if it
   converted to a PLC. Justify your answer.   [6]

Before you continue make sure you are able to

Understand why and how accounts are used:

✓ the needs of different **users of accounts** and **ratio analysis**

✓ how users of accounts and ratio results might use information to help make decisions, for example whether to lend to or invest in the business.

Clues down

2 Gross profit less overheads expressed as a percentage of revenue. This ratio shows how well a business is controlling its running costs (6, 6)

4 These types of accounting ratio show how well a business is using its assets to earn profits (11, 6)

5 A liquidity ratio that measures the ability of a business to pay off its current liabilities from its cash and from money owed to it by its debtors (or accounts receivable) without having to sell off its inventories to do so (4, 4, 5)

6 A business recorded a gross profit of $4 million and overheads of $1.6 million in its income statement and a capital employed of $15 million in its balance sheet at the end of last year. What was its percentage return on capital employed? Answer "fifteen" or "sixteen" (7)

7 In short, this ratio expresses profit as a percentage of the capital employed in a business (4)

8 Another term used to describe the income statements and statements of financial position prepared by a business at the end of an accounting year (5, 8)

10 Term used to describe a business that has insufficient cash, or other current assets it can convert quickly and easily to cash (8)

Clues across

1 Gross profit expressed as a percentage of the revenue of a business. This ratio shows how successful it has been at selling its good or services at a price that exceeds their cost (5, 6, 6)

3 If the revenue of a business last year was $10 million, its gross profit was $4 million and its overheads were $1.6 million, what was its profit margin as a percentage of revenue? Answer "twenty four" or "twenty five" (10)

9 The accounting ratio that measures the ability of a business to settle its current liabilities from its current assets (7, 5)

11 These types of accounting ratio measure the ability of a business to pay its current liabilities as they fall due from its cash and other liquid assets, including from cash it could raise from the sale of its inventories and future payments to be received from its debtors (9, 6)

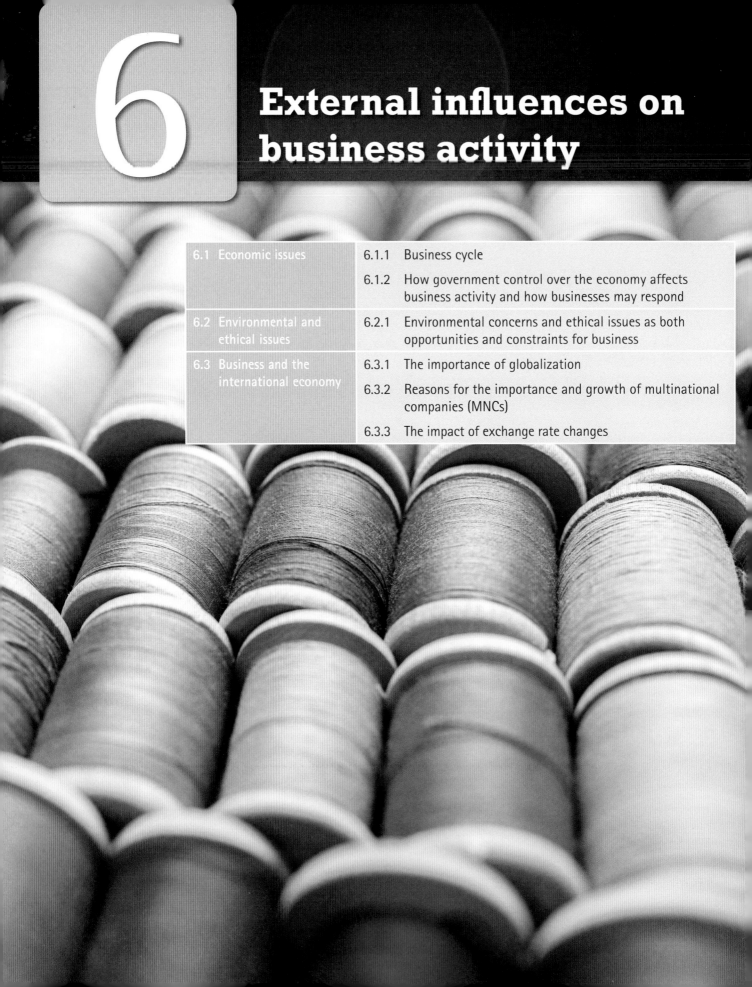

6 External influences on business activity

6.1 Economic issues	6.1.1 Business cycle
	6.1.2 How government control over the economy affects business activity and how businesses may respond
6.2 Environmental and ethical issues	6.2.1 Environmental concerns and ethical issues as both opportunities and constraints for business
6.3 Business and the international economy	6.3.1 The importance of globalization
	6.3.2 Reasons for the importance and growth of multinational companies (MNCs)
	6.3.3 The impact of exchange rate changes

6.1.1 Business cycle
6.1.2 How government control over the economy affects business activity

Key POINTS

▸ Many governments intervene in their national economies to achieve the four main economic objectives of:
  - low and stable price inflation
  - high and stable employment
  - economic growth in national output and income (increased GDP)
  - a favourable balance of international trade and balance of payments.

▸ All governments find it difficult to maintain stable economic conditions year after year. Price inflation, employment and economic growth vary – or fluctuate – over time with the business cycle.

▸ Governments use their economic policy instruments to reduce fluctuations in economic conditions in their economies.

▸ Increasing government spending, cutting taxes and reducing interest rates can increase total demand for goods and services and boost business activity, employment creation and growth during an economic recession.

▸ An economy will recover from recession as consumer confidence and spending returns. During an economic recovery sales and profits will begin to rise and business activity will increase.

▸ During an economic boom sales, profits and business activity will be at their peak but prices may rise rapidly as consumer demand increases faster than total output can expand. Business costs will also rise due to shortages of materials, parts, equipment and skilled labour.

Business BUZZWORDS

Inflation – a sustained rise in the average level of prices in a national economy.

Unemployment – people who are willing and able to work but cannot find paid employment.

Gross domestic product (GDP) – the value of the total annual output of a national economy.

Economic growth – an increase in the total output or GDP of a national economy.

Balance of payments – a record of all the financial transactions between a country and all the other countries with which it trades.

Business cycle – recurrent periods of recession, recovery and boom in business activity and economic growth in a national economy.

Economic recession – a period of declining business activity, falling output, employment and incomes.

Economic boom – a period during which business activity, output and prices increase rapidly.

Policy instrument – a measure used by a government to achieve its economic objectives. They include public expenditures, taxes and interest rates.

Read the news articles and headlines below. Use them to identify why and how different governments try to influence business decisions and activities using economic policies.

Sweden to cut taxes again

Sweden's government said on Saturday it would cut income tax by a total of 10 billion Swedish crowns ($1.45 billion) from next year, a move it said would boost employment.

Higher taxes on car imports to curb deficit

The Vietnam Ministry of Industry and Trade has proposed a rise in import duties on cars and a new luxury tax on mobile phones to narrow its international trade deficit. Payments for imported goods exceeded earnings from exports sold overseas by a record $17.5 billion last year.

Venezuela to increase public spending to boost economy and cut unemployment

The Venezuelan government will increase public spending to boost economic growth and generate employment in response to the global crisis. The government will invest in houses, schools, hospitals, roads and other public works projects the president told the Venezuelan state newspaper.

India raises interest rate to 8% to curb inflation

India's central bank unexpectedly raised interest rates for the first time in 15 months to combat a surge in inflation sparked by rising food and energy costs.

Taiwan cuts interest rates to boost exports

Taiwan announced an emergency cut in its interest rate yesterday after data showed exports falling at a record pace.

The central bank said the slump in exports was having a severe impact on the economy.

"Cutting interest rates will help to increase consumer spending," it said. "It will also help reduce borrowing costs for companies and help boost new investment."

"Exports are a key economic driver and if exports are bad, then it will reduce investments, and force companies to cut their workforce," experts warned.

China launches tax reforms to boost economic growth

China's government announced it would reduce the tax burden on companies by more than 120 billion yuan ($17.6 billion) next year.

The changes will enable companies to get deductions against the taxes they must pay from spending on fixed assets such as new machinery and equipment.

Value added taxes paid by small businesses and the self-employed were reduced to 3% from 6%.

The government said the reforms would help encourage technological upgrading at Chinese companies and boost domestic demand.

Germany wants a million electric vehicles plugged in by 2020

The German government unveiled plans on Wednesday to get one million electric cars on the road by 2020, by offering grants to jump-start national giants like BMW and Volkswagen.

The government will provide grants totalling $162 million to examine how the cars could best be introduced. It also plans to grant about $240 million for research on the batteries that power electric cars and make domestic production a priority.

Government economic objectives

Most governments have four main objectives for their national economies

Most governments want their national economies to expand and prosper and so use economic policies to achieve their objectives. Changes in government economic policies, like the examples in activity 6.1, can have a major impact on business activity.

When Shen Chao learnt the Chinese government was to reduce taxes on business he was very pleased.

"Buying equipment for my business in Nanjing is expensive," he complained.

"We manufacture ball bearings for the growing automobile industry in China. They are used in engines, pulleys, drive shafts, gearboxes and many other applications. Demand has risen significantly and to keep pace I need to invest 20 million yuan (around $3 million) to buy more computers, lathes, grinders, presses and other machinery, but my business is small and does not have enough money to do so. I was at risk of losing my main customer because my business could not supply all the ball bearings it needed."

"However, if I invest I can now claim a reduction in tax on my business turnover. This could be worth up to 8 million yuan to my business over the next year and therefore significantly lowers the cost of buying the new equipment."

"By expanding my business I can increase output and provide more jobs and incomes. This I know will help my government achieve its objective to expand the Chinese economy and improve living standards."

When the Indian government raised interest rates to 8% Ravi Gopan Jindal knew his consumer electronics business was in for a tough time ahead.

"I had just taken out a major variable rate loan with the Andhra Bank to invest in fitting out my new shop," he explained. "As a result of the increase in interest rates my monthly loan repayments rose from 30 000 rupees to 31 200."

Ravi said this increased his annual business costs by over 14 000 rupees, "and at a time when consumer spending was likely to fall".

"People who had already borrowed money had to spend more of their incomes repaying them, while other consumers who had wanted to borrow money to buy a new flat screen television, personal computer or kitchen appliances, decided not to do so."

As a result Ravi decided he would need to increase his prices and cut his shop staff by two to save on wages. "I know the government wanted to reduce price inflation by cutting consumer spending but the impact on business, especially small businesses and employment, was particularly hard."

Most governments have four main objectives for their national economies. These are:

- **low and stable price inflation**
- **high and stable employment**
- **economic growth in the national output and income**
- **a favourable balance of international trade and payments.**

If a government can achieve these objectives it will create an economic environment that is good for business.

1 Low and stable price inflation

What is inflation? A sustained increase in the prices of the vast majority of goods and services available for sale in an economy. If inflation is increasing, it means the rate at which prices are rising is accelerating.

Why is high price inflation bad for business and an economy?

- As prices increase consumers will not be able to afford to buy as many goods or services as they did before so demand and sales will fall. This is because rising prices reduce **real incomes**. Real income is a measure of the purchasing power of money. If a person's income rises by 2% but prices rise by 5%, then that person's real income, and therefore the amount that he or she could have bought with it, will have fallen by 3%.

- Business costs will increase as a result of the rising prices of the goods and services they purchase. Workers may also demand higher wages and salaries so they keep up with rising prices.

- The prices of goods produced in the economy will rise faster than those produced by firms located in countries with lower rates of inflation. As a result, consumers may buy cheaper products from firms located overseas instead. Businesses in the economy will lose sales and jobs will be lost.

Why control inflation? If a government can reduce price inflation and keep it low, it will make it easier for businesses to manage their costs, for exporters to sell their products overseas and for consumers, especially those on low incomes, to continue buying the goods and services they want and need.

2 High and stable employment

What is unemployment? People who are willing and able to work are unable to find work because of a lack of suitable job opportunities.

Why is high unemployment bad for business and an economy?

- As unemployment rises, fewer people will be in work and so fewer goods and services will be produced. Total output in the economy will fall.

- Fewer people will be in paid work so total income will be lower. As a result, consumer spending will fall and businesses will lose revenue.

- The government may have to spend more on welfare or social security payments to support the unemployed and their families. Taxes on businesses and working people may be increased to pay for the additional government spending. This will reduce their disposable incomes and cause demand to fall. Alternatively, the government may have to cut spending on building roads, education or supporting new businesses.

- People who are unemployed for a long time may de-skill (lose their skills).

Why control employment? If a government can reduce unemployment and expand employment opportunities more people will be in paid work and earning regular incomes. As employment increases, total output will expand, consumer spending will rise, more business opportunities will be created and government spending on welfare can be reduced.

What is economic growth? An increase in the total output of goods and services in a national economy. The value of the total output of a national economy each year is measured by its **gross domestic product (GDP)**.

Why is negative growth bad for business and an economy?

Many people are better off today than they were 20 or more years ago because most economies have experienced economic growth over time. However, steady economic growth may not be achieved every year. Sometimes economic growth can turn negative and when this happens the following will occur.

* There will be a sustained reduction in total output or GDP. Fewer people will be employed and so incomes and consumer spending will fall.
* Businesses will lose sales and profits. Many may be forced to close if consumer demand continues to fall.
* There will be fewer business opportunities. Entrepreneurs will not invest in new businesses and may move existing production to other countries where economic conditions are better.
* As incomes and profits fall, government revenue from taxes will fall and government spending on roads, schools and health care may have to be cut.

Why control economic growth? Sustained economic growth will create new business opportunities and jobs. Output, employment and incomes will rise and living standards will improve.

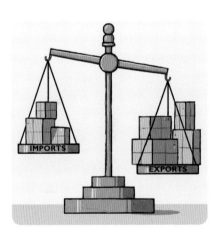

What is the balance of payments? International trade involves the exchange of goods, services and money between residents and firms located in different countries. The **balance of payments** of a country provides a record of the value of all its international trade and financial transactions with other countries.

Why is an unfavourable balance of international trade bad for business and an economy?

No country can produce everything its individual and business consumers need and want. Every country must therefore **import** some goods and services from other countries. In return, the sale of other goods and services to consumers overseas will earn foreign currency. This revenue from the sale of **exports** can therefore be used to pay for imported products. ➤ 6.3.1

If a country spends more on imports than it receives from the sale of exports, its balance of international payments will be in deficit. This can cause the following problems.

* The country may run out of foreign currency to buy imports and may have to borrow money from overseas.
* The national currency may lose value against other foreign currencies. This means it will be worth less than before and this will make imported goods and services more expensive to buy. In turn this can increase price inflation.
* Firms that need to import materials and parts from overseas to produce their own products will face rising costs.

Why control international trade and payments? A favourable balance of international trade and payments provides opportunities for businesses to expand their sales by exporting their goods and services to consumers overseas. It also provides jobs and incomes and ensures the economy can afford to import a wide variety of goods and services to satisfy consumer needs and wants.

ACTIVITY 6.2

Imagine you run a large business selling luxury holidays. Below are some facts about the national economy.

Try to decide what is happening to inflation, real incomes, employment, economic growth and international trade. What impacts could these have on your business?

> Last year average prices increased by 10%. This year prices have gone up by 15%. Over the same period average incomes have risen by only 12%.

> Total output last year was valued at $10 billion. This year it is $11.5 billion but all of this increase has been due to rising prices. Output has not increased.

> Over this year imports have grown by $2 billion while exports have increased by $1 billion.

> The population of working age people has grown by 10 000, while total employment has increased by 6000.

Managing the business cycle

All governments find it difficult to maintain stable economic conditions year after year

The rate of price inflation, employment and economic growth all tend to vary over time. International trade may also be affected by changes in economic conditions.

For example, following several years of strong economic growth and low unemployment many national economies went into deep **economic recession** in 2008 as their national output, spending and incomes fell. The global economic crisis of 2008 resulted in many businesses closing and the loss of many millions of jobs around the world. It started with the collapse of many banks and soon spread to the construction, retailing, tourism and manufacturing sectors as unemployment increased and consumer spending fell rapidly.

Many companies, like Tyco Electronics in the USA, cut their production and workforces in response. Tyco makes electronic connectors used in cars, kitchen appliances, telecommunications equipment and other goods. However, makers of consumer durable goods and their suppliers were hit especially hard as consumers cut their spending on non-essential items in the worst recession in decades. In an attempt to reduce costs Tyco cut its worldwide workforce by 20% or around 20 000 jobs.

Like Tyco, many businesses adopt survival strategies during an economic recession, cutting their costs and reducing their prices to boost sales in order to keep going long enough until there is a recovery in consumer confidence and spending.

Most national economies experience cyclical changes in business activity. Inflation, unemployment, output and trading conditions vary with the business cycle

The **business cycle** (or economic cycle) refers to the recurring pattern of "ups and downs" in business activity and total output that has been observed in many national economies over many years. It is characterized by five main phases and these are shown in the diagram below.

▼ The business cycle

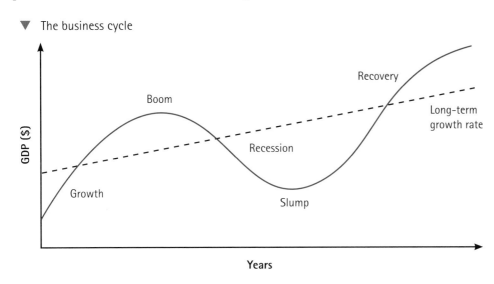

It is normal for national economies to grow over time. This is shown by the steadily rising line labelled long-term growth rate. For example, between 2000 and 2013 the value of the total output or **GDP** of India grew from 21 700 billion rupees to over 100 trillion rupees (the equivalent of $475 billion to $1859 billion). Some of the increase in the value of India's GDP over this period was simply due to rising prices. However, nearly 70% of the growth in GDP was due to an increase in the volume of goods and services produced in the economy. This grew by around 7.1% per year on average between 2000 and 2013.

In some years economic growth in many economies is faster than normal and in others it can be slower than normal or may even turn negative during a recession during which total output falls. The rate of price inflation and total employment will also tend to rise and fall over time.

A complete business cycle involves all five phases shown in the diagram above and can sometimes last for five or more years. The variations in economic growth, inflation and employment that occur over successive phases of the business cycle are called "cyclical fluctuations". Sometimes these fluctuations are relatively mild and short-lived but at times they can be severe and last several years resulting in deep economic recessions or slumps, or periods of uncontrollable price inflation.

Stage of cycle	What happens?
GROWTH (expansion)	Business activity grows. Many businesses enjoy increased sales and profits. New businesses are formed. National output, incomes and employment increase.
BOOM (peak)	Consumer demand, sales and profits peak. There may be rapid inflation as prices rise quickly because consumer demand exceeds the amount of goods and services firms can produce and supply. The economy "overheats". Shortages of materials, parts and equipment increase business costs. Unemployment is low and wages rise as firms compete to employ skilled workers. The government may raise interest rates to control increasing inflation. Consumer confidence and spending may begin to decline due to high inflation and high interest rates.
RECESSION (downturn)	Consumer demand for many goods and services begins to fall. Business activity, sales and profits decline. There is a fall in total output (GDP) as sales decline and firms cut back production. Workers are made redundant and incomes fall, causing consumer spending to fall further. Many businesses cut back their demand for materials, parts and equipment. Total output falls further. Price inflation slows down. Prices may even begin to fall as businesses compete with each other to survive.
SLUMP (trough)	This is a deep and prolonged recession. Business activity, sales and profits may continue to fall or remain low. Many businesses are forced to close down. Unemployment is high and wages may be cut for those still in work. Many people experience falling living standards. The government may increase public spending, cut taxes and reduce interest rates to encourage consumer borrowing and spending.
RECOVERY (upturn)	Business and consumer confidence recovers. Spending on goods and services begins to rise. Sales and profits begin to rise. Firms increase output and employ more workers. New businesses are formed. Unemployment falls and incomes rise boosting consumer spending further. The economy starts to expand again.

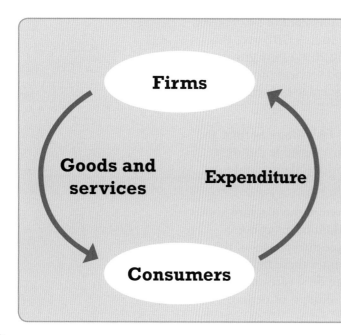

GDP measures the total value of all goods and services produced by business activity within a national economy each year. GDP is also therefore a measure of the national expenditure and national income of an economy.

This is because private and public sector organizations produce goods and services to sell to consumers. Revenue from the sale of goods and services is used by the owners of firms to pay wages and salaries to labour and to pay other firms and individuals to supply capital goods and natural resources. Any money left over after all these payments is profit. The total amount of wages, salaries, payments to suppliers of man-made and natural resources and profits in an economy make up its national income.

Look at the articles and graph below.

▶ What evidence is there of a business cycle in national economies?

▶ What are the main features of an economic recession?

▶ What are the main features of an economic boom?

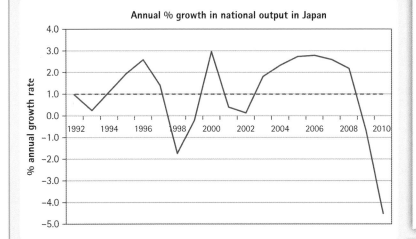

Annual % growth in national output in Japan

US economy: retail sales slide signals recession

The eroding US economy drove retail sales into their longest slump in at least 16 years, even before this month's market collapse signalled a deepening recession.

Consumer purchases fell 1.2% in September, extending the decline to three straight months, the first time that's happened since comparable records began in 1992.

The global recession has raised unemployment rates nearly to double digits in developed countries and to less drastic but still worrying levels in developing countries.

China's strong recovery has brought all sorts of benefits to employees, consumers and business owners but it has also brought rising housing costs and food prices.

Pakistan economic recovery picking up

Economic growth in Pakistan is starting to recover; large-scale manufacturing output has started to increase and the improvement in the global economy has helped boost manufacturing exports.

About 280 small companies are going out of business every week and the number could increase as the downturn continues to bite, according to the Federation of Small Businesses. However, the sector's losses are still well below the nightmare days of the slump in the early 1990s when about 1000 small businesses a week were closing.

Global recession costs 80 000 jobs a day

A rise in car sales during the first half of March is lifting expectations that totals for the month will show the industry's recovery is picking up speed.

How changes in employment, inflation and GDP over the business cycle can affect business

Impact on businesses of changes in employment levels

If employment levels increase, then more people working means higher incomes to spend on goods and services. Businesses sell more and can expand. However, rising employment levels could also mean that wages will increase. This will make labour more expensive and increase business costs. If employment levels fall, then wages may fall and labour becomes cheaper. However, businesses might find it hard to sell goods and services. Falling employment levels could mean lower incomes for consumers. Demand falls for output and business revenue decreases.

Impact on businesses of changes in inflation

Inflation may mean that the costs of production are rising. Resources become more expensive. Some businesses increase prices. Consumers cannot buy as much with their income, so employees ask for increased wages. Businesses can plan for changes in inflation if it is low and stable as it is predictable. If inflation changes are not anticipated, then businesses find that their costs are rising before they can increase their prices. Some businesses may make a loss. Changing prices can be very expensive for a company. New catalogues have to be produced and goods have to have new price labels. This is known as rising "menu costs".

Impact on businesses of changes in gross domestic product (GDP)

Gross domestic product (GDP) is a measure of economic growth. If the economy is growing, it means that more people are employed and businesses can sell more goods and services. Business opportunities expand and investors are more likely to invest in business. Entrepreneurs will find it easier to set up a successful business. A slowdown in economic growth could signal an economy that is entering a recession. Businesses cannot sell all their output, inventories build up, output reduces and some employees are made redundant. There are fewer business opportunities and some businesses may be forced to close down.

The impact of government decisions

Governments use their economic policy instruments to achieve their economic objectives and to reduce the severity of economic recessions and booms

In many countries the government is a major investor, consumer and employer. For example, the government of Denmark accounts for over 57% of total spending on goods and services in the Danish economy and employs around 34% of the Danish workforce.

A government can therefore use its economic power to try to achieve its main economic objectives and to avoid deep recessions and uncontrollable booms in its economy. To do this, a government can use a number of economic **policy instruments**. The main ones are:

- **public expenditure** (or government spending)

- **taxes**

- **interest rates**.

Activity 6.1 showed how different governments were using the above policy instruments to affect change in their national economies through the way they influence or control consumer spending and business activity. It is therefore important for firms to understand how changes in policy instruments can affect them.

How changes in government spending can affect business activity

Many businesses benefit directly from government spending on goods and services

Public expenditure – spending by government authorities and government-owned enterprises – accounts for a large share of total spending in many economies. In most economies, the majority of public expenditure is financed from tax revenues and government borrowing.

The public sector of an economy may spend money on providing health care, education, roads, railways, schools, national parks, a police force, street lights, national defence, wages for public sector workers, welfare or social security payments, financial support for agriculture and industry, equipment for government offices and much more. ➤ **1.5.3**

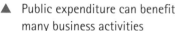
▲ Public expenditure can benefit many business activities

Many businesses therefore benefit directly from different public expenditures or indirectly from their impact on consumer incomes and demand. Here are some examples.

- Construction firms benefit from contracts to build schools and other buildings.

- Office equipment manufacturers benefit from spending on equipping public offices.

- Power companies earn revenue from electricity supplied for street lights.

- The defence industry benefits from orders for defence equipment.

- Small businesses may be given grants to buy equipment and premises.

- Public sector workers use their incomes to buy goods and services from businesses.

- Businesses may receive government grants and subsidies to fund new research and development, to buy equipment and premises, and to train employees.

For example, many governments are increasing grants to businesses to encourage them to invest in electric vehicle development and manufacturing, and in other low-carbon technologies and skills, not only to reduce damage to the environment but also to develop new products they can then sell, including to other countries, to meet growing consumer demand. Just look opposite at how investments by the Chinese government are benefiting Chinese companies and their suppliers.

Raising or cutting public expenditure can therefore have a major impact on business decisions, activities and profitability.

During an economic recession a government may raise its own spending to increase total demand for goods and services in the economy. This will help to create more business opportunities and jobs, increase output and boost economic growth.

In contrast, if prices are rising rapidly during an economic boom a government may cut public expenditure to reduce total demand in the economy. The rate of increase in prices may slow and some prices may even be cut as demand for many goods and services falls.

China goes green

In 2009 the Chinese government launched the world's largest green stimulus plan of $221 billion in support of its state-owned enterprises and private sector to develop the green technology industry.

China's companies have since raced past competitors in Denmark, Germany and the United States to become the world's largest producers of wind turbines. China has also become the world's largest manufacturer of solar panels.

How changes in taxes can affect business activity

Reducing taxes during an economic recession can help to boost consumer spending and business activity

Most governments collect taxes to finance their public expenditures. Taxes are collected either directly from the incomes or wealth of individuals and businesses or indirectly from the money they spend on goods and services.

Increasing the overall level of taxation in an economy will reduce the amount of disposable income people have left to spend on goods and services. This policy may be used when there is high and rising price inflation caused by rapidly rising demand for goods and services. However, as a result business revenues and profits are likely to fall and, following this, output and employment may be cut. In contrast, reducing the overall level of taxation will raise disposable incomes and encourage consumers to spend more on goods and services. This will help to boost business activity during an economic recession.

Different taxes can be used to influence private sector production and consumption decisions

In addition to controlling total spending in the economy a government may also use different taxes to:

- increase the final selling prices of harmful products, such as cigarettes, to discourage their consumption and production

- encourage businesses to invest in new technologies and job creation by cutting or removing taxes on their profits

- protect the natural environment by discouraging activities that create harmful pollution and waste, for example by taxing gasoline and air travel to raise their prices and reduce their consumption ➤ 6.2.1

- reduce inequalities in income and wealth, by taxing people and businesses with high incomes more than those with low incomes

- to restrict the consumption of imported goods to protect domestic firms and employment from international competition.

America's soft drinks industry battles proposals to tax sugary sodas

"Increasing taxes on drinks with high sugar content is the most effective way to reduce consumption," argued researchers at Yale University. They estimate a new tax would reduce the medical costs of treating obesity and dental problems by $50 billion and raise $150 billion in tax revenue in a decade.

However, powerful drinks manufacturers have argued their product should not be singled out over other high fat content food products. "Taxing our industry more will simply harm jobs and people's livelihoods," argued a spokesperson for the industry.

Australian government doubles R&D tax incentives for business

"This is great news for my business," said Faith Ramsay, owner of Outback Logistics in Wollongong.

"Over the last year we invested over $300 000 in new product research and development for our earthquake and disaster survival kits."

"We need to invest to keep ahead of the competition," Faith explained, "but cashflow is a major hurdle in a small business. The new tax incentives will save my business around $25 000 a year, some of which we can use to invest more in new product research and development."

The new tax incentives will double the current rate of government support for research and development conducted by firms turning over less than $20 million.

For example, the article on the previous page reports that US government authorities are considering imposing taxes on sugary drinks to cut their consumption in an effort to reduce health problems in people who drink too many of them. The measure will reduce health care costs but also raise revenue for the government. However, manufacturers of soft drinks are worried about falling sales reducing their profits, leading to possible job losses and closures.

In the same way some countries are increasing taxes on products and activities that cause pollution or harm to the natural environment when they are produced or consumed, including gasoline and industrial waste dumped in landfill sites.

In contrast, many countries, including Australia, Brazil, Puerto Rico, Singapore and Thailand, offer tax credits or concessions to encourage businesses to invest in the research and development of new products and production processes, new technologically advanced equipment and the provision of employee training. Firms that increase their investment in these activities may be offered lower taxes on their revenues or profits and even exemptions from paying taxes on the prices of some products they buy, for example on imported goods.

ACTIVITY 6.4

For each of the images below suggest reasons why a government might impose taxes. What impacts could this have on business activities?

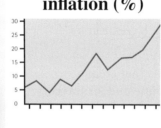
Rate of price inflation (%)

Le Monde

Gap between rich and poor widens according to new report

IT DEL ESSENISL dion heniscinis nullandip estrud ea faci blam, Ibh er ing eui blandipsummy nim zzriusto doloreet, suscilit lamet dolut lamet lum vel utpat Lsisci bla am, quisi estrud te el ut iriureet loreet landre tinci exero et luptatis augue It del essenisl dion heniscinis nullandi estrud ea faci blam, Ibh er ing eui ... rrinsto doloreet,

How much!!??!!

Indirect taxes can be targeted at different products to influence consumer demand for them

Indirect taxes are added to the prices of goods and services and are collected by a government from the sales revenues of businesses. Indirect taxes therefore increase the prices consumers pay for the products they buy. To protect consumers on low incomes, indirect taxes are not usually added to the price of items such as food, baby clothes and educational books, which are considered essential or worthwhile.

Indirect taxes include the following.

- **Ad valorem taxes** such as VAT and other sales taxes are levied as a percentage of the selling price of goods and services or on sales revenues. Some necessities, such as many foods and medicines, may be exempt or zero-rated. Raising VAT will increase the cost of buying goods and services for many consumers.

- **Excise duties** are applied to specific goods such as alcohol, cigarettes, vehicles and petrol. They are normally fixed charges based on the amount sold. For example, some countries have introduced vehicle duties that are greater on large cars than on small cars. This is to encourage consumers to buy smaller vehicles that burn less petrol or gasoline and produce lower engine emissions. In response to changing consumer demand car manufacturers have increased production of small cars with more efficient engines.

- **Import tariffs** are taxes on the value of imported goods entering a country. Tariffs are used to raise the prices of certain imported products to protect domestic firms from overseas competition. Domestic firms producing products that compete with overseas imports should benefit from increased consumer demand for their products. However, domestic firms that must import finished products to sell or raw materials and components to use in their manufacturing processes will face increased costs as a result. ➤ **6.3.1**

- **User charges** include tolls for the use of publicly financed and owned bridges and motorway and air passenger duties.

Raising indirect taxes therefore increases the prices of many goods and services and reduces the real incomes of consumers. As a result, their demand for many goods and services fall. However, some businesses selling cheaper products may benefit from increasing sales as consumers switch their demand away from more expensive items.

▼ Indirect taxes on goods and services include import tariffs and excise duties that may be used to control the demand for specific goods and services

Changes in direct taxes on incomes and profits will affect consumer spending and business investment decisions

Direct taxes are collected directly from the incomes or wealth of an individual or organization. They are normally charged as a percentage of income or the value of wealth held. This may be a fixed percentage so everyone pays the same proportionally or a rising percentage, so wealthier people, businesses or those with higher incomes pay proportionally more in tax than those earning lower incomes.

Direct taxes include the following.

- **Personal income tax** on people's incomes.

- **Payroll taxes** including national insurance or social security contributions collected from the wages and salaries of employees. In some countries the responsibility for paying these taxes is shared between employees and their employers.

- **Corporation tax** on company profits and/or a profits tax on unincorporated businesses such as the profits of sole traders and partnerships. New and small businesses with low profits may pay a low or zero rate of tax to encourage enterprise. ➤ **1.3.1**

ACTIVITY 6.5

In the jumble below try to match up each of the announcements about changes in direct taxes with one of the quotes from business owners and managers about the impact the changes may have on their businesses.

"The tax increase will reduce our incentive to invest in our business. To improve our profits after tax we may have to increase the prices we charge to our customers and cut our costs, especially our wage costs by reducing the size of our workforce."

Corporation tax on company profits to rise by 5%

Payroll taxes on business will rise by 2% from next April

"This change will raise the cost of employing workers and reduce our profit. We will therefore be looking at ways to reduce staff numbers and invest more in new capital equipment to automate more of our production processes."

"The tax change is very welcome. It will leave people with more income after tax and, as a result, they will tend to spend more on goods and services."

Basic rate of personal income tax cut by 1%

For example, when Greece introduced a new higher rate of tax of 45% on personal income over 100 000 euros a year, bookings and takings at the restaurant owned by Demetri Christou in a popular area of Athens fell by 20%.

Demetri explained that while many of his regular customers were wealthy business people, the new higher tax rate had significantly reduced their disposable income and spending. As a result of the downturn in his sales and profits Demetri was considering cutting his restaurant staff and postponing buying new kitchen equipment. "I may even close the restaurant on Mondays to save costs," he explained.

Demetri argued the Greek government needed to do more to help small businesses by cutting corporation tax on their profits: "25% of my profits are taken in tax. If the government took less more people would be encouraged to start small businesses and create jobs and I would have more profit left after tax to invest in my business."

Raising personal income taxes will affect the sales and profits of many businesses.

- This is because it will reduce the **disposable income** of consumers. This is the amount of income a person has left to spend or save after direct taxes have been deducted from their wages, salaries and other incomes. As taxes rise, consumers will have less to spend. Businesses producing luxury items are most likely to be affected as consumers continue to buy food and other essential items but reduce their spending on expensive and non-essential goods and services. ➤ **3.1.2**

- As consumer spending falls the revenues and profits of many businesses will decline. In response, firms will reduce their prices to sell off their inventories and will also try to reduce their costs by cutting their workforces and output. Some businesses badly affected by falling demand may even be forced to close.

In contrast, reducing personal income taxes can help to boost consumer spending and business activity.

Increasing payroll taxes will also reduce disposable incomes.

- They can also increase the cost of employing workers for a business if the responsibility for paying these taxes is shared between employees and employers.

- As the cost of employing labour rises, firms may cut production and the size of their workforces to reduce their costs.

High payroll and income taxes may also reduce labour productivity.

- Workers may not work so hard if more of their wages and salaries are taken in tax.

Lowering these taxes may instead increase employee motivation resulting in higher levels of output. ➤ **2.1.2**

Raising taxes on profits may reduce enterprise and business investment.

- This is because less profit will remain in businesses after tax for owners to share. This will reduce the reward for enterprise and money available to reinvest in expanding their businesses. ➤ **5.3.1**

For these reasons, many countries have been reducing their corporation tax rates over time to help encourage new enterprise, business investment and job creation in their economies.

How changes in interest rates can affect business activity

An interest rate is the cost of borrowing money

In most economies, a person or firm that borrows money from a bank or another lender usually haves to repay the loan with interest charged as a percentage of the loan value. So, for example, a person who borrows $1000 repayable over 12 months at a rate of interest of 10% will repay $1100 in total.

Interest rates charged by banks and other lenders can differ depending on the type and length of the loan and the type of customer. For example, a large loan over ten years to a new, small business may be charged a higher rate of interest than a small loan to be repaid over two years to a person in regular, paid employment. ➤ **5.1.2**

All the different interest rates charged by banks and other lenders in an economy are based on the main interest rate set by the government or its central bank. If the government or central bank in an economy increases its interest rate then banks and lenders will also raise their interest rates. This is because commercial banks regularly borrow money from the central bank. So, if the government or its central bank increases the interest rate it charges them to borrow money, their costs will rise. In turn banks will pass on their increased costs to their customers by raising the interest rates they must pay to borrow money.

Individuals and businesses that have fixed rate loans will be protected from a rise in interest rates. However, people and firms with variable rate loans will have to pay more to repay their loans as interest rates rise.

ACTIVITY 6.6

You are the owner of a small business. You want to borrow $100 000 from a bank to buy new equipment. You have estimated that this investment will increase your profit by $10 000 per year (or 10% of the sum invested) for the next five years. Based on the information provided which loan, if any, will you apply for? Explain your answer.

Accreditable Bank

Loan amount
$100 000

Period of loan
5 years

Fixed annual interest
rate, 11%

Beneficial Bank

Loan amount
$100 000

Period of loan
5 years

Variable annual
interest
rate, currently 9%

So, in activity 6.6 did you decide to borrow $100 000 and, if so, from which bank? If you decided against borrowing money from Accreditable Bank then well done, you made a wise decision. At 11% the annual rate of interest payable on the bank loan is more than the return you expect from additional profits on your investment.

The cost of the loan from Beneficial Bank is currently lower and so could be worthwhile borrowing. However, it is at a variable interest rate and could rise or fall over the next five years. Taking the loan could therefore be very risky for your business. If interest rates rise your costs will increase and your anticipated profit will be reduced.

Raising interest rates to control price inflation can reduce consumer spending and harm business investment

A government may raise interest rates during an economic boom or period when price inflation is rising. This can have the following effects.

Consumer spending will fall.

- Consumers with existing variable rate loans will have to pay higher interest charges. This will reduce the income they have available to spend on goods and services.

- As the cost of borrowing money rises, consumers will be unwilling to take out loans to finance purchases of expensive items such as cars, luxury holidays and new furniture. Businesses making and selling these and other expensive consumer products will be particularly hard hit and may have to reduce their prices, cut output and reduce their workforces.

- As interest rates rise consumers may spend less of their incomes and save more instead. This is because interest rates are also a reward offered by banks for depositing money in savings accounts.

Business costs will rise and investment will fall.

- Businesses with existing variable rate loans will have to pay higher interest charges. This will increase their costs and reduce their profits. Less profit will be available to reinvest in business expansion or to replace old machinery and equipment.

- As the cost of borrowing rises, existing businesses will be unwilling to take out loans to finance their expansion plans or to invest in new technologies to improve their efficiency.

- In addition, there will be fewer business start-ups as consumer spending falls and it becomes more expensive to finance start-up capital with debt.

The balance of international trade and payments may become less favourable.

- If the interest rate is higher than in other countries, it will encourage overseas residents and businesses to transfer their savings to banks located in that country so they can earn a higher return on their money than they could from banks in their own or other countries. To do this they must change their own currencies into the currency of the country receiving their savings. The increase in demand for the currency will increase its value making imports to that country cheaper to buy, but its exports more expensive to buy overseas.

For example, if interest rates are higher in South Africa than in other countries, wealthy residents of other countries may prefer to save their money in South African banks. However, to do this they must buy the South African currency – the rand – with their own currencies. The increase in demand for the rand will push up its price or **foreign exchange rate**, in terms of how much it costs to buy with other currencies. ➤ **6.3.3**

As the value of the rand rises, exports from South Africa will become more expensive to buy overseas and demand for them will tend to fall. However, the price of imported products in South Africa will fall. This may affect consumers and businesses in the South African economy in the following ways.

- Price inflation may fall as imports become cheaper.

- Consumers may buy more imported goods.

- The costs of businesses importing materials, parts or finished goods from overseas will fall.

Cutting interest rates can encourage consumer spending and business investment during an economic recession and also help to boost exports

A government may reduce interest rates during an economic recession in an effort to boost business activity, employment and economic growth. This is because a cut in interest rates could have the following effects.

Consumer spending will increase.

- Consumers with existing variable rate loans will pay lower interest charges and will therefore be able to spend more of their income on goods and services.

- The fall in the cost of borrowing will encourage more consumers to take out loans to purchase expensive items.

- Spending will increase as consumers choose to reduce their savings and spend more instead.

Business costs will fall and investment will rise.

- Businesses with existing variable rate loans will enjoy a reduction in the interest charges they pay.

- Increased spending by consumers will create more business opportunities. The fall in the cost of debt will also encourage businesses to borrow more money to finance their expansion plans and to invest in new machinery and equipment.

The balance of international trade and payments may become more favourable.

- As the interest rate falls, overseas residents and businesses are likely to transfer their savings to banks located in countries that pay higher rates of interest. This will reduce the value of the currency, making imports to the country more expensive to buy and exports cheaper in overseas markets. As a result, demand for imports is likely to fall while demand for exports may rise overseas.

The provision of loans and the charging and payment of interest is not acceptable in some countries

For example, in Islamic countries banking activities must follow the principles of Sharia law. This means banks are forbidden from lending money and charging interest.

- Instead Islamic Banks buy goods on behalf of a customer who then pays a rent for their use over an agreed period of time. At the end of this period ownership of the goods may pass from the bank to that customer. The rental payments will include a mark-up for the bank's profit.

- They also provide finance to new and existing businesses in return for a share of their profits.

This means that the government of an Islamic country cannot use interest rates as an economic policy instrument. Instead, it will control the supply of money available to banks to provide Islamic finance.

For example, during an economic recession the government of an Islamic country may increase the supply of money to banks to finance purchases for customers and make business investments.

In contrast, during a period when consumer demand is rising rapidly and causing prices to increase, it may restrict the supply of money to banks to reduce their ability to finance purchases and invest in businesses.

ACTIVITY 6.7

You own and manage a private limited company that manufactures lighting units and timers for street lamps. Many of the components your company needs to produce the lighting units are imported from a supplier located overseas. Following their production, around 30% of the lighting units are sold to construction firms located overseas. Increasing overseas sales further is a key objective of your company.

▶ Copy the table below. For each economic policy state whether you think it is more likely to cause an "increase" or "decrease" in total spending, output, price inflation and employment in your national economy.

▶ Similarly, in the column marked "Balance of payments" state whether you think each policy will increase or decrease demand for exports and/or imports.

▶ Now add a final column which you should label "Impact on my business". Use this column to identify and explain how each of the policies is likely to affect your company in terms of its:

- total sales and profitability

- pricing and investment decisions.

Economic policy	Likely impact on					
	Total spending	Total output	Price inflation	Total employment	Balance of payments	
					Exports	Imports
Government cuts spending on new road construction	Decrease					
Interest rates are raised					Decrease	Increase
Taxes on profits are cut		Increase				
All indirect taxes are increased						
Income tax payable by high income earners is increased						
Tariffs on imported goods are increased			Increase			

The economy of country A is in recession. To help deal with the problems caused by the recession, the government has cut interest rates. However, the business sector would also like to see the government lower taxes on goods and services to encourage more consumer spending and also to provide more grants and subsidies to private sector firms to help them survive.

a Define "recession".   [2]

b Identify **two** reasons why governments put taxes on goods other than
   to raise revenue to finance their spending.   [2]

c Explain **two** consequences of a fall in interest rates on businesses
   in country A.   [4]

d Explain **three** ways in which a recession might affect businesses in the
   economy.   [6]

e Do you think that governments should give financial support to private
   sector firms to survive in a recession? Justify your answer.   [6]

Before you continue make sure you are able to

Understand the main stages of the **business cycle: growth, boom, recession, slump**.

Understand how government control over the economy can affect business activity:

✓ government economic objectives, for example, increasing **GDP**

✓ the impact of changes in **taxes** and **government spending**

✓ how the impact of changes in **interest rates** can affect business activity

✓ how businesses might respond to these changes.

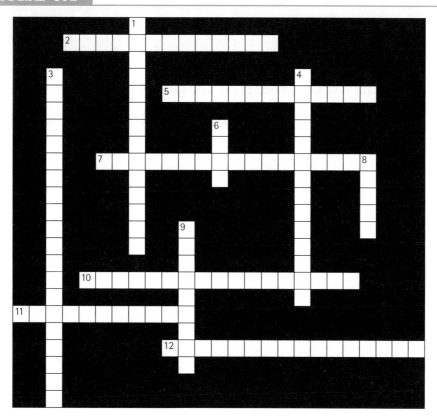

Clues down

1. A sustained rise in the general level of prices in a national economy. Governments aim to keep it low and stable because it can increase business costs and cause hardship for consumers (5, 9)
3. GDP in short. It is the measure used for the value of the combined total output of all organizations in an economy in any given year (5, 8, 7)
4. Governments want to encourage this in their economies because it creates more business opportunities, employment and incomes and raises living standards. It is measured by how much and how rapidly the total or national output of an economy expands (8, 6)
6. A period during which business activity and employment will peak. Price inflation may rise rapidly as increasing demand for goods and services exceeds growth in total output (4)
8. A prolonged period of economic recession caused by low and falling consumer demand for goods and services. Many businesses may close. Output will continue to fall and unemployment will be high (5)
9. A period of declining business activity, falling output, employment and incomes (9)

Clues across

2. These are the cost of borrowing money and a policy instrument many governments can use to influence consumer spending and saving in their economies. For example, lowering them can encourage consumers to save less and borrow more to finance increased spending during an economic recession (8, 5)
5. The term used to describe the recurrent pattern of variations or cyclical fluctuations in business activity and economic growth that has been observed over time in many national economies. It is characterized by five successive phases: growth, boom, recession, slump and recovery (8, 5)
7. This provides a record of all the financial transactions between a country and all the other countries with which it trades. It is considered unfavourable if spending on imports exceeds payments received from the sale of exports (7, 2, 8)
10. Government spending. Increasing it will help to boost total demand for goods and services, employment and output during an economic recession (6, 11)
11. These are collected by a government from the incomes of people and businesses to help finance public sector spending. A government increases them during an economic boom to reduce disposable incomes if consumer spending is expanding significantly and causing prices to rise rapidly (6, 5)
12. A term used to describe an action, such as changing public expenditure, taxation or interest rates, that a government can take in an attempt to control cyclical fluctuations in inflation, employment and economic growth so as to achieve its economic objectives (6, 10)

6.2 Environmental and ethical issues

6.2.1   Environmental concerns and ethical issues as both opportunities and constraints for business

Key POINTS

- ▸ The profit from a business activity is the difference between its private costs and private benefits.
- ▸ Businesses that aim to generate a profit for their owners can also create positive externalities that help to improve social and economic welfare. For example, the creation of new technologies, jobs and skills can provide external benefits to other people and firms.
- ▸ But some business activities may reduce social and economic welfare because they exploit or cause harm to people and the natural environment as it allows them to reduce their costs and increase their profits. Negative externalities, such as pollution and the depletion of non-renewable resources, impose external costs on other people and firms.
- ▸ Sustainable development involves reducing the rate at which we use up natural resources, reducing waste and reducing harmful emissions by changing the way we produce and consume goods and services. Making production more sustainable may impose costs on some businesses but also creates new, profitable opportunities for others in recycling, remanufacturing, renewable energy and new, more "environment-friendly" products.
- ▸ Pressure groups often campaign against businesses that fail to act in socially and environmentally responsible ways.

Business BUZZWORDS

Positive externalities - beneficial impacts on people or businesses resulting from the actions of another.

Negative externalities – detrimental impacts on other people or organizations resulting from the actions of another.

Private costs – the financial (fixed and variable) costs of a business activity.

External cost - a cost imposed by a business activity on other people or organizations.

Social cost – the total cost to society of a business activity: the sum of the private and external costs of that activity.

Private benefits – the financial benefits (sales revenues and other incomes) of a business activity.

External benefit – a benefit created by a business activity that is enjoyed by people or organizations without them having to pay for it.

Social benefit – the total benefit to society of a business activity: the sum of the private and external benefits of that activity.

Non-renewable resources – natural resources that cannot be replaced or reproduced once they have been used up.

Sustainable development – producing goods and services without depleting natural resources and harming the natural environment.

Pressure group – an organization or group of people that aims to change the behaviour of a business that fails to act in a socially or environmentally responsible way through publicity and protest.

Ethical firms - businesses that take account of the impact their decisions and actions can have on other people and organizations, communities and the natural environment.

Business activity and the environment

Business activity contributes to social and economic well-being

When General Motors closed its truck manufacturing plant in Oshawa in Canada it resulted in the immediate loss of 1000 jobs. However, many other businesses and their employees in the region were heavily dependent on the vehicle maker for regular orders of parts and components and the provision of services, including catering and equipment maintenance. Car industry analysts said the closure could ultimately mean the loss of 12 000 jobs including in the parts sector and service providers.

> The closure of the GM truck plant will have a devastating effect on the regional economy which is heavily dependent on the auto sector. It will be extremely painful for a long time in the Oshawa area.

The loss of jobs and incomes following the closure of a major business like General Motors can have a significant impact on social and economic welfare in an economy. This is because it can affect the livelihood of many other people and businesses.

Social and economic welfare, or well-being, will suffer in a national economy where output and incomes are falling, there are high levels of unemployment and if prices are also high and rising. An increasing number of people will face hardship, businesses will lose money and close, causing more unemployment, and living standards will decline.

The health of a national economy, and therefore social and economic welfare, depends crucially on business activity. This is because business activity produces goods and services people need and want, creates jobs and incomes, earns foreign currency from selling exports to overseas consumers and helps to fund the provision of public services from taxes on the incomes and expenditures of businesses, employees and consumers. Many governments therefore actively encourage business creation and expansion in their economies.

However, business activity can also have a negative impact on social and economic welfare because the production of goods and services can create:

- noise, air and water pollution that may affect people's health and well-being

- harmful waste products that have to be carefully disposed of

- lasting damage to the natural environment including to lakes and rivers, woodland and forests, and to plant, sea and animal life.

ACTIVITY 6.8

What do the photographs suggest about the negative impacts of business activity on the natural environment? Are there similar examples of environmental damage from business activity in your economy?

These problems are increasing as the world population expands and global demand for goods and services continues to grow.

Conservationists therefore argue that we must slow the pace at which we are using up resources in the production and consumption of goods and services if we are to protect the natural environment for future generations and avoid irreversible and damaging climate change. Global warming is already having a dramatic effect on the planet as climate change causes more violent storms, droughts and floods.

For example, a report commissioned by the World Wide Fund for Nature says heat waves, droughts, rising sea levels, flash floods, forest fires and disease "could turn profitable tourist destinations into holiday horror stories" including the Maldives, the Seychelles, the European Alps, the eastern Mediterranean, southern Spain, the European lakes, South and East Africa, Australia, Florida and Brazil. Many businesses based on tourism in these areas will lose customers and their livelihood due to **global warming**.

Global warming is also likely to affect food production in many areas. This is because the speed at which global warming is expected to occur is faster than most plant and animal species will be able to cope with. Some species may adapt but others may become extinct.

Growing concern for the environment is creating new opportunities and forcing firms to adopt more sustainable business practices

Growing concern among consumers and some governments about the impact of business activity on the environment is forcing many businesses to change their production methods and the materials and suppliers they use in order to compete for customers and sales. This is increasing the costs of some businesses but it is also creating new profitable business opportunities for others.

Sustainable development involves trying to increase output and economic growth without depleting natural resources and damaging the natural environment, for example by reducing waste and harmful emissions through changes in the way we produce and consume products. For some countries, this means reducing the rate at which they increase their total output and wealth.

Businesses can contribute to the achievement of sustainable development by adopting more **sustainable business practices such as**:

- using **renewable energy** sources including from solar panels, wind turbines and biomass boilers that produce gas for heating and power from sewage and rotting vegetable matter

- increased **recycling** and reuse of waste water and materials from production processes to make more efficient use of resources

- reducing **waste** including packaging waste to cut the amount consumers throw away

- increasing the use of **biodegradable materials** that will decompose quickly after being discarded without damaging the environment

- the increased **remanufacturing** and reuse of items including resharpening tools, replacing covers on armchairs, refilling printer ink cartridges, replacing memory chips and hard drives in computers, retreading worn vehicle tyres and much more. It involves remodelling or replacing old or worn-out parts to restore or update their functionality rather than discarding items and producing new ones.

As more businesses adopt new, more sustainable production methods and practices, new business opportunities are being created in the production and supply of **low carbon and environmental goods and services**, including spray-on solar cells and panels, wind turbines, biofuels and electric vehicles, recycling and waste management services, biodegradable plastics and packaging materials, and new technologies that reduce heat loss and energy use in buildings.

ACTIVITY 6.9

Read the two articles below.

▸ Identify and explain how the changes the two companies are making will help contribute to sustainable development.

▸ What are the likely benefits to the two companies of adopting these new sustainable business practices?

Spier Holdings is a company based in South Africa. It has set environmental goals focused on energy, water and biodiversity as well as financial goals for the agricultural and business estate it manages.

For example, the Adobe Works project is a venture making sun-dried clay bricks without the need for energy-intensive ovens. Spier decided that any new building on the estate should be constructed using these bricks. The bricks are produced on the estate thereby saving transport costs. It has also helped create local jobs and skills.

Its next project is a waste treatment facility to produce its own liquid fertilizer and to help achieve its goal of being a zero-waste business by 2018.

How do you like your computer? With mushrooms and bamboo?

Computer giant Dell is to start using alternative packaging materials for its computers instead of the paper pulp or petrochemical foam that is normally used to protect electronic goods.

They will include "mushroom cushions" developed with partner Ecovative Design. The cushions are produced from fungi grown over five to ten days on a mixture of cotton hulls, rice hulls or wheat chaff, which is otherwise considered agricultural waste.

Dell will also use cushioning made from bamboo pulp. Dell is sourcing its bamboo from a forest in China's Jiangxi Province, which is not near known panda habitats and follows Forest Stewardship Council (FSC) principles and criteria.

Once used the new packaging materials will decompose quickly and can be used for garden compost, reducing the need for disposal.

▲ How business activity is becoming more sustainable and helping the environment

The concept of externalities

Businesses are focused on making profits and may overlook the effects they have on other people and organizations

Most private sector businesses aim to make a profit from their activities. They will therefore be concerned that the revenues and other incomes they earn from producing goods and services exceed their costs of production.

- The income a business earns from it activities are its **private benefits** (or **financial benefits**). This includes revenue from the sale of its goods or services and any interest received on business savings.

- The costs of running that business are its **private costs** (or **financial costs**). These includes the costs of materials, machinery and equipment, the wages and salaries of employees, electricity, insurance premiums and much more.

- If its private benefits exceed its private costs over the same period then the business will have made a **profit**. ➤ **4.2.1**

However, because a business is focused on its own private costs and benefits it may overlook the impacts it has on the natural environment and on other people and organizations. These impacts, or **externalities**, may be positive or negative.

Positive externalities create external benefits that increase social and economic welfare

Positive externalities are beneficial impacts enjoyed by other people or firms as a result of the activities of another business. Economic and social welfare will therefore be improved by activities that create positive externalities.

For example, Swiss multinational Roche Pharmaceuticals recently invested around $182 million in two European production facilities to manufacture a patient-friendly device that will allow people to administer their own cancer-fighting drugs and therefore reduce the time they need to spend in hospital. Roche is a profit-making company but its investments in the advance of medicine and health care can help improve the health and life expectancy of many people, reduce the costs of sick leave and lost production due to staff illness in many other businesses, reduce the cost to governments of providing public health care and create new jobs.

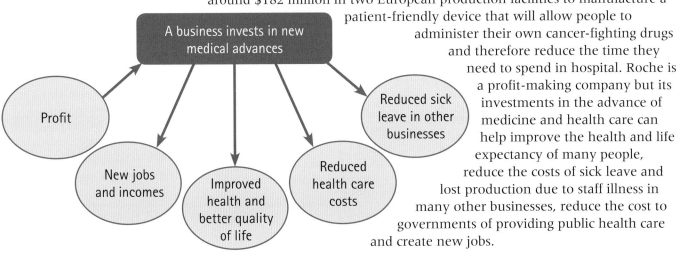

▲ How some business activities can create wider social and economic benefits

In the same way, investments in early laser technologies many years ago, initially at the AT&T (American Telegraph and Telephone) Bell Laboratories, now benefit many millions of other businesses and consumers worldwide. This is because different types of lasers are used in DVD players, for laser light shows, to measure distances accurately, in the cutting and welding of metals, for fingerprint detection, in surgical procedures and much more.

The investments made by Roche and AT&T increased the private costs and benefits of those businesses but in turn they also created **external benefits**, enjoyed by many other people and businesses that they did not have to pay for.

Negative externalities create external costs that reduce social and economic welfare

Negative externalities are detrimental impacts on other people or firms caused by the activities of another business. Economic and social welfare will therefore be reduced by activities that create negative externalities.

When many millions of gallons of thick, toxic crude oil gushed from an oil well two miles below the surface of the sea in the Gulf of Mexico for over two months during 2010, it had a devastating impact on marine life and wildlife, and many communities and businesses located around the US Gulf Coast.

The largest marine oil spill in history occurred after an explosion on an oil drilling platform in the Gulf. Eleven workers were killed and the pipe into the oil reservoir beneath the sea bed was ruptured. Many thousands of businesses in the fishing and tourism industries were unable to continue operating and many millions of dollars in revenue were lost. The loss of lives, the damage to the natural environment and wildlife and the losses suffered by other businesses were the **external costs** of the oil disaster.

The company drilling for oil in the Gulf was BP plc. It had to spend many billions of dollars trying to clean up the oil spill and affected coastline, and paying compensation to people and businesses badly affected. However, the private financial costs to BP may never be enough to fully compensate the external costs of the disaster. This is because the negative impacts of the oil spill may be felt for many more years to come and will be difficult to calculate in financial values.

For example, Mike Voisin, owner of Motivatit Seafoods, Inc. in the state of Louisiana, told reporters he was very concerned about the long-term future of his family business and the fishing industry. He had been unable to fish for shrimps and oysters, and was worried that their damaged populations would not be able to recover for many years.

Negative externalities created by a business activity, such as pollution and damage to the natural environment, impose **external costs** on other people and businesses that they must pay for, for example, in lost incomes and the cost of trying to repair the damage caused.

BP oil spill: worst in history

Most experts now put the economic costs of the disaster at $10–$14 billion – though no one knows for sure.

"Our welfare has been seriously harmed," complained a local business owner. "BP may soon recover its lost profits, but the damage to the environment, to wildlife, the local economy and to society may take far longer to do so."

The full impact of a business activity on social and economic welfare is the difference between its social costs and benefits

Consider the following example.

Curex kills local industry

The river Walden was once teeming with life, both fish and human. Local fishing boats would catch trout and other abundant species in the river to serve in the many local inns and restaurants frequented by a growing number of tourists drawn to the idyllic rural setting each year. But all this has changed. The river today is a dead river.

Over the last few years fish and plant life in the river have been destroyed and the tourists have disappeared. In the last few months alone 25 cattle grazing along the river have also been poisoned. Fears are growing that those local children who play along the banks of the river could be next.

A report has found that a pharmaceuticals plant several miles upstream owned by Curex Chemicals Ltd has heavily polluted the river. Untreated waste chemicals from its production processes have been pumped into the river causing widespread environmental damage and losses to local industries. The report concludes the damage will take many years and many millions of dollars to put right.

Curex employs 300 people at its plant and manufactures biological and medicinal products at a cost of around $10 million per year. Profits last year were $5 million.

In the news article above the private costs of Curex of $10 million per year are not the only costs of its decision to produce pharmaceuticals. Local farmers use water from the river to irrigate their land and for their animals. They have suffered a loss of cattle and crops as a result of pollution from Curex. Local fishermen have also lost their livelihood because the waste has killed all the fish in the river. In addition, tourists no longer visit the area and stay in waterside inns and hotels that have developed along the riverbanks. These external costs are estimated in the table below.

Private costs and benefits	$ (million) per year	External costs and benefits	$ (million) per year
Private costs	10	Lost revenues to farming and costs of restocking	5
▸ wages		Lost revenue from fishing and tourism	2
▸ purchases of chemicals and materials		Cost of cleaning up the polluted river	2
▸ equipment charges			
▸ factory and office rent			
▸ costs of electricity, insurance, transport, etc.			
Private benefits		**Total external costs**	9
▸ sales revenues	15	Health benefits to other people and firms	2
▸ all other revenues		Value to other firms of trained chemical engineers	1
Profit	5	**Total external benefits**	3

Curex makes an annual profit of $5 million for its shareholders from the production of pharmaceuticals, but because it has been dumping waste chemicals in the local river it has imposed external costs on the rest of society (all other people and organizations) of $9 million.

The private costs of Curex, plus the external costs to the rest of society, gives the total social cost of its pharmaceutical production of $19 million, that is:

> **private costs + external costs = social costs**

However, the management of Curex argue that the company also creates many external benefits worth an estimated $3 million each year. These are health benefits enjoyed by the people who use Curex products and a reduction in the costs of sick leave and lost production due to illness of staff in many other businesses. Curex also provides employment for many local people and trains its workers in advanced chemical engineering. These skills may benefit other firms in the future when workers leave and take jobs elsewhere.

The private benefits of Curex and the external benefits to the rest of society give the total external benefit of pharmaceutical production of $18 million, that is:

> **private benefits + external benefits = social benefits**

The social costs ($19 million) of the activities carried out by Curex exceed their social benefits ($18 million). This means society would be better off without these activities, despite the fact that the owners of Curex make a profit. That is, social and economic welfare would be higher if the resources employed by Curex were used to produce other, less harmful, goods and services instead.

Local people, businesses and other stakeholders have therefore complained to the government, asking it to ban production at Curex and force the company to close. However, the government, the employees of Curex and some health care providers are worried that the closure of the factory will result in too many local jobs and external benefits being lost.

Instead the government introduced legislation to ban Curex from dumping waste in the river. If Curex breaks the law it will be fined many millions of dollars. In contrast, the cost of treating waste will increase the private costs of Curex by $1 million per year and its profits will fall to $4 million a year. However, external costs will be greatly reduced in future as a result of the law and the change in production process and waste treatment at Curex.

ACTIVITY 6.10

The government in county A intends to develop a new motorway connecting two major cities. It has contracted a major company to construct the new motorway using $500 million of public funds.

▸ Identify and explain **two** ways the government could finance the new motorway.

▸ Identify and explain **two** potential external benefits of the motorway (during and after its construction).

▸ Identify and explain **two** potential external costs of the motorway (during and after its construction).

▸ Many people believe that it is the role of the government to pass laws to stop firms damaging the environment. Do you agree?

Now consider a decision by a government to use resources to build a new motorway at a cost of $500 million to taxpayers.

Government officials have undertaken a cost–benefit analysis and calculated that the external costs of additional noise nuisance and air pollution to nearby residents over the next ten years will total $100 million. On the other hand, the motorway will improve journey times, reduce costs and cut accidents on other roads for a great many people and businesses. Building and maintaining the new motorway will also create jobs in the construction sector. Together, these external benefits could be worth as much as $1 billion over the next ten years. As the social benefits exceed the social costs of the motorway the government decides to go ahead.

However, protestors against the new motorway point out that the government has failed to consider the loss of agricultural land on which the motorway is to be built and the destruction of wildlife habitats. They also accuse the government of ignoring the impact of increased vehicle emissions on global climate change and argue the government should use $500 million to fund public transport alternatives instead.

Who is right? Do the social benefits of the new motorway exceed its social costs? These are difficult to answer because external costs and benefits are often difficult to value accurately.

Responding to environmental pressures and opportunities

If businesses fail to take account of the negative impact their activities can have on other people, organizations and the natural environment, then tactics to make them change the way they behave include:

- organized protests and the formation of pressure groups

- legal controls on what businesses can and cannot do

- financial penalties on firms that fail to observe legal controls

- taxes on products or activities that create significant external costs

- business grants and other financial incentives to adopt sustainable business practices.

Pressure groups can organize protests, boycotts and publicity campaigns against businesses that fail to act in socially and environmentally responsible ways

If a business is concerned only with the effects of its actions on its profits and ignores the negative impact they can have on others, then anything that damages the reputation, sales and therefore the profits of that business may cause it to change the way it operates for the better. This is the aim of organized groups of people and organizations called **pressure groups**.

Pressure groups can be organized locally, nationally or even internationally depending on the business activity and the scale of the problem it is creating. For example, people from a local community may organize protests against plans to build a new factory or close a railway in their community.

Others such as Greenpeace and Friends of the Earth are well-known international pressure groups that aim to protect the natural environment, marine life and animals by investigating, exposing and confronting environmental abuse by businesses and governments all over the world.

Pressure groups can be very powerful because they can create a lot of bad publicity for a business and persuade many consumers to boycott the purchase of its products. Bad publicity and the threat of falling sales and profits can often persuade some firms to change their business practices. Pressure groups can also show businesses opportunities that can arise from taking action to reduce their impact on the environment such as maintaining customer loyalty and getting good publicity from the changes made.

Pressure groups can often force a business to change the way it operates, especially if:

- the pressure group is well organized and financed
- it has significant public support
- it receives regular television and press coverage
- consumer boycotts result in a significant fall in sales
- the business can be shown to be acting illegally.

However, a business is unlikely to change its practices, for example its production methods or the materials or suppliers it uses, if they are legal and if doing so increases its costs by more than the potential loss of reputation and sales caused by the actions of a pressure group.

Protest drives Nestlé to environmentally friendly palm oil

Nestlé, the world's biggest food manufacturer, says it will make the palm oil in its best-selling chocolate bars more environmentally friendly, after a major campaign against it on the internet.

The Swiss confectionery-to-coffee giant said it would cancel contracts with any firm found to be chopping down rainforests to produce the oil.

The concession followed a three-month campaign by the environmental group Greenpeace, which led to Nestlé being attacked on social networking sites such as Facebook and YouTube.

In each article identify the impacts of business activity and why government action has been taken to support, change or stop the activity.

India to enforce new regulations to curb noise pollution

By and large, Indians embrace noise. Their festivals are a riot of colour and sound, weddings an exercise in high-decibel exuberance and house parties an extreme test of neighbourly tolerance.

But now things have reached such a pitch that the government has decided to step in, beefing up decade-old noise pollution laws and regulations to keep the volume dial turned down.

The Environment Ministry has published a set of guidelines specifying when violations should be considered serious enough to merit police action. They cover a variety of noise sources from industrial processes, construction sites and car horns to living-room stereos and festive firecrackers.

China to impose green tax on heavy polluters

China is to impose an environmental tax on heavy polluters under an ambitious clean-up strategy being finalized in Beijing. The environmental tax – which will levy fees according to discharges of sulphur dioxide, sewage and other contaminants – is intended as a disincentive for polluting industries.

The tax will be part of a package of measures including an ambitious renewable energy scheme in what is likely to be China's biggest, and greenest, five-year plan in modern history.

Nigerian oil and environment reviewed

Ever since the discovery of oil in Nigeria in the 1950s, the country has been suffering the negative environmental consequences of oil development. Oil spills in the Niger Delta since 1960 and gas flaring from oil extraction have resulted in serious air pollution problems in the area.

One of the most visible consequences of this has been the loss of mangrove trees. The mangrove was once a source of both fuel wood for the indigenous people and a habitat for the area's biodiversity. Marine life has also become contaminated in turn creating health problems in local people consuming the fish.

The Nigerian government has recently indicated that it is no longer willing to tolerate this and has taken action to enforce environmental regulations. It also blames the high levels of cancer in the region on exposure to oil spills and has ordered the oil companies to pay $1.5 billion in compensation to local people.

As a result of the more stringent environmental regulations, oil companies that operate in the Niger Delta have begun improving and publicizing their environmental performance.

Food prices will rise following pesticide ban warn farmers

Farmers have warned that the cost of food could rise after the European Parliament voted to restrict the use of many pesticides. The measure is designed to halve the use of toxic products in farming by 2013. Opponents of the move were accused by British Member of European Parliament Chris Davies of ignoring the dangers of pesticides and herbicides to human health and the environment.

Indiana state government offers $500 000 in recycling grants

The Indiana Department of Environmental Management has released a total of $500 000 through its Recycling Market Development Program. Grants will be awarded to businesses with plans to remanufacture recyclable materials into finished products or components.

If businesses fail to control the negative impacts their production and other actions can have on other businesses, communities and the environment, then a government could introduce laws and regulations forcing them to do so. For example, many governments have introduced:

- anti-pollution laws banning the release of untreated waste and chemicals into the sea, rivers and into the air

- planning and building regulations to control where and how new homes, factories, offices and shops are built; these ensure all new constructions are safe, do not use substandard or hazardous materials and are not built in national parks or other environmentally sensitive areas

- regulations designed to phase out and replace the production and sale of products that damage the environment with more environmentally friendly products, for example replacing chemical pesticides with organic pesticides, replacing incandescent light bulbs with low-energy fluorescent and LED light bulbs

- emission standards and caps that set limits on the amount of pollutants that can be released into the environment, including pollutants released by power plants, aircraft, motor vehicles and even small equipment such as lawn mowers and diesel generators.

Businesses that fail to comply with laws and regulations, or breach emission standards, could have to pay significant financial penalties.

Indirect taxes can be used to increase the prices of harmful products to reduce their sales and profitability

For example, when Hong Kong introduced a new "green" tax on plastic carrier bags in 2009, it was designed to stop consumers using so many of them for their shopping. It was estimated that shoppers threw away more than eight billion shopping bags into Hong Kong's landfills every year. Businesses making and supplying plastic bags for the retailing industry complained they would lose sales and their costs would rise, threatening production and many jobs. Shops were also worried that the measure would force more consumers to shop online instead. However, charity shops making cloth bags from waste fabrics and a business specializing in the manufacture and supply of reinforced and reusable shopping bags from recycled plastic welcomed the new tax. Sales of their products have since risen as a result.

Similarly, some countries have introduced "green" taxes on waste disposal, emissions and energy use. Businesses can avoid paying these taxes if they cut their waste, pollutants and energy use. Cars and petrol are also taxed in many countries to reduce consumer demand for large vehicles and to encourage producers to develop and produce "greener" alternatives. ➤ 6.1.1

Making sure business activities comply with laws, regulations and taxes can increase the costs of production in business and therefore the prices of goods and services for many consumers. As a result, businesses may lose sales, cut the production of affected goods and services and reduce their investments in other business activities. Jobs may also be lost and some businesses may even relocate to countries where environmental protection is a lower priority. It is therefore important for a government to ensure that the burden on business of taxes, laws and regulations designed to protect the environment is sensible; otherwise total output, income and employment in its economy may fall.

Grants and subsidies can be used to lower the cost of adopting more sustainable business practices

Grants, subsidies and other financial incentives may be offered by a government to businesses to support and encourage them to adopt and invest in recycling, remanufacturing, renewable energy and other more sustainable activities that create more positive externalities and jobs. ➤ 1.3.1

▼ Should governments use taxes and regulations to control business activities?

No. Taxes and laws to protect people and the environment increase the cost of doing business. This makes business uncompetitive and reduces profits. Prices will be higher and output and employment will be lower as a result. Sales will be lost to businesses in countries with lower taxes and fewer regulations.

Yes. Businesses should act in a socially and environmentally responsible way. If they did there would be no need for high taxes and regulations. These ensure that firms cut their waste and use resources more efficiently. This lowers the cost of doing business. Output and employment will not be lower because businesses will instead employ people to produce products that do less harm to the environment. Consumers will prefer to buy from firms that act responsibly.

▲ Ethical activities?

Ethical issues that a business might face

Profits may sometimes be more important in business than ethical behaviour

Ethics involves making judgments about what is right or wrong. They are the values, standards or morals that govern how we behave and how others judge our behaviours in the communities and countries we live and work in.

Ethical behaviour in business requires business owners and managers to act in ways that their stakeholders consider to be both fair and honest. However, acting ethically could increase business costs, causing a conflict with the objective of making high profits. Shareholders may place a higher priority on high profits rather than a company behaving ethically.

For example, the use of child labour is unlawful in many countries because it is considered to be unethical. However, the use of children as a cheap source of labour is still common in some parts of the world, in factory work, mining, quarrying, agriculture and even prostitution. It has been estimated that up to 13 500 children, some as young as eight, work in carpet-making factories spread across the Punjab province in Pakistan. Like many of the estimated 200 million children being used as cheap labour around the world, they often work long hours in hazardous conditions for very little pay.

There are many other examples of unethical business behaviours. For example, to boost sales and profits, some businesses may mislead consumers about the prices and performance of their products. Others may fail to install health and safety equipment in their factories to protect their employees because it increases business costs and reduces profits.

Some business practices may be perfectly legal but may nevertheless be considered unacceptable by a large number of people. For example, the testing of cosmetics and chemicals on animals is legal in many countries but is disliked by many people who prefer to buy products that have not been tested on animals or from businesses that do not support animal tests.

Consider the following example of unethical business activity.

The price of cheap clothes: 100 die as sweatshop factories collapse

More than 1000 people were injured and 100 people killed when an eight-storey building containing clothing factories collapsed in Bangladesh.

Police said factory owners had ignored a warning to shut after severe cracks were spotted in the building, the construction of which had violated a number of building codes.

Bangladesh is the second biggest exporter of clothes in the world but its £13 billion textiles industry has been plagued by fires and accidents for years, and has been accused of forcing children below the age of 14 to work up to 11 hours each day to produce garments.

The poor working conditions and low wages in its factories have put a spotlight on global retailers such as Benetton, Primark and Matalan that buy cheap clothes from them.

Imagine you are a major shareholder in an international company that purchases cheap clothes from the owners of factories in developing economies where wages and working conditions are poor. Following the disaster in Bangladesh you are concerned that continuing to purchase from these suppliers could damage the reputation and sales of your company. On the other hand, purchasing clothes from other, more responsible suppliers could increase costs and reduce company profits. What should you do?

Continue using the same suppliers?

- Despite the poor wages and working conditions in their factories, they provide jobs and incomes for some of the world's poorest people in least-developed countries. If your company stopped trading with them, many of these people would lose their jobs and have to return to living in poverty.
- Even if the factories stopped employing child labour it is likely that the same children would be forced to work elsewhere and in even worse conditions.
- Your company would have to pay more to buy the products of other, more responsible suppliers. Costs would rise and make the company less competitive.
- Higher costs will mean prices will have to rise. Consumers want low prices, so sales and profits are likely to fall.
- Working with these suppliers to improve conditions in their factories should provide good publicity for your company which will help to maintain sales.

Or stop using the same suppliers?

- Many consumers will be appalled by the use of child labour and the poor wages and working conditions in these factories. Company sales and profits are likely to fall if it continues to buy their products for resale at a profit.
- Pressure groups may organize protests against your company if it continues to sell the products of these factories. A decision to stop trading with the factories will therefore provide good publicity for the business and end any protests or boycotts.
- Customers will be attracted to businesses that behave ethically. This will give your company a competitive advantage over rival firms that do not make ethical decisions. Although the purchase of products from other, more responsible suppliers may be more expensive, sales and profits are likely to be higher.
- Your company is more likely to attract and retain good employees and investors who want to be associated with a business that behaves in an ethical and socially responsible way.

Ethics are therefore about trying to do the right thing.

Some business owners and managers think that acting ethically increases costs and reduces profits. As a result there will be fewer businesses, jobs and incomes created.

However, many other businesses such as The Body Shop, the Fairtrade Foundation and Rainforest Alliance have built strong ethical brand images, believing that customers are prepared to pay more for products that consider the natural environment and ensure employees, including among their suppliers, receive good wages and working conditions. Although costs are higher, sales revenues are also higher. Profits of firms acting ethically can therefore exceed those of firms that do not.

Decisions or actions taken by an **ethical firm** take account of how they could affect other people and organizations, entire communities and the natural environment. In doing so, ethical behaviour can bring significant benefits to a business. For example, it can:

✓ attract more customers to the business, boosting sales and profits

✓ attract and retain the most talented and productive employees, thereby reducing labour turnover and recruitment costs

✓ attract new investors, providing low-cost capital to finance business expansion.

Unethical business behaviour, by comparison, can damage a firm's reputation and make it less appealing to consumers, employees, investors and other stakeholders.

Exam PREPARATION 6.2

Country X's government has decided to invest in a super-fast broadband system which will be available to 95% of the population. Some people are concerned that this will involve a large amount of construction which will disrupt parts of the country as roads are closed to allow fibre optic cables to be laid underground. Some retail employees feel that this will allow online shopping to increase and result in job losses in the retail sector. Taxes may be increased to provide funding for the work. A shortage of skilled workers for the supplying of cables may also mean that some employees may have to work long hours, in dangerous conditions, to meet the deadline set by the government. Employment laws should mean that these workers are protected from long hours and unsafe working conditions.

a   Identify **two** ways that employees may be protected at work by employment laws. [2]

b   Identify **two** reasons why governments put taxes on goods. [2]

c   Explain **two** reasons why many employees in the retail sector are concerned about the decision to provide a super-fast broadband system. [4]

d   Explain **three** social benefits that the provision of faster broadband might create. [6]

e   The management of many businesses in the private sector think employment legislation increases business costs. Do you think society would benefit from a reduction in such laws? Justify your answer. [6]

Learning CHECKLIST

Before you continue make sure you are able to

Show awareness of **environmental concerns** and **ethical issues** as both opportunities and constraints for businesses:

✓ how business activity can impact on the **environment**, for example how it may be contributing to global warming

✓ the concept of **externalities**; possible **external costs** and **external benefits** of business decisions

✓ **sustainable development** and how business activity can contribute to this

✓ how/why businesses might respond to environmental pressures and opportunities; **pressure groups**

✓ the role of **legal controls** over business activity affecting the environment, for example controls on **pollution**

✓ **ethical issues** a business might face; conflicts between profits and ethics

✓ how businesses might react and respond to ethical issues, for example the use of child labour.

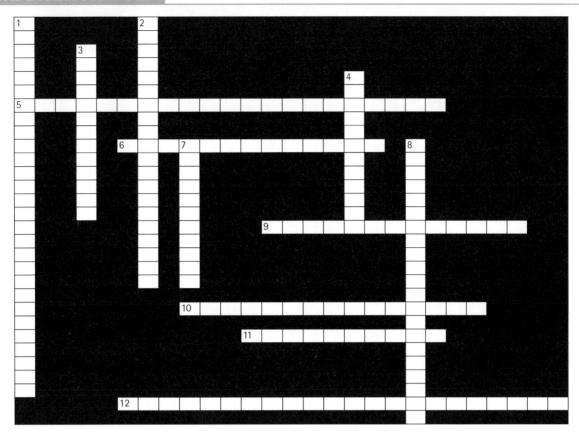

Clues down

1 Collective term used to describe the adoption and use of new production methods and alternative materials and sources of supply in business activity with the aim of reducing the rate of depletion of natural resources and minimizing damage to the natural environment, for example, through the use of recycled materials and renewable energy sources (11, 8, 9)

2 Beneficial impacts enjoyed by other people or firms as a result of the activities of another business, for example, because it creates new technologies, jobs and skills that help to improve social and economic welfare (8, 12)

3 The total benefit to society of a business activity. It is the sum of the private and external benefits created by the activity (5, 7)

4 The financial (fixed and variable) costs of production incurred by a business - not the costs its production may impose on other people and organizations (7, 5)

7 A business that acts in a socially and environmentally responsible way. This is because its decisions will take account of the impacts its activities could have on other people and organizations, communities and the natural environment (7, 4)

8 Natural resources that cannot be replaced or reproduced once they have been used up (3-9, 9)

Clues across

5 Term used to describe the detrimental impacts the activities one or more businesses could have on other people or organizations, for example, through the pollution their production process creates which causes health problems and damage to the environment (8, 12)

6 A farmer loses income because his animals fall ill and die after drinking water from a nearby river that has been contaminated by waste chemicals released into it by a factory further upstream. People suffer breathing problems and lose wages because they have to take days off work due to air pollution in their city caused by industrial activity and traffic congestion. What type of costs do these examples illustrate? (8, 5)

9 A group of people or an organization that will organize protests, publicity and actions against businesses that fail to act in socially and environmentally responsible ways in an attempt to change the way they behave (8, 5)

10 The process of remodelling or replacing old or worn out parts in a manufactured item to restore or update its functionality rather than discarding it and producing an entirely new one. For example, it can include replacing the memory chips and hard drive in a computer or retreading a worn car tyre (15)

11 The total cost to society of a business activity. It is the sum of the private and external costs created by the activity (5, 7)

12 Term used to describe the process of achieving economic growth in total output and income without depleting natural resources and harming the natural environment (11, 11)

6.3.1 The importance of globalization

Key POINTS

- The increasing globalization of production and trade is creating new markets and business opportunities around the world.

- Through international trade, consumers can import a wide variety of goods and services from producers overseas and businesses can expand the scale of their production through the sale of exports to overseas consumer markets.

- Access to international markets also enables firms to find and benefit from the best workforces, resources and technologies worldwide.

- International trade and competition is growing rapidly as more economies develop and their incomes rise. Established businesses in an economy may lose market share and may even be forced to close if they cannot compete with items produced by overseas firms.

- In response, some business organizations are moving their production overseas to be nearer to sources of low-cost materials and labour and new, expanding consumer markets. Jobs and output will be lost in the economies they are leaving.

- A government may use trade barriers to protect national industries from overseas competition. Import tariffs are used to increase the prices of imports to encourage consumers to buy goods produced by firms in their national economy. However, tariffs also raise the costs of domestic firms that need imported goods to continue trading.

- Quotas limit the volume of different imports allowed into a national economy but may cause supply problems for domestic businesses that rely on imported items to process or sell.

Business BUZZWORDS

International trade – the exchange of goods, services and money across national borders.

Globalization – increasing trade, interconnections and interactions between people, firms and governments in different national economies.

Open economy – a country that trades freely with other countries.

Exports – goods and services sold overseas. Their sale involves the receipt of revenues from consumers in other countries.

Imports – goods and services purchased from countries overseas. Their purchase involves making payments to producers in other countries.

Dumping – exporting cheap, subsidized goods to another country to force its firms out of business.

Trade barriers – policy instruments (including import tariffs and quotas) used by a government to protect businesses and jobs in its national economy from global competition.

Import tariff – an indirect tax added to the prices of imported goods to reduce consumer demand for them.

Quota – a limit on the volume of imported goods allowed into a country.

The concept of globalization

The global economy is expanding and increasing international trade and new business opportunities

People often talk about the world "getting smaller". They are referring to the increasing ease with which people can communicate and travel around the world and the fact that our shops are full of a wide variety of products from different countries. However, what they really mean is that the world is getting bigger. That is, the size of the global economy is growing as the incomes and spending power of consumers in different countries are increasing and more and more goods and services are being produced and exchanged internationally.

The term **globalization** is used to describe the increasing international trade, interconnections and interactions between people, firms, governments and entire economies all over the world.

▼ Globalization involves increasing interdependence between countries

China loans Pakistan $6.5 billion to build nuclear plants

Surge in exports spurs Thailand's economic growth

More Filipino workers moving to Europe as demand for manpower continues to rise

Starbucks continues expansion in India with opening of new flagship store in Bangalore

Saudi company invests $133 million in overseas projects

Vietnam spends billions of dollars to import farm produce

Globalization is increasing for the following reasons.

- The global population is increasing, expanding the number of potential consumers in many countries.

- The global economy is growing as industrial output, employment, incomes and consumer spending continue to rise in many economies, especially in rapidly developing economies such as Brazil and China.

- Improvements in the speed and costs of international communications and transport are making it easier and cheaper to discuss business, transport goods and travel all over the world.

- Economies are becoming more open. This means they are exchanging more goods, services, technologies, ideas and capital internationally than ever before. An **open economy** is a national economy that engages in trade with other economies.

- It is becoming easier for workers to move from one country to another for employment, especially within **multinational** organizations with operations in more than one country. ➤ **6.3.2**

International trade involves the exchange of goods, services and money across national borders.

- Goods and services sold by firms located in one country to consumers in other countries are called **exports**. Revenues received from the sale of exports increase the total income of the country.

- Goods and services purchased by consumers in one country from producers located in other countries are called **imports**. The purchase of imports involves making payments overseas which therefore reduces the total income available in the country to spend on goods and services produced locally.

In 1999 the total global value of goods and commercial services exported was $6.82 trillion with the USA, Germany and Japan accounting for 28% of total exports. By 2012 total worldwide exports had risen to almost $18 trillion. The three largest exporting nations in 2012 were China, followed by the USA and Germany, together accounting for 18% of global trade.

Globalization has therefore helped to increase the production and exchange of goods and services internationally, creating many new business opportunities. However, it is also affecting how and where production takes place in the world, and therefore where jobs and incomes are created. Global competition is rising and threatening the market shares of many established businesses in developed economies. ➤ **1.2.1**

Opportunities for businesses in an economy created by globalization and international trade	Potential threats to businesses in an economy from globalization and international trade
✓ The ability to import goods and services from overseas allows businesses in an economy to specialize in products they are best able to produce and to export them all over the world.	✗ Increased competition from cheaper imports may reduce the sales and profits of new and established businesses making the same or similar products. Those unable to increase their efficiency and lower their costs may eventually be forced out of business.
✓ Businesses may increase their revenues and profits through the sale of exports to consumers overseas. Businesses able to do so will be able to expand their production and benefit from economies of scale.	✗ There will be increased competition for sales and skilled employees from overseas organizations that have located business operations in the economy.
✓ Businesses may also find it easier to expand by opening additional business premises to make and sell their products near to new consumer markets. Some may relocate all their production to countries where wages, other costs and taxes are lower.	✗ New and established businesses may find it increasingly difficult to attract and retain highly skilled employees if new and better paid opportunities to work overseas are created. Wages may have to rise to retain skilled workers.
✓ New business opportunities will be created in the distribution and retailing industries from the importation and sale of items produced in other countries.	✗ It may become more difficult for new and established businesses to raise capital if investors are attracted to new and more profitable business opportunities in other countries.
✓ Business organizations finding it difficult to fill their job vacancies may be able to advertise and recruit skilled labour from other countries.	✗ Business closures due to competition with cheap imports, business relocation to other countries and a loss of capital to support new start-ups will result in a loss of output, jobs and incomes in the economy.
✓ Businesses may be able to import the latest technologies, and the materials and components they need for more efficient production, from cheaper foreign suppliers.	

Anglesey Sea Salt goes global

From its origins in a family kitchen, Anglesey Sea Salt has built a loyal UK customer base. Its products are now also on the market in over 20 countries.

Over 40% of company turnover came from exports. Exports are extremely important for future growth, including expansion into new and existing markets as demand for different sea salt products increases in many different countries.

Pure salt is the key export, followed by flavoured salts, oak-smoked water and bespoke gifts. Europe is the most successful export market, followed by North America.

Anglesey Sea Salt is also exported to Japan for use in manufacturing premium quality soy sauce and miso. Company visits to Tokyo and Hong Kong have been well received, with new orders and great potential for future growth.

However, going global has not been without its challenges – the cost of carriage for premium products can price Anglesey Sea Salt out of overseas markets while competition from lower-cost producers in China and India is also increasing. There are also complicated labelling requirements and regulations to comply with in different overseas markets which increase costs.

Adapted from: http://www.fdf.org.uk

▶ How has globalization affected Anglesey Sea Salt?

▶ Identify two benefits and two problems globalization is creating for the company.

Opportunities from globalization and trade

Increased international specialization

No national economy can produce all the goods and services its population needs and wants. However, through international trade, consumers in an economy can import many other goods and services from producers located overseas. The ease with which different goods and services can be imported from overseas allows firms within a country to specialize in producing only those items they are best able to. As they can export them to consumers in other countries, they are able to produce far more than consumers in their home country would be willing and able to buy. ➤ **1.1.1**

US aircraft

For example, many countries in the Middle East specialize in the production of oil because they are located over vast natural oil reserves. Similarly, Japanese industries became world leaders in the design and manufacture of many electronic products and cars because their workers became highly skilled in these activities.

Profits from the sale of exports distributed to business owners and wages earned by the people they employ to produce exports can in turn be spent on the purchase of many imported items.

Spanish olive oil

Through international trade, some countries have become famous for the goods and services they produce, even if in some cases other countries make the same or very similar products. This is because their industries have developed a reputation among consumers worldwide for making certain products cheaper and better than anywhere else.

Swiss watches

Italian shoes

▲ Some examples of international specialization

There are many examples such as Italian shoes and clothes, Belgian chocolates, German beers, Swiss watches, Scottish whisky, Cuban cigars, Spanish olive oil, Japanese electronics, US aircraft and military equipment and many more.

ACTIVITY 6.13

▶ Try to identify and list five or more goods or services that are not produced in your country and have to be imported.

▶ Try to identify and list at least ten goods and services which businesses in your country produce but which are also imported from overseas.

▶ Look at the countries listed below. Which of the products listed do you think each country is best known for?

Saudi Arabia	France	Fish	Beef
Iceland	India	Tea	Lamb
Norway	Jamaica	Timber	Wine
Germany	New Zealand	Oil	Coffee
Argentina	Kenya	Manufactured goods	Tourism

▶ In what ways do you and your family benefit from international trade?

New business opportunities are created from the distribution and sale of exports and imports

Consider the example of Algeria in Northern Africa. Oil, gas and petroleum production is the largest industry in Algeria. Households and businesses in Algeria consume around $20 billion of its output each year but the annual total output of the industry is worth $69 billion. This means the industry exports $49 billion of oil, gas and petroleum products each year to consumers in Europe, Asia and Latin America. Without the ability to export, the Algerian oil and gas industry would not have been able to grow to its present size.

In addition, Algerian businesses export fruit and vegetables, animal products, iron ore and zinc. The output and sale of these items and oil and gas products to overseas consumers increase the total income of the country to around $75 billion each year. In turn, many Algerian businesses use this income to purchase imports including farm machinery, many food and drink products and a wide range of clothes and other consumer goods and services to sell to Algerian consumers.

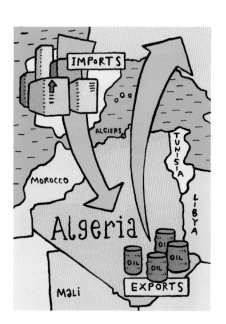

Increasing globalization and international trade has therefore created four major benefits for Algerian businesses.

● They have gained increased revenues and profits from the sale of exports.

● They have been able to expand their businesses, spread their fixed costs over a greater volume of output and benefit from economies of large-scale production. ➤ **1.2.1**

- A fall in consumer demand in Algeria or any one market overseas will have less impact on businesses that are able to sell their products into a number of different consumer markets around the world.

- There are new business and employment opportunities to import a greater variety of different goods and services from suppliers overseas to sell at a mark-up for profit to domestic consumers.

The same gains to business can be observed in many other countries engaged in international trade.

Global businesses can access the best workforces, technologies and resources anywhere in the world

Ease of access to international markets allows a business to find the best and lowest cost sources of materials and components from different producers in other countries. For example, the Airbus 380, the largest passenger aircraft in the world, is assembled in Toulouse in France by the European company Airbus using components from suppliers in Spain, Germany, Japan, the UK, USA, China, India and many other countries. Wages and material costs are lower in developing economies such as China and India than in Europe.

> Dynamatic Technologies Ltd of India produces component parts for Airbus and Ford Motor Co. and plans to invest 900 million rupees ($19.3 million) to expand its factories to meet rising demand. The company intends to focus future production on aerospace as revenue from the market segment has increased significantly as the global demand for passenger air travel and air freight continues to rise.

> Mubadala Aerospace in Abu Dhabi began manufacturing parts for Airbus at its new aerostructures facility in 2010. The company has invested up to $500 million to expand its facilities and import the latest technologies in order to produce components such as spoilers and flap-track fairings for Airbus wings. The company also hopes to eventually develop and manufacture primary aircraft structures.

A business organization can also import the latest equipment and ideas developed in other countries, borrow money from banks overseas offering the lowest interest rates and advertise for foreign workers with the skills it needs if these are lacking in its country's workforce.

A business organization can also move its production, key workers and capital to locations overseas to be near low-cost sources of materials and labour and new, expanding consumer markets. The biggest organizations in the world are no longer national firms but **multinational corporations** with operations in many countries. ➤ **6.3.2**

Threats from globalization and trade

Growing competition from imports and multinationals

Globalization and international trade have increased competition for customers and sales in many markets. The sales, market shares and profits of established businesses in a country may be threatened as follows.

- They may be threatened by increasing imports of goods and services from suppliers overseas, especially if they are cheaper, because overseas producers enjoy lower wages and other costs in their countries. In response, domestic businesses may have to cut their prices and may lose profits or will have to find ways to become more efficient to lower their costs and improve their product quality.

- Overseas producers who have set up factories, offices and shops to produce and sell their products in their country may prove a threat to established businesses there. These overseas firms may be larger and more efficient and therefore able to offer their customers lower prices and better quality.

Business expansion in rapidly developing economies, including China, India and Brazil, is a growing competitive threat to many established businesses in developed economies such as those in the US, Europe and the Far East. Wages and salaries are still relatively low in many rapidly developing economies. This enables many of their businesses to produce goods and services far cheaper than those in more developed economies. They are also rapidly developing the workforce skills and technologies that will help their businesses remain competitive even as the wages of their workers begin to rise due to increasing demand for their labour. ➤ **1.2.1**

Less-developed economies also fear they will be unable to respond to the competitive threat posed by new and expanding firms in rapidly developing economies. Many are trying to develop their own manufacturing and service industries to provide jobs and incomes and to improve living standards, but cheap imports from overseas could prevent them from doing so. This is because their consumers may prefer to buy cheap imports rather than more expensive goods or services produced by local businesses.

Multinational companies are also locating in their economies, attracted by the low wages of their workers and also low taxes in many cases. This again is creating more competition for local businesses. ➤ **6.3.2**

Increasing competition for skilled labour and capital

Capital is becoming more and more mobile internationally. This means it is becoming easier for investors in any one country to move their money around the world to invest in new and expanding businesses in other countries.

Capital will be attracted to those businesses with the greatest potential for profit and growth. Therefore, as more business opportunities are created around the world, competition for capital is also growing. If more capital is attracted to business opportunities in rapidly expanding economies, less may be made available to established businesses in developed economies and start-ups in less-developed economies, especially if they are thought to have less growth potential.

As industries expand globally, demand for skilled labour is also growing. In response, skilled labour is also becoming more mobile internationally and will be attracted to those organizations and jobs that offer the best pay and prospects. Large international firms with business operations in many countries may be able to offer higher wages and more opportunities to travel and work overseas than small national firms. These small firms may not be able to offer such high wages or salaries and could risk losing their most skilled and productive employees, which in turn will reduce their ability to compete for customers, sales and profits.

US "loses" 2.7 million jobs to China

In a recent study, the Economic Policy Institute (EPI) analysed US jobs lost to China between 2001 and 2011. During that time, "trade with China displaced more than 2.7 million US jobs, over 2.1 million of which were in manufacturing," according to the report.

Of the 2.1 million manufacturing jobs lost, more than 1 million were from the computer and electronics industries.

Jobs and incomes may be lost to low-cost economies

The increasing ease with which firms can move or expand their production overseas to be closer to growing consumer markets in other countries or sources of cheaper labour and materials has benefited many established businesses. However, while owners of firms may benefit from moving production overseas, the workforces, suppliers and economy they exit may be left worse off. Employees will be made redundant, suppliers will lose regular customer orders and the economy will lose output. Other businesses in the economy will also suffer falling sales as unemployment rises and consumer incomes fall.

Trade barriers

Some governments attempt to protect national output and employment from overseas competition

ACTIVITY 6.14

Using the article below identify:

▶ different barriers used by governments to restrict international trade and competition

▶ reasons why governments use trade barriers

▶ the impact trade barriers could have on consumers, workers and businesses in different countries

▶ arguments against the use of trade barriers.

More trade barriers as global slump continues

Just over a month ago, world leaders agreed to reject trade protectionism and stick to free trade principles to fight the global economic slowdown. Yet an increasing number of countries are already breaking that promise.

For example, in a move designed to protect its battered manufacturers from foreign imports, Indonesia is slapping restrictions and quotas on another 500 products this month and demanding special licences and new fees on imports. Russia is also increasing tariffs on imported poultry and pork – a move that has angered US farmers: Russia is the single largest market for US poultry producers, which this year exported $740 millions' worth to Russian consumers.

France is launching a government fund to protect French companies from foreign takeovers while Argentina and Brazil are seeking to raise tariffs on products from leather goods and peaches to imported wine and textiles.

The list of countries making access to their markets harder also includes the United States. The US government's $17.4 billion bailout of the US auto industry has been branded an unfair subsidy by many because it puts foreign competitors at a disadvantage. At the same time Russia, the largest car market in Europe, increased taxes on imported foreign cars by 35%.

In hard times, analysts say, nations are more inclined to take steps that inhibit trade, often with dire consequences for consumers, businesses and entire economies.

"Because exporting firms face overseas competition they tend to be innovative, dynamic and capable of generating good job growth," said a US professor of trade policy. "If trade barriers shut these firms down, their suppliers shut down, job losses get worse, and you can quickly have an entire economy spiralling downward."

Increasing global trade and competition, especially from rapidly developing countries, is threatening the sales of many large businesses in developed economies and new, small businesses trying to establish themselves in many of the least-developed economies. For example, the article in activity 6.14 reports that the government of Indonesia has restricted the importation of 500 different products in an attempt to protect its manufacturing industry from competition from producers located overseas.

Like the government of Indonesia, many others around the world are equally concerned that businesses in their national economies may not be able to compete with imports or may relocate to countries where wages and other costs are lower. This will result in a loss of jobs, incomes and tax revenues in their countries and slower or even negative economic growth. As a result, many governments try to restrict international competition to protect businesses and jobs in their economies.

+ **To protect small businesses, new industries and employment from overseas competitors.** New and small businesses may be unable to compete with larger, lower-cost businesses overseas. Protecting them from global competition will allow them to grow and become more established after which they will be better able to compete.

+ **To prevent dumping.** This involves one country "flooding" another with products at prices significantly below their global market price in order to increase their sales and force domestic firms out of business. For example, Australia recently accused Indonesia and China of dumping cheap glass on the Australian market to boost their sales at the expense of Australian producers.

+ **To improve their balance of international trade and payments** by reducing or restricting the demand for imports. **> 6.1.1**

Tariffs and quotas are used to make imports more expensive to encourage sales of home-produced goods

Using policy instruments to restrict international trade and competition is called **protectionism** and involves the use of **trade barriers**. They include the following.

- **Import tariffs** are indirect taxes on the prices of imported goods to make them more expensive to buy than the same goods produced by domestic firms. Sales of home-produced products should therefore benefit. For example, the article in activity 6.14 reported that Russia introduced tariffs on the prices of imported poultry and pork to protect their meat farmers from US farms who were able to supply the same products at lower prices. **> 6.1.1**

- **Quotas** are limits on the quantities of different products that can be imported. These supply restrictions also force up their prices and encourage consumers to purchase from local suppliers instead.

In addition, a government may try to protect businesses and jobs in its economy using the following measures.

- It may pay **subsidies** to firms to reduce their production costs and therefore their prices to below those of overseas firms. For example, the US is among a number of countries that has been accused by others of giving producers in its farming, steel and automotive industries unfair subsidies to lower their costs and prices below those of competitors overseas. **> 1.3.3**

EU trade ban will cause fruit shortage

British supermarkets face severe shortages of oranges, grapefruits and other citrus fruits this summer because of a highly contentious import ban on fruit from South Africa and South America. The ban will "protect" European citrus plants from pests.

- A government may impose an **embargo** or total ban on the importation of a certain good, or all goods, from a particular country. For example, embargoes are often used to control trade in weapons and other products with countries involved in conflicts or abuses of human rights.

Trade barriers can result in increased business costs and retaliation

The use of trade barriers may however cause a number of problems.

- Costs will rise for businesses that rely on the importation of materials, components and equipment from overseas for their factories or the import of finished goods to sell in their shops. Quotas may also result in supply shortages that will hold up production.

- Inefficient businesses that are protected from global competition may continue to produce lower-quality and/or higher-cost products without fear of losing sales to more efficient producers overseas. Consumers in that country will have less choice and pay higher prices as a result.

- Other countries may introduce their own trade barriers in retaliation. Businesses selling exports to these countries will lose sales as a result.

Trade barriers can therefore restrict consumer choice and business and employment opportunities, and are often used to protect large powerful businesses in developed economies at the expense of small businesses in less-developed economies. This has created pressure from many people, businesses and governments around the world to remove trade barriers and to allow all countries to trade freely and fairly.

Exam PREPARATION 6.3

A manufacturer of sporting goods and clothes based in Pakistan wants to export its products to new and expanding markets in Africa. There are already a number of sporting goods and clothes producers in Africa. They are worried cheap imports from Pakistan will harm their businesses and have asked their governments to impose import quotas.

a   Define "import quotas".   [2]

b   Identify **two** ways consumers in Africa could benefit from the importation of sporting goods and clothes from Pakistan.   [2]

c   Identify **two** reasons why African producers believe cheap imports from Pakistan could "harm their businesses".   [4]

d   Explain **three** problems the Pakistani manufacturer could face entering markets in Africa.   [6]

e   Do you think that African governments should protect their businesses from cheap imports? Justify your answer.   [6]

Before you continue make sure you are able to

Understand the concept of **globalization** and the reasons for it:

✓   opportunities and threats of **globalization** for businesses

✓   why some governments might introduce **import tariffs** and **quotas**.

Learning CHECKLIST

▸ Multinational companies are some of the largest businesses in the world, with annual revenues of many billions of dollars and many thousands of employees globally.

▸ Many of the biggest multinational organizations in the world are US-owned corporations with interests in oil and gas exploration and petroleum.

▸ Multinational organizations can benefit from increased sales, low wage costs in low-wage economies and significant economies of scale because of their size and access to overseas markets.

▸ Multinationals can benefit national economies through foreign direct investment (FDI), providing new jobs and incomes through the production and sale of new goods and services including for export.

▸ Governments may offer generous subsidies and tax advantages to multinationals to encourage them to locate business units in their national economies.

▸ Multinationals may also create disadvantages for their host countries. They may force local competitors out of business, exploit low-wage employees and repatriate their profits to countries overseas where taxes on profits are lower or not payable.

Multinational – a company or corporation with business operations in more than one country.

Subsidiary – a company that is completely or partly owned by another company or corporation.

Foreign direct investment (FDI) – direct investment in productive assets in a country by an individual or business of another country, either by buying an established company or by expanding the operations of an existing business in that country.

Multinational companies

Multinationals operate in more than one country and are some of the largest organizations in the world

A key feature of globalization has been the development and growth of multinationals.

A **multinational company** or **corporation** is a truly "global business" with premises and productive operations in more than one country. That is, a multinational owns a number of **subsidiary** companies located in other countries which produce goods and services in those countries. These can then be sold to consumers in these countries or exported around the world. The headquarters of a multinational is normally based in its country of origin.

Multinationals are some of the largest business organizations in the world, often selling many billions of dollars worth of goods and services, and employing many thousands of workers globally. Many of the biggest multinationals are US-based and Chinese government-owned corporations, with interests in oil and gas exploration and petroleum.

In 2018 the largest multinational in the world in terms of sales was Walmart. Its total revenue that year was just under $486 billon. The company is American in origin with subsidiaries in over 28 countries employing 2.3 million staff. However, the most profitable global company in 2018 was US-owned electronics giant Apple with profits of over $48 billion from its operations in 17 countries.

Company Name	Main Industrial sector	Total revenue ($ billion)	Employees	Country of origin
Walmart	Retailing	485.9	2.3 million	USA
State Grid Corporation of China	Electricity supply	315.2	1.9 million	China
Sinopec Group	Oil and gas	267.5	810 000	China
China National Petroleum Corporation	Oil and gas	262.6	1.7 million	China
Toyota Motor	Automotive	254.7	348 000	Japan
Volkswagen	Automotive	240.3	600 000	Germany
Royal Dutch Shell	Oil and gas	240	90 000	Netherlands, UK
Berkshire Hathaway	Conglomerate	223.7	377 000	USA
Apple Inc.	Electronics	215.6	110 000	USA
Exxon Mobil	Oil and gas	205	77 000	USA

▲ The world's ten largest multinationals by revenue, 2018

The revenues of many multinationals are greater than the total income of many countries. For example, of the world's largest 100 economic entities in 2016 in terms of total income, 69 were corporations and 31 were national economies. Royal Dutch Shell, Exxon Mobil, Walmart and Toyota, among others, all ranked above countries such as Austria, Denmark, Argentina, Portugal and Russia in terms of their total annual income. Multinationals are also responsible for around two-thirds of international trade and many global industries are dominated by a handful of these giant businesses.

ACTIVITY 6.15

The following table lists a number of multinational companies. Try to find out their country of origin and their main activities to complete the table. The first one has been done for you.

Company	Country of origin	Main business activities
BNP Paribas	France	Banking and financial services
General Electric		
Siemens		
Gazprom		
Samsung		
Nestlé		
HSBC Holdings		
ArcelorMittal		

Calls from Vietnam animal feed industry for government to protect businesses

Foreign livestock firms now hold over 70% of the animal feed market in Vietnam, pushing out local businesses and making it difficult for them to compete fairly, according to local industry representatives who are calling for the government to step in.

"While local firms are suffering losses, and reducing production, foreign ones are growing in Vietnam, dominating the market and increasing prices unreasonably to earn huge profits," said the Vietnam Animal Feed Association.

Reports claim Walmart's Chinese plants exploit workers

US retailer Walmart Stores, Inc. uses Chinese factories that deny overtime pay and maternity leave to workers and pay less than the local minimum wage, according to three reports from labour monitoring groups released today.

Ecuador's president has called for an international boycott of major US oil corporation Chevron, blaming it for polluting the Amazon.

Toyota to create 800 new jobs in South Africa

Japanese car manufacturer, Toyota, has announced it is to invest R363 million ($51 million) in a parts distribution warehouse in Ekurhuleni, east of Johannesburg, creating about 800 jobs.

Amazon in new UK tax avoidance row

The internet retail giant Amazon is facing fresh claims of tax avoidance after its latest accounts showed it generated sales of £4.3 billion in the UK last year yet paid only £4 million in corporation tax.

When customers order goods from Amazon.co.uk their payments are transferred to its Luxembourg subsidiary, Amazon EU SARL, where corporate taxes on profits are much lower than in the UK.

Amazon has faced fierce criticism from rival retailers, politicians and consumers over the amount of tax it pays in the UK.

Foreign companies boost tax revenues in Xiamen

Thirty-seven subsidiaries of 17 of the top 500 global companies in Xiamen in China, including Dell Inc., Boeing and Toyota, contributed RMB 674 million in taxes in the first seven months of 2011, an 88.27% increase from the previous year.

UK benefits from inward investment

Last year the UK attracted over 1430 foreign companies and investment projects, many in high-technology areas such as software development, advanced engineering, IT and life sciences. More than 94 500 jobs were associated with these investments totalling over £43 billion.

▶ Using the articles, identify as many possible benefits and drawbacks to a country of attracting multinationals to locate and operate within its national economy.

A multinational business has a number of advantages because of its size and access to foreign markets

The global presence and size of many multinational companies give these organizations a number of key advantages. A multinational can:

+ reach many more consumers globally and sell far more than other types of business

+ raise significant amounts of new capital for business expansion, research and development and to employ workers and managers with the highest skills

+ minimize transport costs by locating business operations in different countries to be near to sources of materials or key overseas consumer markets

+ minimize its wage costs by locating business units in countries where wages and other employment costs are low

+ benefit from cost advantages (economies of scale) due to large-scale production **> 4.2.3**

+ avoid trade barriers by setting up operations in those countries that apply tariffs and quotas to imports. **> 6.3.1**

+ as a result of all the above factors, greatly increase the profitability and value of the company for its shareholders.

All stakeholders are affected in some way when a business becomes multinational. The management might be concerned about their jobs or whether they might be moved overseas. Suppliers will be concerned about continuing to supply the company as it might locate cheaper supplies in another country. Employees might be worried about job losses if the business transfers some of its operations overseas. Local communities might welcome the new job opportunities offered by the business operating in their area or they could be concerned about the environmental impact on the local area. Governments might lose tax revenue if profits are transferred overseas.

▲ Royal Dutch Shell and Walmart Stores are among the largest corporations and economic entities in the world

Benefits and disadvantages of multinationals to national economies

Multinationals can increase investment, employment and income

National governments often compete with each other to attract multinationals to their countries for the following reasons.

+ Multinationals provide jobs and incomes for local workers. This helps to reduce unemployment.

+ They invest capital in new or expanded business premises, new machinery and modern equipment. Capital received from overseas that is invested directly into productive assets in a country is called **foreign direct investment (FDI)**. This "inward investment" helps to boost the productive capacity of the economy and, therefore, economic growth. **> 6.1.1**

+ They increase the amount and variety of goods and services available to domestic consumers and compete with domestic firms thereby offering consumers more choice. The increase in competition forces other businesses to improve their efficiency in order to cut their prices and increase product quality to attract and retain customers.

✦ They bring new ideas, technologies and skills into a country which domestic firms and employees can learn and benefit from, helping to increase their productivity.

✦ They pay taxes on their profits and purchases from domestic firms which increases the revenue available to government to finance its public expenditures.

✦ Some of the additional output produced by multinationals may be sold overseas which increases the export earnings of the country.

Multinationals may force local businesses to close, pay low wages and "move" their profits to avoid tax

Many multinationals provide significant benefits to national economies, employees and consumers. However, some multinationals have been criticized for using their size and power to exploit people and businesses in some countries.

For example, in the late 1990s Coca-Cola was accused of bringing in armed groups to intimidate, kidnap and torture trade union leaders who were trying to improve working conditions for employees at their bottling plant in Columbia. Many other US multinationals with factories in Columbia, including Occidental Petroleum and food producer Del Monte, were also accused of similar offences by the Permanent People's Tribunal in Columbia which included professors, human rights commissioners, doctors, judges and social workers from Argentina, Australia, Belgium, Brazil, Chile and a number of other countries.

Elsewhere, in India, Coca-Cola has been accused by the India Resource Center of polluting groundwater and soil, causing water shortages and having high levels of pesticide in its soft drinks.

The multinationals in these examples and many other multinationals deny these and similar claims. However, it is clear that some global corporations may be able to use their power in many developing and less-developed countries to ignore local laws and regulations and to exploit local workers and natural resources in order to minimize their costs and maximize their profits.

– **They may force local competitors out of business.** Multinationals often compete with local businesses. Their cost advantages allow them to sell their products at much lower prices causing local businesses producing and selling the same or similar items to lose sales. As a result, many small local firms may be forced out of business by multinationals. As local competition and consumer choice is reduced, multinationals can begin to raise their prices.

– **They can move their profits between countries to avoid paying corporate taxes.** A multinational may move the profits it has earned in one country to another to reduce the tax it will have to pay in that country on its profits. This involves the transfer or **repatriation of profits** to its headquarters or subsidiary companies overseas. A multinational may even be able to avoid taxes altogether by moving its profits to a country that has no corporation or profits tax, or to some less-developed economies which may have poor tax collection and legal systems.

- **Multinationals may use their power to obtain generous subsidies and tax advantages from host countries.** Multinationals can move their production to the most profitable and advantageous locations anywhere in the world. Due to the investments, jobs and incomes that will be lost if one or more multinationals leave a country, many governments provide generous incentives to encourage them to stay in their national economies. ➤ **4.4.1**

- **Some multinationals may exploit workers in low-wage economies.** Many of the jobs created by multinationals in other countries, particularly in developing economies, involve low-skilled and low-paid work on mass production lines. Workers in less-developed economies may be paid far less to do the same or even more work than employees in more developed economies by their multinational employers. Health and safety standards may also be lower and employment laws weaker in some developing economies.

- **Multinationals may exploit natural resources and damage the environment.** Some multinationals may use up scarce natural resources, create pollution and cause significant damage in their host countries. This is because laws and regulations to protect the natural environment may be weak or not enforced in some developing and less-developed countries.

> ## Nike workers "kicked, slapped and verbally abused" at factories making Converse
>
> New allegations follow years of outrage over child labour and sweatshops in Indonesia.
>
> The sports brand giant claims there is very little it can do to stop it at factories owned by suppliers.

Exam PREPARATION 6.4

The Republic of Ireland is offering generous subsidies to global businesses that locate their headquarters to that country. Acme film company is considering moving to the Republic of Ireland.

a   Define "global business". [2]

b   Identify **two** factors that the Acme film company should consider before moving to the Republic of Ireland. [2]

c   Outline how pressure groups might try and influence Acme's decision to re-locate to the Republic of Ireland. [4]

d   Explain **three** consequences for Acme film company of a rise in the exchange rate of the Euro currency of the Republic of Ireland. [6]

e   Do you think that the Irish government should offer subsidies to encourage companies to move to their country? Justify your answer. [6]

Learning CHECKLIST

Before you continue make sure you are able to

Identify reasons for the importance and growth of **multinational companies**:

✓ the benefits to business of becoming a **multinational** and the impact on its shareholders

✓ potential benefits to a country and/or economy where a multinational is located, including jobs, exports, increased choice and investment

✓ potential drawbacks to a country and/or economy where a multinational is located, including reduced sales of local businesses and the **repatriation of profits**.

6.3.3   The impact of exchange rate changes

- ▸ Payments for imports and exports, and making investments overseas, require the exchange of different national currencies. Currencies are exchanged on the global foreign exchange market.

- ▸ Every national currency has an exchange rate with every other national currency in the world.

- ▸ Businesses engaged in international trade need to be aware of the impact changes in exchange rates can have on their costs, revenues and profitability. For example, an export priced at $10 will sell for 15 euros in Europe if the exchange rate is $1 = 1.5 euros. If the exchange rate falls to $1 = 1.4 euros the same product will sell for 14 euros. The fall in price could help to increase exports to European markets.

- ▸ An appreciation in the value of a national currency will make exports from that country more expensive to buy in overseas markets, but the prices of imports will fall. This will reduce the costs of businesses buying imports from overseas producers.

- ▸ A depreciation in the value of a national currency will make exports from that country cheaper to buy in overseas markets, but import prices will rise. This will increase the costs of businesses buying imports from overseas producers.

Business BUZZWORDS

Foreign exchange market – the global market for buying and selling national currencies. The market determines the price or rate at which one currency can be exchanged for another national currency.

Exchange rate – the market price or value of a national currency in terms of another currency.

Appreciation (in the value of a currency) – a rise in the value or market price of a national currency against another currency or currencies.

Depreciation (in the value of a currency) – a fall in the value or market price of a national currency against another currency or currencies.

International competitiveness – how the prices of items traded internationally compare. For example, an increase in the prices of imported goods will make them relatively less competitive than the same goods produced by domestic firms in the importing country.

The foreign exchange market

International trade involves financial transactions in different national currencies

Have you ever travelled overseas? If so, you may recall that in order to buy things overseas you have to exchange the money you use in your country for the national currency of the country you are visiting. Every country has its own national currency and the amount you get in return for your own currency is called its **exchange rate**.

Similarly, businesses involved in **international trade** must exchange different national currencies and need to be aware of how changes in exchange rates can affect them. This is true for any business that:

IMPORTS	• imports materials, components or finished goods from organizations overseas • buys services from overseas suppliers
EXPORTS	• exports materials, components or finished goods to business, government or individual consumers overseas • sells services to business, government or individual consumers overseas
INVESTS	• buys shares in the ownership of overseas companies • invests in premises and equipment to start and run business units in other countries.

A country buying goods from overseas or making investments in other countries must exchange its national currency for other national currencies. This is done on the global **foreign exchange market**.

For example, every year Egypt imports around $60 billion worth of goods from other countries, of which around $5 billion are imported from the US. To pay for the US imports Egyptian businesses must use Egyptian pounds to buy US dollars. If the value of the Egyptian pound fell by 10% against the US dollar, the cost of the same imports from the US will rise by 10% to $5.5 billion.

The foreign exchange market consists of all those people, organizations and governments wanting to buy or sell national currencies. It is the world's largest financial market.

Many billions of dollars worth of different national currencies are exchanged on the foreign exchange market every day.

Changes in the demand for national currencies and their supply can cause exchange rates to fluctuate

The Egyptian pound, US dollar and all other national currencies each has an exchange rate with every other national currency in the world.

For example, reading down each column of the table on the next page, the rate of exchange or price of 1 US dollar on 17 June 2018 was 0.86 euros, or 68.08 Indian rupees, or 3.67 UAE dirham and so on. In turn this meant that 1 Indian rupee exchanged for just 0.014 US dollars, 1 UAE dirham for 0.27 US dollars and 1 euro for 1.16 US dollars or 4.26 UAE dirhams.

	US dollar US$	Indian rupee Rs	UAE dirham Dh	Argentine peso $	Egyptian pound £	Euro €
US dollar US$	US$1.00	US$0.014	US$0.27	US$0.035	US$0.05	US$1.16
Indian rupee Rs	Rs68.08	Rs1.00	Rs18.53	Rs2.42	Rs3.81	Rs79.04
UAE dirham Dh	Dh3.67	Dh0.053	Dh1.00	Dh0.13	Dh0.205	Dh4.26
Argentine peso $	$28.09	$0.41	$7.65	$1.00	$1.20	$10.43
Egyptian pound £	£17.85	£0.26	£4.86	£0.84	£1.00	£20.07
Euro €	€0.86	€0.013	€0.23	€0.30	€0.04	€1.00

Some exchange rates ▶ on 17 June 2018

The governments of some countries control or fix the exchange rate of their national currency, but most countries have **floating exchange rates**. This means they are determined by global demand for their currencies and their global supply.

Changes in the demand for and supply of a national currency therefore causes its exchange rate to change or "fluctuate".

For example, if Egyptian consumers want to buy more US goods they will need to buy more US dollars to pay for them. This increase in demand for US dollars on the foreign exchange market will increase the price of US dollars. A rise in the price or value of one currency against one or more other currencies is referred to as an **appreciation** in the exchange rate.

On the other hand, if US consumers want to buy more exports from Egypt they will need to exchange US dollars for Egyptian pounds. This will increase the price of Egyptian pounds against the US dollar. This means the US dollar will have fallen in value against the Egyptian pound. This is a **depreciation** in the exchange rate.

A currency might depreciate for these reasons	A currency might appreciate for these reasons
• The country buys more imports than it exports. To do so it must sell its currency to buy other currencies.	• The country sells more exports than it imports. Overseas consumers must sell their currencies to buy exports from that country.
• Interest rates fall relative to those in other countries so people move their savings to banks overseas.	• Interest rates rise relative to those in other countries. This attracts savings from overseas residents.
• Inflation rises relative to inflation in other countries. This makes exports more expensive. Overseas demand for them, and the currency needed to buy them, will fall.	• Inflation is lower than in other countries so exports will become more competitive. Overseas demand for them, and the currency required to pay for them, will rise.
• People and businesses speculate their national currency will fall in value and sell their holdings of the currency.	• People and businesses speculate their national currency will rise in value and buy more of the currency.

How changes in exchange rates can affect businesses

An appreciation in the exchange rate of a currency will reduce the competitiveness of exports from that country

Even relatively small changes in exchange rates between different national currencies may have a significant impact on the **international competitiveness** of firms engaged in overseas trade and therefore on their costs, revenues and profits.

ACTIVITY 6.17

The cartoons below tell a story about two Egyptian businesses engaged in overseas trade. One exports components to US business consumers. The other imports parts from US businesses.

Develop a story to go with the cartoons to describe what is happening to exchange rates and how they are affecting each business.

For example, in activity 6.17 there is an **appreciation** in the value of the Egyptian pound against the US dollar. This means its value has increased and Egyptian pounds will now cost more to buy on the foreign exchange market.

The appreciation in the value of the Egyptian pound had the following impacts on the Egyptian businesses in the activity.

Impact on Egyptian business exporting goods to the US

At £1 = $0.20	At £1 = $0.40
Egyptian exports priced at £100 each will sell for $20 in the US.	The same items priced at £100 each will now cost US consumers $40 to buy. ▷ International competitiveness of Egyptian exports is reduced. ▷ US consumer demand for Egyptian exports could fall.

The rise in the value of the Egyptian pound therefore increased the price of Egyptian goods for sale in the US relative to the prices of the same or similar items produced by firms in the US or other countries.

This is because twice as many US dollars than before must be exchanged for the same amount of Egyptian pounds in order to import the same amount of goods from Egypt. As a result, US consumers are likely to reduce their spending on Egyptian goods. This will reduce the sales revenue, market share and profitability of the Egyptian business exporting its products to the US.

Impact on Egyptian business importing goods from the US

At £1 = $0.20	At £1 = $0.40
US imports priced at $4 each will cost £20 in Egypt.	The same items priced at $4 each will now cost £10 to buy. ▷ International competitiveness of US imports is increased. ▷ Egyptian demand for US imports could rise.

The rise in the value of the Egyptian pound therefore reduced the prices of US goods imported to Egypt relative to the prices of the same or similar items produced by firms in Egypt or other countries. This will reduce the costs of the Egyptian business importing parts from US suppliers. This should allow the company to improve its competitiveness because it will be able to reduce its prices, increase its sales revenue and profitability. **➤ 3.3.2**

A depreciation in the exchange rate of a currency will improve the competitiveness of exports from that country

Consider now how changes in exchange rates can affect the international competitiveness of firms producing pistachio nuts in Iran. Iran is the largest producer of pistachio nuts in the world and each year exports around 100 000 tonnes to countries including Mexico, Spain, Hong Kong and, especially, Germany.

The Hassas Export Co., based in Tehran, is one of Iran's leading exporters of pistachio nuts and each month sends around 4000 tonnes to Germany. Its exports compete internationally with pistachio nuts exported from the US and Turkey.

Atrimex Gmbh in Hamburg Germany is a major importer of pistachios to sell to food processing companies and retail outlets all over Europe. To pay for the nuts it imports from the Hassas Export Co. it needs to exchange the European currency, the euro (€), for Iranian rials.

Iran sells pistachio nuts to Germany

Germany pays for nuts with Iranian rials

Iran sells Iranian rials on foreign exchange market

Germany buys rials with euros

IRAN

GERMANY

Imagine that Atrimex places a regular order with Hassas for 100 tonnes of pistachio nuts each month. Each tonne of nuts has an export market price of 36 000 rials.

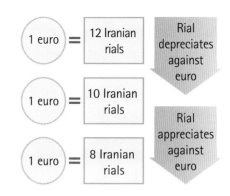

Last month the exchange rate was 10 rials = 1 euro.

- Atrimex had to exchange 3600 euros for 36 000 rials through the company's bank to pay Hassas for each tonne of nuts it imported that month. The total cost of 100 tonnes of imported nuts in euros that month was therefore 360 000 euros (= 3600 euros × 100 tonnes).

This month the rial has depreciated against the euro to 12 rials = 1 euro.

- Atrimex will now only have to exchange 3000 euros in return for 36 000 rials. The purchase of 100 tonnes this month will therefore cost the German company 300 000 euros (= 3000 euros × 100 tonnes) – a saving of 60 000 euros over last month.

  As a result, Atrimex may decide to buy more nuts from Hassas because their imported price has fallen, making them more competitive than the prices of pistachio nuts from the US or Turkey.

  A **depreciation** in the exchange rate of a currency means its market price has fallen and it will now cost less to buy in terms of other currencies on the foreign exchange market. In the above case, 1 euro now buys 12 rials instead of 10 rials. This has reduced the cost to German consumers of importing nuts from Iran.

Now imagine that next month the rial appreciates against the euro to 8 rials = 1 euro.

- It will now cost Atrimex 4500 euros to buy 36 000 rials. The purchase of 100 tonnes will therefore cost the German company 450 000 euros (= 3000 euros × 100 tonnes) – an increase in costs of 150 000 euros over the previous month.

  This rise in costs will reduce profits at Atrimex. As a result, managers at the company may decide to reduce its imports of nuts from Hassas, try to find cheaper suppliers from other exporting countries such as the US or Turkey and/or try to reduce its other costs, for example by cutting its workforce, in order to protect its profits.

Now try activity 6.18. In this activity the sales and therefore the profits of the Thai manufacturer are closely linked to the exchange rate between the Thai baht and the euro because the firm exports all the winter coats it makes to mainland European markets.

A depreciation in the value of the euro against the baht (or an appreciation in the baht against the euro) to 1 euro = 32 Thai bahts will increase the European price of its coats to 125 euros (= 4000 Thai bahts / 32 euros). If demand for the coats in Europe is price elastic sales will decline. If this is permanent the Thai manufacturer will be forced to cut back production and reduce its workforce. ➤ 3.3.2

In contrast, an appreciation of the euro against the baht (or a deprecation in the baht against the euro) to 1 euro = 50 Thai bahts will reduce the European price of its coats to 80 euros (= 4000 Thai bahts / 50 euros). If demand for the coats is price elastic sales will rise and the Thai manufacturer may increase production and create additional jobs in response.

ACTIVITY 6.18

A clothing manufacturer located in Thailand makes and exports winter coats for the European market.

Each coat is priced for sale to shops in Europe at 4000 Thai bahts.

Today's exchange rate is 1 Thai baht = 0.025 euro, or 40 Thai bahts = 1 euro. The price of each coat in euros is therefore 100 euros.

▸ What would be the price of each coat if the euro depreciated against the baht to 1 euro = 32 Thai bahts?

▸ What would be the price of each coat if the euro appreciated against the baht to 1 euro = 50 Thai bahts?

If the demand for winter coats in Europe is price elastic what is likely to happen to consumer demand for the coats and the sales revenue of the manufacturer in Thailand following each change in the exchange rate?

Business and the international economy

A chain of craft shops in the US imports ornate garden pots from Malaysia. The business imports 100 pots each month. The currency of Malaysia is the ringgit (RM).

Each pot costs 30 RM to import.

Today's exchange rate is $1 = 3 RM. The cost of each pot in US dollars is therefore $10. The business sells each pot for $16 which earns a profit margin of $6 per pot.

▶ What would be the total cost of importing 100 pots each month if the US dollar depreciated against the Malaysian ringgit to $1 = 2 RM?

▶ What would be the total cost of importing 100 pots each month if the US dollar appreciated against the Malaysian ringgit to $1 = 4 RM?

If the US business decides not to change the selling price of the pots what will happen to its profits following each change in the exchange rate?

In activity 6.19, the costs and therefore the profits of the US importer are dependent on the exchange rate between the US dollar ($) and the Malaysian ringgit (RM).

A depreciation of the US dollar against the ringgit (or an appreciation of the ringgit against the US dollar) to $1 = 2 RM will increase the cost of each imported pot to $15 (= $30/2 RM). If the US business continues to sell the pots for $16 each, the profit margin on each pot would only be $1 giving a total profit of just $100 from the sale of all 100 pots. The US business may have to raise the selling price of the pots. However, doing so could reduce sales revenues if US consumer demand for the pots is price elastic.

If instead the US dollar was to appreciate against the Malaysian ringgit (or the ringgit fell in value against the US dollar) to $1 = 4 RM, the cost of each pot imported from Malaysia will fall to $7.50 (= $30/4 RM).

If the US business continues to sell each pot for $16 the profit margin on each pot will have increased to $8.50. The US business could therefore afford to cut prices and if demand is price elastic it would sell more pots. However, it would therefore need to import more pots and this would be good news for the Malaysian pot manufacturer.

BSafe PLC is a multinational company based in country A. BSafe PLC manufactures a range of safety equipment for sale worldwide. It imports 40% of the raw materials it uses in production and exports 90% of the component parts to be assembled in various countries overseas. Due to the appreciation of country B's exchange rate, the directors of BSafe PLC are considering moving their headquarters to another country with lower corporation taxes and a more favourable exchange rate.

a Define "exchange rate". [2]

b Identify **two** reasons why a business becomes multinational. [2]

c Explain the impact on two stakeholders if BSafe PLC moves its headquarters overseas. [4]

d Explain **three** ways in which an appreciation of the exchange rate might affect BSafe PLC. [6]

e Consider other ways in which BSafe PLC could respond to the appreciation in country B's exchange rate. Justify your answer. [6]

Before you continue make sure you are able to

Understand the impact changes in **exchange rates** can have on different businesses:

✓ **depreciation** and **appreciation** of an exchange rate

✓ how exchange rate changes can affect businesses as importers and exporters of products, for example their effect on prices, **competitiveness** and profitability (*you will not be expected to carry out exchange rate calculations in your examinations*).

Learning CHECKLIST

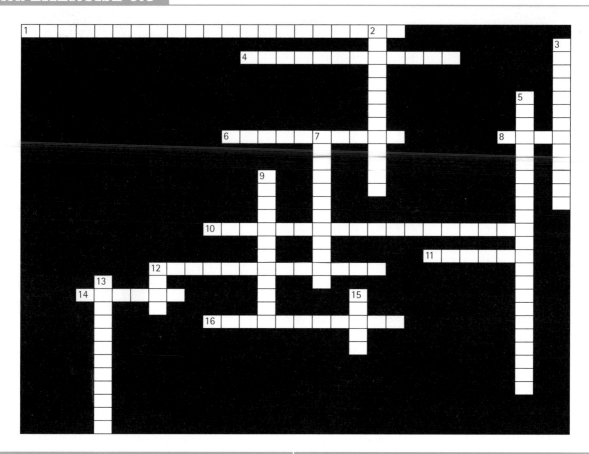

Clues down

2   Policy instruments used by a government to restrict or discourage spending on imports in order to protect domestic firms and jobs from overseas competition (5, 8)

3   Term used to describe the increasing global trade, interconnections and interactions between different people, organizations and national economies (13)

5   Term used to describe capital invested in productive assets in a country by a resident or business of another country, either by buying a company in that country or by expanding the operations of an existing business (7, 6, 10)

7   Term used to refer to a fall in the value of a currency in terms of how much it costs to buy with another currency or currencies (12)

9   Term used to refer to a rise in the value of a currency in terms of how much it costs to buy with another currency or currencies (12)

12 If the UK pound depreciates against the South African currency, the rand, from £1 = 10 rand to £1 = 12 rand, will imports from UK firms become more or less competitive in South Africa? (4)

13 The price or value of one currency in terms of how much it costs to buy using another currency (8, 4)

15 A limit placed on the volume of a particular product that can be imported into a country (5)

Clues across

1   A multinational may move its profits from one country to another via its subsidiaries in order to avoid paying corporation taxes in that country. What term is used to describe this? (12, 2, 7)

4   An indirect tax added to the price of an imported product to make it less competitive (6, 6)

6   A company that is completely or partly owned by another company or corporation (10)

8   If the US dollar appreciates in value against the euro from $1 = €1.5 to $1 = €1.6, will US exports to European countries become more or less competitive? (4)

10 The exchange of goods, services and money between firms and consumers located in different countries (13, 5)

11 A good or service purchased by a resident of a country that has been produced by a firm overseas. The purchase will worsen the balance of payments of the country in which the consumer resides (6)

12 A global company or corporation that owns one or more subsidiary companies producing goods and services in other countries (13)

14 A good or service produced by a firm in one national economy that is sold to a consumer in another. Its sale increases the income of the firm and improves the balance of payments of the economy in which it is located (6)

16 A national economy that trades freely with other countries (4, 7)

Index

absenteeism 93, 325
  reduced 89, 124
accounting 388–92, 416, 422
  accountants 416
  accounting year 386, 416
  accounts payable 396, 400
  accounts receivable 396–97
  final accounts 416–17
  limitations of use of accounts and
    accounting ratios 416, 420–21
  users of financial accounts 416,
    418–20
acquisitions 41–42
advertising 11, 256–59
  informative advertising 254, 256
  job vacancies 135–37
  persuasive advertising 254, 257
after-sales care 263
agents 246, 250
airlines 17, 51, 68, 241, 420
airports 17, 20, 69, 346, 350
annual general meeting (AGM) 61
annual revenues 65, 255, 474
arbitration 122, 126
assets 363
  current assets 301, 396–97, 400–
    401
  fixed assets 397
  liquid assets 376–78
  net assets 401
  net current assets 401
  non-current assets 381, 396–97,
    400–401
  sale and lease back 363
  total assets 400–401
automation 149, 155, 163, 306, 311
autonomation 304

balance of payments 425, 427, 429–
  30, 443–44
balance sheet 396–97, 422
balance sheets 403
bankruptcy 48, 50
banks 38, 80, 361, 364–65, 416
bar charts 218–19
blogging 271
board of directors 61, 105–6

bonus payments 93, 95
borrowing 368, 381
branding 11, 225
  brand awareness 225, 230
  brand image 225, 230, 257
  brand loyalty 230, 257
  brand name 225
  brand recognition 230
break-even analysis 317, 327, 333
  break-even charts 327–30
break-even level of outputs 317,
  326, 328
building regulations 344, 352
business 4, 14
  business expansion 359, 381
  classification 15–19
  closure 391
  purpose 11–13
  specialization 6–8, 467–68
  value added 7–11
business angels 366
business cycle 425, 430–33
business environment 45, 50
business failure 48–50, 53
  causes 50–52
business objectives 13, 72
  key business objectives 79
  setting and meeting business
    objectives 74
business organization 54, 70–71
  franchises 66–67, 289
  joint ventures 54, 66, 285, 289
  limited companies or corporations
    61–65
  partnerships 54, 56, 59–60
  sole traders 54, 57–59
business owners 38, 80
business plans 28, 31–32, 49–50
business start-ups 34–36, 55–57,
  359
business survival 48, 72, 359
business-to-business commerce
  (B2B) 268
business-to-consumer commerce
  (B2C) 268

capital 1, 3, 37–38, 56, 357, 396,
  470
  capital employed 39, 396, 401
  capital expenditure 357, 359
  capital-intensive firms 37, 39
  fixed and working capital
    employed 401
  fixed capital 56, 357, 359
  owners' capital 398
  permanent capital 361, 367
  requirements in business 359
  return on capital employed
    (ROCE) 404, 407, 409–12
  share capital 400
  venture capital 357, 359, 366–67
  working capital 56, 357, 359, 376,
    383, 396, 401
cash 376–78, 384–85, 388
  cash flow cycle 376, 378
  cash flow forecast 376, 379–80
  cash flow management 381–83
  cash flow problems 376–77
  cash inflow 376, 378
    cash outflow 376, 378
    cash reserve 376, 378
    net cash flow 376, 378
change 187, 193, 197
  analysing market trends 188–92
charts 173, 218
  bar charts 218–19
  break-even charts 327–30
  line charts 220
  organizational charts 101, 103–4
  pie charts 222–23
chief executive officers (CEOs) 106
climate 348
closed shops 122
collateral 361, 364
collective bargaining 122, 124–25
commission 93, 95
communication 116, 164, 177–78
  communication barriers 176
  communication breakdowns 164
  effective communication in
    business 165–68
  external communications 164
  formal and informal

communications 170

horizontal communications 164, 168

intended audience 174–75

internal communications 164, 168–69

methods of communication 171–75

one-way communications 170

open communications 164, 170

restricted communications 164, 170

two-way communications 164, 169–70

verbal communications 164, 171–72

vertical communications 164

visual communications 164, 171, 173–74

written communications 164, 171–73

communities 80

companies

joint-stock companies 41, 54, 61

limited companies 54, 56, 61–65, 361, 367

private limited companies 54, 61

public limited companies 54, 61, 64–65

competition 34, 76, 187, 196–97, 464, 472

multinationals 478

non-price competition 187, 193

price competition 187, 193

competitions 261

computer-aided design (CAD) 307, 311

computer-aided manufacturing (CAM) 307, 312

computer-integrated manufacturing (CIM) 312

conglomerates 43

construction 18

consumers 1–2, 8, 38, 80

consumer panels 207, 210, 213, 216–17

consumer protection laws 281–84

consumer spending patterns 187, 190–92, 443–44

consumer spending patterns 190–92

consumption 1–2, 4, 19–21

contracts of employment 140, 156, 158

corporations 54, 61–65

public corporations 22–23, 54, 68–69

cost-effectiveness 263

costs 12, 317, 332–33, 443–44

average costs 317, 323

cost of sales 386

costs of starting and running a business 323

direct costs 317–19

external costs and benefits 448, 453

financial costs and benefits 452

fixed costs 317–19

indirect costs 319

opportunity costs 1, 5

private costs and benefits 448, 452

social costs and benefits 448, 454–56

total costs 317–20, 322–23, 326

variable costs 317–20

credit control 36, 3709

creditors 48, 400

credit unions 364

cultural factors 288

currencies 480–82

appreciation and depreciation 480, 482–86

customers 1, 9, 182, 193

debentures 361, 367

debt finance 361, 364, 368, 382

highly geared businesses 361, 368, 372

debtors 376, 382, 397, 400

defaulting 361, 368

de-industrialization 15, 20

delegation 101, 103–4, 112, 118

delivery lead times 246, 253, 302

developed and developing economies 15, 20

direct mail 261

directors 105–6

disciplinary procedures 149, 153–55

discrimination 156

diseconomies of scale 37, 45, 317, 325, 332–33

dismissal 153–55

unfair dismissal 158–59

distribution 246, 252

diversification 37, 41, 233

donations 260

downsizing 150–51

dumping 464, 472

earnings 93–94

e-commerce 266, 268–71

economic growth 34, 425, 427–28

boom 425

recession 48–49, 425, 430–31, 437

recovery 425

economic systems 19–21

economies 15, 21, 26–27

economies of scale 41, 75, 317, 324, 332–33, 474

external economies of scale 344, 348

efficiency 295–97

embargoes 473

emerging economies 20

employees 38–39, 80, 107, 416

communication 162, 168

contracts 140, 156, 158

dismissal 153–55

employee share ownership 93, 95

financial rewards 93–94

motivation 87–89, 93–97, 99–100

profit sharing 95

redundancy 151–52, 154

selection 128–30

training 144–46, 148

employment 10–11, 128, 425, 427, 429

employment contracts 140, 156–58

full-time and part-time employment 128, 141–42

employment laws 156, 163

dismissal 154

rights and responsibilities of employees and employers 157–62

employment tribunals 156, 158

enterprise 1, 3, 28–29

social enterprise 34, 72, 77–78

entrepreneurs 1, 3, 28–31, 55–57

business activity and the environment 449–51

environmental concerns 448, 452–53, 479

social entrepreneurs 72, 77

equity 368, 398, 401

equity finance 361, 364, 367

ethical considerations 448, 462
exchange rates 480, 488
  exchange rate risks 285, 288
  floating exchange rates 482
  foreign exchange market 480–82
  international competitiveness 480, 486
excise duties 439
exports 464, 466, 468–69
external costs and benefits 448, 453
external impacts of business activity 456
  pressure groups, legal controls and penalties on business activities 459
externalities 452
  negative externalities 448, 453
  positive externalities 448, 452–53

factors of production 1, 3
  factor substitution 307, 313
finance 50, 75, 80, 357–59, 374–75
  banks 361, 364–65
  choosing method of finance 370–73
  debt finance 361, 364, 368, 382
  equity finance 361, 364, 367
  external sources 361–62, 364–68
  internal sources 361–63
  long-term finance 357, 360, 365, 367
  short-term finance 357, 359–60, 365
financial costs and benefits 452
financial economies 325
financial position, statement of 356, 396–402, 406, 410, 416
firms 1, 3
  ancillary firms 344, 348
  ethical firms 448, 462
  market-oriented firms 181, 183, 207–8
  product-oriented firms 181, 183
fit for purpose 334–35
flotations 54
footloose industries 344, 346
foreign direct investment (FDI) 474, 477
foreign exchange market 480–82
franchises 66–67, 289
fringe benefits 93
fundraising events 260

gearing ratio 361
general partners 54, 59
globalization 349–50, 464–67, 473
  opportunities 467–69
  threats 469–71
global warming 450
going concerns 48–49
goods 2–4, 11–12
government 22, 80, 425–26, 446–47
  economic objectives 425, 427–30
  environmental protection 459
  financial support 28, 34–36, 368
  government agencies 22, 136
  government officials 38
  government publications 214
  government spending 425, 435–36
  how governments influence location decisions 350
  multinationals 474
  policy instruments 425
  regional policies 22
grants 28, 34–36, 344, 350, 459
gross domestic product (GDP) 425, 431
gross misconduct 154
growth 37, 72, 74
  can some firms grow too much? 45
  internal and external growth 37, 41
  measuring size of firms 38–40
  why and how firms grow 45
  why some firms remain small 45–47

health and safety laws 156, 161
Herzberg, Frederick 91
hierarchies 101, 110
hire purchase (HP) 361, 366
human resources management 129–30
hygiene factors 91

illiquidity 404
image 193
imports 464, 466, 468–70
  import tariffs 439, 464, 472
income 10–11
  disposable income 187, 190–91

income statements 386, 389, 392–93
incompetence 154
incorporated businesses 54, 62–64
industrial action 122, 125
industrial sector 15–16
industrial structure 15, 21
inflation 382, 425, 427–28
inputs 1, 3, 295–96
insolvency 48, 50, 376, 412
integration 37, 41–44
interest rates 364, 425, 435, 441–45
international trade 425, 427, 429–30, 443–44, 464, 466, 472
  exchange rates 480, 483–86
  foreign exchange market 480–82
Internet 215, 266, 268–72
interviews 138–40, 210
inventories 295, 300
  holding and managing inventories (stocks) 302, 381
investment 443
  foreign direct investment (FDI) 474, 477
  investment banks 364
investors 38

job analysis 128, 131
job applications 137–40
job descriptions 128–29, 131–34
job enlargement 97
job enrichment 97
job rotation 97
job satisfaction 87, 89, 97
joint ventures 54, 66, 285, 289
just-in-time inventory control 295, 304

Kaizen 295, 304–5

labour 1, 3, 470
  division of labour 1, 7–8
  labour diseconomies 325
  labour-intensive firms 37, 39
  labour productivity 295, 298–99
land 1, 3
language barriers 288
leadership styles 112, 119–20
leasing 361, 366
  sale and lease back 363
liabilities 396, 398

current liabilities 396, 398, 400–401
  limited liability 54, 57, 62
  limited liability partnerships
    (LLPs) 59
  non-current liabilities 396, 398,
    400–401
  total liabilities 400
  unlimited liability 54, 57
lifestyle segmentation 201, 203–4
limited partners 54, 59
line charts 220
liquidation 48, 50
liquidity 376, 378
  illiquidity 411
  liquidity ratios 404, 411–13
loans 361, 364, 383, 444–45
local government 22, 69
location 50, 344, 354–55
  choosing business locations
    overseas 350
  how governments influence
    location decisions 350–54
  location factors 345–48
logistics 246–47
loss 52, 327, 386
  loyalty cards and bonuses 261
  profit and loss 390–92

management 50, 101, 112–14
  autocratic management 112, 120
  delegation 101, 103–4, 112, 118
  democratic management 112, 120
  laissez-faire management 112,
    120
  leadership styles 112, 119–20
  management diseconomies 325
  management functions 112, 115
managers 80, 93, 106–7
managing directors (MDs) 101, 106
manufacturing 15, 18
market conditions 187–88
market entry 285, 292
  overseas markets 290
marketing 181
  differentiated marketing 195, 203
  exiting 275
  market-oriented firms 181, 183,
    207–8
  mass marketing 198–200
  niche marketing 198–200, 275
marketing budget 254, 263–65
marketing economies 325

marketing mix 181, 185–86, 225
  branding 230
  product 225–29
  product life cycle analysis 234
  technology 266–67, 272–73
marketing objectives 181, 183–84
marketing strategies 274
  developing 274, 276
  flexibility 277–80
  research 276–77
market leaders 207
market reports 214–15
market research 49, 207, 209, 224,
  290
  accuracy 215–16
  analysis 223
  observation 210
  primary research 207–12
  qualitative data 207–8
  quantitative data 207–8
  questionnaires 211–12, 216
  secondary research 207, 209, 214
markets 181, 349
  contracting and expanding
    markets 187
  niche markets 199
market segmentation 201–6
  market segments 201, 203
market share 37–40, 72, 74–75
  growth 275
market size 37
market trends 187–92
Maslow, Abraham 89
materials 349
mergers 37, 41, 285, 290
  conglomerate mergers 43
micro-finance 361, 370
minimum wage 156
mission statements 72–73
mixed economies 15, 22–25
money-off coupons 261, 271
mortgages 361
motivation 87–89, 93–97, 99–100
  motivational theories 87, 89–92
multinationals 38, 466, 469–70,
  474–77, 479
  benefits and disadvantages
    477–79

nationalization 68–69
needs 2, 8–11, 182
  hygiene factors 91

physiological needs 87, 89
  social needs 87, 90
newly industrialized economies 20
non-price factors 190–92

observation 210
online services 271
open economies 464–65
organizations 101, 167
  centralization and decentralization
    101, 110
  chain of command 101, 103,
    107–8
  departments 101, 104–5
  flat and tall organizations 101,
    108–9
  hierarchies 101, 103, 110
  non-profit organizations 1, 13
  organizational charts 101, 103–4
  roles and relationships 105–7
  span of control 101, 103, 109
  structure 101–5
outputs 1, 3, 38–39, 295–96
  volume and value 38–39
overheads 317–19, 391
overseas markets 288
  overcoming problems 290
overstocking 48
overtime 93–94
overtrading 48, 50

packaging 227–28
partnerships 54, 56, 59–60
performance-related pay 93, 95
personal selling 254, 261–62
person specifications 128–29, 133
phishing 271
piece rate 93–95
pie charts 222–23
place of sale 185, 247
planning 112
planning laws 344, 351
population 191
press releases 260
pressure groups 448, 457
pricing 186, 235–37, 245
  competitive pricing 235
  cost-plus pricing 235
  demand-based pricing strategies
    235, 239–41
  destruction pricing 235, 238
  dynamic pricing 241

penetration pricing 235, 239–40
price competition 187, 193
price elastic demand 235, 244
price elasticity of demand 235, 245
price factors 190
price inelastic demand 235, 244
price skimming 235, 239
price wars 235, 238, 240
promotional pricing 235, 240
psychological pricing 235, 240
selling price 322–23
primary research 207–12
primary sector 15, 17
private costs and benefits 448, 452
private sector 1, 4, 15, 22–23, 54, 57–67
privatization 24
producers 3, 6
production 1, 3–4, 19–21, 295
  chain of productive activity 16–17
  improving productive efficiency 300
  labour productivity 295, 298–99
  lean production 295, 300, 306
  quality production 334–41, 343
  specialization 6–8
production methods 307–10, 316
  batch production 307, 309
  flow production 307–9
  job production 307–8
productivity 295, 297
products 1, 3, 184–85, 225, 295
  benchmarking 225, 228
  endorsements 260
  extension strategies 225, 232
  life cycle analysis 225, 234
  product development 228–29
  product-oriented firms 181, 183
  product placement 260
  product portfolios 225, 233
  products in the marketing mix 226–29
profit 1, 3, 12, 32–33, 72, 317, 322–23, 327, 386, 394–95
  accounting for profit 388–92
  distributed profit 386, 388
  gross profit 386, 390–92
  gross profit margin 404, 407
  importance of making a profit 387–88
  profitability 72, 74, 480

profit after tax 386
profit and loss account 391
profit for the year 392
profit margin 237, 404, 407
profit maximization 72, 74, 193
profit projections 392–93
profit sharing 95
repatriation 474, 478
retained profit 361–62, 386, 388, 400
promotion 185, 254–56, 265
  above-the-line promotion 254, 256
  advertising 254, 256–59
  after-sales care 263
  below-the-line promotion 254, 256, 260–63
  point-of-sale promotions 254, 261
protectionism 472
publications 215
public expenditure 435–36
publicity 260
public relations (PR) 254, 260
public sector 4, 15, 22–25, 69, 72
  business objectives 78–79
purchasing economies 324

quality 334–38
quality assurance 334, 337, 339
quality control 334, 337–39
  marks and standards 342
questionnaires 211–12, 216
quotas 464, 472

ratio analysis 404–6, 415
  accounting ratio 404, 406
  acid test ratio 404, 413
  current ratio 404, 411–12
  financial ratio 404, 406
  limitations 334–35
  liquidity ratios 404, 406, 411–13
  performance ratios 404, 411
  solvency ratios 411
recruitment 128–30
  advertising job vacancies 135–37
  educational institutions 135
  ethical and legal obligations 139
  full-time and part-time employment 128, 141–42
  government employment agencies 136
  headhunting 136

internal and external recruitment 128, 134–37
  interviews 138–40
  job applications 137
  job descriptions 128–29, 131–34
  professional associations 135
  recruitment agencies 135
  shortlisting 128, 138
  sifting 128, 138
redundancy 151–52, 154
research and development 307, 312
resources 1, 3–5, 11–12
  natural resources 17–18
  non-renewable resources 448
retailers 246, 249–50
  return on capital employed (ROCE) 404, 407, 409–11
revenues 1, 12, 32–33
  revenue expenditure 357, 359
  total revenue 390
reverse engineering 225, 228
risk 54, 75

salaries 93, 95
sales 38–39, 193
  growth 274–75
  sales incentives 261
  sales literature 260
sampling 207, 213–14
  quota sampling 207, 213
  random sampling 207, 213
  sampling bias 207, 216
savings 363–64
scale of production 37, 41
search engines 266, 269
seasonal factors 192, 382
secondary research 207, 209, 214–15
secondary sector 15, 18
separate legal identity 54, 57, 62
services 2–4, 12, 18–19
  public services 13, 68
shareholders 41, 61, 80, 367
  shareholders' funds 368, 396, 401
shares 54, 61–65, 361, 367
  rights issue 367
signage 260
silent or sleeping partners 59
social and economic welfare 449, 454–56
social costs and benefits 448, 454–56
social media 266, 271–72

socio-economic groups 201, 204
sole traders 54, 57–59
solvency ratios 323--97
spam 271
specialization 1, 6–8, 467–68
sponsorship 260
stages of production 16–17
stakeholders 38, 80–85
    users of accounts and accounting
    ratios 418–20
start-up costs 318
statement of financial position 4, 11
status quo 275
stock market 54
subsidiaries 474
subsidies 344, 459, 472, 479
supervisors 107
suppliers 76, 80
surveys 210
sustainable development 448,
    450–51

tables 217
takeovers 37, 41–42
targets 72–73
    target markets 201–2
taxes 349, 425, 435
    ad valorem taxes 438
    corporation tax 392, 440
    direct taxes 437–41
    effects of raising 441
    income tax 440–41
    indirect taxes 438–39, 459
    payroll taxes 440–41
    profit after tax 386
Taylor, Frederick 90
teamworking 93, 97
technical economies 325
technology 192, 267, 272–73, 300
    disruptive technologies 307, 312
    modern technology in business
    307, 314
    technological spillovers 307, 312
tertiary sector 15, 18–19
test marketing 207, 211
time rate 93–94
total quality management (TQM)
    334, 337, 339
trade associations 215
trade barriers 349, 464, 471–73
trade credit 80, 361, 365–66
trade shows 260

trade unions 38, 80, 122–25,
    127, 416
    single union agreements 122,
    124–25
trading bodies 23, 68–69
training 144–46, 148
transport 253
turnover 39

unemployment 34, 425
user charges 439

value added 1, 11
vehicle liveries 260
victimization 159

wages 93–95, 349
    minimum wage 156, 162
    wage protection 161
wants 2, 8–11, 182
websites 271
wholesalers 246, 250–52
work 88–89
    Herzberg's motivators and hygiene
    factors 91
    Maslow's hierarchy of needs 89
    Taylor's principles of scientific
    management 90
work-in-progress 301